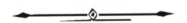

ISBN 978-0-428-81160-0
PIBN 10522213

Attention Scanner:
Foldout in Book!

NORTHERN GERMANY.

MONEY-TABLE.

(Comp. p. XIII.)

English Money.			French Money.		Prussian Money.			South German Money.	
£.	S.	D.	Fr.	Cts.	Thlr.	Sgr.	Pfg.	Fl.	Kr.
1	—	—	25	—	6	20	—	11	40
—	17	1	21	55	5	21	—	10	—
—	16	—	20	—	5	10	—	9	20
—	15	—	18	57	5	—	—	8	45
—	12	—	15	—	4	—	—	7	—
—	10	—	12	50	3	10	—	5	50
—	8	6	10	77	2	25	—	5	—
—	6	—	7	50	2	—	—	3	30
—	4	—	5	—	1	10	—	2	20
—	3	—	3	75	1	—	—	1	45
—	2	—	2	50	—	20	—	1	10
—	1	8	2	15	—	17	—	1	—
—	1	7	2	—	—	16	—	—	57
—	1	—	1	25	—	10	—	—	35
—	—	10	1	8	—	8	6	—	30
—	—	9^{1}|$_{2}$	1	—	—	8	—	—	28
—	—	6	—	62	—	5	—	—	18
—	—	4^{1}|$_{2}$	—	50	—	4	—	—	14
—	—	2^{1}|$_{4}$	—	25	—	2	—	—	7
—	—	2	—	22	—	1	8	—	6
		1	—	11	—	—	10	—	3
		2|3	—	6	—	—	6	—	2
		1|3	—	3	—	—	3	—	1

MONEY-TABLE.

(Comp. p. XIII.)

English Money.			French Money.		Prussian Money.			South German Money.	
£.	*S.*	*D.*	*Fr.*	*Cts.*	*Thlr.*	*Sgr.*	*Pfg.*	*Fl.*	*Kr.*
1	—	—	25	—	6	20	—	11	40
—	17	1	21	55	5	21	—	10	—
—	16	—	20	—	5	10	—	9	20
—	15	—	18	57	5	—	—	8	45
—	12	—	15	—	4	—	—	7	—
—	10	—	12	50	3	10	—	5	50
—	8	6	10	77	2	25	—	5	—
—	6	—	7	50	2	—	—	3	30
—	4	—	5	—	1	10	—	2	20
—	3	—	3	75	1	—	—	1	45
—	2	—	2	50	—	20	—	1	10
—	1	8	2	15	—	17	—	1	—
—	1	7	2	—	—	16	—	—	57
—	1	—	1	25	—	10	—	—	35
—	—	10	1	8	—	8	6	—	30
—	—	9$\frac{1}{2}$	1	—	—	8	—	—	28
—	—	6	—	62	—	5	—	—	18
—	—	4$\frac{1}{2}$	—	50	—	4	—	—	14
—	—	2$\frac{1}{4}$	—	25	—	2	—	—	7
—	—	2	—	22	—	1	8	—	6
		1	—	11	—	—	10	—	3
		$\frac{2}{3}$	—	6	—	—	6	—	2
		$\frac{1}{3}$	—	3	—	—	3	—	1

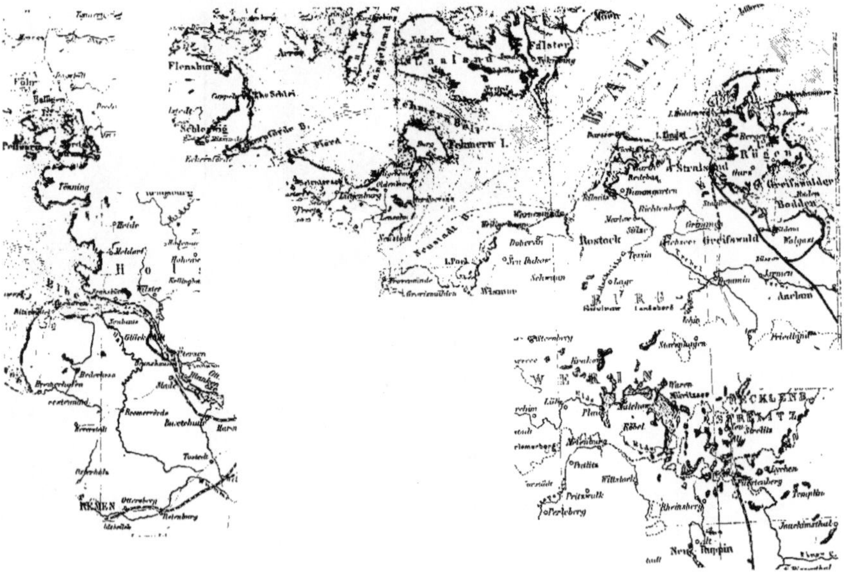

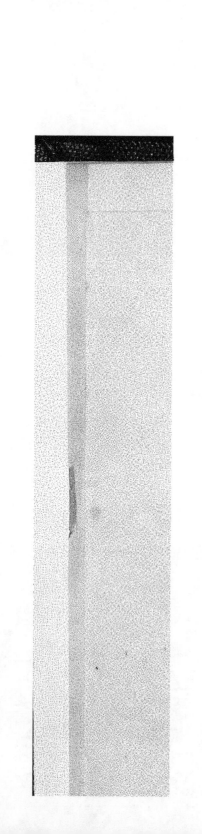

ORTHERN GERMANY.

HANDBOOK FOR TRAVELLERS

BY

K. BÆDEKER.

With 11 Maps and 27 Plans.

FIFTH EDITION, REVISED AND AUGMENTED.

COBLENZ AND LEIPSIC.

KARL BÆDEKER.

1873.

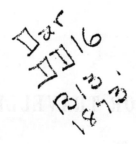

"Go, little book, God send thee good passage,
And specially let this be thy prayere
Unto them all that thee will read or hear,
Where thou art wrong, after their help to call,
Thee to correct in any part or all."

CHAUCER.

PREFACE.

The chief object of this Handbook is to supply the traveller with such information as to render him as nearly as possible independent of hotel - keepers, commissionaires, and guides, and thus enable him the more thoroughly to enjoy and appreciate the objects of interest he meets with on his tour.

The Handbook has been compiled almost entirely from the personal experience of the Editor, and the country described has been repeatedly explored by him with a view to procure the latest possible information: but, as trifling errors and omissions are inevitable, he will highly appreciate any communications with which he may be favoured by travellers, if the result of their own observation. The information already received, which he gratefully acknowledges, has in many cases proved most serviceable.

The *Maps* and *Plans*, on which the most anxious care has been bestowed, will be of essential service to the traveller, and enable him at a glance to ascertain his bearings and select the best routes.

Time Tables. Information as to the departure of trains, steamboats, and diligences is seldom to be relied upon unless obtained from local sources. If Bradshaw is mistrusted, '*Hendschel's Telegraph*' (15 Sgr.), published at Frankfort on the Main, and issued monthly during the summer season, or the official *'Coursbuch'* (20 Sgr.), published at Berlin, and issued seven or eight times a year, will be found useful.

Altitudes are given in English feet (1 Engl. ft. = 0,3048 mètre = 0,938 Parisian ft. = 0,971 Prussian ft.), *Distances* in English miles (except for mountain excursions, in which case the time they occupy is more satisfactory), and the *Populations* from data furnished by the latest census.

Hotels. The Editor has endeavoured to enumerate both the first-class hotels and those of more modest pretensions which may be safely selected by the 'voyageur en garçon', with little sacrifice of comfort and considerable saving of expenditure. The average charges quoted have either been tested by the Editor himself, or have been gathered from the numberless bills with which he has been furnished from various quarters. Hotel charges, as well as carriage fares and fees to guides, are constantly fluctuating; but these items, given approximately, will at least enable the traveller to form a fair estimate of his probable expenditure.

CONTENTS.

Route.   Page.

53. The Thruingian Forest 244

   a. Eastern Portion. From Rudolstadt to Gotha 244
     1. From Schwarzburg to Eisfeld 245
     2. From Ilmenau to Arnstadt 246
   b. Western Portion. From Eisenach to Gotha by Ruhla
      and Liebenstein 247
     1. From Ruhla to the Inselsberg. 249
     2. From the Inselsberg to Eisenach 250
     3. Excursions from Friedrichsroda 252

54. From Gotha through the Thuringian Forest to Hildburg-
    hausen 252

55. From Cassel to Halle (and Leipsic) by Nordhausen. . . 253
     1. From Leinefelde to Gotha. 253
     2. The Kyffhäuser. Rothenburg. Frankenhausen. . . . 254

56. From Brunswick to Nordhausen and Erfurt by Börssum
    (Harzburg, Goslar) 255
     1. From Börssum to Harzburg and Goslar. 255
     2. Scharzfels. Ravenskopf 256

57. From Berlin by Cöthen to Ballenstedt, Thale, Vienen-
    burg (Harzburg, Goslar) 257
     1. The Park of Wörlitz. 257
     2. From Rosslau to Zerbst 257

58. The Harz Mountains 260

   I. The Eastern Harz Mts. 260

    a. Quedlinburg. 260

    b. Selkethal. Mägdesprung. Alexisbad. Victorshöhe.
      Gernrode. Suderode. Lauenburg. 262

    c. Bodethal. Rosstrappe. Hexentanzplatz. Treseburg. 265
     1. From Treseburg to Blankenburg 266
     2. From Thale to Suderode and Gernrode. 267

    d. Blankenburg. Rübeland. Elbingerode 267

    e. Ilfeld. Neustadt unter'm Hohnstein. Stolberg. Jo-
      sephshöhe 268

   II. The Western Harz 269

    a. Goslar. Okerthal 269
     1. The Rammelsberg. 271
    b. Harzburg. Ilsenburg. Wernigerode. 271
     1. From Harzburg to the Okerthal by the Ahrendsberger
       Klippen 265
     2. From Harzburg to Ilsenburg by the Rabenklippen. . . 272
     3. The Steinerne Renne. 274
    c. The Brocken.. 274
    d. Clausthal. Andreasberg. 275

59. From Cassel to Frankfort on the Main 276
     1. Excursions from Marburg. 278
     2. From Giessen to Fulda. 278
     3. From Giessen to Gelnhausen. 278

Maps.

Plans of Towns.

INTRODUCTION.

I. Language.

A slight acquaintance with German is indispensable for those who desire to explore the more remote districts of Northern Germany, but tourists who do not deviate from the beaten track will generally find English or French spoken at the principal hotels and the usual resorts of strangers. If, however, they are entirely ignorant of the language they must be prepared occasionally to submit to the extortions practised by commissionaires, waiters, cab-drivers, etc., which even the data furnished by the Handbook will not always enable them to avoid.

II. Money.

English sovereigns and banknotes may be exchanged at all the principal towns in Germany without loss, unless the rate of exchange be below par (1$l.$ = 6 Thlr. 20 Sgr.). Napoleons are also favourably received (20 fr. = 16$s.$ = 5 Thlr. 10 Sgr.). Those who travel with large sums should carry it in the form of the circular notes of 10$l.$, issued by the London bankers, rather than in banknotes or gold, the value of circular notes, if lost or stolen, being recoverable.

The Prussian currency is employed throughout the whole of Northern Germany, except in the Hanseatic towns of Hamburg, Bremen, and Lübeck, and in a few other districts, the currencies of which are explained in the Handbook. The coins in common circulation are: Friedrichsd'or ($5^2/_3$ Thlr. = 17$s.$), double Friedrichsd'or ($11^1/_3$ Thlr. = 1$l.$ 14$s.$), 20 Mark ($6^2/_3$ Thlr. = 1$l.$) and 10 Mark pieces ($3^1/_3$ Thlr. = 10$s.$) in gold; dollars (3s) and two-dollar pieces in silver; pieces of 10, 5, $2^1/_2$, 2, and 1 Silbergroschen in a mixture of silver and copper; pieces of 4, 3, 2, and 1 Pfennig in copper (12 Pf. = 1 Sgr., 30 Sgr. = 1 Thlr.; 10 Pf. = 1$d.$, 10 Sgr. = 1$s.$). Austrian florins (20 Sgr. = 2$s.$) are also frequently met with. Prussian banknotes (of 1, 5, 10, 25, 50, 100, and 500 Thlr.) are received in all parts of Germany at their full value. The S. German currency consists of florins and kreuzers (1 fl. = 60 kr. = 20$d.$ Engl.; 3 kr. = 1$d.$; 35 kr. = 1$s.$; 11 fl. 40 kr. = 1$l.$). The traveller should also consult the table of comparative values prefixed to this volume.

The expense of a tour in Northern Germany depends of course
on a variety of circumstances; but it may be stated generally that
travelling in Germany is less expensive, and in some respects
more comfortable, than in most other countries in Europe. The
pedestrian of moderate requirements, who is tolerably proficient
in the language and avoids the beaten track as much as possible,
may limit his expenditure to 8—10s. per diem, while those who
prefer driving to walking, choose the most expensive hotels, and·
require the reserves of guides, commissionaires, etc. must be prepared to expend 25—30s. daily.

III. Passports.

In Germany, as well as in Austria, France, Belgium, Holland,
Switzerland and Italy passports are now unnecessary. · It should,
however, be remembered that a passport is occasionally required
to prove the identity of the traveller, procure admission to collections, obtain delivery of registered letters, etc., in countries
where such credentials are otherwise unnecessary. The principal
passport-agents in London are Lee and Carter, 440 West Strand;
C. Goodman, 408 Strand; Dorrel and Son, 15 Charing Cross;
E. Stanford, 6 Charing Cross; W. J. Adams, 59 Fleet Street;
Letts Son & Co., 3 Royal Exchange.

Custom-house formalities at the frontier are generally lenient.
As a rule however, articles purchased during the journey and
not destined for personal use, should be 'declared'.

IV. Railways, etc.

Railway-travelling is cheaper in Germany. than in other parts
of Europe, Belgium excepted, and the carriages are generally clean
and comfortable. Those of the second class, with spring-seats, are
often better than the first in England. The first-class carriages,
lined with velvet, and comparatively little used, are recommended
to the lover of fresh air, as he will be more likely to secure a seat
next the window. The third-class travelling community are generally quiet and respectable, and the carriages tolerably clean. On
a few railways there is even a fourth class, without seats. Smoking
is permitted in all the carriages, except those 'Zum Nicht Rauchen'
and the coupés for ladies. The average fares for the different classes
are $3/5 d.$, $1^1/5 d.$ and $1/5 d.$ per Engl. M. respectively. The speed
seldom exceeds 25 M. per hour, and the enormous traffic carried
on in some parts of England, where many hundred trains traverse
the same line daily, is entirely unknown. These circumstances,
coupled with the fact that the German railways are generally well
organised and under the immediate supervision of government,
render accidents of very rare occurrence. On most lines 20—50 lbs.
of luggage are free, in addition to smaller articles carried in the
hand. Over-weight is charged for at moderate rates. In all cases the

heavier luggage must be booked, and a ticket procured for it; this being done, the traveller need not enquire after his 'impedimenta' until he arrives and presents his ticket at his final destination (where they will be kept in safe custody, several days usually gratis). Where, however, a frontier has to be crossed, the traveller - must see that his luggage is cleared at the custom-house.

Northern and Western Germany are now covered with an extensive network of railways, but an enumeration of their names would probably bewilder the traveller and be of little practical service to him. In planning a railway journey the maps in the Handbook and the railway time-tables should of course be consulted.

Diligence communication in most parts of Germany is well organised and under the immediate control of government. The average speed is 5 Engl. M. per hour, the fare $1^1/_2d$. per M. The vehicles, although cumbrous and uninviting, are tolerably comfortable. A single traveller may sometimes secure a seat by the driver. An 'extra-post' conveyance for one or more persons may generally be obtained on application at the post-offices. The average tariff is 6d. per M. for 1—2, and 1s. per M. for 3—4 pers. Private conveyances may be hired at the rate of 3—5 Thlr. for a one-horse, 4—8 Thlr. for a two-horse carriage per diem.

V. Excursions on Foot.

The pedestrian is unquestionably the most independent of travellers, and the best able, both physically and morally, to enjoy beautiful scenery. For a tour of two or three weeks a couple of flannel shirts, a pair of worsted stockings, slippers, and the articles of the toilette, carried in a pouch slung over the shoulder, will generally be found a sufficient equipment, to which a light Mackintosh and a stout umbrella should be added. Strong and well-tried boots are essential to comfort. Heavy and complicated knapsacks should be avoided; a light pouch or game-bag is far less irksome, and its position may be shifted at pleasure. The traveller should of course have a more extensive reserve of clothing, especially if he intends to visit towns of importance, but even this should be contained in a valise, which may be forwarded from town to town by post.

Northern Germany comprises many attractive and picturesque districts, such as the Saxon Switzerland (R. 39), the Thuringian Forest (R. 52), the Harz (R. 58), the Giant Mountains (R. 29), the environs of Kiel (R. 18), and the island of Rügen (R. 25). The student of art is strongly recommended to visit Dresden, Berlin, and Copenhagen; and the archæologist will find many objects of interest in the ancient towns of Hildesheim, Brunswick, Lübeck, and Dantsic. A perusal of the Handbook will enable the traveller to discover many other interesting places, whether the object of his tour be amusement or instruction.

VI. Hotels.

Little variation occurs in the accommodation and charges of first-class hotels in the principal towns and watering-places throughout Germany; but it sometimes happens that in old-fashioned hotels of unassuming exterior the traveller finds more real comfort and lower charges than in the modern establishments. The best houses of both descriptions are therefore enumerated.

The average charges in the first-class hotels are as follows: bed 2s. 6d., plain breakfast 1s., dinner 2s. 6d., table wine 1s., tea with meat 2s., attendance 1s., light 1s., boots extra.

When the traveller remains for a week or more at an hotel, it is advisable to pay, or at least call for his bill every two or three days, in order that erroneous insertions may be at once detected. Verbal reckonings are objectionable. A waiter's mental arithmetic is faulty, and his mistakes are seldom in favour of the traveller. A habit too often prevails of presenting the bill at the last moment, when mistakes or wilful impositions must be submitted to, from want of time to investigate them. Those who intend starting early in the morning should therefore ask for their bills on the previous evening.

English travellers often impose considerable trouble by ordering things almost unknown in German usage; and if ignorance of the language be combined with want of conformity to the customs, misunderstandings and disputes too often ensue. The reader is therefore recommended to acquire if possible such a moderate proficiency in the language as to render him intelligible to the servants, and to endeavour to adapt his requirements to the habits of the country.

For this purpose *Baedeker's Manual of Conversation* will be found useful.

Valets-de-place generally charge 20 Sgr. or 1 florin for half a day, and 1—1½ Thlr. for a whole day.

Abbrevations.

R. = Room.	N. = North, northern, etc.
B. = Breakfast.	S. = South, etc.
D. = Dinner.	E. = East, etc.
A. = Attendance.	W. = West, etc.
L. = Light.	r. = right.
M. = English mile	l. = left.

ft. = English foot.

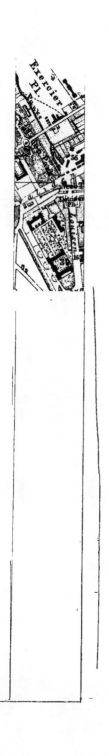

Key to the Plan of Berlin.

1. Chamber of Deputies . . . G. 4.
2. Academy of Art and Science F. 3.
3. Admiralty . . . . E. 5.
5. Anatomy . . . . E. 2.
6. Aquarium . . . . F. 3.
7. Artillery and Engineer School E. 3.

Rail. Stations.

8. Anhalt line . . . . E. 6.
9. Goerlitz . . . . . K. 6. 7.
10. Hamburg . . . D. E. 1. 2.
11. Hanover (Lehrte) . . D. 2.
12. Frankfort . . . . . K. 4.
13. Ostbahn . . . . . . L. 4.
14. Potsdam . . . . . E. 5.
15. Stettin . . . . . . F. 1.
16. Bank of Prussia . . . . G. 4.
17. Bau-Academic . . . . . G. 4.
18. Bellevue, château . . . C. 3.
19. Bethanien . . . . . . I. 6.
20. Library, Royal . . . F. G. 3. 4.
21. Blind Asylum . . . . . F. 6.
22. Exchange . . . . . . G. 3.
23. Borsig's Engine Factory
    and Hothouses . . A. B. 2. 3.
24. Botan. Garden, see Map
    of Environs.
25. Brandenburg Gate . . . E. 4.
26. Cadettenhaus . . . . . H. 3.

Barracks.

27. Artillery Guards F. G. 3, F. 2.
28. Cuirassier Guards . . G. 1.
29. Fusileer Guards . . . E. 1.
30. 1st Dragoon Guards . E. 7.
31. 2nd Dragoon Guards . F. 3.
32. Gardes du Corps . . F. 3.
33. 2nd Infantry Guards . F. 2.
34. Kaiiser Alexander Regt. H. 2.
35. Kaiser Franz Regt. H. 7. 8.
36. Pioneer Guards } K. L. 5. 6.
37. Garde Schützen }
38. 2nd Uhlan Guards . C. D.
39. Charité . . . . E.
40. Circus Renz . . . . . F.
41. Commander, resid. of the G. 2.

Monuments.

42. Frederick the Great . F. 3.
43. Fred. William III. . D. 4.
44. — —, equestr. statue. G. 3.
45. The Great Elector G. H. 3.
46. Generals of Fred. II. F. 4.
47. —, 1813—1815. . . . G. 3.
48. Beuth, Schinkel, Thaer G. 4.
49. Schiller . . . . . . F. 4.
50. Count Brandenburg . E. 5.
51. Obelisk on the Kreuzberg E. 8.
53. Warriors' Monument
    (1848—49) . . . . . E. 1.
54. Monument of Victory E. 2.
55. Column of Peace . . F. 6.
56. Iron Foundry, Royal . . E. 1.
57. Models of Fortresses . . L. 6.
58. Friedrich - Wilhelms - Hospital . . . . K. 3.
59. General Staff . . . . . D. 3.

Embassies.

60. France . . . . E. 3.
61. England . . . . . E. 5.
62. Italy . . . . E. 4.
63. Russia . . . . . . F. 3.
64. Industrial Academy . . H. 3.
65. Industrial Museum . . F. 3.
66. Hausvoigtei . . . . . G. 4.
67. Herrenhaus . . . . . E. 5.
69. Invalidenhaus . . . . E. 1.
70. Kammergericht . . . . G. 6.

Churches.

71. St. Andrew . . . . K. 5.
72. St. Bartholomew . . I. 2.
72a. Bohemian . . . . . F. 5.
73. Christ . . . . . . F. 6.
74. Cathedral . . . . . G. 3.
75. Dorotheenstadt . . . F. 3.
76. Trinity . . . . . . F. 4.
77. English . . . . . . G. 2.
78. French . . . . . . F. 4.
79. Garrison . . . . . . G. 3.
80. St. George . . . . . I. 3.

Key to the Plan of Berlin.

1. Chamber of Deputies . . G. 4.
2. Academy of Art and Science F. 3.
3. Admiralty . . . . E. 5.
5. Anatomy . . . . E. 2.
6. Aquarium . . . . . . F. 3.
7. Artillery and Engineer School E. 3.

Rail. Stations.

8. Anhalt line . . . . E. 6.
9. Goerlitz . . . K. 6. 7.
10. Hamburg . . . D. E. 1. 2.
11. Hanover (Lehrte) . . D. 2.
12. Frankfort . . . . . K. 4.
13. Ostbahn . . . . . L. 4.
14. Potsdam . . . . . E. 5.
15. Stettin . . . . . F. 1.
16. Bank of Prussia . . . . G. 4.
17. Bau-Academie . . . . G. 4.
18. Bellevue, château . . . C. 3.
19. Bethanien . . . . . I. 6.
20. Library, Royal . F. G. 3. 4.
21. Blind Asylum . . . . F. 6.
22. Exchange : . . . . G. 3.
23. Borsig's Engine Factory
    and Hothouses . . A. B. 2. 3.
24. Botan. Garden, see Map
    of Environs.
25. Brandenburg Gate . . . E. 4.
26. Cadettenhaus . . . . . H. 3.

Barracks.

27. Artillery Guards F. G. 3, F. 2.
28. Cuirassier Guards . . G. 1.
29. Fusileer Guards . . . E. 1.
30. 1st Dragoon Guards . E. 7.
31. 2nd Dragoon Guards . F. 3.
32. Gardes du Corps . . F. 3.
33. 2nd Infantry Guards . F. 2.
34. Kaiser Alexander Regt. H. 2.
35. Kaiser Franz Regt. H. 7. 8.
36. Pioneer Guards } K. L. 5. 6.
37. Garde Schützen }
38. 2nd Uhlan Guards . C. D. 2.
39. Charité . . . . . . E. 2.
40. Circus Renz . . . . F. 3.
41. Commander, resid. of the G. 3.

Monuments.

42. Frederick the Great . F. 3.
43. Fred. William III. . D. 4.
44. — —, equestr. statue. G. 3.
45. The Great Elector G. H. 3.
46. Generals of Fred. II. F. 4.
47. —, 1813—1815. . . . G. 3.
48. Beuth, Schinkel, Thaer G. 4.
49. Schiller . . . . . . F. 4.
50. Count Brandenburg . E. 5.
51. Obelisk on the Kreuzberg E. 8.
53. Warriors' Monument
    (1848—49) . . . . . E. 1.
54. Monument of Victory E. 2.
55. Column of Peace . . F. 6.
56. Iron Foundry, Royal . E. 1.
57. Models of Fortresses . L. 6.
58. Friedrich - Wilhelms - Hos-
    pital . . . . K. 3.
59. General Staff . . . . D. 3.

Embassies.

60. France . . . . E. 3.
61. England . . . . . E. 5.
62. Italy . . . . E. 4.
63. Russia . . . . . . F. 3.
64. Industrial Academy . . H. 3.
65. Industrial Museum . . F. 3.
66. Hausvoigtei . . . . G. 4.
67. Herrenhaus . . . . . E. 5.
69. Invalidenhaus . . . . E. 1.
70. Kammergericht . . . G. 6.

Churches.

71. St. Andrew . . . . K. 5.
72. St. Bartholomew . . I. 2.
72a. Bohemian . . . . . F. 5.
73. Christ . . . . . . F. 6.
74. Cathedral . . . . . G. 3.
75. Dorotheenstadt . . . F. 3.
76. Trinity . . . . . . F. 4.
77. English . . . . . . G. 2.
78. French . . . . . . F. 4.
79. Garrison . . . . . G. 3.
80. St. George . . . . . I. 3.

81.	St. Hedwig	G. 4.
82.	Holy Ghost. . . .	G. 3.
83.	St. James . . .	H. 5. 6.
84.	Jerusalem	G. 6.
85.	St. John	B. 2.
86.	St. John Evang. . .	F. 2.
87.	Klosterkirche. . . .	H. 2.
88.	Louisenkirche. . .	H. 5.
89.	St. Luke.	E. 5.
90.	St. Mark	K. 3.
91.	St. Mary	H. 3.
92.	St. Matthew . . .	D. 5.
93.	St. Michael . . .	I. 5.
94.	New Ch. . . .	F. 4.
94a.	St. Nicholas . .	H. 3.
95.	Parochial Ch. . .	H. 3.
96.	St. Peter	H. 4.
97.	Sophienkirche . .	G. 2.
98.	St. Thomas . . .	K. 5.
99.	Werder	G. 4.
100.	Zionskirche . .	G. 1.
101.	Königswache	G. 3.
102.	Hospital, Catholic . .	G. 2.
103.	Kreisgericht.	F. 5.
104.	Military Academy . .	G. 3.
107.	Picture Gallery of the Kunstfreunde	F. 3.
108.	Picture Gallery of the Berlin Artists' Union . . .	G. 6.
109.	Lagerhaus	H. 3.
110.	Agricult. Museum . .	D. 5.
111.	Royal Stables . .	G. H. 3. 4.

Govt. Offices.

112.	Foreign Affairs	E. 4, F. 4.
113.	Finances	G. 3.
114.	Religion and Education	E. F. 4.
115.	Commerce	F. 4.
116.	Royal Household .	E. 4.
117.	Interior	E. 3.
118.	Justice . . .	E. F. 4.
119.	War	E. F. 5.
120.	Agriculture . . .	G. 5.
121.	Navy	E. 4.
122.	Monbijou, château . .	G. 2.
123.	Mint, Royal	G. 4.
124.	Old Museum	G. 3.
125.	New Museum . . .	G. 3.

126.	National Gallery (new building)	G. 3.
127.	Packhof	G. 3.

Palaces.

128.	Emperor William .	F. 3.
129.	Crown-Prince . . .	G. 3.
150.	Prince Adalbert . .	F. 5.
131.	Prince Albert . . .	F. 5.
132.	Prince Alexander .	E. 4.
133.	Prince Charles . .	F. 4.
134.	Police Court	H. 4.
136.	Raczynski's Picture Gall.	E. 3.
137.	Rathhaus	H. 3.
138.	Rauch Museum . . .	H. 3.
139.	Ravené's Picture Gallery	H. 4.
141.	Imperial Diet . . .	E. 5.
142.	Palace, Royal	G. 3.
143.	Seehandlung	G. 4.
144.	Singing Academy . .	G. 3.
145.	Town Court	H. 3.
146.	Royal Printing Office . .	G. 5.
147.	Observatory, Royal .	F. G. 6.
148.	Synagogue, new . . .	G. 2.
149.	Telegraph Office . .	G. 4.
150.	Temple, Israelite . . .	F. 2.

Theatres.

151.	Opera House . . .	G. 3.
152.	Royal Theatre . .	F. 4.
153.	Friedrich - Wilhelmstadt	E. 2.
154.	Wallner	I. 4.
155.	Victoria	H. 2.
156.	Kroll	D. 3.
157.	Woltersdorff . . .	E. 1.
158.	Vorstädtisches. .	G. H. 1.
159.	Residenz	I. 3.
160.	Variété	G. 7.
161.	Louisenstadt . .	H. 5.
162.	Belle-Alliance . . .	F. 7.
163.	Tonhalle	F. 2.
164.	Walhalla	F. 5.
165.	Veterinary School . .	E. 2.
166.	Central Turn-Anstalt .	E. 1.
167.	University Buildings .	F. G. 3.
168.	Prison	D. 2.
169.	Arsenal, Royal . . .	G. 3.
170.	Zoological Garden . .	B. 5.

1. Berlin.

Arrival. A 'controleur' posted at the egress of each railway station hands the traveller a metal ticket with the number of a cab, which is then summoned. Drive from the station into the town, first class carriage 10 Sgr., second cl. 5 Sgr., and 2½ Sgr. in surplus; luggage not exceeding 100 lbs. 5 Sgr., smaller articles under 20 lbs. free (comp. p. 3).

Railway Stations. There are eight railway stations at Berlin. 1. *Anhalt Station*, close to the Anhalt Gate, for Dresden, Prague, Vienna, Leipsic, Halle, the Harz, Thuringia, and Frankfort on the Main. 2. *Potsdam Station* (Pl. 14), outside the Potsdam Gate, for Potsdam, Magdeburg, the Harz, and Brunswick. 3. *Stettin Station* (Pl. 15), outside the Oranienburg and Hamburg gates, for Neustadt-Eberswalde, Freienwalde, Stettin, Stralsund, E. Pomerania, and Dantsic. 4. *Frankfort Station* (Pl. 12), in the Breslauer Strasse, for Frankfort on the Oder, Posen, Breslau, and Vienna. 5. *Ostbahnhof* (Pl. 13), or *E. Station*, adjoining the last, for Cüstrin, Dantsic, and Königsberg. 6. *Hamburg Station* (Pl. 10), outside the Neue Thor, for Hamburg, Mecklenburg, and Holstein. 7. *Görlitz Station* (Pl. 9), in the Köpnickerfeld, for Cottbus, Görlitz, and the Giant Mts. 8. *Lehrte*, or *Hanoverian Station* (Pl. 11), near the Alsenbrücke, for Hanover, Cologne, and Bremen.

Hotels. Those in or near the Linden are best situated for ordinary travellers, and the most expensive: R. from 25 Sgr. to 3 Thlr. and upwards, B. 10, L. and A. 15—20 Sgr., D. at 3 or 4 o'clock 25 Sgr.—1 Thlr. — On the *S. Side:* *Hôtel Royal, Linden 3, at the corner of the Wilhelms-Str., not far from the Brandenburg Gate, patronised by the nobility and diplomatists; Métropole, Linden 20; St. Petersburg, Linden 31; *Meinhardt's, Linden 32, at the corner of the Charlotten-Str.; *Hôtel du Nord, Linden 35, good table d'hôte. *N. Side:* Hôtel de Rome, Linden 39, at the corner of the Charlotten-Str., the largest hotel in Berlin; with handsome dining-room, baths, and restaurant; Arnim's, Linden 44; Victoria, Linden 46, at the corner of the Friedrichs-Str.; *British Hotel, Linden 56. In the *Schinkel-Platz*, between the Schlossbrücke and the Bau-Academic, admirably situated, *Hôtel d'Angleterre; Hôtel de Russie.

The following are somewhat less expensive: Linden-Hôtel, Neustädtische Kirch-Str. 9, at the corner of the Linden; Hohenzollern, Behren-Str. 19; Windsor, Behren-Str. 14; Schmelzer's, Jäger-Str. 13; Markgraf's, Tauben-Str. 16; Hôtel de la Paix, corner of Friedrichs-Str. and Tauben-Str. 12, 13; *Magdeburg, Mohren-Str. 11; Norddeutscher Hof, Mohren-Str. 20; Brandenburg, Charlotten-Str. 59; Schiller-Platz; Bellevue, Mohren-Str. 64, at the corner of the Kanonier-Str.; Scheible's, Markgrafen-Str. 49, Schiller-Platz; *Rheinischer Hof, Friedrichs-Str. 59, at the corner of the Leipziger Str.; *Hotel de France, Leipziger Str. 56, at the corner of the Charlotten-Str.; Kisskalt's London Hotel, Jerusalemer Str. 36, Dönhofs-Platz; Wenzel's Dresden Hotel, Friedrichs-Str. 56, near the Leipziger Str.; Zernikow's, Charlotten-Str. 43, near the Linden.

The following hotels are farther distant from the chief objects of attraction: Töpfer's, Carls-Str. 39, in the medical quarter; Hôtel de Paris, Friedrichs-Str. 137, near the Weidendamm Bridge; *Rother Adlee, Kur-Str. 38, at the corner of the Old Leipziger Str.; *Happold's, Alte Grün-Str. 1; Weissberg's, Dessauer-Str. 38; *Thiergarten, Bellevue-Str. 1, both near the Potsdam Station; Westend, Königgrätzer Str., near the Thiergarten, and not far from the Potsdam and Anhalt Stations.

On the *Right Bank of the Spree*, in the old town (p. 36), the principal business locality: König von Portugal, Burg-Str. 12; *Hôtel de Saxe, Burg-Str. 20 (both on the Spree, opposite the E. side of the palace, and well situated for ordinary travellers); *Stadt Hamburg, Heiligegeist-Str. 18; Deutsches Haus, Kloster-Str. 89; Grossfürst Alexander, Neue Friedrichs-Str. 57; Frankfort, Kloster-Str. 45.

Hotels Garnis. *Schlosser's, Jäger-Str. 17, at the corner of the Friedrichs-Str., a respectable, old established house; Albrecht's, Friedrichs-Str. 72, near the Tauben-Str.; Köhler, Mohren-Str. 37; Gutike, Mohren-Str. 33, recommended to ladies; Frohwerk, Markgrafen-Str. 39; Schulz, Markgrafen-Str. 65; *Dunsing, Jerusalemer-Str. 19; Senior's, Markgrafen-Str. 51; Schmidt's, Karls-Str. 19, near the Hamburg and Stettin Stations; Bartikow, Leipziger Platz 1a, near the Potsdam Station; Frederich's, Potsdamer Str. 12; Bellevue, Mohren-Str. 64; Wieland, Kronen-Str. 51; Negendanck's, Jerusalemer Str. 28; Hohenstein's, Neue Wilhelms-Str. 10; Witt's, Schadow-Str. 2, near the Linden; Böttcher's, Burg-Str. 11; Aschbach's, Heiligegeist-Str. 30; Grüner Baum, Krausen-Str. 56, well situated, moderate. The charges in these houses are somewhat lower than at the regular hotels, and the traveller is more independent with regard to meals. — *Furnished Apartments* may also be procured on reasonable terms in the most convenient quarter of the town, between the Dorotheen and Koch-Strasse.

Dining Rooms. The best are generally styled '*Restaurants*', the less pretending '*Cafés*', while the '*Conditoreien*', or confectioners' shops, are more nearly allied to the coffee-houses of other towns. There are also wine-houses, 'Keller', or luncheon-rooms, and beer-houses innumerable. A few of the best of these various places of refreshment are here enumerated. — **Restaurants.** *Hiller, Linden 62—63, N. side, between the Schadow-Str. and the Neustädter Kirch-Str.; *Borchardt, Französische Str. 48, N. side, near the Friedrichs-Str.; *Ewest, Behren-Str. 26a, S. side, at the corner of the Friedrichs-Str.; *Müller, Linden 4a, near the Wilhelms-Str.; *Europe, Linden 27; *Hôtel Royal, Linden 3; *Hôtel de Rome, Linden 39. These are all first rate, with corresponding charges, and may be visited by ladies. — *Café Zennig, Linden 13, S. side; *Restaurant du Nord, Linden 16, S. side; *Beyer, Jäger-Str. 19, near the Charlotten-Str.; *Bellevue, Bellevue-Str. 1, outside the Potsdam Gate; *Klette, Karls-Str. 27 (all these have open-air dining-rooms); *Theatre Tavern*, Charlotten-Str. 58; Lantzsch, Charlotten-Str. 56 (both near the theatre); Senior, Markgrafen-Str. 51; Deininger, Leipziger-Str. 14; *Kunert, Stechbahn 2, in the 'Rothe Schloss' in the Schloss-Platz. A dinner of four or five courses may be procured at most of these houses for 15 Sgr. at any hour between 1 and 5 o'clock. Beer 2—3 Sgr. per glass, and various kinds of wine. The waiters at the superior restaurants expect a gratuity of 2—3 Sgr. from each person, but less in the others. — A tolerable dinner may be obtained for 10—12 Sgr. at the following houses from 1 to 5 o'clock: *Leipziger Garten*, Leipziger Str. 132; Schmelzer, Dessauer Str. 3, outside the Potsdam Gate; Donny, Krausen-Str. 36, Dönhofs-Platz; Casteeli, Louisen-Str. 34 (these four with gardens); Matz, Leipziger Str. 44; Penkow, Königs-Str. 61. — **Wine Houses**, with dining-rooms: Gerold, Linden 34; Häbel, Linden 30; Wittkopp, Kleine Mauer-Str. 1, between the Linden and the Behren-Str.; Lutter, Charlotten-Str. 49, D. 15 Sgr.; Trarbach, Markgrafen-Str. 48, Schiller-Platz, D. 8 Sgr.; Rähmel, Markgrafen-Str. 45, good red wines; Ilges, Jäger-Str. 52, D. 7½ Sgr.; Haussmann, Jäger-Str. 63a; Dedel, Leipziger Str. 85, opposite the Concerthaus; Beckerath, Leipziger Str. 91; Rubin, Charlotten-Str. 65a; *Kühn, Werderscher Markt 4, D. 10 Sgr., separate room for ladies. — In the Altstadt, Mitscher and Caspary, Königs-Str. 40; Mundt, Königs-Str. 31.

Luncheon Rooms. The *Rathskeller (p. 37), a vast establishment occupying the whole width (100 yds.) of the façade of the Rathhaus towards the Königs-Str., is well worthy of a visit. *Buder, Königs-Str. 1; *Deicke, Königs-Str. 11; Heumann, Jäger-Str. 56; *Höhn's Keller, Markgrafen-Str. 43; Jerusalemer Keller, Jerusalemer Str. 21 (good Hungarian wines); Capkeller, Linden 46, entrance in the Friedrichs-Str.; Niquet, Leipziger Str. 13. —

Genuine imported beer (2¹|₂—3 Sgr. per glass) is a specialty of the following restaurants: *Wagner*, Charlotten-Str. 48; *Lantzsch*, Charlotten-Str. 56; *Olbrich*, Friedrichs-Str. 83, near the Linden; *Dames*, Alexander-Str. 47. — Beer Houses ('Seidel' 1¹|₂, 'Tulpe' 1 Sgr.): *Siechen*, Burg-Str. 7; *Busch*, Spandauer Str. 27, opposite the Rathhaus; *Donny*, Krausen-Str. 36, Dönhofs-Platz; *Gratweil*, Commandanten-Str. 79, a spacious establishment, with numerous billiard-tables; *Becker*, Commandanten-Str. 62; *Jost*, Neue Ross-Str. 13; *Niquet*, Jäger-Str. 41; *Töpfer*, Dorotheen-Str. 85; *Café Suisse*, Dorotheen-Str. 84; *Gärtner*, Dorotheen-Str. 66 (the three last not far from the Linden); *Friedrichs-Garten*, Friedrichs-Str. 229; *Beyer*, Friedrichs-Str. 231; *Kursch*, with garden, Potsdamer-Str. 21. To the N. of the Linden: *Admirals-Garten*, Friedrichs-Str. 103; *Münchener Brauhaus*, with garden, Johannis-Str. 13. — Breweries outside the gates, most of them with spacious saloons and gardens: *Tivoli* on the Kreuzberg (p. 33), military band on Sundays and Wednesdays; *Bockbrauerei* (brewery of 'bock', or strong beer, usually drunk in spring), next to the Tivoli. Towards the N., outside the Oranienburg Gate: *Eiskeller*, Chaussee-Str. 75; *Norddeutsche Brauerei*, Chaussee-Str. 54; *Königsstadt*, Schönhauser Allee 11, 12; *Friedrichshain*; outside the Königsthor; *Friedrichshöhe* and *Böhmisches Brauhaus*, both outside the Landsberg Gate. — The insipid 'Weissbier', once the favourite beverage of the Berliners, is now almost entirely out of vogue. It is sold by *Haase*, Französische Str. 22; *Pupke*, Jerusalemer Str. 8; *Clausing*, Zimmer-Str. 80, etc.

Confectioners (cup of coffee 2¹|₂, chocolate 3—4, ices 5 Sgr.): *Kranzler*, Linden 25, S. side, corner of the Friedrichs-Str.; *Spargnapani*, Linden 50, N. side, to the W. of the Friedrichs-Str.; *Stehely*, Charlotten-Str. 53, Schiller-Platz, well supplied with newspapers; *Josty*, Schlossfreiheit 8; *D'Heureuse*, Kölner Fischmarkt 4 (excellent chocolate); *Schilling*, Koch-Str. 64; *Weiss*, Jäger-Str. 38 (chiefly patronised by ladies); *Hillbrich*, at the corner of the Leipziger and Wilhelms-Str.; *Hofmann*, Bellevue-Str. 21, outside the Potsdam Gate; *Wenghöfer*, Potsdamer Str. 14. — Trinkhallen in various parts of the town, where Seltzer and Soda-water (¹|₂ Sgr., with raspberry or other essence 1 Sgr.) are sold in summer, and tea, etc. in winter.

Cabs. '*First Class*', of a superior build (cabmen wearing white braid), are to be found at a limited number of stands only (Bau-Academie-Platz, Charlotten-Str. 45, corner of the Linden; Universitäts-Str., by the Academy; Pariser Platz; Behren-Str. 1, corner of the Wilhelms-Str.; Ziethen-Platz; Potsdamer Platz, etc.): per drive not exceeding 15 min. (2600 yds.) 1—2 pers. 10, 3—4 pers. 15 Sgr.; for each additional 15 min., without respect to the number of persons 5 Sgr. — '*Second Class*': per drive of 15 min. 1—2 pers. 5, 3—4 pers. 7¹|₂ Sgr.; for each additional 10 min., without respect to the number of persons, 2¹|₂ Sgr. — The tariff applies to drives within the precincts of the city only; longer drives according to bargain. From the railway-stations into the town, or if the carriage be ordered to the theatre, 2¹|₂ Sgr. in surplus are paid. To Charlottenburg, 1st class, 1—2 pers. 15, 3—4 pers. 25, 2nd cl. 10 or 15 Sgr.; Westend 1st cl. 22¹|₂ or 32¹|₂, 2nd cl. 15 or 20 Sgr.; Tegel 1st cl. 30 or 40, 2nd cl. 20 or 25 Sgr. Between 11 p. m. and 6 (in winter 7) a. m. double fares. — Private carriages may be hired at 4 Thlr. a day, or 2 Thlr. per half-day, gratuity 10—15 Sgr.; the best are to be had at the hotels, but at higher charges.

Omnibuses (inside 2, outside 1 Sgr.) traverse the town in every direction at intervals of 5—10 min.; thus from the *Kreuzberg* (Pl. E, 8) through the whole of the Friedrichs-Str. to the *Wedding*, the extreme N. end of the city; from the *Spittel-Markt* (Pl. G, 4) through the Leipziger and Potsdamer Str. to *Schöneberg* (botanical gardens); from the *Lützow-Str.* (Pl. D, 6), at the corner of the Potsdamer Str., through the Leipziger Str. and Gertrauden-Str. to the *Molken-Markt* (Pl. H, 4), where the line divides into three: (1st) to the *Frankfurter Str.* (Pl. K, 3), (2nd) to the *Frankfort Railway* (Pl. K, 4), (3rd) to the *Ostbahn*, or *E. Railway* (Pl. L, 4); then from the *Liesen-Str.* (Pl. E, 1) through the Friedrichs-Str., Schiller-Platz, and Dönhofs-Platz to the *Oranien-Platz* (Pl. I, 6), etc.

Tramway to *Charlottenburg* and *Westend*, (p. 44). A car starts every 10 min. from the Kupfergraben, traversing the Dorotheen-Str., passing the

1*

Brandenburger Thor, and skirting the Thiergarten. Fare for the whole
distance 2½ Sgr. On Sundays the Brandenburger Thor is the point of
departure. Other lines are projected. — Travellers desirous of proceeding
from one of the railway stations to any of the others may now avail themselves of the connecting railway.

Steamboats on the Spree: from the Jannowitz-Bridge (Pl. I, 4) to the
Upper Spree (*Stralau*, *Treptow*, *Eierhäuschen*, *Neuer Krug*, *Sedan*, *Sadowa*,
Köpenick, *Grünau*) every half hour. Generally crowded on Sundays and
in fine weather. Excursionists should avoid delaying their return till the
last boat.

Post-Office. *General Post Office* (Pl. 135), with telegraph station, in
the Königs-Strasse, No. 60, and Spandauer Str. 19, 20. Enquiries in cases
of doubt should be addressed to the porter (3rd door to the l. in the principal entrance from the Königs-Str.). *Poste Restante*, door No. 1 in the
first court. *Money Orders*, door No. 42, opposite. *Letter Boxes* in many
different streets. Letters, books, and parcels are received, and money
orders issued, at all of the 50 branch offices (e. g. Neustädtische Kirch-
Str. 8, close to the Linden; at the 'passage', p. 11, Behren-Str. 52; Behren-
Str. 5, etc. The offices are open from 7 (in winter from 8) a. m. to 8 p. m.;
closed on Sundays and holidays from 9 to 5 o'clock.

Telegraph Offices. Central office, Französische Str. 33c. (Pl. 149;
p. 35), open day and night, and 17 branch offices (e. g. at the Exchange,
at the Potsdam, Brandenburg, and Oranienburg gates), open from 7 or 8
a. m. to 9 p. m. : Telegram within the city 2½ Sgr.

Baths. *Hôtel de Rome*, see p. 1; *Wilhelmsbad* (with Turkish and
vapour baths), Schützen-Str. 18, 19; *Freundliche Bäder* (with vapour baths),
Neue Wilhelms-Str. 2; *Mariannenbad* (with vapour baths), Neue Friedrichs-
Str. 18, 19; *Weidendammer Bad* (with vapour baths), Friedrichs-Str. 136,
near the Weidendammer Brücke; *Ascanisches Bad* (with Turkish and
vapour baths), Königgrätzer Str. 19, near the Potsdam Gate; *Victoria Bad*
(with vapour baths), Neuenburger Str. 15, etc. — Public washing and
bathing establishments (also private baths): Schillingsgasse 7a, August-
Str. 21, etc.

River Baths in the Spree for swimmers at the *Oberbaum* (Pl. L, 5, 6),
outside the Schlesische Thor, and at the Unterbarm (Pl. D, 3), beyond
the old exercising ground. The water at the former, being above the
town, is cleaner. These baths are conveniently reached by steamboat.
River plunge-baths at the Moabiter Brücke. *Winter Swimming Bath* (basin
400 sq. yds. in area) of *Dombernowsky*, Neue Friedrichs-Str. 24, near the
Königs-Str.

Shops. The best are in the Linden, the Leipziger Str., and the Friedrichs, Charlotten, and Markgrafen-Str., between the Linden and the Leipziger Str., in the Oberwall and Jerusalemer-Str., the Hausvoigtei-Platz,
the Werder'sche Markt, the Schlossfreiheit, the Schlors-Platz, the Brüder,
Breiten, and Königs-Str. Less expensive in the Spittel-Markt, the Wall,
and Gertrauden-Strasse. A few of the most noted firms are here enumerated. *Haberdashers:* Gerson, Werder'scher Markt 5; Heese, Alte Leipziger
Str. 1; Bonnwitt & Littauer, Behren-Str. 26a, corner of the Friedrichs-
Str.; Hertzog, Breite-Str. 15; Sy, Jäger-Str. 40. *Silk Mercers:* Baudouin & Co.,
Breite-Str. 3; Lissauer, Jäger-Str. 24. *Drapers:* Goschenhofer & Rösicke,
Leipziger Str. 58; Mezner, Mohren-Str. 32; Israel, Spandauer Str. 28 (less
expensive). *Millinery:* Manheimer, Oberwall-Str. 6; Oppenheim Söhne,
Jerusalemer Str. 20; Selchow, Hausvogtei-Platz 11. *Shawls:* Caspersohn,
Bau-Academie 1, 2; Schröder, Jerusalemer Str. 29. *Lace:* Briet, Jäger-
Str. 28; Bluth, Friedrichs-Str. 176. *Gloves:* Lehmann, Schloss-Platz 14, 15;
Lange, Jerusalemer Str. 32. *Ladies' Bonnets:* Stegemann, Jäger-Str. 27.
Childrens' Clothing: Schlüter, Jäger-Str. 43. *Tailors:* Fasskessel & Münt-
mann, Linden 13; Wilcke, Brüder-Str. 39; Lassalle & Zürcher, Behren-
Str. 57; Eckardt & Son, Krausen-Str. 69, respectable and reasonable.
Hatters: Vassel & Co., Friedrichs-Str. 180; Kaumann, Mohren-Str. 20;
Müller, Friedrichs-Str. 56. *Travelling Requisites:* Ackermann, Königs-
Str. 12; Demuth, Schlossfreiheit 1; Wittig, Linden 27. *Umbrellas:* Prös-
tel & Richter, Leipziger Str. 39; Stegmann, Scharren-Str. 8. *Leather Wares:*

Ackermann, Königs-Str. 62a; Goldschmidt, Linden 58; Mossner, Leipziger Str. 10. *Jewellers:* Friedeberg Sons, Linden 42; Haller & Rathenau, Linden 34; Wagner & Son, Linden 30. *Electro-Plate:* Jürst & Co., Linden 45; Henniger & Co., Stechbahn 2 and Leipziger Str. 103, corner of the Friedrichs-Str. *Bronzes* and *Lamps:* Névir, Linden 14; Rakenius & Co., Linden 62, 63; Berlin Lamp & Bronze Manufactory, Linden 28 and Königs-Str. 55. *Glass* and *China:* Royal Porcelain Manufactory, Friedrichs-Str. 194, corner of the Leipziger Str.; Harsch & Co., Linden 66; Hengstmann, Bau-Academie 6—8; Lange, Jäger-Str. 26. *Marble Wares:* Micheli, Linden 12; Barheine, Jäger-Str. 61a. *Amber Wares:* Hirsch, Linden 26. *Works of Art:* Sachse & Co., Jäger-Str. 29; Lepke, Linden 4a; Amsler & Ruthard, Charlotten-Str. 48, entrance in the Behren-Str.; Schröder, Linden 41. *Bonbons:* Hildebrandt & Son, Friedrichs-Str. 62, corner of the Kronen-St.; Schulz, Linden 19. *Chocolate:* Jordan & Timæus, Friedrichs-Str. 177, branch of a Dresden firm; Gross, Leipziger Str. 23. *Perfumers:* Treu and Nuglisch, Jäger-Str. 33. *Cigars:* Gerold, Linden 24; Gladebeck & Co., Linden 17; Rennert, Linden 54, 55; Weil, Kronen-Str. 44; Schleh, Linden 47 and Leipziger Str. 29.

    Classical Music. *Singacademie* (p. 14); rehearsals on Tuesdays 5—7 p. m., to which visitors are admitted on application to the director Professor Grell (at the building itself). *Stern's Gesangverein* is another musical society of a high class. The *'Symphony Soirées'* are a series of concerts given in winter by the band of the Royal Opera in the concert-room of the opera-house. The performances of these different institutions are unsurpassed in any European capital, and no other branch of art has attained to such high perfection at Berlin. — **Bilse's* admirable orchestra plays daily in winter in the concert-room of the Kaiser-Gallerie (p. 1; 10 Sgr.). *Gungl's* and *Wüerst's* concerts at the Concerthaus, Leipziger-Str. 48 (5 Sgr.). The *Berliner Symphonie-Capelle* plays at different places which are ascertained from the advertisements (5 Sgr., 4—5 tickets at a reduced rate).

    Theatres. There are twenty-five theatres at Berlin (plans may be consulted in the Berlin 'Adressbuch', or Directory), of which the following are the most important:

    1. *Royal Opera House* (Pl. 151) for operas, ballets, and a few of the most celebrated dramas (Faust, Tell, Maid of Orleans). Average charges: best boxes 2 Thlr. 20 Sgr., proscenium by the orchestra 2 Thlr.; 1st balcony and front box-seats 1 Thlr. 25 Sgr.; parquet and parquet boxes (the latter not recommended) 1 Thlr. 15 Sgr.; proscenium, 2nd row, 1 Thlr. 10 Sgr.; upper boxes 25 Sgr., pit 15, gallery 10 Sgr. — Admission higher when some of the greater operas are to be performed.

    2. *Royal Theatre* (Schauspielhaus, Pl. 152), for tragedies, classical and modern dramas (Shakspeare, Schiller, Goethe): best boxes 1 Thlr. 25 Sgr.; proscenium by the orchestra, balcony, or upper boxes 1 Thlr. 10 Sgr.; parquet boxes or parquet 1 Thlr.; pit boxes 22½ Sgr.; 2nd balcony and 2nd boxes 20 Sgr., pit 15, gallery 7½ Sgr.

    Tickets for the opera and theatre are issued on week-days from 10. 30 to 1, on Sundays from 11 to 1. 30 o'clock, for the performance of the same day only. Strangers who are desirous of securing good places should purchase some of the *'Meldekarten'*, or printed forms of application sold by the stationers and music-dealers, write on one of them the number and situation of the seats required, and put it into the box provided for the purpose at the opera-house between 10 and 11 a. m. on the day before the performance. The directors attend to these applications as far as possible, and the tickets bespoken may generally be obtained on the following morning between 9 and 10 (Sundays and holidays between 8 and 9) o'clock, 5 Sgr. extra being paid for each seat. When very popular pieces are about to be performed, a great number of the tickets are purchased by speculators, from whom they can only be obtained at exorbitant prices. In such cases the porter of the traveller's hotel will often be found useful in preventing extortion. The court theatres are closed for one or two months in summer.

    3. *Friedrich-Wilhelmstadt Theatre* (Pl. 153), for comic operas, comedies,

and farces: best boxes 1 Thlr. 20 Sgr.; orchestra boxes 1 Thlr. 10 Sgr.,
1st row of balcony 25 Sgr., parquet 20. There is a 'winter' and also a
'summer' theatre. Admission varies according to the piece to be performed.

4. *Wallner's Theatre* (Pl. 154) for comedies and popular farces: best
boxes 1 Thlr. 10 Sgr., front seats of the other boxes 25 Sgr., parquet 20
Sgr. On Sundays, the principal day of recreation in most parts of the
continent, the tickets are often bought up by speculators and resold by
them at double the above charges.

5. *Victoria Theatre* (Pl. 155), Münz-Str. 20, comprising a winter and
summer theatre, handsomely fitted up, for operas, dramas, farces, etc.:
best boxes in the winter theatre 1 Thlr. 20, front seats 1 Thlr., parquet
20 Sgr.; summer theatre 1 Thlr. 15, 1 Thlr., and 20 Sgr.

6. *Kroll's Theatre*, see below.

7. *Woltersdorff Theatre* (Pl. 157), Chaussee-Str. 27, outside the Oranienburg Gate, for popular farces, parquet 10, pit 5 Sgr.

8. *Vorstädtisches Theater* (Pl. 158), chiefly frequented by the lower
classes.

9. *Residenz-Theater*, Blumen-Str. 9.

10. *National Theatre*, Weinbergsweg 6, 7.

11. *Théâtre Variété* (Pl. 160), to the l. outside the Halle Gate, for
farces and scenes in the café chantant style, admission 3 Sgr. (suitable for
gentlemen only). A great number of small theatres in the same style have
sprung up of late (*Walhalla, Belle-Alliance*, etc.).

Circus, Friedrichs-Str. 141a., to the N. of the Linden, generally occupied by Renz's company: boxes 1 Thlr., parquet 20 Sgr.

Popular Resorts, most of them in the Thiergarten (p. 42): *Kroll*
(Pl. 156), a vast establishment handsomely fitted up, the principal hall
125 yds. in length, 33 yds. in width; good concert and a theatre every
evening. Admission to the garden and theatre 7½ Sgr., seats 15 Sgr. —
The *Zelte*, especially that of *Ley*, to the W. of Kroll, are also much
visited. — The breweries outside the gates attract many visitors (see p. 3).
There are also numerous ball-rooms of more or less dubious reputation.
The handsomest of these is the *Orpheum*, Alte Jacob-Str. 32, near the
Oranien-Str.

Collections, Galleries, etc.

Academies of Science and Art, see p. 12.

Academy, Industrial (p. 37): collection of models Thurs., Sat. 10—12;
technological collection Tuesd., Frid. 10—12.

**Aquarium* (p. 11), daily from 9 a. m. till dusk, on Wed. and Sat.
evenings lighted with gas till 9 p. m., 10 Sgr., Sund. afternoon 5 Sgr.;
catalogue 5 Sgr.

**Arsenal* (p. 15), Wed., Sat. 2—4.

Bethanien (p. 36), strangers admitted daily 10—4; box at the entrance
for contributions.

Börse, or *Exchange* (p. 38), daily 12—2.

Borsig's Palm and Hot-houses at Moabit (p. 40), Tues., Frid. by card
(5 Sgr.) obtained at the office of the manufactory.

**Botanical Garden* (p. 33), daily (except Sat., Sund., and holidays)
8—12 and 2—7. Omnibus, see p. 3.

Cemeteries: Dorotheenstadt, p. 40; Dreifaltigkeit, old and new, p. 33;
French, p. 40; Hedwig's, or Rom. Cath., p. 40; Jerusalem, p. 33; In-
valid, p. 41; St. Matthew, p. 34.

Chamber of the Deputies (p. 35): cards of admission to the meetings
are issued on the previous evenings, 5—7 o'clock, in the room No. 14 on
the ground-floor.

Charité (p. 40), daily 1—4.

Charlottenburg (Mausoleum, p. 44), daily, gratuity at discretion.

Churches: St. Andrew, p. 38; St. Bartholomew, p. 38; Cathedral,
p. 17; Cathedral, German, p. 31; Dorotheenstadt, p. 11; French, p. 31;
Garrison, p. 38; Hedwig's, p. 14; St. James, p. 36; St. John, p. 41;
Kloster, p. 37; St. Luke, p. 33; St. Mark, p. 38; St. Mary, p. 36;
St. Matthew, p. 33; St. Michael, p. 36; Neue Kirche, p. 31; St. Nicholas,

p. 36; Parish, p. 37; *St. Peter, p. 35; *Schlosskirche, p. 17; St. Thomas, p. 36; *Werder, p. 34; Zion, p. 38.

Iron Foundry, Royal (p. 40), daily (except Sund.) 5 Sgr.

Library, Royal (p. 14), daily (except Sund.) 9—4; shown to strangers at 10 a. m.

Library, University (p. 14), daily (except Sat. and Sund.) 2—4.

Mint, Royal (p. 34). The machinery is shown on Tues. and Frid. on application.

Museums. Agricultural (p. 33), Tues., Thurs., Sat. 10—3. — *Anatomical* (p. 13), Wed. and Sat. 2—4, on previous application only. — *Beuth-Schinkel* (p. 34), Tues., Frid. 11—1. — *Christian* (p. 14), Wed. 12—1. — *Historical*, at *Schloss Monbijou* (p. 39) daily 10—5, in winter till dusk. — *Industrial* (p. 40), daily (except Mond.) 10—2, admission on Tues. 5, Sat. and Sund. 1½, Wed., Thurs., Frid. 2½ Sgr. — *Minerals* (p. 13). Wed., Sat. 12—2. — *Ores and Metals* (p. 40), Tues., Thurs., Sat. 8—3, Sund. 12—3. — *Rauch* (p. 37), daily (except Sund., holidays, and the last Sat. of each month) 10—3. — *Royal* (p. 17), daily (except Mond. and the principal festivals), in winter 10—3, in summer 10—4, Sund. (generally crowded) 12—2. Attendants forbidden to accept gratuities. Sticks and umbrellas must be left at the door. — *Weapons*, in the *Palace of Prince Charles* (p. 32) daily 10—5, on application to the Haushofmeister, Wilhelms-Platz 8. — *Zoological* (p. 13), Tues., Thurs. 12—2.

Observatory (p. 33), Wed., Sat. 9—11 a. m.; evening visitors admitted on written application only.

Palaces. *Royal Palace*, or *Schloss* (p. 16), daily 10—4, in winter 12—2, admission 5 Sgr., devoted to a charitable object. The castellan lives in the E. court, to the l. on the ground-floor. — *Palace of the Emperor* (p. 12) shown during the absence of the emperor only, on application to the Haushofmeister. — *Palace of the Crown Prince* (p. 15) shown during the absence of the family, on application to the castellan. — *Palace of Prince Charles*, see above (collection of weapons).

Picture Galleries (public). Pictures in the *Academy*, see National-Gallery, below. — *Berliner Künstler-Verein* (p. 35), daily 10—4, Sund. and festivals 11—3, admission 5 Sgr. — *Kunstfreunde* (p. 11), daily 12—2. — *National Gallery of Modern Pictures* (p. 14), daily (except on high festivals) 11—2; catalogue by Prof. Waagen 5 Sgr. — *Sachse's*, Jäger-Str. 30, modern pictures, 10—4, Sund. and festivals 11—1, admission 5 Sgr.

Picture Galleries (private): *Count Blankensee's*, Linden 70, daily 12—2, by special permission only (222 old masters of different schools). — *Count Raczynski's* (p. 42) daily 11—3; catalogue 7½ Sgr., for the benefit of the attendant. — *Ravené's* (p. 35) Tues., Frid. 11—2. — *Count Redern's* (p. 11) daily 3—5, on previous application.

Potsdam (p. 45). The fountains of Sanssouci usually play on Sundays in summer from noon till dusk; on Thursday afternoons the great fountain only.

Prison (p. 41) daily 3—6, by special permission of the director.

Rathhaus (p. 36) daily (except Thurs. and Frid.) 11—4 gratis, ascent of the tower 5 Sgr.

Reichstag Building (p. 32), or Hall of the Imperial Diet, may be inspected daily, except when the Diet is sitting. Cards of admission to the meetings are obtained at the office to the l. in the inner court on the previous evening, 5—7 o'clock. Early application recommended.

Sanssouci, see Potsdam, above.

Synagogue, New (p. 39), daily.

Temple, Israelite, see p. 39.

Zoological Garden (p. 43) daily, 10 Sgr., Sund. 5 Sgr.

Diary (fuller particulars, see above; consult also the daily newspapers):

Daily. *Royal Museum* (p. 17; Mond. and high festivals excepted) 10—3 or 10—4, Sund. 12—2. — *National Gallery of Modern Pictures* (p. 14; high festivals excepted) 11—2. — *Royal Palace* (p. 16) 10—4, in winter 12—2. — *Historical Collection* (p. 39) 10—5. — *Royal Library* (p. 14; Sund. and festivals excepted) 10 a. m. — *Industrial Museum* (p. 40; Mond. excepted) 10—12. — *Rauch Museum* (p. 37; Sund. and festivals excepted)

10—3. — *Raczynski's Picture Gallery* (p. 42) 11—3. — *Exhibition of the Berliner Künstler* (p. 35) 10—4, Sund. and festivals 11—3. — *Exhibition of the Kunstfreunde* (p. 11) 12—2. — *Borsig's Engine Factory* (p. 40; Sund. and festivals excepted) 12—2. — *Collection of Weapons* of Prince Charles (p. 32) 10—5. — *Aquarium* (p. 11) from 9 till dusk. — *Zoological Garden* (p. 43) 9 till dusk. — *Botanical Garden* (p. 33) 8—12 and 2—7. — *Mausoleum* at Charlottenburg (p. 44) daily till dusk. —: *Palaces* of the *Emperor* (p. 12) and *Crown Prince* (p. 15) shown during their absence only. — *Reichstag Building* (p. 32), except during the sitting of the Diet. — *New Synagogue* (p. 39).

Sundays. *Sanssouci* (p. 47); fountains from 12 till dusk. — *Rathhaus* (p. 36) 11—4. — *Museum of Ores and Metals* (p. 40) 8—3.

Mondays. *Rathhaus* (p. 36) 11—4. — *Models of Fortresses* (p. 36) 9—2. — Royal Museum closed.

Tuesdays. *Beuth-Schinkel Museum* (p. 34) 11—1. — *Ravené's Picture Gallery* (p. 35) 11—2. — *Borsig's Hothouses* (p. 40) till dusk. — *Industrial Academy*, technological collections (p. 37) 10—12. — *Agricultural Museum* (p. 33) 10—3. — *Museum of Ores and Metals* (p. 40) 8—3. — *Zoological Museum* (p. 13) 12—2. — *Rathhaus* (p. 36) 11—4. — *Royal Mint* (p. 34) on previous application.

Wednesdays. *Observatory* (p. 33) 9—11. — *Christian Museum* (p. 14) 12—1. — *Cabinet of Minerals* (p. 13) 12—2. — *Arsenal* (p. 15) 2—4. — *Rathhaus* (p. 36) 11—4. — *Aquarium* (p. 15) by gas-light from dusk to 9 p. m.

Thursdays. *Sanssouci* (p. 47), great fountain in the afternoon. — *Museum of Ores and Metals* (p. 40) 8—3. — *Models of Fortresses* (p. 36) 10—12. — *Agricultural Museum* (p. 33) 10—3.

Fridays. *Beuth-Schinkel Museum* (p. 35) 11—1. — *Ravené's Picture Gallery* (p. 35) 11—2. — *Borsig's Hot-houses* (p. 40) till dusk. — *Industrial Academy*, technological collections (p. 37) 10—12. — *Zoological Museum* (p. 13) 12—2. — *Royal Mint* (p. 34) on previous application.

Saturdays. *Museum of Ores and Metals* (p. 40) 8—3. — *Observatory* (p. 33) 9—11. — *Agricultural Museum* (p. 33) 10—3. — *Cabinet of Minerals* (p. 13) 12—2. — *Arsenal* (p. 15) 2—4. — *Industrial Academy*, collection of models (p. 37), 10—12. — *Rathhaus* (p. 36) 11—4. — *Aquarium* (p. 11) by gas-light from dusk till 9 p. m.

English Church Service in the *English Chapel* (p. 39). — *American Chapel*, 5 Junker-Strasse.

Berlin (99 ft. above the sea-level), the capital of Prussia, residence of the Emperor of Germany, and seat of the imperial government, as well as of the highest Prussian authorities, with 828,013 inhab. and a garrison of 21,000 soldiers, is situated in an extensive sandy plain, about half-way between the extreme S.W. and N.E. extremities of the Empire (460 M. from Mülhausen in Alsace, and 414 M. from Memel). The town consists of ten different quarters and six suburbs, which have sprung up at different periods. The oldest quarters are *Alt-Berlin*, with the Rathhaus, on the r. bank of the Spree, bounded by the Königsgraben, and *Köln*, with the Royal Palace, on an island in the river. Adjoining these on the W. are the *Friedrichswerder* with the Arsenal, on the l. bank of the Spree, surrounded by the fosse of the old fortifications, the *Dorotheenstadt*, or *Neustadt*, with the Linden, to the N.W. of the Friedrichswerder, extending N. as far as the river; the *Friedrichsstadt* to the S. of the Neustadt, with the Wilhelms-Platz and the Schiller-Platz; then from W. to E. along the r. bank of the Spree, the *Friedrich-Wilhelmstadt*, the *Spandau Quarter*, the *Königsstadt*,

and the *Stralau Quarter*; and finally the *Louisenstadt* on the l.
bank, to the S.E. of the Friedrichswerder. The six suburbs are now
increasing rapidly in extent, especially in the neighbourhood of the
railway stations. The old town wall which formerly enclosed these
ten quarters was about 9 M. in circumference. The boundaries
of the city having been extended in 1861, it now covers an area
of 23 sq. M., of which however about one-third only is occupied
by buildings. The town contains about 480 streets, 58 squares, 700
public buildings (including 60 churches) and 15,000 private houses
(comprising 169,000 dwellings or suites of apartments). The commerce and manufactures of Berlin have increased so rapidly of late
years that it now ranks among the most important mercantile places
of continental Europe. The staple commodities are grain, spirits,
and wool; the principal branches of industry are engine-building,
iron-casting, and the manufacture of woollen and silk goods and
fancy articles.

At the time of the Wends the site of Berlin was occupied by two
fishing villages, into which the Margraves of Brandenburg introduced
German settlers in the 12th cent. The name of *Köln* is mentioned for
the first time in a document of 1238, that of Berlin in 1244, after which
it soon began to be regarded as one of the most considerable towns in the
March, next to Brandenburg, the residence of the Margraves. After the
union of the towns in 1307, the importance of the place increased. During
the troubles in which the land was involved after the extinction of the
Ascanians (1320), Berlin and Köln placed themselves at the head of a
league of towns of the March, formed for the more effectual advancement
of their common interests; and having about 1340 become members of the
Hanseatic League, they attained to a still more powerful and independent
position. Notwithstanding these advantages the attacks of the predatory
nobles, in league with the Pomeranians, ever increasing in violence,
frequently menaced the sister towns with ruin, but the *Hohenzollern*
family, who became masters of the March in 1411, at length succeeded in
restoring order and tranquillity. The nobles were kept in check, but on
the other hand Berlin was deprived of its independence as a town of the
empire. On several occasions the town rebelled against the severer
measures of the new government, especially when Elector *Frederick II.*
'*of the Iron Tooth*' (1440—1470) erected a fortified castle at Köln, but its
opposition was soon overcome, and the towns of Berlin and Köln were
again disjoined by the nomination of a separate council for each. *John
Cicero* (1486—1499), who had originally resided at Spandau, at length took
up his permanent abode at Köln, and since that period the fortunes of the
town have been closely bound up with those of the Hohenzollern family
and the country at large. In 1539 the townspeople and the Elector
Joachim II. (1535—1571), by whom the Schloss was altered, embraced the
reformed faith. Berlin sustained a serious reverse during the Thirty Years'
War, but gradually recovered from its disasters under the fostering care
of the great Elector Frederick William (1640—1688). The *Friedrichswerder*,
which had sprung up prior to his reign, was now endowed with municipal
privileges, and the *Neustadt* was founded and named *Dorotheenstadt* after
the wife of the Elector. In consequence of the introduction of numerous
foreign settlers, especially French Protestants (in 1685), the population of
the town increased to 20,000. *Frederick I.* (1688—1713), who became King
of Prussia in 1701, built the *Friedrichsstadt*, constituted Berlin the royal
residence, and united the administrations of the five hitherto separate
quarters of the town. To his reign Berlin is indebted for some of its
handsomest edifices, such as the Schloss, the Arsenal, the French, and the
New Church. *Frederick William I.* (1713—1740), after his despotic fashion,
was indefatigable in embellishing and extending the city, an object

which he attained partly by the reception of.Bohemian and Salzburg Protestants, and partly by compelling private individuals to erect numerous buildings according to his directions. At the close of his reign the population had reached 90,000. *Frederick II.*, the *Great* (1740—1786), although not particularly partial to Berlin, contributed materially by the brilliance of his reign to the prosperity of the town, and after its reverses during the Seven Years' War (when it was occupied and laid under contribution by the Croatians in 1757, and by the Russians in 1760) he never lost sight of its interests. The Opera House, the Library, and the Rom. Cath. Hedwigs-Kirche are monuments of his reign. At his death the population amounted to 114,000, and in 1800 to 172,000. After the catastrophe of 1806 and the temporary subversion of the Prussian monarchy, a new era of progress began with the promulgation of a new municipal code on 18th Nov. 1808, and the foundation of the university. Although in 1806 the entry of the French had been regarded with some degree of indifference, yet in the general rising of 1813, Berlin, as well as the Province of Prussia, set a noble example of patriotic zeal to the rest of the country, and the Battle of Grossbeeren was afterwards fought chiefly by the 'Landwehr' of Berlin. After the peace of 1815 the city increased rapidly, and being the central point of the government and the army of a number of as yet unconsolidated provinces, and at the same time a zealous patron of the arts and sciences, a considerable manufacturing place, and a vigorous upholder of German nationality, it gradually rose to a position which fairly entitles it to its present rank as the capital of the Empire of Germany.

a. *Unter den Linden. Platz am Opernhaus.*
Platz am Zeughaus.

The handsomest and busiest part of Berlin is the long line of streets extending from the Brandenburg Gate to the Royal Palace, consisting of *Unter den Linden, the *Platz am Opernhaus*, and the *Platz am Zeughaus*, terminated by the *Schlossbrücke*, with the Palace and *Lustgarten* beyond it (see Plan). The Linden, a street 55 yds. in width deriving its name from the double avenue of lime-trees (interspersed with chestnuts) in the middle, resembles the Boulevards of Paris, although inferior in length, and is flanked with handsome palaces; spacious hotels, and attractive shops, between which the long vistas of a number of side streets are visible at intervals. The most striking part of the street, and indeed the finest point in the entire city, is by the monument of Frederick the Great (p. 11). A view is here disclosed of the Opernplatz and its environs: to the r. is the Palace of the Emperor, the Library, the Hedwigskirche, the Opera House, the Palace of the Crown-Prince, and the Bau-Academie; to the l. the Academy, the University, the Königswache (or royal guard-house), the Arsenal, and beyond the Schlossbrücke the Palace and Museum, with numerous intervening monuments. These important buildings may be viewed almost simultaneously from this point, while the extensive Schiller-Platz, with its two churches surmounted with domes and the theatre, is in the immediate vicinity. The length of this line of streets from the Brandenburg Gate to the Palace is about 1 M.

The *Brandenburg Gate (Pl. 25), at the W. end of the Linden, forms the entrance to the town from the Thiergarten. It was erected in 1789—1792 by *J. G. Langhans* in imitation of the Propylæa at

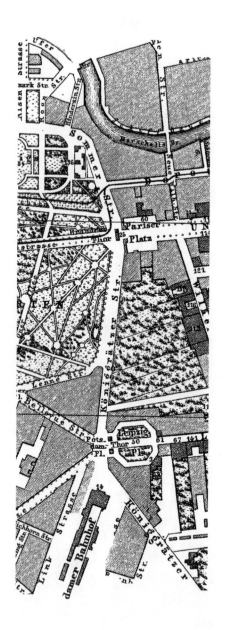

Prussia and Duke Ferdinand of Brunswick on the E., and Generals Zieten and Seydlitz on the W., between which are placed spirited groups of other contemporaries and officers of the king (thus on the E. side Prince Augustus William and Keith, on the N. side Kleist, Winterfeld, and Tauentzien, on the S. side Leopold of Dessau and Schwerin, on the W. side Lessing and Kant, all life size). The *lower* section contains names of other distinguished men, chiefly soldiers of the time of Frederick. The basement is of polished granite. The foundation-stone was laid on 31st May, 1840, the hundredth anniversary of the accession of Frederick to the throne of Prussia, and the monument was completed and inaugurated in 1851.

To the r. of the statue is situated the **Palace of the Emperor William** (Pl. 128; adm. see p. 7), erected by *K. F. Langhans* in 1834—36 (a flag is hoisted when the emperor is residing here). The building extends behind the Royal Library as far as the Behren-Str., and contains a suite of apartments sumptuously fitted up, a reception room 75 yds. in length, and a summer and winter garden. The apartments near the Opera House are those occupied by the emperor. A good photograph taken from the corner window may be purchased at the principal shops.

Opposite the palace is the **Academy Building** (Pl. 2), erected in 1690 and re-modelled in 1749, containing the *Academy of Art* and the *Academy of Science*, founded in 1699 and 1700 respectively by Frederick I. in accordance with a plan of Leibnitz, each of them possessing a library and various collections. The latter holds public sessions on the birthdays of the reigning king (22nd March), of Frederick II. (24th Jan.), and Leibnitz (5th July), and under the auspices of the former, grand *Exhibitions of Art* take place every alternate year (1872, 1874, etc.), from 1st Sept. to 31st Oct. The * **National Gallery of Modern Pictures** now in course of formation, consisting of 340 paintings, chiefly by German masters, most of them bequeathed to the state in 1861 by the consul Herr Wagener, is at present preserved here, but will be transferred to the building mentioned at p. 19 which is now approaching completion. Admission see p. 7. The entrance is by No. 7 Universitäts-Str. (2nd floor). Catalogue 5 Sgr.

ANTE-ROOM. This room and the following contain pictures recently added to the Wagener collection. 7. *C. Becker*, Visit of Emp. Charles V. to Fugger; *1. *A. Achenbach*, Ostend; 36. *Kolbe*, Emp. Charles V. on his flight from Innsbruck to Trent; 9. *Brendel*, Returning home to the village; 46. *Rottmann*, Bavarian mountain-scene; 19. *Graef*, Patriotism in 1813; 31. *Hoguet*, The last mill on the Montmartre; 16. *Cretius*, Captive cavaliers before Cromwell.

I. ROOM. Entrance-wall: *49—54. *Schirmer*, Six double landscapes with scenes from Scripture-history; 15. *Camphausen*, Dybbol after its capture by storm; *29. *J. Hübner*, The golden age; 47. *W. Schadow*, Christ and the disciples on the way to Emmaus. By the l. window: 17. *Daehling*, Prince entering his castle; 44. *Passini*, Canons in St. Peter's, a watercolour. Right window: *59. *Tischbein* (d. 1799), Portrait of Lessing. 3rd wall: 32. *Ittenbach*, Holy Family.

II. ROOM. 1st Cabinet. r. *202. 203. *Schinkel*, Landscapes; *Ahlborn*, 5. View of Wernigerode, 6. View of Florence; *200. *Schinkel*, Gothic cathedral; 66. *Hampe*, Luther's room at Wittenberg; 156. *M. Müller*, Scene from the Tyrol. 2nd wall: 91. *Hildebrand*, A robber; 248. *Wach*, Psyche; *90. *Th. Hildebrand*, Warrior and child; 234. *Sohn*, Lute-player; 28. *Bürkel*,

Passage of ships; 193. *Rottmann*, The Ammersee; 176. *Quaglio*, Fish-market at Antwerp; *201. *Schinkel*, Old French château. 3rd wall: 17. *Biermann*, View of Finstermünz in the Tyrol; *137. *Lessing*, Defence of a mountain pass; 237. *Steinbrück*, Girls bathing; 99. *Jordan*, Death of the pilot; 221. *Schrader*, Portrait of the consul Wagener; 247. *Wach*, Virgin. 2nd. Cab. r. 98. *Jordan*, Proposal of marriage in Heligoland; 82. *P. Hess*, St. Leonhard's day on the Schliersee; 115. *Kolbe*, Street in an old German town; 45. *Ebers*, Smugglers coming ashore; 64. *Gurlitt*, Scene from the Alban mounts. 2nd wall: 163. *Pistorius*, Lady in a satin dress; 217. *Schorn*, Pope Paul III. before the portrait of Luther; 79. *Henning*, Girl of Frascati; 226. *Schrödter*, Scene at a forge. 3rd wall: 153. *Monten*, Poles leaving their country in 1832; *Calame*, 32. Lake of Lucerne, 33. Storm among the Alps; *224. *Schrödter*, Don Quixote.

3rd Cab. r. *Schrödter*, 222. Tasting the Rhenish of 1830, 225. Scene from Shakspeare's Henry V.; *38. *Cornelius*, Hagen throwing the treasure of the Nibelungen into the Rhine; 189. *Riedel*, Peasant women of the Alban mountains; 173. *Preyer*, Vase of ivory. 2nd wall: 147. *Meyer of Bremen*, Girl lulling her sister to sleep; 199. *Schiavone*, Penitent Magdalene; 167. *Plüddemann*, Columbus. 3rd wall: 133. *Lessing*, Castle on a rock; 223. *Schrödter*, Rhenish tavern; 109. *Klöber*, Invention of the reed-flute.

4th Cab. r. 24. *Bossuet*, A street at Seville. 2nd wall: *71. *Hasenclever*, Reading room; 112. *Köhler*, Semiramis receiving the news of the rebellion at Babylon; 70. *Hasenclever*, Wine tasting. 3rd wall: 258. *Werner*, Interior of the cathedral at Cefalù; *155. *Mücke*, St. Elizabeth of Thuringia giving alms; 238. *Steinbrück*, Fairy scene; 1. *Achenbach*, Forest scene.

5th Cab. r. 190. *A. Robert*, Consecration of baptismal water in St. Mark's at Venice. 2nd wall: 89. *E. Hildebrandt*, Sea-coast; 100. *Jordan*, Fishermen on the coast of Normandy; *104. *N. de Keyser*, Death of Marie de Medicis; *183. *Rahl*, Persecution of the Christians in the catacombs at Rome. 3rd wall: *154. *Mücke*, Body of St. Catherine borne by angels; *58. *Gallait*, Count Egmont with his confessor on the night before his execution; 249. *Wagenbauer*, Mountain lake.

III. Room. r. 129. *Ch. Landseer*, Cromwell at the battle of Naseby reading a letter of Charles I. to his queen; 44. *D'Unker*, Scene at a police-office; *251. *Waldmüller*, Closing of the village school; *219. *Schrader*, Charles I. of England taking leave of his children before his execution; *139. *Leys*, Albert Dürer at Antwerp drawing the portrait of Erasmus; 144. *Maes*, Roman woman praying to the Virgin for her child; *289. *Stilke*, Richard III. separating the sons of Edward from their mother; 138. *Leys*, Sermon in a Gothic church; *148. *Meyerheim*, Target shooting in Westphalia; 220. *Schrader*, Esther and Ahasuerus; 172. *Preyer*, Still life; 57. *Gallait*, Capuchin; 174. *Preyer*, Fruit piece; 14. *Biard*, Incident in Linné's youth; 197. 198. *Schendel*, Market scenes; *15. *De Biefve*, Compromise of the nobles at Brussels in 1566, a small duplicate of the celebrated picture; 140. *Leys*, Party. — Window-wall: 56. *Schadow*, Girl reposing, in marble.

The ***University Buildings** (Pl. 167), formerly the palace of Prince Henry, brother of Frederick II., erected in 1754—64, and presented in 1809 by Frederick William III. to the then recently founded university, contain the lecture-rooms and scientific collections (2000 stud.). The *Zoological Museum* (adm. p. 7) is one of the most valuable in Europe, and contains a remarkably fine collection of birds. Among the curiosities of the *Mineral Cabinet* (adm. p. 7), the most extensive collection of the kind on the continent, may be mentioned a piece of amber weighing upwards of 14 lbs., found 100 M. from the Baltic, and numerous meteorolites. The objects brought by Humboldt from S. and Central America form an additional ornament to the collection. The *Anatomical Museum* (adm. p. 7) is also very valuable. The *Christian Museum* (adm. p. 7) contains copies and casts of Christian monuments of art. The *University Library* (adm. p. 7), containing 90,000 vols., is in a separate building (Tauben-Str. 29). By the chestnut plantation at the back of the university is a bust of *Hegel*, erected in 1871.

The **Royal Library** (Pl. 20; adm. p. 7), entered from the Opern-Platz, erected in 1775—80 from designs by *Unger*, is said to be indebted for its form to a caprice of Frederick the Great, who gave the architect a cabinet with drawers as a model. The ground floor contains the maps on the r., and the reading-room on the l. (open on week-days from 9 to 4). The library on the upper floor is shown daily at 10 o'clock.

The Library contains 700,000 vols. and 15,000 MSS., among which may be mentioned the MSS. and first impressions of *Luther's* translation of the Bible, *Melanchthon's* report of the Diet of Worms, *Gutenberg's* Bible on parchment of 1450, the first book printed with moveable types, the *Codex Wittekindi*, a MS. of the Gospels of the 8th cent., said to have been presented by Charlemagne to the Saxon duke Wittekind, miniatures by *Lucas Cranach*, 36 vols. of portraits and autographs of celebrated characters, Chinese books, a small octagonal Koran, important musical works, &c.

Opposite the University is the **Opera House** (Pl. 151), erected by *Knobelsdorff*, the architect of Frederick the Great, the largest in Germany (for 1800 spectators), with the exception of its rival the court-theatre at Munich. The interior was destroyed by fire in 1843, but was soon restored with increased magnificence. The tympanum contains an admirable *group in zinc, designed by Rietschel: in the centre the muse of music; on the r. the tragic and comic muse with the bantering satyr, the dramatic poet with the arts of painting and sculpture; on the l. a dancing group with the Three Graces.

At the back of the Opera House is situated the Roman Catholic **Church of St. Hedwig** (Pl. 81), another monument of the reign of Frederick the Great, erected in 1747—73 in imitation of the Pantheon at Rome, with a spacious dome and a portal borne by six Corinthian columns.

Five *Statues** (Pl. 47) by *Rauch*, over life-size, embellish the Opern-Platz. Between the palace of the crown-prince and the Opera House is that of *Blücher* (d. 1819), erected in 1826; at his r. hand *Gneisenau* (d. 1831), at his l. *York* (d. 1830), both erected in 1855; all three in bronze. In front of the guard-house *Bülow* (d. 1816) and *Scharnhorst* (d. 1813), both in marble, erected in 1822. The pedestals are adorned with reliefs referring to the events of 1813—1815.

The ***Royal Guard House** (*Königswache*, Pl. 101) opposite the Opera, was constructed by *Schinkel* in the Doric style in 1818 in the form of a Roman castrum. Adjoining it are three large cannon captured in 1814. Military music here daily 11—12 o'clock.

At the back of the guard-house is the **Singing Academy** (Pl. 144), the members of which meet for rehearsals on Tuesday evenings 5—9 o'clock (adm. p. 5). It was founded by *Fasen* (d. 1800) in 1791, and is now under the management of Prof. *Grell.*

The Palace of the Crown-Prince (Pl. 129; adm. p. 7) adjacent to the Opera, erected in 1687, was once occupied by Frederick the Great, when heir-apparent, and afterwards by Frederick William III. till his death in 1840. The upper storey was added in 1857. The palace contains a number of apartments tastefully fitted up and adorned with good modern pictures. A circular memorial hall is embellished with the bronze busts of seven generals of 1813—15; above are medallion reliefs in marble of eight citizens of Berlin distinguished in science, art, and commerce, and various allusions to England. The arch over the Oberwall-Strasse leads to the so-called *Palace of the Princesses*, the residence of the Princess Liegnitz, second consort of Fred. Will. III., till her death in 1873.

The Arsenal (Pl. 169; adm. p. 6; entrance at the back), adjoining the guard-house, erected in 1685—1706 under Frederick I., whose bust is placed over the principal portal, is a massive square structure, each side of which is 71 yds. in length, with a quadrangle in the middle. The keystones of the windows consist of heads of expiring warriors, remarkable for the vigour of their expression. In the centre of the court is placed the lion of Flensburg (p. 114). The ground-floor is occupied by cannon of every description; among them two Swedish leather field-pieces of the Thirty Years' War, guns captured from the Austrians in 1866, and numerous French pieces, including specimens of the destructive mitrailleuse and the huge Ste. Valérie from the Mont Valérien near Paris. The first floor contains 100,000 muskets and fire-arms, captured French and Austrian flags, trophies, etc. The *Residence of the Commandant* is opposite the Arsenal. Farther towards the S.E. is the Bau-Academie (p. 34).

b. *The Schloss-Brücke and Schloss.*

The * Schloss-Brücke (palace-bridge), constructed in 1824 from designs by *Schinkel*, crosses the arm of the Spree which separates Alt-Köln from the Friedrichs-Werder. It is adorned with eight groups in marble, over life-size, illustrative of the life of a warrior. On the S.: 1. Victory teaches a boy the history of the heroes (by *E. Wolff*); 2. Minerva instructs the youth in the use of weapons (by *Schievelbein*); 3. Minerva presents the combatant with arms (by *Möller*); *4. Victory crowns the conqueror (by *Drake*). On the N.: 5. Victory raises the wounded warrior (by *Wichmann*); 6. Minerva inciting him to a new contest (by *A. Wolff*); *7. Minerva protecting and aiding a combatant (by *Bläser*); 8. Iris conducts the victorious fallen warrior to Olympus (by *Wredow*).

To the l. beyond the bridge extends the Lustgarten, a square 247 yds. in length, and 220 yds. in width, which at the time of Frederick William I. was the drilling ground of the 'Long Guard'.

It is .now planted with trees and is enclosed by the Royal Palace, the Cathedral, and the Old Museum (p. 17). In the centre, on a pedestal of granite 20 ft. in height, rises the equestrian **Statue of Frederick William III.** by *A. Wolff*, inaugurated on 16th June, 1871, during the festival in celebration of the victories over the French. Beyond the statue, in front of the steps of the old Museum, is a huge *Granite Basin*, 22 ft. in diameter, and 75 tons in weight, hewn out of a solid erratic block of ten times the weight found near Fürstenwalde.

The ***Royal Palace** (Pl. 142; adm. p. 7) was founded by the Elector Frederick II., re-erected by Joachim II. in 1540, and completed in its present form chiefly by *Schlüter*, the most eminent architect of his time, and *E. v. Gœthe*, in 1697—1716, under the kings Frederick I. and Frederick William I. Its extension in various styles of architecture corresponds closely with the growth and development of the Prussian state. The edifice is in the form of a rectangle 158 yds. in length, and 94 yds. in width, and comprises two extensive courts. It is entered by five portals, two towards the Lustgarten, two towards the Schloss-Platz, and the principal portal on the W. side towards the Schlossfreiheit. This last is an imitation of the triumphal arch of Septimius Severus.

The Portal from the Lustgarten by which the public are admitted to the palace is adorned by the *Horse-Tamers*, two large groups in bronze, by Baron Clodt of St. Petersburg, presented by the Emp. Nicholas in 1842. The first court is adorned with St. George and the dragon, a colossal group in bronze by *Kiss*, erected in 1865.

***Interior.** Admission see p. 7. Visitors apply to the castellan in the inner court, on the ground-floor to the l., and are generally conducted into the palace by the large portal, erected by *Schlüter*, on the E. side of the quadrangle. The building contains about 600 apartments.: The Schweizer-Saal, the Königs-Saal (with full-length portraits of the kings of Prussia), and the Rothe Adler-Saal are first entered. One of these contains a handsome silver memorial of the foundation of the Order of the Iron Cross, designed by *Burger*, and presented to King William in 1870 by the senior members of the order. — The Ritter-Saal, or Thron-Saal, contains the royal throne entirely wrought in silver, 8 ft. in height, presented to the emperor by the officers of the army and navy in 1867 on the 60th anniversary of his admission to the military service; also vases and tankards in silver and gold, &c. — The Schwarze Adler-Saal, where the meetings of the Order of the Black Eagle are held, contains a large picture by *Camphausen*, representing Frederick the Great surrounded by his generals. — The Picture Gallery, a hall 70 yds. in length, which also serves as a reception room on festive occasions, contains some good modern pictures: *Steffeck*, King William at the Battle of Sadowa; *Menzel*, Coronation of the king at Königsberg in 1861, with numerous portraits; *Camphausen*, King William presenting the crown-prince with the order 'pour le mérite' after the Battle of Sadowa; *Eybel*, The Great Elector at the Battle of Fehrbellin in 1675; *David*, Buonaparte crossing the St. Bernard. Older pictures: at the entrance Portrait of Sultan Soliman II. by *Lievens*, at the egress Charles I. of England and his queen by *Van Dyck*. — The *White Saloon altered in 1857, 36 yds. in length, 17 yds. in width, and 42 ft. high, contains marble statues of the twelve Electors of Brandenburg and an admirable *Victory in a sitting posture by *Rauch*.

In niches above are eight statues emblematical of the eight provinces of the Prussian state; beneath are Caryatides with armorial bearings, above them eight appropriate paintings. — The adjoining STAIRCASE is embellished with marble statues of the emperors Justinian, Constantine, Charlemagne, and Rudolph II. by *Eggers*, and reliefs by *Schlüter*. — The *PALACE CHAPEL, sumptuously fitted up in 1848—54, 126 ft. in height, and 88 ft. in diameter, is lined and paved with marble, and adorned with frescoes by distinguished modern masters, representing scriptural subjects, members of the royal family, reformers, &c. The altar is of Oriental alabaster, with a lofty crucifix gilded and set with precious stones. On the r. and l. are ambos!, or reading desks, in Carrara marble. Ten columns in marble serve as candelabra. The chapel is capable of containing 1500 persons, and is used by the royal family on the occasion of church festivals.

The *White Lady*, a spectre which traditionally haunts the palaces of Baireuth and Berlin, and periodically appears to portend the death of a member of the royal family of Brandenburg, is said to be the ghost of the Countess Agnes of Orlamünde, who murdered her two children in order that she might be enabled to marry the Burggrave Albert of Nuremberg, ancestor of the Electors of Brandenburg. The apparition is said to have been observed last in Feb. 1840 in the palace at Berlin, and Fred. Wm. III. died in the summer of the same year.

On the E. side of the Lustgarten, between the palace and the Museum, is situated the insignificant **Cathedral** (Pl. 41), erected in 1747 under Frederick the Great, and restored in 1817, with a large and two smaller towers covered by domes. It contains a monument to the Electors John Cicero (d. 1499) and Joachim I. (d. 1535), cast by Vischer of Nuremberg in 1540, and the handsome sarcophagi of the Great Elector and King Frederick I. Beneath the church are the burial vaults of the Prussian royal family.

The adjoining burial-hall, an imitation of the *Campo Santo* at Pisa, for which the distinguished painter *Cornelius* designed his spirited compositions illustrative of the Christian views of Sin, Death, and the Redemption, is uncompleted.

c. *The Royal Museums.*

The ** Old Museum (Pl. 124; adm. p. 7), on the N.W. side of the Lustgarten, an admirable building in the Greek style, the finest at Berlin, with an Ionic portico of eighteen columns, and approached by a broad flight of steps, was erected by *Schinkel* in 1824—28 (length 94 yds., depth 28 yds., height 62 ft.).

The central part of the structure, rising above the rest of the building and corresponding with the rotunda in the interior, is adorned at the corners with four colossal groups in bronze: in front, the Horse Tamers of the Monte Cavallo at Rome, a copy by *Tieck*; at the back, Pegasus refreshed and caressed by the Horæ, by *Schievelbein* and *Hagen*. The steps are adorned with two large groups in bronze: r. *Amazon on horseback, defending herself against a tiger, by *Kiss*; l. *Lion combat, by *A. Wolff*.

The vestibule contains marble statues of *Schinkel* (d. 1841) by Tieck, *Rauch* (d. 1857) by Wichmann, and *G. Schadow* (d. 1850) by Hagen. The *Frescoes designed by *Schinkel* (p. 34) and exe-

cuted under the direction of *Cornelius* represent (on the l.) the
development of the world from chaos, and (on the r.) the progress
of human culture, pourtrayed in the ancient style.

Left: Uranus and the Dance of the Constellations. Saturn and the
Titans retire to the obscurity of the primitive age. The flock of the
moon-lit clouds cross the sky, recalling the reign of Saturn. Jupiter or-
ganises the new course of the world, diffusing the life-giving fire; the
Dioscuri, the first distributors of light, precede him; Prometheus steals
the fire for the inhabitants of earth. Selene (Luna) drives her chariot to
illumine the night; heavenly figures aid in spreading forth the broad
curtain of night. Night unfolds the mantle from which the figures crowd
forth, her children repose around her. Elements of manifold varieties of
life are developed; maternal love; war still slumbers; joyful Peace with
Muse; a child waters the earth with fruitful rain. Elements of science,
impeded by the forces of nature. Fructification. A cock proclaims the
dawn, with which care begins. Rise of the Sun. Venus and Cupid. The
Sun in his chariot rises from the ocean. The Graces soar upwards.

Right: 1st Group. Morning and Spring of life; shepherds; prize
contests; the Muse and Psyche in the hut of the poet stringing his lyre;
the Genius of the poet inspires him. — 2nd Group. Summer and Noon;
harvest and its joys; a youthful hero draws inspiration; Music. — 3rd
Group. On the clouded heights of Helicon, beneath the hoof of the winged steed, springs the fountain of imagination, from which mankind derives
refreshment; behind the veil of water, the powers which regulate the
eternal laws of life shimmer in the bosom of the earth; happy beings
hover in the element of the beautiful. — 4th Group. Music of the Forest;
rejoicing in the winged steed; Nymphs pour water into the fountain from
which the poet draws; a lawgiver approaches. — 5th Group. Evening
and Autumn; vintage; art of Sculpture (Schinkel is represented as a
sculptor). Architecture, the acanthus embraces the outline of the Corinthian capital; heroes return victorious; Psyche; festival of the wine-press
by the fire-side; age rejoicing in the dance of the Muses; the wise man
fathoms the course of the stars; the sailor drifts out to the moon-lit sea;
Night and Winter; Luna descends into the sea. — Beginning of a new
day. Mourning by the tumulus.

Beneath these are smaller mural paintings: on the l. the myth
of Hercules, on the r. that of Theseus.

A double stair leads from the vestibule direct to the second floor
of the Museum. The staircase is adorned with a copy of the celebrated ancient Warwick Vase in England, and with busts of the
ministers *v. Altenstein* (d. 1840) and *W. v. Humboldt* (d. 1835).
In the upper passage, at the entrance to the Rotunda, are frescoes
also designed by *Schinkel* (p. 34), representing the struggle of civilised mankind against barbarians and the elements: on the l. wild
horses penetrating into a shepherd's dwelling, on the r. the distress
of an inundation. On the lateral walls the peaceful avocations of a
civilised people: on the l. the domestic hearth, on the r. summer
in the open air.

At the back of the Old Museum, to the N.W., and connected with
it by a short passage crossing the street, is situated the *New Museum* (Pl. 125; entrance see pp. 19, 25), erected by *Stüler* in the
Renaissance style in 1843—55, and adorned with Greek details (length
116 yds., depth 44 yds.; height of the central part, with the principal portal, which is still closed, and the grand staircase, 102 ft.).
The principal façade, with the inscription, 'Museum a patre bea-

tissimo conditum ampliavit filius 1855', is on the E. side, facing the *National Gallery*, now in course of construction from designs by *Stüler*, in the form of a Corinthian temple. The houses between these buildings are to be removed, and an open space will thus be left between them.

The *Royal Collections of Art (adm. p. 7) contained in these buildings are inferior to those of Dresden, Munich, and indeed to those of most other European capitals, a natural result of the lateness of their foundation (1820); but they are so extensive and admirably arranged, as to afford the student an excellent and comprehensive survey of the history of sculpture and painting.

The collections are arranged as follows : —

The Old Museum contains the *Antiquarium (p. 21), a collection of ancient coins, gems, implements, vases, &c. on the *Ground Floor;* the ancient and mediæval *Sculptures (see below) on the *First Floor;* and the *Picture Gallery (p. 22) on the *Upper Floor.*

The New Museum contains the handsome *Staircase* (p. 25) adorned with *Kaulbach's Mural Paintings; the *Egyptian (p. 29) and *Northern Antiquities* (p. 28) and the *Ethnographical Museum* (p. 29) on the *Ground Floor;* a valuable collection of *Casts of ancient, mediæval, and modern sculptures (p. 26) on the *First Floor;* and the *Kunst-Kammer* and *Cabinet of Engravings* (p. 29) on the *Upper Floor.*

The *National Gallery* (see above) is destined for the reception of the collection of pictures now in the Academy (p. 12), the cartoons of Cornelius (p. 17), and various other works of art.

The Entrance (adm. p. 7) is in the vestibule of the Old Museum, which is reached by a broad flight of steps from the Lustgarten (comp. Plan, p. 20). Passing through a massive bronze winged door, the visitor first enters the *Rotunda* (see below), beyond which is the *Hall of the Gods and Heroes* (p. 20), adjoined by the *Greek and Assyrian Sculptures* (see below) on the r., and the *Kaisersaal* (p. 21) and *Mediaeval Sculptures* (see below) on the l. From the Hall of the Gods, opposite the entrance to the Rotunda, a stair descends to the ground-floor where the *Antiquarium* (p. 21) is placed, while a double stair ascends to the connecting passage (p. 21) leading to the *New Museum* (p. 25), and in the opposite direction, a few steps higher, to the *Picture Gallery* (p. 21).

1. *Collections in the Old Museum.*

The *Gallery of Original Sculptures is chiefly indebted for its origin to Frederick the Great, to whose collection purchased at Rome by Bianconi that of Cardinal Polignac was afterwards added. It contains about 1000 objects, most of them of mediocre merit, belonging to the later Roman Empire, and freely restored, but many deserving of inspection, and a few of great value. The arrangement begins with the

ROTUNDA, a large circular hall covered with a glass cupola, rising to the full height of the building. Between the columns supporting the gallery are eighteen ancient statues, the best of which are (beginning from the l.): 9. Satyr; 7. Polyhymnia; 4. Minerva; 2. Jupiter; 17. Æsculapius; 18, 1. Victories; (without No.) *Amazon; 14. Juno. Above is the Raphael tapestry (p. 22).

On entering the Hall of the Gods and Heroes, the visitor is recommended at once to turn to the r. and proceed to the end of the hall of the GREEK, ROMAN, AND ASSYRIAN SCULPTURES. The *Assyrian Reliefs*, in grey alabaster, once adorned the royal palaces of ancient Nineveh erected

2*

about B.C. 900 and 750 respectively, and situated near the modern Nimrud and Kouyundschik, and represent kings, demons, hunting and battle scenes, &c. (comp. the casts, p. 27). The most interesting of the *Greek and Roman sculptures*, which occupy the three sections divided by columns next to the entrance, are: 1st section: 802. Helius; 803. Venus; 746. (by the window) Amymone, daughter of Danaus (a torso); 399. Berenice, in black marble. 2nd section: 769. Thorn extractor; 758. Vespasian, in porphyry, the flesh parts gilded, a modern restoration; 757. Male torso. 3rd section: 33. Meleager; 747. Venus; 343. Sella of white marble.

Plan of the First Floor of the Old Museum

(Gallery of Original Sculptures).

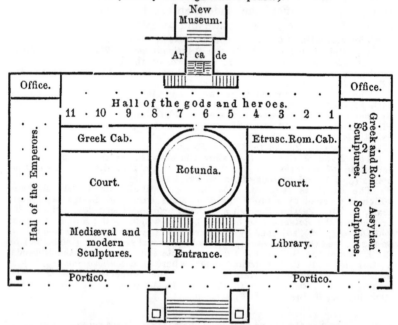

HALL OF THE GODS AND HEROES. 1st Section: 124. Head of Pallas; *112. Apollo Citharœdus with four Muses; **111. Polyhymnia, an admirable draped statue; 79. Urania; *80. Euterpe; 98, 36, 59, 856. Busts of Demosthenes, Pericles (?), Themistocles (?) and Euripides. — 2nd: **140. Boy praying, in bronze, probably by Boëdas son of Lysippus, found in the Tiber and purchased by Frederick the Great for 1500*l.*; 217. Son of Niobe. — 3rd: 121. Victoria standing on a globe; 107. Flora. — 4th: 140a. Youthful genius ('bonus eventus'?), in bronze, found in the Rhine near Xanten in 1859; *74. Girl sitting, playing with dice. — 5th: 131. Large Roman basin from the Thermæ of Diocletian; 275. Isis; 78. Juno. — 6th: 325. Vase in alabaster. — 7th: 151. Venus; 155. Granite basin (like No. 131); 154. Bacchus and Ariadne; *150. Satyr and Hermaphrodite. — 8th: 855, 164. Silenus. — 9th: 180. Ganymede; 58. Alexander the Great; 22. Venus. — 10th: 218. Bacchus; 141. Head of Pallas; 226. Male torso, restored as an archer; 160. Hermaphrodite; 227. Athlete. — 11th: 159. Cupid bending his bow; 235. Apollo and Mercury; 236. Antinous as Mercury; 264. Antinous.

GREEK CABINET. In the centre, *146. Torso of Cupid; 25. Group of Bacchus; 270, 69. Two archaic reliefs: Apollo crowned by the goddess of victory, and Apollo contending with Hercules for the tripod; *219. Mercury, restored as a hero; *483. Torso of Marsyas.

ETRUSCAN-ROMAN CABINET. In the centre, 542. Sarcophagus. In the·
l. corner *539. Urn in shape of a house; 519. Clay-sarcophagus, on the lid
a recumbent figure and a woman. To the r. Roman cinerary urns and
sarcophagi. — The visitor next enters the Kaisersaal, or

HALL OF THE EMPERORS, containing numerous busts of Roman emperors and empresses. 1st Section: 340. Germanicus; *295. Cæsar in a toga;
293. Augustus; 299. Tiberius; 301. Caligula. — 2nd: 304. Vitellius; 419.
Seneca; 307. Vespasian, a colossal head; 308. Domitian. — 3rd: 411. Barbarian head of a Dacian from the forum of Trajan; 395. Marciana; 316.
Hadrian. — 4th: 359. Trajan as Jupiter, sitting;· 362. Sabina, as Pietas;
363. Statue of Marcus Aurelius. — 5th: 322a. L. Verus; 368. Sacrificers. —
6th: nothing worthy of note. — 7th: *873. Statue of Augustus, opposite
that of Cæsar. — Then the Hall of the

MEDIÆVAL AND MODERN SCULPTURES: *414. Napoleon I. as a Roman
emperor·, executed by *Chaudet*, the best existing likeness of the emperor;
696a. Mercury sitting, by *Pigalle* (d. 1785); *719. Hebe by *Canova* (d. 1822);
687. Ephebe as Hyacinth, recumbent figure in bronze by *Bosio* (d. 1845).
By the window: 740. Cosimo dei Medici, a relief in marble by *Andr. Verocchio* (d. 1488); 675. Macchiavelli; 674. Lorenzo de' Medici, 'Il Magnifico';
668. Pier Soderini, opponent of the Medicis (three coloured busts); 656.
Virgin and Child with four Saints by *Sansovino;* 621. Virgin and Child by
Luca della Robbia, and several other terracottas of his school. — The
visitor now returns to the Hall of the Gods, and descends by the stair to
the l. to the

*Antiquarium. At the bottom of the stair, under glass, the instructive
model of an ancient quinquereme.

On the *left* is a suite of rooms containing antique vases, terracottas,
mosaics, and bronzes. Many of the *Vases* (about 1600 in number) are valuable and important in the study of Greek painting and mythology. The
small *Bronzes*, consisting of idols, weapons, statuettes, domestic utensils,
&c., afford an insight into the public and domestic life of the Greeks and
Romans.

On the *right* are the *Cabinet of Coins* and *Collection of Gems (Intaglios*,
receding, and *Cameos*, raised), comprising several works of the highest artistic
value. Casts of the chief treasures of other collections and mural paintings from Pompeii are suspended on the wall. Here, too, is preserved the
Silver Treasure found at Hildesheim (p. 57), consisting of Roman plate,
probably of the time·of Augustus. Some of the articles possess great artistic merit, especially four round flat dishes with reliefs at the bottom :
*Minerva, Young Hercules, Deus Lunus, and Cybele; and several wide
goblets with feet.

The CABINET OF COINS (upwards of 40,000 in number) is chronologically
arranged. The mediæval and modern coins are in a separate apartment,
to which access is obtained by application at the office of the director.
Casts and imitations of the best gems may be purchased of the custodians.

The double stair from the Hall of the Gods ascends to the PASSAGE
connecting the old and new Museums, where several casts of ancient portrait-statues are placed. The passage leads to the Roman Cupola Saloon
(p. 27), instead of proceeding to which, the visitor now turns in the opposite
direction and ascends a few more steps to the upper or **Second Floor** of
the Old Museum, containing the picture gallery (see Plan, p. 22). Another
(the old) approach to the picture gallery is from the vestibule of the Old
Museum towards the Lustgarten, by the double stair leading direct to the
gallery of the Rotunda (comp. p. 22).

The *Picture Gallery, although, as already observed, inferior to the
other great continental collections, is admirably adapted for the study of
the history of the art. It is divided into 37 apartments, each bearing
a number. To the r. of the entrance from the connecting passage, and
to the l. of the approach from the Rotunda, the Italian school begins in
the 4th, and the Dutch school in the 5th saloon, one of which may be
conveniently taken as a starting-point. Each of these is marked in the
Plan as No. 1, and the following enumeration begins with No. 1 of the
Italian School. A list of the pictures in each room hangs on the wall

(about 1400 in all). The number, author, and subject of each of the finest
works are here given, while of the less important the number and painter
only are mentioned. Catalogue 15 Sgr.

Upper Floor of the Old Museum
(Picture Gallery).

```
                          Ar | ca | de
 ┌──────────┬──┬──┬─────┬─────┬────Entr.──┬──┬─────┬─────┬──────────┐
 │ Office.  │2 Germ.│Dutch│Ital.│Sch│ools│   │ I│ta│lian│Sch│ools│ Office.  │
 │          │  │  │  1  │ 1 │ 2 │ 3 │ 4 │ 5│ 6│ 7│ 8 │ 9 │    10    │
 ├──────────┼──┴──┴─────┴───┴───┼──┬────┬──┼──┬──┴─────┴───────┤
 │German Schools 3 4 5 6 7      │Incu nabu la.│      │Umb r.  In cun.│ Italian Schools 11 12 13 14 │
 │          │              │      Rotunda     │Scho ol.│            │
 │   and    │              │    Raphael's     │        │            │
 │          │              │    Gobelins      │        │            │
 │ Dutch 8 9│ Du tch │ and │              ║Entrance║│17th and 18th   │ Ec-lec- │
 │          │ Ger man│ Sch.│              ║        ║│   cent.        │ tics. 15 16 │
 │          │  10    │ 11  │  12          ║        ║│French.  Spa-   │         │
 │          │        │     │              ║        ║│       17 niards│         │
 └──────────┴────────┴─────┴──────────────┴────────┴────────────────┴─────────┘
```

     As already mentioned, the upper walls of the ROTUNDA are hung
with the celebrated * *Tapestry* woven at Arras for Henry VIII. in the 16th
cent. from designs by Raphael, being like that at Dresden a repetition of
the famous tapestry in the Vatican. The colours are unfortunately faded.
It was once in the possession of Emp. Charles I., then in that of the
Dukes of Alva, and was purchased by Frederick William IV. in 1844.
The subjects, with which every one acquainted with the cartoons or the engravings from them is familiar, are from the Acts of the Apostles: 1. Death
of Ananias; 2. Christ giving Peter the keys of heaven; 3. Paul and Barnabas
at Lystra; 7. The sorcerer Elymas struck with blindness; 5. Conversion
of St. Paul; 6. Paul preaching at Athens; 7. Stoning of St. Stephen; 8.
Miraculous draught of fishes; 9. Peter and Paul healing the lame man.
(The 10th, Paul in prison at Philippi, unfortunately no longer exists.)
     After inspecting the tapestry, the visitor should proceed to the l. to
the 1st Italian Saloon and examine the finest works of the *Italian, Spanish,*
and *French* schools in their order.

Italian School.

     EARLY PERIOD (1430—1520). 1st Room. Venetians. 1st wall: 15. *Cima
da Conegliano,* Miracles of St. Amianus; 21. *Mantegna,* Judith; 5. *Antonio
da Murano,* Adoration of the Magi; 2. *Cima,* Virgin and SS. 2nd wall:
20. *M. Basaiti,* Virgin and SS.; 18. *Antonello da Messina,* Portrait; *Mantegna,* 27. Virgin, *28. The body of Christ supported by two weeping angels. 3rd wall: 38. *L. Vivarini,* Virgin and SS.; 41. *P. degli Ingannati,*
Virgin.
     Lombard and Tuscan Schools. 2nd Room. 1st wall: 1. 51. 52. *Ambr.
Borgognone,* Inthroned Virgin; 58. *Fra Filippo Lippi,* Virgin. 2nd wall: 60.
Fra Angelico da Fiesole, Virgin and Child between St. Dominicus and Peter
the Martyr; 61, 62. *The same,* Legends of St. Francis; *69. *Fra Filippo
Lippi,* The Madonna adoring the Infant Christ; *70 *The same,* Mary with
a goldfinch; *73. *Pollajuolo,* Annunciation. 3rd wall: 47 a. *Unknown master,*
Assumption of the Virgin.

3rd Room. 1st wall: 1. *79. *Luca Signorelli*, Six Saints (two wings of an altar-piece of which the central scene is missing); 82. *Filippino Lippi*, Virgin. 2nd wall: 104. *Andrea Verocchio*, Virgin with Christ and St. John; 90 a. *Leonardo da Vinci*, Madonna and Child; 93. *P. di Cosimo*, Meeting of Christ and John the Baptist; 94. *Filippo Lippi*, Same subject in a forest landscape; 92. *Lor. di Credi*, Adoration of the Magi; 96. *Filippino Lippi*, Christ on the cross.

4th Room. 1st wall: *Sandro Botticelli*, 106. Madonna and Child with saints, *102. Madonna with seven candle-bearing angels; 107. *Piero di Cosimo*, Venus and Mars; 109. *B. Peruzzi*, Caritas; 108. *Pesello*, Madonna; 103. *L. di Credi*, Magdalene; *100. The same, Madonna adoring the Child. 2nd wall (School of Bologna previous to 1520): 111. *Cosimo Tura*, Virgin; 112. *L. Costa*, Presentation in the Temple.

5th Room. 1st wall: 1. 117. *L. Longhi*, Madonna with St. Sebastian and Francis; 114. *L. Co·ta*, Presentation in the Temple. 2nd wall: 120. *Timoteo della Vite*, Madonna with the two SS. James; *121. *F. Francia*. Pietà; The same, *122. Madonna inthroned, *123. Madonna, 127. St. John the Bapt. and St. Stephen.

A room to the r. with pictures which chronologically belong to this period is opened by the attendant on application. It contains early Christian pictures on a gold ground, interesting as the first attempts at painting in various countries, and also a number of valuable works of the Umbrian school (1460—1520) and from the early period of Raphael. *135. *Raphael*, Christ at the Sepulchre; *150. *Giovanni lo Spagno*, Adoration of the Magi, in water-colours on linen, half-obliterated; 140 a. *Giovanni Santi* (Raphael's father), Madonna; 132. *G. B. Bertucci*, Adoration of the Magi; 140. 146. *Perugino*, Madonna.

BEST PERIOD (1500—1540). 6th Room. Venetians. 1st wall: 1. 156, 152. *Giorgione* (?), Portraits. 2nd wall: *Titian*, *163. Portrait of himself; **166. Portrait of his daughter Lavinia (the other pictures bearing Titian's name are by masters of his school only). 165. *Pordenone*, Washing of the feet; 169. *Bordone*, Chess-players. 3rd wall: 180. *Bordone*, Venus; 174. *Palma Vecchio*, Portrait.

7th Room. 1st wall: 1. 187. *Moretto*, Adoration of the Shepherds. 2nd wall: *Bordone*, Virgin and saints; 198. The same, Female portrait; 183. *Palma Vecchio* (?), Holy Family; *196. *Pordenone*, Christ and the adulteress; 197. *Moretto*, Holy Family; *197 a. *Palma Vecchio*, Portrait of his daughter; 190. *H. von Calcar*, Portrait. 3rd wall: 200. *Bonifazio*, Christ and the adulteress.

8th Room. Lombard School. 1st wall: 1. 217. *B. Luini*, Madonna; *207 a. *Correggio* (?), Thorn-crowned head of Christ, formerly in the private chapel of Frederick William III., the favourite picture of that monarch; 204. *G. Ferrari*, Adoration of the Shepherds. 2nd wall: *216. *Correggio*, Io embraced by Jupiter in the form of a cloud (probably an old copy of the original picture at Vienna); 224. *Luini*, Madonna; *218. *Correggio*, Leda and the swan; 222. *Melzi*, Pomona and Vertumnus.

9th Room. Florentine and Roman School. 1st wall: 1. 234. *Seb. del Piombo*, Portrait of P. Aretino; 240. *A. del Sarto*, The painter's wife; 236, 241. The same, Legends of St. Antony of Padua; 239. *Pontormo*, Portrait of A. del Sarto; **141. *Raphael*, Madonna reading, and the Child holding a thistle-finch; *237. *S. del Piombo*, Body of Christ with Joseph of Arimathea and Magdalene; *145. *Raphael* (early period), Virgin with SS. Jerome and Francis. 2nd wall: 246. *A. del Sarto*, Madonna with saints; **247 a. *Raphael*, Madonna and Child, with the two Johns ('Madonna coi Bambini'), a work of Raphael's first period, purchased at Naples for 6750l.; *249. *Fra Bartolommeo*, Assumption of the Virgin.

10th Room. 1st wall: 1. *265. *Giulio Romano*, Diana and Calisto (a fresco transferred to canvas); 233. *Pontormo*, Venus kissing Cupid. 2nd wall: **248. *Raphael*, 'Madonna di Casa Colonna', so called from the palace at Rome in which the picture was formerly preserved, purchased for 3000l.; 259. *S. del Piombo*, Crucifixion (on marble).

PERIOD OF DECLINE (after 1570). 11th Room. Venetians. 2nd wall:

298, 299. *Tintoretto*, Two procurators of St. Mark; *The same*, 301. Portrait, 300. Maria Gloriosa.

12th Room. 2nd wall: 309. *P. Veronese*, Minerva arming Mars; 311. *The same*, Apollo and Juno; 316. *Tintoretto*, St. Mark and three procurators. * Ceiling-painting (326) by *P. Veronese*.

13th Room. 1. 337. *Vasari*, Grandduke Cosimo dei Medici.

14th Room. Florentines and other Italians of the 16th and 17th cent., naturalists and eclectics. 1st wall: *Caravaggio*, 365. St. Matthew the Evangelist, 359. The mount of olives; 362. *Domenichino*, St. Jerome. 2nd wall: 375. *Domenichino*, Portrait of the architect Scamozzi; 377. *G. Reni*, Venus. 3rd wall: *G. Reni*, Fortune; 385. *Domenichino*, The deluge.

15th Room. Italian, German and Dutch eclectics. 1st wall: 1. 423. *C. Dolci*, St. John the Evangelist. 2nd wall: 483. *Mengs*, Holy Family.

16th Room. 1st wall: 491. *Mengs*, Portrait of his father; 499. *A. Kauffmann*, Her own portrait; 502. *A. v. d. Werff*, Madonna. 2nd wall: *The same*, Lamentation; 492. Pastoral scene.

17th Room (lighted from above), principally Spanish and French masters. 1st wall: 1. *Spagnoletto*, Martyrdom of St. Bartholomew; 428. *Claude Lorrain*, Landscape; 405. *Murillo*, Spanish woman. 2nd wall: 494. *Greuze*, A girl; *Watteau*, 474. Musical performance in the country, 470. Masquerade at night, 468. Minuet; 489. *Pesne*, Frederick the Great; 475. *Clouet*, King Henry III. as a youth. 3rd wall: 421. *S. Rosa*, Shipwreck; 369. *Caravaggio*, Cupid; 465. *Mignard*, Maria Mancini, niece of Card. Mazarin; 353. *Caravaggio*, Entombment; 471. *Lebrun*, The Jabach family at Cologne, mentioned in Goethe's 'Truth and Fiction'; *413. *Velasquez*, Card. Azzolini; 404 a. *Zurbaran*, Exhibition of the miraculous crucifix; *408. *Murillo*, Magdalene. 4th wall: *414. *Murillo*, St. Antony of Padua with the Infant Christ.

The visitor should now retrace his steps to the first room of the Netherlands and German Schools.

FIRST CULMINATING PERIOD, from Hubert and John van Eyck to Hans Holbein and the pupils of Albert Dürer (1420—1550). 1st Room: **512—523. *John* and *Hubert van Eyck* (the gem of the collection), twelve paintings on six panels which formed the wings of the celebrated altar-piece of the 'Adoration of the Spotless Lamb' in the church of St. Bavon at Ghent. There were originally thirteen panels, which were carried off by the French and fell into the hands of a dealer; six are now in Belgium, six here, purchased for 15,000 *l.*, the thirteenth has disappeared. 1st. The just judges; the old man on the magnificently caparisoned grey horse is the painter Hub. van Eyck (1366—1426), at the side in a black robe his brother John (1400—1445); 2nd. Champions of Christ, St. Sebastian, St. George, and St. Michael the foremost; 3rd and 4th. Singing and playing angels; 5th. Hermits; 6th. Pilgrims. The following six are painted at the back of the above (the panels are turned every three days; a second visit therefore necessary): 7th. John the Baptist; 8th. Portrait of Jodocus Vyts, burgomaster of Ghent, for whom the picture was painted; 9th and 10th. Annunciation, the angel Gabriel, and the Virgin; 11th. Wife of Jodocus Vyts as St. Elizabeth; 12th. St. John the Evangelist. The sketches by the window afford a clue to the connection between the pictures. — In the same Room: *Mich. Coxcie*, 524, 255. Copies of the above-mentioned altar-piece at Ghent; *J. van Eyck*, 528. Head of Christ, painted in 1438; *Memling*, 528 h. Madonna; 533. The Prophet Elisha visited by an angel; *Rogier van der Weyde*, * 534 b. Three scenes from the life of John the Baptist; 534 a. Life of Mary (a triptych); 535. Altar-piece with wings, Nativity, Adoration of the Magi, the Sibyl of Tibur and the Emp. Augustus adoring the Virgin; 530. *Hugo van der Goes*, Annunciation; 539. *Memling*, Jewish family celebrating the Passover; 539 a. *P. Christophsen*, Annunciation and Nativity; 529 b. *The same*, The day of judgment.

2nd Room. German Schools. 1st wall: r. 563 a, b, c, d. *Hans Holbein the Younger*, Eight saints; 561 a. *Zeitblom*, St. Peter; 564. *L. Cranach the Elder*, Apollo and Diana, 566. Adam and Eve. 2nd wall: 577. *H. Holbein*, Portrait of the Imp. General Frundsberg; 583. *Amberger*, Portrait of Seb. Münster the geographer; 589. *Cranach*, Card. Albert of Brandenburg; *586.

H. Holbein, Portrait of M. Gyzen, a London merchant; 590. *Cranach*, Portrait of Duke John Frederick of Saxony; *The same*, 594. Venus, 593. The spring of youth.

3rd Room. *Cranach*, 567. Adam and Eve, 618. Luther disguised as Junker George; 619 a, b. *Beham*, Four saints; *Mabuse*, 642. Adam and Eve, 648. Neptune and Amphitrite.

4th Room. Netherland Schools. 1st wall: r. 688. *Breughel* and *Rottenhammer*, Festival of Bacchus. 2nd wall: 721. *P. Breughel,* Procession to Mount Calvary; 731. *P. Brill*, The tower of Babel.

5th Room. 1st wall: 750. *Th. de Keyser*, Family piece; 743. *J. G. Cuyp*, Portrait of an old woman; 744. *Rubens* and *Snyders*, Stag-hunt. 2nd wall: *Rubens*, 758. Portrait of his second wife Helena Fourment, 762. Coronation of Mary; *Van Dyck*, 770. Christ scourged, 768. Portrait, 786. Portrait, 787. Nuptials of St. Catherine, 771. The Infant Christ and St. John.

6th Room. 1st wall: r. 778. *Van Dyck*, The dead Christ mourned over by Mary Magdalene, St. John, and an angel; *Rubens*, *783. Lazarus, 781. St. Cecilia; 796. *Metsu*, Medical visit; 785. *Rubens*, Perseus and Andromeda; 779. Christ and St. John as children; 782. *Van Dyck*, Portrait of Prince Thomas of Carignan. 2nd wall: 790. *Van Dyck*, Children of Charles I. of England; *G. Terburg*, 791. Paternal admonition, 793. Genre-piece; 795. *J. Steen*, Garden of an inn; 800. *F. Hals*, Portrait. 3rd wall: 797. *Rubens,* Three cavaliers; 798. *Rubens* and *Snyders*, Christ with Mary and Martha.

7th Room. 1st wall: r. 811. *Rembrandt*, Moses; 823. *J. J. van Vliet,* Pluto and Proserpine; *Rembrandt*, 808, 810. Portraits of himself; *802. Duke Adolphus of Guelders threatens his captive father; 815. *Govaert Flinck,* Abraham banishes Hagar.

8th Room. 1st wall: r. *840. *A. van der Neer*, Conflagration at a Dutch sea-port; 832. *Van der Helst*, Portraits. 2nd wall: 852. *Everdingen*, Waterfall; 856. *D. Teniers*, Peasants playing cards; 854. *G. Dow*, Cook. 3rd wall: 879. *J. Jordaens*, 'When the old quarrel the young squeak'.

9th Room. 1st wall: r. 884. *J. Ruysdael*, Sea slightly agitated. 2nd wall: 899. *A. Ruysdael*, Landscape; 911. *W. van de Velde*, Quay.

10th Room. Period of Decline. 2nd wall: 948. *Pierson*, Still life. 3rd wall: 955. *Van Thulden*, Triumph of Galathea.

11th Room. 1st wall: l. 963. *De Heem*, Festoons of fruit; in the centre, Virgin and Child by *C. Begas*. 2nd wall: 974. *Snyders*, Contest between bears and dogs.

12th Room. 1st wall: l. 998. *Huysum*, Flowers. 2nd wall: 1014, 1014 b. *Denner*, Portraits of two old men; 1023 a. *Dietrich*, Tivoli.

2. Collections in the New Museum.

Approaching the New Museum from the Old by the connecting passage, the visitor is recommended to traverse Rooms X., XI., and XII. (see Plan, p. 26) and enter the spacious ***Staircase** (Pl. II.), 44 yds. in length, 19 yds. in width, and 102 ft. in height, which forms the centre of the building. A single stair leads from the ground-floor to the first storey, a double from the first to the second. The steps are of Silesian marble.

Six magnificent ****Mural Paintings by Kaulbach**, executed in 1847—66, representing important epochs in the history of mankind, adorn the upper walls of the staircase.

1. *Fall of Babel*, King Nimrod in the centre, in the foreground the division of the tribes, on the l. the Shemites with their flocks, in the centre the idolatrous descendants of Ham, on the r. the children of Japhet, the founders of the Caucasian race. Slaves stone the architect. — 2. *Prosperity of Greece.* Homer approaches the shore of Greece in a boat and sings to the listening people, on the l. poets, sculptors, architects, &c., on the r. warriors dancing around the altar, in the foreground Thetis,

risen from the sea, also in a listening attitude. On the rainbow above, Jupiter, Juno, and the gods of Olympus, Apollo with the Muses and Graces. — 3. *Destruction of Jerusalem* by Titus, in the foreground the High Priest killing his family and himself, on the l. Ahasuerus, the wandering Jew, fleeing, on the r. a Christian family retreating, the most beautiful group. Above, the four prophets who predicted the destruction of the city. — 4. *Battle of the Huns*, considered the finest of the six paintings. According to a legend, the combatants were so exasperated that the slain rose during the night and fought in the air. Rome, which is seen in the background, is said to have been the scene of this event. Above, borne on a shield, is Attila with a scourge in his hand, opposite him Theodoric, king of the Visigoths. — 5. *The Crusaders before Jerusalem* under Godfrey de Bouillon. At their head Godfrey, presenting the crown of Jerusalem to the Saviour; beneath are Pierre of Amiens and other crusaders; the group on the l. is an embodiment of minstrelsy, which was so intimately associated with the chivalry of the middle ages. — 6. *Age of the Reformation*, comprising numerous historical personages. In a Gothic church Luther at the altar, holding up the Bible, with Melanchthon, Zwingli, Calvin, and Bugenhagen; sitting in a semicircle are Wickliffe, Huss, and other early Reformers; on the wall behind them the 'Last Supper' of Leonardo da Vinci; l. Huguenots with Coligny; Elizabeth of England; r. Gustavus Adolphus; in the aisles, l. Copernicus, Galileo, Kepler, Newton, Columbus, &c.; r. Dürer, Holbein, Leonardo da Vinci, Raphael, Gutenberg, Shakspeare, Cervantes, Petrarch, &c.

Adjoining and between the great paintings are several figures on a gold ground, over the doors Tradition and History, Science and Primitive Art (poetry). Between the large pictures the lawgivers Moses, Solon, Charlemagne, Frederick the Great; above them Egypt, Greece, Italy, Germany. On the window-walls the arts of Sculpture, Painting, Architecture, and Engraving.

Around the entire hall, beneath the richly decorated pendent work, runs a *Frieze*, bearing a humorous representation (in grisaille) of the history of the development of mankind, terminating with Humboldt leaning on his Cosmos, the whole hardly intelligible without a detailed explanation.

First Floor of the New Museum

(Collection of Casts).

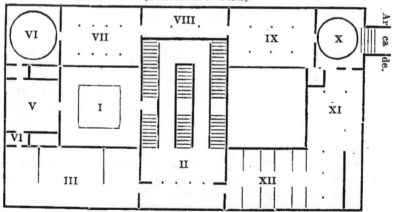

The **First Floor**, or central storey, of the **New Museum**, which is first entered by the connecting passage from the Old, is entirely occupied by the very extensive and valuable *Collection of Casts, arranged in twelve saloons. Similarity of subject was the chief principle on which the rearrangement of 1871 took place, while in the general grouping of the collection a chronological order has been observed. Detailed catalogue of the antiques 15 Sgr., extract 2¹|₂ Sgr.

I. GALLERY OF THE N. COURT (entrance see Plan). This room contains casts of the most ancient works of the plastic art: Assyrian reliefs (*B.C. 1200—700*); early Greek statues (among them the Lions from Agamemnon's castle at Mycene, etc.). Early Greek metopæ (about *B.C. 600*) and tombstones. Also reliefs, metopæ, and friezes of the best period of Greek art (about *440*), e. g. from the Parthenon, from the Theseum at Athens, and from the temple of Zeus at Olympia.

Returning by the (II.) Staircase the visitor now enters the

III. GREEK SALOON. Tympanum groups from the Temple of Minerva at Ægina at the upper end of the saloon (dating from the time of the Persian wars) show the transition from the rigid early Greek style to the spirited and natural beauty of the golden period (about *B.C. 440*, Phidias and his pupils). To the latter period belong the tympanum groups and frieze of the Parthenon at Athens; then reliefs and tombstones of the same period. The ten *Mural Paintings*, beginning from the entrance from the staircase, represent: 1. Ancient Athens; 2. Temple of Zeus at Olympia; 3. Monument of Lysicrates at Athens; 4. The Acropolis at Athens; 5. Temple of Zeus at Ægina; 6. Sacred grove at Olympia; 7. Temple of Apollo Epicurius at Phigalia; 8. View of ancient Syracuse; 9. Lycian tombstones; 10. Altar of Zeus Lyciæus in Arcadia.

IV. ANTE-CHAMBER: Laocoön group, the well known work of the Rhodian school, 3rd cent. B.C.

V. SALOON and CABINET, containing heroic representations: Group of the Farnese Bull, a work of the Rhodian school; Amazons. Mythological: Representations of Apollo, and of Artemis, from the earliest period down to the conquest of Greece, *B.C. 146*, and the time of Augustus, *A.D. 14*. Then examples of the Ionic and Doric orders of architecture. In the corner to the l. a model of the Acropolis in its present form.

VI. GREEK CUPOLA SALOON: Figures of Pallas Athene of different periods (among them 664. Athena-Medici, now in the Ecole des Beaux Arts at Paris, and probably appertaining to the Parthenon sculptures). Figures of Hercules; Menelaus with the body of Patroclus, of the Rhodian school. *Mural Paintings*: Theseus slaying the Minotaur, Hercules capturing the Arcadian stag, Bellerophon slaying the Chimæra, Perseus releasing Andromeda.

VII. NIOBE SALOON, containing various heroic and mythological representations. By the long wall, Group of the Children of Niobe, probably from the tympanum of a temple of Apollo, copy of an earlier work of the Attic school of Scopas and Praxiteles (*B.C. 400—325*); Zeus of Otricoli, copy of a celebrated work by Phidias (*500—432*); Hera Ludovisi, copy of the Hera of Polycletes (*460—400*); Discus thrower; Borghese gladiator; Wrestler of the Rhodian school; Dying Gaul, of the school of Pergamus (about *B.C. 200*); Colossal figure of the Nile, of the same period; Thornextractor, a genre sculpture of the same period. Then, along the wall to the r., numerous portrait-busts of Greek poets and generals, most of them Roman copies of Greek originals. *Mural Paintings:* Greek heroic and mythological scenes.

VIII. SALOON. Cabinets on the r. contain small casts, chiefly from Pompeii; on the l. figures of animals, of Greek and Roman workmanship. The door leading to the staircase from this room is closed.

IX. SALOON. Representations of Aphrodite and Dionysus; figures of satyrs, chiefly of Græco-Roman origin; Sleeping Ariadne, 1st cent. B.C. Then portrait-busts of the Roman empire. — The walls are embellished with seventeen encaustic (wax) paintings of ancient Roman localities, designed by Stüler, Pape, and Seiffert.

X. ROMAN CUPOLA SALOON: Roman portrait-statues; along the wall reliefs from the Arch of Constantine and the Column of Trajan at Rome. Three large *Mural Paintings*: Consecration of the Church of St. Sophia by Justinian, by *Schrader;* Subjugation of Wittekind by Charlemagne, designed by Kaulbach and executed by *Gräf;* Christianity adopted as the religion of the state, by *Stilke.*

XI. MEDIÆVAL SALOON. Casts of sculptures and mouldings in German, French, and English churches. On the l. Tomb of St. Sebaldus at Nuremberg, by Vischer; St. Hippolytus, from the Lateran; Font at Hildesheim. In the cupolas portraits of German Emperors.

XII. MODERN ART SALOON (divided into ten sections). Immediately to the l. Ghiberti's doors of the Baptistery at Florence, with scenes from the Old Testament; St. George, by Donatello; Mercury by Giovanni da Bologna; Entombment by Kraft; r. Michael Angelo's monuments of the Medicis at Florence, Pietà, youth in fetters, Moses. The last section contains reliefs, a Venus, and Hope, by Thorvaldsen; Victoria, by Rauch.

In the STAIRCASE (Pl. II.), as already mentioned, a flight of steps descends to the **Ground Floor** of the New Museum, which contains the collection of Northern Antiquities, the Ethnographical Collection, and the Greek Court on the r., and the Egyptian Museum on the l.

Ground Floor of the New Museum.

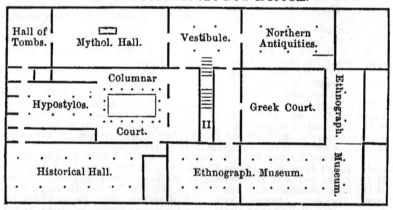

The **Northern Antiquities**, arranged in twelve cabinets and along the walls, consist of various kinds of weapons, household utensils, cinerary urns, gold and silver trinkets, &c., provided with the names of the places where they were found. Most of them were found in tumuli and belong to various periods, ranging from the flint to the bronze and the Roman. The stereochromatic (water-colours glazed with a solution of silica) *Mural Paintings* by *Bellermann, Müller*, etc. illustrate the mythology of the North. *W. Wall*, beginning opposite the entrance: 1st window: Hertha, the Ceres, and Odin, the Jupiter of the North; above them day and night. 2nd window: Baldur, the northern Apollo, and Hulda, the goddess of domestic life. 3rd window: Freyr, god of spring, and Freya, his sister, goddess of love; above them dwarf ship-builders. 4th window: Odur and Freya on the battle-field, marking with blood the dead who are worthy of Walhalla (paradise of the heroes), in the centre Walkyries (fates) conducting the dead to Walhalla, r. Tyr, god of war. — Above the door: Odin, the universal father, l. the Walhalla, r. Helheim, the abode of those who have died a natural death. — *E. Wall:* wicked deities. By the first window l. Hela, r. Loke; by the 2nd window Nornas (fates); by the 3rd window water-sprites, the griffin, and contest of the giants with the dragon; by the 4th window Titania and elves; Thor, god of thunder, in a chariot drawn by mountain goats.

The visitor next enters the room containing the geographically arranged **Ethnographical Collection**, comprising numerous objects illustrative of the manners and habits of foreign nations, arranged in thirty-four cabinets, provided with the names of the different countries.

On leaving the Ethnographical Museum the visitor passes through a door to the r. leading to the so-called **Greek Court**, containing a *Frieze by *Schievelbein*, representing the destruction of Pompeii, and a number of modern copies of ancient and modern works of art in bronze (from the Berlin Industrial Institution) and plaster.

The ***Egyptian Museum** (see Plan), one of the most important collections of the kind, founded by *Passalacqua*, and greatly extended by *Lepsius* in 1845, is arranged in five saloons, the artistic embellishment of which contributes materially to explain the nature of the different objects. Instructive catalogue by Lepsius, 2½ Sgr.

I. The MYTHOLOGICAL SALOON is chiefly occupied by sarcophagi and mummies. The most valuable of the former, placed under glass in the centre, was found at Thebes. The mural paintings afford a survey of the principal forms of the Egyptian gods.

II. SALOON OF THE TOMBS. The **Tomb Chambers* here, entirely covered internally and externally with hieroglyphics, were brought in fragments from the Necropolis at Memphis by Professor Lepsius and reconstructed in their original forms. They all belong to the ancient Egyptian kingdom, dating from between 3000 and 2000 years before Christ.

III. HYPOSTYLE. On the walls between the columns are papyrus MS. preserved under glass. A niche in the background contains the colossal statue of King Horus.

IV. The PASSAGE ROOM to the historical saloon also contains papyrus rolls, as well as tiles of the clay of the Nile.

V. The HISTORICAL SALOON contains figures of gods, kings, priests, and dignitaries of the kingdom, monuments, altars, inscriptions, mural paintings, &c., chiefly of the later kingdom, B.C. 1650—525. The glass cabinets contain various smaller objects of a religious and domestic nature, utensils, heads of mummies, mummies of sacred animals, cats, fish, crocodiles, frogs, ibises, grasshoppers, amulets, cut stones, trinkets, coins, fruit. The mural paintings beginning on the E. side, and continuing towards the l., present a chronological review of the different periods of the history of Egypt: 1—17. The old kingdom, 18—40. The later kingdom.

VI. The COLONNADE COURT, together with the contiguous hypostyle and the niches terminating the latter, the central of which is occupied by the colossal figure of King Horus, represents the main features of an Egyptian temple. In the centre of the entrance-court stands an altar. In front of the hypostyle are two colossal figures of kings in a sitting posture, in porphyry; to the l. Ramses II., termed Sesostris by the Greeks, entirely uninjured; to the r. Usortesen I. (B.C. 2000), consisting chiefly of fragments reunited and supplemented. In the centre two ram sphynxes (that on the r. a cast). The hieroglyphics on the entablature record in the Egyptian language that these monuments were arranged here in 1848 by order of Frederick William IV. The mural paintings by *Schirmer*, *Pape*, and others, represent Egyptian landscapes.

A COLLECTION OF CASTS, upwards of 200 in number, also belongs to this department.

In the PASSAGE OF THE SECOND FLOOR is the entrance to the

Collection of Engravings, open to the public on Sundays only, on other days to students. It comprises upwards of 500,000 engravings, 20,000 drawings, miniatures, etchings, &c. A number of the most important impressions in an historical point of view are exposed to view in glazed frames, while the rest are preserved in portfolios in the cabinets. The visitor is recommended to proceed to the end of the saloon and begin with an inspection of the cabinets on the W. side. On the six cabinets on the W. side of the *Blue Room* are Germans and Netherlanders, beginning with the 'Master of 1464', down to Wille, Chodowiecky, and Bause, the Netherlanders extending down to the 'peintres-graveurs' of the 17th cent. The cabinets on the E. side contain Italian, French and Spanish, English and Russian masters. — On the walls of the *Green Room* are a number of admirable engravings and drawings of every school and period in contemporaneous frames. — The *Brown Room* contains drawings, chiefly by Dürer, water-colours, and miniatures. The portfolios are on request placed before visitors for inspection. A niche here contains a bust of Dürer.

The **Kunstkammer**, or Chamber of Art, entered to the r. from the passage of the upper floor (see above), contains the *Historical Collection* and the *Smaller Objects of Art.*

I. *Room.* Artistically finished furniture; small models of celebrated monuments; in the glass cabinets numerous *models of buildings architecturally interesting, chiefly in N. Germany.

The *Niche* adjoining contains relics and memorials of the royal family of Prussia, e. g. the life-size figure of the Great Elector, beside which are those (in wax) of kings Frederick I. and Frederick the Great in the clothes usually worn by them, the hat of the Great Elector worn by him at the Battle of Fehrbellin, pipes used by Frederick the Great's father in his 'Tabakscollegium', Frederick's flute, drawings by him, &c.; hussar uniform and 'Kolpak' of General Ziethen; Napoleon's orders, hat, and pistols, captured in his carriage at Genappe after the Battle of Waterloo; Blücher's orders, &c.

II. *Room.* Majolicas and glasses, most of them of Italian workmanship, of the 16th and 17th cent.; Nuremberg glasses of the 17th cent.

III. *Room.* Smaller objects of art, carved ivory and wood, tankards, vases, glasses, enamelled ornaments, &c., historically arranged.

IV. *Room.* Ecclesiastical antiquities, crucifixes, monstrances, reliquaries.

The *Packhof* (Pl. 127) adjoining the Museum is a modern building, designed by Schinkel.

d. *Schiller - Platz.   Wilhelms - Strasse.   Wilhelms - Platz. Leipziger Strasse. Leipziger Platz. Potsdam Suburb. Belle-Alliance-Platz. Kreuzberg.*

With the Behren-Strasse to the S. of the Linden begins the Friedrichs - Stadt (p. 8), the most regularly built quarter of Berlin, founded by Frederick I. and Frederick William I. It was formerly a dull part of the town, but the N. part of it next the Linden is now the great centre of business and the principal rendezvous of travellers. The most important streets intersecting it are the *Friedrichs-Strasse*, running from N. to S., and the *Leipziger Strasse*, from E. to W., the junction of which is probably the busiest spot in the city. The Friedrichs-Str., the longest in Berlin, with its prolongation to the N. of the Linden, measures 2½ M. from the Oranienburg to the Halle Gate.

In the Schiller - Platz (or *Gensdarmen-Markt*), a few paces only from the Linden and the Platz am Opernhaus, are situated the Schauspielhaus, the French, and the New Church.

The *Schauspielhaus*, or Theatre (Pl. 152), 84 yds. long, 55 yds. in depth, and 125 ft. in height, was erected by *Schinkel* in 1819—21 in the Greek style, to replace the original building which was burned down in 1817, and is one of that master's finest works. The principal façade towards the E. is embellished with an Ionic portico, approached by a prominent flight of steps. At the sides of the steps are two groups in bronze by *Tieck*, genii riding on a panther and a lion. The tympanum of the portico contains a Group of the Children of Niobe in sandstone, by the same sculptor. The summit of the principal part of the building is crowned with an Apollo in a chariot drawn by two griffins, a group in bronze by *Rauch* and *Tieck*, in the tympanum beneath which are Melpomene and Polyhymnia. On the W. summit of the building, corresponding to the Apollo, is a Pegasus in copper. The N. tympanum contains the *triumphal procession of Bacchus with Ariadne; in the S. tympanum, *Orpheus and Eurydice, both by *F. Tieck.* Besides the theatre, in which seats are provided for 1500 spectators, the building contains two concert-rooms, the larger of which can accommodate 1200 persons.

In front of the steps of the theatre stands the **Monument of Schiller**, 19 ft. in height, consisting entirely of Carrara marble, by *Begas.* The figure of the poet, 9 ft. in height, partially enveloped in a long mantle, stands on a pedestal originally destined to serve as a fountain, and adorned at the corners with allegorical figures of lyric and dramatic poetry, historical composition and philosophy.

To the N. of the theatre is the *French Church* (Pl. 78), to the S. the *New Church*, or German Cathedral (Pl. 94), both built at the beginning of last century in the Renaissance style, and provided by *Gontard* in the reign of Frederick the Great with handsome towers covered with domes and surrounded with detached columns. .

In the Gensdarmen-Markt, at the corner of the Jäger-Strasse, opposite the theatre, is also situated the building of the *Seehandlung*, an institution founded in 1772 for the promotion of trade, now a species of bank under the control of the minister of finance. The Bank of Prussia is in the vicinity.

The *WILHELMS-STRASSE (Pl. E, F, 4—6), which forms the W. boundary of the Friedrichs-Stadt, diverges from the Linden near the Pariser Platz towards the S.E., and like the Friedrichs-Strasse terminates in the Belle-Alliance-Platz (p. 33). The N. half of this street is considered the most aristocratic quarter of the city. No. 70, on the r. (approaching from the Linden), is the residence of *Herr Hansemann;* No. 72, the *Palace of Princes Alexander and George of Prussia*; No. 73, that of the *Minister of the Household*; No. 65, opposite, the residence of the *Minister of Justice.* Then on the r., No. 76, the *Foreign Office of the Empire of Germany* and *Residence of the Chancellor of the Empire*; No. 77, *Palace of Prince Radziwill*; No. 79, *Minister of Trade and Public Works.*

On the l. side of the street is the WILHELMS-PLATZ, adorned with flower-beds and with **Statues** of six heroes of the three Silesian wars of Frederick the Great: *Schwerin*, who fell at Prague in 1757; *Winterfeldt*, Frederick's favourite, who fell at Moys, near Görlitz, in 1757; *Seydlitz*, the hero of Rossbach, who died in 1773; *Keith*, who fell at Hochkirch in 1758; the gallant *Ziethen*, who died in 1786; and *Prince Leopold of Anhalt-Dessau*, the victor at Kesselsdorf, who died in 1747. The marble statues (p. 38) with which the Platz was formerly embellished were replaced by bronze statues in 1862, Schwerin and Winterfeldt newly designed by *Kiss*, the others copied from the original figures, of which Ziethen and Leopold of Dessau were by *Schadow*. .

On the N. side of the Wilhelms-Platz is the **Palace of Prince
Charles** (Pl. 133), erected in 1737, and remodelled by *Schinkel* in
1827. The *Museum of Weapons* (adm. p. 7; visitors apply to
the major-domo, Wilhelms-Platz 8) on the ground-floor, containing
among other curiosities some admirable specimens of Italian workmanship of different centuries, is well worth seeing. — Adjoining
the Wilhelms-Platz on the E. is the small *Ziethen-Platz*, connected
with the Schiller-Platz by the Mohren-Strasse. On the r. in
the latter is the *Church of the Trinity*, of which Schleiermacher,
the eminent preacher and philosopher, was incumbent from 1809
until his death in 1834.

A few paces to the S. of the Wilhelms-Platz the traveller
reaches the busy *LEIPZIGER STRASSE, about 1 M. in length,
running parallel with the Linden, and leading from the Dönhofs-
Platz (p. 35) to the Potsdam Gate. At the S.W. corner of its
intersection with the Friedrichs-Strasse is the attractive depôt of
the *Royal Porcelain Manufactory*, on the first floor. To the W. of
the Wilhelms-Strasse, No. 5 in the Leipziger Strasse, on the l., is
the *War Office*, an imposing edifice, restored in 1847. The four
figures in sandstone at the portals represent a hussar, a gunner, a
grenadier, and a cuirassier. No. 4, adjacent, is the temporary
Reichstags-Gebäude or **Hall of the Imperial Diet** (Pl. 141), hastily
erected in 1871 on the site of the old porcelain manufactory.

The **Interior** (adm. p. 7) is worthy of a visit. The entrance to
the assembly hall is by the central door. The *Vestibule* is adorned with
medallion portraits of distinguished Germans (Stein, Fichte, Arndt, Dahl-
mann, Mathy, Uhland, Schiller, and Scharnhorst). The *Assembly Hall*,
lighted from above, contains seats for 400 deputies and the 44 members of
the Imperial Council. The building contains seven other halls, and numerous apartments for committee meetings, for the Imperial Chancellor, the
President of the Diet, the President of the Council, &c. The entrance to
the galleries is not by the central door, but in the court, into which the
gateway on the l. leads, and where the office is situated (cards of admission to the sessions, see p. 7).

Adjoining the Hall of the Diet is the *Herrenhaus*, or Upper
Chamber (Pl. 67), beyond which the Leipziger Str. expands into
the octagonal LEIPZIGER PLATZ, adorned with grounds. No. 11
on the S. side of the latter is the *Palace of Prince Adalbert*, Admiral
of the German navy (d. 1873). No. 12 on the N. side is the *Navy-
Office*. On the r. side of the street which intersects the Platz rises
the bronze statue of the Prussian general and premier *Count Brandenburg*, erected in 1862.

The **Potsdam Suburb**, outside the *Potsdam Gate*, one of the
most attractive quarters of Berlin, is the residence of the wealthier
portion of the community. The N. half, lying between the canal
and the Thiergarten, is chiefly remarkable for its handsome
dwelling-houses and villas, most of them designed by *Stüler* and
other eminent architects. The streets skirting the Thiergarten are
a favourite winter promenade (p. 42).

·The POTSDAMER PLATZ lies immediately outside the Potsdam Gate·; on the l. side of it is the station of the *Berlin*, *Potsdam*, *and Magdeburg Railway*. The *Bellevue-Strasse*, with its continuation the *Bellevue Allée*, leads from this Platz direct to Schloss *Bellevue*, on the N. side of the Thiergarten, comp. p. 43.

The *Potsdamer Strasse*, leading S.W. from the Platz, is the old high road to Potsdam. No. 24, at the corner of the Schöneberger Ufer, is the **Agricultural Museum** (Pl. 110; adm. p. 7), interesting chiefly to farmers and mechanicians. Near it is *St. Matthew's Church* (Pl. 92), a brick edifice by *Stüler*, completed in 1845; in front of it a colossal figure of the evangelist in terracotta, by *Wolff*.

The *Botanical Garden (adm. p. 6) is situated at the village of Schöneberg, which also .lies on the Potsdam road, 1 M. from the gate (omnibus see p. 3; comp. Map of Environs in the large Plan). It is one of the most extensive in Europe, and contains upwards of 20,000 species of plants in thirty-one different hothouses. The palms and cacti are particularly fine.

The quarter between the Potsdam and the *Anhalt Gate* is the residence of many of ·the higher government officials. The *Anhalt-Station* (Pl. 8) and the *Church of St. Luke* (in the Bernburger-Str., a brick edifice by *Stüler*) are situated here.

The S. Half of the Friedrichs-Stadt· is comparatively dull and uninteresting.

In the Wilhelms-Str., No. 102,· opposite the Koch-Str., is the *Palace of Prince Albert* (Pl. 131), erected in 1738, and remodelled by Schinkel in 1832. The entrance-court is .separated from the street by a colonnade.

In the Enke-Platz, at the end of the Charlotten-Str., is situated the *Observatory* (adm. p. 7), erected by *Schinkel* in 1835, with a handsome·dome. Opposite to it, Linden-Str. 15, is the *Kammergericht* (Pl. 70), the appeal court of justice for the Berlin and Potsdam district. The court contains a marble statue of Baron Cocceji (d. 1765), chancellor and president of the supreme court of justice under Frederick William I. and Frederick the Great.

The Wilhelms, Friedrichs, and Linden-Strasse converge in the circular BELLE-ALLIANCE-PLATZ (Pl. F, 6), the centre of which is embellished with the *Friedens-Säule*, or **Column of Peace**, 197 ft. in height, erected in 1840 to commemorate the 25th anniversary of the peace of 1815. It consists of a column of granite with a marble capital, placed on a lofty pedestal, and is crowned with a Victory by *Rauch*, holding a twig of palm in her left hand, and presenting the victor's wreath to the city with the right.

Outside the HALLE GATE, opposite the large *Barracks* of the 1st Dragoon Guards, lie the old and the new **Jerusalem Cemeteries**, where several distinguished Germans are interred. Adjoining it is the *Old Trinity Cemetery (Dreifaltigkeits-Kirchhof)*, in the N.W. corner of which *Mendelssohn* is buried.

The Belle-Alliance-Str. leads from the Halle Gate (omnibus see p. 3) to the (³|₄ M.) *Kreuzberg (213 ft. above the sea-level), a sand-hill rising about 100 ft. above the city, of which, being the only eminence in the environs, it affords a fine survey. On the top rises a Gothic *Obelisk* in ron, 62 ft. in height, dedicated by Frederick William III. to his people, and inaugurated in 1821. It was designed by *Schinkel;* statues and reliefs by *Rauch, Tieck,* and *Wichmann.* The invalid custodian shows the monument (5 Sgr.). — The extensive *Tivoli* brewery is situated on the Kreuzberg.

In the *Tempelhofer Feld*, an open piece of ground extending from the Kreuzberg to the S. to the village of *Tempelhof*, grand reviews of the Berlin garrison take place annually from spring to autumn.

To the E. of the Kreuzberg lies the **Hasenhaide**, with the infantry rifle galleries and a large gymnastic ground in which a statue of *F. L. Jahn* (d. 1852), the German 'Turnvater' (father of gymnastics), was erected in 1872. The *Carlsgarten* here contains monuments to the guardsmen who fell in 1866 and 1870—71. — In the new **Dreifaltigkeits-Kirchhof**, or *Trinity Cemetery* (Pl. G, 8), repose *Schleiermacher* (d. 1834), *Neander* (d. 1850), and other eminent persons. — The distinguished philologists *Jacob* and *Wilhelm Grimm* are buried in the **Matthäi-Kirchhof**, or *Cemetery of St. Matthew*, which lies between the Kreuzberg and the Botanical Garden.

e. *Bau-Academie. Ravené Picture Gallery. Louisenstadt.*

To the S. of the Schlossbrücke (p. 15) rises the ***Bau-Academie,** or *Academy of Architecture* (Pl. 17), a lofty square edifice of four storeys, constructed in brick with remarkable skill and taste by *Schinkel* in 1835. The ground-floor is occupied by shops. The entrance to the upper floors is on the N. side towards the Schinkel-Platz. The passage is adorned with a colossal bust of the chief government architect Mellin (d. 1860). The first floor contains the lecture rooms of the academy, which is attended by about 600 students. On the upper floor is the **Beuth-Schinkel-Museum* (adm. p. 7), an extensive collection of architectural sketches, plans, etchings, the designs of the frescoes in the vestibule of the Old Museum (p. 7), etc., comprising the finest and most important of Schinkel's works.

The Schinkel-Platz on the N. side of the Bau-Academie, is adorned with three statues in bronze. In the centre that of **Schinkel* (d. 1849), with Science, Architecture, Sculpture, and Painting as Caryatides at the four corners of the pedestal, the whole designed by *Drake.* On the r. that of *Thaer* (d. 1828), the agriculturist, *Rauch's* last work; on the l. that of *Beuth* (d. 1853), to whose efforts Prussia has been much indebted for her advance in industrial pursuits, designed by *Kiss.*

In the Werder Market, adjoining the Academy, is the *Werder Church* (Pl. 99), a Gothic building with two flat towers, erected by Schinkel in 1824—30. The altar-piece is a Resurrection by *Begas;* at the sides the Four Evangelists by *W. Schadow.* — No. 5 in this Platz is *Gerson's* extensive clothing and haberdashery shop.

Opposite the church is situated the **Mint** (Pl. 123; adm. p. 7), built in 1794, and recently enlarged by the addition of a handsome brick structure, the sandstone frieze of which over the ground-floor is embellished with reliefs by *Schadow* representing the processes of obtaining and treating the metals.

In the vicinity , Französische Str. 33c., at the corner of the
Oberwall-Str., is the *Telegraph Office* (Pl. 149), a large building
completed in 1863, the central station for Northern Germany. A
little to the S., Jäger-Str. 34, is the *Bank of Prussia* (Pl. 16), recently extended, adjoining which is the *Hausvoigtei*, or prison.

From the Hausvoigtei-Platz the traveller may now proceed by
the Jerusalemer Str. to the DÖNHOFS-PLATZ, where the *Abgeord-
neten-Haus,* or *Chamber of the Prussian Deputies* (Leipziger Str. 75)
is situated (adm. p. 6).

No. 77—79 in the Kommandanten-Strasse, which diverges from
the Dönhofs-Platz to the S.W. (on the l. side, opposite the Linden-
Str.) is Geber's extensive industrial building, a large saloon in which
contains the *Picture Gallery* of the 'Verein der Berliner Künstler',
or Artists' Association (entrance by the 2nd portal; adm. p. 7).
Adjoining the gallery are several spacious assembly rooms and other
apartments tastefully decorated by members of the association.

At Nos. 92, 93 Wall-Strasse, to the W. of, and not far from the
Dönhofs-Platz, is *Ravené's Picture Gallery* (Pl. 139; adm. p. 7),
a choice collection of 147 works by modern German and French
masters, and admirably lighted. Entrance by No. 93 ; visitors ring
on the upper floor. Catalogues for consultation.

Large Room. Wall on the r.: 60. *Hübner*, Game Law; 9. *Begas*, Moor-
washing; 67. *Knauss*, Peasant girl gathering flowers; *22. *Gallait*, Bohemian
musicians; *131. *Tidemand*, Norwegian funeral scene; 111. *Ritter*, The
drowned fisher-boy; 46. *Hildebrandt*, Winter amusement. — Entrance
wall : 130. *Tidemand*, The slain wolf. — Wall to the l.: 34. *Hasenclever*,
Jobs (a dunce) undergoing examination; 94. *Meyerheim*, Going to church;
33. *Hasenclever*, Jobs as a nightwatchman; 35. *Hasenclever*, Portrait of himself; 62. *Jordan*, Burial of the youngest child; 32. *Hasenclever*, Wine-
tasting; 37. *Hasenclever*, Jobs as a schoolmaster. Between the two columns: 47. *Hildebrandt*, Bay of Rio de Janeiro by moonlight. Then in
the second division of the room: 125. *Schreyer*, Attack of Prussian hussars on artillery; 62. *H. ten Kate*, Genre piece; 80. *Lessing*, Landscape;
10. *Brendel*, Sheep leaving the stable; 89. *Menzel*, Frederick the Great
travelling; 122. *Schmitson*, Transport of Hungarian mares; 1. *A. Achenbach*, Norwegian coast; 14. *Auguste* and *Rosa Bonheur*, Landscape with
cattle. — Short wall: 41, 42, 45. *E. Hildebrandt*, Landscapes; 142. *Robert
Fleury*, Massacre of Jews on the coronation day of Edward the Martyr
of England in 975; 137. *Horace Vernet*, Zouave acting as a nurse; 66.
Krauss, Girl playing with cats. — Long wall: 135. *Troyon*, Dogs leashed
together; 17. *Couture*, Noble youth playing with falcons; 25. *Graeb*, Interior
of the cathedral at Halberstadt; 3. *Achenbach*, Sea piece. — The adjoining
cabinets contain drawings, water-colours by *Graeb, Gudin, Preyer, Brendel*,
&c. In the first, 104. *Preyer*, Sparrow's breakfast; 90. *Meissonnier*, Man
reading. In the cabinet of the entrance wall, 126. *Schröder*, Jester in
the character of a baker's assistant; 12. *Biard*, Fight with polar bears.

On quitting the gallery the traveller may proceed to the N. by
the Grünstrassen-Brücke, the Petri-Platz, and the Brüder-Strasse
to the Schloss-Platz (p. 36). In the Petri-Platz is situated the
Gothic *Church of St. Peter* (Pl. 96), erected from designs by *Strack*
in 1846—53 to replace an earlier structure. The bold vaulting has
a span of 49 ft., being about 5 ft. wider than that of the cathedral
at Cologne. Tower 311 ft. in height.

3 *

The LOUISENSTADT extending to the S. of the Wall-Strasse, which has chiefly sprung up within the last 25 years, is now the largest and most populous, but least interesting quarter of Berlin. In an open space about the middle of this quarter rises the *Church of St. Michael (Pl. 93), a Romanesque edifice designed by *Soller*, and erected in 1856 as a Rom.- Cath. garrison church. The tympanum is adorned with a St. Michael by *Kiss;* the statues and decorations are in terracotta. — A little farther to the S.W. rises the imposing castellated Bethanien (Pl. 19; adm. p. 6), with its two towers and long façade, completed in 1847, comprising an admirably organised hospital and an institution for Protestant sisters of charity. — The adjacent *Church of St. Thomas* was completed in 1868.

The *Jacobikirche*, or Church of St. James (Pl. 83) in the Oranien-Str., No. 133, designed by *Stüler*, and completed in 1845, is a brick edifice in the basilica style, with a detached tower and an entrance court with colonnades containing a statue of St. James.

At No. 11 Köpenicker-Strasse, not far from the barracks of the pioneer guards, is a collection of eighteen *Models of French Fortresses* (adm. p. 8), brought from Paris in 1815. — Near the pioneer barracks is the *Swimming Bath* by the Oberbaum, mentioned at p. 4.

Outside the *Köpenick Gate* (Pl. K, 6) is the station of the *Berlin and Görlitz Railway* (comp. p. 1), opposite which, on the r. bank of the Spree, are the Berlin *Water Works* (p. 38).

f. *Kurfürsten-Brücke. Rathhaus. Rauch Museum. Stralau Quarter. Königs-Stadt.*

From the SCHLOSS-PLATZ (p. 16), to the S.W. of the Palace, the *Lange*, or *Kurfürsten-Brücke* (i. e. Bridge of the Elector) leads to the old town of Berlin. The bridge is adorned with an equestrian *Statue of the Great Elector (d. 1688) in bronze, designed by *Schlüter*, and erected in 1703, with four slaves at.the corners, a clever and artistic group, with a Latin dedication by Frèderick I.

The Königs-Strasse, which begins beyond the bridge, and intersects the *Old Town*, is a great artery of traffic, presenting almost as busy a scene as the Leipziger Strasse. No. 60 in this street is the extensive *Imperial Post Office* (Pl. 135; comp. p. 4). — To the S., in the neighbourhood, is the *Church of St. Nicholas* (Pl. 94a), the oldest in Berlin, dating from the 13th cent., and containing the tomb of the celebrated jurist Puffendorf (d. 1690). On the outside is the tomb of Spener (d. 1705). In the Molken-Markt are situated the *Police Court* and the *Criminal Court* (Pl. 134). — To the N. of the post-office, near the Neue Markt, rises the *Marienkirche* (Pl. 91), an edifice of the 14th cent., with a tower 296 ft. in height added in 1790. It contains the finely executed tombstone of Count Sparr, a field marshal under the Great Elector, by *Quellinus*, and a pulpit by *Schlüter*.

Farther on in the Königs-Strasse, nearly opposite the post-office, is the Rathhaus (Pl. 137), an imposing brick edifice in the mediæval (chiefly Romanesque) style, resting on substructions of Silesian granite, designed by *Waesemann*, and erected in 1860—70. The principal façade is towards the Königs-Strasse, with a tower 276 ft. in height, to the second storey of which the.-handsome

the Great which formerly adorned the Wilhelms-Platz (p. 31) are
also preserved here.

To the E. of the old town of Berlin, on the r. bank of the Spree, and
reached by the *Stralau Bridge*, lies the STRALAU QUARTER, another
modern part of the town, with numerous factories, where the **Wallner**-
Theatre (Pl. 154; p. 6) is situated. — To the N. of it, in the Weber-
Strasse, rises the Romanesque *Church of St. Mark (Pl. 90), with its massive dome, erected in 1848—55 by *Stüler; frescoes in the interior by *Peters,:
Schultz, and *Stürmer*. — No. 17 Frankfurter Strasse is the extensive *Fried-
rich-Wilhelms-Hospital*.

At the S.E. end of this part of the town lie the stations of the *Ostbahn*
and the *Niederschlesisch-Märkische Bahn* (comp. p. 1). Near the latter is
the *Church of St. Andrew*, erected by *Strack* in 1854—56.

Farther towards the S.E., outside the *Stralau Gate*, are the] extensive
Water Works, with twelve steam engines in constant operation, by means
of which the city is supplied with water from the Spree.

Beyond the *Königsbrücke* and the Alexander-Platz (Pl. H, 3) the Königs-
Strasse runs N,E. through the KÖNIGSSTADT to the *Königs-Thor* (Pl. I, 2).
On a height to the r. near the gate stands the *Church of St. Bartholomew*
(Pl. 72), a Gothic building in brick, with a tower 223 ft. in height, erected
by *Stüler* in 1854—58.

Outside the Königs-Thor, to the r., and towards the S.W. as far
as the Landsberg Gate (Pl. K, 2) extends the **Friedrichshain**, a pleasant
park affording good views of the town, laid out under Frederick William
IV. A slight eminence here is adorned with a bust of Frederick the Great.

To the N.W. of the Königs-Thor, outside the Rosenthal Gate (Pl. G,
1), is the *Zionskirche*, erected by *Orth* in 1866—69, a Gothic structure in
brick, with rich tracery.

g. *Exchange. Monbijou. Synagogue.*

Opposite the Museum (p. 17), on the other side of the Spree,
and at the corner of the Burg-Str. and the Neue Friedrichs-Str., is
situated the imposing new Börse, or *Exchange (Pl. 22), erected in
1850—63 in the Renaissance style from designs by *Hitzig*, 92 yds. in
length, 67 yds. in depth. The chief façade towards the Spree is embellished with a double colonnade, above which, in the centre, is a group in
sandstone by *C. Begas*, representing Borussia as the protectress of agriculture and commerce; on the wings are smaller groups and figures,
emblematic of the most important commercial towns and countries.
Entering from the Burg-Strasse, the visitor passes through the
ante-chamber, adorned with a statue of the present king by *Siemering*, to the great hall, the largest at Berlin, 74 yds. in length, 28^1/$_2$
yds. in width, and 66 ft. in height. It is divided by arcades into
two halves, one of which is the money, the other the corn-exchange,
both adorned with appropriate frescoes by *Klöber*. During the business hours, 12—2, visitors are admitted to the gallery, which affords
the best survey of the busy scene. Entrance by the first door to the
r. in the Friedrichs-Strasse, by a stair to the first floor, then by
the first door to the l. (no fees).

In the vicinity, Burg-Strasse 19, is the *Military Academy,*
founded by General Scharnhorst in 1810. In the Neue Friedrichs-
Strasse, between Nos. 45 and 46, is the *Garrison Church* (Pl. 79),
built during the last cent., containing a Crucifixion by *C. Begas* and

several pictures representing the death of generals of the Seven
Years' War.

Proceeding to the N.W. of the new Exchange, and crossing the
Hercules-Bridge, so called from two sandstone groups by *Schadow,*
the traveller reaches the royal château of **Monbijou** (Pl. 122), which
stands in a beautiful garden always open to the public. It was
erected by *E. v. Goethe* for Queen Sophia Dorothea, wife of Frederick William I., and is now the residence of Princess Louise,
daughter of Prince Charles of Prussia. The palace contains an
English Chapel and an *Historical Museum* (adm. p. 7), where
numerous memorials of the Brandenburg and Prussian history
are preserved in 14 saloons: e. g. battles, representations of
ceremonies, portraits, models of palaces, weapons, uniforms, relics,
etc. The 4th Room is dedicated to the memory of Frederick William IV., the 5th to that of Frederick William III. and Queen
Louise. The last, the *14th, comprises in four sections reminiscences of the Great Elector, King Frederick I., Frederick William
I., and Frederick the Great.

On the N.W. side of the Monbijou garden runs the busy Oranienburger Strasse, in which (No. 30) is situated the **New Synagogue**
(Pl. 148; sacristan's dwelling in the building itself), an imposing
edifice in the Moorish style, designed by *Knoblauch,* 31 yds. in
length, 106 yds. in depth, and the principal dome 165 ft. in height.
The façade is constructed of yellow bricks with intervening layers
of different colours. The *interior, sumptuously decorated in the
Alhambra style, is entered by three bronze doors separated by
columns of green granite. A vestibule leads to the *Small Synagogue,*
in which minor religious rites are performed, beyond which is the
magnificent *Principal Synagogue,* with seats for 3000 persons. The
most richly decorated part is by the ark of the covenant, carved in
wood. During the evening service (Fridays at dusk) the 'dim religious light' from the stained glass and the cupolas produces a
remarkably fine effect.

No. 67 Oranienburger-Str., to the l. farther on, indicated by a granite
slab, is the house which the celebrated Alexander v. Humboldt occupied
from 1842 to 1859. Near the Oranienburg Gate the Oranienburger Str. unites
with the Friedrichs-Strasse (comp. p. 40).

The *Israelite Temple* (Pl. 150) in the Johannis-Str., employed by the
Old Jewish community, designed by *Stier,* possesses a handsome dome.

The *Rom. Cath. Hospital* (Pl. 102) in the Hamburger-Str., erected in
1854, is conducted by sisters of charity.

The new *Jewish Hospital,* August-Str. 15, was completed in 1861 from
designs by *Knoblauch.*

h. *N. Friedrichs–Strasse. Oranienburg–Suburb. Louisen--Strasse. Warriors' Monument. Moabit.*

The FRIEDRICHS-STRASSE (p. 30) continues in a straight direction towards the N. from the Linden to the Oranienburg Gate,

about half-way to which it crosses the Spree by the *Weidendamm-Bridge* (Pl. F, 3). Near the latter, on this side of the river, at the corner of the Georgs and the Stall-Strasse, is the **German Industrial Museum** (entrance Stall-Str. 7; adm. p. 7), comprising specimens of all kinds of products from different countries, most of them purchased at the Paris Exhibition of 1867, and since gradually augmented. A *Modelling* and *Drawing School* and a good *Library* are connected with the Museum. In the Kupfergraben opposite is the extensive *Barrack* of the Field Artillery Guards.

To the r., farther on in the Friedrichs-Strasse, on the r. bank of the Spree, is the *Barrack* of the 2nd Infantry Guards. On the l., to the S. of the Carls-Strasse, is the *Market Hall*, built in 1867, a spacious structure of glass and iron, designed for the purpose of concentrating all the markets of the city, but still closed.

Outside the ORANIENBURG GATE, to the r. in the Chaussee-Strasse, is **Borsig's Engine Factory** (adm. p. 6), a vast establishment where 160 locomotives are manufactured annually. (Borsig's other establishments and hothouses, see p. 41.)

Opposite the factory is the Rom. Cath. **Hedwig's Cemetery**, where the eminent painter *Cornelius* (d. 1867) is interred. — Farther on, beyond the Invaliden-Strasse, which to the r. leads to the *Stettin Station* (Pl. F, 1) and to the l. to the *Hamburg Station* (Pl. D, E, 1, 2; comp. p. 1), are situated the three handsome *Barracks* of the Fusilier Guards (Pl. 29). — Still farther is the **Cemetery of the French Colony**, where *Ravené* (p. 35), the wealthy merchant and patron of art, is interred (sarcophagus and life size figure); then the **Old Dorotheenstadt Cemetery** with the graves of *Schinkel*, the architect (d. 1842), *Schadow*, the sculptor (d. 1850), with a statuette, *Hegel* (d. 1831) and *Fichte* (d. 1814), the philosophers, the latter with a lofty triangular obelisk, *Rauch*, the sculptor (d. 1857), *Stüler*, the architect (d. 1868), &c.

The N. prolongation of the Wilhelms-Strasse (p. 31), running parallel with the Friedrichs-Strasse, intersects the FRIEDRICH-WILHELM-STADT, and leads to the New Gate (Pl. E, 2). As far as the *Marschalls-Brücke* it is termed the *Neue Wilhelms-Strasse*, beyond it the *Louisen-Strasse*. No. 56 in the latter is the *Veterinary School* (Pl. 165), erected by *Hesse* in 1840, originally founded in 1798, and now attended by 80—100 students. It possesses good collections relating to the veterinary art. At the entrance a copy of the Florentine dogs. Garden open to the public.

To the l., opposite the Veterinary School, and entered from the Unterbaum-Str. No. 7, is the **Royal Charité** (Pl. 39), the largest hospital at Berlin, capable of accommodating 1400 patients, and chiefly designed for the gratuitous reception of the poor.

Outside the NEW GATE, immediately to the N., Nos 45, 46 Invaliden-Strasse, is the **Royal Iron Foundry** (Pl. 66; adm. p. 7), an establishment worthy of a visit, where iron wares of all descriptions, from the largest objects down to ornaments, statuettes, etc. are manufactured. In the court is a *Museum of Ores and Metals* (adm. p. 7), a choice and well arranged collection.

To the W. of the Foundry, to the l. of the traveller quitting the New Gate, is situated the **Invalidenhaus** (Pl. 69), erected by Frederick the Great in 1748 'læso et invicto militi', and surrounded by a pleasant park. In the latter, opposite the principal entrance of the hospital, rises the **Warriors' Monument**, a Corinthian column of iron 120 ft. in height, on a pedestal of granite 19 ft. in height, and decorated with allegorical groups in high relief by *Wolff*. The monument, which is crowned with the Prussian eagle, was erected in 1854 to the memory of soldiers who fell during the revolution of 1848—49. A winding iron stair (adm. 9—12 and 4—5 or 3—6 o'clock) of 181 steps leads to the top, which commands a good survey of Berlin, especially the modern part of the city: to the S. the Invalidenhaus, the Hamburg Station, the Prison, the Uhlan Barracks, and the manufacturing village of Moabit in the background; to the N. the three large barracks are most conspicuous. The city itself is concealed by the smoke of manufactories. In the vicinity, also within the hospital grounds, is an obelisk of Silesian marble, 31 ft. in height, commemorating the loss of the Prussian training corvette *Amazone*, in 1861, erected by the parents of the cadets who perished in the ill-fated vessel.

The adjoining **Invaliden-Kirchhof** is the burial-place of many distinguished officers, among whom is *Scharnhorst* (d. 1813), over whose grave a marble monument 18 ft. in height, crowned with a recumbent lion in iron, was erected in 1826 'by his comrades of 1813'.

Opposite the cemetery, towards the N.E., is the '*Central Turn-Anstalt*', an institution for training teachers of gymnastics.

To the W. of the Invalidenhaus, beyond the canal which is crossed by the Invaliden-Strasse and connected with the Spree by means of the *Humboldts-Hafen*, is situated the *Hamburg Station* (Pl. D, 1). Beyond it is the *Zellengefängniss*, or **Prison** (Pl. 168; adm. p. 7), a model establishment for the reception of 820 inmates, consisting of a central structure with wings radiating from it in the form of a star. Then the extensive *Barracks* of the 2nd Uhlan Guards. Opposite is the new *Lehrte Station* (p. 1), extending as far as the Spree, handsomely fitted up.

Beyond the latter lies the suburb of **Moabit**, so named by French immigrants, chiefly gardeners, who on account of the sandy and sterile nature of the soil termed the country '*Pays de Moab*'. Several favourite places of recreation for the lower classes are situated here, as well as some important manufactories. Among the latter is that of **Borsig** (p. 40), with interesting *Hothouses* and *Palmhouses* (adm. p. 6). The neighbouring *Johanniskirche* (Pl. 85) was erected by *Schinkel* in 1834.

i. *Königs-Platz. Thiergarten. Zoological Garden. Charlottenburg.*

Outside the Brandenburg Gate the Sommer-Strasse to the r. leads past the Thiergarten to the *KÖNIGS-PLATZ (Pl. D, E, 3), which with its environs is destined to be one of the most imposing parts of the city. The Platz, which is to be laid out in grounds, is bounded on the W. by *Kroll's Establishment* (p. 43), and on the E. by the *Raczynski Palace* (p. 42). The **Monument of Victory** in the centre, 190 ft. in height, now approaching completion, stands on a massive square pedestal adorned by Professor *Siemering* with reliefs commemorating the great victories of 1870—71 and others of earlier campaigns, and consists of a 'hall of victory' surrounded with Doric columns, and terminating in a circular tower adorned with captured cannon. A Victory by *Drake*, 42 ft. in height, is destined to crown the whole.

The above mentioned Raczynski Palace (Pl. 136), Königs-Platz No. 2, contains the choice * **Picture Gallery of Count Raczynski** (adm. p. 7), consisting chiefly of modern works.

On the stair a Ganymede by *Thorvaldsen.* — The gallery is divided by a partition into two sections, the walls of which are furnished with numbers. No. I.: *1. *Cornelius*, Christ in hell; 2. *Kaulbach*, Tradition; *3. *Kaulbach*'s cartoon of the Battle of the Huns (p. 26), occupying almost the entire wall; *4. *Cornelius*, Allegorical group; *5. *Overbeck*, Sposalizio; 7. *Führich*, Triumph of Christ; *8. *Schnorr*, The poet of the Nibelungen; 10. *Steinle*, Salutation; 11. *Bendemann*, Sapientia; 12. *Makart*, Queen of the elves; *14. *Deger*, Adam and Eve; 15. *H. Hess*, Adoration of the Shepherds and Magi (a sketch). On the window-wall, *17. *Schwind*, Father Rhine. — No. II.: 28. *Schadow*, A Templar; *32. *Preller*, Ulysses and Nausicaa in the island of the Phæacians; 34. *Meyerheim*, Woman and children in a landscape; 35. *Schadow*, Daughter of Herodias; 36. *Hübner*, The beautiful Melusina watched; *37. *Hildebrandt*, The sons of Edward; 38. *Preyer*, Breakfast; 41. *Stilke*, Pilgrims in the desert; 45. *Becker*, The wounded poacher; 47. *Rottmann*, Nauplia; 58. *Sohn*, The two Leonoras; *60. *Kaulbach*, Shepherd boy at Rome; 61. *Bendemann*, Shepherd and shepherdess; 63. *Steinbrück*, The elves; 65. *Lessing*, Confession in the wood. — No. III.: Early Italian and a few early German pictures: 72. *Botticelli*, Virgin and Child; 87. *Bellini*, Holy Family; 97. *Garofalo*, Jupiter and Io; 99. *Domenichino*, Madonna. — No. IV.: Spanish and Netherlands masters: 115. *Murillo* (?), Madonna; 119. *Zurbaran*, Madonna adored by monks; 120, 121. *Velasquez*, Blind woman, Dog, presented by the King of Spain to Count Raczynski in 1854. — No. V.: 132. *Cretius*, Cromwell surrounded by his adherents; 133. *Lepoitevin*, Fishermen on the shore; 139. *Riedel*, Nurse with child; 140. *Verboeckhoven*, Bull in a landscape; 142. *Madrazo*, Portrait of Count Raczynski; 144. *Loewenthal*, Death of Rizzio; *147. *Paul Delaroche*, Pilgrims at Rome; 149. *Ary Scheffer*, Charity; 153. *Schnetz*, Pope Sixtus V. having his fortune told by a gipsy; *155. *L. Robert*, Reapers. Also busts of Frederick William III. and IV. by *Rauch*.

To the N. of the Königs-Platz a new and handsome quarter of the town bounded by the Spree is fast springing up, consisting of the *Alsen, Bismarck, Moltke, Herwarth, Roon*, and other streets. In the Moltke-Strasse are situated the new buildings of the *General Staff*, containing the residence of Count Moltke, field-marshal and chief of the staff. The handsome *Alsenbrücke* in the vicinity crosses the Spree to the Wilhelms-Ufer and Alexander-Ufer on the Humboldts-Hafen (p. 41).

To the S. of the Königs-Platz, and immediately outside the *Brandenburg Gate*, extends the * **Thiergarten**, the largest and most attractive park near the town, shaded by fine old trees and enlivened by sheets of water, about 2 M. in length and 3/4 M. in breadth, and bounded by the Königs-Platz and the Spree on one side and the Lenné and Thiergarten-Strasse on the other. The pleasantest parts of the park are near the lakes on the W. side, at some distance from the town, but in winter the road and walks on the side next the town, leading to the S.W. of the Brandenburg Gate, are a fashionable promenade from 2 to 4 p. m. The road (p. 43) leading

from the Brandenburg Gate to Charlottenburg divides the Thiergarten into two unequal parts. On the N. side, beyond *Kroll's
Establishment* (p. 6) are the popular places of recreation known
as the *Zelte* (Pl. D, 3). In the same direction, about ³/₄ M. farther,
on the bank of the ·Spree, is situated the royal château of *Bellevue*
(Pl. C, 3), now the residence of Duke William of Mecklenburg, to
which the *Bellevue Allee*, intersecting the Charlottenburger Strasse
at the *Kleine Stern*, leads from the Potsdam Gate. Opposite the
château, on the r. bank of the Spree, lies the suburb of *Moabit*
mentioned at p. 41. From the *Grosse Stern* (Pl. B, C, 4) several roads radiate. The *Hofjäger Allee*, leading from this point to
the S., is a favourite and fashionable drive in spring. The lakes and
canals intersecting the Thiergarten afford capital skating in winter,
the neighbourhood of the *Rousseau-Island* (Pl. C, 4) being the
favourite point. — Near the *Louisen-Insel*, on which a small monument by Schadow commemorates the return of Queen Louise from
Königsberg in 1809, rises the marble **Monument of Frederick
William III.* (Pl. 43), admirably executed by *Drake* in 1849. The
pedestal, 18 ft. in height, is adorned with *reliefs representing
the blessings of peace. The monument is covered in winter.

The **Zoological Garden* (Pl. 170; adm. p. 7), which has
recently been much extended, lies at the S.W. end of the Thiergarten, and about 2¼ M. from the Brandenburg Gate. The me-
nagerie formerly kept in the Pfaueninsel at Potsdam was transferred
to this garden in 1844 and formed the nucleus of the collection.
The extensive, well shaded grounds attract numerous visitors, and
concerts are frequently given in the afternoon (**Restaurant* to the
l. of the entrance). Near the cages of the beasts of prey is a bust
of Prof. Lichtenstein, the founder of the garden. — On the N.W.
lies the *Hippodrome*.

The *Charlottenburg Road* (see Map of Environs on the larger
Plan) leads from the Brandenburg Gate to (3 M.) Charlottenburg,
to which a *Tramway* runs from the Kupfergraben (in ½ hr., car
every 10 min.; fare 2½ Sgr.). The cars start on Sundays from the
Brandenburg Gate only. *Omnibuses* also run to Charlottenburg in
summer from the Lustgarten every half-hour. *Fiacres*, see p. 3.
The precincts of the city extend as far as the Charlottenburg Bridge,
from which the palace is 1½ M. distant.

Charlottenburg (*Zipter*, Berliner Strasse 114, is the best of the
numerous cafés) is a dull town with 19,518 inhab., the principal
street of which, 1½ M. in length, lies on the Berlin and Spandau
road. The site was formerly occupied by the village of *Lietzen*, where
Sophia Charlotte, wife of Frederick I., founded a country residence
at the end of the 17th cent., after which the name was changed.

The royal *Palace*, erected in 1699 by *Schlüter*, is covered with
a handsome dome, and flanked with wings. On the r. and l. at the
entrance to the court are copies of the Borghese Gladiator in bronze.

— Between the two barracks opposite the palace are two groups in
bronze representing soldiers of the Gardes du Corps.

The entrance to the pleasant *Palace Garden* is near the small
guard-room, adjoining the W. wing. Crossing the orangery to the
r., turning to the l. on the farther side, and then following an
avenue of pines to the r., the visitor reaches (in 10 min. from the
entrance) the *Mausoleum, designed by *Schinkel* in the Doric style,
where Queen Louise (d. 1810) and her husband Frederick William
III. (d. 1840) repose. The custodian (p. 6) shows the tomb. The
recumbent figures of the illustrious pair, executed in marble by
Rauch's masterly hand, are strikingly impressive. At the sides are
beautiful candelabra, that on the r. with the three Fates by *Rauch*,
that on the l. with the three Horæ by *Tieck*; the crucifix by *Achtermann* of Rome. The heart of Frederick William IV. is placed at the
feet of his parents in a marble casket. Divine service is celebrated
here on the anniversaries of the deaths of the king and queen, the
7th June and 19th July respectively.

In the Louisen-Platz, at the upper end of Charlottenburg, is the
large *Winter Garden* of the Flora society, with a spacious palm
house in course of construction. About $1/2$ M. to the S.W. of the
Schloss-Platz lies the *Witzleben Park* on the *Lietzen-See*, well stocked
with flowers. — March's pottery works, Sophien-Strasse 1, also
deserve a visit.

On an eminence on the Spandau road, beyond Charlottenburg, lies
Westend, a group of villas and country houses which have sprung
up within the last few years. A small open space is adorned with
a colossal bust of the Emp. William.

The *Spandauer Bock*, $3/4$ M. farther, the terminus of the tramway (p.
3), is a much frequented beer-garden commanding a view of Spandau.
Pleasant walk hence through the N. end of the Spandau Forest to ($1^1/2$ M.)
Pichelsberg, situated among woods on a basin of the *Havel*, opposite the
Pichelswerder, an island which may also be visited. — The shooting lodge
of *Grunewald*, situated on the lake and in the forest of that name, $3^1/2$ M.
to the S. of Charlottenburg, is another favourite point for excursions. The
road passes the Witzleben Park.

k. *Environs of Berlin.*

(See Map on large Plan.)

The pleasantest points have already been mentioned, viz. the *Thiergarten* (p. 43), *Charlottenburg* (p. 43), the *Zoological Garden* (p. 43),
Schöneberg and the *Botanical Garden* (p. 33), *Moabit* (p. 41), *Pichelsberg*
(see above), the *Kreuzberg* and *Tempelhof* (p. 33). Then *Stralow* and
Treptow, villages on the Spree, 2 M. to the S.E. of the Köpenick Gate,
reached by omnibus or steamboat (p. 4).

To the N., $1^1/2$ M. beyond the Rosenthal Gate, is the *Gesundbrunnen*,
with a park and restaurants. About 3 M. from the Schönhausen Gate are
situated *Pankow* and *Schloss Schönhausen* with its park.

Pleasant excursion by carriage to (9 M.) *Tegel*, the residence of the
Humboldt family, originally a hunting lodge of the Great Elector, but
altered by *Schinkel* in 1822 in imitation of a Roman villa. On the four
corner towers the winds are represented in relief. In the niches of the
central part of the building towards the garden are Diana, Minerva, an

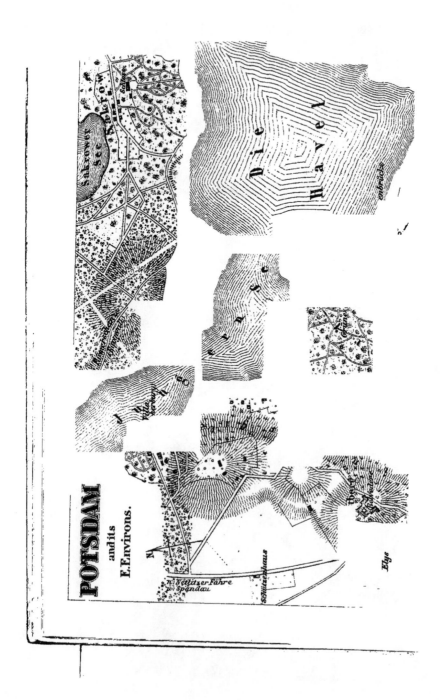

POTSDAM
and its
F. Environs.

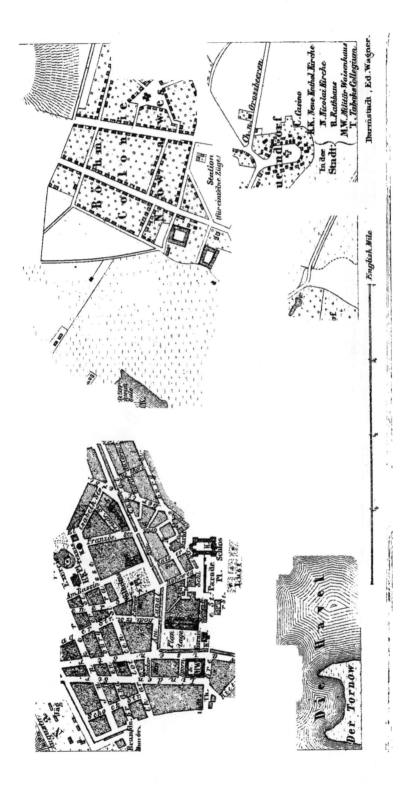

Station
(für einzelne Züge)

Böhm. Colonie

Gr. zu Grossbeeren

Neuendorf

C. Casino
K.K. Neue Kathol. Kirche
N. Nicolai Kirche
R. Rathhaus
M.W. Militär Waisenhaus
T. Tabaks Collegium

In der
Stadt:

Darmstadt, Ed. Wagner.

English Mile

Franzos. Str.

Parade
Pl.

Schloss

Der TORNOW

Der TORNOW

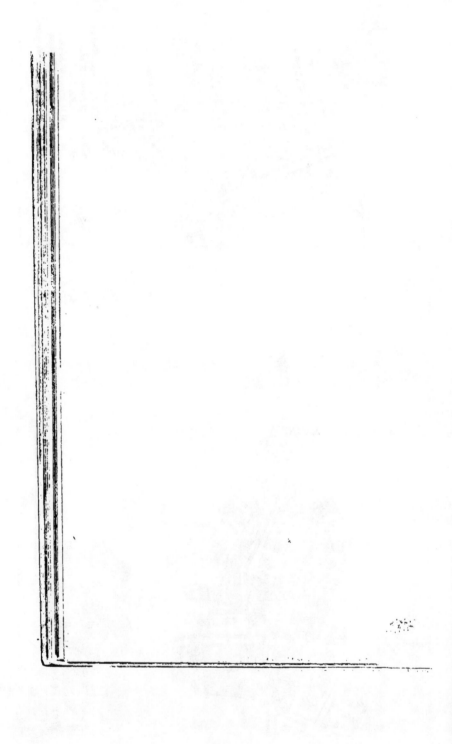

Amaz0n, and a Faun. The interi0r is decorated with admirable works of art. The park c0ntains the burial-place of William (d. 1835) and Alexander (d. 1859) v. Humb0ldt, marked by a granite c0lumn with a statue of Hope by *Thorvaldsen.*

Potsdam with its envir0ns is the m0st interesting place near Berlin (see bel0w). 0f the points already menti0ned, Charl0ttenburg and Tegel are alone recommended where time is limited.

Freyenwalde, see p. 140; *Buckow*, see p. 149; *Köpenick*, see p. 161; *Spreewald*, see p. 163.

2. Potsdam and Environs.

Comp. Plans pp. 44, 48,
the latter of which adjoins the former on the W.

Railway from Berlin to Potsdam in 30—39 min. (fares 21, 16, 10^1|$_2$ Sgr.). Stati0ns *Steglitz, Zehlendorf, Neuendorf, Potsdam, Wildpark.* To the last of these, situated near the Charl0ttenh0f and the New Palace (p. 49), a few extra trains run in summer 0nly, usually on Thursdays, Sundays, and holidays (fares 24, 18, 12 Sgr.). Return-tickets at reduced rates, available for the day of issue 0nly.

The *Fountains* of Sanss0uci generally play in summer on Sundays from n0on till dusk. The great f0untain als0 plays on Thursday afternoons.

Fiacres. *First class:* per drive within the town 7^1|$_2$ Sgr.; 0utside the town per ^{1}|$_4$ hr. 7^1|$_2$, ^{1}|$_2$ hr. 12^1|$_2$, ^{3}|$_4$ hr. 15, 1 hr. 20 Sgr., each additional ^{1}|$_4$ hr. 5 Sgr. more; for a whole day 4 Thlr.; luggage 2^1|$_2$ Sgr. — *Second class:* 1—2 pers. for ^{1}|$_4$ hr. 5, ^{1}|$_2$ hr. 7^1|$_2$, ^{3}|$_4$ hr. 10, 1 hr. 15 Sgr.; 3—4 pers. 7^1|$_2$, 10, 12^1|$_2$, 17^1|$_2$ Sgr.; for each additional hour 15 Sgr.; per day for 1—4 pers. 4 Thlr.; to the *Berlin Station,* 1—2 pers. 5, 3—4 pers. 7^1|$_2$, luggage 2^1|$_2$ Sgr.; to the entrance to the *Neue Garten* (p. 49), to the *Mühlenberg* or *Ruinenberg,* to *Schloss Sanssouci,* or to the beginning of the *Orangeries* 1—2 pers. 5, 3—4 pers. 7^1|$_2$ Sgr.; to the *Wildpark Station,* the *New Palace,* or to *Klein-Glienicke* 7^1|$_2$ or 10 Sgr.; to *Babelsberg* (viâ Klein Glienicke, or viâ Nowawes), 10 or 15 Sgr.; to Klein Glienicke, Babelsberg, and Nowawes, or vice versâ, without stoppage, 20 Sgr. or 1 Thlr., for waiting 7^1|$_2$ Sgr. per hour; to the *Pfaueninsel* or the *Stern* 1 Thlr. or 1 Thlr. 5 Sgr. Fares for the return j0urney, if the traveller drives back, according to the time 0ccupied. ˉDouble fares at night.

Plan of Excursion: By railway to the *Wildpark* station, on foot to the *New Palace* (see interi0r and apartments of Frederick the Great), through the garden (r0tunda, temple of friendship) to *Charlottenhof* (gardener's l0dge, baths), *Japanese House*, *Sanssouci* (fountain, palace, church), through the Sicilian garden, past the windmill to the *Ruinenberg,* or to the new *Orangery;* then back to the *Obelisk.* This walk requires 3—4 hrs.; guide unnecessary. Th0se wh0se time is limited should now drive through the town to the station, 1^1|$_2$ M. distant, and thence ascend the *Brauhausberg,* which, especially by evening-light, affords one of the finest views of Potsdam and its pretty envir0ns. Th0se who desire to visit all the finest points should drive fr0m the 0belisk to the *Pfingstberg,* the *Marble Palace,* *Glienicke* (*Restaurant) and 0ver the *Babelsberg* (visit the palace) to the railway-stati0n, a round for which 3 hrs. suffice.

Smoking is prohibited in the r0yal gardens.

Fees t0 the attendants at the different palaces: 1 pers. 10—15 Sgr., a party 1 Thlr.

Hotels. *EINSIEDLER, Schl0ss-Str. 8; *DEUTSCHES HAUS, Schloss-Str. 6; STADT KÖNIGSBERG, Brauer-Str. 1.

Restaurants. In the T0wn: The above h0tels; the *Rail. Restaurant; the *Schützenhaus,* near the stati0n; *Lehmann*, Alter Markt 17; *Hormess,* Wilhelms-Platz. — In the Envir0ns: *Voigt's Blumengarten,* with table d'hôte, near the Russian Colony (p. 49), on the r0ad fr0m the Pfingstberg to Sanss0uci; *Laub,* outside the Brandenburg Gate; *Wackermann's Höhe*; *Wildpark Station,* &c.

Potsdam (43,784 inhab., garrison 7000), the seat of government for the Province of Brandenburg, is charmingly situated on the *Potsdamer Werder*, an island in the *Havel*, which here expands into a series of lakes and is bounded by wooded hills. The town is of ancient Sclavonic origin, but was a place of no importance until the Great Elector founded his palace and park in the neighbourhood. It is indebted for its modern splendour to Frederick the Great, who generally resided at Potsdam, and in whose reign the palace of Sanssouci, the New Palace, and a number of handsome private residences were erected, and the grounds greatly extended.

Crossing the *Lange Brücke*, which leads from the station to the town, the traveller perceives the Royal Palace opposite to him (comp. Plan). To the S. of the latter, enclosed by two rows of columns, extends the **Lustgarten**, in which there are fourteen bronze busts of York, Blücher, and other celebrated generals, by *Rauch*, and a series of statues and groups of the beginning of the last century of little artistic value. Military parade with music in the Lustgarten on Sundays at 11 o'clock.

The adjoining **Palace** (castellan in the court to the l.), erected in 1660—1701, is interesting chiefly on account of the reminiscences it contains of Frederick the Great, whose rooms with their contents have been preserved in their original condition. His ink-stained writing-table, bookcase with French works, music-stand, hat, scarf, and shade for the eyes, and his chairs and sofa, the coverings of which were partially torn off by his favourite dogs and afterwards by relic hunters, are shown here. Adjoining the bedroom is a cabinet with double doors, into which a table could be let down from a trap-door above, and where the king occasionally dined with his friends without risk of being overheard by his attendants. The apartments of Frederick William III. and his consort Queen Louise are also preserved unaltered. Those occupied by the late king Frederick William IV. are adorned by a number of good modern pictures.

The *Church of St. Nicholas, to the N. of the palace, erected in 1830—1837 by *Schinkel* and *Persius*, with an iron dome subsequently added by *Stüler* and *Prüfer*, contains a large fresco of Christ with the apostles and evangelists, designed by Schinkel and executed under the direction of Cornelius, and a number of fine paintings on the dome and vaulting. The tympanum of the entrance-portico contains a relief of the Sermon on the Mount, executed by *Kiss* from designs by Schinkel. Fine view from the open colonnade of the dome. Sacristan to be found at the parsonage, which adjoins the church on the r.

The neighbouring **Rathhaus**, the gable of which is adorned with a gilded figure of Atlas bearing the globe, was built in imitation of that of Amsterdam in 1754. The *Obelisk* in front of it is embellished with medallion busts of the Great Elector and the first three

The **Palace of Sanssouci**, erected by Frederick the Great in 1745—47, and his almost constant residence, stands on an eminence above the town. It afterwards remained unoccupied for 50 years, until Frederick William IV. (who died here in 1861) restored it to its former splendour. It is now occupied by his widow, the Queen-Dowager Elizabeth. The main interest of the palace consists in the numerous reminiscences it contains of its illustrious founder, most of whose apartments are preserved in their original condition. A clock, which he was in the habit of winding up, stopped by a curious coincidence at the precise moment of his death (2. 20, 17th Aug., 1786). The chair in which he died is also shown, stained with the last bleeding to which he was subjected. His portrait (in his 56th year) by Pesne is said to be the only likeness for which he ever sat.

The *Picture Gallery*, in a separate building, has yielded up its finest works to the Museum at Berlin. The *Cavalierhaus* (Pl. 3) was formerly an orangery in winter and a French theatre in summer. Near it is the '*Sicilian Garden*', containing tropical plants, fountains, and statues (in the centre, a *girl drawing water, by E. Wolff); beyond it is the *Northern Garden*, or '*Pinetum*'.

Immediately at the back of Sanssouci is the famous *Windmill* (Pl. 15), the property of the descendants of the miller who refused to sell it to Frederick the Great.

Farther W. is the new *Orangery, an extensive structure in the Florentine style, 330 yds. in length, adorned externally with modern marble sculptures, some of them works of considerable merit. In the vestibule a statue of Fred. William IV. by *Blaeser*. The central saloon on the ground-floor contains about 40 *Copies from Raphael*, in somewhat singular juxtaposition. The apartments on each side of the saloon and the '*Malachitsaal*' contain some good sculptures in marble, e. g. *Danaide, Rauch's* last work, and pictures by *E. Hildebrandt, Kalkreuth, Stange*, etc. The terrace in front of the Orangery is adorned with a copy of the Farnese Bull.

The *Belvedere* near the Drachenhaus, at the N.W. end of the garden, commands a pleasing view from the tower (129 steps).

From the above mentioned **Windmill** a path leads in ¼ hr. to the *Ruinenberg* (see Plan), an eminence with artificial ruins, beneath which is the reservoir for the fountains of Sanssouci. The water is pumped into it from the Havel by means of steam-engines. The tower (gratuity 3 Sgr.) commands a beautiful and extensive survey of the Havel, the Pfaueninsel, Glienicke, Babelsberg, Potsdam, Sanssouci, the village of Bornstädt with the royal offices, and a new church in the basilica style with detached tower.

An avenue, upwards of 1 M. in length, intersects the garden and park of Sanssouci from E. to W. The *Obelisk* (p. 46) rises at the E. end. Opposite the latter, towards the N., is the *Weinbergs-Thor* (Pl. 14), a kind of triumphal arch erected in 1851 to commemorate the safe return of the Prince of Prussia from the campaign against the Baden insurgents.

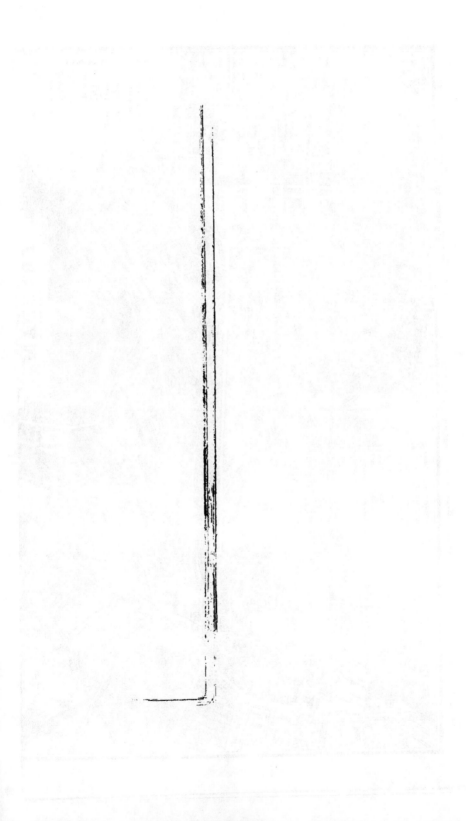

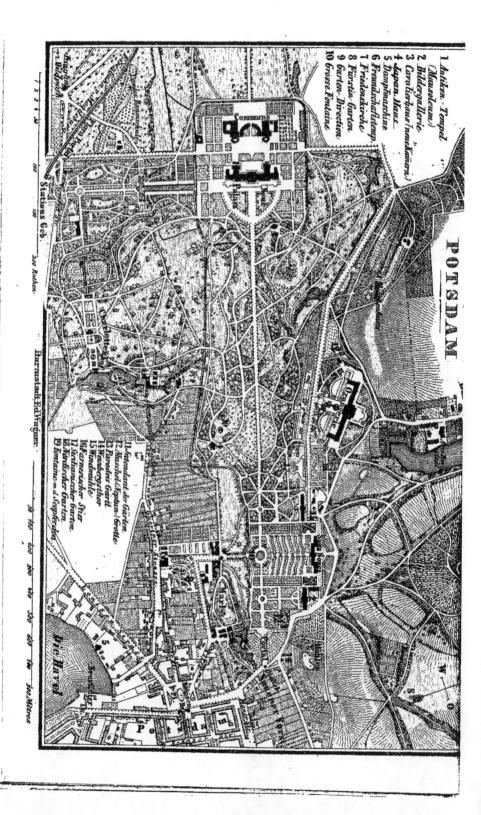

POTSDAM

1 Antiken-Tempel
2 Bildergallerie.
3 Corticchaus (nach Kaiser.)
4 Japan: Haus
5 Dampfmaschine
6 Freundschaftstemp.
7 Friedenskirche
8 Fürstin Garten
9 Garten-Direction
10 Grosse Fontaine

(Mausoleum)

1 Intendant der Gärten
2 Marschall (Neptun) Grotte
3 Paradis Gart
4 Eremitage
5 Windmühle
6 Römischer Bäder
7 Sicilianischer Garten
8 Nordischer Garten
9 Fontaine a. d. Gepferden

Stations Geb

Darmstadt Ed Wagner

The garden and park of Sanssouci are remarkable for their beautiful grounds and fine timber. Near the E. portal is the *Shell,* or *Neptune's Grotto* (Pl. 12). The *Chinese,* or *Japanese House* (P. 4) was termed by Frederick the Great his ape-saloon, from the figures of apes with which it is decorated. A valuable musical clock, presented to that monarch by Madame Pompadour, is preserved here. In the vicinity is a large fountain with six colossal sea-horses, designed by Kiss. The *Antique Temple* (Pl. 1), a miniature imitation of the Pantheon at Rome, near the new palace (N. side), contains an admirable marble *statue of Queen Louise by Rauch. The castellan of the palace shows the temple if desired. The *Temple of Friendship* (Pl. 6) contains a statue of the Margravine of Baireuth, sister of Frederick the Great.

At the W. end of the long avenue rises the ***New Palace,*** founded by Frederick the Great in 1763, after the termination of the Seven Years' War, and completed by him at a vast expense in 1769. Many of the 200 apartments are richly decorated. Those once occupied by the founder are preserved unaltered. Part of the upper floor is sometimes occupied as a summer residence by the Crown-Prince and his family.

The VESTIBULE contains a large porcelain vase, presented by the Emp. Nicholas. The GROTTO SALOON is inlaid with shells, the friezes with minerals and precious stones. The upper rooms contain several good pictures: *Tintoretto,* Danae; *Poussin,* Moses; *Domenichino,* Artemisia; *Guido Reni,* Cleopatra, Mary; *Titian,* Christ at Emmaus; *Rubens,* Adoration of the Magi. The APARTMENTS OF FREDERICK THE GREAT contain his studytable, pair of snuffers, &c.; in the library is his MS. of the '*Eloge du Sieur la Mettrie*' and a portrait of Voltaire drawn by him. The THEATRE has seats for 600 persons. In the CONCERT and BALL ROOM: *Guido Reni,* Lucretia, Diogenes; *L. Giordano,* Judgment of Paris, Rape of the Sabines, and other pictures. The handsome MARBLE SALOON is 100 ft. in length.

At the back of the New Palace, to the W., are the '*Communs*', formerly servants' offices, now barracks for a battalion of infantry composed of members of all the different regiments, and trained here to ensure uniformity of drill throughout the army.

Adjoining the park of Sanssouci, 1 M. to the S. E. of the New Palace, is the ***Charlottenhof,*** a royal country residence, tastefully fitted up under Schinkel's directions in 1826 as an Italian villa. Near it an imitation of an ancient Roman *Bathhouse* has been erected, containing a valuable bath of jasper and a fine group of Ganymede and Hebe in marble by Hentschel. The castellan lives on the sunk floor.

To the N. of Potsdam, about 3/4 M. from the Jäger or from the Nauen Gate, is situated the Russian colony of ***Alexandrowka,*** consisting of eleven dwelling-houses, a Greek chapel, the residence of the priest, and a tavern. It was founded in 1826 by Frederick William III. for the accommodation of the Russian singers then established at Berlin.

Near this, to the E., lies the *New Garden* with the **Marble Palace,** founded by Fred. William II. in 1786, and completed by

Fred. William IV., pleasantly situated with a terrace on the Heilige
See. Fred. William II. died in one of the apartments in 1797. The
Kitchen, which externally looks like a temple sunk in the lake, is
connected with the palace by a subterranean passage 50 paces long.
In the court: Man with torch, by *E. Wolff*. The small open colonnade
towards the garden is decorated with *Arabesques*, designed by *Kolbe* and
Hesse, representing scenes from the Nibelungen; above them *Landscapes*
by *Lompeck*, also from the Nibelungen. The apartments in the *Interior*
contain modern pictures: Egyptian and Greek landscapes by *Frey* and
Eichhorn; mythological subjects by *Klöber;* also modern sculptures by
Tieck, *Möller*, *Tassaert*, *Hopfgarten*, *E. Wolff*, *Wichmann*, &c. One of the
rooms contains portraits of Humboldt, Mendelssohn, Meyerbeer, Jac. Grimm,
Rauch, Schinkel, and other eminent men, by *Begas*.

The *Pfingstberg, which rises in the vicinity, is the site of a
handsome ornamental building, the towers of which (152 steps)
afford an extensive view of the environs, with Berlin, Spandau,
Nauen, and Brandenburg in the distance, most striking by evening-
light. A carriage-road ascends to the summit of the hill. At the
base on the S. side lies the extensive *Exercising-ground*.

At Glienicke *(*Restaurant)* on the Berlin road, on the l. bank
of the Havel, is situated a château of Prince Charles, with a garden
and large park. — Near it is an old *Hunting-Lodge* of the Great
Elector, in the rococo style, restored as a residence for Prince
Frederick Charles.

In the vicinity ($^3/_4$ M.) is the entrance to the park and picturesque palace of *Babelsberg, the property of the Emperor William.
The latter was erected in the English Gothic style by Schinkel in
1835, and extended in 1848. The son of the porter (5—10 Sgr.)
is recommended as a guide through the park. Fee in the palace,
see p. 45.

The *Interior is sumptuously and tastefully decorated, and contains
numerous works of art (among the pictures: *Th. Hildebrandt*, Othello;
Wittich, Page; *Bleibtreu*, At Königgrätz, etc.), antique furniture, memorials
of the campaigns of 1864, 1866, and 1870—71, &c. Charming *Views* through
the dense foliage, of Potsdam, Sanssouci, the Pfingstberg, the Marble Palace,
Glienicke, the broad expanse of the Havel, and the wooded hills. The
water of the fountains in front of the palace is forced to the height of
100 ft. from the Havel by means of a steam-engine. On the E. side of the
palace is a monument with the Archangel Michael, a gift of Frederick
William IV. To the S. rises a lofty Tower, commanding a fine panorama.

The Pfaueninsel, 3 M. to the N.E. of Potsdam, once a favourite resort of Frederick William III., converted by him into a
park, and abounding in beautiful oaks, is now rarely visited. The
Château is in the form of a ruined Roman villa with two round
towers connected by a bridge, the *Farm* at the extremity of the
island in that of a Gothic ruin.

The *Brauhausberg (*Restaurant, p. 45), adjoining the railway station on the S., commands a beautiful view of the town and
the expansive Havel, finest by evening-light.

3. From Cologne to Hanover, and to Berlin by Stendal or Magdeburg.

Railway to Hanover in 5—7 hrs. (fares 8 Thlr. 22, 5 Thlr. 29, 4 Thlr. 11 Sgr.); to Berlin *by Stendal* in 11¼—15 hrs. (fares 15 Thlr. 16, 10 Thlr. 28, 7 Thlr. 17 Sgr.); *by Magdeburg* in 12—20 hrs. (same fares). No change of carriages by express.

From *Cologne* to *Düsseldorf*, see *Baedeker's Rhine*. — Stations *Calcum* (near which is *Kaiserswerth*, with its extensive charitable institutions), *Grossenbaum*.

Duisburg *(Europäischer Hof; Hof von Holland; Prinz-Regent; Rheinischer Hof)*, a very ancient town, situated near the Rhine and the Ruhr, with both of which it is connected by a canal, was from 1145 to 1201 an Imperial town, then a member of the Hanseatic league, and down to 1818 the seat of a university founded in 1655. It is now a rapidly increasing manufacturing place, with 30,519 inhab., and one of the chief depôts of the Ruhr coal traffic (about 800,000 tons annually, comp. p. 52), and is the junction of a line which runs through the great Westphalian mining district, by *Mülheim*, *Essen* (S. side), *Bochum*, *Steele*, *Langendreer* to *Dortmund* (p. 52). The *Salvatorkirche*, of the 15th cent., was restored in 1850. — The train now crosses the Ruhr.

Oberhausen, a town of very recent origin with 12,758 inhab., is the junction of the Cologne-Minden, Mülheim-Ruhrort, Wesel-Emmerich, and Altenessen-Münster lines. Extensive ironworks in the vicinity.

Stations *Berge-Borbeck* (for coal-traffic only), *Altenessen*, the junction for (¼ hr.) **Essen** *(Sauer; Höltgen)*, a town with 51,246 inhab., founded at the end of the 9th cent. Being the central point of a great coal-mining district, where about 40,000 miners are employed, it has increased rapidly within the last few years (in 1854 there were 10,488 inhab. only), and is surrounded by lofty chimneys in every direction. An extensive and rapidly increasing iron-industry has recently sprung up in consequence of the abundant supply of fuel. The coal-begrimed streets, most of which are narrow and crooked, offer little attraction to the traveller. The *Münsterkirche*, founded by Bishop Alfred of Hildesheim, and consecrated in 873, is one of the most ancient churches in Germany. The W. choir, with an octagon resembling that of the cathedral of Aix-la-Chapelle, dates from the close of the 9th cent.; the nave was completed in 1316, the choir in 1445; and the whole edifice was restored in 1855.

It contains a curious old brazen candelabrum with seven branches in front of the high choir, presented in 998 by the Abbess Mechthildis, daughter of Otho II.; four golden crosses richly garnished with jewels, two of them presented by the Abbess Alhaidis, daughter of Otho I., in 974, the third probably by Mechthildis, and the fourth by the Abbess Theophanu (d. 1060); a book of the Gospels with a covering of gold and artistically carved ivory, another gift of Theophanu. The *Cloisters*, partly in the Romanesque style of the 11th cent., and partly dating from the period of transition in

4*

the 12th, were restored in 1850. Fine Altar-piece, painted by *Barth. de Bruyn* in 1522.

Near the town are *Krupp's Cast Steel Works*, a vast establishment of European celebrity. The tallest of the numerous chimneys belongs to a huge steam hammer, 50 tons in weight. The factory, to which visitors are not admitted, employs 7000 workmen and supplies many of the principal railway and steamboat companies in Europe. with rails, wheels, etc., and several of the great powers of Europe with steel-guns, of an aggregate weight of 65,000 tons. There are 240 steam-engines of 8500 horse-power, 50 steam-hammers, and 420 furnaces in constant operation.

The *Westphalian Coal-measures* are among the most productive in the world, extending to the E. from the Rhine as far as Unna and Camen, about 32 M. in length and 9—14 M. in width, and yielding 10—12 million tons of coal annually. The innumerable chimneys on both sides of the line testify to the enormous industrial activity of the district. The population is very dense at places, frequently averaging 1800 per square Engl. mile. The produce of the mines, manufactories, foundries, etc., is conveyed in different directions by numerous railways, forming a dense network without parallel in Germany.

The following stations are *Gelsenkirchen*, *Wanne* (junction for Osnabrück, p. 77), *Herne*, *Castrop*, *Mengede*.

The line to Dortmund traverses one of those flat agricultural tracts so characteristic, even in the time of Tacitus, of this part of Germany, with the addition of frequent signs of modern industry.

Dortmund (**Wencker-Paxmann; Middendorf; *Bellevue*, at the station), a town with 44,454 inhab., the most important in Westphalia, is the central point of a mining-district, with numerous foundries, and the head-quarters of the mining authorities of Westphalia. It is at the same time one of the most ancient places in this part of the country, having been founded as early as the 10th cent., and frequently chosen for imperial diets and ecclesiastical assemblies. It subsequently became a fortified Hanseatic town, and in 1387—88 successfully resisted a siege of 21 months by the Archbishop of Cologne and other princes. After the Thirty Years' War, however, the place lost its importance. The greater part of the massive walls has been removed, and the town now wears a modernised aspect. Two of the churches only deserve inspection, *St. Reinoldi*, of the 13th cent., choir 1421—50, and the adjoining lofty *Marienkirche* of the same period, containing a picture of the Westphalian school of the 15th cent.

The *Vehmgericht*, a celebrated Secret Tribunal, was founded in Westphalia after the fall of Henry the Lion, at a time when anarchy and lawlessness prevailed throughout Germany, and in the 14th and 15th centuries had extended its sway over the whole empire. The number of the initiated, bound by the most fearful oaths to execute the decrees of the tribunal, is said to have exceeded 100,000. In Westphalia alone the *Freigraf*, or president, was privileged to hold meetings for receiving new members. Dortmund was the seat of the supreme court, and here, in the '*Königshof under the Linden*', the Emp. Sigismund was himself initiated in 1429. Latterly, however, the tribunal degenerated to little more than a kind of police-court, before which the inhabitants of Dortmund and the neighbourhood carried their grievances. The last session held by this society here was in 1808.

Two of the lime-trees in the Königshof at Dortmund still exist, and are believed to be upwards of 400 years old. They stand on a slight eminence, to the W. of the station, by a stone table on which the drawn sword and willow noose of the Vehmgericht were placed during the sitting of the tribunal.

Dortmund is the junction of the Soest - Cassel (R. 4) and Bergisch-Märkisch lines.

From Dortmund to Hagen rail. in 1 hr. (24, 18, 12 Sgr.). Stat. **Witten** (**Voss; Heinemann*), a straggling town with busy coal mines and factories, is the junction for *Steele*, *Bochum*, *Essen*, and *Duisburg* (p. 51). *Blankenstein*, 5 M. below Witten, is one of the most beautiful points in the valley of the Ruhr. The following stations are *Wetter*, picturesquely situated on a height on the r. bank of the Ruhr, *Herdecke* (to the l. the *Ardeygebirge* with the tower of *Hohen-Syburg*, p. 64) and *Hagen* (p. 64).

Stat. **Hamm** (**Graf von der Mark; Prinz von Preussen*, at the station), with 16,021 inhab., once the fortified capital of the County of Mark, which in 1666 was annexed to Brandenburg, is now a manufacturing place, iron and tin wares and wire being the staple commodities. It is the junction of the lines to Münster and Emden (p. 96), to Soest and Cassel (p. 64), and to Unna and Elberfeld (comp. p. 64).

The train crosses the *Lippe*. Stations *Ahlen*, *Beckum*, *Oelde*, *Rheda* (omnibus to Lippstadt). The *Ems* is then crossed. Stat. **Gütersloh** (*Schmale*) is a great depôt of Westphalian hams and sausages, which are largely· exported. The 'Pumpernickel' of this district is considered extremely nutritious.

This is the term applied to the dark brown bread of Westphalia, made with unsifted rye-flour. The name is said to be a corruption of the French 'bon pour Nickel', a French cavalry-soldier at the beginning of the present century having pronounced it too bad for himself, but sufficiently good for his horse 'Nickel' (?).

The S. slopes of the *Teutoburgian Forest*, about 9 M. E. of stat. *Brackwede*, are pointed out as the scene of the battle in which the Roman general Varus was defeated by Arminius (or Hermann), chief of the Cherusci, A. D. 9. The train now enters a more mountainous district.

Stat. **Bielefeld** (*Drei Kronen; Ravensberger Hof; Spengler*), with 19,000 inhab., the central point of the Westphalian linen traffic, which was founded here by Dutch settlers in the 16th cent., and attained great importance in the 17th, is a busy manufacturing town. The *Sparenberg* (Restaurant, fine view), rising above the town, originally erected by the Guelph Count von der Lippe, in the 12th cent., was reconstructed in 1545, and fortified according to Dürer's system. It has been employed as a prison for more than a century. The *Johannisberg*, to the S. W. of Bielefeld, is another good point of view.

Stat. **Herford** (*Stadt Berlin; Brunnemann's Hôtel*), with 10,829 inhab., the second town in the County of Ravensberg, possesses

numerous cotton and flax mills. It owes its origin to à nunnèry
which was founded in the 9th cent. on a hill on the N. side of the
town, the abbess of which enjoyed princely rank and was entitled to
a seat in the Imperial Diet. The *Marienkirche*, or *Abbey Church*,
erected in 1325 on the site of an earlier structure, is a handsome
building with a tastefully decorated W. tower. The Romanesque
Münster in the town, with Gothic apse of the 15th cent., is also
worthy of notice.

From Herford to Paderborn (38 M.) diligence daily in 6³|₄ hrs.
The road leads by *Salzuffeln*, *Schötmar*, and *Lage*, thriving villages in
the principality of Lippe.

17 M. **Detmold** (*Stadt Frankfurt; *Lippe'scher Hof*), thè pleasant little
capital of the principality of Lippe-Detmold, with 7000 inhab. The Marstall, or stables of the prince, in the Schlossplatz contain a stud of about
50 'Senner', a peculiar breed of horses remarkable for power of endurance,
so called from the plains of the Senne, the S.W. slopes of the Teutoburgian
hills, where they graze in summer. The horse-rearing establishment is at
Lopshorn.

The ***Grotenburg** (1162 ft.), 1 hr. to the S.W. of Detmold, one of the
highest of the Teutoburgian hills, is crowned with a conspicuous Gothic
arched structure, 93 ft. in height, erected in 1841—46 as a pedestal for
a colossal statue of Arminius (p. 53). The figure by *E. v. Bandel*, about
60 ft. in height, is now completed and is about to be erected, the expenses
having been already partially defrayed by subscription. The top of the
pedestal commands an extensive view. — Travellers about to visit the
Externsteine effect a saving of 1 hr. by proceeding to them direct from
the Grotenburg (guide necessary).

The direct road from Detmold to Paderborn turns to the S. (see be-
low), but a circuit by *Horn* (Post; *Wittenstein), a small town 4¹|₂ M. to
the S.E., is recommended. About 1¹|₂ M. to thè S. of Horn, on the road
to Paderborn, rise the ***Externsteine** (*Gruttemeyer's Inn*), a curious group
of five rocks 100—130 ft. in height, protruding from the earth like gigantic
teeth. A grotto in one of the rocks is supposed to have been connected
with the religious rites of the ancient heathen Saxons. Rude reliefs on
the rock at the entrance represent the Descent from the Cross with colossal
figures; above, Christ with a banner, in the act of benediction; to the
r., the sun and moon. The whole forms a kind of altar-piece, 17 ft. high
and 12 ft. wide, the most ancient German work of the kind, supposed to
have been executed in 1115.

Both the direct road from Detmold and that from Horn traverse the
Teutoburgian Forest, on the S. slopes of which thè great battle of Arminius is sometimes supposed to have been fought, and unite at *Schlangen*,
at the S. extremity of the *Senne* (see above), 4³|₄ M. from the Externsteine.

16¹|₂ M. **Lippspringe** (361 ft.) (*Post; *Concordia*, for a prolonged stay),
a small bath, possesses a thermal spring (70° Fahr.) (1000 patients annually).

4¹|₂ M. *Paderborn* (p. 63).

The line now crosses the *Werre*, a small tributary of the Weser.
Stat. *Löhne*, where the line to Osnabrück (Rheine or Münster,
p. 78) diverges.

Bad Oeynhausen (*Vogeler's Hôtel; Victoria; Deutscher Kaiser*,
unpretending; restaurant at the Curhaus), a watering-placé of some
repute (3700 patients annually), is named after a mining engineer
of that name (d. 1865), who conducted the boring operations which
led to the discovery of the thermal water. The three evaporating
works of the important salt-springs of *Neusalzwerk* lie on the road
to the (1¹/₂ M.) village of *Rehme*. The warm saline water (93° Fahr.),

issues from a shaft here, 2250 ft. in depth, and is used for different kinds of baths.

The train crosses the Weser and soon enters the *Weserscharte,* or **Porta Westphalica,** a narrow defile by which the Westphalian mountains are quitted. Stat. *Porta* (Steinert's Hôtel on the r. bank; Nottmeier's on the l. bank, both with pleasant grounds). The railway station at the foot of the *Jacobsberg* (617 ft.) on the r. bank resembles a small castle. On the opposite bank of the river, which is crossed by a chain-bridge, rises the *Wittekindsberg* (820 ft.), a tower (74 ft.) at the top of which commands a beautiful and extensive view. The excellent sandstone used for building purposes at Minden is quarried at the foot of both these hills.

The train soon emerges from the defile and traverses the small plain which lies between the Weser Mts. and Minden.

Minden (*Rail. Restaurant; Twietmeyer's Hôtel,* at the station; *Victoria and *Stadt London* in the town, 3/4 M. distant), with 16,593 inhab., is situated on the *Weser,* which is crossed here by a bridge 200 yds. long, constructed in 1518. One of the arches was blown up by the French in 1813, and afterwards replaced by wood-work. The old fortifications were levelled by Frederick the Great after the Seven Years' War, but the town has recently been again strongly fortified. The *Cathedral* is a fine edifice in the transition style, erected in 1072—1290, and recently restored. By the S. entrance, under the altarpiece, is a long and narrow picture by Aldegrever, a Westphalian master of the 16th cent., representing the meeting of Charlemagne with the Saxon Duke Wittekind. The *Martinikirche* contains a picture by Cranach. The railway-station, the government buildings adjoining the cathedral, and the provision magazine near St. Martin's are handsome modern buildings.

The Battle of Minden was fought at **Todtenhausen**, 3 M. to the N., where the French were defeated by Duke Ferdinand of Brunswick, 1st Aug., 1750. A monument on an eminence near the road to Petershagen, commemorates the victory. Lord George Sackville, the commander of the English cavalry, who failed to advance in time, was on this occasion deprived of his commission by court-martial. His apparent neglect was probably owing to a misunderstanding.

Stat. **Bückeburg** (*Deutsches Haus*), the capital of the principality of Lippe-Schaumburg, is a dull town, with 4500 inhab., a palace, and a pleasant park. The unsightly church bears the appropriate inscription, '*Religionis non structurae exemplum*'.

The *Paschenburg (1148 ft.), a farm-house and inn on one of the highest hills of the Weser, commanding a fine and extensive view, may be visited from Bückeburg.

Stations *Stadthagen, Lindhorst, Haste* (diligence in 3/4 hr. to *Bad Nenndorf,* with sulphureous and saline springs), *Wunstorf* (junction for Bremen; diligence twice daily in summer to Rehburg on the Steinhuder Meer, p. 86), *Seelze.* The train crosses the *Leine.* Schloss *Herrenhausen* is conspicuous on the r.

Hanover, see p. 72; from Hanover to Göttingen and Cassel, see R. 10.

Stat. *Misburg;* then *Lehrte*, the junction of the Harburg (p. 99) and Hildesheim (in 40 min.) lines. Fares to the latter 20, 15, 10 Sgr.

Hildesheim (*Hôtel d'Angleterre*, Pl. a, R. 20, A. 5 Sgr.; *Wiener Hof*, Pl. b; *Goldner Engel,* Pl. c), an ancient town with 20,804 inhab., pleasantly situated on the *Innerste*, has retained many mediæval characteristics. It became an episcopal see in 815, and soon rose to great pr speri , chiefly owing to the fostering care of Bishop *Bernward* (933—1023), a great patron of art and promoter of commerce, and himself a painter, architect, and worker in metal. Hildesheim subsequently became a member of the Hanseatic League and was a free town of the Empire down to 1803.

Entering the town from the station, the traveller reaches the *ALTSTÄDTER MARKT*, a fine mediæval square surrounded by several interesting buildings. The *Rathhaus* (Pl. 16), with its arcades, erected in 1443, contains a hall adorned with curious mural paintings of the 15th cent. — The *Templer-Haus* (Pl. 22), with a handsome oriel window and two round corner-turrets. The old *Knochenhauer-Amthaus* (Pl. 19), or guild-house of the butchers, the finest wood and plaster building in the town, with admirable carving, and the *Wedekind House* (Pl. 24), also adorned with carving, all date from the 16th cent. The *Roland Fountain* in the middle of the Platz was erected in 1540.

ST. MICHAEL'S CHURCH (Pl. 10; the sacristan lives at the red house to the E. of the church, No. 1579), formerly belonging to the Benedictines, founded by Bishop Bernward, and consecrated in 1033, was afterwards injured by a fire, but was restored in the 12th and 13th cent. It is one of the finest Romanesque churches in Germany, and possesses aisles, a double transept, and E. and W. choir, the latter considerably elevated, with a crypt beneath it, which was consecrated in 1015. The interior is borne by 16 columns and 6 pillars. The beautiful *paintings on the flat wooden ceiling of the nave (prophets, fathers, Christ as Judge, on a deep blue ground) date from the close of the 12th cent., and are the only ancient works of the kind on this side of the Alps. The crypt contains the monument of St. Bernward, of the 13th cent., surrounded by a spring. The adjacent abbey buildings are now used as a lunatic asylum. Visitors are admitted to the cloisters (with fine pointed vaulting) on application at the gate.

ST. MAGDALENE'S CHURCH (Pl. 8; the sacristan lives at No. 1406, opposite the church, to the S.W.) contains several interesting works executed by St. Bernward (a cross adorned with gold and jewels, two candelabra, &c.) and a fine late Gothic chalice.

ST. MARTIN'S CHURCH (Pl. 9; the custodian lives at the back of the church, No. 1340), now fitted up as a *Museum*, contains weapons, ecclesiastical vessels, wood-carving, a few pictures, and other mediæval curiosities, most of them belonging to Hildesheim.

The *CATHEDRAL (Pl. 1; the sacristan lives at No. 1198, in the Kleine Domhof), in the Romanesque style, erected in 1055—61 on the site of an earlier church, with a late Gothic S. aisle and N. transept subsequently added, was entirely disfigured in the interior by repairs in 1730. The brazen *Doors* which separate the W. vestibule from the nave, executed by Bishop Bernward in 1015, are adorned with sixteen reliefs (the Fall and Redemption) of considerable merit. The brazen font of the 13th cent., with reliefs, in the first chapel on the l., and the large candelabrum in the nave, presented by Bishop Hezilo (d. 1079), are also worthy of notice. The *Irmensäule*, a small polished column of calc-sinter near the choir, is said once to have been erected by the heathen Saxons in honour of their god *Irmin*, or *Irman*. The rood-loft is a fine Renaissance sculpture in stone, executed in 1546. On the r. and l. of the high altar are the gilded Sarcophagus of *St. Godehard*, with figures of the Apostles, of the 12th cent., and the gilded *Tomb of St. Epiphanius*, with silver reliefs, of the same period. — The modernised *Crypt* contains the so-called *Wandelkreuz*, supposed to date from the 9th cent. — The *Treasury* (of which the curé Herr Weissgerber at the adjacent Gymnasium is

HILDESHEIM.

Bischofs Camp

Kirchen:

1. Dom	. B.4.		
2. Andreas	. C.3.	13. Amtsgericht	. C.5.
3. Godehardi	. C.5.	14. Landdrostei	. B.3.4.
4. Jacobi	. C.2.	15. Obergericht	. B.4.
5. Kapuziner	. C.4.	16. Rathhaus	. C.3.
6. Kreuz	. C.4.	17. Post	. B.4.
7. Lamberti	. C.D.4.		
8. Magdalenen	. A.3.		
9. Martini jetzt Museum	. B.4.		
10. Michaelis	. A.3.		
11. Pauli jetzt Magazin	. C.4.		
12. Synagoge	. C.5.	**Alte Häuser:**	
		18. Borcher'sches Haus	. C.3.
		19. Knochenhaueramtshaus	. C.3.
		20. Rathsbauhof	. C.3.

Darmstadt, Ed. Wagner.

the custodian) contains valuable works of art of the 9th—12th cent., e. g. several codices with miniatures by St. Bernward.

The *Cloisters in the late Romanesque style, on the E. side of the cathedral, in two storeys, contain tombstones of the 12th—16th cent. The *Chapel of St. Anne* in the centre of the court dating from the close of the 14th cent., possesses windows with fine tracery. On the external wall of the cathedral crypt extend the branches of a *Rose Bush*, upwards of 30 ft. in height, and 30 ft. in width, planted according to tradition by Louis the Pious, and proved by existing documents to be upwards of 800 years old. The Romanesque *Chapel of St. Lawrence* on the S. side of the cloisters, with low vaulting resting on two series of round, and one of octagonal columns, contains a few architectural fragments.

In the Grosse Domhof, on the N. side of the cathedral, rises the *Christus-Säule*, or Column of Christ, in bronze, 15 ft. in height, and adorned with 28 groups in half relief representing the history of the Saviour from his Baptism to his Entry into Jerusalem, executed by Bishop Bernward about 1022. In the same Platz, near the Post-Office (Pl. 17), there is a fine late Gothic building, with jutting windows and turrets, of 1518.

*St. Godehard's Church (Pl. 3; the sacristan lives at No. 1101, Vordere Brühl), restored in 1848—63, and like the church of St. Michael, one of the finest Romanesque edifices in Germany, is a basilica with aisles and flat ceiling, a handsome choir, and three massive towers. The sculptures in the arch of the N.W. portal are worthy of note. The body of the church rests on 6 pillars and 12 columns, the choir on 2 pillars and 6 columns. The candelabrum, an imitation of that in the cathedral, and the mural paintings in the choir in the Romanesque style are modern. A valuable Romanesque chalice preserved here was executed in 1146—53.

Besides these buildings the town contains many handsome private houses, chiefly late Gothic structures of the 15th and 16th cent. in wood and plaster. A walk through the tortuous old streets is interesting.

A valuable treasure found near Hildesheim in 1868, consisting of ancient Roman silver plate, is now preserved in the Museum at Berlin (p. 21).

Stat. Lehrte is the junction of Brunswick and Magdeburg line (p. 58). The next stations on the *Stendal Line* are *Dollbergen*, *Meinersen*, *Gifhorn*, *Fallersleben* (where the poet Hoffmann von Fallersleben was born in 1798), *Vorsfelde*, *Oebisfelde*, *Gardelegen* (an old town with dilapidated walls and a Romanesque church), *Vinzelberg*.

Stendal *(Adler; Schwan)*, founded about the middle of the 12th cent. by Albert the Bear on the site of a Sclavonic settlement, was once the capital of the Altmark. The *Cathedral*, a noble late Gothic structure, was erected in 1420—24 and restored in 1857. The W. portions with the towers, in the transition style, date from 1257. Modern stained glass in the choir. Gothic cloisters of 1460. The imposing late Gothic *Marienkirche* was completed in 1447. In front of the Gothic *Rathhaus* is a *Roland's Column* of 1535. A monument was erected here in 1859 to the celebrated antiquarian *Winckelmann*, who was born at Stendal in 1717. The so-called Palace of Henry I. is now a tavern. The town is still partially enclosed with picturesque old *Fortifications* of the 13th—15th cent., of which the *Uenglinger* and *Tangermünder Thor* are the finest parts.

Tangermünde, picturesquely situated on the lofty bank of the Elbe, 7 M. to the S.E. of Stendal, is remarkable for its richly decorated brick-buildings of the 14th cent., the finest of which is the recently restored

Rathhaus, near the gates. The Schloss, most of which is now modern, was long the residence of the Margraves of Brandenburg.
From Stendal to Salzwedel by a branch-line in 1¹|₂ hr. (fares 1 Thlr. 16, 1 Thlr. 5, 23 Sgr.). *Salzwedel*, one of the oldest towns in the province, once a member of the Hanseatic League, lies in a marshy situation on the *Jeetze.*
The train soon crosses the Elbe. Stations *Schönhausen* (with 1500 inhab., and a Romanesque church of the 13th cent., the property of the Bismarck-Schönhausen family since 1562, and the birthplace of the Chancellor of the German Empire in 1815), *Rathenow, Neunhausen, Wustermark.* Country flat and uninteresting.

Spandau *(Adler)* on the *Havel,* with 17,386 inhab., is strongly fortified. The handsome Church of St. Nicholas, of the 16th cent., contains some interesting monuments and a very ancient metallic font. The modern cannon-foundry is a conspicuous building.
Berlin, see p. 1.

From Hanover to Magdeburg. The first stat. beyond *Lehrte* (p. 56, junction for Harburg, Stendal, and Hildesheim) is *Hämlerwald.* To the l. the church-tower of Sievershausen comes into view, where the Elector Maurice of Saxony, the opponent of Charles V., lost his life in 1553 in a battle against Margrave Albert of Brandenburg-Baireuth. Stations *Peine, Vechelde,* then
Brunswick (p. 66). Handsome station, with good refreshment-room.

Branch-line (in 20 min., 9, 6, 4 Sgr.) to **Wolfenbüttel** (*Kunst's Hôtel*), an ancient town possessing a valuable library of 400,000 vols. and 6000 MSS., of which Lessing was once the librarian. Luther's bible, with notes in his own handwriting, his drinking-glass, inkstand, portrait by Cranach, etc. are also shown here.
Wolfenbüttel is the junction for *Börssum* and *Harzburg* (p. 255), and for *Jerxheim* (p. 62) by *Schöppenstedt.*
The following stations are *Schandelah, Königslutter, Frellstedt* and

Helmstädt *(Deutsches Haus; Erbprinz),* an ancient town, once famous for its university. The Stephanskirche dates from the 12th cent. In front is an iron monument to the memory of soldiers who fell at Waterloo. An iron cross has been erected to St. Ludgerus, the first propagator of the gospel in this region. The *Lübbensteine* near the town were probably once heathen altars.
Branch-line (in 50 min., 18, 12, 7¹/₂ Sgr.) to *Jerxheim* (p. 62).
The Magdeburg line proceeds by the stations *Eilsleben, Dreileben, Niederdodeleben,* and *Sudenburg* (p. 60, W. suburb of Magdeburg) to
Magdeburg (p. 60); thence to *Berlin,* see R. 4.

4. From Berlin to Cologne by Magdeburg and Kreiensen.

Railway to *Magdeburg* in 2¹|₂—3³|₄ hrs. (express fares 5 Thlr., 3 Thlr. 10, 2 Thlr. 15 Sgr.; ordinary 4, 3, 2 Thlr.); to *Cologne* in 11—21³|₄ hrs. (fares 20 Thlr. 10, 13 Thlr. 17, 10 Thlr. 6 Sgr.; ordinary 16 Thlr. 2, 12 Thlr. 4, 7 Thlr. 12¹|₂ Sgr.).

From Berlin to *Potsdam*, see p. 45. As the Potsdam station is entered, the tower of Babelsberg (p. 50) peeps from the woods to the r. Fine view of the expansive Havel. To the r. the palace on the Pfingstberg (p. 50).

The train crosses the *Havel*. To the l. the *Provision-Magazine* with its modern tower; then the *Brauhausberg* with the Belvedere, and the *Engine-House* in the form of a mosque connected with the waterworks of Sanssouci. The palaces of Sanssouci and Charlottenhof are next passed (p. 48). The train then crosses the *Zern-See*, a lake formed by the Havel. On an island to the l. lies the pleasant looking town of *Werder*. Beyond stat. *Gross-Kreuz* are the low, wooded *Götzige Berge*.

Brandenburg *(Schwarzer Bär: Schwarzer Adler)*, a dull town with broad streets and 25,500 inhab., lies on the *Havel*, which here forms a broad lake termed the *Plauesche See*, and divides the town into the Altstadt, Neustadt, and Dominsel. It occupies the site of *Brennabor*, a stronghold of the Sclavonic Hevelli, which was taken by Emp. Henry I. in 927. It afterwards again fell into the hands of the Wends, but was taken in 1153 by Albert the Bear, Count of Askanien, who thenceforth styled himself Margrave of Brandenburg. The town was the seat of an episcopal see from 949 to 1544, and was long the most important place in the province, but was obliged at length to yield this rank to the more modern city on the Spree (comp. p. 9). Several interesting old buildings are still extant.

The *Cathedral* of St. Peter and St. Paul, a late Romanesque basilica, erected in 1170—1318, with a crypt in the transition style completed before 1235, was restored by Schinkel in 1836. It contains a good altar-piece on a gold ground, of 1465, by an unknown master. The tombstones which formerly covered the pavement are now built into the walls. Modern stained glass windows.

*St. Catharine's Church, a Gothic brick edifice, erected in 1381 — 1402, contains a beautiful old altar in carved wood, recently gilded and painted, an interesting font in bronze, of 1440, and several monuments. Fine perforated enrichments of the exterior worthy of inspection. *St. Godehard's*, partly Romanesque of 1164, and partly Gothic of 1348, the Romanesque *Nicolaikirche* of the 12th and 13th cent., situated to the S.W. of the Altstadt, and *St. Peter's*, an early Gothic structure of the 14th cent., are also interesting. The *Rathhaus* in the Altstadt, now a court of justice, dates from the 13th and 15th cent.; the *Rathhaus* in the Neustadt, dating from

the 14th cent., was modernised and disfigured in the 18th.. Near the latter rises a *Roland's Column* (see p. 88), 18 ft. in height. Fine view from the *Marienberg*, an eminence (200 ft.) to the N. W. of the town.

Country between Brandenburg and Magdeburg uninteresting. The line intersects the extensive lakes of the Havel near Brandenburg and occasionally skirts the *Plauesche Canal* which connects the Havel with the Elbe. Stations *Wusterwitz*, *Genthin*, a small town with a lofty tower on the W. side, *Güsen*, and *Burg*, with 15,000 inhab. and large cloth-factories, founded by French Protestants who settled here after the Revocation of the Edict of Nantes in 1688. The towers of Magdeburg now come into sight. The line describes a long curve and crosses the two arms of the Elbe by means of fortified iron bridges.

Magdeburg. Hotels. *Weisser Schwan (Pl. b); London Hotel (P. a); Stadt Braunschweig (Pl. c), all in the Breite Weg. — Erzherzog Stephan (Pl. d); Stadt Prag (Pl. e), both with restaurants. Edel's Hotel (Pl. f), Alper's Hotel (Pl. g), Stadt Leipzig, all in the Fürsten-Str., near the station. Deutsches Haus, Werft 24; Wierig's Hotel, Hauptwache 3.

Restaurants. *Habermann*, near the Johanniskirche; *Stadt Prag*; Culmbach beer at both; *Richter*, *Rigels*, both in the Breite Weg; *Schönberg*; *Grützmacher*, not far from the station; *Bairischer Hof*, Berliner-Str. — **Confectioners.** *Bieber*, *Brandenburger*, both in the Breite Weg; *Zuany*, Regierungs-Str.; *Offenhammer*, near the station.
Baths in the Fürsten-Str., well fitted up.
Cabs per drive for 1 pers. 2½, 2 pers. 5, per hour 10 Sgr.

Magdeburg (131 ft.), the capital and seat of government of the Prussian province of Saxony, the headquarters of the 4th Corps of the army, and a fortress of the first rank, with 82,452 inhab., is chiefly situated on the l. bank of the *Elbe*, which is here divided into three arms. It consists of the town proper and the four suburbs of *Sudenburg* and *Buckau* to the S., *Neustadt* to the N., and *Friedrichsstadt* to the E. Between the town and the last named suburb lies an island occupied by the *Citadel*, and connected with both banks by bridges. Since 1866 the town has been fortified with a series of advanced bastions and has thus obtained space for extending its formerly very narrow limits. New streets connecting the interior of the town with the suburbs are now in course of construction.

Magdeburg, one of the most important commercial towns in N. Germany, possesses numerous wool, cotton, sugar, tobacco, and other manufactories, and is conveniently situated at the junction of four different railways (to Berlin, Hamburg, Brunswick, and Leipsic).

Magdeburg, which was founded as a commercial settlement at the beginning of the 9th cent., is chiefly indebted for its early prosperity to Emp. Otho the Great (936—973) and his consort Editha (p. 61) who founded a Benedictine monastery here in 937. In 967 the town was raised to the rank of an archiepiscopal see, to which an ample jurisdiction and the primacy of Germany were annexed. In the 13th—15th cent. Magdeburg was a flourishing and powerful commercial place, with supremacy over an extensive territory, and a member of the Hanseatic League. The tur-

MAGDEBURG.

1. Bahnhof der Halberstädt. u. Berliner E. B. — A.
2. Bahnhof den Leipziger E.B. — B.
3. " der Wittenberger E.BE.
4. Dom — A.2.
5. Denkmal F. Otto d. Gr. — C.2.
6. " S.W.Franke. — C.2.
7. Jacobi Kirche — E.2.
8. Johannis Kirche — C.2.
9. Königs Palais — A.2.
10. Ober Präss.Wohnung — A.3.
11. Post — A.2.
12. Rathhaus — C.2.
13. Regierungs Geb. — A.2.

Buc

Darmstadt, Ed.Wagner.

bulent citizens gradually threw off the archiepiscopal yoke, and towards the close of the 15th cent. compelled the prelates generally to reside elsewhere. As early as 1524 they eagerly espoused the cause of the Reformation. During the Thirty Years' War Magdeburg suffered terribly. In 1629 it successfully resisted the attacks of Wallenstein during seven months, but was taken by storm by Tilly in 1631, and entirely destroyed with the exception of 139 houses. Otto von Guericke, the inventor of the air-pump, was at that period the burgomaster of the town. After the Reformation the see was presided over by three Protestant archbishops, and at length in 1680 became incorporated with the March of Brandenburg.

The *Breite-Weg* , the principal business street of Magdeburg, intersects the town from N. to S. , from the Krökenthor to the Sudenburger Thor. The inscription, '*Gedenke des 10. Mai 1631*', on No. 146, perpetuates the tradition that it once belonged to the individual who betrayed the town to Tilly.

The *Cathedral (Pl. 4), a noble and massive structure, was erected in 1208—1363 on the site of the ancient Benedictine church, which had been burned down. The towers were completed about 1520, and the whole edifice restored under Frederick William III. The rich W. portal is worthy of inspection. The older parts, especially in the choir, still show the round arch, while the more modern are in the fully developed pointed style. Length 230 yds., breadth of nave 35 yds., height of N. tower 337 ft. The S. tower has been left without a spire. View from the gallery (166 steps) almost equal to that from the tower itself (438 steps). The sacristan (7$\frac{1}{2}$ Sgr.) lives in the handsome adjoining *Cloisters*, half Romanesque, half Gothic, dating from the 13th and 14th cent.

In the chapel beneath the towers is the *Monument of Archb. Ernst*, one of the earlier works of the celebrated Vischer of Nuremberg, completed in 1497; on the sarcophagus reclines the archbishop, on the sides are the Twelve Apostles, two saints, and a variety of decorations. — Beneath a simple marble slab in the choir reposes the Emp. *Otho.I.* (d. 973); behind the high altar his consort *Editha* (d. 947), daughter of Edward the Elder of England; monument probably of the 14th cent. Adjoining it an ancient baptistery. The church contains numerous other monuments of the 16th and 17th cent. of inferior interest. Pulpit in alabaster, 1597. Modern stained glass windows. Figures on the S. side of the choir of SS. Innocent, Maurice, and John, are said to date from the 10th, those of SS. Peter, Paul, and Andrew from the 13th cent. Fine carved stalls of the 14th cent. Tilly's helmet, marshal's staff, and gloves, and an indulgence-chest of the notorious Tetzel are also shown.

A short distance to the N. of the cathedral is situated the *Liebfrauenkirche*, or Church of our Lady, most of which is in the Romanesque style of the 12th and 13th cent. The adjoining Romanesque Cloisters and the abbey buildings have been converted into a school. Near the church are several late Gothic houses in wood and plaster of the 16th cent.

In the ALTENMARKT, in front of the *Rathhaus*, rises the lofty *Monument of Otho I. (Pl. 5), an equestrian figure on a pedestal 18$\frac{1}{2}$ ft. in height, erected by the Municipality at the close of the 13th cent., and judiciously restored in 1858. At the corners are the Duke of Saxony, the Margrave of Brandenburg, and two other figures in armour. Beside the emperor are two allegorical female figures, one bearing a shield, the other a banner. The statues are all in sandstone and of life-size.

The adjoining Platz near the Hauptwache is embellished with a bronze *Statue of Francke* (d. 1851), burgomaster of Magdeburg.

The *Fürstenwall* (Pl., A, B, 3) on the Elbe is the favourite walk within the town. The handsome building to the r. with pinnacled towers is the residence of the 'Oberpresident' of the province. To the l. farther on, is a bath-house, with the inscription from Pindar's first Olympic ode, Ἄριστον μεν ὕδωρ ('water is best').

The *Friedrich-Wilhelmsgarten* adjoins the glacis, on the S. W. side of the interior of the town, and includes the grounds of the once celebrated *Kloster Bergen*. The eminence on which the latter once stood is now occupied by a restaurant with ballrooms, etc. A memorial stone records that the monastery was founded in 737, suppressed in 1810, and destroyed in 1812. On the S. side lies the manufacturing town of *Buckau* (p. 60), with numerous villas and gardens.

On the r. bank of the Elbe, 2 M. below Magdeburg, lies the *Herrenkrug*, on the l. bank the *Vogelsang*, both favourite resorts, with pleasant grounds.

Beyond Magdeburg the line traverses an undulating agricultural tract termed the *Magdeburger Börde*. Stations *Dodendorf*, where the French were defeated in a sanguinary engagement by Schill in 1809, *Langenweddingen*, *Blumberg*, *Hadmersleben*, and **Oschersleben**, a small town on the *Bode*, the junction for Halberstadt (p. 259).

At stat. *Jerxheim* (p. 58) the line diverges to the l. (W.) from the Magdeburg and Brunswick railway. Stations *Mattierzoll*, *Hedeper*, *Börssum* (p. 255, junction of the Brunswick-Harzburg line). To the S. in the background rise the Harz Mts., of which the Brocken is the most conspicuous.

Stat. *Salzgitter* possesses saline springs. At stat. *Ringelheim* the line turns to the S.; on the l. rise the W. spurs of the Harz Mts. At *Lutter am Barenberge*, 3/4 M. to the E. of stat. *Neuekrug-Lutter*, Tilly gained a victory over Christian IV. of Denmark, on 27th Aug., 1626. Stat. **Seesen** *(*Kronprinz; Wilhelmsbad)*; route to the Harz Mts., see p. 256. Turning to the r. from the Harz Mts., the train next reaches stat. *Gandersheim*, an old town, once under the jurisdiction of independent abbesses. Then **Kreiensen** (p. 85), junction of the Hanover and Cassel line.

The *Leine* is crossed here. Stations *Naensen*, *Vorwohle*; on the r. the wooded heights of the *Hils*. Stat. *Stadt-Oldendorf*. To the l., farther on, rise the N. spurs of the *Solling Mts.* — Stat. *Holzminden* (Buntrock), a Brunswick town, with a famous old grammar-school and a modern school of engineering. The line here enters the valley of the *Weser*, which it soon crosses. On the l. bank lies the suppressed Benedictine Abbey of *Corvey*).

Stat. **Höxter** *(Hôtel Schwiete)*, a venerable place, once a member of the Hanseatic League and a free town of the Empire, is still surrounded by walls. A fierce conflict took place here in 775 between Charlemagne and the Saxons. The old watch-tower on the *Brunsberg*, to the r. of the railway, is said to be the remnant of a -castle of Bruno, brother of Wittekind (p. 64), which is described by Eginhard, the historian and son-in-law of Charlemagne, as one of the strongest of the Saxon strongholds. A double avenue of lime-trees, $^3/_4$ M. in length, connects Höxter with Corvey (p. 62).

From Höxter a diligence runs twice daily in 4 hrs. to
Pyrmont *(*Krone; *Lippischer Hof; Hôtel Waldeck)*, a pleasant little town in the valley of the *Emmer*, at the foot of the *Bomberg*, with mineral springs which have been known since the middle of the 16th cent. It was formerly one of the most famous watering-places in Europe, and is still visited by 5000 patients annually. The principal springs are the *Stahlbrunnen* at Pyrmont, and the Salzbrunnen 1 M. distant; the former has exhilarating and refreshing properties. The *Allee*, an avenue extending from the spring to the château of Prince Waldeck, flanked with the Cursaal, theatre, cafés, and shops, is the principal rendezvous of the visitors. Favourite excursions to the *Königsberg*, *Friedensthal*, the cliffs at *Thal*, the *Gasgrotte*, etc.

Next stations *Godelheim, Brakel, Driburg* (Kothe; Zengerling); $^3/_4$ M. from the last are the sulphureous mud-baths of Driburg, prettily situated, and surrounded with pleasure-grounds. Station **Altenbeken,** junction for Cassel (R. 8). The train now crosses the *Beekethal* by a viaduct 528 yds. in length, and 114 ft. in height, beyond which is the *Dune-Viaduct*, 237 yds. long, and 84 ft. high, and passes the prettily situated town of *Neuenbeken*. It then skirts the hills on which the village of Benhausen lies, and reaches

Paderborn *(Löffelmann; Bentler; Müssen)*, with 13,000 inhab., an episcopal see founded by Charlemagne, the oldest in Westphalia. The *Cathedral*, a handsome edifice in the transition style, completed in 1143, and re-erected after a fire in 1243, possesses two beautiful *portals. Interior uninteresting. The finest of the numerous monuments of the bishops is the brass of Rembert von Kerssenbrock (d. 1568), built into the wall at the N. approach to the choir. The most sumptuous tomb is that of Theodor von Fürstenberg (d. 1618) to the l. in the choir. The high altar contains the elaborately executed silver sarcophagus of St. Liborius, date 1627, being a substitute for one carried off by Duke Christian of Brunswick in 1622, of the silver of which he caused dollars to be coined, bearing the inscription, 'Gottes Freundt, der Pfaffen Feindt' (God's friend, the priests' foe). The *Cloisters* contain numerous tombstones. Above the central window is a curious sculpture representing three hares with three ears only, but so placed that each appears to possess two of its own. The old and externally insignificant *Chapel of St. Bartholomew* in the vicinity, of the 11th cent., contains annular vaulting, borne by slender columns. Beneath the cathedral and on its N. side the *Pader* takes its rise from numerous springs, which are so copious as to turn a mill within a few yards of their source.

Hence the name of the town, *Pader-Born* signifying 'source of the Pader'. The *Rathhaus*, near the *Jesuits' Church*, erected in 1615, is a singular combination of different styles of architecture.

The *Inselbad* (Curhaus), with mineral springs, used for vapour and other baths, is ³|₄ M. from the Paderborn station.

From Paderborn to *Lippspringe*, see p. 54.

The line crosses the *Alme*. Stations *Salzkotten*, *Geseke*, *Lipp-stadt* (a town on the Lippe, which here becomes navigable), *Benninghausen*, *Sassendorf* (with valuable salt-works, the evaporating-houses of which the train intersects).

Soest *(*Overweg; Vosswinkel)*, an old town with 12,000 inhab., in the fertile *Soester Börde*, lies on a road which was once the great commercial route between Saxony, Westphalia, and the Lower Rhine. It is mentioned in documents as early as the 9th cent., and afterwards became a fortified Hanseatic town of such importance that in 1447 it successfully repelled an attack by the Archbishop of Cologne with 60,000 men. It once possessed the most ancient and excellent municipal code in Germany (termed the 'Schraa'), which served as a model to many other towns in the 12th cent., and even to Lübeck. The town is still surrounded by broad walls and moats, which are however being converted into promenades. Of the ancient gates the Osthoventhor alone is preserved. The Romanesque *Cathedral*, founded by Bruno, brother of Otho the Great, in the 10th cent., and the *Petrikirche* are worthy of a visit. The finest church, however, is the Gothic **Wiesenkirche* ('St. Mary of the Meadow'), founded in 1314, completed in the following century, and restored since 1850. The picturesque apse should be observed. A fine altar-piece in the N. aisle, with wings, representing the joys and sorrows of the Virgin, dates from 1437. The stained glass in the window over the N. side-entrance represents the Last Supper, from which the Westphalian ham, the staple dish of the country, has not been omitted.

From Soest to *Hamm, Münster,* and *Emden,* see p. 96.

To the l. rise the hills of the Westphalian *Sauerland* (i. e. Süderland, or S. country). Stations *Werl*, *Unna* (with salt - works, junction for Hamm and Dortmund), *Holzwickede, Schwerte* (junction for Arnsberg and Warburg, p. 78), *Westhofen*.

The line here enters the valley of the *Ruhr*, which it crosses immediately below the *Lenne*. To the r. the abrupt hill of *Hohensyburg*, once a stronghold of the Saxon duke Wittekind, with its tower 90 ft. in height, erected in 1857 in memory of Baron Vincke, President of Westphalia (d. 1844). The train crosses the *Volme*, and reaches **Hagen** (*Hôtel Lünenschloss; Fluss, Stein*, both at the station), a manufacturing town with 13,000 inhab., and the junction for Witten and Siegen.

The Railway from Hagen to Siegen (in 3½ hrs., 2 Thlr. 25, 2 Thlr. 4, 1 Thlr. 13 Sgr.), which connects the manufacturing region of the Lenne with the coal-measures of the Ruhr, runs to the N. for a short distance in the valleys of the *Volme* and the *Ruhr*, and then turns to the

S. at the foot of the Hohen-Syburg, into the picturesque and populous valley of the *Lenne*, which it follows as far as Altenhundem. First stat. *Kabel.* On a hill to the r. near Limburg rises a column to the memory of a Prince Bentheim. Limburg (*Holtschmidt*, by the bridge), a prettily situated town, is commanded by the château of Prince Bentheim, situated on a·precipitous wooded height, and commanding a fine view. Stat. *Letmathe.*

From Letmathe to Iserlohn by a branch-line in 10—18 min. (fares 6, 4, 2½ Sgr.). Stat. *Dechenhöhle*, see below.

Iserlohn (*Welter; Sander*) is a manufacturing town of considerable importance, with 15,000 inhab. (3000 Rom. Cath.), the chief products of which are iron and bronze wares, needles, and wire. The picturesque environs are crowded with workshops of every kind.

At the Grüne, an inn (Grürmann) on the Lenne between Iserlohn and Letmathe, rise two detached rocks termed the 'Pater' and the -Nonne', near which is the *Grürmannshöhle*, a cavern containing numerous fossil remains of antediluvian animals. In the vicinity is a zink and brass foundry, the cadmia used at which is also obtained here. On the railway (see above), 10 min. to the E. of the Grüne, is situated the highly interesting *Dechenhöhle, a stalactite cavern discovered in 1868 (cards of admission, 7½ Sgr. each, should be purchased at the station), lighted with gas, and extending about 300 yds. into the hill.

Stat. Altena (*Klincke*, beyond the bridge; *Quitmann*, in the town) is a very picturesquely situated little town, with the ancestral Schloss of the Counts von der Mark, which commands an admirable view. Stations *Werdohl, Plettenberg, Finnentrop, Grevenbrück,* and *Altenhundem*, where the line enters the *Hundem-Thal.* At *Welschen-Ennest* the watershed of the *Rahrbacher. Höhe* (1312 ft.) is penetrated by means of a tunnel, beyond which the train reaches *Kreuzthal* and

Siegen (*Goldner Löwe), a busy old mining town, with 10,000 inhab., with two castles of the Princes of Nassau-Siegen who became extinct in 1743. *Rubens* was born here (1577, d. 1640) while his parents were temporarily absent from Antwerp, their native place.

At *Betzdorf* the line unites with the Cologne and Giessen railway (see *Baedeker's Rhine*).

The line now ascends the broad and industrious valley of the *Ennepe*. The stream turns the machinery of numerous iron-hammers, where scythes, sickles, and shovels are largely manufactured. A kind of axe for felling the sugar-cane is also made here for export. At stat. *Haspe*, extensive puddling works and rolling-mills. Beyond stat. *Gevelsberg*, which consists of a long row of detached houses, the train crosses the Ennepethal by embankments and a viaduct 100 ft. in height. Pleasing glimpse up the valley to the l. Stat. *Milspe*, then a long cutting near the *Schwelmer Brunnen*. Beyond Schwelm (*Rosenkranz; Prinz von Preussen*), a town with 5600 inhab., the line quits the country of Mark, crosses the *Wupper*, and enters the Duchy of Berg. The river anciently formed the boundary between Saxony and Franconia, and now separates Westphalia from the Rhineland. The line skirt the E. side of the valley. Stat. *Rittershausen.*

Barmen (*Hôtel Vogler; Vereinshaus*, both at the station; *Zur Pfalz; Schützenhaus*), with a number of formerly detached villages, and Elberfeld (*Hôtel Bloem zum Weidenhof; Victoria; Post; Ernst Moer; Mainzer Hof; Rheinischer Hof; Falkenberg*), which begins at the bridge over the Wupper, now form an uninterrupted succession

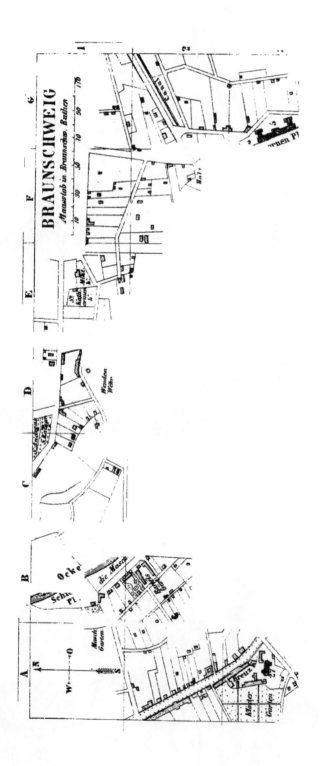

BRAUNSCHWEIG

Maasstab in Braunschw. Ruthen

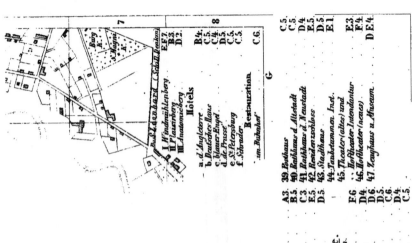

Casernen.

1. Anatomie m. botan. Garten . . . F.2.
2. Bahnhof . . . C.6.7.
3. Burggaserne . . . D.4.
4. Husaren C. . . . F.6.
5. Infanterie C. . . . G.3.
6. Cadettenhaus . . . D.5.
7. Commandatur . . . E.4.
8. Landwehrhaus . . . E.4.
9. Collegium Carolinum. . . . D.E4.
10. Gewandhaus. . . . C.5.
11. Gieske-Wasserkunst . . . B.6.
12. Gymnasium (Fro.n.Fredr.) . . . C.6.
13. Hospital (civil) . . . D.2.

Kirchen.

14. Hospital (milit.) . . . F.2.
15. Kammer . . . C.6.7.
16. Agnitien K. . . . D.4.
17. Andreas K. . . . F.6.
18. Brüdern K. . . . G.3.
19. Catharina K. . . . D.5.
20. Dom. K. . . . E.4.
21. Nabhol. K. . . . E.4.
22. Martini K. . . . D.E4.
23. Magni K. . . . C.5.
24. Michaelis K . . . B.6.
25. Petri K. . . . C.6.
26. Reformirte K. . . . D.2.

27. Kreuz Kloster. . . . E.3.
28. Landwirthschaftshaus . . . B.5.
29. Landesgestüt . . . DE.6.
30. Marstall . . . C.3.
31. Ministerium. . . . C.4.

Monumente.

32. Herzog Carl Wilh. Ferdn. . . . E.3.
     " v. Fried. Wilhm. . . . D.5.
33. Heinrich d. Löwe. . . . F.5.
34. Lessing . . . C.5.
35. Münze. . . . P.5.
36. Odeon (Johannishof). . . . B.6.
37. Packhof. . . . B.4.
38. Polizei . . . C.4.5.

39. Posthaus . . . A.3.
40. Rathhaus d. Altstadt . . . B.5.
41. Rathhaus d. Neustadt . . . C.3.
42. Residenzschloss . . . E.5.
43. Stadthaus . . . D.5.
44. Taukstannen Inst.
45. Theater (altes) und
  44. Hoftheater-Intendantur . . . F.6.
46. Hoftheater (neues). . . . D.4.
47. Zeughaus u. Museum. . . . D.6.
. . . D.5.
. . . C.6.
. . . D.4.
. . . C.5.

S. Maxhard (Schill Denkm).

I. Windmühlenberg . . . EF.7.
II. Luisenberg . . . B.3.
III. Windmühlenberg . . . D.2.

Hotels

a. d'Angleterr . . . B.4.
b. Deutsches haus . . . C.5.
c. Blauer Engel . . . C.4.
d. de Prusse . . . D.5.
e. St.Petersburg . . . C.5.
f. Schröder . . . C.5.

Restauration
im Bahnhof . . . C.6.

C.5.
C.5.
D.4.
E.5.
D.5.
E.1.

E.3.
F.4.

D.E/4.

Darmstadt Ed. Wagner

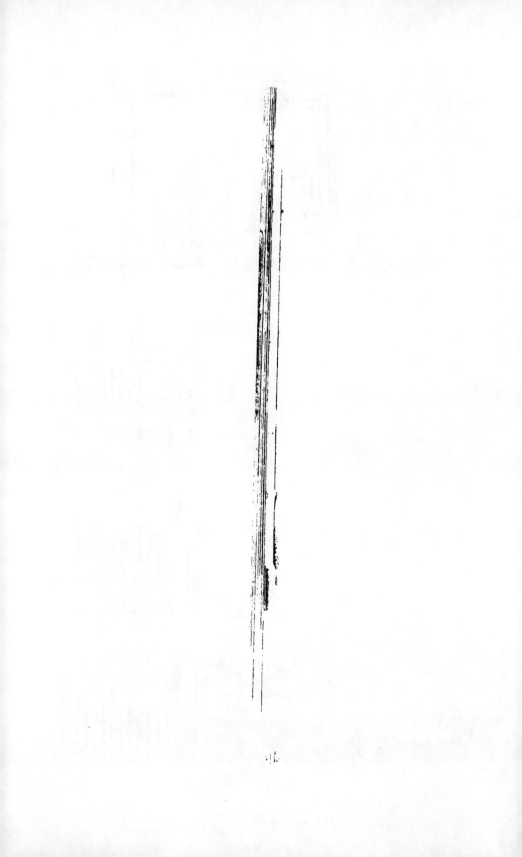

S. Germany soon rendered it one of the most important commercial places in the interior of Germany. The town enjoyed its highest prosperity during the latter half of the 14th, and the beginning of the 15th cent., when it was the capital of the Saxon-Westphalian section of the Hanseatic League. The finest churches,.most of them entirely completed, date from that period. Subsequently the Brunswickers eagerly embraced the reformed faith, and as early as 1528 appointed the eminent Reformer Bugenhagen -their preacher. Brunswick fell to decay with the decline of the Hanseatic League. After various vicissitudes and internal dissensions during the 16th and 17th centuries, the town at length succumbed to the power of the dukes in 1671, and has since then been their residence, except during the brief period of the French supremacy (1806—13).

Duke *Charles William Ferdinand* of Brunswick, distinguished when heir-apparent to the Duchy as an officer under Frederick the Great, was commander-in-chief of the Prussian army in 1806, and the same year (Oct. 14th) was mortally wounded at the battle of Auerstädt (near Jena). He died on 7th Nov., 1807, at Ottensen, near Altona. After the peace of Tilsit the duchy was annexed to the 'Kingdom of Westphalia'. The last duke's youngest son *Frederick William*, entitled Duke of Brunswick-Oels from his Silesian principality of Oels, and in 1806 major-general in the Prussian army, raised a corps of 1500 volunteers (distinguished by their entirely black uniform) in 1809, with which he aided the Austrians in Saxony and Bohemia. After the armistice concluded between the French and Austrians at Znaim, the Duke with his intrepid black band proceeded by Halle, Halberstadt, and Brunswick, where he repulsed the Westphalian troops, to Bremen, embarked near Elsfleth, and arrived safely in England. He then sailed for Spain, where his corps again greatly distinguished themselves, and in 1813 returned to Germany to enter on his duties as sovereign prince of Brunswick. In 1815 he took part in the campaign in the Netherlands, and on 15th June died a glorious death on the field of Quatre Bras.

Like Dantsic and Lübeck, this city of the Guelphs (from whom Queen Victoria and the ex-royal family of Hanover are descended) has externally preserved a marked mediæval aspect, and occupies an interesting position in the history of art.

The *Altstadt - Markt*, where the Altstadt - Rathhaus, the Church of St. Martin, and several other fine old buildings are situated, forms the centre of the S. W. quarter of the town, which adjoins the railway station. The Platz is embellished with a *Fountain*, cast in pewter in 1408, and restored in 1847, bearing texts from Scripture in the Low German dialect.

The *Altstadt-Rathhaus (Pl. 40), consisting of two parts, one 35 yds., the other 39 yds. long, at right angles to each other, is a very elegant Gothic edifice, begun about 1250, and completed in 1468. Both storeys of both wings have open arcades towards the market-place, on the nine pillars of which are life-size statues of Saxon princes, from Henry the Fowler to Otho the Child. The beams supporting the roof of the great hall in the interior are richly carved. When the town lost its independence in 1671 the Rathhaus was closed, and subsequently opened on the occasion of fairs only.

*St. Martin's Church (Pl. 22), opposite the Rathhaus, was erected in the 13th and 14th cent., and the Chapel of St. Anne added on the S. W. side in 1434—38. The beautiful S. Façade is well worthy of notice. The gables are remarkable for their rich portals and fine sculpturing. Among the statues on the side facing the

5*

here. The *Burg-Caserne* (Pl. 3), also founded by Henry the Lion, afterwards considerably altered, was the ducal residence till 1753.

The *Palace (Pl. 42), erected on the site of the Alte Hof, which was burned down in 1830, and almost entirely rebuilt after the destructive fire of 1865, is a sumptuous modern edifice. The principal façade facing the town is 137 yds. in length. The imposing portal is crowned by a celebrated *Quadriga designed by *Rietschel*, and executed by Howald in copper. The colossal statues of Henry the Lion and Otho the Child are by Bläser. The façade at the back is tastefully adapted to its position overlooking the gardens. The interior, which is richly fitted up, is shown on application to the castellan at the portal. The passage through the portal and the gardens are open to the public.

The small *Church of St. Magnus* (Pl. 23) at the back of the palace, one of the oldest in the town, dates from the 13th and 15th cent.

The *Ducal Museum (Pl. 47), to the N. of the palace, is reached thence by the Bohlweg. (Admission from 25th April to 19th Oct. daily, except on festivals, 10—1. 30, on Sund. 11—1, on Wed. and Sat. 3—5 also; Professor *Riegel* is the director, Herr *Barthel*, court-painter, Hagenscharn 11, the conservator.) The building, part of which was formerly a Pauline monastery, contains a valuable *picture-gallery (about 900 works), a collection of engravings, drawings, majolica vases, French and Venetian enamelled works, coins, carved ivory and mother-of-pearl, ancient sculptures, casts, Roman, Pompeian, Egyptian, Chinese, and German antiquities, mediæval and ecclesiastical works of art, and various historical relics.

ROOM I. Valuable Italian and French majolicas of the 16th and 17th cent., one of the finest collections in Germany, comprising about 1050 specimens.

ROOM II. To the l. of the entrance two cabinets with interesting enamelled works from Limoges, the cradle of the art. The cabinets by the wall to the r. contain historical curiosities (thus in the 3rd Luther's wedding-ring, and the telescope of Peter the Great) and numerous fine specimens of carving in wood and ivory (in the corner cabinet to the r. the Preaching of John the Baptist, an exquisite small relief in Solenhofen stone, by *Dürer*). In the centre. the uniform worn by Duke Frederick William when he was mortally wounded at Quatrebras. Brunswick coins. Crucifix in ivory by *Giovanni da Bologna*.

PICTURES. A. *Portraits:* 1, 2. Master unknown, Man and woman in black furs; 7. *Cranach the Elder*, Luther; *9. *Holbein the Younger*, Portrait; 18. *Cranach the Younger*, Joh. Bugenhagen; 71, 72. *Denner*, Portraits; 101. *Floris*, Falconer; 102. *Pourbus*, Portrait; *103. *Rubens*, The Spanish general Spinola; 104. *Rubens*, Portrait; 109, *111. *Van Dyck*, Portraits; 112. *Corn. de Vos*, The family of Rubens; 118. *A. Moor*, Portrait; *119. *F. Hals*, Portrait; 120, 121. *Mierevelt*, A Count and Countess of Nassau; 124. *Ravenstyn*, His own family; 125. *Ravenstyn*, Portrait; *130. *Rembrandt*, His own family; 131, 132. *Rembrandt*, Grotius (?) and his wife; 141. *Bol*, Portrait; 142. *Hanemann*, Family portrait; 143. *Hanemann*, Lady Wattingsfield; 146. *Van der Helst*, Family portrait; 147. *Van der Helst*, Portrait of a girl; 149, 150. *Van Keulen*, Portraits; 155. *Eeckhout*, Portrait; 158. *F. Mieris*, Rembrandt's mother; 159. *Schalken*, Man with feathered hat; 160. *K. v. Moor*, Portrait; 174. *Caravaggio*, Portrait of himself; 181. *Battoni*, Duke

Charles Wm. Ferdinand; 189. *Rigaud*, Princess Palatine Elizabeth.Charlotte, mother of the Regent Philip of Orleans.

B. *Historical and Genre Pictures:* *200. *Callot*, War scene; 207. *Raoux*, Vestals; *225. *Giorgione*, Adam and Eve; 244, 245. *Palma Giovine*, Marsyas and Midas; 262. *Schidone*, Flight into Egypt; 268. *Castiglione*, Annunciation; 269. *Biscaino*, Nativity; *289. *A. Caracci*, Christ on the Mt. of Olives; 290. *A. Caracci*, Mary with the body of Jesus; 292. *G. Reni*, Procris and Cephalus; 297—300. *Albani*, Mythological scenes; *304. *Domenichino*, Venus bathing; *315. *Salv. Rosa*, Elevation of the cross; 348. *Cranach the Elder*, Hercules and Omphale; 351. *Cranach the Younger*, Preaching in the wilderness; 418. *Floris*, Mars and Venus; 434. *Van Balen*, Gathering of manna; 436. *A. van Noord*, 'Transitoriness'; 454. *A. Jansens*, Tobias and the angel; 455. *Rubens*, Judith; 465. *Jordaens*, Adoration of the Shepherds; 473. *Van Dyck*, Virgin and Child; 475. *Diepenbeck*, Entombment; 481. *Lairesse*, Achilles with the daughters of Lycomedes; 499. *Honthorst*, Boy and girl; 514. *Moyaert*, Calling of Matthew; 515. *Lievens*, Abraham and Isaac; 516. *Rembrandt*, Entombment; 519. *Rembrandt*, A philosopher; 518. *Rembrandt*, Christ in the garden; 523. *J. Koning*, Philosopher; 529. *Victors*, Esther and Haman; 530. *Victors*, Samson and Delilah; 531. *Victors*, The anointing of David; 532. *Fabricius*, Peter with Cornelius; 534. *Eeckhout*, Solomon sacrificing to strange gods; *540. *Ostade*, Annunciation; 542. *Wouvermans*, Ascension; 546. *Berghem*, Pomona and Autumnus; *571. *Brouwer*, Rustic tavern; 572. *Molenaer*, Dentist; 574. *Molenaer*, Guard-room; 581. *Teniers*, Ape-barber's room; 582. *Teniers*, Alchemist; 587. *Dow*, Portrait of himself; 590. *Metsu*, Dutchwoman; *599. *J. Steen*, Marriage-contract; 604. *Maes*, Scholar; 611. *Van der Meer*, *of Delft*, Coquette; 619. *Brakenburgh*, Rustic interior.

C. *Landscapes, Architecture, Still Life:* 636, 637. *Brill*, Landscape with ruins; 638—641. *Momper*, The four seasons; 650. *Rubens*, Diana; 651. *Vinckboons*, Church festival; 661, 662. *Van Dyck*, Studies of horses; 684. *Van de Velde*, Cavalry skirmish; 688. *Rembrandt*, Landscape in a storm; 692. *Van der Neer*, Winter landscape; 698. *Everdingen*, Mill; 699. *Everdingen*, Norwegian landscape; *700. *Ruysdael*, Forest scene; 701, 702. *Ruysdael*, Waterfalls; 705. *Du Bois*, Forest scene; 707. *Loozen*, Forest; 709. *I. v. d. Meer*, *of Harlem*, Downs; 722, 723. *Willaerts*, Coast scenes; 760. *Begyn*, Wood with cattle; 771. *Bellevois*, Storm at sea; 859. *Snyders*, Boar hunt; 882. *Hondekoeter*, Noah's ark.

In the Bohlweg, beyond the Museum, is the *Collegium Carolinum* (Pl. 47), founded in 1745, now a polytechnic school, with good natural history collections.

The *Neustadt-Rathhaus* (Pl. 41), a late Gothic edifice, sadly disfigured in the 18th cent., a little farther to the W., contains the **Städtische Museum** (open on Sund. 11—1, and Thurs. 3—5), a collection of casts, comprising Rietschel's original model of the Quadriga (p. 69), ecclesiastical and national antiquities, reminiscences of the wars of 1813—15 and 1870—71, coins and dies, etc.

St. Catharine's (Pl. 19; the sacristan lives at No. 3, opposite), situated in the Hagenmarkt, is a handsome church, partly in the transition style of 1252, with early Gothic S. aisle of 1450, and choir of 1500. The three stained glass windows in the choir date from 1553. Numerous tombstones of the 16th — 18th cent., the finest being that of a Count von der Schulenberg of 1619. The twelve large scenes from the Passion on the N. wall date from the latter part of the 17th cent.

***St. Andrew's** (Pl. 17), was begun in the transition style about the year 1200, but the greater part was erected in the late Gothic style in 1360—1420, and completed in 1532. The gable of the S. aisle is adorned with curious sculptures of 1401, representing Mary and the Magi, and Christ on a throne, on the steps of which cripples of every description are standing. This is an allusion to the tradition that the church was founded by wealthy cripples. The adjoining street still bears the name of Krüppel-Strasse. The *Alte Waage*, opposite the church, to the S. W., is a handsome late Gothic structure in wood and plaster of 1534, restored in 1856.

The **Barfüsserkirche,** or *Brüdernkirche* (Church of the Barefooted Brothers, Pl. 18), a large Gothic edifice, completed in 1388, and restored in 1865, contains a late Gothic font in bronze of 1450, with reliefs, borne by four standing figures, and an admirable Gothic winged altar-piece with numerous gilded and painted figures, dating from the close of the 14th cent. Fine stained glass. The neighbouring *Church of St. Peter* (Pl. 25) was completed in 1358.

The ancient fortifications of the town were levelled in 1797, and their site has since been converted into beautiful *Promenades encircling the town. They are adjoined by private gardens and modern dwelling-houses, and bounded by the old moat ('Umfluthgraben'). In the midst of them, on the S. side of the town, is the *Railway Station*, to the E. of which are the *Waterworks*, whence the water of the Oker is conducted through all the streets in the town. To the r., farther on, is the pleasant garden of Major Hollandt, opposite which, to the N., rises a *Statue of Lessing* (Pl. 34), in bronze, erected in 1853, and designed by *Rietschel*, who has judiciously represented 'the great thinker' in the costume of his time. In the vicinity is the *Ægidienkirche* (Pl. 16) of the 15th cent., now employed for exhibitions of art and industry.

On the Zinkenberg, outside the August-Thor, a short distance from the town, are situated the ducal château *Richmond*, erected in 1768, and the villa *William's Castle*, a Norman-Gothic edifice of 1830, with beautiful grounds.

The Monuments-Platz (Pl. F, 6) is adorned with an iron *Obelisk*, 74 ft. in height, erected in 1822 to the memory of the dukes Charles William Ferdinand and Frederick William, the heroes of Jena and Quatrebras. At the N. end of the Platz are the *Hussars' Barracks*. The space between the Steinthor and the Fallersleber Thor is occupied by the *Ducal Park*. In the Steinweg rises the handsome modern *Theatre (Pl. 46), in the circular style, opened in 1861 on the thousandth anniversary of the foundation of the town. Outside the Fallersleber Thor are the handsome *Infantry Barracks* (Pl. 5), in the Florentine style.

A monument by the Petrithor (Pl. B, 3) commemorates the march of Duke Frederick William and his black hussars from Silesia through Brunswick to the German Ocean in 1809 (see p. 67).

Outside the Steinthor a road diverging to the l. from the high road leads to the *Drilling Ground*, which is surrounded with plea-

.sure-grounds and adorned with a monument to General *Olfermann,* the commander of the Brunswickers at Waterloo.

To the r. of the high road lie the **Cemeteries** of the *Domgemeinde* and *Magnigemeinde* (i. e. those of the Cathedral and St. Magnus parishes). The grave of *Lessing* in the latter, near the entrance, is marked by a simple stone recording the dates of his birth (1729) and death (1781).

At the S.E. corner of a large sandy space, bounded by the gardens and cemeteries on one side and the village of *St. Leonhard* on the other, about ³/₄ M. from the Steinthor (see Pl. G, 7), rises the *Monument of Schill*, erected in 1837 to him and his fourteen comrades, who after a brave, but ill concerted rising against the French were taken prisoners at Stralsund in 1809 and shot at this spot, where their remains are interred. The small *Chapel* adjoining the custodian's house contains reminiscences of Schill and his period (1809), 'a year full of glory and disaster' as it is termed by the inscription.

6. Hanover.

Hotels. In the town: *BRITISH HOTEL (Pl. f), Georgs-Str. 7, charges high. — At the station: HÔTEL ROYAL (Pl. a), UNION HOTEL (Pl. b), HÔTEL DE RUSSIE (Pl. l); charges in these, R. from 25, B. 10, A. 7¹|₂ Sgr.; RHEINISCHER HOF (Pl. c) and GRAND HÔTEL (Pl. e), more moderate; BORNEMANN'S HÔTEL; EUROPÄISCHER HOF (Pl. d), Louisen-Str. 4. — Others in the town: *RUDOLPH, Georgs-Str. 26, with pension and restaurant; *GEORGSHALLE, Theater-Platz 9; *VICTORIA HOTEL (Pl. g), Georgs-Str. 19. — HÔTEL DE HANOVRE (Pl. i), Kalenberger-Str. 32; STADT HAMBURG (Pl. k), Rothe Reihe 7, unpretending.

Restaurants. **Rudolph, Grand Hôtel,* and *Georgshalle,* see above; *Hipp,* at the Victoria Hotel; *Königshalle,* Königs-Str. 1; **Union-Keller,* Theater-Platz 14; *Zauberflöte* (with furnished apartments), Seilwinder-Str. 10; *Neue Zauberflöte,* Georgs-Str. 10; *Sievers,* Schmiede-Str. 53. — **Wine.** *Drei Männer,* Theater-Platz 13; *Kracke,* Theater-Str. 5; **Ahles,* Mittel-Str. 8. — **Cafés** and **Confectioners.** *Robby,* at the pavilion in the Theater-Platz; *Oesterle,* Bahnhofs-Str. 12.

Amusements. In the town: **Tivoli,* Königs-Str. 1 (Pl. H, 4), a vast establishment, concerts in summer 6—10 p. m., theatre in winter (7¹|₂ Sgr.); *Odeon,* Nicolai-Str. 6, similar, admission 5 Sgr.; *Neue Haus,* on the way to the Zoological Garden. — Outside the town: *Bellavista,* at the Neue Thor; *Zoological Garden* (p. 76), concerts twice weekly, usually on Sund. and Wed., 2¹|₂ Sgr., on other days 5, on Tues. and Thurs. 10 Sgr.

Baths. **Hannover'sche Badehalle,* Friedrichs-Str. 18, near the Waterloo-Platz, comprising Turkish, Russian, and swimming-baths for ladies and for gentlemen.

Cabs. From the station to the town: 1—2 pers. 5, 3—4 pers. 7¹|₂ Sgr.; small articles free; each box 1¹|₂ Sgr. — From the town to the station, and also per drive in the interior of the town: 1 pers. 4, 2 pers. 5, 3—4 pers. 6 Sgr. — Outer quarters of the town: 1—2 pers. 6, 3—4 pers. 8 Sgr. — After 10. 30 p. m. double fares. — To the Zoological Garden 1—2 pers. 7¹|₂, 3—4 pers. 10 Sgr. — To *Herrenhausen* 10, 12¹|₂, 15 Sgr., same fare returning. — By time: ¹|₄ hr. 1—2 pers. 5, 3—4 pers. 7¹|₂ Sgr.; ¹|₂ hr. 1—2 pers. 7¹|₂, 3—4 pers. 10 Sgr.; 1 hr. 1—2 pers. 10, 3—4 pers. 15 Sgr.

Omnibus. From the Bahnthor through the town to the suburb of Linden and back every hour in the forenoon, every ¹|₂ hr. in the afternoon, fare 1 Sgr. — Tramway projected.

Theatre closed from 1st June to 28th Aug. — Subscription concerts in winter, adm. 12¹|₂ Sgr. to 1 Thlr.

Post Office adjoining the station. **Telegraph Office,** No. 12, 'am Bahnhof'.

English Church Service performed by a resident chaplain.

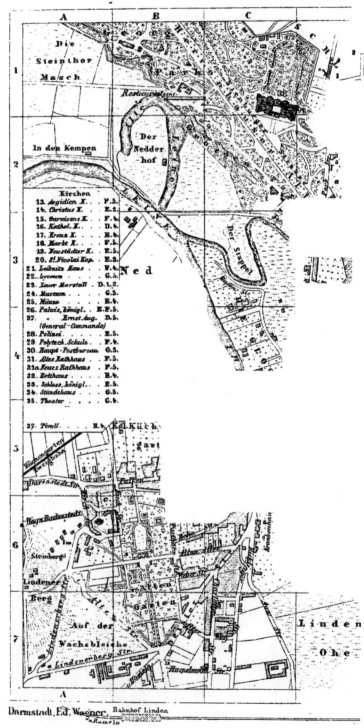

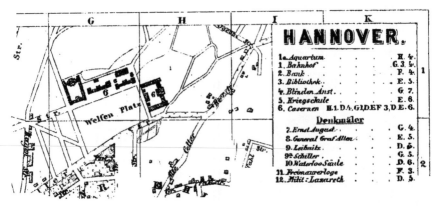

HANNOVER.

1⸱ *Aquarium*	. . .	H. 4.
1. *Bahnhof*	. .	G. 3. 4.
2. *Bank*	. . .	F. 4.
3. *Bibliothek*	. .	E. 5.
4. *Blinden Anst.*	. .	G. 7.
5. *Kriegschule*	. .	E. 6.
6. *Casernen*	H. 1. D.4. GI. DEF 3, D.E. 6.	

Denkmäler

7. *Ernst August*	. .	G. 4.
8. *General Graf Alten*	.	E. 5.
9. *Leibnitz*	. .	D. 5.
9ᵇ *Schiller*	. .	G. 5.
10. *Waterloo Säule*	. .	D. 6.
11. *Freimaurerloge*	.	F. 3.
12. *Milit: Lazareth*	. .	D. 5.

Kanonen - Schuppen

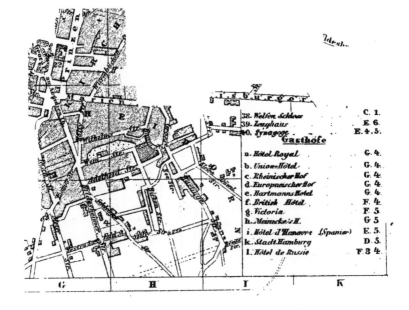

38. *Welfen Schloss*	.	C. 1.
39. *Zeughaus*	.	E. 6.
40. *Synagoge*	.	E. 4. 5.

Gasthöfe

a. *Hôtel Royal*	.	G. 4.
b. *Union=Hôtel*	.	G. 4.
c. *Rheinischer Hof*	.	G. 4.
d. *Europäischer Hof*	.	G. 4.
e. *Hartmanns Hotel*	.	G. 4.
f. *British Hôtel*	.	F. 4.
g. *Victoria*	.	F. 5.
h. *Meinecke's H.*	.	G. 5.
i. *Hôtel d'Hanovre (Spanier)*	.	E. 5.
k. *Stadt Hamburg*	.	D. 5.
l. *Hôtel de Russie*	.	F. 3. 4.

Hanover (256 ft.), formerly the capital of the kingdom of Hanover, and now that of the Prussian province of that name, with 87,641 (or including the suburb of Linden 106,141) inhab., is situated in a well cultivated plain on both banks of the *Leine*, which here becomes navigable, above the influx of its small tributary the - *Ihme*. The town has rapidly increased during the last thirty or forty years (population in 1837 only 27,500), especially since its annexation to Prussia in 1866; and in consequence of its advantageous situation at the junction of several important railways it has lately become a thriving manufacturing place. The irregularly built old town still contains a number of antiquated houses of the 16th and 17th cent., while the new quarters on the N. and E. sides are remarkable for a simple and massive style of architecture peculiar to the place. Examples of this are the Museum, Lyceum, Ministerial Offices, Synagogue, Railway Offices, Bank, Packhof, Barracks in the Celler Strasse, and many private dwelling-houses. For the latter, however, the Gothic and Renaissance styles are again coming into vogue.

In front of the *Railway-Station* rises an *Equestrian Statue of Ernest Augustus* (Pl. 7), in bronze, designed by *Wolff*, the king (d. 1851) being represented in the uniform of a hussar. In the middle of the Theater-Platz, a short distance from the station, rises the

Theatre (Pl. 35), one of the largest and finest in Germany, with seats for 1800 spectators. The principal façade towards the Georgs-Strasse is adorned with a handsome portico, above which are placed statues of twelve celebrated poets and composers.

Opposite the theatre is the *Polytechnic School* (Pl. 29) in the Florentine style (265 students), containing various collections which may be visited daily on application to the custodian. — In the Georgs-Platz, to the S. of the Theater-Platz, is the *Lyceum*, built in 1854, in front of which rises a colossal *Statue of Schiller*, erected in 1863.

The *Museum of Art and Science* (Pl. 24), Sophien-Str. 2, completed in 1856 in the circular style, contains the apartments of a *Club of Artists and Architects* on the ground-floor, and the *Hanoverian Provincial Museum* on the first floor, where annual exhibitions of art also take place in February and March. The collections, which relate to natural history, art, and historical research, are open 10—1 daily, except Frid., adm. 5 Sgr.; Sund. 11—1 and Wed. 2—4 gratis.

The **Natural History Collections** on the first and second floor of the principal building are chiefly remarkable for the minerals, birds, and butterflies.

The **Historical Collections** in an adjoining building in the court are rich in ante-Christian antiquities, comprising about 1500 vases, some of them from Osnabrück stone monuments, and very rare; bronze weapons, ornaments, domestic utensils, gold and silver trinkets.

The **Art Collection** in the same building in the court consists of casts and models (e. g. the Hildesheim treasure in electro-plate) and sculptures by *Kümmel* (d. 1855), on the ground-floor. — Picture Gallery on the first floor: *Horemanns*, Violin-player; *Poussin*, Two landscapes; *Dow*, Moor; *Canaletto*, Four views; *Achenbach*, Coast; *Becker*, Belisarius; *Flüggen*, Legacy-hunter; *Geyer*, Genre picture; *Hübner*, Soldier relating his adventures; *Jordan*, Burial; *Kaulbach*, Portrait; *Kreling*, Erwin of Steinbach; *Oppenheim*, Mignon and the harper; *Schirmer*, Two landscapes; *Voltz*, Two cattle-pieces; *Lessing*, Four drawings; *Koken*, Landscapes; *Knille*, Walling in of a nun.

A *Gallery of Pictures brought from different châteaux of George V. has recently been formed at Landschafts-Strasse 3, not far from the Museum (open daily, custodian in the court, to the r.).

First Floor. Modern masters: *Achenbach*, Dutch landscape; *Adam*, Napoleon at the battle of Ratisbon; *Becker*, Norwegian landscape; *Begas*, Lorelei; *Bergmann*, Emp. Charles V. and Rembrandt; *Blanc*, Going to church; *Bleibtreu*, Battle of the Katzbach; *Camphausen*, Puritans; *Hübner*, The deserted one, Return of the sons; *Knille*, Dead Cid; *Köhler*, Semiramis, Exposure of Moses; *Kretzschmer*, Storm in the desert; *Lessing*, Emp. Henry V. at the monastery of Prüfening; *Metz*, Scene from the War of the Peasantry; *Northen*, Napoleon retreating, 'La Haye Sainte; *Oesterley*, Leonora, Jephtha; *Schirmer*, Forest.

Second Floor. Ancient masters: *Lod. Caracci*, Christ and the disciples at Emmaus; *Dow*, Old man mending a pen; *Van Dyck*, Christ and the lame man; *Van der Helst*, Portraits; *Holbein the Younger*, Prince Edward, Melanchthon (medallion); *Mierevelt*, Portrait; *Panini*, Piazza Navona, St. Peter's at Rome; *Poussin*, Rape of the Sabine women; *Rubens*, Rape of Dejanira; *Snyders*, Bear; *Snyders* and *Rubens*, Man cutting up a deer; *Ruysdael*, Ruins; *Teniers*, Slaughter-house; *Titian*, Portraits; *Veronese*, Christ.

In the centre of the *Altstadt* is the market-place with the *Marktkirche* (Pl. 18) of the 14th cent. On the outside are several tombstones of the 16th cent. The interior, restored in 1855, contains fine modern stained glass and a modern altar carved in oak. Tower 297 ft. high. The handsome old **Rathhaus** (Pl. 31), erected in the late Gothic style in 1439—55, has a modern wing facing the Köbelinger Strasse.

The Markt-Strasse and Köbelinger Strasse running to the S. from the market-place, and the Knochenhauer-Strasse and Schmiede-Strasse to the N., contain a number of picturesque late Gothic brick buildings with lofty gables, of the 15th and 16th cent. No. 10 in the last named street, at the corner of the Kaiser-Strasse, was once **Leibnitz's House**, a Renaissance building in stone, of 1652, with a jutty adorned with sixteen reliefs from Scripture. The neighbouring *Kreuzkirche* (Pl. 17) contains a good altar-piece.

The **Palace** (Pl. 33), an edifice of considerable extent, with its back to the Leine, is situated in the Lein-Strasse, to the S. W. of the market-place. It was built about the middle of last century and altered in 1817. The interior (accessible daily 9—5 o'clock; entrance by Portal No. 2) has recently been fitted up as an occasional residence for the Emperor and Empress of Germany. The chapel contains an altar-piece by *L. Cranach*, representing the Crucifixion, and frescoes of the Ascension by *Oesterley*.

Opposite the palace is the *Alte Palais* (Pl. 26), formerly the residence of King Ernest Augustus. To the l., a short distance hence, at the corner of the Friedrichs-Strasse, is the old palace of George V., now the *Rathhaus* (Pl. 31a).

At the back of the Palace flows the Leine, beyond which stretches an extensive drilling-ground termed the Waterloo-Platz, at the farther end of which rises the *Waterloo-Column*, 150 ft. in height, erected 'by the grateful Fatherland' to the Hanoverians who fell at the battle of Waterloo. Good survey of the town from the top. To the r. and l. are barracks, and to the l. is also the spacious *Arsenal* (1846). At the N. end is the *Statue of Count Alten* (d. 1840), the Hanoverian general at Waterloo, and commander of the Foreign Legion in Spain. In the grounds between this and the barracks is a temple (Pl. 9) with a bust of *Leibnitz* (d. 1716), who is interred in the neighbouring Neustädter Kirche (Pl. 19). His grave is marked by a marble slab with the words 'Ossa Leibnitii'.

At the back of General Alten's monument is the *Royal Library* (Pl. 3), containing 170,000 vols. and 3000 MSS., comprising those left by Leibnitz (open on week-days 12—1, Wed. and Sat. 12—2).

The *Poor House* in the Neue Strasse bears an inscription to the effect that the Duke of Brunswick dined here (the house being then an inn) when on his expedition from the Erzgebirge to the North Sea.

The *Picture Gallery of King George V., Holzmarkt 4, contains a number of good works by Italian, Flemish, and Old German masters. The senator Herr *Culemann*, Oster-Str. 54, possesses a collection of mediæval works of art, autographs, early typography, etc., to which connoisseurs are readily admitted.

The *Aquarium (adm. 5 Sgr.), near the Tivoli, and not far from the station, consists of 22 reservoirs of sea-water in a kind of subterranean grotto, lighted from above.

The *Gewerbe-Ausstellung*, or Industrial Exhibition, Georgs-Str. 34, consisting of machinery, manufactures, models, etc., is open daily 11—3 (adm. $2\frac{1}{2}$ Sgr.), and in winter on Sund. also 6—8 (1 Sgr.). No. 1 in the Lange Laube, the N. E. extension of the Georgs-Strasse, is the so-called *Haus der Väter*.

The *Christuskirche (Pl. 4), a handsome modern Gothic church, with good stained glass, is worthy of a visit (sacristan Oberstrasse 1).

An *Avenue of Limes, upwards of 1 M. long, leads on the N. W. side of the town to ($1\frac{1}{2}$ M.) Schloss Herrenhausen. On the E. side of it is the imposing *Welfenschloss*, or Palace of the Guelphs (Pl. 38), in the circular style, with five towers. The interior is unfinished. On the other side of the avenue is the *Georgen-Park* (with a café). **Schloss Herrenhausen**, at the farther end of the avenue, was the favourite residence of George I. (d. 1727), George II. (d. 1766), and George V. The garden, 120 acres in area, is laid out in the French style, and contains an open-air theatre, fountains, and hothouses. The jet of the principal fountain rises upwards of 100 ft. Adjoining the château is a building containing

At Zutphen the line to *Zwolle* and *Leeuwarden* (Friesland)
.diverges. Our line crosses the Yssel, traversing a district intersected by numerous canals. Five unimportant stations. Branch
lines diverge from stat. *Hengelo*, N. to *Almelo*, S. to *Enschede* and
Glanerbeck. Beyond stat. *Oldenzaal* the line crosses the Prussian
frontier. The custom-house·is at stat. **Bentheim,** a small town
(2000 inhab.) with an old château and a cold sulphureous spring.
Next stations *Schüttorf, Salzbergen* (junction for Emden, p. 98),
and **Rheine** (p..98) (**Rail. Restaurant)*, the junction for Münster
and Hamm, where carriages are changed.

The Osnabrück line crosses the *Ems*. Stations *Hörstel, Ibben-
büren* (with valuable mines), *Velpe*. The wooded chain of hills on
the l., the N.W. spurs of the Teutoburgian Forest (p. 54), enhance
the picturesqueness of the scenery. On a slope covered with sum-
mer-houses and orchards, on the l. as the station is entered, stands
the lunatic asylum of *Gertrudenberg*, formerly a Benedictine nunnery
.(suppressed in 1803).   :

Osnabrück *(*Schaumburg*, at the station ; **Dütting's Hôtel)*, the
capital of a bishopric founded by Charlemagne in 783, but suppressed in 1803 (governed alternately by a Rom. Cath. and a Protestant
prelate after the Peace of Westphalia), has since 1858 again been
the seat of a Rom. Cath. bishop (23,306 inhab., 1/3 Rom. Cath.).

The *Cathedral* (Rom. Cath.) of the 12th cent., a spacious cruci-
form structure, possesses three towers (the oldest on the N. side),
that over the choir being octagonal in form. The N. Portal (walled
up) dates from the period of the foundation. The W. Portal was
restored in 1840.

The large Platz on the N. of the cathedral is adorned with a
Statue of Justus Möser in bronze, designed by Drake, erected in
1836. This patriot (d. 1794), the 'Franklin of Westphalia', is interred in the Marienkirche.

The (Prot.) **Marienkirche*, or Church of St. Mary, is a noble
Gothic structure of moderate dimensions, borne by very lofty, slender columns. The nave was erected in the 14th, the choir in the
15th cent. The altar-piece is a beautiful and elaborate specimen
of **wood-carving, executed in the 15th cent., and gilded, resembling the altar-piece of St. Michael's Chapel in the cathedral of
Cologne. It is divided into 9 sections, representing scenes from the
life of the Saviour (the 'Seven Sacraments') and the Crucifixion,.
admirably grouped. The eight contemporaneous winged paintings,
probably of the old Westphalian school (p. 52), recal the style of
John van Eyck.

Adjacent is the *Rathhaus* (custodian at the police guard-house),
erected at the close of the 15th cent., where the negociations for
the Peace of Westphalia were carried on from 1643 to 1648. The
'Friedenssaal' contains portraits of princes, ambassadors, and other
reminiscences of that period (comp. p. 97).

The railway from *Osnabrück* to *Bremen* is now completed. The next stations beyond Osnabrück are *Wissingen* and *Melle*. The *Dietrichsburg*, a château 2¹/₄ M. to the N. of Melle, possesses a conspicuous modern tower commanding an extensive prospect. At its foot lies the estate of *Ostenwalde*.

Stations *Bruchmühlen*, *Bünde*, *Kirchlengern*, and *Löhne*, where the Cologne and Hanover line is reached. Thence to Hanover, see p. 54.

8. From Düsseldorf to Cassel.

Express in 6, ordinary trains in 9 hrs.; fares 7 Thlr. 1, 5 Thlr. 9, 3 Thlr. 16 Sgr.

Stat. **Gerresheim** possesses a fine church of the 12th cent. From a nunnery here Archbishop Gebhard of Cologne abducted the beautiful Countess Agnes of Mansfeld in 1582. After passing *Erkrath* (hydropathic estab.), the train ascends to *Hochdahl* (large ironfoundry of *Eintracht*), 494 ft. higher than Düsseldorf.

Stat. **Vohwinkel** is the junction of the *Deutz* line to the S. (R. 4), and the *Steele-Vohwinkel* line to the N., the latter being principally used for the coal traffic. At *Sonnborn* the train suddenly enters the valley of the *Wupper*, traverses it, then skirts the hill-side, commanding a view of Elberfeld below.

Elberfeld, and thence to *Schwerte*, see R. 4.

The Cassel line diverges here from the Berlin railway and follows the valley of the *Ruhr*. Stations *Langschede*, *Fröndenberg* (branch line to *Menden*, an industrious place), *Wickede*, and *Neheim-Hüsten*, where the *Möhne* falls into the Ruhr to the r., and the *Röhr* to the l. *Schloss Herdringen*, 1 M. to the W., erected by Zwirner, the late talented architect of the Cathedral of Cologne, is the seat of Count Fürstenberg.

Arnsberg *(*Husemann; Weipert)*, once the capital of the ancient Duchy of Westphalia, and greatly extended since 1815, is prettily situated on a height skirted by the Ruhr. The hill is crowned with the ruins of a castle, which fell to decay after the Seven Years' War; it commands a charming prospect. Another excellent point of view is the *Eichholz*, a park on the S. side of the town. The former Præmonstratensian abbey of *Weddinghausen* at the foot of the hill is now a grammar school.

The following stations are *Oeventrop* and **Meschede** *(Schäffer)*; ¹/₄ hr. to the W. the château of *Lahr*, the seat of Count Westphalen. At stat. *Bestwig* the valley of *Ramsbeck*, with productive lead mines, opens to the S. Beyond stat. *Olsberg* the line quits the picturesque valley of the Ruhr (to the r. the *Bruchhauser Steine*, a curious group of rocks) and penetrates the watershed between the Rhine and Weser by a long tunnel. Stat. *Brilon-Corbach*; 1 hr. to the N. the old town of **Brilon** *(Krüper)*, with venerable church, said to have been founded in 776 by Charlemagne.

The line then descends the narrow and wooded *Höpke-Thal*.

KASSEL.

1. Bellevue Schloß mit der Bildergallerie ——— D.4.
2. Garde du Corps-Casernen ——— C.3.4.
3. Infanterie- ——— C.12.
4. Neue Artillerie C. ——— C.12.
5. Castell ——— C.3.
6. Fürstenhaus ——— C.4.
7. Gymnasium ——— B.3.
8. Kriegschule ——— E.4.
9. Kattenburg ——— E.3.4.

Kirchen
10. Bruder K. ——— F.G.3.
11. Garnison K. ——— E.3.
12. kathol. K. ——— E.3.
13. Luther. K. ——— F.3.

Kirchen
14. St Martins K. ——— F.2.
15. Br. Neust. K. ——— B.4.
16. Frie.Neustädt.K ——— B.3.4.
17. Marmorbad ——— E.3.
18. Palais ——— DE.3.
21. Polizey ——— F.3.
22. Post ——— F.2.
23. Rathhaus ——— F.4.
24. Palais ——— F.4.
25. Standbild Friedrich II ——— D.4.
26. Synagoge ——— F.1.
27. Theater(Königl.) ——— D.3.
28. Zeughaus ——— C.1.2.

10. Museum mit Landes-
Bibliothek ——— E.3.4.
19. Museum Casino ——— D.4.
20. Orangerie ——— F.5.
20.* Theater ——— C.1.

A   B   C   D   E   F   G   H

Darmstadt, J:d. Wagner.

Near stat. *Bredelar* are extensive iron works, established in a former monastery. The *Diemel* is crossed, into which the Höpke here empties itself. The railway then skirts the hill, on which the old town of **Stadtberge** or *Marsberg* is situated, once a strong fortress, which was destroyed during the Thirty Years' War. This was the site of the ancient Saxon fortress *Eresburg*, which was captured and destroyed by Charlemagne in 772. Stat. *Nieder-Marsberg*, at the N. foot of the hill, is the seat of the provincial lunatic asylum.

Beyond Marsberg the valley of the Diemel expands. Stat. *Westheim, Scherfede.*

Warburg *(*Bracht)*, the junction of the line to Paderborn and Soest (R. 4), an ancient and once powerful Hanseatic town on the Diemel, is picturesquely situated on the slope of an eminence.

Diligence from Marsberg and from Warburg twice daily to (15 M. from either station) Arolsen *(Römer)*, with 2000 inhab., the seat of Prince Waldeck, where a valuable collection of antiquities from Herculaneum and Pompeii is preserved. Rauch, the celebrated sculptor, and Kaulbach, the no less distinguished painter, were both born at Arolsen. The Church contains three statuettes in marble by the former.

On the l. beyond Warburg rises the ruined castle of *Desenberg.* The *Diemel* is crossed. Stations *Liebenau, Hümme.*

Branch Railway from Hümme (in 3|4 hr.; fares 13¹|2, 9, 5¹|2 Sgr.) to the N., viâ *Trendelburg* on the Diemel, and *Helmarshausen*, commanded by the ruins of the *Kruckeburg*, to **Carlshafen** *(Schwan)*, a small town prettily situated at the influx of the Diemel into the Weser. It was founded in 1704 by the Landgrave Karl, with a view to provide his dominions with a harbour on the Weser. Fine view from the (10 min. *Juliushöhe* (tavern on the top).

Steamboats on the Weser from Carlshafen 2—3 times weekly in summer up to Münden, and down to Minden. The river scenery is picturesque at places.

Stat. *Hofgeismar* (Schwarzer Adler) is a small watering-place with a chalybeate spring. Stat. *Grebenstein*, with ancient watch-towers and a ruin on the Burgberg. To the S. in the distance rises the *Dörnberg* (1940 ft.), above a group of wooded hills. Last stat. *Mönchehof* (thence to Wilhelmsthal, see p. 84).

Cassel, see below.

9. Cassel and Environs.

Hotels. *Kœnig von Preussen (Pl. a), next to the post-office; *Hôtel Schirmer (Pl. b), both in the Königs-Platz, which is remarkable for its sixfold echo; Prinz Friedrich Wilhelm (Pl. c); Victoria Hôtel (Pl. d); Hôtel du Nord (Pl. e); Deutscher Kaiser, Bahnhofs-Str. 1; these four are all near the station. *Rheinischer Hof, Hedwigs-Str.; Russischer Hof, Königs-Str. 56, with restaurant. — Second class: *Ritter (Pl. f), Mittelgasse; Hessischer Hof, Martins-Platz. — *Schombardt's Hôtel at *Wilhelmshöhe* (p. 84) is much frequented, R. from 20, D. at 1 o'clock 20, at 5 o'clock 30 Sgr., also a pension; carriages to meet the trains. At *Wahlershausen*, near Wilhelmshöhe, *Zur Station Wilhelmshöhe*, unpretending.

Restaurants. *Bohne, Krech*, both in the Friedrichs-Platz. Beer at the *Café Wulp*, at the corner of the Museum-Str. and Stände-Platz, at *Schaub's Garden*, where concerts are frequently given in the evening

(Pl. 27). The S. side is open, and a view is obtained through the handsome *Friedrichs-Thor* of the Augarten, the valley of the Fulda, and the distant hills, of which the Meissner to the l. is the most prominent.

The ***Museum Fridericianum** (Pl. 18), erected in 1779 by the Landgrave Frederick II., contains a collection of curiosities and objects of art founded by the Hessian princes at the close of the 16th cent. and greatly extended in the 18th. Admission gratis; in summer Mon., Tues., Thurs., Frid. 10—1, in winter Tues. and Frid. 10—1; at other times on application to the inspector, fee for 1—4 pers. 1 Thlr., catalogue 5 Sgr.

I. HALL OF THE FOUNDERS. 1. Bust of Landgrave Frederick II.; on the r. and l. busts of the Napoleon family, some of them attributed to Canova. — II. ANCIENT SCULPTURES (to the r. of the first). On the r. and l. of the entrance: *1. Youth about to anoint himself, a Greek work; 2. Nymph with a shell. Between the columns are eight large statues: 4, 5. Apollo; 7. Pallas Athene. On the r. and l. of the egress: 11. Faun, 12. Youth, Greek works. By the wall at the back, to the l. of the entrance: 19, 20, 21. Draped female statues. — III. ANTICAGLIAS. On a column opposite the entrance a celebrated *Victoria, a Greek statuette in bronze. The nine cabinets contain Egyptian, Græco-Roman, and Germanic antiquities. In Cabinet D, 3rd compartment, *38. Statuette of Minerva, 44. Statuette of Diana. By the window, between the two last cabinets, casts of the Hildesheim treasure (p. 21). In the centre two stands with coins, and two with gems (2500 specimens). A number of the latter are antiques; e. g. in the 1st stand sections 5, 7, 13, in the 2nd 1, 2. — IV. PRECIOUS CURIOSITIES. 1st Cabinet (to the l. of the entrance): 564 objects, comprising gold and silver plate, ivory goblets, agates and gems, porcelain paintings, fancy weapons, etc. 2nd Cabinet: works of art in ivory, e. g. 96. Vessel with Bacchanalian procession, and 115. Vase with the Battle of Alexander, both by *Dobbermann*; 154. Two tablets with the history of the Passion in six sections, ascribed to *Albert Dürer*; 155. Crucifix by *Michael Angelo* (?); 167. Early German embodiment of Venus. 3rd Cabinet: amber articles. 4th and 5th Cabinets: Miscellaneous works of art. 6th Cabinet: modern works of art in bronze and marble. About 8200 modern silver medals are also preserved in thirteen stands in this room. — V. CLOCK ROOM. Curious clocks, automata, chronometers, etc.; in the centre of the room, 130. Clock worked by two balls, alternately relieving each other, manufactured by Campani at Rome in 1730 as a 'perpetuum mobile'; 133. Astronomical clock according to Ptolemy's system. — VI. MOSAICS. Roman and Florentine mosaics, works in scagliolo (imitation mosaic), and specimens of stones polished in Hessen. — The visitor now returns to Room II., and from it enters the *Collection of Casts* on the r., occupying four rooms, and arranged chronologically: VII., first gallery of the casts, earliest period; VIII., circular room, culminating period of Greek art in the 5th cent. B. C. (Phidias, Myron, Polycletes); IX., 4th cent. (Scopas and Praxiteles); X., works from the Alexandrine period down to that of Hadrian. — XI. ROOM: Models in cork of ancient Roman buildings, executed by Chichi at the close of last century. — The NATURAL HISTORY COLLECTIONS occupy four rooms on the ground floor, XII—XV. (mammalia, birds, amphibious animals, fish, insects), and three more on the first floor XVI—XVIII. (plants; in the 16th room, specimens of 546 different kinds of wood, in the form of bound books; then corals, fossils, and minerals). — XIX. ARMOURY (on the second floor). Old weapons, goblets, trinkets, hunting accoutrements, historical curiosities.

The LIBRARY (open daily, 10—1), occupying a large hall on the first floor of the building, in front, contains 200,000 vols. and many MSS. (e. g. the oldest of the 'Hildebrandlied', 9th cent.).

BÆDEKER's N. Germany. 5th Edit.   6

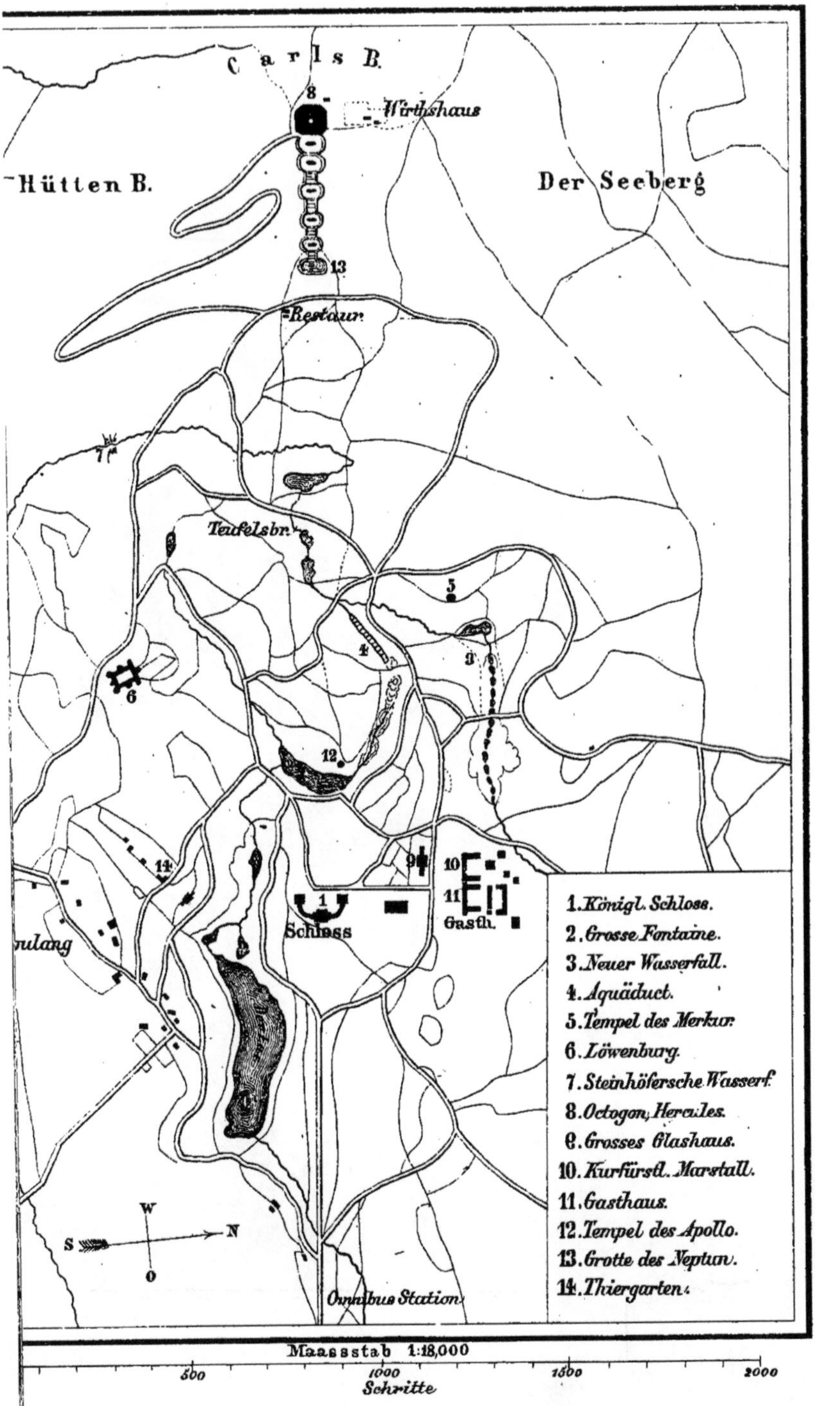

Carls B.

8

Wirthshaus

Hütten B.

Der Seeberg

13

Restaur.

7

Teufelsbr.

5

4

3

6

12

14

9

1

10

11

Schloss

Gasth.

1. Königl. Schloss.
2. Grosse Fontaine.
3. Neuer Wasserfall.
4. Aquäduct.
5. Tempel des Merkur.
6. Löwenburg.
7. Steinhöfersche Wasserf.
8. Octogon, Hercules.
9. Grosses Glashaus.
10. Kurfürstl. Marstall.
11. Gasthaus.
12. Tempel des Apollo.
13. Grotte des Neptun.
14. Thiergarten.

rulang

W N

S

O

Omnibus Station.

Maassstab 1:18,000

500   1000   1500   2000

Schritte

head of Holofernes; *384, 385. *Terburg*, Woman with a lute; 51, 52. *Holbein the Younger*, Portraits of men; 504. *Weenix*, Fruit piece; *183. *Rubens*, Portrait of a Greek; 592. *Netscher*, Italian theatrical masks; *23. *Titian*, Cleopatra; 25. *Titian*, Portrait of Alphonso d'Avalos; 380, 381. *Adr. Brouwer*, Peasants; 352. *Rembrandt*, Portrait; 586. *Netscher*, Mad. de Maintenon; on the opposite wall, 447. *Metsu*, Lady giving alms; 625. *Weenix*, Dead hare; 200. *Snyders*, Fox with its prey attacked by dogs; 448. *Metsu*, Woman tuning a lyre, with a man behind her; 511. *Eeckhout*, Circumcision; 399. *Ostade*, Rustic party; 526. *Potter*, Cattle piece; 224. *Hals*, Portrait of a man; 294. *Van Dyck*, Counsellor of Antwerp; 459. *Gonzales*, Family picture; 350. *Rembrandt*, Old man; *366. *Rembrandt*, Woodcutter's family; *364. *Rembrandt*, The burgomaster Six; 458. *Gonzales*, Young scholar in Spanish costume with his wife; 225. *Hals*, Young woman; 854a. *Jan van Eyck*, Altar piece; 578. *Hondekoeter*, Cock fight; *371. *Rembrandt*, Civic guardsman.

The Prot. Church of St. Martin (Pl. 14) in the Gothic style, with nave of the 14th and choir of the beginning of the 15th cent., was judiciously restored in 1842. Sacristan's address, Hohenthor-Str. 18.

The *Monument of Philip the Generous* (d. 1567) and his wife, erected by their son William IV., in black marble with white reliefs and profuse gilding, occupies the place of the high altar. The *Monument of the Landgrave Moritz*, in coloured marble, was erected in 1662; opposite to it a monument in bronze, with a likeness of the Landgravine Christina (d. 1549). — The *Tower* (231 ft.) overlooks the red roofs of the town and the environs as far as Wilhelmshöhe. Visitors ring at a small door to the r. of the W. portal.

The eminent historian Johann von Müller (d. 1809) is interred at the N.W. corner of the *Old Cemetery* (Pl. E, 2), where a monument was erected to his memory in 1852 by King Lewis of Bavaria. The great composer *Spohr* (d. 1859) reposes in the *New Cemetery* outside the Holländische Thor.

The *Auegarten, or *Carlsaue*, near the Friedrichs-Platz, and bounded by the Fulda on the E., the favourite promenade of the inhabitants, was planned by *Le Nôtre*, the French landscape gardener, in 1709, and contains beautiful trees. Descending from the Friedrichsthor, the visitor soon reaches the large *Orangery* (Pl. 20), which has been recently restored. The pavilion adjoining it on the W. is the **Marmorbad** (Pl. 17), a large bath-room adorned with marble sculptures, chiefly by *Monnot*, a French sculptor of the last century. Among the statues may be mentioned the Faun, the dancing Bacchante, Bacchus, and Leda; among the scenes from Ovid's Metamorphoses, the reliefs of Apollo and Daphne, and Andromeda and Perseus. The custodian, who lives in the opposite (E.) pavilion, is generally on the spot (fee 5—10 Sgr.).

From the *Wilhelmshöher Thor* (Pl. B, C, 4) a fine avenue of limes, flanked with many handsome dwellings, leads by the village of *Wahlershausen* to (3¾ M.) *Wilhelmshöhe (railway, omnibus, and carriages, see p. 80), formerly the residence of the Elector of Hessen, and celebrated for its park and fountains. The beautiful grounds, partly laid out at the beginning of the 17th cent., are chiefly indebted to the Landgrave Carl (d. 1730) and the Elector William I. (d. 1821) for their present extent.

The **Schloss** (Pl. 1), erected at the end of last century, and oc-

6*

cupied by Napoleon III. during the latter part of the Franco-Prussian war in 1870—71, is a somewhat heavy building, the body and wings of which are disposed in the form of a semicircle. The interior is sumptuously fitted up, and contains a collection of Chinese and Japanese porcelain, and several good pictures, principally portraits of Hessian princes. The castellan lives on the ground-floor, close to the entrance. Near the Schloss is the *Marstall*, or stables of the château, which have been converted into a hussar-barrack, and adjoining it *Schombardt's Hôtel* (p. 79).

A visit to the finest points in the **Park**, which requires about 4 hrs. (guide 10 Sgr., hardly necessary), may be made in the following order.

From the inn good paths lead to the r. past the *Hothouses* (Pl. 9) to the *New Waterfall* (Pl. 3), 130 ft. in height. Ascend thence to the l. to the *Temple of Mercury* (Pl. 5), and proceed by wood-paths to the *Riesenschloss*, or *Octagon* (Pl. 8), the highest point in the grounds, 1360 ft. above the Fulda, a strange-looking vaulted structure in three storeys, surmounted by a colossal statue of the Farnese Hercules in copper (room in the club for 9 pers.). The *Grotto* in front of the Octagon, to the r., contains a water puzzle.

The *Cascades* descending from the Octagon are 300 yds. in length, with large basins at intervals of 50 yds. Pleasant walks descend to the r., passing the *Steinhöfer'sche Wasserfall* (Pl. 7), to the *Löwenburg* (Pl. 6), a modern imitation of an ancient castle, but in bad taste. The view from the platform of the tower is the chief attraction here.

In front of the Schloss is the **Great Fountain*, the highest in Europe, and the chief boast of Wilhelmshöhe, which sends up a jet of water 1 ft. in thickness and 200 ft. in height. Near it, to the l., is the *Teufelsbrücke*; to the r. the *Aqueduct* (Pl. 4), with a fine waterfall. The *Grosse Lac*, another large pond to the E. of the château, near the road to Cassel, is one of the finest points.

The *Fountains* play on Ascension-day, then from Whit-Monday till October (the 'Cascades' and the 'New Waterfall' on Sund. only) on Sund. at 3, and on Wed. at 2.30 o'clock. The visitor is recommended to be at the foot of the Cascades at the appointed hour, and to follow the course of the water thence (to the Teufelsbrücke, Aqueduct, Great Fountain, and New Waterfall), as the supply of water is limited and the exhibition therefore of brief duration.

Wilhelmsthal, a château of the former Electors of Hessen in the Italian palatial style, with handsome rococo decorations in the interior, lies in a beautiful park, 7½ M. to the N.W. of Cassel, and 1½ M. of *Mönchehof* (p. 79), the first station on the Cassel and Hofgeismar railway.

10. From Cassel to Hanover.

Railway in 4¹|₄—5 hrs.; express fares 5 Thlr. 5, 3 Thlr. 20, 2 Thlr.
15 Sgr.; ordinary 4 Thlr. 15, 3 Thlr. 11, 2 Thlr. 7¹|₂ Sgr.

Soon after leaving Cassel the train crosses the *Fulda*, and for
a long distance skirts the picturesque banks of the stream.

Stat. **Münden** *(Goldner Löwe; Hessischer Hof; Hôtel Schmidt;
Rail. Restaurant), charmingly situated on a tongue of land at the
junction of the *Fulda* and *Werra*, the united waters of which form
the *Weser* (steamboats to Minden and Bremen), is an old-fashioned
place of some commercial importance. The *Church of St. Blasius* is
of the 14th cent. The extensive *Schloss*, built by Duke Erich II. of
Brunswick-Lüneburg in 1571, is now a barrack, near which is the
recently founded *Forst-Academie*. Picturesque views from *Andree's
Berggarten* (10 min.), and from the *Tivoli*, near the station and the
town. — Railway to *Nordhausen* and *Halle*, see R. 55.

The train crosses the *Werra*, follows the valley of the *Weser*
for some distance, ascends gradually to stat. *Dransfeld*, the
culminating point of the line, and finally descends to the valley of
the *Leine*.

Stat. **Göttingen** (424 ft.) *(Krone; Gebhard's Hôtel*, near the
station), with 14,534 inhab., is remarkable for nothing but its university (700 stud.), founded by George II. of Hanover in 1737. The
Library is very valuable (350,000 vols., 5000 MSS.). The anatomical
(remarkable collection of skulls), natural history, and other collections may be visited by the scientific.

From Göttingen to Arenshausen by a direct line from Cassel,
in 35 min., ascending the broad valley of the Leine. Thence to *Gotha*,
Erfurt, and *Halle*, see R. 55.

Beyond stat. *Bovenden* is the ruin of *Plesse*, with beautiful wooded
environs. Above stat. *Nörthen* rises the imposing ruin of *Hardenberg* and a modern château, beyond it a slender watch-tower on an
eminence.

Northeim *(Sonne)*, an old town, with a good church of 1519
(old carving at the altar; in the window of the choir, remnants of
fine stained glass of 1404), is the station for travellers intending
to explore the Harz from this side.

From Northeim to Herzberg railway in ³|₄ hr. (22, 17, 11 Sgr.).
Stations *Catlenburg*, *Hattorf*. *Herzberg*, and thence to *Nordhausen* and *Erfurt*, see p. 256.

Salzderhelden, with a saline spring and ruined castle, is the
station for *Eimbeck*, 2¹/₄ M. to the N.W., an old town famous for
its beer.

Stat. **Kreiensen** is the junction for Cologne, Brunswick, Magdeburg, and Berlin (R. 4). Stat. *Freden* is situated in one of the
prettiest parts of the valley of the Leine, on which the ruins of
Freden and the *Winzenburg* look down from the heights. Stat. *Al-
feld* lies at the base of the *Sieben Brüder*, a group of hills, the
highest of which is 1480 ft. above the sea-level. The mountainous
district is now quitted. Stat. *Banteln*.

Beyond stat. *Elze* the Leine is crossed. On an eminence to the
l. rises *Schloss Marienburg*.   Stat. *Nordstemmen* is the junction for
Hildesheim (p. 56).

Hanover, see p. 72.

11. From Hanover to Bremen.

Railway in 3—3¹|₂ hrs.; fares 3 Thlr., 2 Thlr. 7¹|₂·, 1 Thlr. 16 Sgr.

At stat. *Wunstorf* (p. 55) the Bremen line diverges from the
line from Hanover to Minden. The district traversed is poor, flat,
and sandy.

Near stat. *Neustadt*, to the W., is situated the *Steinhuder Meer*,
an inland lake 2 M. in width, on an artificial island in which Count
Wilhelm von der Lippe (d. 1777) erected the *Wilhelmstein*, a small
model fortress where he established a military school. General
Scharnhorst (p. 14) received his first military training here. *Rehburg*, on the W. bank, is a pleasant watering-place, with baths and
whey-cure.

Stations *Hagen, Linsburg, Nienburg, Rohrsen, Eistrup, Döverden*.
Near stat. *Verden*, with its cathedral destitute of tower, where
Charlemagne founded an episcopal see, the line crosses the *Aller*,
which falls into the Weser below Verden. Stations *Langwedel,
Achim, Sebaldsbrück*.

Bremen.

Money. Since 1st July, 1872.: 1 Mark=100 Pfennige = 1 shilling English (1 Prussian Thaler=3 Marks). The old currency was 1 dollar in
gold (=1 Thlr. 3 Sgr. Prussian) = 72 Grote = 3 sh. 3¹|₂ d. English (21²¹|₃₁
Grote = 1 Mark). The grote (a little more than ¹|₂ d.) is still in common use.

Hotels. *HILLMANN's (Pl. d), Heerdenthor-Steinweg 39, at the corner
of the Wallpromenade; *HÔTEL DE L'EUROPE (Pl. c), opposite Hillmann's; * GRAND HÔTEL DU NORD (Pl. a), Bahnhofs-Str. 14; three large establishments, with high charges. *STADT FRANKFURT (Pl. e), Domshof 18;
*HOTEL SIEDENBURG (Pl. f), Wall 175; ALBERTI, Bahnhofs-Str. 27; HAN-
NOVERSCHES HAUS (Pl. g), a hotel and boarding-house, Dechanat-Str. 15, near
the Osterthor; SCHAPER (Pl. h), CASPER, and BELLEVUE (Pl. i), all in the
Bahnhofs-Str., R. 1¹|₂ M. and upwards.

Restaurants. *Rathskeller (p. 88); *Rheinischer Keller*, under the Hôtel
de l'Europe; *Alberti* and *Hôtel du Nord*, see above; *Börsen-Restaurant* in
the Exchange passage; *Hasselmann*, Seemann-Str. 15; *Jacobihalle*, Jacobi-
kirchhof 13 (in the restored choir of a church); *Kapff's Keller*, Wacht-
Str. 43, by the Weser Bridge; *Kirchner*, Wacht-Strasse 40; *Siedenburg*,
see above; at the *Bürgerpark*, see p. 90. — **Cafés.** *Hillmann's* and *Café de
l'Europe*, see above. — **Beer.** *Haake & Co.*, Kirchen-Str.; *Dornkiste*,
Martini-Str. 41a; *C. H. Haake* and *Feldmann*, Wacht-Str.; *Kaune*, in the
Market; *Engelhardt*, Langen-Str.; *Schaper*, Bahnhofs-Str.; *Hoppe*, Wall 161.

Cabs (with two horses) per drive within the city, 1—2 pers. 12 Grote,
to Saltzmann's Garten 18, Bürgerpark 36, each additional pers. 3 Gr.; for
¹|₄ hr. 16, ¹|₂ hr. 24, ³|₄ hr. 32, 1 hr. 40 Gr., each additional ¹|₄ hr. 8 Gr.;
small packages free; each box 6 Gr.

Theatre daily. Performances in winter at the *Stadttheater* (Pl.
34). Open air theatres in summer at *Saltzmann's Garten* and the *Tivoli*.

Post Office at the Stadthaus, on the N. side in the Domshof. Office
for money-orders and diligence passengers in the Violen-Str. **Telegraph
Office** at the Exchange,

A

Darmstadt Ed. Wagner.

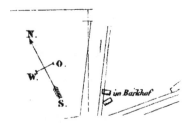

im Barkhof

5

BREMEN.

Arbeitshaus	E.56	23 St. Rembert K. u. Stift . . G3
2 Bahnhof	E.2	24 Stephani B4
3 Bank	E.4	25 Museum E.4
4 Börse	E.4	26 Nachw. Bur. f. Auswand. Nr. E2
5 Börsenhalle	F.E.4	27 Norddeutsch. Lloyd . . . E.4
6 Bürgerschule u. Stadtbibliothek E.4		28 Omnibus u. Dilig. B. . . . F.4
7 Casernen CD.7		29 Post (nordd.) E.4
8 Centralhalle C.2		30 Rathhaus E.4
9 Colosseum C.2		31 Rolandsäule E.4
10 Conventgarden G3		32 Schütting E.4
Denkmäler		33 Stadthaus E.4
11 Gustav Adolph F.4		34 Stadttheater E.3
12 Olbers G.4		35 Telegraphen E.3.4
13 Detentionshaus G.4		36 Tonhalle C.3
14 Kunsthalle G.4		37 Union G.4
15 Künstlerverein F.4		38 Urne E.3
Kirchen		39 Waisenhaus F.4
16 St. Ansgarii K. . . . D.4		
17 Dom F.4		
18 St. Johannis K. . . . F.5		
19 Liebfrauen K. . . . E.4		
20 Martini K. . . . E.5		
21 St. Michaelis B.3		
22 St. Pauli E.6		

6

7

G   H   I

Baths in the ·Weser by the Osterdeich, outside the Osterthor. — *Swimming Bath* in the Kleine Weser, outside the Werderthor. — Warm Baths: *Spilcker*, Altenwall 22; *Muth's* Russian baths, Wall 133.

Steamboats from *Bremerhaven* to *London* (40 hrs.) and *Hull* (36 hrs.) once or twice weekly; to *New York* weekly in 15 days (of which travellers returning to England may avail themselves as far as Southampton); to *Norderney*, see p. 91; to *Heligoland*, see p. 108.

Bremen, the second in importance of the three independent Hanseatic cities, with 82,990 inhab., and the principal commercial place in N. Germany next to Hamburg, lies in a sandy plain on both banks of the *Weser*, 65 M. from its influx into the German Ocean. On the r. bank is the *Altstadt*, formerly enclosed by ramparts, round which the *Vorstädte* are situated, and on the l. bank the *Neustadt*. Many well preserved old buildings testify to the mediæval importance of the place, while the numerous handsome edifices erected within the last twenty or thirty years entitle it to a respectable rank among the modern cities of Europe.

The Bishopric of Bremen was founded in 788 by Charlemagne. In the 10th cent. the town, which had already received certain privileges and a constitution, began to flourish as a seaport and a commercial place. In 1284 it became a member of the Hanseatic League, but proving intractable on several occasions it was more than once excluded from the society. In 1522 Bremen embraced the Reformation, and in 1547 gallantly repelled an attack by the Imperial army. The citizens bravely defended themselves against the Swedes also, who had obtained possession of the episcopal see by the Peace of Westphalia, and stoutly maintained the position of Bremen as a free city of the Empire. Bremen is now chiefly indebted for its importance to its seaport Bremerhaven (p. 91), which is annually entered by 3300 vessels. Value of imports about 21 million, of exports 20 million pounds sterling. The staple commodities are tobacco, petroleum, rice, and cotton. The merchants of Bremen possess about 265 sea-going vessels and 30 steamers. Bremen is one of the principal starting points of German emigrants to America, upwards of a million of whom have quitted their Fatherland by this port within the last twenty years.

The * **Promenades** laid out on the old ramparts, and separating the old town from the suburbs, constitute the principal ornament of the city. The picturesque groups of trees, the broad moats, and the rich vegetation of the opposite bank, on which a number of handsome residences rise, present a succession of pleasing pictures. At the Heerdenthor (Pl. E, 3) is a *Vase* adorned with reliefs by *Steinhäuser*, representing the 'Klosterochsenzug', a procession which takes place annually·in October.

Traversing the Sögestrasse, and then turning to the l., the traveller reaches the MARKT (Pl. E, 4), which is surrounded by the Rathhaus, the Exchange, and the Schütting, and is adorned with a 'Roland Monument' in the centre.

The * **Rathhaus** (Pl. 30) was erected about 1410, and the S. façade, with its magnificent jutting storey and beautifully decorated arcades and galleries, added in 1612. The façade is adorned with statues of the Emperor and seven Electors. From the lower corridor a wooden stair (open to the public) ascends to the great hall, 180 ft. in length, and 45 ft. in width, which has recently been restored and handsomely decorated. On the ceiling are medallion portraits of

German emperors from Charlemagne to Sigismund. The stained
glass windows contain names and armorial bearings of counsellors of
Bremen. In a corner of the hall stands a *Statue of Smidt* (d. 1857),
burgomaster of Bremen, in Carrara marble, also by Steinhäuser. The
Güldenkammer, where the women formerly assembled on the occasion of grand processions, is approached by a finely carved staircase.

On the W. side is the entrance to the celebrated *Rathskeller, which
contains Rhine and Moselle wines exclusively. It is open daily till 10. 30
p. m.; on Sundays not before 3 p. m. Wine may be purchased by the glass
or bottle; oysters and variou cold viands are also supplied. The oldest
casks are the 'Rose' (dating from 1624) and the 'Twelve Apostles', which
are kept in another part of the cellar, and are shown to the curious. The
'Rose' derives its name from a large rose painted on the ceiling, beneath which
the magistrates are said in ancient times to have held their most important sessions, such deliberations '*sub rosa*' being kept profoundly secret.

In front of the Rathhaus stands the *Roland (Pl. 31), a colossal
figure in stone, erected in 1412 on the site of an earlier figure of
wood, a symbol of free commercial intercourse and supreme criminal jurisdiction, and the palladium of civic liberty. In his left hand
the giant bears a shield with the imperial eagle, and a naked sword
in his right, while the head and hand of a criminal at his feet are
emblematical of the extent of the municipal jurisdiction.

On the S.E. side of the market rises the *Exchange (Pl. 4), designed by *H. Müller*, and completed in 1867, an imposing edifice in
the Gothic style. The W. façade is adorned with six figures emblematical of the different branches of commerce and manufacture. At the
N. portal, on the l. Fortune, on the r. Prudence. The handsome
Hall, with a fretted ceiling, and richly decorated with gilding, has
double aisles supported by 12 columns. A mural painting by *Jensen*,
representing the foundation of Riga by the inhabitants of Bremen
in 1201, is now approaching completion. Business - hour 1 o'clock;
strangers admitted only when accompanied by a member of the Exchange.

To the W. of the Exchange, and S. of the Rathhaus, is the
Schütting (Pl. 32), or *Chamber of Commerce*, erected in 1594; to
the N.W. is the *Liebfrauenkirche* (Pl. 19), dating from the 13th
cent., recently restored on the side facing the market. The modern
Stadthaus (Pl. 33), with the *Guard-House* and *Post-Office*, adjoins
the Rathhaus on the N.E. side.

The *Cathedral (Pl. 17), a Romanesque edifice with double
choir, the main parts of which belong to the original building, was
begun in the 11th cent. and greatly altered in the 13th. The
N. aisle, which is of equal height with the nave, was added in the
16th cent.

The INTERIOR (visitors enter through the house of the sacristan,
Domshaide 8) has been restored and fitted up for Protestant worship. Admirable *Organ*. Of the fine old *Screen* the stone sculpturing in front of
the organ is the sole remnant. *Windows* with stained-glass portraits of
Luther and Melanchthon, recently executed at Nuremberg. Rococo *Pulpit*,
presented by Queen Christina of Sweden. In the low S. *Aisle* is a me-

tallic *Font,* said to be 900 years old. A few steps here descend into the *Bleikeller* (i. e. lead-cellar, where the lead for the roof was melted), which contains several mummies, the oldest having been 400, the most recent 100 years in this undecayed condition. This vault still possesses the property of preventing decomposition, a proof of which is afforded by the dried poultry suspended in it some years ago.

In the *Domshof*, an extensive Platz on the N. side of the cathedral, is the *Museum* (Pl. 25), dedicated to social and scientific purposes, and containing good natural history and ethnographical collections (admission gratis in summer on Mon. and Thurs. 11—2, and Sat. 3—5; at other times by payment of a fee).

On the S. side of the Cathedral, at the back of the Exchange, lies the *Domshaide*, which is adorned with a *Statue of Gustavus Adolphus (Pl. 11), designed by the Swedish sculptor Fogelberg, and cast in bronze at Munich. It was destined for Gothenburg, but the vessel in which it was conveyed having been wrecked, the statue was rescued by boatmen of Heligoland, purchased by merchants of Bremen, and presented to their native city in 1856.

Opposite the statue, on the N. side, is the handsome Gothic building of the *Künstlerverein* (artists' association, Pl. 15), dating from the 13th cent., now fitted up in the mediæval style, and containing concert and ball rooms, etc. Strangers must be introduced by a member.

The Rom. Cath. *Johanniskirche* (Pl. 18) is a lofty edifice, with a nave 60 ft. in height, borne by eight slender columns.

Near the Osterthor, in the public grounds already mentioned (p. 82), is situated the new Kunsthalle (Pl. 14), containing pictures, chiefly modern, and a few sculptures, as well as a meritorious collection of old engravings, woodcuts, etc. (admission daily by payment of a fee).

GROUND FLOOR. *Leutze, Washington's passage of the Delaware; on the r. a number of sculptures in marble and casts by *Steinhäuser*, *Hirt*, and others. — STAIRCASE. *Stilke's cartoons of the frescoes at Stolzenfels: King John of Bohemia at the battle of Crécy, and Emp. Frederick II. receiving is bride Isabella of England. — FIRST FLOOR. *Steinhäuser*, Psyche, Pandora, sculptures in marble; *Saal*, The sun at midnight in Norway; *Schwerdgeburth*, Departure of the Salzburg Protestants from their native country; *Zimmermann*, Forest scene; *Achenbach*, Westphalian mill; *Meyer of Bremen*, Penitent daughter; *Bamberger*, English church near Hastings; *Calame*, Swiss mountains; *Ritter*, The son's last letter. Also several Dutch, early German, and Italian works. Seapieces by *Gruyter* and *Koekkoek*. Violin-player, Mignon, etc., sculptures by *Steinhäuser*.

The *Altmannshöhe* (Pl. G, 5), at the S. end of the promenades, affords a pleasant view of the busy Weser and the opposite Neustadt. — In the promenades, to the N. of the Kunsthalle, rises the *Statue of Olbers (d. 1840), a distinguished physician and astronomer, in Carrara marble, by *Steinhäuser*. Farther N. is the *Stadttheater* (Pl. 34), near the Bischofsthor.

The new quarters of the town outside the *Osterthor* and *Bischofsthor* contain many handsome private houses. The Körner-Markt (Pl. H, 4) is embellished with a *Statue of Theodore Körner*, in bronze, by Deneys of Bremen. The modern Gothic *Rembertikirche* (Pl. 23) is also noticeable.

The **Ansgariikirche** (Pl. 16), erected in 1229—1243, with an altar-piece by Tischbein, has been recently restored aud adorned with stained glass windows. The tower, 357 ft. in height, commands an extensive view. Opposite the W. portal is a group in sandstone by *Steinhäuser*, representing St. Ansgarius, the apostle of this district, and first archbishop of Bremen and Hamburg (d. 865), in the act of releasing a heathen boy from the yoke of paganism. Beyond it is the *Gewerbehaus*, erected in 1619 as a guild-hall of the cloth merchants, with a well preserved Renaissance façade in sandstone. The interior is restored, and has been employed for commercial purposes since 1863.

In the Hutfilter-Strasse, in the vicinity, is the old *Haus Seefahrt*, an asylum for aged mariners and widows, bearing the quaint inscription, 'Navigare necesse, vivere non est necesse'.

Two **Bridges** (a third is in course of construction) connect the Altstadt on the r. with the Neustadt on the l. bank of the Weser. In the centre of the town the *Grosse Brücke* crosses from the Wacht-strasse to the Werder, from which a smaller bridge crosses the *Kleine Weser* to the Neustadt. The former commmands a pleasing view of the town, the Weser, and the *Schlachte*, a wharf on the r. bank where the principal shipping traffic is carried on.—At the lower (W.) end of the town the river is crossed by the *Railway Bridge* (p. 94), open to pedestrians also, part of which can be opened to admit of the passage of vessels.

To the N.E. of the town, about ¼ M. from the principal Railway Station (Pl. E, 1, 2), is situated the **Bürgerpark**, 180 acres in area, which has been laid out since 1866, and is now a favourite resort of the citizens, especially on evenings when concerts are given. The road to it crosses the new Osnabrück and Hamburg railway.

From Bremen to Bremerhaven. Railway to Geestemünde in 1½ hr. (fares 1 Thlr. 20, 1 Thlr. 7½, 25 Sgr.). Steamboat daily in 5 hrs. (fares 28, 19 Sgr.).

Scenery uninteresting. Railway-stations *Burg-Lesum* (branch-line in ¼ hr. to **Vegesack,** a pleasantly situated town with a harbour), *Ritterhude, Osterholz-Scharmbeck, Oldenbüttel, Stubben* (diligence to *Stade*, p. 108), *Loxstedt.*

Geestemünde *(Hôtel Hannover*, opposite the quay of the Norderney and Heligoland steamers, R., B., and A. 1 Thlr. 7½ Sgr. ; *Meyer*, at the upper end of the town ; *Wehring*, at the station), situated on the l. bank of the *Geeste*, at its influx into the Weser, was founded by the former Hanoverian government as a rival of Bremerhaven, and provided with a harbour in 1863. On the opposite bank of the Geeste lies

Bremerhaven *(Beermann's Hotel, Steinhoff's*, and *Löhr's*, all in the market-place; *Winter's*, on the quay), the seaport of Bremen, founded by the advice·of the burgomaster Smidt on a small piece of land purchased from Hánover in 1827, is now a rapidly increasing town with 10,802 inhab. and extensive shipping traffic. The *Docks* are commodious and well organised. A large dry-dock of the 'Bremer Lloyd' was completed in 1871. A visit may be paid to one of the large Transatlantic steamers usually lying here (tickets at the Lloyd Office gratis). The *Lighthouse* commands a good survey of the environs. The lofty open spire of the modern Gothic church is a conspicuous object for many miles around.

From Bremerhaven to *Heligoland*, see p. 108; to *Spiekeroog* and *Norderney*, see below.

12. The East-Frisian Islands.

Spiekeroog. Norderney. Borkum.

Comp. Map, p. 114.

From. Geestemünde (Bremerhaven) to *Norderney* a steamer three times a week in 6—8 hrs., fare 2½, return 4 Thlr.; to Spiekeroog by the same vessel in 4—5 hrs., 2½ Thlr. — *From Emden* to *Norderney* a steamer daily in 4—5 hrs. (fares 2, 1⅓ Thlr.; return 3, 2 Thlr.), starting three times a week from Leer (p. 98) (same fares). Norderney may also be reached from Emden viâ *Norden*. Diligence to Norden three times daily in 3¾ hrs. (25½ Sgr.), also an omnibus. From Norden either by omnibus to the coast n ½ hr. (5 Sgr.), and thence by steamboat in ½ hr. to Norderney (10, 5 Sgr.), r by the diligence which runs daily direct from Norden to Norderney at w tide in 3½—5 hrs. (21 Sgr.). — *From Emden* to *Borkum* a steamer our times a week in 4 hrs.; fare 2, return 3 Thlr. — Return-tickets by all these steamers are available for the entire season.

From Geestemünde to Norderney. The steamboat-pier is on the Geeste, ½ M. from the railway-station. The coast soon disappears. In the distance are seen the *Bremen Light-ships* and the *Bremer Bake* (buoy). A line of islands then becomes visible to the l. The first of these is *Wangeroog (Ooy, Oye, Ey,* the Rhenish *Au,* and Scandinavian *Ö*, signify island), formerly much frequented as a sea-bathing place.

The steamer steers through the *Watt*, a strait with numerous sandbanks, which separates the islands from the E. Frisian coast, and is passable for carriages at low tide at the S. E. end (p. 92). On the mainland, towards the S., *Cärolinen Siehl*, with its windmills, *Neuharlinger-Siehl*, and the churches of *Wittmund* and *Esens* successively come into view. The steamer touches at **Spiekeroog** (passengers for which are landed in small boats), visited as a sea-bathing place by several hundred persons annually (accommodation unpretending), and passing *Langeroog*, which also begins to attract sea-bathing visitors, and *Baltrum*, stops at the S. W. point of Norderney.

From Emden to Norderney (comp. p. 99). The steamer describes a long curve towards the S., and then steers towards the

N.W. through the *Dollart*, a bay of 120 Sq. M. in area, formed by an inundation of the river in 1277, which occasioned the destruction of a town and numerous villages. On the r. are the villages of the E. Frisian coast, on the l. the Dutch province of *Groningen*, where the small fortified harbour of *Delfzyl* is conspicuous. The vessel then turns to the N.E. To the l. appear the islands of *Borkum* (p. 94) and afterwards *Juist*, to the r. the lofty church of Norden (see below). Arrival at Norderney, see below.

Land Route (diligence and omnibus, see p. 91). *Norden* (Dippel), a small manufacturing town with 6500 inhab., 20 M. from Emden, has a pleasant market planted with trees and a Protestant church of the 15th. cent.

Omnibus in 1/2 hr. from Norden to the *Norderdeich*, whence a steamboat crosses once or twice daily to Norderney at high tide in 1/2 hr. — The diligence from Norden to Norderney (4—5 hrs.) runs by (6 M.) *Hilgenrieder Siehl*, and then crosses the *Watt*, which is nearly dry at low tide, a tedious, but not unpleasant journey.

Norderney. Arrival. Carriages are in waiting at the pier to convey travellers to the Conversationshaus (2¹|₂ Sgr. each person). The services of an '*Ordonnanz*', or commissionaire, may then be engaged (2¹|₂ Sgr. each errand) to facilitate the search for apartments, but from the middle of July to the end of August accommodation can rarely be procured unless previously ordered. *Luggage* is conveyed from the steamer to the *Lagerhaus* in the Marien-Str. (for which 1—7¹|₂ Sgr. per package is charged), where it is afterwards reclaimed by its owners.

Hotels, Apartments, etc. Table d'hôte daily at 1 o'clock at the **Conversationshaus* and the *Strandhalle, adults 17¹|₂, children 12¹|₂ Sgr.; at 3 o'clock 25 and 15 Sgr.; suppers *à la carte* after 8 p. m. Dinners at 25 and 15 Sgr. may also be sent for by those who prefer to dine in private, if ordered early in the day. Apartments are not let at these establishments, but at the *Grosse and *Kleine Logirhaus, near the Conversationshaus, and in the upper part of the *Bazaar*. — The hotels *DEUTSCHES HAUS, *SCHUCHARDT, BELLEVUE, MEYER'S and KROLL'S are generally crowded in July and August. — *Private Apartments* very unpretending, but generally clean, may be hired in most of the streets at 5 Thlr. and upwards per week. Everything in Norderney used to be strictly regulated by *tariff*, from the doctor's fee and the price of a dinner down to the gratuity payable to the boots, but this system was found to paralyse all attempts at improvement, and the rules have recently been somewhat relaxed. — *Music Tax*. For a family 2—5 Thlr., a gentleman 1¹|₂—3, a lady 20 Sgr. to 1 Thlr.; for the serenade with which visitors are usually greeted on the morning after their arrival 1 Thlr.

Bath Tickets for the machines drawn by horses 10, for the others 7¹|₂ (children 4) Sgr., issued at the Conversationshaus and the Giftbude (p. 93). If all the machines are occupied, a ticket is handed to the intending bather, who must then wait until his number is called out. Towels and bathing dresses are distributed on the beach; charge for their use 15 Sgr. per week. The inexperienced bather who requires a bath-attendant ('Rothhosen') in the water pays 10—15 Sgr. a week for his services. — Bathing hours from 5 a. m. to 2 p. m. The highest tides, at the new and full moon, are about 10, at the time of half-moon 4 o'clock, and each following day about 50 min. later (tide-tables at the bazaar 3 Sgr.). — All these rules and formalities and petty payments will probably prove irksome to the vigorous and practised bather, but it must be borne in mind that the visitors are numerous, the space limited, and most of the bathers inexperienced. — At the *Warmbadehaus* fresh-water, shower, and other baths may be had.

Physicians. The 'Sanitätsrath' *Dr. Fromm* and *Dr. Kirchner*.

Post Office, Louisen-Str. 8.; *Telegraph Office* near the church. *Bath, Police,* and *Enquiry Offices* at the old Conversationshaus.

Norderney, i. e. 'northern island', about 9 M. long, and 5 broad, is the largest and the most populous of the East Frisian islands, and like the rest of the gro..p is sandy and almost entirely destitute of vegetation. The village, which has recently become the most frequented of the German sea-bathing places (nearly 6000 visitors annually) lies at the S. W. angle of the island and consists of about 300 small houses, almost all of which are let during the season. The footpaths are all paved with brick.

At the S. end of the village is the *Conversationshaus,* surrounded by grounds, and containing dining, ball, billiard, and reading rooms. Near it is the *Bazaar* with its shops, the new *Warmbadehaus,* and the *Kleine* and *Grosse Logirhaus.* The latter lies to the S. of the Conversationshaus. Beyond it lies the 'Neue Polder', the principal pasture at Norderney. From the Conversationshaus towards the E. runs the *Marien-Strasse,* commanding a view of the opposite coast and the roads where a number of fishing-boats are generally anchored. Along the downs towards the N. W. extends the new *Victoria-Strasse,* facing the sea. At the N. end of the latter is the new *Strand-Halle,* similar to the Conversationshaus, but better fitted up.

The *Beach* to the N. of the village is the principal rendezvous of the visitors. The W. part is the *Damenstrand* (from which gentlemen are excluded till 2 p. m.), near the Strandhalle, and separated from it by a slight eminence termed the *Marienhöhe;* the E. part is the *Herrenstrand,* near which is the *Georgshöhe,* commanding a pleasant view. The *'Giftbude'* is a small restaurant on the Herrenstrand, where a band plays twice a week in the evening.

The island is bounded on three sides by *Dünen,* or sandhills, 30—50 ft. in height, formed by the action of the wind, and presenting a barrier to the encroachments of the sea. The W. side of the island, however, has frequently suffered seriously from storms, and in 1855 the village itself was endangered. A breakwater 880 yds. in length has therefore been constructed opposite the beach for the protection of the place, while seven bulwarks projecting into the water are designed for the consolidation of the Dünes. The *Ostdünen,* or E. downs, lie to the E. of the Georgshöhe.

At the S. E. end of the village, towards the mainland, is the *Schanze,* an intrenchment thrown up by the French in 1811, now converted into pleasure-grounds. A short distance to the N.W. is the *Bake,* a scaffolding erected on an eminence, serving as a landmark to sailors, and affording a good survey of the island. The *'Ruppertsberger Kamp',* a small grove of alders, encircling an eminence, $3/4$ M. farther to the E., may also be visited.

At the E. end of the island, 3 M. farther, is the *Weisse Düne* (carr. 2 Thlr.), a hill of white sand affording an extensive prospect of the sea and part of the island.

Pleasure-boats may be hired at 1 Thlr. per hour.   A seal-hunt-
ing or dolphin-fishing expedition (in which success is not invari-
able!) may also be undertaken (3 Thlr.).

From Emden to Borkum (comp. p. 99).   Steamer, see
p. 91.   The vessel traverses the Dollart (p. 92), then steers towards
the N. W., and touches at the S. coast of the island.

Borkum, situated at the mouth of the Ems, 9 M. from the
Dutch coast and between the channels termed the *Ooster Ems* and
Wester Ems, is the most western of the Frisian islands.   Like Nór-
derney the island is sandy and barren, and encircled with a belt of
downs.   It is $4^1/_2$ M. long and 2 M. broad, and consists of the Ost-
land and Westland.   The principal village lies in the latter and is
visited by about 1000 sea-bathers annually.   Tolerable apartments
may be procured for 3—6 Thlr. per week, and there are three inns
(Bakker; Köhler; Visser).   Excellent beach for bathing, 1 M. from
the village, but suitable at high tide only (machine 4, tent 2 Sgr. ;
attendant 1 Thlr. per month).

13. From Bremen to Oldenburg and Emden.

Railway from Bremen to *Oldenburg* in $1^1/_4$ hr. (fares 1 Thlr. 1 Sgr.,
19, or $12^1/_2$ Sgr.); from Oldenburg to *Leer* in $1^1/_2$ hr. (fares 38, 23, 16 Sgr.);
from Leer to *Emden* in $3/_4$ hr. (fares 21, 16, 10 Sgr.).

The train describes a long circuit round the town, intersects the
promenades, crosses the Weser, and halts at *Bremen-Neustadt.* The
district traversed is at first well cultivated, but afterwards barren
and unattractive.   Stations *Huchtingen, Delmenhorst*, the first place
in the Duchy of Oldenburg, *Gruppenbühren, Hude*, with picturesque
ruins of a monastery, and *Wüsting.*

Oldenburg *(*Hôtel de Russie*, R. 20, B. 10 Sgr. ; **Erbgrossher-
zog*, similar charges; *Neues Haus*, beer; *Buitjadinger Hof)*, the capital of the Grand Duchy of that name, is a quiet and pleasant town
on the *Hunte*, with 13,400 inhab., surrounded by handsome avenues and modern dwelling houses, which have superseded the old
ramparts.   In the market-place is the old *Rathhaus.*

The grand-ducal *Palace* at the S. end of the town, erected in
the 17th and 18th cent., contains some modern pictures (Greek
landscapes by *Willers*, scenes from the Iliad by *Tischbein*, young
Circassian girl by *Riedel*, Arabian and camel by *Kretzschmer*, etc.)
and a library of 120,000 vols. — To the E., between the Hunte
and the Garten-Strasse, lies the *Palace Garden.*

Crossing the Hunte and pursuing a straight direction, the traveller observes the *Palais*, the residence of the Grand Duke, on the
l., which also contains a number of good modern pictures.   On the
r. is the

*Augusteum, a handsome edifice in the late Renaissance style,
containing the valuable grand-ducal picture gallery of old masters
(admission daily 11—2, Sund. 12—2).

SECTION I. (by the entrance-door): *37. *Beltraffio*, Head of a girl; *38. *Solario*, Herodias; 31, 32. *Gaud. Ferrari*, Madonna; 33. *Borgognone*, 55. *Franc. Francia*, Madonnas; .*30. *Lombard School*, John the Baptist; 4. *Garofalo*, St. Catharine; 17. *Pontormo*, Portrait of a woman; 7. *Fiesole*, Madonna. — SECTION II. (continuing to the l.): 87. *Zurbaran*, Portrait of a man; 88. *Murillo*, Madonna as the good shepherdess; 89. *Velasquez*, Portrait of the Cardinal Infanta Fernando. — SECTION III.: 66. *Cariani*, The jealous man; 64, 65. *Bellini*, Madonnas; 82. *P. Veronese*, Venus, Cupid, and young woman; 81. *Veronese*, Portrait of a lady; *77. *P. Bordone*, Venetian lady; *71. *Moretto*, Noble of Bergamo; 68. *Seb. del Piombo*, Body of Christ with angels; 18. *Al. Allori*, Portrait of Bianca Cappello; 70. *Lor. Lotto*, Cavalier. — SECTION IV.: Works by *Tischbein* and other painters of last century, and several early German pictures. Returning to the entrance, the visitor now proceeds to the r. to — SECTION V.: 130, 129. *Teniers*, Peasants; 115. *Van Dyck*, Counsellor of Antwerp; 107. *Rubens*, St. Francis of Assisi; .106. *Rubens*, Head of a man. — SECTION VI.: 120, 121. *Snyders*, Poultry; .103. *Pourbus the Younger*, Bust of a knight; 90. *Mabuse*, Madonna; 155. *Wouvermans*, Alms; *Rembrandt*, *169. Landscape; 167. Portrait of a man, 166. Old woman, 170. Old man; 171, 172. *F. Bol*, Man and woman; 161—164. *Ruysdael*, Landscapes. — SECTION VII.: *139. *Lucas van Leyden*, Count Etzard I. of E. Friesland; 143. *Mierevelt*, Bust of a woman; 203. *Jan Steen*, Party; 202. *Honthorst*, Tavern; *196. *Backhuysen*, Sea-piece; 185. *Van der Helst*, Portrait of a man; 205. *Hondekoeter*, Unbidden guests; 104. *Rubens*, Prometheus.

The *Museum* in the Hafen-Str. contains ornithological, geological, and botanical collections of considerable value.

From Oldenburg to Wilhelmshaven railway in 1³⁄₄ hr. (fares 36, 22, 15 Sgr.). The district traversed is monotonous and barren. Stations *Rastede*, *Jaderberg*; then **Varel** (*Hôtel Eboli*, *Müller*), a cheerful little town (extensive cotton-mill at the station). At the W. angle of the Jade-Busen, 3 M. to the N., is *Dangast*, a sea-bathing place with 'Cursaal', etc. (living not expensive). At stat. *Ellenser-Damm* the line approaches the Jade-Deich, over which masts are seen in the distance. The scenery assumes the Frisian character, viz. that of interminable pastures occasionally enlivened by cattle and farm-houses. Stat. *Sande* (branch-line to *Jever* in 40 min.). Then

Wilhelmshaven (*Hôtel Denninghof*, R. and B. 22¹⁄₂, A. 5 Sgr.; *Keese*), the second war harbour of Germany on the N. Sea, constructed by the Prussians in 1855—69, near the Oldenburg village of *Heppens* on the N.W. side of the Jade-Busen. This basin, formed in 1528 by an inundation, is upwards of 60 sq. M. in area, and is connected with the N. sea by a channel 2 M. wide. The *Entrance* to the harbour, protected by piers 120 yds. long, is shut off by a huge dock-gate from the *Outer Harbour*; a second gate and a canal then lead to the *Inner Harbour* (400 yds. by 240 yds.). Connected with the latter are three dry docks and two slips for the construction of iron-clad vessels. This vast establishment, although still in an unfinished state, deserves a visit. The works are still progressing, and fortifications are being erected for their protection.

Beyond Oldenburg woods and moor are traversed. Stations *Zwischenahn* (pleasantly situated on a lake, a favourite resort of the citizens of Bremen), *Ochholt*, and *Apen*, on the Apen Diep. The line intersects the extensive *Hochmoor* (p. 98). Beyond *Augustveen* (with large iron-works) the line crosses the Prussian frontier, and the scenery changes its character. Pleasant meadows intersected by cuttings are traversed, while sails are occasionally visible in the distance. Stations *Stickhausen*, *Nortmoor*. At **Leer** (p. 98) the Oldenburg line unites with the Westphalian. From Leer to Emden, see p. 98.

14. From Hamm to Emden.

Railway to Emden in 6—7½ hrs.; fares 5 Thlr. 28, 4 Thlr. 10, 2 Thlr. 27 Sgr.

Stations *Drensteinfurt, Rinkerode,* and

Münster (*König von England,* R. 20, D. 17½, A. 5 Sgr.; *Rheinischer Hof; *Moormann,* and *Deutscher Kronprinz* of the second class), situated on the brook *Aa,* in a flat district, the ·capital of the Prussian province of Westphalia, with 25,452 inhab. and a garrison of 3300 men, is like Osnabrück and Paderborn an episcopal see of great antiquity. In the 13th and 14th cent. it was a prosperous Hanseatic town, and even carried on commerce beyond seas on its own account; at the time of the Reformation it was the scene of the fanatical excesses of the Anabaptists (see below), and in 1661 it finally succumbed to the episcopal yoke of the warlike Bishop von Galen. The town still retains many mediæval characteristics, which are most marked in the 'Principal' and Roggen-Markt with their arcades and picturesque old gabled houses, and in the Church of St. Lambert on the one side and the Rathhaus on the other. The residences of the wealthier nobility, in the palatial style of the 18th cent., such as the *Erbdrosten-Hof* and *Romberger Hof,* also form a peculiar feature of Münster.

The most conspicuous object from the railway is the handsome *Church of St. Maurice,* a Romanesque structure of the 12th cent., with three towers and Gothic choir of 1451, restored and enlarged in 1859. The chapel on the W. side, erected in 1371, contains the monument of the founder Bishop Erpho (1084—97). Near it is the modern Gothic *Hospital* and the monasteries 'Vom guten Hirten' and 'Kindlein Jesu'.

The next object of interest is (l.) the **Ludgerikirche** (Pl. 12), with a *tower terminating in a picturesque lantern. The original Romanesque structure of 1170 was rebuilt and extended in the Gothic style after a fire in 1383, and the whole judiciously restored in 1856—60. The coloured decorations of the nave and choir, the carved altars, and the modern (Romanesque) pulpit should be inspected. The three principal windows are filled with fine modern stained glass. In the choir eight statues, dating from 1600.

On the l. as the town is entered from the station, is the *Church of St. Servatius* (Pl. 14), erected as a chapel in the Romanesque style in 1197, rebuilt in the 15th cent., restored and decorated in 1854, and provided with a new spire in 1858.

The beautiful Gothic *Church of St. Lambert (Pl. 10) of the 14th cent. contains a fine open staircase in the choir. On the outside, over the S. portal, is represented the genealogy of Christ. From the S. side of the tower, which is considerably out of the perpendicular, are suspended the three iron cages in which the bodies of the fanatics John of Leyden, Knipperdolling, and Krechting, the leaders of the Anabaptists, were placed after they had been tortured to death

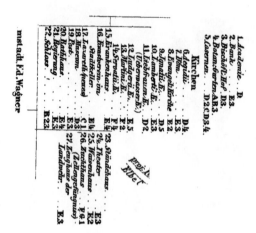

1. *Academie* . . .	D . E3
2. *Bank*	E3
3. *Bischöfl:Hof* .	D3
4. *Botan:Garten* AB3.	
5. *Casernen* . .	D2.C.D3.4.

Kirchen

6. *Ägidii* . . .	D4.
7. *Dom* . . .	E3.
8. *Evangel:Kirche*	E2.
9. *Ignatii* E. .	D.5
10. *Lamberti* E. .	E3
11. *Liebfrauen* E. .	D2.
(*Uebernnasen* E.)	
12. *Ludgeri* E. .	E5.
13. *Martini* E. .	E3.
14. *Neubau* E. .	F2.
14½ *Peruti* E. .	F4.

15. *Krankenhaus* .	E4
16. *Festbrunn im* .	
Rathkeller . .	F4.
17. *Lazareth (neues)* .	C1
18. *Museum* . .	D3
19. *Post* . . .	D3
20. *Rathhaus* . .	E3
21. *Regierung* . .	E4
22. *Schloss* . .	E3

23. *Ständehaus* .	
24. *Theater* . .	E3
25. *Waisenhaus* .	E2
26. *Zuchthaus* . .	F4.1
27. *Zeughaus der*	
(*Zellengefängniss*)	
Landwehr. . .	E3

Würzburg

mst adt. F. d. Wagner

in 1536 with red-hot pincers. Portraits of John of Leyden and his executioner are preserved in the library of the Academy.

The *Anabaptists*, a sect widely spread over Germany and the Netherlands about the beginning of the Reformation, added at that period to their rejection of infant-baptism a number of other startling and pernicious doctrines. · One of their most fanatical adherents was Thomas Münzer, leader of the insurgent peasantry. In Holland they were known, and still exist, under the name of Mennonites, derived from their founder Menno Simons. In 1533 a number of Dutch Anabaptists, headed by John Bockhold, a tailor from Leyden, and Matthiesen, a baker from Haarlem, settled at Münster, where with the aid of the Pastor Rottmann and Counsellor Knipperdolling they succeeded in establishing their supremacy in the town and in banishing the episcopal party. Bockhold (John of Leyden) was proclaimed king of the 'New Sion' in 1534. A reign of terror now began, polygamy was introduced, and many atrocities committed, while famine and pestilence devastated the town. The following year, however, Münster was compelled to capitulate by the bishop and his army, and Bockhold, Knipperdolling, and Krechting, the leaders of the Anabaptists, were cruelly tortured and executed.

The *Rathhaus (Pl. 20) of the 14th cent. with a beautiful Gothic façade contains the 'Friedenssaal' where the Peace of Westphalia was signed on 24th Oct., 1648. Picturesque chimney-piece of 1577; portraits of several ambassadors and princes, present at the conclusion of the peace, most of them by Terburg. Some of the cushions on which they sat still exist. Another chamber contains old armour, etc., and the pincers with which the Anabaptists were tortured before their execution.

The *Cathedral (Pl. 7), erected in the 13th—15th cent., has remarkably low aisles. The S. vestibule contains old Romanesque sculptures and columns. Several parts of the exterior exhibit a combination of Gothic and Romanesque.

Interior. The ancient decorations were almost entirely destroyed by the Anabaptists. In the W. part of the nave, a *Pietà by Achtermann of Rome, 1850. Over the S. portal the Last Judgment in relief, 1692. Opposite to it, over the N. portal, the remains of an old painting of the 14th cent., Frisians offering tribute to St. Paul. The *Apostelgang is a rich screen in the Flamboyant style, separating the choir from the nave, executed in 1542. — Choir Passage. Achtermann's *Descent from the Cross, a fine group in marble. On the wall an astronomical clock, constructed in 1400. Behind the high altar the chapel and monument of he warlike Bishop Galen (d. 1678), who for many years, particularly during the war with France and the Netherlands, maintained an army of 42,000 infantry, 18,000 cavalry, and 200 artillery, and was a formidable opponent of his Dutch neighbours. — Choir. Tombstones of bishops. Ciborium of 1536. The credence table was used as a draught-board by the Anabaptists.

In the Domplatz is the *Episcopal Residence* (Pl. 3); adjoining it the *Museum of Ecclesiastical Antiquities* (Pl. 18). Opposite the cathedral, the *Ständehaus* (Pl. 23), or Chamber of the Estates; at the entrance, the statues of *Arminius* and *Wittekind*.

The noble Gothic *Liebfrauen, or Ueberwasser-Kirche (Pl. 11), possesses a fine tower, the spire of which was removed by the Anabaptists (1533—35), in order that 'everything exalted might be brought low!' The Twelve Apostles and the Virgin over the W. portal are modern.

St. Ægidius (Pl. 6), of the 18th cent., is adorned with frescoes by Steinle, Settegast; and Mosler.

St. Ignatius (Pl. 9) is a modern Gothic Jesuit church (1857—58). Stained glass from Paris, in the style of the 16th cent.; Gothic carved altars.

St. Martin (Pl. 13), a Gothic structure commenced in 1187, but dating in its essential parts from the 14th cent., was judiciously restored in 1859.

The *Stadtkeller* at the corner of the Clemens-Str., contains the collections of the *Kunstverein* (Pl. 16), comprising several fine old Italian and German pictures.

At the back of the **Schloss,** which was formerly the episcopal palace, built in 1767, are well kept grounds, a favourite place of resort, and the *Botanical Garden* (Pl. 4), the property of the Academy. The fortifications of the town were converted into promenades after the Seven Years' War. The *Academy*, comprising theological and philosophical faculties, is the remnant of a former university.

In the promenade at the Ludgerithor rises a *Germania*, erected as a monument to Westphalians who fell during the Franco-German campaign of 1870—1871.

The next stations beyond Münster are *Greven, Emsdetten, Mesum,* and

Rheine (**Rail. Restaurant; *Hôtel Schultze*, in the town), a busy commercial town on the *Ems*, with fine old Gothic church and several new buildings near the station, the junction of the line to Osnabrück and Hanover (p. 77). Station *Salzbergen* (Overhues), junction for Arnheim, and *Leschede*, beyond which the *Ems* is crossed to *Lingen* (Hüvett). Country flat and barren. Several unimportant stations; then *Papenburg*, the largest settlement on the *Hochmoor*, a marshy district of 120 sq. M., intersected by canals. **Leer** (*Möller's Hotel; Voogdt*) a busy mercantile place, with 8800 inhab., situated on the *Leda*, at its union with the Ems, in the most fertile part of Ostfriesland. (Railway to Oldenburg and Bremen, see p. 95. Steamboats to Norderney, comp. p. 91.) Stations *Neermoor, Oldersum.*

Emden (**Weisses Haus*, nearest the steamboat-quay; **Prinz von Preussen; *Goldne Sonne)*, with 13,000 inhab., a free town of the Empire down to 1744, formerly situated on the Ems, but now $1^1/_2$ M. distant from it, is a prosperous, Dutch-looking place, with navigable canals in the streets, connected with the Ems, and at high tide 12 ft. in depth. The **Rathhaus*, a rich Renaissance structure of 1575, contains a remarkable **Arsenal*, where a number of very curious old fire-arms are preserved. They are said to have been captured by natives of Emden, together with the vessel in which Count Mansfeld (d. 1628), a celebrated general during the Thirty Years' War, was conveying his booty to England. The

tower commands a good survey of the town and environs. Fee 5 Sgr.
— The *Grosse Kirche* contains the marble monument of Count
Enno II. of E. Friesland. The *Natural History Museum* contains
a fine collection of specimens of amber. The Museum of Art and
Antiquity contains a small picture-gallery.

Emden is a good starting-point (steamer daily in 4—5 hrs.) for the
islands of **Norderney** and **Borkum**, two of the most frequented German sea
bathing-places (comp. p. 91). From Bremerhaven to Norderney, see p. 91.

15. From Hanover to Hamburg.

Railway in 4¹|₂—5 hrs.; fares 4 Thlr. 7¹|₂, 3 Thlr. 6, 2 Thlr. 4¹|₂ Sgr.
Passengers from Hamburg are lable to custom-house examination.

Hanover, see p. 72. 'Stat. *Misburg;* then **Lehrte**, the junction
of the Berlin-Hanover-Cologne (p. 56), the Magdeburg-Brunswick-
Hanover (p. 58), and the Hildesheim (p. 56) lines. Stations *Burg-
dorf, Ehlershausen*.

Stat. **Celle** *(Hannov. Hof; Sandkrug, Adler; Bockstöver's
Hotel)*, on the *Aller*, with 16,300 inhab., possesses an old *Schloss*
now restored, with an interesting chapel of 1485. The 'French
Garden' contains a monument to Queen Caroline of Denmark (d.
1775), sister of George III. of England. There is an extensive horse-
rearing establishment here.

Stations *Eschede, Unterlüss, Suderburg, Uelzen* (where there
are several large blocks of stone covered with a kind of roof, probably of Druidical or early Saxon origin), *Bevensen, Bienenbüttel*,
beyond which the dreary *Lüneburger Heide* is traversed.

Stat. **Lüneburg** *(*Wellenkamp's Hôtel; Deutsches Haus; Hoff-
nung)*, an old town of some importance, with 14,500 inhab., on the
navigable *Ilmenau*,- possesses many picturesque buildings of the
15th and 16th cent., among which the *Fürstenhaus* and the *Rathhaus
in the market-place deserve notice. The 'latter contains some good
wood-carving of the 16th cent., old silver plate, and stained glass.
The churches are also worthy of inspection. **St. John's*, with its
double aisles, *St. Michael's*, and *St. Lambert's* date from the 14th
cent.; *St. Nicholas* from the 15th. The Russians and Prussians
gained a victory over the French near Lüneburg in 1813. Extensive salt-works. Fine view from the Kalkberg.

Branch Line. to *Lauenburg, Büchen*, and *Lübeck* in 3¹|₂ hrs. (Hanover
to Lübeck 6³|₄ hrs.).

Beyond Lüneburg the train passes *Bardewieck*, once the chief
commercial town of N. Germany. It was destroyed by Henry the Lion
in 1189, and fragments of the vast cathedral now alone remain.

Harburg *(*König von Schweden*, R. 20, L. 4, A. 5 Sgr.;
**Weisser Schwan; *Rail. Restaurant)*, an increasing town with
16,506 inhab. Beyond Harburg the line crosses the Elbe by the
new railway-bridge (p. 103) to

Hamburg (see below).

7*

16. Hamburg.

Money. 16 Schillings ($) = 1 Mark = 1s. $2^1|_2 d$. Engl.; 5 $ = $4^1|_2 d$. English banknotes and sovereigns, as well as Prussian paper and silver, are everywhere received at the full value: 3s. = 1 Thlr. = $2^1|_2$ Marks.

Hotels. The best are on the Alster-Bassin: Hôtel de l'Europe (Pl. b), Alsterdamm 39; *Streit's Hôtel (Pl. a), Jungfernstieg .19; *Victoria (Pl. c), good cuisine, Jungfernstieg 10; Schadendorf's Hôtel, in the promenades near the Alster-Bassin, at the corner of the Steindamm and the Grosse Allee (Pl. H, 3). Charges at these: R. 2, D. (generally at 4 p. m. 2 M., B. 12 $, A. 12 $. — *Hôtel St. Petersburg (Pl. d), Jungfernstieg 1; *Kronprinz (Pl. h), Jungfernstieg 8; Belvedere (Pl. e), Alsterdamm 40; Alster Hôtel (Pl. f), Alsterdamm 32; *Hôtel de Russie (Pl. g), Jungfernstieg 15. — Hôtel du Nord, at the corner of the Neue Jungfernstieg and the Günsemarkt. Charges at all these: R. from $1^1|_2$, D. 2 M., A. 8—12 $. — Near the Alster-Bassin: *Waterloo Hotel, Dammthor-Str. 14. — Hôtel Royal, Grosse Bleichen 12; Scheller's Hotel, Dammthor-Str. 16. — Wiezel's Hotel at St. Pauli, on the quay, with fine view; Hôtel de Bavière, Plan 5; *Zingg's (Pl. k), R. 1, D. $1^1|_2$ M.; Kaiserhof, Ness 10; Weidenhof, Grosse Burstah 54; Bartel's, Post-Str. 14; *Hoefer's, at the Berlin station; Grossherzog von Mecklenburg, Schweinemarkt.

Restaurants. * Wilkens, Berg-Str. opposite the S. end of the Binnen-Alster; Grube, Alte Jungfernstieg 9, with fine view of the Binnen-Alster; Streit's Hôtel, see above; Bargstedt, English cookery, Admiralitäts-Str. 2; Schadendorf's Hotel; Pöhl, Zollenbrücke 3; Wiezel, on a rising ground by the quay, opposite the Harburg landing-place, fine view. Zingg's Hotel; Luzi, Grosse Johannis-Str. 9, both near the Börse. — Oysters. *Ulesch, Alsterdamm 42; Cölln, Brodschrangen 7; Iden, Alte Jungfernstieg 1c; Zeppenfeld, Alte Jungfernstieg 2; London Tavern, Neale, and Kolbe in the Hafen-Str., at St. Pauli, less expensive. — Hamburg Beef (smoked), which is much esteemed, may be purchased of Fett, Hopfenmarkt 14, or Hess, Grosse Burstah 8. — Fish at Meyer's, Königs-Str. 9, 10. — Beer. *Gebhardt, Kleine Bäcker-Str. 15; at the 'Casemate', Alster-Arcaden 12; Heitmann, Pferdemarkt; Steinbach, Berg-Str. 22. — At St. Pauli, outside the Millernthor: Mutzenbecher, Reeperbahn 100; Hantelmann & Zethner, Marien-Str. 32; Stelzer, Reeperbahn 69. Concerts at the Conventgarten, Neust. Fuhlentwiete 59, and at Sagebiel's, Grosse Drehbahn. — Cafés. Alster-Pavillon, Alte Jungfernstieg; at Schadendorf's Hotel; Sagehorn, Berg-Str. 2; at Zingg's Hotel.

Baths in the Elbe. John's Swimming Bath, on the Grasbrook, 5 $.; Krüger's Swimming Bath, on the Steinwärder (steamboat from St. Pauli every 5 min.); Möller, by the Lombardsbrücke, in the Aussen-Alser 4 $., much frequented, baths of all kinds. — Warm Baths. Flamm, Königs-Str. 3; Glissmann (vapour), Pferdemarkt 54; Vachez, Grosse Bleichen 36; Turkish Bath (1 Thlr.), Theater-Str. 41.

Theatres. Stadt-Theater (Pl. 44), beginning at 6.30 p. m., best seats 3, stalls $1^1|_2$, pit 1 M. — Thalia-Theater (Pl. 45), chiefly for comedy, much frequented, boxes 2, stalls $1^1|_4$ M., pit 10 $. — Schultze's Theatre at St. Pauli, farces and local pieces, well acted. — Damm's Tivoli in the Schulterblatt, outside the Holstenthor. — *Centralhalle at St. Pauli, for concerts and theatrical performances; Odeon, at St. Pauli.

Newspapers from every part of the world at the Börsenhalle (Pl. 7), to which strangers are admitted gratis for a few days if introduced by a member; Harmonie, Grosse Bleichen 19, introduction by a member, four weeks gratis; at the reading-rooms of the Vereinigte Gesellschaften, the Verein für Kunst und Wissenschaft, and the Patriotische Gesellschaft (introduction necessary in each case).

English physician Dr. F. Oppert M. D., M. R. C. P. Lond., Pelzer-Str. 3.

Cabs. Per drive in the town, 1—2 pers. 8 $.; 1 hr. in the town 1 M., $1|_2$ hr. 10 $.; 1 hr. beyond the town $1^1|_4$ M., each additional hour 1 M; to St. Pauli and the steamboat-piers 12 $., with ordinary luggage 1 M., each additional box 4, small packages 2 $.; to the station at Altona 1 M., each

A

HAMBURG.

1. Apollo Saal . . . . . D.2.
2. Bahnhof (Berliner) . G.H.4.
3. Bahnhof (Lübecker). I.3.4.
4. Bank . . . . E.4.
5. Bazar . . . . E.3.
6. Bibliothek (Stadt) . . F.4.
7. Börse . . . . E.4.
8. Botanischer Garten . D.1.2.
9. Conventgarten . . . D.3.

Denkmäler.
10. Adolph von
       Schaumburg . . . . G.3.
11. Büsch . . . . F.2.
12. Meyer . . . . G.4.
13. Repsold . . . . B.4.
14. Elbhöhe . . . . B.5.
15. Elbpavillon . . . . . B.4.
16. Johanneum . . . . . . F.4.

Kirchen.
17. Anschar Cap. . . . . D.3.
18. Dreieinigkeits K. . . G.2.
19. Deutsch. reform. . . E.3.
20. Engl. bischöffl. . . . C.4.
21. St. Jacobi . . . . . . F.4.
22. St. Katharina . . . . F.5.
23. Gr. Michaelis . . . . C.4.
24. Kl. Michaelis . . . . D.4.
25. St. Nicolai . . . . . E.4.5.
26. St. Petri . . . . F.4.
27. Klett's Gesellschaftsgart. D.3.

Klöster.
28. St. Johannis . . . . . G.4.
29. Maria M. dalena . G.3.

30. Krankenhaus . . . . . I.1.
31. Krankenhaus der
       „ Israeliten . . . . A.4.
32. Kunsthalle im Bau . . G.2.
33. Markthalle . . . . . . F.3.
34. Neuer Israel. Tempel . . C.3.

Post.
35. Mecklenburg'sche . . D.3.
36. Postgebäude . . . . . E.3.
37. Preussische . . . . . D.3.
38. Rathhaus . . . . . . D.5.
39. Rathhaus (im Project) E.4.
40. Seefahrer Armenh. . . D.5.
41. Seemannshaus . . . . B.5.
42. Stadt Wassermühle . E.3.
43. Sternwarte mit . . . B.4.
       Navigationschule

Theater.
44. Stadttheater . . . D.E.2.
45. Thalia . . . . F.3.
46. Tivoli . . . . H.3.
47. Verwaltungs Geb. . D.E.3.
48. Wasch. u Badeanst. . G.4.
       Zoolog. Garten . C.D.1.
50. Denkm. v. Schiller F.2.

Hôtels
a. Streit . . . . E.3.
b. de l'Europe . . . . . F.3.
c. Victoria . . . . E.3.
d. de St. Petersburg . . E.3.
e. Belvedère . . . . . . E.3.
f. Alster H. . . . . . . F.3.
  de Russie . . . . . . E.3.
  Kronprinz . . . . . . E.3.
i. de Baviere . . . . . . E.4.
k. Zinggs H . . . . . . E.4.
l. Weidenhof . . . . . . E.4.

Stein

Meter od.1 Kilometer.

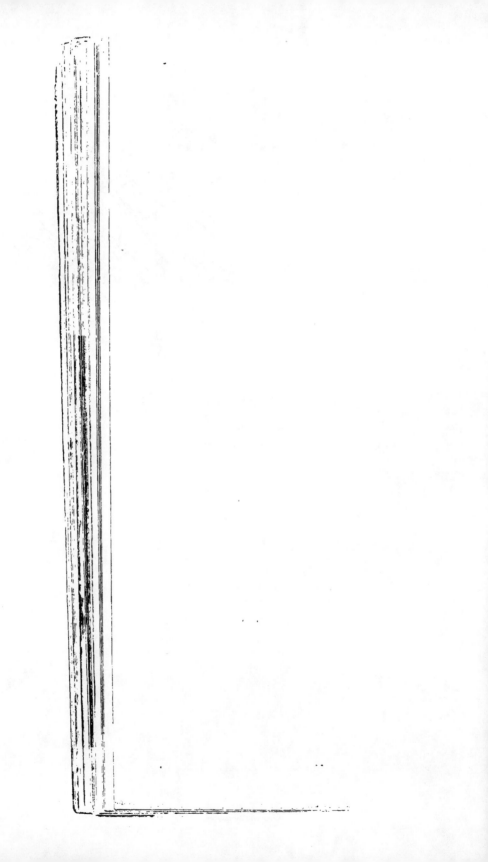

box 4 ſ.; from the Berlin-Hamburg to the Altona station 1 M.; Flottbeck
2¼ M.; suburb of St. George 10 ſ.; Grasbrook 12 ſ.; Wandsbeck 1½ M.
— Between 10 and 11 p. m. one-half more; from 11 p. m. to 5 a. m.
double fares.

Post Office (Pl. 36), Post-Str. Fifteen branch-offices in different parts
of the town. **Telegraph Office** at the General Post Office.

Omnibus every 7 min. from the Schweinemarkt (Pl. G, 3) to *Altona*
(p. 110), by a different route alternately, fare 3 ſ., half the distance 2 ſ.;
to *Hamm* and *Horn* (p. 108) from the Rathhausmarkt every ¼ hr.; to *Eppendorf* (p. 107) and *Locksledt* in summer every hour, in winter every 2
hrs., from Berg-Str. 19; to *Harburg* three times daily from Schlüter, near
St. Peter's (14 ſ., with luggage 20 ſ.).

Tramway (starting from the Rathhaus-Markt, Pl. E, 4). 1. To *Wandsbeck* (p. 108) every 12 min., 3 ſ.; 2. To *Barmbeck* every ½ hr.; 3. To
Eimsbüttel every ½ hr.; 4. To *Hoheluft*, eight times daily.

Junction Railway ('Verbindungsbahn') between Hamburg and Altona:
15 trains daily from the Berlin station at the *Klosterthor* (Pl. G, H, 4) to
the station of the Blankenese and Kiel railway at *Altona* (p. 110). The
intervening stations are the *Dammthor* (Pl. F. 1), *Sternschanze*, and *Schul-
terblatt* (comp. Map, p. 106).

Steamboats (comp. advertisements). 1. *On the Alster*. Small screw-
steamers, leaving the Jungfernstieg every 10 min., touch at the Lombards-
brücke, and then at *Alsterglacis, Rabenstrasse*, and *Eppendorf* on the W.
bank of the Aussen-Alster, and at *St. George* (at two places), *Uhlenhorst*
(at three places), and *Mühlenkamp* (comp. p. 107, and Map) on the E. bank;
fares 2, 3, 4 ſ. — 2. *On the Elbe*. To *Blankenese* (p. 108) several times
daily; to *Harburg* (p. 99) 12—14 times, viâ Altona; to *Stade* (p. 108)
twice daily; to *Cuxhaven* (p. 108) several times a week; ferry from *St.
Pauli* to the *Steinwärder* at frequent intervals during the day. — *Deep
Sea Steamers*. To *Heligoland* see p. 108. Communication with European
and foreign ports, see advertisements at the Exchange.

English Church (Pl. 20), near the Millern-Thor.

Hamburg, with 270,000 inhab., is the largest of the three free
Hanseatic towns of the German Empire, and next to London, Liver-
pool, and Glasgow, the most important commercial place in Europe.
It is advantageously situated on the broad lower *Elbe*, in which the
tide rises twice daily so as to admit of the entrance of vessels of
considerable tonnage, and is also connected by railways with every
part of Europe. The town consists of the *Altstadt* and *Neustadt*,
formerly surrounded by fortifications, and the suburbs of *St.
George* (N.E.) and *St. Pauli* (W.), adjoining which a new quarter
has recently sprung up on the N., outside the Dammthor. Hamburg
also lies on the *Alster*, a small stream from the N., which forms a
large basin outside the town, and a smaller one within it, termed
the *Aussen* and *Binnen-Alster* respectively, and is then discharged
through locks into the canals (Fleete) and branches of the Elbe which
flow through the lower part of the town.

Nothing certain is known of the origin of Hamburg, but it is probable
that the advantages of its site were appreciated at a very early period.
In 805 *Charlemagne* founded a castle here, to which he soon added a
church, presided over by a bishop, whose mission was to propagate Christianity in these northern regions. In 831 the diocese was elevated to
the rank of an archbishopric by *Louis the Pious*. During the following
centuries the town was frequently pillaged by Danes, Normans, and Wends.
In the 12th and 13th cent. the *Counts of Holstein*, within whose jurisdiction Hamburg was situated, and particularly *Adolph IV.*, became great
benefactors of the town, and procured for it from the emperors many of
those privileges and immunities which formed the foundation of its sub-

sequent independence. In 1241 Hamburg entered into a treaty with Lübeck, an alliance which was afterwards extended to other towns and de
veloped into the powerful *Hanseatic League* (p. 118). In the campaigns of
the League the Hamburgers distinguished themselves greatly in suppress-
ing the piratical 'Vitalienbrüder', whose leader Störtebecker they captured
and beheaded in 1402. They subsequently succeeded in repelling repeated
attacks of the Danes, who were then in possession of Holstein. In 1529
they adopted the reformed faith, and at the same time established a free
political constitution. Hamburg fortunately remained unaffected by the
Thirty Years' War, and during that period greatly extended her commercial relations, which now embraced the newly discovered continents
of America and East India. Dissensions, however, which arose between
the Council and the citizens in 1672 and were not allayed till 1712, proved
very detrimental to the welfare of the city. Towards the middle of the
last century her prosperity began to return, chiefly owing to the establishment of that direct communication with America, which to this day forms
the mainspring of her commercial importance; but at the beginning of
the present century the citizens were doomed to an overwhelming reverse.
In 1810 Hamburg was annexed to the French Empire, and the citizens
having in 1813 attempted to rebel against the foreign yoke, Davoust wreaked
his vengeance on them with unexampled barbarity. During those years
of disaster, from 1806 to 1814, the direct loss sustained by the city is
estimated at upwards of 13 million pounds, an enormous sum in pro-
portion to the population and the value of money at that period. After
the Peace of Vienna Hamburg rapidly increased in extent, and notwithstanding the appalling fire which raged from 5th to 8th May, 1842, and
destroyed nearly a quarter of the city, and the temporary disasters occasioned by frequently recurring commercial crises, she has never ceased
to prosper since she regained her independence.

Down to the beginning of the present century Hamburg enjoyed considerable literary reputation. In 1678 the first theatre in Germany for
comic operas was founded here; in 1767 *Lessing* visited Hamburg with a
view to assist in the foundation of a national theatre; and the talented
Klopstock resided in the Königs-Strasse here from 1774 to 1803.

Hamburg cannot boast of architectural monuments or scientific
or other collections commensurate with its wealth and antiquity.
The history of the city, together with the enterprising character of
its inhabitants, sufficiently account for the almost entire disappea-
rance of all relics of the past, and its thoroughly modern aspect.

The *Harbour, where numerous vessels from all quarters of the
globe generally lie, presents a busy and picturesque scene. The
quays, recently extended, now stretch along the r. bank of the
Norder-Elbe from Altona to the Billwärder Neuendeich (see Map,
p. 106), a distance of 3 M., and accommodate upwards of 400 sea-
going vessels and as many barges and river craft. The W. end of
the quay, opposite St. Pauli (Pl. A, 5) is chiefly occupied by English coal vessels and the steamers of the Hamburg and American
Co. Adjacent is the *Niederhafen*, destined principally for the
reception of sailing vessels during the season of floating ice, consisting of the outer harbour and the Binnenhafen, and connected
with the Elbe by several outlets ('*Gatts*'). The numerous *Fleete*, or
canals, which intersect the town and fall into the Niederhafen are
navigated by the '*Schulen*', or flat-bottomed boats used for conveying wares to the magazines and warehouses. Farther E. are the unfinished *Sandthor-Hafen*, 1100 yds. in length, and 100—140 yds.

in width, and the *Grasbrook-Hafen*, destined for the reception of
steamers, and provided with steam cranes and rails in connection
with the principal lines. Still farther E. are the *Brookthor-Hafen*
and the *Oberhafen*, for the accommodation of river craft, and finally
the *Holzhäfen*, or wood-harbours for the storage of timber, which
occupy an area of 400 acres. The visitor may explore these different
harbours by boat (for 1—3 pers. 1 M. per hour) and thus obtain an
idea of their extent. A visit may also be paid to one of the large
American steamers (ticket 4 ʃ).

Statistics. About 5000 steam and sailing vessels of an aggregate burden
of upwards of 2,000,000 tons enter and quit the port of Hamburg annually,
while 6000 barges and 100 rafts of timber arrive from the upper Elbe.
The chief articles of commerce are coffee, sugar, spirits, dyes, wine, iron,
grain, butter, hides, and fancy goods, the last five of which constitute the
most important exports. The average imports are valued at 64 million
pounds sterling annually. The annual number of emigrants who embark
here is 27,442. The Hamburgers are proprietors of 439 sailing vessels and
37 deep-sea steamers. The English trade with the north of Europe is
chiefly carried on viâ Hamburg. The port of *Altona* (p. 110), which both
commercially and politically forms a part of Hamburg, is entered by 893
sea-going vessels annually, *Harburg*, which lies opposite, by 661.

Between the Brookthor-Hafen and the Oberhafen is situated the
large new *Station* of the uncompleted Bremen and Osnabrück Railway, the extension of which viâ Wesel and Mastricht will afford direct communication between Hamburg and Paris. Near it are extensive warehouses and custom-house offices. About 1 M. above
the station the line crosses the Elbe by a handsome *Iron Bridge*;
and then turns towards the S. to Harburg, which is reached by a
second bridge. The *Baakenwärder*, an island to the S. of the
station is occupied by warehouses for combustible goods.

The *Steinwärder* and *Kleine Grasbrook*, islands opposite the
Niederhafen, to which steam-ferryboats cross frequently, possess
wharves, dry-docks, and ship-building yards, and afford a good survey of the Hamburg quays. On the Steinwärder is the new *German
Seamen's School*, to which visitors are admitted daily 10—12 and
3—5 o'clock.

The *Elbhöhe (Pl. 14), locally termed the *Stintfang*, above the
landing-place of the Harburg ferry, commands one of the finest
views near the harbour, embracing the Elbe, with its numerous islands, forest of masts, and gaily coloured pennons, St. Pauli, and
Altona. On the height beyond the moat rises the *Seemannshaus*,
where unemployed mariners are accommodated at a cheap rate, and
the aged and sick are received gratuitously. The adjoining height
is occupied by *Wiezel's Hotel* (p. 100).

St. Pauli, the suburb contiguous to Hamburg on the W., better
known as *Hamburger Berg*, is principally frequented by sailors, for
whose amusement booths and shows of every description abound. The
scene witnessed here on a Sunday afternoon is a highly characteristic phase of Hamburg low life. Hawkers and itinerant vendors of
every kind also thrive here.

The visitor may now return by the Zeughausmarkt and the Neue and Alte Steinweg, the Jews' quarter, where brokers' shops abound. — A few paces to the S. rises the *Grosse Michaeliskirche* (Pl. 23), erected in 1750—65 in the degraded taste of that period, with one of the loftiest towers in Europe (450 ft., that of Strassburg 465 ft.), which commands a very extensive prospect. (Visitors apply at Engl. Planke No. 2, near the W. portal, 1 pers. 1, 2 pers. 1½, 3—8 pers. 2 M.)

The *Exchange, or *Börse* (Pl. 7), is the great focus of business, where four or five thousand brokers, merchants, and ship owners congregrate daily between 1 and 3 o'clock. The noisy crowd may best be surveyed from the gallery (admission gratis, except between 1.15 and 2.15, when 4 ſ. must be paid). The building itself, completed shortly before the great fire, escaped, while the surrounding houses were reduced to ashes. The groups surmounting the edifice on either side of the pediment are by *Kiss*. On the first floor is the *Börsenhalle* (p. 100), with a reading-room, restaurant, etc., much frequented before and after business-hours. The *Commercial Library* (40,000 vols.) contains numerous works on geography, political economy, statistics, and history.

Nearly opposite the Exchange is the *Bank of Hamburg*, erected after the conflagration of 1842, an establishment founded in 1619 for the simplification of commercial account keeping.

·   To the S.E. of the Adolphs-Platz, between the Börsenbrücke and the Forstbrücke, are situated the brick buildings of the *Patriotische Gesellschaft*, erected in the Gothic style after the great fire, and now the seat of the 'Vereinigte Gesellschaften' (p. 100). In the vicinity is the

*Church of St. Nicholas (Pl. 25; visitors admitted gratis daily from 12.30 to 2.30 o'clock, at other times on application to the sacristan, Neueburg 28, second floor, opposite the transept), erected after the fire of 1842 by *Gilbert Scott* in the rich Gothic style of the 13th cent. The decorations of the exterior and interior are still uncompleted. Altar, pulpit, and font in white marble, designed by *Scott*; altar-piece, the Resurrection, by *Steinfurth*. In the choir the Twelve Apostles under canopies by *Winck* and *Neuber*. In the S. aisle of the choir are fine stained glass windows. The beautiful intarsia work of the door of the sacristy, by *Plambeck*, also deserves notice. — In front of the W. façade of the church lies the *Hopfenmarkt*, the principal market place at Hamburg, where fish of all kinds, meat, vegetables, and fruit are sold. — *St. Catharine's Church* (Pl. 22), to the S.E. of St. Nicholas, on the opposite side of the broad canal, escaped destruction in 1842. It contains a modern altar artistically executed, above which is a window with stained glass from Munich (Christ and the Apostles), designed by *Overbeck* and *Schwind*.

Near the Exchange, to the N.E. rises *St. Peter's Church*

(Pl. 26), which was burned down in 1842, and has since been erected in the Gothic style of the 14th cent. The choir contains stained glass by *Kellner* of Nuremberg. Altar - piece, a Resurrection by *Steinfurth.* To the l. in the altar-niche an Entombment in relief, — by *Schubert* of Rome. The granite columns once belonged to the cathedral of Hamburg, which was taken down at the beginning of the present century. — To the S.E., opposite the church, is the **Johanneum** (Pl. 16), a spacious edifice in the Italian style, erected in 1834, where the chief educational institutions of Hamburg are established, viz. the college of that name founded in 1529, the Gymnasium, or grammar-school, founded in 1611, and the Real-schule, or commercial school. The S. wing (Pl. 6) contains the admirably arranged *Town Library*, consisting of 250,000 vols. and 5000 MSS., and comprising various curiosities, such as the biblical literature bequeathed by the Orientalist Wolff. On the ground-floor is the *Natural History Museum* (Sund. to Wed. 11—1 gratis, Thurs. 8 ʃ.), containing numerous skeletons and one of the most valuable collections of conchylia in Germany. Here also is the *Museum of Hamburg Antiquities*, where among other curiosities is preserved an old tombstone representing an ass blowing the bagpipes, with the quaint inscription, 'De Welt heft zik umekert, darume zo hebbe ik arme eezel pipen ghelert.'

In the Pferdemarkt is the *Thalia Theatre* (Pl. 45), a tasteful Renaissance edifice erected in 1842, with seats for 1800 spectators. Near it is the *Jacobikirche* (Pl. 21), which with a number of the surrounding houses survived the fire of 1842. The difference between old and modern Hamburg is here very noticeable, the buildings of the former with their numerous windows being meanly constructed and somewhat resembling Dutch houses, while the latter are handsome and substantial edifices of the 19th century.

The ***Binnen-Alster** and its environs, usually termed the *Alster Bassin* (Pl. E, F, 2, 3; comp. p. 101), is unquestionably Hamburg's greatest attraction. This sheet of water, upwards of 1 M. in circumference, is bounded on three sides by quays planted with trees and flanked with palatial hotels and handsome private dwellings, termed respectively the *Alte* and *Neue Jungfernstieg*, and the *Alster-damm*, while the fourth side towards the Aussen - Alster is formed by promenades connected by means of the *Lombards-Brücke*. The surface of the water is enlivened by numerous diminutive screw-steamers, rowing-boats, and groups of swans, and the banks are a favourite promenade, especially on fine summer evenings. The *Alte Jungfernstieg*, where the *Alster-Pavillon* (p. 100) and the *Bazaar*, a glass-covered arcade, are situated, is the scene of the busiest traffic. Adjoining the Alte Jungfernstieg on the S.E. are the *Alster Arcades* with attractive shops, which run parallel with the most eastern of two arms of the Alster issuing from the 'Bassin', and extend from the Reesendamm-Brücke to the Schleusen-Brücke.

The ramparts near the *Lombards-Brücke* command a charming view of the expansive Aussen-Alster to the N., with its banks studded with villas, and the Binnen-Alster to the S. with the towers of the city in the background. On the W. rampart rises an *Obelisk* (Pl. 11) to the commercial writer Prof. Büsch (d. 1800); on the E. a *Statue of Schiller* (Pl. 50), erected in 1866, by *Lippelt*.

On the Alsterhöhe, to the S.E. of these monuments, rises the **Kunsthalle** (Pl. 32), erected in 1863—69 in the early Italian Re-naissance style. The niches and medallions of the exterior contain statues and reliefs of distinguished artists. (Admission daily except Mond., from 1st Apr. to 30th Sept. 10—5, the rest of the year 11 —4; catalogue 6 ſ.)

The GROUND FLOOR contains *Sculptures* by modern masters, casts of ancient and Renaissance works, and a valuable *Collection of Engravings*, the most important of which are exposed to view. — The marble steps in the handsome staircase, which is borne by 10 Corinthian columns, lead to the UPPER FLOOR. In.the corridor four allegorical figures and two praying angels by *Lippelt*. Opposite the visitor is the I. ROOM. Beginning on the 1. : 401. *Verboeckhoven*, Sheep; 186. *Calame*, Fall of Handeck; 187. *Camp-hausen*, Puritans; *Max Michael*, Knitting-school at Rome; *399. *Vautier*, Toasting of the bride; 205. *Eberle*, The pledge; 196. *Conräder*, Tilly before the battle of Breitenfeld in 1631; 354. *Ruths*, The Campagna of Rome; 201. *Decaisne*, Caritas; *180. *Brendel*, Interior of a sheepfold. — Then to the r. the II. ROOM. 306. *Marsland*, Politicians; 285. *Kirner*, The im-provisatore; 207. *Ehnle*, Reception of a boy at the orphan-asylum of Harlem; 331. *Northen*, Storming of Planchenois; 313. *Melby*, Ship laying to. — III. ROOM. Chiefly Netherlands, early German, and Italian pictures. — The saloon adjoining the last on the l. contains the permanent *Exhibition of Art*. — I. and II. CABINETS. Small Netherlands and Italian works. — III. CABINET. Modern French and Netherlands masters: *Verboeckhoven*, 400. Sheep, 402. Donkey and sheep; *202. *P. Delaroche*, Oliver Cromwell by the body of Charles I. — IV. CABINET. Modern German masters: 286. *Kraus*, Drinker; 369. *Schlesinger*, Holstein peasants; 364. *Scheuren*, Château by the waterside; 396. *Tidemand*, Wolfhunter.

The *ANLAGEN laid out on the old fortifications, and extending round the interior of the city from the Elbhöhe (p. 103) to the Ber-lin Railway Station, also afford pleasant walks. Near the Kunsthalle, to the E., is an iron Monument (Pl. 10) to the memory of Adolph IV., Count of Holstein, the founder of the liberties of the city. — In the Dammthor-Strasse, near the *Esplanade*, a handsome street with a double avenue of trees (Pl. E, 2) is situated the *Stadt-Theater*, designed by Schinkel, with seats for 2500 spectators. — In the Valentinskamp is the *Anschar-Capelle* (Pl. 17), a tasteful structure consecrated in 1860.

On the l., immediately outside the Dammthor, lies the **Botani-cal Garden** (Pl. 8), open daily, one of the best in Germany, and possessing a Victoria Regia house. A little beyond it is the ***Zoolo-gical Garden** (admission 12 ſ., aquarium 8 ſ.), one of the most extensive and best organised in Germany; the gardens were laid out by the landscape gardener *Jürgens* of Ottensen. The most interesting points are the Eulenburg (view) with the bears'

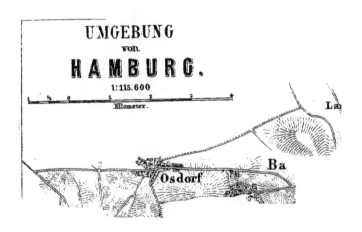

UMGEBUNG
von
HAMBURG.
1:115.600

Kilometer.

Osdorf   Ba   La

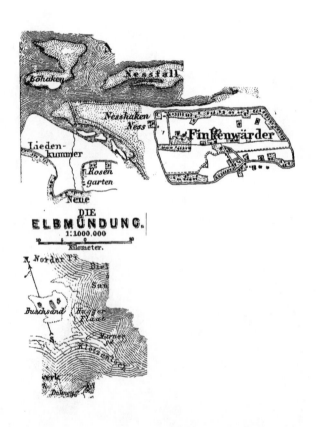

Bohaken   Nessfall

Nesshaken
Ness

Lieden-
kummer   Finkenwärder

Rosen
garten

Neue

DIE
ELBMÜNDUNG.
1:1000.000

Kilometer.

N. Norder P?   Biel
Swa

Buschsand   Hagger
Flaat

Kurze
Klotzenbrg

werk
Dalneige

Darmstadt, Ed. Wagner.

den, the cascade grotto, the *aquarium, the terrarium, and the still
unfinished Ernst-Merck-Halle with the bust of the founder of the
gardens, adjoining which is the *Restaurant.

Opposite the Zoological Garden, to the S.W., near the Sternschanze
railway station, is situated the new and spacious Zollvereins-Niederlage,
a vast depôt for goods from the Zollverein' (now almost the whole of
Germany, where the customs-dues are uniform), with a railway-station,
post, and telegraph office. The merchandise stored here may be sold to
any other part of the Zollverein without payment of duty, whereas if
once admitted to the free port of Hamburg where no customs are levied,
it would be as liable to duty on re-entering any part of the Zollverein as
if imported from foreign countries.

The *Cemeteries* in the neighbourhood are laid out as gardens. On the
N. side, opposite the Petrikirchhof, is a sarcophagus, brought from Ottensen in 1841, commemorating the melancholy fate of 1138 citizens of Hamburg, 'who, having been banished by Marshal Davoust, together with
many thousands of their fellow citizens during the severe winter of
1813—14, fell victims to starvation and disease'.

Charitable Institutions abound at Hamburg. The most important are
the large public *Hospital* (Pl. 30) at St. George, one of the most admirable establishments of the kind (in the chapel, Christ on the Mt. of
Olives, a good picture by Overbeck); the *Poorhouse* on the road to Barmbeck (accommodating 1000 adults and 100 children); the *Waisenhaus*, or
orphan-asylum on the Uhlenhorst; the *Friedrichsberg Lunatic Asylum* between Barmbeck and Wandsbeck; the *Gasthaus* at St. George; the *Schrö-
derstift* outside the Dammthor; the *Oberaltenstift* by the Mühlendamm. At
St. Pauli are the *Jewish Hospital* (Pl. 31) and the *Seemannshaus*.

Beyond the Berlin station, 1½ M. from the Dammthor, are the extensive *Water Works* by which the whole city is supplied. They command
a fine view, and their construction is also interesting. Visitors admitted
gratis.

The *Environs of Hamburg (comp. Map), which are sprinkled with
country-houses, gardens, and parks in almost every direction, especially in
the neighbourhood of the Aussen-Alster and near the Elbe between Altona and Blankenese, afford some pleasant excursions.

The banks of the *Aussen-Alster, with their green meadows and scattered villages, which chiefly consist of country-seats, are most conveniently visited by one of the small screw-steamers (p. 101) which ply the
whole day between the Jungfernstieg and the N. end of the lake. The favourite points are the *Uhlenhorst* (concerts at the Fährhaus frequently),
Harvestehude, where the lime-tree of the poet Hagedorn (d. 1754) rises on
the Licentiatenberg, and *Eppendorf* (Restaurant at the *Andreasbrunnen*).

A double avenue leads from the Millern-Thor at Hamburg, past the
taverns and booths of *St. Pauli* (p. 103) to the Nobisthor (so called from
the inscription, 'Nobis bene, Nemini male') of Altona (p. 110); carriages,
omnibuses, and railway thither, see p. 101.

At the N. end of Altona, adjacent to the town, lies the village of Ottensen, in the churchyard of which Klopstock (born 1724, d. 1803) and
his two wives are interred. Their grave is shaded by an old lime, a few
paces from the church-door.

From Altona to Blankenese by railway in 25 min. (fares 9, 6,
3¾ Sgr.); from Hamburg to Altona, and thence to Blankenese about 1 hr.
(fares 13, 9, 6 Sgr.). Stations *Bahrenfeld*, *Flottbeck*, *Blankenese*. — As the
scenery is pleasing, a drive to Blankenese in an open carriage is far preferable to the railway. Cab from Altona to Klein-Flottbeck, 1—2 pers.
1½ M., to Blankenese 2½ M. (or 1 Thlr.). Omnibus between Altona (starting from the Pallmaille, near the theatre) and Blankenese several times
daily, fare 6 ſ. — Even pedestrians will be rewarded by a walk along the
bank of the Elbe to (8 M.) Blankenese, passing numerous villas and gardens, the pleasantest part of the route being from Klein-Flottbeck (about
half-way) onwards. — The traveller may then return by the steamboat
(p. 101), which commands fine views of the banks of the river.

At the end of the pleasant village of *Neumühlen* is situated the castel-lated villa of Consul Schiller. *Booth's* gardens at **Flottbeck** and the park of Senator Jenisch with their extensive hothouses merit a visit. Between *Parish's* garden at **Nienstädten** (*Jacob's Restaurant) and Godeffroy's park at *Dockenhuden*, lies Senator Godeffroy's château on the abrupt bank of the Elbe. The finest view of the Elbe is obtained from the **Süllberg** (250 ft.; tavern at the top), one of the peaks of the group of hills at the base of which the fishing village of **Blankenese** (tavern at the *Fährhaus*) is situated, 1¹⁄₂ M. from the railway station. Baur's garden at Blankenese also affords beautiful views. All these grounds are open to the public.

Those interested in evangelical missions should visit the *Rauhe Haus* at *Horn*, 3 M. to the E. of Hamburg, on the Bergedorf road, a most use-ful establishment (Omnibus, see p. 101; cab 1¹⁄₂ M.).

Wandsbeck (railway, see p. 101; tramway, p. 101; cab 1¹⁄₂ M.), a town in Holstein (*Hôtel zum Posthause*), with 8000 inhab., 3 M. to the N.E., was the home of the talented Matthias Claudius (d. 1815), the 'Wands-becker Bote', who is buried in the churchyard here. A simple monument has been erected to his memory in the park of Count Schimmel-mann.

17. Heligoland.

Comp. Maps, pp. 106, 114.

Steamers viâ Cuxhaven to Heligoland three times a week in sum-mer in 7—8 hrs.; fare 5 Thlr., there and back within a week 8 Thlr. — From *Bremerhaven-Geestemünde* (p. 90) to Heligoland steamer three times a week in summer in 4 hrs.; fare 4 Thlr., there and back within a week 6 Thlr.

A steamboat-trip on the Lower Elbe is one of the pleasantest river excursions in N. Germany. Soon after starting, the vessel com-mands a fine retrospect of the imposing city with its forest of masts, and of *Altona* (p. 110), almost a suburb of Hamburg. Numerous villas on the hills peep from the midst of parks and pleasure-grounds, which extend for a considerable distance below *Blankenese* (see above). Inland to the l. is seen the town and fortress of **Stade**, connected with the Elbe by a canal; then on the r. bank *Glückstadt* (p. 110). The banks now recede.

Cuxhaven (*Belvedere; Bellevue; Baben*, unpretending), fre-quented by Hamburgers as a sea-bathing place, is situated in the small Hamburg bailiwick of *Ritzebüttel*, the castle of which, once strongly fortified, is visible from the Elbe. (Diligence daily to Bremerhaven; carr. 6 Thlr.). The steamer next passes the island of *Neuwerk* with its lighthouse, originally erected in 1290 as a castle for protection against pirates.

At the mouth of the Elbe two light-ships, and between them the *Pilot-ship* are passed, beyond which the open sea is reached. The sea-passage occupies 2¹⁄₂—3 hrs. only.

From Bremerhaven to Heligoland. The steamboat-pier is ¹⁄₂ M. from the railway-station at Geestemünde (p. 90). To the r., as the steamer quits the *Geeste*, lies the district of *Wursten*, to the l. the *Butjadinger Land*, a peninsula between the estuary of the Weser and the Jahdebusen (p. 95). After 2 hrs. the light-ships are passed and the open sea is reached. Sea-passage about 2 hrs. more.

At **Heligoland** (comp. Map, p. 114) passengers are landed in boats, and scrutinised as they pass by numbers of the visitors who assemble to see the arrival. Disembarcation 12 ſ.; luggage is conveyed to the Conversationshaus; thence to the Unterland 2 ſ., to the Oberland 4 ſ. for each package.

Hotels. *City of London and *Queen of England in the Oberland; Hôtel Krüss in the Unterland. Table d'hôte at these, and in the Conversationshaus at 3 p. m., 32 ſ. (for subscribers 24 ſ.); board and lodging 4—5 Marks per day. — **Lodgings,** where breakfast only is usually supplied, are also easily obtained. The best are on the Falm (see below) in the *Oberland,* at 15 M. per week and upwards; those in the back streets without view are cheaper. Those in the *Unterland* are also cheaper. — **Restaurants.** In the Unterland: *Conversationshaus*, with dining and reading rooms, etc.; *Fremdenwillkomm*; *Deutscher Hof; Dünenpavillon*; *Erholung*, by the steps to the Oberland. In the Oberland: *Janssen*, by the church; *Meier*, Leuchtthurm-Str. — The *Pavillon* on the beach is much visited as a café in the afternoon. — Rain collected in cisterns is used for drinking-water; good spring-water is obtained at the Brewery (4 ſ. weekly). — The Bathing-Place is on a small sandy island, 1 M. to the S.E.; ferry there and back 4 ſ.; bath 11 ſ.; bath and ferry tickets at the bath-house, where warm and other baths are also to be had. — *Theatre* during the season. — Considerable improvements in the arrangements have recently been effected by the English government, by which the privileges of the bath were purchased from the shareholders in 1872. — **Boats.** Small boat for 1—4 pers. 3 M.; excursion round the island 1—2 pers. 2, 3—4 pers. 2½ M.; illuminations of the rocks and grottoes take place several times during the season.

Heligoland (i. e. 'holy land'), which formerly belonged to Schleswig, was taken by the English in 1807, and still continues under their supremacy. During the blockade of 1812 it was a great resort of smugglers. On three sides the island, which consists of hard red clay and marl, rises nearly perpendicularly from the sea to a height of 150 ft., forming a long and narrow triangle about 1 M. in length, and ⅓ M. in breadth, termed the *Oberland*. On the S.E. side only a low, flat bank of sand rises from the water, called the *Unterland*. The island contains 2000 inhabitants of Frisian extraction, whose dialect, habits, and costume are in many respects peculiar. The bathing-season and lobster fishing are their chief sources of gain. The German language is employed in the schools and church.

The visitor to the island lands on the Unterland, on which a Bath-house, Conversationshaus, chemist's shop, theatre, restaurants, etc. are situated. The principal streets are the Dünen-Strasse, or *Gesundheits-Allee*, on the N.E. side of the group of houses, and the *Bindfaden-Allee*, which runs parallel to the cliffs from N.E. to S.W. At the end of the latter is the '*Rothe Meer*', a bathing-place so called from the colour with which the red clay tinges the waves, and resorted to when the passage to the bathing-island is impracticable.

From the Unterland an easy flight of 190 wooden steps ascends the rock to the Oberland, a plateau planted chiefly with potatoes, and intersected by the *Kartoffel-Allee*. The pastures support goats and about 300 sheep only. The principal street in the village termed the *Falm*, skirting the S.E. margin of the cliff, commands a fine view of the Unterland, the downs, and the sea. The best views of the cliffs are obtained at the *Sathurn* (Südhorn) and *Nathurn* (Nordhorn). The *Lighthouse* merits a visit (fee 2 ʃ). An excursion round the island is very interesting. Many of the rocks have received fanciful names, such as the Nun, Monk, Pastor.

Opposite the Unterland, and separated from it by a strait ¹/₂ M. in width and 12—16 ft. deep, is the *Düne*, or *Sandinsel* (ferry), on the N. (l.) side of which is the gentlemen's, and on the S. (r.) side the ladies' bathing-place. Between the two is situated the Dünen-Pavillon (p. 109).

The luminous appearance of the sea at night is more frequently observed at Heligoland than elsewhere, especially in sultry weather, with a S. wind and a clouded sky. When the water is struck by the hand, each particle resembles a fire-fly or glow-worm. This phenomenon, as is well known, is occasioned by innumerable mollusca, almost invisible to the naked eye, which emit a phosphorescent light when in motion.

18. From Hamburg to Kiel and Flensburg.

Railway from Altona to Kiel in 2¹/₂—3 hrs. (fares 2 Thlr. 24, 2 Thlr., 1 Thlr. 12 Sgr.); Altona to Flensburg in 5—7 hrs., fares 5 Thlr. 11¹/₂, 3 Thlr. 27, 2 Thlr. 17 Sgr. — A line connecting the Berlin station with that of Altona, with several stations (the most convenient at the Dammthor), describes a circuit round Hamburg. At Altona a halt of ¹/₄ hr. Omnibus from Hamburg to Altona see p. 101; cab from the Alster 1 Mark, box 4 ʃ. Examination of luggage at the custom-house at the Altona station. Hamburg and Prussian money is current in the duchies, and Danish pieces, especially of 4 Skillings = 1¹/₄ ʃ. (about 1 d.), and 15 Sk. = 5 ʃ., are frequently met with.

To Altona from the Millernthor at Hamburg ³/₄ M., thence to the station ³/₄ M. more.

Altona (*Königlicher Hof; *Holsteinisches Haus*, unpretending; *Bahnhofs-Hôtel*, also a restaurant and café), on the N. bank of the Elbe, with 74,131 inhab., is a well-built modern town. Like Hamburg it is a free port and a prosperous commercial place, but of course very inferior in life and importance. Its situation on the lofty bank of the Elbe, encircled with gardens and villas, is picturesque, especially when viewed from the river. The *Palmaille*, planted with lime-trees, and affording pleasant glimpses of the Elbe, is adorned with a statue of *Count Blücher*, who was president of Altona from 1808 to 1845.

Stat. *Pinneberg*; near it on the r. lies *Rellingen*, with one of the finest country-churches in Holstein. *Tornesch* is the station for the borough of *Uetersen*. Stat. *Elmshorn* (6617 inhab.), on the *Krückau*, a wealthy town in a fertile district.

Branch-Line from Elmshorn in 1¹/₄ hr. (fares 30, 18, 12 Sgr.), traversing a bleak and marshy district, to Glückstadt (*Stadt Hamburg*) on the Elbe, a dull place with 6100 inhab., fortified by Christian IV. in 1620, and regarded as the key of Holstein. It was unsuccessfully besieged by Tilly in 1628, and by Torstenson in 1643; but in 1814 was surrendered to the Allies, and in 1815 dismantled. Harbour neglected. — In 38 min. more the train reaches

Itzehoe (*Helmund's Inn*; *Dühring*) on the *Stoer*, with 7300 inhab., the most ancient town in the Duchy, founded as early as the 9th cent., and formerly the place of assembly of the Holstein Estates. Church of

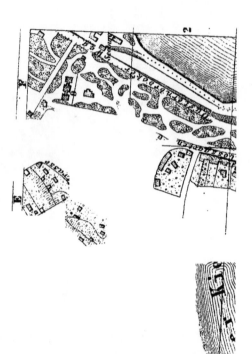

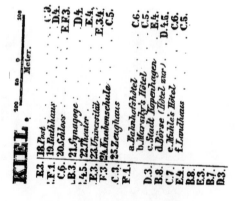

KIEL.

E.3. 18. Post . . . . . . C.3.
F.1. 19. Rathhaus . . . . D.4.
C.6. 20. Schloss . . . . E.F.3.
B.3. 21. Synagoge . . . . D.4.
4.5. 22. Theater . . . . . E.4.
E.3. 23. Universität . . . E.3.4.
F.3. 24. Knabenschule . . . C.5.
C.3. 25. Zeughaus . . . . . C.5.
F.1.
      a. Bahnhofshôtel . . . C.6.
D.3. b. Marsily's Hôtel . . C.5.
B.8. c. Stadt Kopenhagen . . E.4.
C.7. d. Börse (Hôtel zur) . D.4.5.
E.4. e. Mühle's Hôtel . . . C.6.
B.8. f. Landhaus . . . . . C.5.
E.3.
B.7.
D.3.

100 50 0 100
Meter.

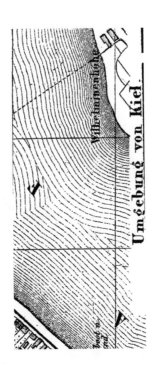

Umgebung von Kiel.

St. Lawrence of the 12th cent. Pleasant excursion of 1 hr. to Schloss *Breitenburg* on the Stoer, the handsome château of Count Rantzau. The fertile fen-district, extending 20 M. to the N.W., from Glückstadt on the N. Sea as far as the Eider, is the land of the *Ditmarsch Peasants*, celebrated for their fierce and intrepid opposition to the supremacy of the Dukes of Holstein, who in 1559 at length succeeded in gaining the mastery. Niebuhr, the traveller, and his son, the historian (b. at Copenhagen in 1776, d. at Bonn in 1831), once resided at *Meldorf*, one of the principal places in this district.

Next stat. *Horst.* On a height to the l. of stat. *Wrist*, rises the ancient round tower of *Kellinghusen.* Stat. **Neumünster** (**Harm's Hôtel)*, a town with considerable cloth-factories, is the junction of the lines to Kiel, to Ploen and Neustadt, and to Rendsburg, Schleswig, and Flensburg.

The next station on the line to Kiel is *Bordesholm*, once a richly endowed monastery, prettily situated on the lake of that name. The church contains monuments of Frederick I. of Denmark (d. 1533) and his Queen Anna; of Duke Christian Frederick of Holstein-Gottorp, ancestor of the present imperial family of Russia, etc. The country becomes more attractive. Near Kiel the picturesque *Eiderthal* is traversed, beyond which the harbour and the distant Baltic become visible.

Kiel. BAHNHOFS-HÔTEL (Pl. a); STADT KOPENHAGEN (Pl. c); MARSILY'S HÔTEL (Pl. b); charges at these, R. 1$\frac{1}{2}$ M. and upwards, F. 12 $\int$. — HÔTEL ZUR BOERSE (Pl. d), MUEHL'S GASTHOF (Pl. e), LANDHAUS (Pl. f), and STADT HAMBURG (Pl. g) are of moderate pretension. — For a stay of several days the **HÔTEL BELLEVUE* and HÔTEL DÜSTERNBROOK (p. 112) are recommended. — *Fiacre* per drive in the town 6 $\int$.; to Bellevue 12, Neumühlen 24, each additional person 12, each package 2 $\int$.; per hour 12, beyond the town 16, each additional pers. 4 $\int$. — *Boat* per hour, for 1—2 pers., 16, each additional person 4 $\int$. — Small *Steamers* also ply in all directions at very moderate fares: to Wilhelminenhöhe every 5 min., 2 $\int$.; Ellerbeck every $\frac{1}{2}$ hr., 2 $\int$.; Neumühlen every hour, 2 $\int$.; to Laboe by Bellevue, Schrevenborn, Möllenort, and Friedrichsort, six times daily.

Kiel, one of the oldest towns in Holstein, with 31,750 inhab., the seat of government for Schleswig - Holstein, and the German naval head-quarters on the Baltic, with a naval academy, etc., is picturesquely situated at the S. end of the *Kieler Föhrde*, one of the best havens in Europe and the chief war - harbour of Germany. Kiel was a member of the Hanseatic League as early as the 14th cent., and is now a commercial place of considerable importance, being a great depôt of the trade between the Danish islands and the continent. Extensive harbour fortifications, quays, and docks are in course of construction.

The *University* (Pl. 23), founded in 1665 (250 stud.), possesses collections of some merit, especially that of *National Antiquities* in the Kehden-Strasse and the *Mineralogical Museum*. The *Museum of Art*, in the palace (Pl. 20), open on Sat. and Sund., 12$\frac{1}{2}$—1$\frac{1}{2}$ o'clock, contains casts from antiques. The hall of the *Kunstverein* (Pl. 15) contains some good modern pictures. — Visitors may be introduced by a member to the reading - room of the *Harmonie.* — The collection of Schleswig - Holstein **Wood Carvings* of Professor

Thaulow, Lorentzendamm 23, deserves a visit (Wed. and Sat. 11—12, Sund. 1—2).

*Environs. The harbour is picturesque, and a trip by steamer or small boat as far as *Laboe* is recommended.

On the W. Bank (comp. Pl. F, 1, 2, and small Map of Environs) a picturesque road flanked with pleasant country-houses leads through beautiful beech woods to the (1¹/₂ M.) *Hôtel Düsternbrook* and the *Hôtel Bellevue* (R. in July and August 4—16, D. 5 Thlr. per week, less expensive earlier and later in the season; warm sea-baths), two favourite sea-bathing places. The latter lies on a hill, and commands a beautiful and extensive view over the Föhrde. Beyond the Bellevue is the hotel and pension *Marienhöhe*. A little inland is the forest-nursery of *Düvelsbeck*. From the Bellevue the traveller may follow the coast by the village of *Wiek*, to *Holtenau*, at the mouth of the Schleswig-Holstein Canal, 20 M. in length, constructed in 1777—84 for the purpose of connecting the Baltic with the N. sea by means of the Eider, but navigable for vessels of small tonnage only. A delightful walk hence is by the canal and the Holtenau Lock to the park of *Knoop* (good rustic inn at the second lock). Distance from Kiel to Holtenau 3 M., thence to Knoop 2 M.; direct route back to Kiel 3 M. (fiacres, p. 111). *Friedrichsort*, a fortress 3 M. farther, with the works on the Branneberg and the opposite batteries of *Möltenort* and *Laboe*, command the entrance to the harbour. Steamers see p. 111.

The E. Bank of the harbour is also attractive. The *Wilhelminenhöhe* (or *Sandkrug*), opposite the station (comp. Plan; steamers, see p. 111), commands an admirable view of the town and the wooded W. bank. Between this height and the fishing-village of *Ellerbeck* are the premises of the *N. German Shipbuilding Co.* and the uncompleted *Government Docks*. A pleasant footpath leads hence over the *Koppeln*, to *Neumühlen*, at the mouth of the *Schwentine*. Farther distant is the *Schrevenborn* wood; then, between the villages of *Alt-Heikendorf*, *Möltenort*, and *Laboe*, the 'Gründe', affording charming wood-excursions on the slopes of the coast. Laboe belongs to the *Probstei*, an extremely fertile district, 40 sq. M. in area, the property of the monastery of *Preetz*, where primitive habits and costumes are still to some extent prevalent. Popular festivals take place at Whitsuntide.

To *Eckernförde* (p. 114) diligence twice daily in 2³/₄ hrs. (fare 22¹/₂ Sgr.), by *Luchsdorf* and *Gettorf*.
To *Copenhagen*, see p. 125.
Steamers to *Sonderburg* (p. 115), Stettin, and Christiania.

The traveller proceeding to Flensburg returns to the *Neumünster* junction (p. 111).

Rendsburg (*Stadt Hamburg and Lübeck*, in the Altstadt, moderate; *Pahl's Hôtel*, in the Neuwerk; *Nordischer Löwe*, unprètending), a fortified town with 11,514 inhab., was unsuccessfully besieged by the Swedish General Wrangel in 1645. The fortress formerly consisted of three works separated by the *Eider*, the *Altstadt* on an island, the *Neuwerk* to the S., and the *Kronwerk* to the N. The Eider falls into the N. Sea at Tönning, and is also connected with the Baltic by means of the Schleswig-Holstein Canal.

Stations *Owschlag*, *Klosterkrug*. As Schleswig is approached a fine view is suddenly disclosed of the broad estuary of the Schlei and the town itself.

The *Danewerk* (or *Dannevirke*), an intrenchment which formerly defended the Danish frontier, stretching across the level country, was stormed by the Prussians in 1848. The works were subsequently restored, and greatly extended and strengthened by the Danes, so that in 1864 they constituted a barrier from the mouth of the Schlei to Friedrichsstadt, a distance of 46 M., which might easily have been defended, had the Danish army been sufficiently numerous. Their forces were, however, totally unequal to the task. The result was inevitable. The united troops of Austria and Prussia, notwithstanding the gallant resistance of their enemy, stormed the advanced positions in rapid succession, while a Prussian division proceeded to force the passage of the Schlei, in order to attack the Danes in the rear. The Danish General de Meza, seeing the impossibility of preventing this, at once abandoned his position and retreated rapidly in order to save his army from total annihilation. — The intrenchments have since been entirely levelled.

Schleswig (*Stadt Hamburg*; **Raven's Hôtel*, in the Altstadt, R 24 ʃ, A. 6 ʃ; *Stehn's Hôtel*, near the station; **Stadt Kiel*, small; omnibus to the town 4, with luggage 6 ʃ), an ancient town, founded in the first half of the 10th cent. after a campaign of Emp. Henry I. against the Danes, and afterwards the residence of the Dukes of Schleswig, is a charmingly situated place with 13,000 inhab., and consists of a single street 3½ M. in length extending round the W. end of the arm of the sea termed the *Schlei*. The different parts of the town are termed *Friedrichsberg*, *Lollfuss*, *Holm*, and *Altstadt*. The finest *view is commanded by the *Erdbeerenberg*, on the S.W. side, near the station.

At Friedrichsberg, the part of the town next the station, is situated the old ducal *Schloss Gottorp*, now occupied by government offices, behind which are beautiful oak and beech woods.

In the Altstadt is the *Dom* (sacristan opposite the S. Portal, No. 68, fee 15 ʃ), dating from the 10th cent., but frequently restored, and of unprepossessing exterior. The **altar-piece, formerly in the monastery of Bordesholm, a work executed in carved oak by Brüggemann in 1521, represents the history of the Passion in 14 sections, and is by far the finest work of art in the Duchies. To the l. in the choir is a font of 1480, on the r. the tombstone of King Frederick I. Adjacent is the chapel of the Dukes of Gottorp, and in the nave are those of several noble families.

The *Mövenberg* (sea-gull's hill), a small island near the town, is densely covered with sea-fowl, which regularly take possession

of it on 12th March, covering the entire surface like a white
mantle, and leave it again in autumn. They are shot in July, when
great numbers of the surrounding population assemble to enjoy the
sport.

Steamboat twice daily, except Sund., in 2³|₄ hrs. to **Cappeln** (*Roh-
weder's Inn*), on the picturesque banks of the *Schlei*, a charming excursion,
which may also be made in a rowing-boat. At *Missunde*, the narrowest point of the Schlei, commanded by seven Danish intrenchments, an
engagement took place on 2nd Feb., 1864, between the Danes and the
Prussians, after which the latter effected the passage of the bay at *Arnis*.
The result of this was the abandonment of the Danewerk by the Danes
(see above). The district of *Angeln*, a fertile peninsula between the Schlei
and the Bay of Flensburg, presents a somewhat English appearance with
its high hedges, which are not common on the continent. The finest survey of the district is obtained from the *Schiersberg*.

Diligence daily in 2¹|₄ hrs. from Schleswig to **Eckernförde** (*Götze*),
near which is *Borby*, a small sea-bathing place much visited by Hamburgers.

Stat. *Jübeck*, the junction for Husum (route to Wyk and Sylt)
and Tönning, see p. 116. Then *Eggebeck*, *Tarp*, and *Nordschleswig'-
sche Weiche*, whence a branch line (the main line goes on to Denmark) conveys the traveller to

Flensburg (* *Stadt Hamburg*, in the Südermarkt; **Bahnhofs
Hôtel*; charges at both, R. 1¹/₂ M., A. 6 ƒ), a thriving town with
21,325 inhab., beautifully situated at the S. end of the *Flensburg
Fjord*, one of those deeply indented bays ('fjords') which form
the excellent harbours of Schleswig-Holstein. Fine view from the
Bellevue, a café on the hill to the W., near the windmills. The
Cemetery, prettily situated on the same height, contains a number
of monuments to soldiers who fell in the German – Danish wars.
The '*Lion of Flensburg*', placed here by the Danes to commemorate
the victory of Idstedt in 1850, was removed to Berlin in 1864
(p. 15).

At *Oeversee*, 6 M. to the S. of Flensburg, on the road to Schleswig, a
fierce conflict took place between the rear-guard of the retreating Danish
army and the pursuing Austrians in 1864. Farther to the S., 3 M. to the
N. of Schleswig, is the village of *Idstedt*, where the Danes gained a victory over the Schleswig-Holstein army in 1850.

**Excursion to Düppel and Alsen*. Steamboat from Flensburg
four or five times a day, alternately by *Nübel* (whence an omnibus runs
to Düppel and Sonderburg), and direct round the *Broacker* peninsula, to
Sonderburg. One of these routes may be taken in going, the other in returning. Fare by either 25 ƒ., return-ticket 40 ƒ.

The ***Flensburg Fjord** is a fine sheet of water enclosed by gentle
slopes, partly wooded, and partly covered with pastures, and enlivened by
the red roofs of scattered farm-houses. Stations (touched at alternately
only) *Mürwick*, *Collund*; then **Glücksburg**, on the S. bank, ³|₄ M. from the
shore, and not visible thence, with a Schloss of the 16th cent. containing
the burial vault of the older Glücksburg line of dukes, who became extinct in 1799. *Sandacker* on the N. bank is the station for the village of
Rinkenis, situated on the high road. On the trip to Nübel the steamer
proceeds towards the N., traverses the narrow *Eken-Sund*, and touches at
Gravenstein, the Schloss of which was the headquarters of Prince Charles
of Prussia during the Dano-Prussian war. Then *Nübeler Mühle*, where
an omnibus for Sonderburg is in waiting. Pleasant walk to (³|₄ M.) *Nübel*
(Inn), where the Flensburg and Sonderburg road is reached. From Nübel

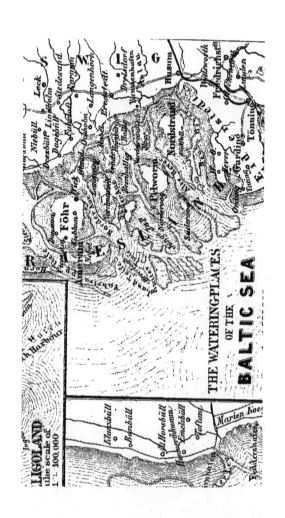

THE WATERINGPLACES OF THE BALTIC SEA

to Sonderburg 6 M. The road ascends gradually, passing a number of graves of fallen Danes and Prussians. To the r. rise the two conspicuous towers of the village of *Broacker*, on the peninsula of that name. To the l. the spire of *Satrup*. The village of *Düppel*, or *Dybbol*, lies to the l. of the road. On the hill rises the recently completed Gothic *Obelisk*, commemorating the storming of the intrenchments of Düppel. *** View** to the _E. of the island of *Alsen;* to the S., beyond the Wenningbund, the peninsula of *Broacker;* farther W. the village of Broacker; then the fertile hills of the *Sundewitt;* and finally to the N. the distant Baltic.

A little farther the road passes the *Intrenchments of Dybbol*, a connected series of bastions forming a semicircle round the point of the Sundewitt opposite Sonderburg, and extending from the Alsen Sund to the *Wenningbund*. They were taken by the Prussians in 1864 after a siege of two months, and have since been refortified. The road now descends to (1 M.) the narrow *Alsen-Sund*, which is crossed by a bridge of boats to

Sonderburg (**Holstein'sches Haus; *Stadt Hamburg*, unpretending), the pleasant little capital (4000 inhab.) of *Alsen*, an island 200 sq. M. in area. The old Schloss of the Duke of Augustenburg is now a barrack. A walk round the town is recommended. — On the Alsen-Sund, about 3 M. to the N. of Sonderburg, rises a *Monument* commemorating the passage of the Prussians at this spot in 1864. — Towards the E., about $4^1\!/_2$ M. from Sonderburg, lies the village of *Augustenburg* (Jürgensen's Inn), with the ancestral château of the Dukes of Schleswig-Holstein-Sonderburg-Augustenburg, now a barrack, prettily situated on the deeply indented *Augustenburg Fjord*. Near *Adzerballig*, $4^1\!/_4$ M. farther, rises the *Hüge Berg* (233 ft.), which commands a survey of the island, the sea, Fühnen, Aröe, &c.

. On the direct steamboat trip from Flensburg to Sonderburg, the vessel steers from Sandacker (see above) to the S., stops at *Brunsnis* on the W. coast of the peninsula of Broacker, and steams round the S. end of the peninsula, on which rise the conspicuous towers of the village of Broacker. The pier at Sonderburg is at the S. end of the town, near the lofty Schloss.

Steamer from Sonderburg to *Apenrade* (see below) several times a week.

From stat. Nordschleswig'sche Weiche (p. 114) the main line runs due N.; country uninteresting. Stat. *Tingleff* (branch-line to Tondern, for Sylt, see below); then *Rothenkrug*, whence a branch-line runs in $1/_4$ hr. to *Apenrade* (Bahnhofs-Hôtel; De Vos), a small trading town and sea-bathing place on the beautiful *Apenrad Fjord*. From stat. Woyens another branch-line runs in 24 min. to *Hadersleben* (**Petersen's Hôtel), a small commercial town on the fjord of that name. At stat. *Sommerstedt* the Prussian frontier is reached (see p. 124).

19. The N. Frisian Islands Föhr and Sylt.

W. Schleswig.

Wyck in the island of *Föhr*, and *Westerland* in *Sylt*, two much frequented bathing-places, are most easily reached from *Husum* and *Hoyer* respectively. *Railway* from Hamburg (Altona) viâ Jübeck (p. 114) to Husum in $4^3\!/_4$ hrs. (fares 4 Thlr. 17, 3 Thlr. 9, 2 Thlr. 5 Sgr.). *Steamboat* thence to Wyck in 3—4 hrs. (fare 1 Thlr. 27 Sgr.); from Wyck to Sylt in 2 hrs. (fare $1^1\!/_2$ Thlr.); from Husum to Sylt 3 Thlr. (by carriage from the landing-place to Westerland in 2 hrs.). — *Railway* from Hamburg (Altona) via Tingleff (see above) to *Tondern* in $5^3\!/_4$ hrs. (fares 6 Thlr. 5, 4 Thlr. $12^1\!/_2$, 2 Thlr. 27 Sgr.); by carriage or diligence to *Hoyer* in $1^3\!/_4$

hr.; and thence by steamboat to *Sylt* in $2\frac{1}{2}$ hrs. (fare 25 Sgr.); carriage from the landing-place to W.esterland in $\frac{1}{2}$ hr. The departure of the steamers depends on the tide. Through-tickets may be óbtained at Berlin, Hamburg, and Altona.

From Hamburg to *Jübeck*, see R. 18. The Husum line diverges to the I. here. Stations *Sollbrück, Ohrstedt.* Near Husum begins the marshy district of *Eiderstedt*, with its excellent pastures, whence cattle are largely exported to London.

Husum (*Thoma's Hôtel*; **Stadt Hamburg*, not expensive), situated on the *Husumer Au*, which here empties itself into the German Ocean by means of the 'old' and the 'new' *Hever*, is a dull seaport, with an old château and park of the former dukes. About $\frac{1}{2}$ M. from the town are extensive *Oyster Parks*, from which 60,000 oysters on an average are taken daily during the season and exported at 4*l.* per thousand.

FrOm Husum the railway runs to the S. to *Friedrichsstadt* and *Tönning*.

The *S t e a m b o a t* threads its intricate passage between numerous islands and sandbanks. Some of the latter, termed '*Hallige*', although covered by spring tides, are inhabited, the buildings being erected on embankments of earth. On the l. the large island of *Nordstrand*, on the r. *Nordstrandisch Moor*; then *Pelworm* on the l. The steamer steers between numerous '*Hallige*', and the large island of *Föhr* soon comes in view.

Wyck (**Conversationshaus*, on the Sandwall, R. 4—6 Thlr. per week, D. 18 Sgr. for subscribers; **Redlefsen*, on the Sandwall, with terrace, same charges; **Hansen*, Sandwall, cheaper. — Applications for apartments should be addressed to Herr Weigelt, the proprietor of the baths), the principal village (200 inhab.) on the island of Föhr, lies on the S.W. coast. The *Sandwall*, a road parallel to the beach, and shaded with a double avenue, where the Conversationshaus (music morning and evening), the hotels, the landing place, etc., are all situated, is the favourite promenade. The bathing beach is at the S. end. The sea is generally smooth, and the water unusually salt.

From Wyck to Sylt 2 hrs. by steamboat; the landing-place is at the *Nösse*, on the S.E. side of the island (trifling fee to the boatmen), where carriages are in readiness to convey passengers to Westerland (1—2 pers. 2, 3—4 pers. $2\frac{1}{2}$ Thlr.).

From Hamburg to *Tingleff*, see R. 18. *Branch-Line* thence to **Tondern** (**Stadt Hamburg*, in the town; *Bahnhofs-Hôtel*, at the station; *Stadt Copenhagen*), an old town with 3500 inhab., and the capital of the district. — The *High-Road* to Hoyer ($8\frac{1}{2}$ M.; diligence once daily; carr. for 1—4 pers. $2\frac{1}{2}$ Thlr.) traverses extensive pastures on which a fine breed of cattle is reared. *Mögeltondern*, with a château and park of the Countess Schack, is about half-way. **Hoyer** (*Paulsen's Hôtel*) lies $\frac{3}{4}$ M. from the sea shore.

The small *Steamboat* starts from Hoyer, and steering for the N. end of the island of *Sylt*, turns to the S. towards the lighthouse

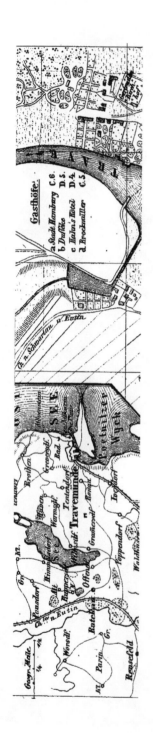

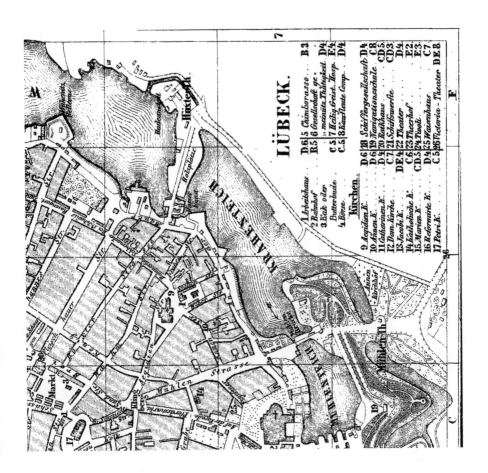

LÜBECK.

1 Arbeitshaus	D6	5 Chimborasso B3
2 Bahnhof	B5	6 Gesellschaft ge-
3 Kiek oder		meinütz. Thätigkeit D4
Butterbude	C5	7 Heilig-Geist. Hosp. E4
4 Börse.	C5	8 Kauffleute Comp. D4

Kirchen.

9 Aegidien K.	D6	18 Seher Pflegegesellschaft D4
10 Annen K.	D6	19 Navigationsschule. C8
11 Catharinen K.	D4	20 Rathaus CD5
12 Dom-Kirche.	C7	21 Schiffswerfte CD3
13 Jacobi K.	DE4	22 Theater D4
14 Katharine K.	C6	23 Theerhof E2
15 Marien K.	CD5	24 Tivoli E3
16 Reformirte K.	D4	25 Waisenhaus C7
17 Petri K.	C5	26 Victoria - Theater DE8

near Wenningstedt. At the landing-place at *Munkmarsch* (tavern) carriages are in waiting to convey passengers to Westerland (in 1/2 hr., 1—4 pers. 1 Thlr.).

Westerland (**Hôtel Royal*, pension from 15 Thlr. per week; **Deutscher, Kaiser*; *Strand-Hôtel* and *Dünenhalle*; *Stadt Hamburg*; *¯Steffensen*; *Westendhalle*, moderate. *Bath* arrangements defective, each bath 7¹/₂ Sgr.), a scattered village, frequented as a sea-bathing place since 1858, lies on the W. side of the island of *Sylt*, and is separated from the sea by a range of sand-hills, across which a wooden pathway leads to the beach (at the top is the *Erholung* restaurant). To the r. (N.) is the gentlemen's, to the l. (S.) the ladies' bathing place. Sea generally rougher than at the other sea-bathing places on this coast.

20. From Hamburg to Lübeck and to Schwerin.

Railway to Lübeck in 1³/₄—2 hrs.; fares 1 Thlr. 20¹/₂, 1 Thlr. 7¹/₂, 25¹/₂ Sgr.—From Lübeck to Schwerin in 2¹/₄ hrs.; fares 2 Thlr. 9, 1 Thlr. 8, 28 Sgr.

The journey presents few objects of interest. Stations *Wandsbeck* (p. 108), *Alt-Rahlstedt*, *Ahrensburg* (with château and park of Count Schimmelmann), *Bargteheide*, *Oldesloe* (a picturesquely situated watering-place with saline baths). Beyond stat. *Reinfeld* the ancient and imposing Lübeck becomes visible. The railway-traveller enters the town by the handsome *Holstenthor*, completed in 1477, and restored in 1871, a good specimen of an ancient structure of this description.

Lübeck. Hotels. STADT HAMBURG (Pl. a), on the Klingberg; **DÜFF-KE's HOTEL* (Pl. b), at the corner of the Meng-Str. and Breite-Str., commercial; **HAHN's HOTEL* (Pl. c), Breite-Str.; charges in all, R. from 1¹/₂ M., D. 1¹/₂ M.; BROCKMÜLLER's HOTEL (Pl. d), in the Kohlmarkt. — Wine at the *Raths-Weinkeller*. — Money as at Hamburg (p. 100). — *Theatre* (Pl. 22) in winter only; *Tivoli Theatre* (Pl. 24), with concerts, etc., summer and winter. — *Cab* for 1—2 pers. 6, each additional pers. 2 ʃ.; per hour 1 M. small articles of luggage 4 ʃ. — Money, the old English 'marchpane', is a kind of macaroon for which Lübeck is famous.

Lübeck, with 49,183 inhab., the smallest of the three independent Hanseatic towns of the German Empire, and the seat of the appeal court for these towns, was once at the head of the League, and is still a busy commercial place. It lies 9 M. from the Baltic, on the *Trave*, the channel of which has been deepened so as to afford access to vessels of considerable size. The town still contains reminiscences of its mediæval greatness in its lofty towers, its ancient gabled houses, fortified gateways, Gothic churches, and its venerable Rathhaus.

' *Lübeck* was founded in 1143 by Count Adolph II. of Holstein, on the site of an earlier town of the Wends, and shortly afterwards ceded to Henry the Lion, under whom it prospered so greatly that it was declared a free town of the Empire in 1226 and invested with important municipal privileges. In 1227 Lübeck in alliance with the Holsteiners signally defeated the Danes at *Bornhöved*, thus releasing the surrounding country from their yoke, and in 1234 they gained the first German naval victory on record at *Travemünde*, which overthrew the naval supremacy of the

Danes. Lübeck's enterprising spirit, coupled with the increasing activity of the neighbouring towns (Rostock, Wismar, Greifswald, Stralsund, Hamburg), gave rise to the foundation of the *Hanseatic League* (from 'Hansa', i. e. association), an alliance of the great commercial towns of N. Germany, which formed a peace-loving, but powerful bond of union between Western and Eastern Europe. The first alliances were indeed soon dissolved, but in the 14th cent. they were eagerly renewed in consequence of the Danes having by the conquest of the ancient colony of Wisby in the island of Gothland in 1361 threatened to monopolise the trade of the Baltic. The war resolved on by the first general *Hanseatic Diet* at Cologne in 1367 soon raised the League to the zenith of its power. They conquered S. Sweden and Denmark and permanently garrisoned several important places within these countries, and by the *Peace of Stralsund* in 1370 they even became entitled to ratify the election of the kings of Denmark. The League enjoyed marked prosperity for upwards of a century, and embraced eighty cities in all, from Reval to Amsterdam, and from Cologne to Breslau and Cracow, which according to their situation belonged to one of four sections, viz. the Wendish, the Prussian, the Westphalian, and the Gothlandish, and had their factories at Bergen, Novogorod, London, and Bruges. Lübeck at that period numbered 80—90,000 inhab., and held undisputed precedency over the other members of the League. Towards the close of the 15th cent. the increasing power of the Northern and the Russian empires proved detrimental to the League, and its decline was accelerated by the new commercial relations of Europe with America and India, which were chiefly carried on through the medium of England and Holland. Notwithstanding this, Lübeck again endeavoured to assert her ancient supremacy over the Baltic, and the enterprising burgomaster *Jürgen Wullenwever* conceived the bold project of establishing a democratic hegemony over the Scandinavian kingdoms (1531—35). But these schemes proved abortive, and a war against Sweden in 1563—70, although not unattended with glory, led to no practical result. Lübeck's power thenceforth declined, but she preserved her position as a free city of the Empire, and continued to enjoy a considerable share of commercial prosperity, although her population gradually dwindled to one-third of its ancient number.

The Holsten-Strasse leads straight to the MARKET. The *Rathhaus (Pl. 20), situated here, a Gothic edifice constructed of red and black bricks, with five curious towers, was almost entirely completed in 1444. The arcades and the Renaissance staircase in stone, towards the street, were added in 1594. The *Audience Chamber* and the *Kriegsstube* ('War Chamber') ,with wood-carving of the end of the 16th cent. , are worthy of inspection. The ancient Hanseatic Hall, in which the diets were held, has been converted into public offices.

Under the N. wing is the entrance to the **Rathskeller** (see p. 117), which was completed in 1443, and is remarkable for its fine well-preserved vaulting. The *Chimney Piece* in the apartment where bridal festivities were wont to be celebrated bears the quaint inscription, 'Menich Man lude synghet, wen me em de Brut briniet; weste he wat men em brochte, dat he wol wenen mochte' (many a man sings loudly when they bring him his bride; if he knew what they brought him, he might well weep). The *Admiral's Table* is said to be made of a plank of the last admiral's ship of Lübeck (1570).

The *Pranger* (pillory), termed *Kaak* in Low German, a Gothic structure of brick in the market-place, has lately been restored and converted into market-stalls.

A few paces to the N. of the market rises the *Church of St. Mary (Pl. 15) (open 10—1 o'clock; the sacristan, who lives at Meng-Str. 4, usually shows the church about noon), the finest edifice at Lübeck, and one of the most admirable examples of the grave Gothic style peculiar to the shores of the Baltic. It is constructed of brick, and was completed in 1304. The nave is of unusual height (123 ft.); spires 409 ft. high.

The S.W. Portal, by which the church is usually entered, leads into the 'BRIEFCAPELLE' (chapel of letters), so termed from indulgences having once been sold there, with groined vaulting supported by two slender monoliths. — At the W. end of the nave is a FONT of 1337. — Beyond it is the CHAPEL OF THE BERGENFAHRER, with the 'Mass of St. Gregory' (in distemper). Altar with scenes from the life of the Virgin; altarpiece with Descent from the Cross and Saints. The DANCE OF DEATH, in a closed chapel on the l., is erroneously attributed to Holbein. — In the following chapel the *Taking leave of the body of the Saviour, painted at Rome by *F. Overbeck*. — .The SACRISTY contains some good carving. — Farther on, against a pillar on the l., hangs an admirable old winged picture, the Nativity, Adoration of the Magi, and Flight into Egypt, painted in 1518, ascribed to *Jan Mostaert*. — Among the lower of the stone reliefs opposite is a black mouse gnawing at the roots of an oak, the ancient emblem of the city. — The *Clock* at the back of the high altar, dating from 1405, from which at noon the Emperor and Electors step forth, move past the Saviour, and disappear on the other side, always attracts numerous spectators; beneath it an astronomical dial, repaired in 1860, which gives eclipses of the sun and moon and various other data down to the year 1899. — The so-called BEICHTCAPELLE, to the E., at the back of the choir, contains *Overbeck's* Entry of Christ into Jerusalem, painted in 1824. The *stained glass in this chapel was executed by a Florentine in 1436. — HIGH ALTAR of 1697, beside it the graceful Gothic *ciborium of 1479. Some wood-carving on the benches and several brasses of the 15th and 16th cent. are also worthy of notice. — Fine modern organ (5134 pipes and 80 stops).

To the S.W., in the vicinity of the market, is the **Church of St. Peter** (Pl. 17; sacristan, Petri-Kirchhof 307), a Gothic edifice with double aisles, erected on the site of a Romanesque church about the year 1300. A few circular arches of the original building of 1170 are still left. The monumental brass of the burgomaster Clinghenberch, a work executed in the Netherlands in 1356, merits inspection.

The ***Cathedral** (Pl. 12 ; sacristan, Hartengrube 743), founded by Henry the Lion in 1173, re-erected in 1276, was completed in 1334; towers 394 ft. high. The *E. Portal, transept, choir, and nave are in the Romanesque, the rest of the edifice in the Gothic style. The church is generally entered by the N. Portal.

FONT of 1445 in the chapel behind the organ. — Brazen lamp of the 15th cent. — An elegant railing surrounding the pulpit is attributed by tradition to the workmanship of the devil; the pulpit itself dates from 1568. — In the CHOIR the recumbent bronze *figure of Bishop Bockholt (d. 1341), founder of the choir. HIGH ALTAR of 1696; in front of it the tombstone of Gerold, the first Bishop of Lübeck (d. 1163). — The ARCHIEPISCOPAL CHAPEL to the l. of the choir contains sarcophagi of the last archbishops. — In the next CHAPEL the *monument of the bishops von Serken and von Mull, Netherlands workmanship of the 14th cent. — The GREVERADEN-CAPELLE contains the finest work of art in Lübeck, an **altar-piece of 1491, by Memling: on the external shutters the Annunciation, in grisaille, on the inner shutters SS. Blasius, Ægidius with the deer, John the Baptist, Jerome with the Lion; in the interior the history of the Passion in 23 scenes, from the Mt. of Olives to the Ascension; the Crucifixion forms the great central scene.

The *Ægidienkirche* (Pl. 9) is a somewhat cumbrous structure of the 14th cent. — The eminent painter *Friedrich Overbeck* (d. at Rome in 1870) was born at No. 894 Königs-Strasse. — *Dr. Gaedertz* (No. 876 Königs-Str.) possesses a cabinet of valuable paintings by old masters, to which strangers are readily admitted.

The now disused *Church of St. Catharine* (Pl. 11), an admirable structure in the early Gothic style, possesses an elegant choir borne by columns, where a collection of ecclesiastical antiquities is now preserved (open Mond. and Thursd. 12—1). The buildings of the monastery are occupied by a grammar-school *(Gymnasium)* and Library, containing several historical treasures. — The *Gesellschaft zur Beförderung gemeinnütziger Thätigkeit*, Breite-Str. 786, also possesses a collection of Lübeck antiquities (adm. Mond., Wed., Frid. 12—1).

The *Natural History Cabinet*, Breite-Str. 805, includes a collection of gorillas, presented to the city by the traveller Heinrich Brehmer, and said to be the most complete in Europe.

The **Jacobikirche** (Pl. 13; sacristan Breite-Str. 770, a corner house), a Gothic building of the 14th cent., contains a chapel (the Brömsencapelle) with a remarkable *Altar* of the latter part of the 15th cent., representing the Crucifixion in relief in the centre, and the family of the donor, the Burgomaster Brömse, on the wings.

Opposite the W. Portal of the church is the handsome house of the *Schiffergesellschaft* (Pl. 18), with interior little altered, an interesting example of the old guild-houses. — The third house from it, that of the **Kaufleute-Compagnie** (Pl. 8), Breite-Str. 800, contains some admirable wood-carving, particularly in the old *Fredenhagen-Room*, executed by an unknown master in 1585, and transferred hither (open Thursd. 1—2; at other times apply at Engelsgrube 536).

The **Hospital zum Heiligen Geist** (Pl. 7), on the Kuhberg is an admirably organised institution. A fine early Gothic chapel, dating from the early part of the 14th cent., and now rarely used for divine service, serves as an entrance-hall. The chapel and its ancient mural-paintings were restored in 1866. — A short distance hence, in the Grosse Burg-Str., is the old *Burgkloster*, a fine, but sadly dilapidated brick edifice of the 13th cent.

The **Burgthor**, the N. gate of the town, is a lofty brick structure of 1444. In the vicinity, on 6th Nov. 1806, several severe engagements took place between Blücher, with the wreck of the Prussian army which had survived the battle of Jena and retreated to Lübeck, and the pursuing French marshals Bernadotte, Soult, and Murat.

The house No. 298 on the Trave contains a *Weinstube*, or tap-room, curiously carved in wood in 1644.

Walks on the old ramparts, the pleasantest outside the Holstenthor; to the N. of the station is the 'Chimborasso' (Pl. 5), an emi-

nence commanding a fine *survey; the harbour also affords a picturesque view.

To the N.E. of Lübeck (steamer several times daily) lies (9 M.)
Travemünde (*Kurhaus; Hôtel de Russie; Stadt Lübeck; Stadt Hamburg, &c.*),
a sea-bathing place, and the port of Lübeck before the deepening of the
river.

From Lübeck to Copenhagen, see p. 125; there are also numerous
steamboats to the different ports of the Baltic.

From Lübeck to Kiel. Diligence to Eutin twice daily in 4¼ hrs.,
fare 28½ Sgr. (railway in progress); railway from Eutin to Kiel in 1¾ hr.;
fares 1 Thlr. 9, 28½, 19½ Sgr. (Or an excursion from *Kiel* to Eutin and
its environs and back should be undertaken by travellers who do not wish
to proceed thence to Lübeck.)

Eutin (**Stadt Hamburg*; Hotel Bellevue*), pleasantly situated between
the *Grosse* and *Kleine Eutiner See*, now belongs with its *Schloss* and pretty
*grounds to the Duke of Oldenburg. Weber (d. 1826), the great composer,
was born here.

The **Environs** of Eutin, as far as Ploen and Preetz towards the
W., and Lütjenburg towards the N.E., are the most picturesque part of
Holstein. Good village inns. About 1¼ M. to the N. of Eutin is the
picturesque *Kellersee*, a path along the bank of which leads partly through
pleasant beech woods to (¾ hr.) *Sielbeck*. The charming *Ukleisee, 7 min.
to the E. of Sielbeck, should next be visited; the walk round it occupies
1 hr.; the inn and the forester's house afford refreshments and unpretending accommodation. Cart-roads lead from the Uklei inn towards the N.E.
in 1¼ hr. to the *Bungsberg* (570 ft.). the highest point in the district, the
tower on which commands an extensive prospect. Thence 12 M. (or direct
from Eutin by the loftily situated village of *Kirchnüchel* about 18 M.) to
Lütjenburg (*Stadt Hamburg*), from which the charmingly situated sea-
bathing place *Hassberg* (not expensive) is 3 M. distant. Thence in 2 hrs.
by the *Stöss* farm and the N. bank of the *Selenter See* to *Panker*, seat of
the Landgrave of Hessen-Cassel. Near it rises the *Pielsberg (446 ft.),
with the tower of *Hessenstein*, which commands one of the most extensive
prospects in N. Germany. Farther to the W. is *Salzau*, with the château
and park of Count Blome; then the *Probstei* (p. 112). — A road leads on
the S. bank of the Selenter See through the wooded estate of *Neuhaus* and
past the *Blomenburg* to *Rasdorf* (see below).

The next station beyond Eutin is *Gremsmühlen* (*Inn), charmingly
situated on the *Dieksee*, along which a beautiful footpath leads to Ploen
in 2½ hrs.

Stat. Ploen (*Stadt Hamburg; Prinz*) is very picturesquely situated between the *Grosse* and *Kleine Ploener See* (pleasant steamboat trip on the
former to Ascheberg, see below). The Prussian military school was once
a royal Danish château. Fine view from *Lange's Anlagen* (Apartments
and Pension), 8 min. from the station, on the road to Lütjenburg.

The railway skirts the N. bank of the Grosse Ploener See. Stat.
Ascheberg, on Count Ahlefeldt's estate of that name, junction for Neumünster (p. 111). The Kiel line turns to the N. and skirts the *Lanker
See*. Stat. **Preetz** (*Stadt Hamburg*) possesses a convent for ladies of noble
birth, founded as early as 1220. A walk of ½ hr. may be taken hence
to *Rasdorf*, with a beautiful park in the valley of the *Schwentine*, which
forms the outlet of the Ploener See; then in 2 hrs. down the valley by
the *Rasdorf Papermill* and *Oppendorf* to Neumühlen (p. 112).

Kiel, see p. 111.

Beyond Lübeck begins the Mecklenburg line. Stations *Schönberg, Grevismühlen, Bobitz* and *Kleinen* (Rail. Rest.) whence there
are branch-lines to Wismar and to Schwerin.

Branch-line (in ½ hr.) to **Wismar** (*Stadt Hamburg*), a Mecklenburg town with 14,000 inhab., possessing an excellent harbour and
several fine churches. *St. Mary's dates from 1339. The Fürsten-

hof, formerly a ducal palace, is now the seat of the municipal authorities. — Near Wismar is the little sea-bathing place *Bolten-hagen.*

Schwerin (**Hôtel du Nord,* Pl. a; **Stern's Hôtel,* Pl. b; **Hôtel de Russie,* Pl. c; **Louisenhof,* Pl. d; the two last in the Louison-platz, more moderate than the first two, R. 20, B. 8 ∫.—Confectioner, *Krefft.* — Restaurants : **Cohen* in the Königs-Str.; *Dabelstein* and *Frohleke* in the Salz-Str. — *Cab* 8 ∫ per drive), an ancient settlement of Wends, and an episcopal see from 1170 to 1624, is now in its modern parts a well built town with 25,100 inhab., and the capital of the Grand Duchy of Mecklenburg Schwerin, prettily situated on the *Lake of Schwerin* (14 M. long, 3½ M. broad) and several smaller lakes.

The **Cathedral* (Pl. 6) in the Altstadt, a fine brick edifice in the Baltic style, begun in the middle of the 14th cent. and completed in 1430 on the site of an earlier building, has recently been restored.

The '*Chapel of the Holy Blood*' at the back of the high altar, contains tombs of the grand-ducal family. The stained glass windows, representing the Ascension, with seven figures of apostles and evangelists, were designed by Cornelius. The N. side of the choir contains a *Monument* of Duke Christopher (d. 1595). *Altar-piece,* a Crucifixion, executed under the directions of Cornelius. By one of the S. pillars is an *Epitaphium* of the Duchess Helena (d. 1524), executed in bronze by the celebrated Peter Vischer of Nuremberg. The four remarkable monumental *Brasses,* 10 ft. in height, date from 1473.

From the cathedral the traveller crosses the market-place, and traverses the Königs-Str. and the Schloss-Str., at the end of which is the *Collegiengebäude* (Pl. 4), on the r., containing government offices. Beyond it is the Alte Garten, an open space, where a *Monument to Grand Duke Paul Frederick* (Pl. 15), designed by Rauch, stands near the *Theatre* (Pl. 21).

On the opposite side rises the grand-ducal **Palace* (Pl. 19), beautifully situated on an island between the Schweriner See and the Burgsee, begun in the early Renaissance style in 1845, and completed by *Stüler* in 1857. It is an imposing and extensive structure, with irregular wings flanked with lofty towers, and encloses a pentagonal court-yard, the whole producing a very picturesque effect. As early as the beginning of the 12th cent. a palace of the princes of Mecklenburg occupied this site. It was rebuilt in the 15th and 16th cent., and parts of this mediæval edifice have been skilfully and tastefully incorporated with the modern palace. The **Interior,* decorated chiefly by *Stüler* and *Strack,* is open on Sundays and holidays at noon, on week-days at 10, 1, and 5. 30 (from 1st Sept. to 31st March at 3) o'clock. On the ground-floor is the *Waffensaal;* on the first floor are the spacious *Festsaal,* the *Thronsaal,* and the tasteful Gothic *Chapel.* Fine views from the windows. The *Burggarten* adjoining the Schloss is also worthy of inspection. The extensive **Schlossgarten* is reached hence by a bridge.

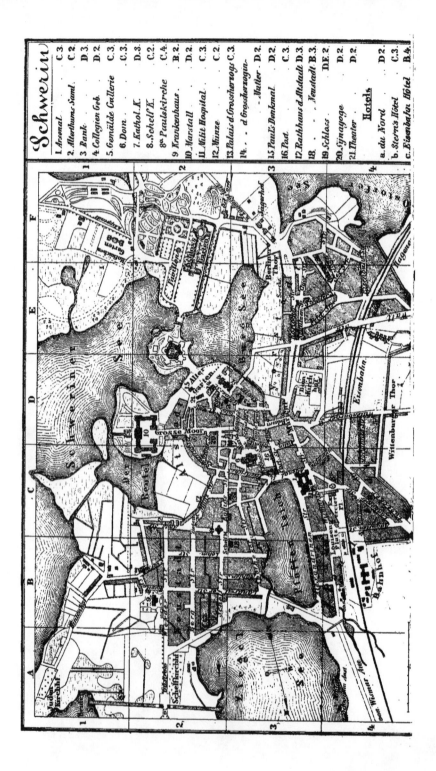

Schwerin

1. Arsenal. — C. 3.
2. Alterthum. Saml. — C. 2.
3. Bank. — D. 3.
4. Collegien Geb. — D. 2.
5. Gemälde Gallerie — C. 3.
6. Dom. — C. 3.
7. Kathol. K. — D. 3.
8. Schelf K. — C. 2.
8ᵉ Paulskirche — C. 4.
9. Krankenhaus — B. 2.
10. Marstall — D. 2.
11. Milit Hospital. — C. 3.
12. Münze. — C. 2.
13. Palais d Grossherzogs — C. 3.
14. .. d Grossherzogin- —
   Mutter. — D. 2.
15. Pauls Denkmal. — D. 2.
16. Post. — C. 3.
17. Rathhaus d Altstadt. — D. 3.
18. .. Neustadt. — B. 3.
19. Schloss — D. E. 2.
20. Synagoge. — D. 2.
21. Theater — D. 2.

Hotels

a. du Nord — D. 2.
b. Stern's Hôtel — C. 3.
c. Eisenbahn Hôtel — B. 4.

The Anna-Strasse leading from the Alte Garten to the S. to the *Ducal Stables* (which also deserve a visit) contains a number of handsome houses. Around the Pfaffenteich (Pl. B, C, 3) there are also some good modern buildings, the finest of which is the *Arsenal* (Pl. 1). Opposite to it is the *Gymnasium*.

Near the station rises the new Gothic *Church of St. Paul* (Pl. 8a).

The grand-ducal **Picture Gallery** (Pl. 5), at the corner of the Alexandrinen-Str. and Wilhelms-Str., is open daily (except Tuesd. and Sat.) 11—12, on Sund. and holidays 12—2. Engravings and sculpture in the same building, Sund. 12—2 only. Lists of the pictures are hung up in each room.

The *Antiquarium (Pl. 2), in the Amts-Str., contains the valuable and well arranged collections of the Mecklenburg Antiquarian Society.

*Walk to *Zippendorf*, and along the bank of the lake to *Rabensteinfeld*, where the grand duke has a villa. Steamboat on the lake in summer. The *Kaninchenwerder* (Restaurant), or rabbits' island, is much visited. — *Parchim*, the birthplace of the celebrated Prussian field-marshal Count Moltke (b. 1800), is a small town 25 M. to the S.E. of Schwerin.

From Schwerin to Rostock by railway in $2^1|_2$—$3^1|_2$ hrs. (fares 1 Thlr. 19, 1 Thlr. 5 Sgr., 25 Sgr.) viâ stat. *Kleinen* (see p. 121), *Blankenberg*, *Bützow*, and *Schwaan*.

Rostock (*Hôtel de Russie; Sonne; *Stadt Hamburg; restaurants of *Friedmann*, Friedrich Franz-Str., and *Ahrens*, Hopfenmarkt; *Bellevue*, *Tivoli*, *Tholia-Theater*, &c. are places of popular resort), on the *Warnow*, with 32,000 inhab., once a prominent member of the Hanseatic League, is the most important place in the Duchy of Mecklenburg, possessing the most considerable commercial fleet on the Baltic. The astronomer Kepler once taught at the University here (founded 1419; 200 stud.), having been appointed professor by Wallenstein during his brief supremacy in 1629. The handsome new *University Building* is a Renaissance structure in brick. The *Marienkirche*, a fine edifice erected in the Baltic-Gothic style in 1398—1472, contains numerous tombstones, chiefly of the Meerheimb family. A stone in the church marks the spot where the learned Grotius, who died here in 1645 on his way as Swedish ambassador to the French Court, was buried; his body was afterwards removed to Delft in Holland. The lofty tower of *St. Peter's Church* (430 ft.) serves as a landmark to mariners. The *Rathhaus* and a number of private dwellings are interesting examples of the secular architecture of the 15th cent. The Blücherplatz is adorned with a bronze *Statue of Blücher*, who was born in the Blücher-Strasse. The reliefs are in allusion to the marshal's defeat at Ligny and his victory at Waterloo.

[*Gebhard Lebrecht v. Blücher*, born at Rostock in 1742, first entered the Swedish, then the Prussian military service. When captain of cavalry in 1772, in consequence of a delay in his promotion, he applied for his discharge, which was granted in the characteristic words of Frederick the Great, 'Der Rittmeister v. Blücher soll sich zum Teufel scheeren', i. e. may betake himself to . . . . &c. After Frederick's death he re-entered the service as major in 1787, distinguished himself against the French in 1793, and in 1806 became general of the advanced guard of the army. After the disastrous battle of Jena he retreated to Lübeck, where after a determined resistance he was at length compelled to capitulate. In 1813 he was appointed to the command of the Silesian army (40,000 Prussians and

Russians), defeated the French at the Katzbach (p. 163), and paved the way for the victory of Leipsic by the battle of Möckern, on 16th and 18th Oct. On New Year's Day, 1814, he crossed the Rhine at Caub, defeated Napoleon on 1st Feb. at La Rothière, and on 31st March took the Montmartre at Paris by storm. At Paris Blücher was created marshal and Prince of Wahlstadt by the King of Prussia, and afterwards accompanied him to England, where among other marks of distinction the degree of D.C.L. was conferred on him by the University of Oxford. After Napoleon's return in 1815 Blücher commanded the Prussian army of 115,000 men, and was repulsed by the French at Ligny on 16th June. He succeeded, however, in rallying his army with wonderful rapidity, and on the memorable 18th, arriving on the field of Waterloo at 4. 30 p. m., decided the victory. On the termination of the war Blücher retired to his estates in Silesia, where he died on 12th Sept. 1819.]

The *Warnow*, the channel of which is 12—15 ft. in depth, forms an excellent harbour for vessels of moderate burden. Pleasant walk of ³|₄ hr. along the bank, past the walls of the town, and through the grounds laid out on the old ramparts. The new hospital is passed on the way. Near the new school-house rises a monument to Mecklenburgers who fell in France in 1870—71.

Steamboat from Rostock (in summer 6—12 times a day, in 50 min.) to **Warnemünde**, a seaport on the Baltic 9 M. to the N., which is entered and quitted by about 700 vessels annually. The sea-bathing attracts about 4000 visitors in July and August.

Diligence from Rostock twice daily to **Dobberan** (*Logierhaus; Lindenhof*), on the Baltic, 10 M. to the W. of Rostock, a sea-bathing place with a chalybeate spring. The palace with its park and the Gothic *Church, completed in 1368, are the principal buildings. The bathing-place is at the *Heiligendamm*, 1¹|₂ M. distant, delightfully situated. Omnibus thither 12 ſ.

The Mecklenburg line proceeds from Bützow by *Güstrow*, *Malchin*, *Neubrandenburg*, to *Strasburg*, the junction of the Prussian line to *Stettin*, see p. 142.

21. From N. Germany to Copenhagen.

a. *From Hamburg through Schleswig, Jutland, and the Danish Islands.*

Railway the whole way, with the exception of the short ferries to Fünen and Zealand. Through train in 17¹|₂ hrs.; fares 15 Thlr. 2, 11 Thlr. 21, 7 Thlr. 29 Sgr.

From Hamburg to stat. *Sommerstedt*, the Prussian frontier, see R. 18. Stat. *Vamdrup* is the Danish frontier station (luggage booked for Copenhagen is not examined till the capital is reached). Stat. *Kolding*, with the imposing ruin of *Koldinghuus*. At **Fredericia** (*Victoria Hôtel*), which is surrounded by an extensive girdle of decaying fortifications, there is an interesting bronze *Statue of a soldier in commemoration of the victory of the Danes over the Schleswig-Holstein besiegers in 1849. Passengers cross the *Little Belt* by a steamboat to **Fünen**, Dan. *Fyen*, and land at *Strib*, near *Middelfart*. Several unimportant stations. Then **Odense** (*Postgaard*), the capital of the island, with 15,000 inhab., the birthplace of Andersen, the author. The *Cathedral of St. Knut*, erected in 1086—1301, contains monuments of the kings John and Christian II. The Fünen railway terminates at **Nyborg**; the quay is 7 min. from the station (omnibus 1 Mark = 4 Sgr.). The steamer departs 1/2 hr. after the arrival of the train, and crosses the *Great Belt* to **Zealand** in 1 1/4 hr. The starting point of the Seeland line is **Korsör** *(Hôtel Store Belt)*, with 3000 inhab. Then stations *Slagelse*, *Sorö* (on the lake of that name, surrounded by beech woods), *Ringsted*, *Borup*.

Roskilde *(*Hôtel Frederikstad*, at the station; *Rail. Restaurant)*, an old town on the deeply-indented fjord of that name, was the capital of the kingdom down to 1448 (comp. p. 129), and the residence of the Bishop down to the Reformation, and once numbered 100,000 inhab., but now contains 5000 only. The only relic of its ancient glory is the fine **Cathedral* (sacristan, Dan. 'Graver', nearly opposite the W. portal, 1—3 pers. 6 M.), consecrated in 1084, restored after a fire in 1282, and at subsequent periods, and finally in 1868. It contains the tombs of the Danish kings, all of whom, from Harold I. (d. 985) down to Frederick VII. (d. 1863) repose here, the earlier in vaults, the more recent in chapels added to the church in 1615—42 and 1772—1825. Some of their monuments are worthy of inspection. The small gate opposite the N. side of the church leads to grounds which command a pleasing view of the fjord. The S. Zealand railway diverges here.

The railway journey from Roeskilde to Copenhagen occupies 1 hr. more. Last stat. *Frederiksberg* (p. 136). The station of Copenhagen is outside the Vester-Port, near the Tivoli (see Plan).

b. *From Kiel to Copenhagen by Korsör.*

Steamer to *Korsör* (see above) every evening on the arrival of the last train from Hamburg (R. 18) in 6—7 hrs., cabin-fare 3 Thlr. 22 1/2 Sgr.; in the reverse direction every evening on the arrival of the last train from Copenhagen. *Railway* from Korsör to Copenhagen in 3 1/4 hrs.; fares 4 Rd. 24, 3 Rd. 16, 2 Rd. 12 ſ. Dan. currency. *Through tickets* from Hamburg to Copenhagen: 1st class railway and cabin 9 Thlr. 27, 2nd class and cabin 8 Thlr. 15, 3rd class and steerage 4 Thlr. 1 1/2 Sgr.; from Kiel to Copenhagen 6 Thlr. 22 1/2, or 5 Thlr. 25 Sgr.

Kiel, see p. 111 (steamboat-quay, comp. Pl. E, 5). The pretty *Kiel Fjord* is unfortunately generally traversed at night. The vessel steers between the islands of *Laaland* on the E. and *Langeland* on the W., and arrives at Korsör about 7 a. m. (steward's fee 5—10 ſ. Hamburg currency). From Korsör to Copenhagen, see above.

From Kiel to Copenhagen by steamboat direct, twice weekly in 16 hrs.; fares 5 Rd. 16 ſ., 3 Rd. 64 ſ. Departure in the evening.

c. *From Lübeck to Copenhagen.*

Steamboat from 1st April to 30th Sept. daily in 16 hrs.; fares 6 Thlr. 5, 5 Thlr. 8, 3 Thlr. 22 1/2 Sgr.

The steamer usually starts from Lübeck about 4 p. m. (Pl. D, 3). The descent of the *Trave* is uninteresting. In 1 1/2 hr. *Travemünde* (p. 121) is reached. The *Travemünder* or *Neustadter Bucht* is then traversed. The chalk cliffs of the Danish island of *Möen* and the coast of Zealand come in sight about 4 a. m.; then the light-house of *Falsterbö* on the Swedish coast, opposite which, on the Danish side, is the *Kjöge Bugt*, where the Danes under Niels Juel gained a great naval victory over the Swedes in 1677.

The vessel steers round the fertile island of *Amager*, on which the village of Dragör is situated. To the r. on the Swedish coast lies Malmö (p. 139). The island of *Saltholm* is next passed, and the towers of Copenhagen at length become visible. The *Lunette* and *Tre Kroner* batteries, which proved so destructive to the English fleet on 2nd April, 1801, are passed, and about 6 a. m. the *Harbour* of Copenhagen, defended by the citadel of *Frederikshavn*, is reached (steward's fee 10—15 ſ. Hamburg currency).

The formalities of the custom-house take place at the *Toldbod*. Porterage for each package from the steamer to the custom-house, and thence to a cab, 1 M. — Cabs, see p. 127.

d. *From Stralsund to Copenhagen by Malmö.*

Steamboat to *Malmö* (p. 139) three times a week in summer in 8 hrs. (fares 5, 3½, 2 Thlr.). From Malmö to Copenhagen in 1½ hr. (fares 72, 48 ſ. Danish).

The steamer (which generally starts about daybreak) traverses the Strela Sund, the narrow strait between Pomerania and the island of Rügen (see Map, p. 144). In about 6 hrs. the Swedish coast comes in sight. The promontory of *Falsterbö* with its lighthouse is rounded, and **Malmö** (p. 139) reached about noon. Another steamer is here in waiting to convey passengers across the Sound to Copenhagen, where they are landed near the *St. Annae-Plads* (Pl. 42). Cabs, see p. 127.

e. *From Stettin to Copenhagen.*

Steamboat every Saturday in summer in 15—20 hrs.; fares 5, 3½, 2 Thlr., return-tickets 8, 6, 3 Thlr.

The steamboat generally starts at noon, and about 5 p. m. touches at Swinemünde (p. 141). About 3 a. m. the chalk cliffs of the island of Möen come in sight. Approach to Copenhagen and arrival, see above, R. c.

22. Copenhagen.

Language. English is spoken at all the principal hotels and shops. A brief notice of a few of the peculiarities of the Danish language may however prove useful.

The pronunciation resembles that of German more nearly than that of English: *a* is pronounced like ah, *e* like ā, *i* like e, *aa* like a long o, *œ* like ā, *o* and *œ* almost like oo, *ø* or *ö* like the German ö or French eu, *y* like the German ü or French u; *d* is generally mute after l, n, r, sk, st, t, and in the terminations ds, dse, e.g. Kilde, a spring, pron. Kille, Plads, a place, pron. Plass; *g* is often mute, or pronounced like y, e.g. Pige, a girl, pron. peayäh, Segl, a sail, pron. sayel, Fugl, a bird, pron. fool; *gn* has a slightly nasal round, e.g. Vogn, a carriage, pron. almost like vong, Regn, rain, pron. raing; *j* is like the English y; *j* after k is mute, e. g.

B

44.Klampenborg Station ... C.5.

A

armstadt, Ed.Wagner.

Kjöd, meat, pron. Köd; *sj* is like the English sh. The Danish article is *en* for the masculine and feminine, and *et* for the neuter; when definite it is suffixed, when indefinite prefixed to the substantive, e.g. Fisken, the fish, en Fisk, a fish; Skibet, the ship, et Skib, a ship. But if the substantive be qualified with an adjective, the article is *den* (m. and f.) and *det* (n.) in the singular, and *,de* in the plural, e.g. den smukke Pige, the pretty girl. The plural of substantives is sometimes formed by adding *e* or *er*, while in other cases the singular remains unaltered. To be *være;* I am, &c.: *jeg* (pron. yai-ỹ) *er;* du er; *han, hun, det, man er; vi, i, de er.* To have *hafve;* I have, &c.: *jeg har; du har; han, hun, det, man er; vi, i, de har.* The third pers. pl. *De* (pron. dee) is commonly used instead of the second pers. sing. or pl. (like the German *Sie*), the dative and accusative of which is *Dem.*

Cardinal numbers: *een* or *eet, to, tre, fire, fem, sex, syv, otte, ni, ti, élleve, tolv, tretten, fjorten, femten, sexten* (pron. sayisten), *sytten, atten, nitten, tyve, een og* (g mute) *tyve,* &c., *tredive,* and so on. The Ordinals: *den, det förste; den anden; or det andet; den, det tredie; den, det fjerde, femte, sjette, syvende, ottende, niende, tiende,* &c.

Ja, yes; *nei* (pron. nai-ỹ) no; *ikke,* not; *Tak,* thanks.

Har de Øl? Have you beer? *Giv mig* (pron. mai-ỹ) *et Glas Viin eller Porter!* Give me a glass of wine or porter. *Bring mig Sup, Kjöd, og Grönt!* Bring me soup, meat, and vegetables. *Kartoffel,* potato; *Rödviin,* red wine; *Vand,* water; *Bröd,* bread; *Smør,* butter; *Ost,* cheese; *Middagsmad,* dinner; *Frokost,* breakfast. *Hvormeget er jeg Dem skyldig?* How much do I owe you? *Hvormeget koster det?* What does this cost? *Jeg beder, hvilken Vei förer til Banegaarden?* Pray, which is the way to the station? *Ligefrem,* straight on; *paa venstre,* to the left; *paa höire,* to the right; *bag,* back. *Er det Toget til K.?* Is that the train to K.? *Hvorledes kaldes denne Station* (pron. stashoon)? What is this station called? *Jernbane,* railway; *Dampskib,* steamer; *By,* town; *Gade,* street; *Torv,* market; *Nytorv,* new market; *Gammeltorv,* old market; *Halmtorv,* straw market; *Port,* gate; *Bro,* bridge; *Höibro,* high bridge; *Holm,* island; *Have,* garden; *Havn,* harbour; *Kjøbenhavn,* Copenhagen, i. e. merchants' harbour; *Kong,* king; *Dronning,* queen; *stor,* great; *liden, lille,* small; *gammel,* old; *ny,* new.

Money. Rix-dollars, marks, and skillings are the current coins of Denmark; 1 Rd. = 6 m., 1 m. = 16 sk.; 1 Rd. = 2 *s.* 3 *d.*, 1 m. = 4¹/₂ *d.*; 3¹/₂ sk. = 1 *d.*, nearly. Prussian money is favourably received: 1 Thlr. = 8 m.; sovereigns and Napoleons also realise their full value.

Hotels. *HÔTEL ROYAL (Pl. a),* opposite the Christiansborg; HÔTEL D'ANGLETERRE (Pl. c), Kongens Nytorv 34; PHŒNIX (Pl. b), Bredgade 37; charges at these, R. from 5, L. 2, D. 6, B. 2¹/₂ m. — Second class: JERNBANE-HÔTEL (Pl. d); SCANDINAVISK HÔTEL (Pl. e); PRINZ KARL, Store Kongensgade; KONG AF DANMARK (Pl. f); *KRONPRINDS (Pl. g);* NORDISK HÔTEL (Pl. h); STADT LYBAEK (Pl. i); DANNEVIRKE (Pl. k), near the station. — UTTENREITER's HÔTEL GARNI, Store Kongensgade 3.

Restaurants. *A. Vincent Junr.,* on the Holmens-Canal, D. 4—6 m. and upwards; *Vincent,* Kongens Nytorv 21; *Schwalbe,* Lille Kongensgade 1; *Bechmann,* Pilestrade 15; *Hansen,* Store Kjöbmagergade 20; *Toldbod-Viinhus,* near the custom-house, reasonable, with view of the harbour. — **Beer.** *Ryberg,* Östergade 13; *Ginderup,* Vimmelskaftet 38; *Svanholm,* Gammel Kongevei; *Figaro,* Vesterbrogade, concerts in the evening.—**Confectioners.** *Porta,* Kongens Nytorv 17; *Richardt,* Norgesgade 4; *Gianelli,* Kongens Nytorv 23, &c.

Fiacres and Cabs (the latter for 2 pers. only). Per drive within the town 1 m. 12 ſ.; to Christianshavn, the Tivoli, or the railway-station 2 m., box 12 ſ.; to Vesterbro as far as the Frederiksberg-Allee, Nörrebro as far as the cemetery, or Österbro as far as the Triangle 2 m. 8 ſ.; Frederiksberg and Söndermarken (p. 136) 3 m.; by the hour ('tiineviis') 4 m.

Tramway, Dan. *Sporvei.* The three chief lines are: 1. The *Slukefter-Vibenshus-Frederiksberg,* 5 M. in length, consisting of two branches diverging from the *Kongens Nytorv* (Pl. F, 4); the *W. Branch* leads by the Större Strade, Holmens Bro, Slotsplads, Storm-Gade, Vester Port, *Tivoli,*

Vesterbrogade, and then either through the Frederiksberg Allee (p. 136), or through the Pile Allee to the entrance of the *Frederiksberg-Have* (palace-garden), in all a drive of ¹|₂ hr.; the *N. Branch* leads by the Norges Gade, the St. Annae Plads, *Gröningen* (p. 136), Osterbrogade, and the Strandvei to *Vibenshus* in the suburb Österbro, and thence to Slukefter, near the railway station Hellerup (p. 137), 3 M. to the N. of Copenhagen; fare from station to station (those printed in Italics) 4 ʃ. — 2. From the Kongens Nytorv by the Slotsplads, *Tivoli*, past the station, and over the Sporveis-Bro to the *Parcelvei.* — 3. From the *Kongens Nytorv* by the Gothers Gade, *Norre Port*, and the Norrebro Gade to the end of the *Lyg-levei.*

Omnibuses. The only lines in the town likely to be serviceable to the traveller are those from the *Amagertorv* near the Höibroplads (Pl. E, 5) to the Toldbodvei (Pl. G, G, 3), near the Lange Linie, and to Frederiksberg (Pl. 121), fares 4 and 8 ʃ. — In the *Environs*, those from the Hôtel du Nord, Kongens Nytorv 13, several times daily to *Charlottenlund, Bellevue, Klampenborg*, and *Taarbaek* (see p. 137).

Boat from the Nyhavn to Christianshavn 4 ʃ., Toldbod 24 ʃ., Knippelsbro and Exchange 12 ʃ., Langebro 12 ʃ.

Baths. *Ryssensteen*, by the Lange Bro, all kinds of baths, including Russian; at the *Commune Hospital* (Pl. D, 3), open to the public in the afternoon only; at the *Frederiks Hospital* in the Amalie Gade; *Drachmann & Schytte*, Gammeltorv 18, Turkish and other baths. — The *Sea Baths* of *Engelbrecht, Baëk*, &c., and 'those at Klampenborg (p. 137) near the Lange Linie (Pl. G, 1), are recommended.

Post Office. Kjöbmagergade 33; poste-restante to the r. in the court. Branch offices at the Toldbod and the railway-station. — *Telegraph Office* at the post-office.

Thorvaldsen's Sculptures. Beautiful copies at the *Royal Porcelain Factory*, Kjöbmagergade 50; *Bing*, at the corner of the Kronprindsensgade and the Philestræde; *Brix*, Nygade 2; *Ipsen*, Norgesgade 31. — Photographs. *Wagner, Tryde*, both in the Östergade. Casts of these celebrated works may also be purchased.

Military Parade daily about noon in the Kongens-Nytorv when the king is residing at the Amalienborg.

Theatre (Pl. 36) in the Kongens Nytorv from 1st Sept. to 31st May, good acting and ballet. *Casino Theatre* (Pl. 37), much frequented. *Popular Theatre* (Pl. 38).

***Tivoli** (Pl. 39; admission 1 m., and on grand occasions 1¹|₂ m.), outside the Vester-Port, is a very extensive and interesting establishment, comprising all kinds of amusements, concerts by *Lumby's* excellent band, &c. — The **Sommerlyst* and other places of recreation of the same description are all situated in the Frederiksberg Allee.

Steamboats (see also the 'Reiseliste for Kongeriget Danmark', published twice monthly, 8 ʃ.) to *Helsingör* in 2¹|₂ hrs. (fares 64, 48 ʃ.), and *Helsinborg* in 2³|₄ hrs. (fares 1 Rd. 16, 88 ʃ.), twice daily, starting from the quay near the St. Annæ Plads (Pl. 42); pleasure trips on Sundays at reduced fares ('Tour og Retour'). To *Malmö* (p. 139) four times daily in 1¹|₂ hr., fares 96, 72 ʃ.; to *Bellevue* near *Klampenborg* (p. 137) several times daily in ³|₄ hr., fare 24 ʃ. — To *Kiel, Lübeck, Stralsund*, and *Stettin*, see R. 22. — To *London, Hull*, and *Leith* generally once weekly. — The larger vessels start from the Toldbod.

Railway (see also the 'Reiseliste for Kongeriget'). The station (Dan. *Banegaard*, Pl. C, 5) lies outside the Vester Port, near the Tivoli. There are four lines in Zealand: 1. The *Western Line* to Korsör (see p. 125); 2. The *Southern Line*, which diverges from the first at Roskilde (p. 125); 3. The *Northern Line* to Helsingör (p. 138); 4. The *Line Klampenborg* (p. 137), a short branch of the last. Trains on the Klampenborg line start from the *Klampenborg Station* (Pl. 44), a little way to the N. of the principal station, every hour on week-days, and every half-hour on Sundays.

English Church Service by a resident chaplain.

Diary (comp. the 'Erindringsliste' in the *Dagbladet* or any other newspaper, as the hours are frequently changed).

Anthropological Museum (p. 135) on Saturdays in summer, 9—11.
**Antiquities, Northern* (p. 134), from 1st May to 30th Sept, Thursd. and Sat. 12—2, Tuesd. 5—7 (in Sept. 3—5); from 1st Oct. to 30th April Sund. and Thursd. 12—2.
Antiquities, Royal Collection of (p. 134), Tuesdays 12—2.
Arsenal (p. 132), Wednesdays 1—3.
Botanical Garden (p. 130) Thursdays 8—2 and 4—7, open to scientific men daily.
Christiansborg, Palace of (p. 131), daily.
Coins and Medals, Royal Collection of (p. 134), from 1st May to 31st Oct. Mondays 12—2, open to scientific visitors on Wed. and Frid. also, 12—3.
Engravings, Royal Collection of (p. 134), Tuesd. and Fridays 12—2.
**Ethnographical Museum* (p. 134), from 1st May to 30th Sept. Sat. 12—2 and Wed. 5—7 (in Sept. 3—5); from 1st Oct. to 30th April Sund. 12—2.
Exhibition of Art at the Charlottenborg (p. 130) daily 9—6.
*Fruekirke (Church of Our Lady, p. 130) daily 9—11.
Natural History Museum. (p. 131), Sund. and Wed. 12—2.
Picture Gallery, Royal (p. 131) from 1st May to 31st Oct. Sund. 11—2, Tuesd. 3—7 (in Sept. 2—6, in Oct. 1—5), Frid. 11—3.
Picture Gallery, Moltke's (p. 135), daily.
Rosenborg, Palace of (p. 135) daily, on application made the day before, fee 3 Rd. for 12 pers.
***Thorvaldsen Museum* (p. 132) from 1st May to 30th Sept. Sund. 11—2, Tuesd. 2—3, Thursd. 9—12, Sat. 12—3; in winter Wed. 11—2.
Zoological Garden (p. 136) daily.
Principal Attractions. Fruekirke (p. 130), Thorvaldsen Museum (p. 132), Northern Antiquities (p. 134), view from one of the towers mentioned at pp. 131, 135, 138, walk along the Lange Linie (p. 136), an evening at the Tivoli (p. 128), and if possible an excursion to Helsingör (p. 138).

Copenhagen, Dan. Kjøbenhavn, the capital of the kingdom of Denmark and the residence of the king, with 181,291 inhab. (exclusive of the suburb Frederiksberg, with 19,000 inhab.), lies on both sides of the *Kallebostrom*, a narrow and deep strait of the Sound which separates Zealand from the small island of *Amager*. The N. and broader part of the strait forms the excellent *Harbour*, to which the city was indebted for its early commercial prosperity.

Copenhagen was founded in the 13th cent. by Axel, Bishop of Roeskilde, on the site of a fishing village (whence its original name *Axelhuus*), and increased so rapidly in consequence of its trade that King Christian III. constituted it his capital and residence in 1448. It was extended by Christian IV., chiefly by the foundation of the Christianshavn quarter on the island of Amager. Thenceforward the city steadily increased, notwithstanding the numerous reverses it sustained in the wars with the Hanseatic League, Norway, Sweden, England, and Holland. Copenhagen suffered severely from two well-known events at the beginning of the present century, the naval battle of 2nd April, 1801, and the bombardment of the city and capture of the fleet by the English, 2nd—5th Sept., 1807. The occasion of the former was the alliance concluded by Denmark with Sweden and Russia, of the latter the necessity of preventing the Danish fleet from falling into the hands of the French. The business of the place has at length recovered from these shocks and has been considerably extended of late. It now possesses about 470 vessels. The number of vessels which annually enter the port is 9000, chiefly of small tonnage (in 1843 the number was 4800 only). The staple commodities are grain, leather, wool, and train oil.

The commercial harbour, situated on the Zealand side, is separated from the war-harbour by a barrier across the Kallebostrom.

The warehouses and magazines are in the Christianshavn quarter. The *Orlogshavn*, or war-harbour, adjoins the small islands of *Nyholm*, *Frederiksholm*, *Arsenalö*, and *Christiansholm*, on which the naval depôts are situated.

Down to 1864 Copenhagen was carefully fortified, but the works on the land side have since been removed. Those on the side towards the sea, the citadel of *Frederikshavn*, the advanced batteries of *Trekroner* and *Lynetten*, and the *Sextus* and *Quintus* batteries in Amager are still capable of being defended.

Apart from its picturesque situation and environs, Copenhagen is chiefly interesting from its having given birth to the greatest master of modern sculpture, *Albert* (Dan. *Bertel*) *Thorvaldsen* (b. 1770, d. 1844), all of whose works are represented by casts, or in some cases preserved in the original, within the precincts of his native city.

The centre of the city and chief focus of business is the **Kongens Nytorv** (king's new market, Pl. F, 4, 5), from which thirteen streets radiate. The theatre, the palace of *Charlottenborg* (Academy of Art, Pl. 23), the chief *Guard-house* (Pl. 9), and the principal hotels are situated here. In the centre rises the *Equestrian Statue of Christian V.* (d. 1699), cast in lead. Adjoining the Charlottenborg is the *Botanic Garden* (Pl. 3), with palm-houses, etc., open to the public on Thursdays only, 8—2 and 4—7 o'clock, to professional men daily (entrance from the Nyhavn).

The *Østergade* and beyond it the *Vimmelskaft* lead from the Kongens Nytorv to the *Gammel og Nytorv* ('old and new market'). In the corner to the l. is the *Town-Hall* (Pl. 31), erected in 1815, with a portico; in the tympanum are the words with which the Jutland Code of 1240 begins: *'Med Lov skal man Land bygge'* ('with law one must establish the land').

Turning hence again to the r., the traveller passes a fountain erected by Christian IV., and soon reaches the Prot. ***Fruekirke** ('Church of Our Lady', Pl. 21), the metropolitan church of the Danish dominions, a simple but impressive structure in the early Renaissance style, replacing one which was destroyed by the bombardment in 1807. On the r. and l. of the entrance are statues of Moses and David. The tympanum contains a group of John the Baptist preaching in the wilderness, in terracotta; over the entrance door, Christ's Entry into Jerusalem in stucco, both by Thorvaldsen.

*Interior (open daily 9—11). The sole ornament of the interior consists of the exquisite *marble groups designed and partially executed by *Thorvaldsen:* a Risen Christ and the Twelve Apostles, over life-size; a Kneeling Angel of striking beauty, with a shell as a font; over the altar and in the two chapels, reliefs of the Bearing of the Cross, Baptism, and Last Supper; above the alms-basins the Guardian Angel and Charity. St. Paul, with the sword, entirely executed by the great master himself, is probably the finest of the apostles; SS. John, James, Matthew, and the pensive Thomas are the next in point of excellence. All these plastic works form a cycle of Scripture history, commencing with John the Baptist; and terminating with the Risen Saviour.

The tower commands a view similar to that from the Round Tower (p. 135).

Opposite the church is the **University** (Pl. 41), founded in 1479 (burned down in 1807), and attended by 1000 students, more than half of whom study theology. In the vestibule, by the entrance, Apollo and Minerva in marble; above, frescoes by *Hansen.* Next door is the *University Library* (300,000 vols.) and the extensive and valuable *Natural History Museum* (Pl. 27), containing a separate department for whales. Entrance in the Krystalgade (Sund. and Wed. 12—2).

Between the university and the Fruekirke are monuments to the naturalist *Schouw* (d. 1852) and the organist *Weyse* (d. 1842).

The Raadhuus-Stræde leads from the Fruekirke and the Gammel og Nytorv towards the S.W. to the **Christiansborg Palace** (Pl. E, F, 5, 6), situated on an island, which was fortified by Bishop Axel (p. 129) in 1168. On the site of the ancient **Axelhuus,** which had been frequently restored and altered, Christian VI. caused a magnificent palace to be erected in 1732—40, but that building was burned down in 1794. The present palace, designed by *Hansen,* and completed in 1828, is a spacious and lofty edifice, which with its numerous offices and dependencies of itself forms a small quarter of the city. The handsome façade towards the Slots-Plads is adorned with several sculptures by *Thorvaldsen.* Above are four reliefs: Minerva and Prometheus, Hercules and Hebe, Jupiter and Nemesis, Æsculapius and Hygeia. The niches adjoining the portal contain four large allegorical figures in bronze, of Wisdom, Power, Justice, and Health, by Bissen. The castellan Zeltner lives at Töihuusgade 16, near the Prindsensbro. The finest apartments in the interior are the spacious Hall of the Knights, the Chamber of the Council of State, which contains a copy of *Thorvaldsen's* *Procession of Alexander (at the Villa Sommariva on the Lake of Como), and the Throne Room. The caryatides on each side of the throne are by *Thorvaldsen*; the walls are embellished with four scenes from Danish history by *Eckersberg.* The palace also contains the halls in which the Upper and Lower Chamber assemble, the picture gallery, the court chapel, the *Royal Library* (500,000 vols., comprising many valuable works on Scandinavia), etc.

The **Royal Picture Gallery** (or *Kongelige Maleri-Samling*) is on the upper floor of the palace. Entrance by the chief portal in the Slotsplads, then ascend the stair to the l. (Admission see p. 129. Catalogue in Danish 1½, in French 3 m.)

Towards the *Court-Yard.* I. Room. 20. *Cignani*, Joseph and Potiphar; 64. *Salv. Rosa*, The prophet Jonah. II. Room. 255. *Jordaens*, Hercules; *F. Bol*, The women at the tomb of the Saviour. III. Room. 382. *Rubens*, Solomon's Judgment. From the 2nd Room the visitor enters the nine rooms facing the *Slots-Plads.* Passing through the two rooms to the r., he will reach the last of the suite, which according to the present plan may be termed the — 1st Room. 304, 305. *Mierevelt*, Man and woman; 115. *Bloemart*, Niobe sheltering her children from the arrows of Apollo and Diana; 178. *Everdingen*, Waterfall. — 2nd Room. 388. *Ruisdael*, Torrent;

229. *Honthorst*, Effect of light; 430. *Jan Steen*, Miser; 419. *Slingeland*, Young Dutchwoman with parrot. — 3rd ROOM (that by which the suite has been entered).   215. *Van der Helst*, Portrait of a man; 306. *Mierevelt*, Portrait of a man; 249. *Huysum*, Flower piece; 443. *Teniers*, Temptation of St. Antony. — 4th ROOM.   167. *Van Dyck*, Portrait of a lady; 489. *Weenix*, Game; 366. *Paul Potter's School*, Cows at milking time; 405. *Schalcken*, Holy Family; 490. *Weenix*, Game. — 5th ROOM.   123. *F. Bol*, Dutch lady; 166. *Van Dyck*, Holy Family; 296. *Mieris*, The order; 160. *G. Dow*, Physician and lady; 370. *Rembrandt*, Christ at Emmaus; 124. *F. Bol*, Admiral de Ruyter; 297, 298. *Mieris the Elder*, Portraits of men; 383. *Rubens*, Portrait of the Abbot Irselius; 384, 385. *Rubens*, Portraits of Francis I. of Tuscany and his Duchess; 418. *Slingeland*, Family picture. — 6th ROOM. 371, 372. *Rembrandt*, Portraits. — 7th ROOM.   *Cranach the Elder*, 146. Luther, 147. Catharine Bora, &c.; 406. *Schalcken*, Dutchwoman sealing a letter; 454. *Rembrandt's School*, Portrait of a woman. — 8th ROOM.   79. *Luini*, St. Catharine; 60. After *Raphael*, Adoration of the Magi; 51. *Moretto*, Portrait; 34. *Garofalo*, Adoration of the Magi; 14. *Caravaggio*, Gamblers.   Beyond the 8th Room is a dark corridor, from which the visitor turns to the r. into the — 9th ROOM.   35. *Luca Giordano*, Cain slaying Abel. — The other *Six Rooms* contain modern pictures by *Danish Masters*, the collection being annually extended by purchase: 541, 542. *Carstens*, Bacchus giving wine to Cupid, and Fingal fighting with Loda; 564. *Exner*, The difficult choice; 565. *Exner*, Grandmother greeting her convalescent granddaughter; 577. *Gurlitt*, View of Skanderborg; 578. *Gurlitt*, Scene in Jutland; 594—597, 602—604. Portraits by *Jens Juel*; 618. *Köbke*, Coast of Capri; 624. *Lund*, Battle of Fridericia; 641. *Marstrand*, The visit; 643, 644. *Melby*, Sea pieces; 687, 688. *Sonne*, Battle of Dybbol in 1848, and that of Idsted in 1850.

A wing of the Christiansborg contains the *Royal Stables*. The *Palace Chapel* is on the N. side. The *Arsenal* is open to the public on Wednesdays, 1—3 o'clock.

On the N.W. side of the palace rises the **Thorvaldsen Museum (Pl. 40), a somewhat gloomy edifice erected in 1839—48 in the style of the Pompeian and Etruscan tombs.   Over the pediment of the façade is a goddess of victory in a quadriga, in bronze, designed by Thorvaldsen and executed by *Bissen*.   The other three sides of the building are adorned with a series of scenes in plaster, representing the reception of the illustrious master at Copenhagen on his return after an absence of eighteen years, bringing with him a number of works destined for the Museum.   The inner quadrangle contains Thorvaldsen's tomb (d. 1844).   Visitors (adm. see p. 129) usually enter by the small door opposite the palace.

Besides *Thorvaldsen's Works* (copies and photographs, see p. 128) the Museum contains his collections of ancient and modern objects of art, all bequeathed by him to his native city.   The whole of the master's own works, which are the most interesting part of the collection, are represented here, both by the original models and designs and by excellent copies, some of them in marble (by himself or his pupils), others in plaster.

VESTIBULE (entered from the corridor).   r. 128. Elector Maximilian I. of Bavaria, a model of the monument at Munich; l. 123. Poniatowsky, designed for Warsaw (two colossal equestrian figures); 142—45. Monument of Pius VII. at Rome; 135. Schiller, Mayence; 113. Copernicus, Warsaw; 253. Marble bust of Horace Vernet. — CORRIDOR.   On the l. and r. of the entrance from the vestibule: 55, 56. Caryatides from the Christiansborg; l. 119. Dying lion, protecting the French fleur de lys, Lucerne; r. 122. Lion reposing; continuing to the r., 575—578. The Four Evangelists, reliefs in marble; 59—70. Preaching of John the Baptist in the tympanum of the Fruekirke. In returning through the corridor, the visitor should observe the artistic · tomb reliefs on the pillars between the windows. — CABINETS: *1st.* · 40, 42. Ganymede. — *2nd.* 27. Cupid and Psyche; 426. Ages of love; 430. Cupid awakens Psyche; 585, 587. Genii, reliefs. — *3rd.* 29. The Graces and Cupid; 340. Dance of the Muses on Helicon, relief; 371, 396, 397, 375, 393. Five reliefs, Cupid in different attitudes. — *4th.* 11. Venus with the apple of Paris; 414, 410, 412. Winter, Summer, and Autumn, reliefs. — *5th.* · 51. Jason with the golden fleece; 489, 492, 493, 495. Scenes from the life of Achilles.· — *6th.* 38. Hebe; 321—324. Hercules and Hebe, Æsculapius and Hygeia, Minerva and Prometheus, Nemesis and Jupiter, reliefs. — *7th.* 6. Mars and Cupid; 499, 501. Scenes from the Iliad. — *8th.* 46. Hope; 367, 368. Day and Night,· a relief. — *9th.* 8· Vulcan; 497. Athene awards the arms of Achilles to·Ulysses, a relief. — *10th.* 4. Mercury as the slayer of the Argus; 352, 354, 407, 416. Groups of Pan, satyrs, and Cupid. — *11th.* 166. Countess Ostermann; 171. Princess Bariatinski; 451.

Cupid and Hymen; 618 a. Death of the Baroness Schubert.— *12th.* 124. Equestrian statue of Prince Poniatowsky ; 207. Count Bernstorff; 234. Prince Metternich, 272. Count Somma-riva, busts in marble. — The CHRIST SALOON (the 'cella') contains the models of the sculptures in the Fruekirke (p. 130). — The corridor is next traversed. The model of the Procession of· Alexander serves ·as a frieze. On the pillars between the windows are tasteful reliefs; l. 252. Apotheosis of Napoleon, a bust in marble ; 233. Lewis I. of Bavaria; 255. Walter · Scott. — CABINETS. *13th;* 121. Lion reposing; 130. 131. Lord Byron, and a

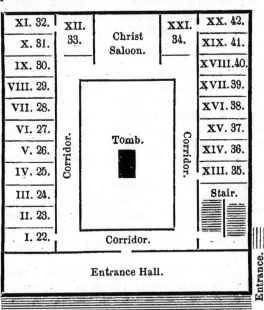

I.—XXI. Ground Floor.   22.—42. First Floor.

relief; 343. Cupid listening to the singing of Erato; 365. The three Fates, a relief. — *14th.* 44. Ganymede with the eagle of Jupiter; 389. Cupid on the lion; 391, 417, 424. Groups of Cupid, reliefs ;. 484. Hylas carried off by Nymphs. — *15th.* 155. Prince Wladimir Potocky; 359. Victory noting a heroic exploit on her shield; 514. Alexander the Great induced by Thaïs to set· fire to the Temple of Persepolis. — *16th.* 22. Cupid triumphant; 377—80. Four reliefs, Cupid as ruler· of the elements; 395, 454. Groups of Cupid. — *17th.* 53. Adonis; 480. Nessus embracing Dejaneira, a relief. — *18th.* 31. The three Graces with the arrow of Cupid. — *19th.* 176. Shepherd-boy; 482. Hylas carried off by Nymphs, a relief; 638—41. The four ages and seasons. — *20th.* 162 A. Thorvaldsen, a statue in marble; 232. Lewis I. of Bavaria. — *21st.* 150. Conradin, the last of the Hohenstaufen (from the original tomb at Naples). — On the staircase leading to the UPPER FLOOR, Hercules, from the portal of the Christiansborg (p.·131). Then in the upper CORRIDOR to the l.: 508. Alexander's entry into Babylon, reduced,·with variations; 509. Variation of the central piece. Then along the side of the corridor a number of models and casts. Cabinets *22nd—32nd* contain Thorvaldsen's picture gallery, comprising works by *Overbeck*, *W. Schadow*, *Leop. Robert*, *Richter*, *Horace Vernet*, &c. Then several statues by Thorvaldsen. In the *24th* a triumphant Cupid, in the *25th* Georgina Russell, 'la fanciulla', in the *26th* a dancing girl, in the *27th* Cupid playing the lyre, in the *29th* Cupid with the bow, in the *31st* Psyche. The *32nd* contains a selection of engravings and drawings from Thorvaldsen's valuable collection. *33rd.* Sketches and designs by Thorvaldsen. *34th.* 649. Marble chimney-piece after Thorvaldsen, relief sketches and designs. The *35—40th* contain Thorvaldsen's collection of antiquities, the 41st his library, the 42nd his unfinished works, his furniture, and his bust by *Bissen*.

On the Frederikholms-Canal, to the S.W. of the Christiansborg, beyond the bridges, is situated the **Prindsens-Palais** (Pl. 29), once an occasional residence of the Danish crown-princes, and now containing several interesting collections.

1. The *Museum of Northern Antiquities* ('Nordiske Oldsager'; admission, see p. 129) is the finest of its kind in existence, and invaluable to the historian of early civilisation, especially in Scandinavia. The objects it contains, 40,000 in number, consist of weapons, tools, implements, domestic utensils, hunting gear, wooden coffins, cinerary urns, musical instruments, trinkets, Runic inscriptions, ecclesiastical vessels, armour, tombstones, etc., all admirably arranged in chronological order. There are five leading departments. 1st. The *Flint Period* (Rooms 1—3; down to B. C. 1500); 2nd. The *Bronze Period* (Rooms 4 and 5; down to A. D. 250); 3rd. The *Iron Period* (Rooms 6—9); 4th. *Mediaeval Christian Period* (Rooms 10—15; from about 1030 to 1536); 5th. *Modern Period* (Rooms 16—19; down to about 1660). The two last departments are on the first floor. Interesting catalogue in French 3 1/2 m. On the second floor is the antiquarian-topographical museum, open on Tuesd., Thursd., and Sat., 12—2 o'clock.

2. The *Ethnographical Museum* (admission, see p. 129), which is also one of the most extensive in Europe, occupies 35 rooms. The two chief departments are: 1st. *Ancient Times*, comprising European antiquities (except those of the North), Asiatic, African, and American; 2nd. *Modern Times*, comprising objects from primitive or barbarous non-European nations, illustrative of their arts of war and peace (Greenland and E. India are particularly well represented). Danish catalogue 2 m.

3. The *Royal Collection of Antiquities* (admission, see p. 129) contains Egyptian, Assyrian, Phœnician, Etruscan, Greek, and Roman antiquities, of no great value.

4. The *Royal Collection of Coins and Medals* (admission, see p. 129) contains 30,000 specimens in five sections: 1st. Greek; 2nd. Roman and Byzantine; 3rd. Mediæval; 4th. Modern; 5th. Oriental.

5. The *Royal Collection of Engravings* (admission, see p. 129) consists of upwards of 80,000 plates.

On the quay, on the E. side of the Christiansborg, is situated the **Exchange** (Pl. 4), erected in 1615 in a degraded style, with a tower 150 ft. in height, the summit of which consists of four dragons with entwined tails. The hall is to be embellished with paintings from the history of Denmark; opposite the entrance is the statue of Christian IV. in bronze, by *Thorvaldsen*. The lower part of the building is occupied with shops, offices, etc. Business hour 1. 30 to 2. 30 daily.

The *Knippelsbro* at the back of the Exchange crosses the harbour to the *Christianshavn* quarter (p. 129), where the singular tower of **Vor Frelsers Kirke** (*Church of Our Redeemer*, Pl. 20), erected in 1749, rises conspicuously (286 ft. in height). A winding stair on the exterior ascends to the summit, which is crowned with a figure of the Redeemer. Extensive *view. *Graver* (sacristan), Dronningensgade 67; fee 6 m. for 1—4 pers.

Opposite the Exchange, beyond a branch of the harbour, rises the *Holmens-Kirke* (Pl. 15), erected at the beginning of the 17th cent. and recently restored, containing the tombs of several Danish naval heroes (Niels Juel, d. 1687; Peter Tordenskjold, d. 1720, etc.).

At the W. end of the Gothersgade, which diverges from the Kongens Nytorv, is situated the handsome **Rosenborg** (Pl. 32), a handsome royal palace with three towers, erected in 1604, partly in the Gothic, and partly in the Renaissance style. The interior, resembling the 'Green Vault' at Dresden, is worthy of inspection. It contains a great number of valuable curiosities, jewels, weapons, ivory carving, furniture, &c. (6—12 pers. 3 Rdlr.; application must be made on the previous day; entrance from the Osterwall).

The palace is enclosed by moats, and is bounded on the E. by the *Rosenborg-Have*, a pleasant park, and on the S. by the *Esplanade*. On the Osterwall, opposite the Rosenborg, rises the new *Observatory*. Beyond the ramparts is the extensive *Hospital*.

A short distance from the Rosenborg, at the corner of the Landemærke and the Store Kjobmagergade, is situated the *Church of the Trinity* (Pl. 33), with its **Round Tower** 116 ft. in height, which commands an admirable survey of the city and environs. The tower is ascended by means of a broad and winding causeway. (Visitors knock at the door; fee 2 m.)

The *Aristocratic Quarter* of Copenhagen lies to the N.E. of the Kongens Nytorv, and consists of the *Norges-Gade* or *Brede-Gade*, the *St. Annae Plads*, and the *Amalie-Gade*. At No. 15 Norges-Gade (to the r. in the court) is the *Picture Gallery of Count Moltke*, consisting of 500 works by Dutch and German masters of the 17th and 18th cent. At No. 46 in the same street is an *Anthropological Museum*, open in summer on Sat., 9—11 o'clock. The *St. Annae Plads* is adorned with a bronze statue of the Danish poet *Oehlenschläger*. The Amalie-Gade is broken by the octagonal

Frederiks-Plads, which is embellished with an equestrian *Monument of Frederick V.* (d. 1766) in bronze, erected in 1771 by the Asiatic Trading Company. The four buildings enclosing the Plads are the *Amalienborg* (Pl. 1), which is now the principal residence of the reigning monarch Christian IX., and the residences of the Queen Dowager, the Crown Prince, and the minister of the exterior. Travellers who have the misfortune to be overtaken by illness may obtain private apartments and good medical advice on reasonable terms at the Frederiks-Hospital in the Amalien-Gade.

The *Nyboder* ('new buildings'), a series of parallel streets of one-storeyed houses erected at the beginning of the 17th cent. under Christian IV., to whom the city is also indebted for various other buildings, and extended during the last century, are inhabited chiefly by sea-faring men and their families.

Walks. Besides the Rosenborg Garden (p. 135), the *'Gröningen'* esplanade (Pl. G, 2, 3) between the citadel and the town, and its continuation towards the N., termed the **Lange Linie* (Pl. 1, 2), afford a pleasant promenade, with a view of the sea. A little farther to the N. are the bathing-places and a large *Blind Asylum.* — Near the Vester Port is the so-called *Philosopher's Walk* (Pl. D, E, 6), laid out on the old ramparts of the city.

The **Environs,* as well as the entire N.E. part of Zealand, are very attractive. The rich corn-fields, green pastures, and fine beech-forests, contrasting with the blue-green water of the Sound, are enlivened with numerous châteaux, country-houses, and villages. A few of the finest excursions are here mentioned.

The **Frederiksberg,** a royal palace 1½ M. to the W. of the town, may be reached by tramway or by omnibus. Outside the Vester Port, at the entrance to the Tivoli (p. 128), rises the *Friheds-Stötten,* or Column of Liberty (Pl. 8), an obelisk of reddish granite erected in 1778 to commemorate the final abolition of serfdom. On the l., farther on, is the new *Industrial Hall.* The road then leads through the *Frederiksberg-Allee,* with its numerous pleasure-gardens. At the entrance to the *Frederiksberg-Have,* or palace garden, rises a *Statue of Frederick VI.* (d. 1839) by Bissen. The palace, erected in the Italian style under Frederick IV. (d. 1730), lies conspicuously on an eminence. The chief attraction is the view from the platform. Adjoining the palace on the S. is the beautiful shady park of *Söndermarken,* containing the large basin whence Copenhagen is supplied with water. In the vicinity is the *Zoological Garden.*

Roskilde, 17 M. farther to the W., see p. 125.

To the N. of the city, 2 M. from the Oster-Port, is the royal château of **Charlottenlund,** generally occupied by the crown-prince in summer, situated in a beautiful park, ¾ M. from Slukefter, the terminus of the tramway. A fine avenue leads from Charlottenlund to the N.W. to (1½ M.) the château of *Bernstorff,* the autumn residence of the royal family, also situated in a park, and the hamlet

Maassstab 1:500.000

Darmstadt, Ed. Wag

of *Jägersborg* (Inn). The railway stations Gjentofte and Lyngby mentioned below are respectively 3/4 M. and 1 1/2 M. distant.

A very favourite excursion is to the *Dyrehave, or deer-park, a beautiful forest of oaks and beeches. At the entrance, 3 M. to the N. of Charlottenlund, is the *Bellevue-Hotel*, the landing-place of — the steamers from Copenhagen (p. 128). In the vicinity is the water-cure and sea-bathing establishment of **Klampenborg** (railway p. 128; omnibus to Taarbæk, p. 128), which attracts numerous visitors in summer (*Hotel and restaurant, commanding a fine view). The numerous villas of *Taarbæk* and *Ny-Taarbæk*, farther on, are chiefly let as summer quarters. On a height, a little inland, stands the *Eremitage*, a shooting lodge, near which groups of stags. and deer are frequently observed. The *Dyrhaves Bakken* ('deerpark hill'), on the S. side of the park, is a favourite resort of the lower classes in summer. The costumes of the peasant women are often very becoming. Near the spring termed the *Kirsten-Piils Kilde* are grouped numerous booths and popular shows of all kinds, which with the beautiful neighbouring woods afford a pleasant picture of humble life 'al fresco'.

The *Railway to Helsingör* (in 2 hrs.; fares 1 Rd. 32, 1 Rd., or 72 ∫; steamboat see p. 128) affords the traveller a good opportunity of visiting several points farther inland. Stations *Hellerup*, junction for Klampenborg; *Gjentofte* (château of Bernstorff, see above); *Lyngby*, near which are the châteaux of *Sorgenfri*, with beautiful rose-garden, and *Frederiksdal; Holte*, also with pleasant environs, comprising the *Dronninggaard* on the *Fuur-Sø; Birkerød, Lillerød*.

At stat. **Hillerød** *(Rasmussen's Inn)*, the principal town in the district of Frederiksborg, is situated the handsome palace of **Frederiksborg**, the summer residence of the king, re-erected after a fire in 1859. The palace church, in which the Danish kings were once crowned, is worthy of a visit. The palace lies in the middle of a small lake, surrounded by beautiful oak and beech woods, termed the *Indelukket*, through which a road leads to the N.W. to the (4 1/2 M.) **Fredensborg**, another favourite summer seat of the royal family, near the picturesque *Esrom-Sø*. This château was built in 1720 in commemoration of the peace ('Freden') which had shortly before been concluded between Denmark and Sweden. The village of *Fredensborg* (*Jansen's Restaurant) is also a railway-station.

Next stations *Kvistgaard* and *Helsingör* (see below). The railway-station (refreshment-room) is on the E. side of the town.

The *Steamboat Journey* to Helsingör (in 2 1/2 hrs.; see p. 128) is preferable to the railway route, as it affords a view of the picturesque coast of Zealand. The vessel touches at *Bellevue* (see above), *Taarbæk* (see above), *Skodsborg*, and *Vedbæk*; then, leaving the Swedish island for *Hveen* to the r., at *Rungsted* and *Humlebek*.

Helsingör, or *Elsinore.* (**Hôtel Øresund; Hôtel du Nord)*, a small and very ancient commercial town with 8500 inhab., lies on the Sound at its narrowest part, which separates Zealand from the Swedish province of Skaane. The Gothic *Raadhuus* in the principal street was restored in 1855.

' The ***Kronborg**, a picturesque fortress rising conspicuously on the N.E. side of the town, was constructed in 1577—85, and surrounded with ramparts and broad moats. After the fall of the Hanseatic League: the Danish government assumed a right to levy toll here on all vessels passing through the Sound, but in, 1857 agreed to a commutation of the obnoxious Sound dues for a payment of 3½ million pounds sterling by the commercial nations chiefly interested. The Danish batteries were moreover. unable without cooperation from the Swedish side, effectually to prevent the passage of vessels, as was proved on two different occasions by the English fleet. The *Flag Battery*, where the Dannebrog, or national banner, is planted (open to the public; turn to the l. on entering the fortress by the W. gate), commands a beautiful view of the Sound, the island of Hveen, and the promontory of *Kullen* (see below). This battery is said to be the 'platform of the castle of Elsinore' where the ghost appeared to Hamlet. The Kronborg is also the scene of other interesting legends connected with Denmark. Thus the tutelary genius of the country, Holger Danske, who is familiar to the reader of Andersen's fables, is said to repose beneath the castle, ready to arise when Denmark is in danger. The pulpit and choir-stalls in the castle chapel were carved by German masters, Two rooms contain a few pictures by Danish masters. The flat roof of the S.W. tower commands the most extensive inland view (castellan in the court to the l. ; fee for a party 1 Rd.).

Marienlyst, a sea-bathing place, lies ³/₄ M. to the N.W. of the Kronborg. The château of that name, situated on a hill, is now a 'Curhaus'. A small column near it, without inscription, is said to mark Hamlet's grave (reached through the Curhaus, fee 2 m.). Nearer the beach is the *Badehôtel.*

Pleasant walk hence along the wooded coast to (4½ M.) **Helle-bæk**, another sea-bathing place. On the Swedish coast opposite the red château of *Sophienro* and the coal mines of Höganäs (see below) are conspicuous.

Swedish Coast. Opposite the Kronborg lies -the small town of **Helsingborg** (**Hôtel de Mollberg*), an uninteresting seaport with 7000 inhab. — The baths of *Ramlösa*, used as a remedy for gout and rheumatism, are situated 5 M. S'. of Helsingborg.

The pleasantest excursion from Helsingborg is to the **Kullen**, a conspicuous promontory about 14 M. to the N. with a lighthouse at its extremity (carr. to *Kullagaard*, 3 M. from the lighthouse, about 12 Dan.-or 24 Swed. dollars). The road passes the coal-mines of *Höganäs*. The traveller may now return to Copenhagen viâ Malmö on the Swedish coast.

Railway in 2 hrs. by *Billeberga* (junction for the fortified seaport *Landskrona*) to *Eslöf*, the junction of the Helsingborg, Stockholm, Ystadt, and Malmö lines. Thence to Malmö in 1 hr. Stat. **Lund**, with 10,000 inhab., an ancient episcopal see with a celebrated cathedral in the Romanesque style, possesses a university founded in 1666, where the poet *Esaias Tegnér* (d. 1846) was a professor. A monument was erected to him in 1853.

Malmö (**Krämer's Hotel*, a German house; *Gustaf Adolf; Svea Hotel*) is a busy seaport with 21,000 inhab. The station is near the harbour. Steamboats to Copenhagen several times daily, see p. 128.

23. From Hamburg to Berlin.

Railway in 6—8 hrs.; express fares 10, 7 Thlr.; ordinary 7 Thlr. 15, 5 Thlr. 20, 4 Thlr. 5 Sgr.

Custom-house formalities at the Hamburg station. Stat. **Bergedorf**, where peasant-women wearing a peculiar and picturesque costume offer fruit and flowers for sale, belongs to Hamburg. *Reinbeck* and *Friedrichsruh*, in the Sachsenwald with its fine beeches, are favourite resorts of the Hamburgers. At *Schwarzenbeck* the wood is quitted. At stat. **Büchen** the line to Lübeck diverges. Several châteaux and parks with deer are passed. Stations *Boitzenburg*, *Brahlsdorf*, *Pritzier*, and *Hagenow* (junction for Schwerin and Rostock, R. 20).

Stat. **Ludwigslust** (**Hôtel de Weimar*) is an occasional residence of the Duke of Mecklenburg-Schwerin. The château contains some good Dutch pictures and a collection of Sclavonic antiquities. Extensive grounds. The Russian chapel contains the tomb of the Grand Duchess Helena, a Russian princess (d. 1803). At *Wöbbelin* on the road to Schwerin, 5. M. to the N., is the grave of the poet *Theodore Körner*, who fell in battle in 1813 at Gadebusch, near Schwerin.

At stat. **Wittenberge** (**Rail. Restaurant*) on the Elbe, the Magdeburg line (p. 223) diverges. Stat. *Wilsnack* possesses the most ancient church in this district. Stations *Glöven, Zernitz* (station for *Kyritz* and *Wittstock*), *Neustadt* (where the *Dosse* is crossed). Stat. *Friesack* is 9 M. from *Fehrbellin* (E.), where the Great Elector of Brandenburg with 5000 cavalry defeated 11,000 Swedes in 1675. Stations *Paulinenaue, Nauen, Seegefeld*.

At stat. **Spandau** (*Adler*), a strongly fortified town, with 17,386 inhab., the *Havel* is crossed, near its union with the *Spree*. The Church of St. Nicholas, a fine edifice of the 16th cent., contains some remarkable monuments and a very ancient metal font. Near the park of *Charlottenburg* the line crosses the Spree.

Berlin, see p. 1.

24. From Berlin to Stettin.

Railway in 2³|₄—3¹|₂ hrs.; express fares 4 Thlr. 15, 3 Thlr. 10 Sgr.; ordinary 4, 3, 2 Thlr.

Shortly after leaving Berlin, the train passes *Bernau*, a small town which was gallantly defended by its inhabitants against the Hussites in 1432. Armour said to have been captured on that occasion is shown at the Rathhaus. Stat. *Biesenthal;* then *Neustadt-Eberswalde* (*Rail. Restaurant), a busy town on the *Finow Canal,* the seat of the Prussian Foresters' Academy.

    Branch Railway to Wriezen (in 50 min.; 27, 20, 13 Sgr.). Stat. *Falkenberg;* then **Freyenwalde** *(Post; Alexandrinenbad),* a small watering-place in the prettiest part of the Province of Brandenburg. Stat. **Wriezen** is a small town on the *Alte Oder.*

    Beyond Neustadt the Finow Canal is crossed. To the r. the picturesquely situated old monastery of *Chorin*, now a farm, soon becomes visible. The fine early Gothic abbey-church is now in a ruinous condition. Near *Angermünde*, an ancient town with a lofty church, the line skirts the *Paarsteiner See.* The line to Stralsund diverges here (R. 25).

    Schwedt on the Oder, 12 M. to the E. of Angermünde, was once the seat of the Margraves of Brandenburg-Schwedt, descendants of the 'Great Elector', who became extinct in 1788.

    The line traverses the valleys of the *Randow* and *Welse*, and intersects extensive and well-cultivated fields of beet, from which sugar is manufactured. Views of the large *Damm'sche See* are occasionally obtained to the r.

    Stettin. Hotels. *Hôtel de Prusse, Louisen-Str.; Hôtel du Nord, *Drei Kronen, and Deutsches Haus, in the Breite-Str.; at all these, R. 20, D. 20, B. 7½ Sgr.; Wold's Hotel, near the station; Fürst Blücher, Grosse Wollweber-Str.; Zwei Goldne Anker; Hôtel de Russie. —'**Restaurants.** *Hoeven* (formerly *Truchot*), under the Hôtel de.Prusse; *Herbing, Reifschlager-Str. 18, 19; *Tessendorf*, Kl. Dom-Str. 10; *Grand Restaurant*, Schuh-Str. 12.— **Beer.** *Zum luftdichten Schneider*, Breite-Str. 39; *Leichsenring*, Gr. Dom-Str. 13; *Spielvogel*, Kl. Dom-Str. 21; *Louisengarten*, belonging to the Hôtel de Prusse. — *Jenny*, confectioner, with garden, Kleine Dom-Str. — **Baths.** *Moritz* (river, Russian, and other baths) and *Pioneer Swimming Bath* on the r. bank of the Oder. — **Cab** for 1—2 pers. 5, 3—4 pers. 7½ Sgr.

    Stettin, a fortress of the first class, and the capital of the Province of Pomerania, with 76,149 inhab. and a garrison of 6000 soldiers, originally belonged to the Dukes of Pomerania, who became extinct in 1637, then to Sweden from 1648 to 1720, and has subsequently been Prussian. It is a commercial and manufacturing town of great importance, situated on the l. bank of the *Oder*, and connected with the suburb of *Lastadie* (i. e. 'wharf') by four bridges.

    The *Quay*, extending from the station to the steamboat-pier, is the scene of brisk traffic, the water being sufficiently deep (16 ft.) for vessels of considerable size. Stettin possesses 200 sea-going craft. The chief exports are corn, wood, and spirit, valued at 6,000,000 *l.* annually; the imports (averaging 7,000,000 *l.* per annum) are petroleum, train-oil, French wines, and herrings. Since the abolition of the Sound dues (p. 138) the trade of the place has been nearly doubled.

    The town contains little to interest the traveller. The modern *Neustadt* possesses a number of handsome buildings, among which is the *Hauptwache* (Pl. 2). The terrace above the railway station

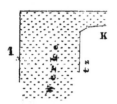

K

1

Werbe

tz

N

S

Stadt

STETTIN.

1. Börse.	C. 2.
2. Hauptwache.	A.B. 2.
3. Jacobikirche.	B. 2.
4. Johanniskirche.	B. 1.
5. St Peter-u.Paulskirche.	B. 3.
6. Kreisgericht.	A.B. 2.
7. Post.	A. 2.
8. Rathaus.	C. 2.
9. Schloss.	C. 1.
10. Standbild Friedr. d. Gr.	B. 2.
11. — Friedr. Wilh. III.	B. 1.
12. Theater.	B. 1.
13. Turnhalle (Gemäldesammlg.)	A. 3.

DIE INSELN
USEDOM & WOLLIN
1:800.000

Kilometer.

Usin

dorf

W See

commands a fine view. The *Turnhalle* (Pl. 13) contains a small collection of *Modern Pictures*, open to the public on Sund. 11—12, and at other times by payment of a fee.

The conspicuous old *Schloss* (Pl. 9), erected in 1575, once the seat of the Dukes of Pomerania, is now occupied by courts of judicature and government-offices. The church contains the burial-vault of the dukes. The painting over the altar represents Duke Bogislaw X. entering Venice on his return from the Holy Land in 1497. The grotesque face of the clock in the tower of the S. wing turns its eyes at each stroke of the pendulum. The tower commands the finest view of the town and environs.

The *Town Hall* (Pl. 8) contains a collection of Russian medals dating from the time of Catharine II. (1729) and Mária Feodorowna (1759), wife of the Emp. Paul, both of whom were born at Stettin. Their fathers (Princes of Anhalt and of Wurtemberg respectively) were Prussian governors of the town. The new *Exchange* (Pl. 1; open 12½—2) is opposite the town-hall.

The Königs-Platz is adorned with a fine marble *Statue of Frederick the Great* (Pl. 10) by Schadow, erected in 1793. In front of the new *Theatre*, also situated in this Platz, stands the marble *Statue of Frederick William III.* (Pl. 11), by Drake.

The *Church of St. James* (Pl. 3) is an important-looking structure on an eminence in the centre of the town. The oldest part dates from the 13th cent., and the whole was remodelled after the siege of 1677. — *St. Peter and St. Paul* (Pl. 5), the most ancient church in Pomerania, was founded in 1124, and after various vicissitudes restored in 1816. The modern stained glass was presented by Frederick William IV. and William I.

The *Logengarten*, 1 M. beyond the Königsthor, a fashionable promenade in the afternoon, commands a pleasant view.

Steamboats to *Copenhagen*, see p. 126). To *London, Hull,* and *Leith* several times a month, the voyage in each case occupying 4—5 days.

To Swinemünde a steamer daily in summer at 12. 30, in 4 hrs (fares 1 Thlr. 15 Sgr.; 1 Thlr.), a pleasant trip. Immediately after starting, *Frauendorf,* a place of popular resort, is visible among the trees on the l. The boat next passes the *Damm'sche See,* enters the broader *Papenwasser,* and then the *Stettiner Haff,* 2 hrs. from Stettin, a fresh-water basin 75 M. in circumference, divided into the *Grosse* and *Kleine Haff,* from which the Oder empties itself into the Baltic by means of three channels, the *Peene, Swine,* and *Dievenow,* thus forming the two large islands of *Usedom* and *Wollin.* The steamboat enters the Swine. To the r. rise the wooded *Lebbiner Sandberge;* on the l., farther on, is the *Friedrichsthaler Forst,* which extends as far as Swinemünde.

Swinemünde (*Hôtel de Prusse; Hôtel de l'Europe; Drei Kronen*), the capital of the two islands, with 7000 inhab., situated in *Usedom,* 1½ M. above the mouth of the Swine, was founded in 1740, and is now the seaport for the heavier vessels trading with Stettin. At the mouth of the *Swine,* which is protected by fortifications, are two massive breakwaters, ¾ M. in length, forming the entrance to the harbour. On the E. bank are new docks and a lighthouse 210 ft. in height, commanding an extensive view. Swinemünde is also a sea-bathing place. The beach, 1 M. to the N. of the town, is reached by a shady road through the *Plantage,* passing the *Wilhelmsbad.*

The road to *Heringsdorf*, 4¹|₂ M. from Swinemünde (one-horse carr.
1 Thlr.) passes the fishing village of *Ahlbeck* (Inn), a small sea-bathing
place.

Heringsdorf *(Lindemann's Hotel; *Gesellschaftshaus;* lodgings generally
full in the season),* charmingly situated in the midst of beech woods, is a
favourite sea-bathing place (2000 visitors annually). Fine view from the
Kulm. The beach and the wooded heights near it afford pleasant walks.
Extensive prospect from the *Streckelberg* (164 ft.),-7 M. to the N.W.; near
which is *Koserow* (*Karstädt's Inn).

Vineta, the traditional fortress and prosperous capital of the Wend
settlers on the coast of the Baltic, is said to have been situated at the
base of the Streckelberg, until at a very remote period it was overwhelmed
by the sea. The imaginative may still distinguish its vast towers and
palaces far beneath the surface of the water.

From Stettin to Misdroy. Steamboat to Latzig daily during the
bathing season, except Sund., at 12. 30, in 4 hrs.; fares 1 Thlr. 5, 25 Sgr.;
from Latzig to Misdroy 1¹|₂ M., Omnibus 2¹|₂ Sgr. — Steamboat route as
far as the entrance to the Swine, see above; the vessel then steers to the
N. and stops at *Latzig*.

Misdroy *(*Deutsches Haus; *Herzberg's Hotel;* lodgings often full),* very
pleasantly situated between two wooded heights on the N.W. coast of the
island of *Wollin*, is a well organised bathing-place. Pretty walks near
the conspicuous new church, on the beach, to the Kaffeeberg (view), to
the Jordansee (4 M.), &c.

To Wollin and Cammin a steamboat also runs daily from Stettin,
except Sund. — From *Wollin*, the ancient, but now unimportant capital of
the island, a diligence runs to Misdroy and Swinemünde.

25. From Berlin to Stralsund. Rügen.

Railway in 5¹|₂–6¹|₂ hrs.; fares 7 Thlr., 5 Thlr. 8, 3 Thlr. 15 Sgr.
The route is the same as the preceding as far as *Angermünde*
(p. 140). Next stations *Greiffenberg, Wilmersdorf, Seehausen.*

Prenzlau *(Hôtel de Prusse; Deutsches Haus; Schneyer's Hotel),*
on the *Ucker*, the ancient capital of the Uckermark, with 16,000
inhab., lies at the N. end of the *Uckersee*, a lake 3¹|₄ M. in length
and of nearly equal breadth. The Gothic *Church of St. Mary,* dating
from 1340, is one of the finest brick structures in this district.
Handsome town-gate.

Stat. *Nechlin;* then **Pasewalk** *(Stuthmann's Hotel),* the junction
of the lines to *Stettin* and to *Schwerin* and *Hamburg* (R. 20). Several small stations.

Anclam *(*Traube; Böhmer),* with 13,000 inhab., on the *Peene,*
which is here navigable for small sea-vessels, and was formerly the
frontier between Prussia and Sweden, contains several picturesque
old houses. The tower of the Steinthor is particularly fine. The
Hohe Stein, an ancient watch-tower 2 M. from the gate, was erected to protect the town against the Counts of Schwerin. — Diligence
by the *Pinnow Ferry* to Swinemünde daily.

Stat. *Züssow* is the junction for *Wolgast* (reached in ¹/₂ hr.),
a busy commercial town on the *Peene*, and the ancestral seat of the
Dukes of Pomerania.

Greifswald *(*Deutsches Haus; Hôtel de Prusse; Hôtel du Nord),*
a town with 17,208 inhab., possesses a university founded in 1456

(300 students), and several picturesque gabled houses, especially in the market. The *Monument* in the Universitäts-Platz commemorates the 400th anniversary of the foundation of the university. In the vicinity are salt-works of some importance. The small river *Ryck*, or *Hylde*, connects Greifswald with the *Greifswalder Bodden*, a broad arm of the Baltic, 2¼ M. distant. Near the mouth of the river are the ruins of the Cistercian monastery of *Eldĕna*, destroyed by the Swedes, and the buildings of an agricultural school of that name. — Steamboat to *Rügen*, see p. 145.

From stat. *Miltzow* a diligence runs by *Stahlbrŏde* and the *Glewitz Ferry* to *Garz* in the island of Rügen; see p. 145.

Stralsund (**Goldner Löwe; *Hôtel de Brandebourg; Römischer Kaiser; Hôtel Bismarck*, near the post-office), the capital of a province of that name, and a fortress of the second class, with 26,731 inhab., lies in a plain on the *Strelasund*, a strait 2 M. wide, which separates Rügen from the mainland. The town is entirely surrounded by water, being connected with the mainland by three bridges only. The lofty gabled houses, the towers, and the Gothic churches of brick resemble those of Rostock and Lübeck.

Stralsund was founded in 1209, and soon attained to such prosperity that in the 14th cent., of the Hanseatic towns on the Baltic, it was second in importance to Lübeck alone. The citizens adopted the reformed faith at an early period, and were therefore on the side of Sweden during the Thirty Years' War. In 1628, aided by Danish and Swedish vessels, they gallantly defended their town against Wallenstein, who had sworn to take it, 'though it had been attached by chains to heaven', but was compelled to abandon the siege after sustaining a loss of 12,000 men. By the Peace of Westphalia in 1648 the town, together with the province of Vor-Pommern and the island of Rügen was ceded to Sweden, to which, notwithstanding its capture by the Great Elector in 1678, and by the Prussians, Danes, and Saxons in 1715, it continued to belong down to 1815, when it became Prussian.

On leaving the station, the traveller passes through the Tribseer Thor and reaches the *Neue Markt* in a straight direction. The *Marienkirche*, situated here, erected in 1416—78, is a vast brick structure with a transept, aisles, and a series of chapels between the flying buttresses. Two modern stained glass windows were presented by Frederick William IV. The tower affords a fine survey of the peculiar, insulated position of Stralsund, part of the island of Rügen, etc. (Sacristan at the back of the church, No. 18).

Opposite the Marienkirche, to the N., a broad street leads to the l. to the *Alte Markt*; a fine mediæval Platz. The handsome *Rathhaus* here, with its rich façade, was erected in 1316, and enlarged in the 18th cent. The provincial museum on the upper floor contains a collection of Northern antiquities of some value.

Beyond the Rathhaus rises the *Nicolaikirche*, a church resembling the Marienkirche, but on a smaller scale. The high-altar, carved in wood in the 15th cent., represents the Passion. A bronze slab to the memory of a burgomaster of Stralsund dates from 1357. Benches of the 16th cent.; at the entrance to those of the Krämer, or mer-

chants, is the polite intimation : ' Dat ken kramer ist de blief da
buten, oder ick schla em up de Schnuten' (literally,. 'He that's no
merchant stay without, or else I strike him on the snout!'). The
sacristan lives opposite the S.W. tower.

From the Alte Markt the *Fährstrasse* (see below) descends to
the Fährthor, outside which is the steamboat quay.

A stone built into the wall, near the *Frankenthor*, bears a
Swedish inscription recording that Charles XII. defended the town
at the siege of 1715. In the Strelasund, to the S.E. of the Frankenthor, is the small fortified island of *Dänholm*.

In 1809, when the war between France and Austria broke out, Major
Ferdinand v. Schill, a distinguished Prussian officer of hussars, quitted Berlin with his regiment without the knowledge of the king, with a view to
effect a patriotic rising against the French in N. Germany. His noble
effort was however premature and met with little response, and he and
his corps were eventually driven back to Stralsund by the Westphalian
and Dutch allies of the French. The town was taken by storm, and after
a heroic defence Schill and most of his corps were killed in the streets.
Eleven captured officers were afterwards shot at Wesel by order of Napo-
léon. The spot where Schill fell is indicated by an inscription in the
pavement of the Fährstrasse (opposite the house A. No. 67). His head was
preserved in spirit at Leyden till 1837, when it was finally interred at
Brunswick. His body reposes in the *Kneiper Cemetery*, 3|4 M. from the
gate of that name. The grave, in the N.E. angle, was originally marked
by a simple iron slab without a name, bearing the inscription, partly from
Virgil (Æn. II. 557):

> *Magna voluisse magnum.*
> *Occubuit fato: 'jacet ingens litore truncus,*
> *Avolsumque caput: tamen haud sine nomine corpus.'*

A monument has since been erected to the memory of the intrepid soldier.
Steamer to Malmö in Sweden 3 times a week in 8—9 hrs.; railway
thence by *Jönköping* and *Falköping* to *Stockholm* in 1¹|₂ day.

Rügen.

Comp. Map.

Plan of Excursion. Steamboat in the afternoon to *Lauterbach*, walk
or drive to *Putbus*, and spend the night there. 1st Day. Drive in 1¹|₂, or
walk in 2¹|₂ hrs. to the *Jagdschloss;* walk in ¹|₂ hr. to Binz and *Aalbeck*,
row or sail thence to *Sassnitz* in 2¹|₂ hrs., and walk to *Stubbenkammer* in
3 hrs. — 2nd Day. Walk in 2¹|₂, or drive in 1¹|₂ hr. to Sagard, and return
thence to *Stralsund*, either by steamboat viâ *Polchow*, or by carriage viâ
Bergen. — If the traveller have three days at his disposal, he may drive
on the second by the *Schaabe* to *Arcona* in 7 hrs. (or walk to *Lohme* and
row or sail thence), and return to Stralsund on the third from *Breege* (by
steamboat, arriving at 9 a.m.), or by *Vieregge* and Bergen (see p. 149).
Arcona, however, is inferior to Stubbenkammer, and should either be seen
first, or entirely omitted.

The above mode of exploring the island is the pleasantest, and affords
considerable variety, but a carriage may be hired for the whole excursion
at Putbus, Bergen, Polchow, or Sagard.

Putbus and *Sassnitz* are the most attractive places for a prolonged stay.

Carriages with two horses may be hired at Putbus, Bergen, Alte Fähre,
and Sassnitz., and at Polchow and Stubbenkammer if ordered previously.
Usual charges from *Putbus:*. to the pier at Lauterbach 15, Friedrich-Wil-
helmsbad 20, per hour 25 Sgr.; to the Glewitz Ferry 3 Thlr. 10, Neuencamp (p. 146) 1 Thlr., Garz or Bergen 1 Thlr. 20, for each hour of wait-
ing above 2 hrs. 5 Sgr.; Jagdschloss and back in ¹|₂ day 2¹|₂ Thlr.; to
Stubbenkammer and back in one day 6, or by the Jagdschloss and back

THE ISLAND OF RÜGEN

500 000

English Miles

armstadt, Ed. Wagner

in two days 8, or back by Bergen 9 Thlr.; either of these three last routes by Sassnitz 1 Thlr. more; to Stubbenkammer by the Jagdschloss and by Bergen to Alte Fähre 12 Thlr.; to Arcona and back by Stubbenkammer and the Jagdschloss in three days 13 Thlr. (tolls included in each case.

Sailing Boats. From Lauterbach to the island of Vilm, with stay, 1 Thlr., to Mönchgut $2^1/_2$ Thlr.; from Aalbeck to Sassnitz 3, to Stubben- kammer 4 Thlr.; from Sassnitz to Stubbenkammer 4 Thlr.; from Lohme to Arcona $3^1/_2$ Thlr.

Diligence between Stralsund and Bergen, Stralsund and Garz, and Stralsund and Putbus twice, between Miltzow and the same places once daily; between Bergen and Putbus once, between Bergen and Sagard twice daily. In summer a post-omnibus also runs between Putbus and Sassnitz.

Steamboat from *Eldena (Greifswald)* to *Lauterbach (Putbus)* in summer daily, except Sund., in 2 hrs., fares 30, 20 Sgr.; Omnibus from Lauterbach to Putbus 3 Sgr. — From *Stralsund*, from 15th June to 15th Aug. daily at 2.45 p.m. (after the arrival of the Berlin express train) by *Breege* (arrival at 6 p.m.; to Arcona, see p. 148) and *Polchow* (arr. 8 p.m.) to *Ralswiek* (arr. 8.30 p.m.), 3 M. from Bergen; returning from Ralswiek at 6.45 p.m., arr. at Stralsund at noon. Before 15th June and after 15th Aug. the steamers depart from Stralsund on Tuesd., Thursd., Saturd., from Rals- wick on Mond., Wed., and Frid. Fare for the single trip 1 Thlr. $2^1/_2$ or $17^1/_2$ Sgr.

Ferries. Steamboat hourly between Stralsund and the Alte Fähre in 10 min.; sailing-boat between Stahlbrode ($4^3/_4$ M. to the N. of *Miltzow*, p. 143), and Glewitz in 30—40 min., 5 Sgr.

Rügen, the largest island belonging to Germany (400 sq. M.), with 45,677 inhab., is separated from the mainland on the S.W. by the *Strelasund*, which at the narrowest part is $1^1/_2$ M. in breadth. The deep bays by which the island is indented in every direction form a number of peninsulas, connected with it by narrow strips of land only. The most important of these are *Wittow* and *Jasmund* on the N. and *Mönchgut* on the S. side of the island. Rügen, which was originally inhabited by the Germanic Rugii, was afterwards oc- cupied by a Sclavonic race, who resisted the influences of Christ- ianity and civilisation down to the middle of the 14th cent. In 1478, after the native princes had become extinct, the island was annexed to W. Pomerania, the vicissitudes of which it thenceforward shared (comp. p. 143). The blue bays, the magnificent beech forests, and the traditionary traces of the heathen rites of the ancient Germans (p. 148) invest Rügen with a peculiar interest. Stubbenkammer, the most beautiful point, will amply repay the traveller.

Putbus (**Fürstenhof*, in the Promenade; **Bellevue*, in the Cir- cus; **Hôtel du Nord*, at the corner of the Promenade and the Circus; charges in all, R. 20, L. 6, A. 5, B. $7^1/_2$ Sgr.; *Adler*, unpretending. At Lauterbach, the **Victoria Hotel*, and near it the **Badehaus*, the latter for a prolonged stay), a handsome modern watering-place, founded in 1810 by the proprietor, the Prince of Putbus, whose estates are 120 sq. M. in area and contain 13,000 inhab., lies about 2 M. from the sea. The town consists chiefly of the *Promenade* and the *Circus*, the latter of which is adorned with a monument to the founder.

The *Palace*, in the park, was erected in the late Renaissance

style on the site of an older building, which was burned down in
1865. Fine terrace at the back. In front of it rises a *Statue* of
the late prince, by Drake. The park, with its beautiful walks, contains the handsome mausoleum of the princely family. The bathing-places are $2^1/_4$ M. distant (after $1^1/_2$ M. the road to the l. must
be followed), near *Lauterbach* (hotels, see above), which is charmingly situated on the *Rügen'sche Bodden*. Omnibus thither 5—6
times daily (3 Sgr.). The beautiful island of *Vilm* (boat see above),
with its magnificent oaks and beeches, should be visited.

Near *Neuencamp*, on a small peninsula, 3 M. to the S. of Putbus, is a *Monument* to the 'Great Elector', erected on the spot where
he landed with his army in 1678 for the purpose of wresting the island from the Swedes.

To the *Jagdschloss*, $7^1/_2$ M., a good and well shaded road,
on which lies ($1^1/_2$ M.) *Vilmnitz*, with a church containing the burial-place of the Counts and Princes of Putbus. At *Gross-Stresow*,
to the r. near the coast, there is a monument to Frederick William I.
of Prussia. The *Granitz*, a beautiful deer-park in which the Jagdschloss (or 'hunting château') is situated, is entered by a gate (carriage $2^1/_2$ Sgr.).

The **Jagdschloss**, erected from designs by Schinkel in 1835—
46, and situated on an eminence, contains several good modern
pictures by *Kolbe* and *Eibel*, and a collection of Rügen antiquities.
The platform, to which an iron stair ascends, commands a fine *view
(fee $7^1/_2$ Sgr., for a party 20 Sgr. to 1 Thlr.). The forester keeps a
small *Inn* at the foot of the hill. The *Kieköwer* and other points in
the park can only be visited by permission of the forester, and under
the guidance of an under-keeper ($2^1/_2$ Sgr. per hour).

The rugged peninsula of **Mönchgut** may be visited from Putbus
by boat (see p. 145); view from the *Grosse Pehrd*, the E. extremity
of the peninsula, 7 M. from the Jagdschloss; also from the Baken-
berg in *Gross-Zicker*, whence the curious indentations of Mönchgut
are best observed, and from *Thiessow* on the S. extremity.

From the Jagdschloss a road descends to the N. (r.) to the ($1^1/_2$
M.) hamlet of *Binz*, which with *Aalbeck*, a hamlet to the r. nearer
the coast, is frequented as a bathing-place. The beach is the best in
Rügen. Sailing-boat to Sassnitz 3 Thlr. The road next passes the
picturesque *Schmachter See*, bounded on the W. by wooded hills,
traverses the isthmus termed the *Schmale Heide*, and then unites
with the road from Putbus to Sagard, not far from the (3 M.) forester's house of *Prora*.

A slight digression may be made to the *Schanzenberg*, near (1 hr.)
Lubkow, an open eminence in the midst of the woods, commanding an extensive view. Immediately beyond the Schmachter See follow the road to
the l. to *Dollahn* and *Lubkow*, turn to the r. from the latter on the Putbus
and Sagard road for $3/_4$ M., then ascend to the l. by an oak to the top of
the hill in 5 min. The forester's house of Prora (see above) is $1/_2$ M.
beyond this point.

: *Neu-Mucran* (poor inn), 4½ M. from the forester's house, is next reached. The road divides here. That to the l. leads to (3¾ M.) Sagard, see p. 148. — That to the r. leads by *Mucran* and the estate of *Lanken* to *Crampas* and **Sassnitz** (**Paulsdorff's Hôtel; *Küster; Gothan*, all often crowded in summer; another new *Hôtel* opened in 1873). The latter, prettily situated at the mouth of a ravine, is a sea-bathing place. Best survey from the *Fahrenberg*, a wooded hill between Crampas and Sassnitz, on the slope of which Paulsdorff's Inn is situated.

   From Sassnitz to Stubbenkammer, about 8 M., either by sailing-boat (2 Thlr.), or on foot through beautiful beech forest, the path being indicated by finger-posts, and commanding occasional glimpses of the rocky and romantic coast. Another path recommended to the traveller is that by the **Wissower Klinken*, a series of chalk cliffs resembling those of Stubbenkammer. A finger-post in the wood, 2 M. from Sassnitz, indicates the route thither to the r.; beyond the cliffs the beach is followed, and the routes then unite at the *Kieler Bach*. Near Stubbenkammer the Victoria Sicht and Wilhelm I. Sicht (see below) are passed.

   *Stubbenkammer (from the Sclavonic *stopien*, steps, and *kamien*, a rock) (*Inn*, often full, R. 20, D. 20, B. 7½, L. 5 Sgr.; tolerable quarters at *Eichstädt's* at *Nipmerow*, 2 M. from Stubbenkammer, or at *Lohme*, p. 148), the finest point in Rügen, situated on the E. coast of the peninsula of *Jasmund*, is a furrowed chalk cliff, rising to a height of 420 ft. almost perpendicularly from the sea, the summit of which, termed the **Königsstuhl*, commands a beautiful view. To the l. is a rugged precipice of chalk; in the distance the lighthouse of Arcona (p. 148); to the r. the *Kleine Stubbenkammer*. The latter, termed the *Wilhelm I. Sicht* since the visit of the king in 1865, commands a fine survey of the Königsstuhl itself. A third point, named the *Victoria Sicht* since 1865, is a few minutes' walk farther. Between the Königsstuhl and the Kleine Stubbenkammer a winding path descends, passing the clear and cool *Golcha-Quelle*, in 10 min. to the foot of the cliffs, of which an imposing survey is obtained from below.

   An illumination of the cliff at night by means of red hot charcoal produces a striking effect (each spectator 5 Sgr.). In 1864 a naval engagement between Prussian and Danish vessels took place off Jasmund.

   The E. side of the peninsula of Jasmund is clothed with beautiful beech-forest, termed the *Stubbenitz*, extending along the coast for 12 M., and said to have been regarded as sacred by the ancient Rugii. In this forest, about ¼ hr. from Stubbenkammer (finger-post on the road to Sassnitz, to the r., 10 min. from the inn), lies the **Herthasee**, a small lake about 200 yds. in diameter, on the W. bank of which rises the *Herthaburg*, a semicircular mound, 50 ft. in height. Several 'altars' found in the neighbourhood appear to mark this as the scene of ancient religious rites. One of these, near the foot of the Herthaburg, about a hundred paces to the r. of the path from the road to the lake, is provided with runlets supposed to have been designed for the escape of the blood. Tacitus (Germ. 40) mentions the mysterious rites of the goddess Hertha, or Nerthus, but the tradition which points out this spot as the scene of her worship is probably unfounded.

From Stubbenkammer to Arcona. A boat for this excursion should be hired at *Lohme* (inn tolerable), a fishing village 1½ M. to the N. of Stubbenkammer, and sometimes visited as a sea-bathing place, or at *Glowe*, at the S. end of the Schaabe (see below). The voyage occupies 2—4 hrs., according to the wind. The fatiguing *Road* (20 M.) leads by the *Schaabe*, a narrow, sandy isthmus 5 M. in length, connecting the peninsulas of Jasmund and *Wittow*. The usual route to Arcona now runs inland by *Altenkirchen* (Inn), where a figure built into the wall of the church is said to be that of the idol Swantewit, but the coast road by *Goor* and *Vitte*, is far preferable. At Vitte the pastor of Altenkirchen preaches on eight consecutive Sundays during the herring-fishery to the fishermen assembled on the beach by their boats.

The promontory of **Arcona**, the most N. point of Rügen, 206 ft. above the sea, is crowned with a lighthouse (which is also a good inn), 75 ft. in height. The view embraces the coast of Jasmund, the island of Hiddensöe, and the Danish island of Möen in the distance. Here once stood the ancient stronghold of the Wends, consisting of a circular intrenchment 20—40 ft. high, and containing the temple of their four-headed idol Swantevit. It was taken and destroyed by the Danes under Waldemar I. in 1168.

The traveller is recommended to return from Arcona by Altenkirchen (see above) and (7½ M.) *Breege*, a large fishing-village on the N. shore of the Breeger Bodden (steamboat to Stralsund, or to Polchow, or Ralswiek, see p. 145). From Breege a sailing-boat may be taken direct to *Vieregge* (in 1 hr., 1 Thlr.), or the traveller may cross by the ordinary ferry from *Cammin* (3 M. from Breege) to *Vieregge* in ¼ hr. Between Vieregge and (1½ M.) *Neuenkirchen* (Inn) rise the *Hochhilgord* hills, employed in ancient times as places for sacrifice and burial, whence a view of the N. part of the island is enjoyed. Bergen (p. 149) is 9 M. distant. The regular carriage-road from Arcona to Bergen by *Altenkirchen* (Inn), *Wieck*, the *Wittow Ferry*, and *Trent* is uninteresting.

Most travellers prefer to return direct from Stubbenkammer to Stralsund. A tolerable road leads by *Nipmerow* (Inn), *Poissow*, and *Volksitz* to (7½ M.) **Sagard** *(Fürstenkrone)*, from which a diligence runs twice daily to Bergen; or the traveller may proceed to *Polchow*, about 2½ M. from Sagard, and return thence to Stralsund by steamboat (see p. 145). To the N. of Sagard and E. of *Quoltitz* is a so-called 'Opferstein', or altar, resembling those already mentioned

(p. 148). To the S. of Sagard, immediately to the l. of the Bergen road, is the *Dubberworth*, the largest tumulus, or 'giant's grave', in Rügen. The road from Sagard to (10½ M.) Bergen crosses the narrow passage between the Grosse and Kleine Jasmunder Bodden by a bridge at the *Lietzow Ferry*.

Bergen (**Prinz von Preussen; *Rathskeller; Goldner Adler*, unpretending), a town with 4000 inhab., is the capital of Rügen and the neighbouring islands. The conspicuous church with its lofty tower is partly in the late Romanesque style and dates from the 12th cent. The *Rathhaus* contains a small collection of Rügen antiquities. To the N.E., ¼ hr. from the town rises the **Rugard** (490 ft.) the highest point in the island, crowned by an intrenchment, the sole vestige of a stronghold which was destroyed in 1316. The view is very extensive and strikingly picturesque, especially by evening light. The entire island, with its deeply indented coast, its promontories, wooded heights, and extensive bays, lies like a relief-map at the spectator's feet. Stralsund, Greifswald, Wolgast, and the island of Usedom with its sombre pine-forests are also visible. The tower in course of construction here is a monument to the poet *Arndt*.

Steamboat from *Ralswiek* to Stralsund, see p. 145.

Good roads lead from Bergen to Putbus (6 M.), and to Stralsund (16 M.). Diligence see p. 145. At *Samtens*, halfway to Stralsund, the road unites with the Stralsund and Putbus road, on which, about 4½ M. to the S.E., lies *Garz* (Hôtel du Nord), the ancient *Carenza*, formerly the capital of the island, destroyed by the Danes in 1168. A well-preserved circular wall here is a relic of heathen times. *Schoritz*, 2 M. to the S., on the road leading to the Glewitz Ferry, was the birthplace of the poet Arndt (b. 1790, d. 1860).

26. From Berlin to Dantsic and Königsberg.

Railway to *Dantsic* in 10½—13¼ hrs. (express fares 14 Thlr. 2, 10 Thlr. 25 Sgr.; ordinary 13 Thlr. 2, 9 Thlr. 24, 6 Thlr. 16 Sgr.); to *Königsberg* in 12¾—16 hrs. (express fares 17 Thlr. 28, 13 Thlr. 24 Sgr.; ordinary 16 Thlr. 17, 12 Thlr. 13, 8 Thlr. 9 Sgr.).

The country traversed is flat and uninteresting. Stations *Neuenhagen, Straussberg, Dahmsdorf-Müncheberg*.

Diligence from Müncheberg once daily to (7 M.) **Buckow** (*Hoffacker*), a small town situated in a pretty district termed the '*Märkische Schweiz*'. Stations *Trebnitz, Gusow, Golzow*.

Cüstrin (*Kronprinz; Adler*) is a strongly fortified town with 10,000 inhab. at the confluence of the *Warthe* and *Oder*. Frederick the Great, when crown-prince, was once imprisoned by his stern father in the castle here; and on the ramparts, in view of the room where he was confined, his friend Lieut. v. Katte, who was to have accompanied Frederick in his intended flight to England, was beheaded on 6th Nov., 1730.

At **Zorndorf**, 4¹|₂ M. to the N., Frederick the Great and Seydlitz with 30,000 Prussians defeated 50,000 Russians under Fermor, 25th Aug., 1758. The line crosses the Oder and the navigable Warthe. Stations *Tamsel, Vietz, Döllens, Düringshof.*

Landsberg *(Lüdke's Hôtel; *Rail. Restaurant)*, with 19,000 inhab., and a brisk river traffic, is picturesquely situated on the Warthe. At stat. *Zantoch* the *Netze* falls into the Warthe. Stations *Gurkow, Friedeberg, Alt-Carbe.* The sandhills near stat. *Driesen* are planted with vineyards. At stat. **Kreuz** *(Rail. Restaurant)* the lines to Stettin and Posen diverge.

Kreuz lies about half-way between Stargard and Posen, on the Stettin and Breslau Railway.

From Stettin to Posen in 4¹|₄—6 hrs. (5 Thlr. 29, 4 Thlr. 17, 3 Thlr. 6 Sgr.). Near Stettin the line crosses the Oder, and near Damm the *Reglitz,* an arm of the Oder, which falls into the *Lake of Damm.* Beyond stat. *Carolinenhorst* the train passes the *Madü-See,* the largest lake in Pomerania, and famous for its lampreys.

Stargard *(Hôtel Daniels; Stadt Petersburg),* on the navigable *Ihnà,* the most important town in E. Pomerania, with 18,000 inhab., is surrounded by a well-preserved wall, with handsome towers and gateways. The *Marienkirche,* of the 14th and 15th cent., is richly adorned, externally, and of imposing dimensions in the interior. The *Rathhaus* of the 16th cent. and the *Protzen'sche Haus* adjoining the church deserve notice.' — To the S. of Stargard lies the small town of *Pyritz,* where the *Ottobrunnen* has been erected in honour of St. Otho, the apostle of this district. Pretty environs, termed the *Weitzacker;* picturesque costumes.

Several unimportant stations; then *Kreuz,* beyond which the journey is uninteresting.

Posen *(Hôtels de Dresde, de Rome, de France, de l'Europe, du Nord; Bazar.* — Cab from the station to the town for 1 pers. 5, 2 pers. 7¹|₂ Sgr.)', Pol. *Poznán,* the capital of the province of that name, and a fortress of the first rank, with 56,464 inhab. (more than ¹|₂ German, about ¹|₄ Prot., and ¹|₄ Jews), and a garrison of 7000 men, lies at the confluence of the *Cybina* and *Warthe.* It is the most ancient town in Poland, having been the residence of the Polish kings down to 1296. It was also important as a great depôt of the trade between Germany and the East, and was a member of the Hanseatic League in the middle ages. The new part of the town has been erected since it came into the possession of Prussia in 1815. The station is ¹|₂ M. from the Berliner Thor. Massive fortifications. The *Wilhelms-Platz* with the *Theatre* and the *Raczynski Library,* is a handsome square. The oldest building is the *Rathhaus,* in the round-arch style, 1512—30. The *Dom,* or Cathedral, on the r. bank of the Warthe, re-erected in 1775, contains several treasures of art (sacristan to the r., at the corner of the chief façade). On four pillars four **Brasses* of the 15th cent., among them that of the Woywoda, or governor, Gurka (d. 1472); *Monuments* of bishops; sumptuous **Golden Chapel,* erected in 1842 by a society of Polish nobles, in the Byzantine style, adorned with paintings and mosaics and fine gilded bronze statues of the two first Christian Polish Kings, by Rauch; monument in the chapel, adjoining the latter on the r., of the Powodowski family, 1585. — **Fort Winiary,* the citadel of the fortifications, affords the best survey of the environs (tickets at the office of the commandant, Wilhelmsplatz).

From Posen to Breslau in 4¹|₄ hrs., an uninteresting journey.

Bromberg *(Hôtel Moritz; Englisches Haus; *Rios; Schwarzer Adler)* on the *Brahe,* with 28,000 inhab., is the seat of the government of this district. The town owes its commercial importance to Frederick the Great, who caused a canal to be constructed from the Brahe to the Netze, thus connecting the Vistula and the Oder, two

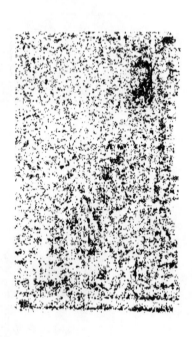

of the greatest rivers in Europe. A monument to him adorns the market place.

From Bromberg to Thorn by railway in 1³|₄ hr. (fares 40, 30, 20 Sgr.). **Thorn** (**Hôtel Sanssouci; Marquardt; Drei Kronen*), with 17,000 inhab., is an old fortified town of some importance on the *Vistula*. The handsome *Rathhaus* of the 14th and 16th cent., the *Krumme Thurm* (i. e. crooked, or leaning tower), the *Kulmer Thor* (with the ancient insignia of the town, a cook with a spoon), the old *Schloss* (erected in 1260, destroyed by the townspeople in 1420), and the *Katzenschwanz*, a handsome watch-tower, are all worthy of inspection. The *Church of St. John* contains a monument to Copernicus (d. 1543), who was born at Thorn in 1473. The *Marienkirche* contains good wood-carving of the 14th cent.

To Warsaw express in 7¹|₄ hrs.; *to Posen*, a direct line is in course of construction.

The line follows the course of the *Vistula*, at a distance of 4—6 M. from it. Stations *Kotomierz, Terespol, Laskowitz, Warlubien, Czerwinsk.*

From Terespol diligence four times daily to **Culm** (*Schwarzer Adler*), an ancient stronghold of the Teutonic Order (p. 156), on the lofty r. bank of the *Vistula*. — A diligence also runs from Terespol to *Schwetz*, 4¹|₂ M. N. of Culm.

From Warlubien diligence five times daily to (9 M.) **Graudenz** (*Gold. Löwe*), a strong fortress, picturesquely situated on the r. bank of the Vistula, which successfully resisted the French in 1807.

From Czerwinsk diligence four times daily to (11¹|₂ M.) **Marienwerder** (**Heltzner*), the seat of government for the district and of a public horse-rearing establishment. *Cathedral* of 1348, and *Schloss* founded in 1233, with two remarkable projecting towers.

Stat. *Pelplin*, the residence of the Bishop of Culm, has a fine cathedral.

Dirschau (*Kronprinz*), where the passage of the Vistula in winter was formerly often attended with great difficulty, now possesses a handsome *Railway Bridge*, completed in 1857, nearly ¹/₂ M. in length.

As the train approaches Dantsic the country becomes more picturesque. Last stations *Hohenstein* and *Praust.*

Dantsic. Hotels. *Englisches Haus (Pl. a), once the English cloth-makers' hall, fine view from the old tower; *Hôtel du Nord (Pl. b); *Walter's Hôtel (Pl. c); Hôtel de Berlin (Pl. d), nearest the station; Drei Mohren (Pl. e); Scheerbart, new, Hundegasse 17; Kronprinz (Pl. f); Deutsches Haus, Holzmarkt 12.

Restaurants. *Leutholz* No. 11, and *Denzer* No. 12 Langemarkt; *Fuchs*, Brodbänkengasse 40; *Rathskeller*, under the Artushof. — **Beer.** *Schneider*, Hundegasse 86; *Gambrinus-Halle*, with garden, at the Ketterhager Thor, near the Hôtel de Berlin; *Heyn*, Kohlenmarkt, adjoining the theatre. — *Selonke*, Langgarten 31, outside the Grüne Thor, with theatre, concerts, &c. — **Confectioners.** *Sebastiani*, Langgasse 66; *Grentzenberg* No. 32, and *a Porta* No. 8 Langemarkt.

Amber. *Hoffmann*, Altstädtischer Graben 92; *Jantzen*, Heil. Geistgasse 114; *Alter*, Breite-Str. 79.

Goldwasser, a specialty of Dantsic, is a liqueur prepared by *Isaac Wedling Widow and Eydam Dirck Hekker*, Breitegasse 52, a firm founded in 1598; ordinary quality 16 Sgr., superfine 1¹|₂ Thlr. per bottle.

Cabs. Per drive 1—2 pers. 5 Sgr., 3 pers. 7¹|₂, 4 pers. 10 Sgr.; luggage to or from the station 2¹|₂ Sgr. for each person. For ¹|₂ hr. 7¹|₂, 10, or 12 Sgr., 1 hr. 12¹|₂, 15, or 17¹|₂ Sgr. At night double fares, but no extra charge for luggage.

Railways. There are two stations at Dantsic, the *Prussian E. Railway*

Station at the *Legethor* (Pl. B, 6) for the line to Dirschau, Marienburg, and Königsberg (pp. 151, 156), and the *Berlin and Stettin Railway Station* outside the *Hohe Thor* (Pl. A, 3), for the line to Neufahrwasser and to Oliva, Zoppot. Stettin, and Berlin (pp. 155, 156).

Steamboats (the quay is outside the Johannisthor, at the end of the Johannisgasse, Pl. C, 3) to *Neufahrwasser* (p. 156) hourly in summer, $2^1|_2$, $1^1|_2$ Sgr.; to *Elbing* (p. 157) by the Vistula and the Frische Haff three times a week, in 8 hrs., 20, $12^1|_2$ Sgr.; to *Stettin* (p. 140) by Neufahrwasser and Swinemünde six times monthly in 28 hrs., 3, $1^1|_2$ Thlr.

Post-Offfce, Pl. 23. *Telegraph Office* (Pl. 27) at the entrance to the Kürschnergasse, near the Langenmarkt.

Sea Baths. The most frequented are at *Brösen*: steamboat hourly in $^3|_4$ hr. ($2^1|_2$ Sgr.) to Neufahrwasser (or by railway, see above), and omnibus thence to Brösen in 20 min. ($1^1|_4$ Sgr.) The *Westerplatte*, beyond the harbour canal, and *Weichselmünde* (p. 155) are also bathing-places.

Chief Attractions. Langemarkt and Langgasse, Rathhaus, Artushof, Marienkirche, view from the Bischofsberg (p. 155), and excursion to the Johannisberg.

Dantsic, or *Dantzig*, Pol. *Gdansk*, with 89,121 inhab., including a garrison of 7000 men, lies near the influx of the united *Mottlau* and *Radaune* into the *Vistula*. The Mottlau flows through the town in two branches, and separates the *Altstadt*, *Rechtstadt*, and *Vorstadt*, the older parts of the town on the l. bank (enumerated from N. to S.), from the modern *Niederstadt* and *Langgarten* on the r. bank; between the branches is the *Speicherinsel* (p. 153). The Radaune enters the town by an artificial channel near the Hohe Thor, and then separates the Altstadt from the Rechtstadt.

Dantsic was originally a Sclavonic-Danish settlement and became the capital of the Duchy of *Pommerellen* as early as 997. In 1310 it came into possession of the Teutonic Order, whose fostering care inspired the town with new life. The German *Rechtstadt* was then added to the still half Sclavonic *Altstadt* and soon became the centre of the business of the city. About 1360 the citizens of Dantsic joined the Hanseatic League and took an active part in the wars of their allies against the Northern kingdoms and the pirates, in which they were aided by the Teutonic knights. With the latter, however, they soon quarrelled, and in 1454, when the Order began to decline, they were induced to place themselves under the protection of Poland. Repeated attempts were made to re-establish the authority of the Grand Master, but they were as often repressed. As an independent state, under Polish supremacy, the city enjoyed extensive privileges, and absorbed almost the entire trade of Poland. When the Hanseatic League took part in the English wars of the Roses, the ships of Dantsic frequently returned home laden with booty. The city embraced the Reformation at an early period, but continued its connection with Roman Catholic Poland. During the incessant wars in which the kingdom was involved in the 16th—18th cent. the town was frequently besieged, but never surrendered, except to the Russians in 1734. The second division of Poland in 1793 at length restored Dantsic to German supremacy. In 1807 the Prussian Marshal Kalkreuth surrendered the town, after an obstinate resistance, to the French Marshal Lefebvre, who in consequence of this success was created 'Duke of Dantsic'. Although retaining the semblance of a free city, Dantsic then became an important French arsenal, especially during the Russian campaign of 1812. In 1814 it was surrendered by the French Marshal Repp to the Russian and Prussian armies under the Duke of Wurtemberg, and when peace was concluded it was again awarded to Prussia.

The town owes its importance as a *Seaport* to its situation at the mouth of the Vistula, which forms the great highway of the extensive Polish corn-trade. This river affords excellent anchorage for vessels of moderate tonnage, while smaller craft and barges penetrate into the heart of the town by means of the Mottlau. In 1840 the Vistula forced a new passage for itself into the sea at *Neufähr*, 7 M. to the E., but strong bulwarks have since been erected to prevent the recurrence of such an event. The corn-trade of Dantsic is the most extensive in Europe, with the exception of that of Odessa. The vast magazines on the *Speicher-Insel* are capable of containing 2¹/₂ million bushels. The timber-trade, the depôts of which are in the *Langgarten* quarter, to the E. of the Speicher-Insel, is also very considerable. Amber is also a specialty of Dantzig. The *Lange Brücke*, a quay on the Mottlau, is the principal resort of the bargemen, most of whom are Poles, wearing picturesque costumes.

Dantsic was the cradle of the infant navy of Germany, the headquarters of which were removed to Kiel and Wilhelmshaven in 1865.

The town still contains many interesting memorials of its past history. While the lofty Church of St. Mary and the Rathhaus recall the period when Dantsic was under the supremacy of the Teutonic Order and a member of the Hanseatic League, the rich façades and interiors of many of the old houses bear testimony to the subsequent prosperity of the merchant-princes of the place.

The RECHTSTADT is the most interesting quarter to strangers. The *Langemarkt and Langgasse (Pl. B, 4) form a single broad street intersecting the town, flanked with many handsome edifices, some of the façades of which were imported from Italy and Portugal. Each house was formerly provided with a 'Beischlag', or landing-place approached by a flight of steps, but this peculiarity of mediæval Dantsic is rapidly disappearing.

The handsome *Rathhaus (Pl. 24), dating from the beginning of the 14th cent., with a beautiful slender tower added in 1561, has recently been admirably restored in the interior (custodian to the l. in the corridor, 5 Sgr.).

GROUND FLOOR. To the l. the *Sommer-Rathsstube* (council-chamber), with good carving on the ceiling and frieze, and fine inlaid work on the windows and doors dating from the 16th cent.; chimney-piece of 1593; among the mural paintings is one representing a listener and a man enjoining secrecy, in allusion to the use of the apartment. Adjacent is the *Winter-Rathsstube*. To the r. on the ground-floor is the *Remter*, the (modern) vaulting of which rests on a single octagonal column of granite. — An ingenious winding stair of wood ascends to the FIRST FLOOR, containing the *Empfangszimmer*, or reception-room, which resembles the Sommer-Rathsstube in its decorations, but is of later date, and the handsome *Arbeitszimmer* of the burgomaster, &c.

The *Neptune Fountain* in the Langemarkt, opposite the corner of the Rathhaus, was cast in Holland about the middle of the 17th cent.

Beyond the fountain a broad flight of steps ascends to the *Artushof, or Junkerhof (Pl. 1), now the Exchange, the former name being derived from the mediæval tradition of King Arthur, and intended to indicate the festive purposes of the building, the latter from the 'Junker', or wealthy merchants of Dantsic, who formerly met here to transact business. The present building dates from the 16th cent.

The *HALL (generally open in the forenoon, entrance by the adjoining house on the l.; business hours 11—2) with fine groined-vaulting, borne by four slender pillars of granite, is very quaintly decorated with pictures, reliefs, and statues from subjects derived from Christian and pagan traditions. In the centre Augustus III. of Poland, in marble. To the r. of the entrance a Last Judgment by *Möller*, 17th cent.; Madonna by *Stech*; Actæon, a strange combination of painting, relief, and antlers; Head of Christ, by *Stech*; Siege of the Marienburg in 1410 (p. 156); Departure of mediæval warriors, a small, but good picture; frieze representing the history of the 'Children of Haymon'; Orpheus playing to his spell-bound audience (with a cleverly painted burning light), &c.

The Langemarkt is terminated on the E. by the *Grüne Thor*, and the Langgasse on the W. by the *Langgasser-Thor*, erected in 1612. Opposite the latter is the lofty *Stockthurm*, now a prison, and adjoining is the *Hohe Thor* (Pl. A, 4), a handsome fortified gateway erected in 1588.

In the neighbouring Kohlenmarkt is the *Old Arsenal* (Pl. 30), a curious Dutch-looking edifice of 1605. The *Altstädtische Rathhaus*, on the opposite bank of the *Radaune*, now a court of justice, is a similar building.

The *Church of St. Mary (Pl. 17), a noble pile, begun in 1343, and completed in 1503, possesses aisles and a transept flanked with chapels between the flying buttresses. Massive W. tower, 248 ft. in height, and ten slender turrets on the gables. The beautiful and varied vaulting of the interior is borne by 28 pillars. The church contains several treasures of art (sacristan, Korkenmachergasse No. 4, to the r., opposite the N. tower).

Gothic *HIGH ALTAR, carved in wood by *Michael Schwarz* in 1517, representing the life of the Virgin in ten sections; fine candelabra of the same date. To the r. a tasteful Gothic ciborium. Modern stained glass at the back of the altar presented by Frederick William IV. 1844. A chapel on the S. side of the choir contains a * *Crucified Christ*, admirably carved in wood. The Dorotheen-Capelle in the N. aisle contains the gem of the cathedral, a large altar-piece with wings, painted in 1467, a bold and grand conception of the * *Last Judgment*, by Memling, formerly ascribed to John van Eyck. It is said to have been painted for the Pope, captured by pirates on its way from Bruges to Rome; re-captured by a vessel of Dantsic, and presented to the church of St. Mary. The French carried it to Paris in 1807, but it was restored after the war. Large FONT, cast in the Netherlands in 1554. Two well executed *Candelabra* in brass, in the nave. The Reinholds-Capelle, to the N.W. of the font, contains a small altar with fine carving. The Allerheiligen-Capelle and 'Spruchstube' contain a valuable *COLLECTION of sacerdotal vestments and ecclesiastical vessels of the 12th—16th cent.

The TOWER commands a good survey of the town (tickets at 40 Heil. Geistgasse, 2½ Sgr.).

The other churches, all brick structures in the Gothic style, are inferior in interest to St. Mary's. *St. Catharine's* (Pl. 11); erected in 1326, and extended in the 15th cent., possesses musical bells. *St. John's* (Pl. 15), completed in 1465, is of noble proportions, but disfigured by restoration. *Trinity* (Pl. 18), completed in 1514, has a curious, richly decorated W. gable. Adjoining it is the old *Franciscan Monastery* (Pl. 32), recently restored, a fine brick edifice in the Baltic style, the ground-floor rooms of which, covered with bold vaulting, are destined for the reception of a museum of Dantsic antiquities, while the upper floor is to be fitted up as a picture gallery.

Kabrun's Picture Gallery in the Handels-Academie, Hundegasse 10, contains about 350 works, chiefly of the Netherlands schools, 2000 drawings and water-colours, and 10,000 engravings and woodcuts (Sund. 11—1).

Herr *Kupferschmidt*, Breitegasse 52, possesses a valuable collection of carved furniture and other objects of art of the 16th, 17th, and 18th cent., to which strangers are readily admitted.

View of the picturesque town and its environs from the *Bellevue* inn, at the entrance to the fort on the *Bischofsberg*, an ascent of $1/_4$ hr. from the Hohe Thor (p. 154). To the l. rises the fortified *Hagelsberg*.

The *Environs of Dantsic surpass those of any other German seaport. The finest points are easily reached by railway or steamboat.

Mouth of the Vistula. By steamboat (p. 152) to Neufahrwasser, and back by railway (p. 152). The steamer starts from the Mottlau, passes the fortified island of *Holm* and the fortress of *Weichselmünde*, from the green ramparts of which a very ancient tower rises, and stops at Neufahrwasser, the seaport of Dantsic for vessels of heavy burden. Two or three hours may be devoted here to inspecting the piers and lighthouse, and enjoying a bath.

To Langfuhr, Oliva, and Zoppot by the Stettin Railway. Stat. Langfuhr, a suburb of Dantsic, with numerous villas, is connected by a double avenue of fine limes with the Olivaer Thor. A road to the l. in the middle of it ascends to the *Johannisberg* (on the slope of which is the *Bellevue*, or *Zinglershöhe* inn), the top of which (300 ft.) commands a noble and extensive prospect, most beautiful towards sunset. Descend for variety by the pretty *Jeschkenthal.*

At stat. Oliva, a village $3^1/_2$ M. to the NW. of Langfuhr, there is a once celebrated *Cistercian Abbey* suppressed, in 1829, the *Church* of which, dating from 1581, is now that of the parish. The choir contains figures of Polish kings and Dukes of Pomerellen, the S. transept good carving of 1619. The *Refectory* is adorned with portraits of all the abbots from 1170, the date of the foundation of the abbey. The peace which terminated the sixty-one years' Northern war was concluded here between Sweden and Poland on 3rd May, 1660. The *Schloss* of the abbots, the last of whom was a Prince of Hohenzollern, with its *Garden*, is now the property of the emperor.

The *Carlsberg (350 ft.), immediately at the back of Oliva, is a favourite point of view. The survey of the environs is remarkably picturesque, in some respects surpassing the view from the Johannisberg.

Stat. Zoppot (*Kutzbach's Hôtel; Hochbaum's; Curhaus* on the beach), $2^1/_2$ M. farther N., is a sea-bathing place, near which are the *Thalmühle, Elisenhöhe*, and *Königs-Höhe*, all good points of view. The *Adlershorst* (200 ft.), a promontory $2^1/_2$ M. to the N., commands a charming survey of the bay of Zoppot and of another bay farther N., formed by the prominent *Oxhöfter Spitze.*

The *Carthaus*, or suppressed Carthusian monastery of *Marien-Paradies*, $18^1/_2$ M. to the S.W. of Dantsic, with the village of that name, lies in a wooded and hilly lake-district. The *Schönberg* (1120 ft.), 9 M. farther S., is one of the highest hills between the Harz and Ural Mts.

From Dantsic to Königsberg. **Dirschau**, see p. 151. The train now traverses a fertile plain, and crosses the *Nogat*, an arm of the Vistula. This district lies below the highest level of these rivers, and is protected from inundation by embankments.

Marienburg *(*König von Preussen; Hochmeister)*, an ancient town on the *Nogat*, with 8000 inhab., was anciently the seat of the powerful knights of the Teutonic Order. The market-place, flanked with handsome arcades, contains the Gothic *Rathhaus*, erected at the end of the 14th cent. The handsome *Town Gates* are of the same period. At the N. end of the principal street rises a small modern Gothic *Obelisk* to the Burgomaster Blume (see below).

The **Schloss*, the grandest mediæval secular edifice in Germany, was at once the residence of the Grand Master and a fortress. The N. and W. façades (the latter best viewed from the bridge over the Nogat) are the finest. It consists of three parts, the *Alte*, or *Hohe Schloss* (Pl. A), the *Mittelschloss* (Pl. B), and the *Vorburg*, which is no longer extant. Principal entrance on the N. side (Pl. e). The sacristan of the Marienkirche lives at the school at the end of the town; the castellan, who shows the Mittelschloss, in the W. wing of that building (Pl. f).

The Teutonic Order, founded in 1191, began in 1231 under the auspices of the Grand Master *Hermann v. Salza* to undertake the conquest and conversion of the heathen Prussians. Each conquered piece of land was protected by castles and provided with German colonists. In this manner *Marienburg* was founded in 1274, at first merely as the seat of a commander of the Order. In 1309, however, *Siegfried v. Feuchtwangen* transferred the residence of the Hochmeister hither, and the castle was extended so as to render it worthy of its new dignity. In 1335 *Dietrich v. Altenburg* began to erect the *Mittelschloss*, which was magnificently completed under *Winrich v. Kniprode* (1351—82). This was the golden age of the Order, after which it rapidly declined. Its moral foundations were sapped by luxury and internal dissensions, and at the same time Poland became its bitter and implacable enemy. Disputes with regard to the frontier caused the outbreak of hostilities in 1407, and in 1410 the Grand Master *Ulrich v. Jungingen* fell at the bloody battle of *Tannenberg*. The greater part of the Teutonic dominions now succumbed to the Polish yoke; and although the *Marienburg* under the gallant *Heinrich v. Plauen* (1410—1413) with the remnant of his knights successfully resisted a siege, and the Peace of Thorn was concluded in 1411, the power of the Order was irretrievably gone. The incursions of barbarian hordes became more frequent, and numbers of the towns and noblesse went over to Poland. The mercenaries employed by the Order moreover rebelled when their pay was in arrear, and one castle after another was pledged to them. At length in 1457 the Marienburg itself thus fell into their hands and was sold to the Poles, who at the same time took possession of the whole of W. Prussia. The Grand Master escaped to Königsberg, and thenceforth retained E. Prussia only as a fief from the king of Poland. The town of Marienburg, however, under its faithful and undaunted burgomaster *Bartholomew Blume*, continued to resist the attacks of their enemy, and did not succumb until three years later. During the Polish supremacy (down to 1772) the Marienburg fell to decay and was frequently altered and disfigured, but in 1817—20 the venerable Mittelschloss was restored. The Hochschloss is still in a ruinous condition, while the site of the Vorburg is now covered with modern buildings and intersected by the railway.

The HOCHSCHLOSS (Pl. A), next to the town, encloses a quadrangle, formerly surrounded with cloisters, and contains the **Marienkirche* (Pl. a), a pure Gothic structure, but disfigured by the Jesuits, which the visitor enters by the elegant 'Golden Gate'. It contains the old choir stalls of the knights. A niche on the exterior, on the E. side, contains an inlaid **Statue* of the Virgin, 26 ft. in height. The *Chapel of St. Anna* beneath the church contains the ancient burial vault of the Grand Masters,

The *MITTELSCHLOSS (Pl. B), adjoining the Hochschloss, forms an irregular quadrangle, about 100 yds. in length and 90 yds. in width, and contains the sumptuous apartments of the Grand Master and knights, and the three 'Remter' or halls. A long passage leads to the *Master's Great Hall (Pl. b), the bold vaulting of which is borne by a single granite pillar 19 in. thick and 38 ft. in height. During the siege of 1410 this pillar formed the principal aim of the Polish cannon, a ball from which is still to be seen built into the wall. Stained glass illustrating the history of the Order. Over the door and on the E. wall are portraits of celebrated Grand Masters and generals. The *Master's Small Hall (Pl. c) is also borne by a single column of granite. The *Chapel* of the Grand Master contains the field altar of the Grand Master probably lost at the battle of Tannenberg, but discovered at Gnesen in 1823. One of the finest apartments in the Schloss is the *Convent Remter* (Pl. d), or assembly hall, with remarkably light and elegant groined vaulting, borne by three granite pillars, 16 in. thick. Stained glass windows with subjects relating to the Order. The pinnacles of the Schloss afford a good survey of the environs. The vast *Cellars* are also worthy of inspection.

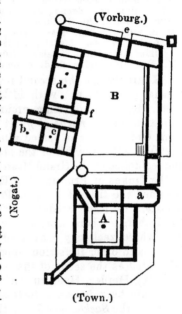

(Vorburg.)

(Nogat.)

(Town.)

The train now traverses the fertile plain of Marienburg and Elbing. Stations *Altfelde*, *Grunau*.

Elbing (*Hôtel de Berlin; *Königlicher Hof), a commercial town on the *Elbing*, with 31,000 inhab., somewhat resembling Dantsic in the older parts, contains nothing to detain the traveller. *Vogelsang* and *Dambitzen* are fine points in the environs. Pleasant excursion by steamboat to *Kahlberg*, a small watering-place; or by *Reimannsfelde* (water-cure) to the deserted monastery of *Cadienen*.

From Elbing by steamboat in 2½ hrs. to the small town of *Frauenburg* (*Zum Copernicus*), the seat of the Bishop of Ermeland, whose modern palace lies on the height. The conspicuous *Dom, fortified with towers and walls, externally a fine Gothic edifice of brick of the 14th cent., is decorated in the interior in the bad taste of the 17th and 18th cent. The celebrated Copernicus, who died here as a canon in 1543, is said to have erected the tower containing the machinery for supplying the cathedral and vicinity with water.

Next stations *Güldenboden*, *Schlobitten*, *Mühlhausen*, *Tiedmannsdorf*, *Braunsberg*, a town on the *Passarge* (Rheinischer Hof; Schwarzer Adler), *Heiligenbeil*, *Wolitnik*, *Ludwigsort*, *Kobbelbude*, *Seepothen*.

Königsberg. Hotels. *DEUTSCHES HAUS (Pl. a); *HÔTEL DE PRUSSE (Pl. b); *BRITISH HOTEL (Pl. c), new; HÔTEL SANSSOUCI (Pl. d), at the station; charges in all, R. 20, D. 20, B. 10 Sgr. — *KÖNIGLICHER HOF (Pl. e); HÔTEL DE BERLIN (Pl. f); SCHWAN; HOTEL DU NORD, Steindamm 117.

Restaurants. *Skibbe*, Kneiphöf'sche Langgasse; *Scharschmidt,* at the
Königliche Hof (Pl. e); *Schwarz*, Kneiphöf'sche Langgasse 27. *Blut-Gericht,* in
the Schlosshof, good wines. *Bellevue*, on the Schlossteich, pleasant view.
— **Confectioners.** *Zappa,* Französische Str. 14; *Steiner*, Junker-Str.; *Po-
matty*, Altstädtische Kirchen-Str. 19, S. side of the palace; *Bucella*, Post-
Str. 3, sells the best 'marchpane', a specialty of Königsberg.
    Amber Wares. *Liedtke*, Altstädtische Kirchenplatz.
    Chief Attractions. Palace, Monuments of Kant and Frederick William
III., New University, Stadt-Museum, Dom.

Königsberg, the second town in Prussia, and seat of the provincial government, with 112,123 inhab. and a garrison of 6680
men, lies on undulating ground on the *Pregel*, 4¹/₂ M. from its
influx into the *Frische Haff*. It was originally a fortress of the Teutonic Order, and was named after their ally King Ottocar of Bohemia
(1255). After the fall of the Marienburg (p. 156) the town became
the residence of the Grand Master, and afterwards (1525—1618) that
of the Dukes of Prussia. The Elector Frederick III. of Brandenburg
assumed the title of king of Prussia here in 1701, and after the
disasters of 1806 Frederick William III. and his court retired to
Königsberg, where schemes for the salvation of the tottering kingdom where zealously canvassed by Baron Stein, W. v. Humboldt,
York, and other illustrious men of the period. Königsberg is also
celebrated as the scene of the labours of the philosopher Kant (1724
—1804), Herder, Hamann, and other distinguished scholars.

    Königsberg is now a fortress of the first rank. The principal
gates are the *Sackheimer Thor*, the *Rossgärter Thor*, and the *Königs-
Thor*, which last is adorned with statues of King Ottocar of Bohemia,
Duke Albert of Prussia, and King Frederick I.

    The lofty *Granaries* on the bank of the river testify to the com-
mercial importance of the place, while the *Harbour* generally contains
a number of steamboats, small sea going craft, and Polish barges.
The staple commodities are grain, flax, hemp, and spirits.

    The **Palace** (Pl. 19), an extensive building, enclosing a large
quadrangle, with a lofty Gothic tower, situated nearly in the centre
of the city, was formerly the seat of the Teutonic Order, and was
re-erected in 1532—54. It now contains the apartments of the royal
family, government offices, and the Archives (open daily 9—1).
The W. wing contains the *Schlosskirche*, where Frederick I. of
Prussia was crowned in 1801, and William I. in 1861. The Province of Prussia is the cradle of the 'Landwehr', the names of
numerous members of which, who fell in 1813, are recorded on the
walls of the church. Above the church is the spacious *Moscowiter-
Saal,* employed for festivals, exhibitions of art, etc. (custodian in
the E. wing, opposite). The *Tower*, the summit of which is 330 ft.
above the Pregel, commands an extensive prospect (custodian in
the S.W. corner of the court).

    The **Statue of Frederick I.** (Pl. 4) in front of the E. portal of
the palace, was erected in 1801.

    The ***Monument of Kant** (Pl. 6), in bronze by *Rauch*, near the

0   200   400   600   800   1500 Schritt

1. Bank	E 5.	12. Kathol. K.	G. 4.
2. Bibliothek	H 3.	13. Neue Altstädt. K.	F. 3.
3. Börse	E. 5.	14. Neurossgärt. K.	D. 3.
Denkmäler		15. Polnische K.	E. 3.
4. Friedrich I.	F. 4.	16. Maler Academie	H. 3.
5. Friedrich Wilhelm III	F. 3.	17. Post	F. 3.
6. Kant	F. 4.	18. Schauspiel Haus	F. 3.
7. Hospital	G. 5.	19. Schloss	F. 4.
8. Kant's Haus	F. 3.	20. Städt. Museum	H. 3.
		21. Sternwarte	C. 3.
Kirchen		22. Universität neue	F. 3.
9. Dom	E. 5	23. " alte	F. 5.
10. Deutsch. Reform. K.	G. 4.	24. Zoolog. Museum	D. 2.
11. Französ. K.	H. 4.		

land.

H   **I**   **K**

N.W. corner of the palace, completed in 1864, represents the philosopher in his 30th year. The house No. 3 Prinzessin-Str. (Pl. 8), in the vicinity, was occupied by Kant from 1793 to 1804. The *Post-Office* (Pl. 17) is situated opposite Kant's house, and adjoining it the modern *Altstädtische Kirche* (Pl. 13).

In the vicinity is the *Parade-Platz*, or *Königs-Garten*, bounded on the N.E. by the *Theatre* (Pl. 18), and on the N.W. by the New University, and embellished with an equestrian *Statue of Frederick William III. (Pl. 5), by *Kiss*, erected by 'grateful Prussia' in 1851.

Reliefs. 1. Domestic life of the king at Königsberg in 1807—9; 2. The king delivers to Hardenberg the new laws enacted during these years, Scharnhorst and Stein approving; 3. Foundation of the Landwehr in 1813; York between Dukes Alexander and Lewis Dohna gives a musket to a student; Bardeleben leaning on his sword; to the r. in the corner the burgomaster in the Landwehr uniform; to the l. a soldier of the national cavalry regiment. The 4th and 5th scenes represent the blessings of peace.

The **New University** (Pl. 22), completed in 1862, is a fine Renaissance structure by *Stüler*. The façade is adorned with an equestrian figure in relief of *Duke Albert* of Prussia, the founder of the 'Hochschule' in 1544. Below are niches containing statues of Luther and Melanchthon; above, medallion portraits of celebrated Königsberg professors.

Interior. Handsome staircase, borne by marble columns. The SENATE HALL contains a portrait of the Crown Prince as rector, by *Lauchert*, and a bust of Kant in his 80th year, by *Schadow*. The adjacent *AULA is adorned with admirable frescoes, representing the different branches of art and science, and pleasing allegories in the arches above. The carved chairs are also worthy of notice.

The Schlossteichgasse leads from the Königsgarten to the E. to the **Schlossteich**, a small lake intersecting half the town from S. to N., and surrounded by public and private gardens (Bellevue, see p. 158). The bridge across it (Pl. G, 3) at the end of the Schloss-teichgasse is for foot-passengers only. Traversing the Weissgerber-gasse and crossing the Rossgärtsche Markt, the traveller enters the long Königs-Strasse, where a column rises to the memory of the Prussian minister v. Schön. No. 57, near the monument, is the *Kunst-Academie* (Director Prof. Rosenfelder), containing on the upper floor the

*Stadt-Museum (Pl. 20), a choice collection of 300 pictures, chiefly modern (Sund. 11—2, Wed. 11—1; at other times fee 10 Sgr.; custodian Landhofmeister-Str. 2, l. side, a street nearly opposite the museum).

ENTRANCE CABINET. Engravings of the finest pictures in the collection. *Right:* 1st ROOM. *157. *Campanella*, Choir of S. Maria della Concezione at Rome; 272. *Scherres*, Landscape in E. Prussia; 273. *Piloty*, The Abbess of the Chiemsee Nunnery defending it against plundering soldiers of the Thirty Years' War; 114. Portrait of Bessel (p. 160); 110. Portrait of Hamann. — 2nd ROOM. *173. *Köhler*, Finding of Moses; 62. Portrait of an old woman, after Rembrandt; 254. *Brendel*, Flock of sheep; 263. *Hiddemann*; Quartett; 167. *Hübner*, Distress; 195. *C. Sohn*, Lady with a mirror; 278. *Schmidt*, Forest scene; 178. *Maes*, Roman woman praying; 274. *Pauwels*, Persecution of Protestants in the Netherlands; 215. *Gudin*, Sea-piece. — 3rd ROOM. 220. *Hollstein*, Alpenglühen; 226. *Robert*, Woman of Procida; 191.

Schrödter, Jester and cellarman; 255. *W. Sohn,* Gipsy; 192. *Schultz;* Choir of the cathedral of Königsberg; 181. *Pistorius,* Village fiddler; 217. *Gudin,* African coast; 218. *Gudin,* Neighbourhood of Antibes; 258. *Achenbach,* Beach at Scheveningen; 252. *Count Kalkreuth,* Lake in the Pyrenees; 224. *Pistorius,* Cellarman; 179. *Perrot,* Naples. This and the following room also contain a number of old Italian and small Netherlands works. — 4th Room. 270. *Nordgreen,* Scene in Swedish Lapland; 261. *Schleich,* Landscape near Munich; 246. *Watelet,* Rainy day; *210. *Delaroche,* Night of St. Bartholomew; 153. *Blanc,* Going to church. — *Left:* 1st Room. 115. *Wach,* Minister v. Schön; 277. *Dücker,* Coast of the Baltic; 242. *Voltz,* Cattle on the Benedictinerwand in Bavaria; 276. *Brausewetter,* Lady at the grave of her husband; 150. *Adam,* Horses; 259. *Bodom,* Norwegian landscape. — 2nd Room. 188. *Schorn,* Cromwell foretelling the victory at Dunbar; *253. *Lessing,* Monk praying at the coffin of Henry IV.; 262. *Camphausen,* Blücher and Wellington at Belle-Alliance; 243, 244. *Wagenbauer,* Valley of the Inn between Rosenhain and Kufstein; 264. *Tidemand,* Holy Communion in a Norwegian cottage. — 3rd Room. 169. *Jacobs,* Story in the Arabian Nights; 200. *Vennemann,* Nap; 222. *Isabey,* Ships; 160. *Van der Eycken,* Winter landscape; 203. *Waldmüller,* Sunday afternoon; 225. *Preyer,* Still life; 174. *Kolbe,* Battle of the Lechfeld; 141. *Hobbema,* Water-mill; 248. *Girardet,* Souvenir de Suisse; 240. *Verboeckhoven,* Man with a calf; 216. *Gudin,* Sea-piece. — 4th Room. 182. *Lepoittevin,* Bay of Naples; 183. *Quaglio,* Cathedral of Frauenburg; 154. *Blechen,* Ruin of a chapel; *267. *Knaus,* Gipsies reposing; 250. *Leu,* Norwegian scene; *269. *Vautier,* Sunday afternoon in a Swabian village; *189. *Schotel,* Shipwreck. — 5th Room. *249. *Rosenfelder,* Occupation of the Marienburg (p. 156); 198. *Stilke,* Departure of Syrian Christians after the destruction of Ptolemais in 1291; 187. *Schirmer,* Repose after a stormy day; 251. *Weber,* Forest scene; 247. *Behrendsen,* Morning among the Alps; 152. *Bellermann,* Evening on the Manzanares; 177. *Leu,* Waterfall in Norway.

No. 65 in the same street is the *University Library* (Pl. 2), containing 250,000 vols. and MSS. of Luther, etc. (Tuesd., Thursd., and Frid. 11—4, Wed. and Sat. 2—4). Farther on is the *Königs-Thor* (p. 158).

In the quarter termed the *Kneiphof,* on an island in the Pregel, rises the Gothic **Cathedral** (Pl. 9), begun in 1335 (sacristan Dom-Str. 15, S. of the church).

The CHOIR, now disused, contains ancient monuments, the chief of which is that of Albert I., Duke of Prussia (d. 1568), the founder of the university, and a most important personage in the annals of the city. On the N. side the tomb of the Chancellor Kospoth. A number of Grand Masters of the Teutonic Order and Prussian princes are interred in the vaults.

The '*Stoa Kantiana*' adjoining the cathedral, on the N. side of the choir, contains the grave of the illustrious thinker.

The *Old University* (Pl. 23) and the *Kneiphof Gymnasium* adjoin the cathedral.

The *Observatory* (Pl. 21), on an old bastion to the W. of the city, built in 1811—13, was fitted up by the talented astronomer Bessel (d. 1846). Near it are the *Botanical Garden,* Butterberg Nos. 2—3 (in summer Wed. and Frid. 2—6), the valuable *Zoological Museum* (Pl. 24), Sternwart-Str. 5—6 (Wed., Frid. 2—5; strangers admitted on Mond. and Thursd. also), and the *Chemical Laboratory* of the university.

From Königsberg to Pillau by railway in 1³/₄ hr. (fares 1 Thlr. 6, 27, 18 Sgr.). Stations *Metgethen;* to the l. the *Caporn'sche Haide,* an extensive forest, in the centre of which rises the Vierbrüdersäule; *Powayen.*

whence the Galtgarben is visited; *Fischhausen*, 1½ M. from the *St. Adalbert Cross* at *Tenkitten*, which marks the spot where the saint was murdered by the heathen inhabitants in 997; *Lochstedt*, an ancient castle of the Teutonic Order; *Neuhäuser*, a bathing-place surrounded by woods. Then **Pillau**, a fortress at the mouth of the Frische Haff, with a harbour and lighthouse. — *Steamboat* from Königsberg to Elbing by Pillau daily in 8 hrs. (1 Thlr., or 20 Sgr.), a pleasant trip.

Samland (see Map after the Index) is a fertile and wooded district, with several lakes, lying to the N. of Königsberg. The highest point in the Galtgarben (365 ft.), the top of which, reached in 1 hr. from stat. Powayen viâ *Medenau*, is crowned with a large iron cross in commemoration of the War of Independence. Most of the villages on the N. coast are frequented as bathing-places. **Cranz**, the chief of these, lies 20 M. to the N. of Königsberg (diligence daily in 3¾ hrs.), at the S. end of the *Kurische Nehrung*, a sandy tongue of land running N. to Memel, a distance of 69 M. The sand-hills of the Nehrung, attaining a height of 200 ft., are sometimes visited. **Schwarzort**, a bathing-place on the Nehrung, 14 M. from Memel, is chiefly remarkable for its amber-diggings, which yield about 80,000 lbs. annually, worth on an average 27,000 *l.* To the W. of Cranz lie *Neukuren*, *Rauschen*, *Georgenswalde*, and *Warniken*, the environs of the last of which vie in grandeur with Stubbenkammer (p. 147).

Amber of a remarkably pure and solid consistency is found at *Brüsterort*, at the N.W. angle of Samland, where divers are employed in the search. The whole of the W. coast of Samland has for more than a thousand years been celebrated as the '*Amber Coast*'. The yield is most abundant after storms. In 1862 about 4000 lbs., valued at 1800 *l.*, were found near *Palmnicken* and *Nodems* in a single morning. Dantsic is now the principal depôt of this highly prized antediluvian gum. It is exported to the East for pipe mouthpieces, as well as to America, Africa, etc. The right to collect amber, formerly a privilege of the Teutonic Grand Master, and subsequently a royal monopoly, protected by severe laws, is now farmed to private individuals. It is found among the seaweed, and also dug out on the coast, sometimes at a considerable distance from the water. Fragments ½ oz. in weight are valued at 1 *s.* 6 *d.* to 2 *s.*, those of 1 lb. at 15 *l.* and upwards. The milky amber is most esteemed.

From Königsberg to Memel. Railway in 4½ hrs. by *Insterburg* to Tilsit (**Hôtel de Russie; Hôtel du Nord*), a town with 20,336 inhab. on the *Memel*. On a raft below the bridge of boats the peace of 1807 was concluded between Napoleon, Alexander, and Frederick William III., by which Prussia was deprived of one-half of her dominions. From Tilsit by diligence in 15—20 hrs. to

Memel (*Weisses Ross; British Hotel; Victoria Hotel; Weisser Schwan*), a seaport with 19,019 inhab., at the entrance to the Kurische Haff, the most N. town in Prussia, and the central point of the Baltic timber trade.

From Insterburg to *Eydtkuhnen*, the Prussian frontier station, by railway in 2 hrs.; thence by *Kowno* and *Dünaburg* to *St. Petersburg* by express in 24 hrs.

27. From Berlin to Breslau.

a. By Frankfort on the Oder and Kohlfurt.

Railway in 7½—10½ hrs.; express fares 10 Thlr. 9, 7 Thlr. 7½ Sgr.; ordinary 9 Thlr. 15, 7 Thlr. 5, 4 Thlr. 22 Sgr.

Scenery unattractive. Stations *Rummelsburg*, *Köpenick*, where Frederick the Great was tried by court-martial when crown-prince, *Erkner* (to the S. rise the *Müggelsberge*), *Fürstenwalde*, *Briesen*.

Frankfort *on the Oder* (*Deutsches Haus; Goldner Adler; Prinz von Preussen;* restaurants of **Ludwig* and *Eckhardt* in the market), the capital of the district of that name, with 43,211 inhab., and

the largest town in the Province of Brandenburg after Berlin and
Potsdam, was founded by the Wends, annexed to Brandenburg in
1250, and notwithstanding its repeated capture during the Hussite, the Thirty Years', and the Seven Years' wars was always an-
important station on the commercial route to Poland. The Marga-
retha, Reminiscere, and Martini fairs are still much frequented by
Poles. The streets are broad and well built. The *Oberkirche*, or
Church of St. Mary, is a handsome brick structure of the 14th cent.;
the external aisles were added subsequently. Carved altar, richly
gilded, of 1717. Old stained glass. Candelabrum with seven branches,
with reliefs of the 14th cent. A picture by the S. entrance represents the finding of the body of Prince Leopold of Brunswick,
nephew of Frederick the Great, who perished in 1785, while at-
tempting to rescue a family from the Oder during an inundation.
— The handsome **Rathhaus* in the market-place, near the Oberkirche, was erected in 1607. On the S. gable is seen the device of
the Hanseatic League, an oblique iron rod, supported by a shorter
one (thus ⟨). *Theatre* in the large Platz near the railway. The
park on the S. side of the town contains a monument to the poet
Ewald von Kleist, who fell at the battle of Kunersdorf in 1759.

Railways diverge here to *Cüstrin* (p. 149) and to *Posen* (p. 150).

At stat. *Finkenheerd* the *Müllroser Canal*, which unites the
Spree and Oder, is crossed. Stations *Fürstenberg, Neuzelle, Wellmitz*,
Guben (with 16,000 inhab., cloth-factories, and vineyards).

From Guben to Cottbus, see p. 164.

From Guben to Bentschen railway in 3³|₄ hrs., viâ *Crossen*, at the
confluence of the Bober and Oder, the capital of an ancient duchy of the
name which was annexed to Brandenburg in 1538, and **Rothenburg**, another
town on the Oder.

From Rothenburg to Liegnitz by railway in 5 hrs., viâ *Grünberg*,
prettily situated, where sparkling wine is largely manufactured, and **Glogau**
(*Deutsches Haus; Westphal's Hotel*), a fortress on the Oder, with 17,000
inhab. *Liegnitz*, see below.

Beyond Guben the line crosses the *Neisse*. Stations *Jessnitz,
Sommerfeld, Liebsgen*, and **Sorau** (*Länger's Hôtel; Stern*), a manufacturing place with a royal Schloss. Then *Hansdorf*.

From Sorau or *from Hansdorf to Glogau* by railway in 2¹|₄ hrs., viâ
Sagan, the property of the Duke of Sagan and Valençay.

The line intersects the extensive woods of Görlitz. Stations
Halbau, Rauscha, and **Kohlfurt** (**Rail: Restaurant*), where the
lines to Dresden and to Hirschberg (p. 172) diverge. Travellers may
proceed by the latter direct to the Giant Mts. (comp. p. 171). The
Bober is now crossed by a long viaduct.

Bunzlau (*Schwarzer Adler; Kronprinz*), with 8000 inhab., is
famous for its pottery. Monument in the market to the Russian
General *Kutusoff* (d. 1813). About 3 M. E. is the Moravian colony
of *Gnadenberg*. The country becomes fertile and undulating. At
stat. *Haynau* the Prussian cavalry defeated the French in 1813.

Liegnitz (*Rautenkranz; Schwarzer Adler; Krone*), at the confluence of the *Katzbach* and *Schwarzwasser*, with 20,069 inhab.,

formerly the capital of a principality, is now that of a province of
the name. The *Schloss* near the station, rebuilt since 1835, contains the government offices. Museum of industrial products on the
upper floor. The *Rom. Cath. Church* contains monuments of the
princes, who formed the last branch of the ancient Polish Piast
family, and became extinct in 1675. *St. Peter's*, *St. Mary's*, and
two huge towers all date from the 14th cent.

From Liegnitz to Königszelt by railway in 1½ hr., intersecting
(between *Neudorf* and *Brechelshof*) the field of the *Battle of the Katzbach*,
in which, on 26th Aug., 1813, Blücher signally defeated the French and
took 100 pieces of cannon and 18,000 prisoners. A monument was erected
on the field by Frederick William III. Near this spot Duke Henry of
Liegnitz conquered the heathen Mongolians in 1241, but fell in the battle.
His mother St. Hedwig erected a chapel here, on which the monastery of
Wahlstatt, now a military school, was afterwards founded. Next stat.
Jauer, famed for its sausages. — Stat. *Königszelt* (king's tent), the junction
for Breslau, Freiburg, and Frankenstein, derives its name from the tent
of Frederick the Great having once been pitched here during the Seven
Years' War.

From Liegnitz to Hirschberg, 35 M., diligence twice daily in
7½ hrs., viâ *Goldberg* and *Schönau*, through a picturesque hilly district.
Fine view from the *Capellenberg, halfway between Schönau and Hirschberg; finer from the *Hohgulje, or *Hugolie* (2350 ft.), to the r. of the road.
Hirschberg, see p. 172.

Beyond Liegnitz the Breslau train crosses the *Katzbach*. To the
l. the *Kunitzer See*. Stat. *Maltsch*. The *Zobten* (p. 166) is conspicuous in the distance, especially near stat. *Neumarkt*. Stat.
Nimkau. At *Leuthen*, near stat. *Lissa*, Frederick the Great with
33,000 Prussians defeated 90,000 Austrians under Prince Charles
of Lorraine in 1757. On the evening of the same day Frederick surprised a number of Austrian officers in the château of *Lissa* (l. of
the stat.) with the enquiry, 'Good evening, gentlemen! Any room
for me here?' —

Breslau, see. p. 167.

b. By Görlitz and Hirschberg.

Railway to *Görlitz* in 4¾—5½ hrs. (5 Thlr. 18, 4 Thlr. 6, 2 Thlr.
24 Sgr.); thence to *Altwasser* in 4¾ hrs. (3 Thlr. 16½, 2 Thlr. 20, 1 Thlr.
23 Sgr.); from Altwasser to *Breslau* in 2 hrs. (1 Thlr. 23, 1 Thlr. 7½,
26½ Sgr.).

Scenery at first uninteresting. To the l., near stat. *Grünau*, is
Schloss Köpenick (p. 161); the neighbouring *Müggelsberge* and
Müggelseen are often visited from Berlin. Beyond *Brand* begins the
Spreewald, which the line skirts for 25 M. Stations **Lübben** *(Stadt
Berlin)*, at the confluence of the *Berste* and *Spree*; *Lübbenau*
(Braunes Ross), with a château of Prince Lynar; *Vetschau*.

The **Spreewald** is a wooded and marshy district, about 28 M. in length
and 2—5 M. in width, intersected by a network of upwards of three
hundred branches of the Spree. Part of it has been drained, but the
wilder parts are only accessible by boat in summer. The inhabitants are
a Wendish race, who still retain their Sclavonic dialect, costumes, and
manners. The *Untere* Spreewald lies to the N.W. of *Lübben*, the *Obere* to
the N.W. of *Vetschau*. A visit to the latter is not without attraction.
Walk from Vetschau to the (4½ M.) *Gasthaus zum Spreewald* near the

11*

village of *Burg;* walk or row to the (3 M.) *Buschmühle* (2 M. distant is the
Weinberg, a good point of view near Straupitz); row to the (¹|₂ hr.) *Forst-
haus Eiche,* and thence by the village of (¹|₂ hr.) *Leipe* to (³|₄ hr.) *Lübbenau*
(see above).

Cottbus *(Lossow's Hotel; Ansorge's; Goldener Ring),* a busy
town on the Spree, with 18,000 inhab., the junction for Dresden
(p. 190), and for Guben (p. 162), contains considerable cloth-
factories and a mediæval Schloss. The château of *Branitz,* a seat of
Prince Pückler, is 2¹/₂ M. distant. Stat. *Spremberg* (Grundig),
pleasantly situated in part on an island in the Spree; then *Weiss-
wasser.*

   Branch-line in ¹|₄ hr. to **Muskau** *(Grüner Baum; Stadt Berlin)* on
the *Neisse,* where Prince Frederick of the Netherlands possesses a beautiful
**Park,* 2750 acres in area, laid out by the former proprietor Prince Pückler,
and including an **Arboretum.* Modern *Schloss* in the Renaissance style.
The pine-cone and mineral baths of *Hermannsbad* are also situated here.
The shooting lodge of *Hermannsruh* is situated amidst magnificent woods,
7 M. from Muskau.

   The next stations are *Rietschen, Uhsmannsdorf,* and

   Görlitz (*Victoria Hôtel,* Post-Platz; *Rheinischer Hof,* near the
station; *Herbst's* and *Stadt Dresden,* opposite the station; *Preuss.
Hof* and *Gold. Krone* in the Obermarkt; *Prinz Friedrich Karl;
König Wilhelm,* near the station, new; *Strauss,* Marien-Platz), a
busy and rapidly increasing town with 42,732 inhab., situated on
the *Neisse,* and on a very ancient commercial route to Poland. In
1346 it was at the head of the alliance between the six towns of
Upper Lusatia (Görlitz, Bautzen, Löbau, Kamenz, Lauban, and
Zittau), but was afterwards annexed to Bohemia and was frequently
involved in the religious wars of Bohemia and Germany in the
15th—17th cent. In 1635 it became Saxon, and in 1815 Prussian.
The fine Gothic churches, the handsome gateways, the sculpturing
on many of the houses, and the Rathhaus in the Altstadt, all testify
to the age and ancient importance of the town, while the broad and
well-built streets of the new quarters betoken its modern prosperity.

   Leaving the station the traveller proceeds straight through the
Packhofs-Str. and Salomons-Str. and across the Post-Platz, to the
Marien-Platz, where the *Frauenkirche,* erected in 1449—94 and
recently restored (fine portal) is situated. Opposite to it rises the
Statue of the Burgomaster Demiani (d. 1846), to whom the town was
indebted for its rapid development. The neighbouring *Frauenthurm*
with the arms of the town dates from the end of the 15th cent.
Near the Marien-Platz, to the l. (W.) lies the Demiani-Platz, with
the modern *Theatre* and the **Kaisertrutz,* a massive bastion of 1490,
now used as a guard-house and arsenal. Opposite is the Industrial
Museum. To the E. of this Platz is the Obermarkt, with the
Trinity, or *Abbey Church,* of the 13th and 14th cent., which contains some fine wood-carving. Beyond the church is the modern
Gothic *Gymnasium,* occupying the site of the old abbey. A short
distance hence, in the Untermarkt, which is partly enclosed by

arcades, rises the *Rathhaus* of the 14th cent., at the corner of the
Brüder-Str.; the entrance steps with a statue of Justice and the
court should be inspected; on the tower (view) are the arms of the
Hungarian King Matthew Corvinus, with whom Görlitz was allied
against king George of Bohemia. Proceeding towards the N. through
the Peters-Str. the traveller next reaches the

Church of St. Peter and St. Paul, erected in 1423—97, with
earlier W. portal and crypt, one of the most remarkable Gothic
edifices in E. Germany. Interior, with double aisles, borne by 24
slender palm-like pillars. The wooden bridge over the Neisse to the
E. of the church commands a good survey of the choir.

At the *Kreuzcapelle*, to the N.W. of the town, is an imitation of the 'Holy Sepulchre', constructed at the end of the 15th cent.
by a burgomaster of Görlitz, who undertook two journeys to Jerusalem for the purpose.

A beautiful *Park*, beginning on the lofty l. bank of the Neisse
to the S. of the Altstadt, extends round the entire S.E. angle of
the Neustadt. Between the park and the Altstadt is the modern
Rom. Cath. Church in the Romanesque style, to the S. of which is
the *Ständehaus* in the Renaissance style. In the grounds near the
latter is a *Monument of Humboldt*. Best survey of the Neissethal
and the viaduct (see below) from the *Blockhaus* at the S. end of the
promenades, near which is a *Monument to Schiller*.

The *Landskrone* (1421 ft.), a basaltic hill 5 M. to the S.W., with a
castellated inn and belvedere on the top occupying the site of an ancient
robbers' stronghold, commands a fine view. To the *Kreuzberg* near *Jauer-
nick* also 5 M. — To the *Königshainer Berge* 9½ M. — To the Cistercian
Nunnery of *St. Marienthal* near *Ostritz*, in the pretty valley of the Neisse,
9½ M. — At *Moys*, 2¼ M. to the S.W. of Görlitz, *General v. Winterfeld*,
the favourite of Frederick the Great, fell in 1757 in a battle against the
Austrians.

Görlitz is the junction for Kohlfurt (p. 162) and Dresden (p.
185). The line to Breslau ('Silesian Mountain Railway') now crosses
an imposing *Viaduct* of 34 arches over the Neissethal, ¼ M. in
length and 70 ft. in height. Pleasing retrospect. Stations *Nicolaus-
dorf*, *Lichtenau*, and **Lauban** *(Rother Hirsch)*, where another line
to Kohlfurt diverges. Stat. **Greiffenberg** *(Spohn's Hôtel; Dietzel's)*,
prettily situated ¼ M. to the r. of the railway; 1 M. to the S. rises
the ruined castle of *Greiffenstein* (1400 ft.), on a wooded hill, a fine
point of view.

Roads lead from Greiffenberg and Rabishau (see below) to the S., passing the Greiffenstein and the small town of *Friedeberg* to (11 M.).

Flinsberg (1116 ft.) *(Neues Brunnenhaus; Schubert*, poor), a straggling
village in the *Queisthal*, with mineral baths. The oldest spring, discovered
in 1572, is termed the 'Heilige Brunnen'. The *Geierstein* (2648 ft.), 1 hr.
to the E., is a fine point of view. To the S. rises the *Iserkamm*, of which
the highest points are the *Heufuder* (3543 ft.) and the *Tafelfichte* (3629 ft.),
reached in 2½ and 3 hrs. respectively from Flinsberg. At the foot of the
latter lies Bad *Schwarzbach*, 1 hr. from Flinsberg. The *Hochstein* (p. 174)
may be reached hence by ascending the wooded Queisthal, with a guide.

A footpath leads from Flinsberg to the W. in 3½ hrs. to the small
baths of *Liebwerda* (Adler), charmingly placed in the valley of the *Wittig*,

at the foot of the Tafelfichte, with a château of Count Clam-Gallas. Thence
to Friedland (p. 188) 6 M., or by the direct road from Flinsberg 13¹|₂ M.
(see Map, p. 170).

A view of the Giant Mts. to the r. is gradually developed. Stations *Rabishau*, *Altkemnitz*, and *Reibnitz* (omnibus and diligence
several times daily to *Warmbrunn*, 5¹/₂ M., see p. 172), beyond
which one of the finest parts of the journey begins. The *Bober* is
crossed twice, and a succession of views is enjoyed.

Hirschberg, see p. 172. Omnibuses daily to *Warmbrunn* (p. 172)
and to *Schmiedeberg* (p. 174).

Stat. *Schildau*, with a château of the Princess of the Netherlands (omnibus to *Schmiedeberg*, *Jannowitz*, and *Merzdorf*). The
Bober is crossed several times. At stat. **Ruhbank** the line to *Trautenau* and *Pardubitz* (p. 180) diverges.

The train now traverses the valley of the *Lässig* to *Gottesberg*
(1805 ft.), the highest place in this mountain district, and descends
to *Dittersbach*.

Waldenburg (1385 ft.) (*Schwarzes Ross*, R. and B. 20 Sgr.;
Deutsches Haus; *Gelber Löwe*), a busy manufacturing town with
5000 inhab., lies on the *Polsnitz*, and is the centre of a coal-mining
district in the principality of Schweidnitz. Krister's china factory
at the station employs 1500 workmen. There are also considerable
flax mills and linen factories here. Handsome modern Rathhaus in
the Gothic style.

To *Adersbach*, see p. 178. Diligence three times daily from Waldenburg to *Charlottenbrunn*, see p. 182.

Altwasser (1368 ft.) (*Villa Nova*, at the station; *Berger's Hotel*),
with 3000 inhab., possesses mineral springs containing salt and
iron, which have been known since the 14th cent. and attract a
number of visitors, extensive brown-coal mines, iron-foundries, and
a porcelain factory.

To *Salzbrunn*, see p. 181; the Wilhelmshöhe, p. 182. From Altwasser to *Charlottenbrunn* diligence three times daily, see p. 182.

Freiburg (906 ft.) (*Schwarzer Adler; Burg; Schwarzer.Bär;
Rother Hirsch*), a small town, with several weaving factories, is
prettily situated on the hill-side. On the opposite bank of the
Polsnitz lies the village of *Polsnitz*. — To *Salzbrunn*, see R. 31.

Hohenfriedberg, 4³/₄ M. to the N.E. of Freiberg, was the scene of a
celebrated victory gained by Frederick the Great over the united Austrians
and Saxons under Prince Charles of Lorraine. The tower on the *Sieges-
höhe* commands a fine panorama (inn).

Stations *Königszelt*, an important junction (p. 182); *Saarau*,
with foundries and chemical works; *Mettkau*, the station for the
Zobten. To the l. a château of Count Pinto.

From Mettkau diligence twice daily in 2 hrs. to *Zobten am Berge*
(Hirsch), at the base of the Zobten. Near it are *Gorkau* (Inn), prettily
situated, with granite quarries, and the *Rosalienthal* (Inn). Paths easily
found lead from Zobten and from Gorkau to the (1¹|₂ hr.) summit of the
*Zobten (2215 ft.), the finest point of view in Silesia. Chapel, small inn,
and a few fragments of an old castle, destroyed in 1471. Best view from
an open space, about 300 paces from the chapel: to the E. and S.E. the
Moravian-Silesian Mts., among which is the distant three-peaked Altvater;

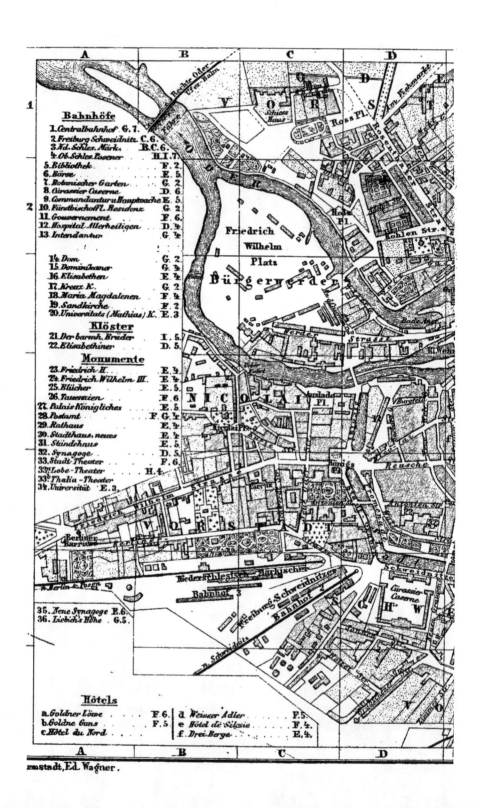

Bahnhöfe
1. Centralbahnhof G. 7.
2. Freiburg Schweidnitz C. 6.
3. Nd. Schles. Märk. B. C. 6.
4. Ob. Schles. Posener H. I. 7.
5. Bibliothek F. 2.
6. Börse E. 5.
7. Botanischer Garten G. 2.
8. Cürassier Caserne D. 6.
9. Commandantur u. Hauptwache E. 5.
10. Fürstbischöffl. Residenz G. 2.
11. Gouvernement F. 6.
12. Hospital Allerheiligen D. 4.
13. Intendantur G. 4.

14. Dom G. 2.
15. Dominikaner G. 3.
16. Elisabethen E. 4.
17. Kreuz K. G. 2.
18. Maria Magdalenen F. 4.
19. Sandkirche F. 2.
20. Universitäts (Mathias) K. E. 3.

Klöster
21. Der barmh. Brüder I. 5.
22. Elisabethiner D. 5.

Monumente
23. Friedrich II. E. 4.
24. Friedrich Wilhelm III. E. 4.
25. Blücher E. 5.
26. Tauenzien E. 6.
27. Palais Königliches E. 5.
28. Postamt F. G. 4.
29. Rathaus E. 4.
30. Stadthaus, neues E. 4.
31. Ständehaus E. 5.
32. Synagoge D. 5.
33. Stadt-Theater F. 6.
33b. Lobe-Theater H. 4.
33b. Thalia-Theater E. 3.
34. Universität E. 3.

35. Neue Synagoge E. 6.
36. Liebich's Höhe G. 5.

Hôtels
a. Goldner Löwe F. 6.
b. Goldne Gans F. 5.
c. Hôtel du Nord
d. Weisser Adler F. 5.
e. Hôtel de Silesie F. 4.
f. Drei Berge E. 4.

rmstadt, Ed. Wagner.

S. the Mts. of Glatz, the large rounded Schneeberg, the Heuscheuer, the Hohe Eule, the fortifications of Silberberg, then above Schweidnitz the Riesenkamm; W. the Riesenkoppe as far as the Tafelfichte; N. the populous Silesian plain. — *Schweidnitz* (p. 182) is 9¹/₂, *Strehlen* (p. 182) 14 M. from the foot of the Zobten.

Next stat. *Canth.* At *Kryblowitz*, 3 M. to the S.E., there is a monument to Prince Blücher, who died here in 1819 at the age of 77. Last stat. *Schmolz.* To the r. as Breslau is entered are the cuirassier barracks and Reich's hospital.

28. Breslau.

Hotels. *GOLDNER LÖWE (Pl. a), Tauentzien-Platz, R. from 20, B. 10, D. 25 Sgr.; *GOLDNE GÁNS (Pl. b), Junkern-Str., similar charges; *WEISSER ADLER (Pl. d), Ohlauer-Str. — *HÔTEL DU NORD (Pl. c), opposite the Central Station, R. 15 Sgr.; HÔTEL DE SILÉSIE (Pl. e); DREI BERGE (Pl. f). — *DEUTSCHES HAUS, Albrecht-Str. 22, and *WEISSES ROSS, Nicolai-Str. 10, 11, both unpretending; STADT BRANDENBURG, Berliner-Platz 6; GEBAUER'S HOTEL, new.

Restaurants. *Hansen*, Ohlauer-Str. 9; *Wittig*, Junkern-Str. 11; *Philippi*, Albrecht-Str.; *Lange*, Junkern-Str. 10. — **Beer.** *Kissling*, Junkern-Str. 9; *Börsenkeller*, at the new Exchange; *Friebe*, Schweidnitzer Keller, below the Rathhaus; *Weberbauer*, Zwinger-Str. 5; *Hôtel de Rome*, with reading-room; *Hermann*, Ohlauer-Str. 75; *Labuske*, Ohlauer-Str. 79; *Lowitsch*, Carl-Str. 41. — **Public Gardens** outside the gates: *Wintergarten*, with theatre; *Liebich*, *Weiss*, *Volksgarten*, etc., at all of which concerts are frequently given. — **Confectioners.** *Perini*, Junkern-Str. 2; *Monatschal*, Ring 18; *Steiner*, Albrecht-Str. 33; *Brunnies*, Junkern-Str. 30. — *Liebigshöhe* (p. 168), restaurant, with beautiful view.

Baths. *River Baths:* *Riesenwellenbad, by the mills; others by the Matthiaskunst, outside the Ohlauer-Thor, etc. — *Warm Baths:* Malitzki, Weidendamm 3; Georgenbad, Zwinger-Str. 8 (also vapour). — *Turkish Baths:* at Malitzki's, and at Baron's, Friedrich-Wilhelm-Str. 66.

Theatres. *Stadttheater* (Pl. 33), burned down in 1871; *Lobetheater* (Pl. 33 a), for comedies and minor operas; *Thalia-Theater*, *Vaudeville*, etc.

Post Office (Pl. 28), Albrechts-Str.; also several branch-offices. **Telegraph Office** at the new exchange.

Railway Stations. 1. *Central Station* (Pl. 1) for the Upper Silesian and Posen railway, and for the express trains of the 'Niederschlesisch-Märkisch' line. 2. *Niederschlesisch-Märkisch Station* (Pl. 3), for the ordinary trains of this line. 3. *Freiburg Station* (Pl. 2), for the Freiburg and Schweidnitz line. 4. *Station for the Right Bank of the Oder*, N. of the city (comp. Pl. D, 1).

Cabs. Per drive in the town, for 1 pers. 3, 2 pers. 5, to the station 5 Sgr.; per hour 10 Sgr.

Breslau (391 ft.), the second city in Prussia, the capital of Silesia and seat of government for the province, and the residence of a Rom. Cath. bishop of princely rank, with 208,025 inhab. (50,000 Rom. Cath., 20,000 Jews, 8000 soldiers), lies in a fertile plain on both banks of the *Oder*, at the influx of the *Ohlau*. The islands formed here by the Oder are connected with the banks by numerous bridges. The city consists of the *Altstadt*, *Neustadt*, and five suburbs. The latter were burned down during the siege of 1806, but have been re-erected in a modern style; the *Schweidnitzer Vorstadt* is particularly well built.

Breslau, Lat. *Wratislavia*, Pol. *Wraclaw*, a town and episcopal see as early as the year 1000, is of Sclavonic origin, and with Silesia belonged

to Poland down to 1163, after which it became the capital of the independent Duchy of Silesia. On the extinction of the dukes in 1335 it was
annexed to Bohemia and became subject to the emperors of the Luxemburg
family, who took the city under their special protection. Charles IV. introduced the then famous municipal law of Magdeburg, which, in spite of the
storms of the Hussite wars and of the following centuries, favoured the
development of an independent German element. In 1523 Breslau embraced
the Reformation, and although it was annexed to Austria in 1527, it succeeded in maintaining its privileges, which were farther secured by the
Peace of Westphalia. In 1741 Frederick the Great marched into Silesia and
took Breslau by surprise. In 1757 the town was again occupied by the
Austrians, but was re-captured by Frederick after the battle of Leuthen
(p. 163). In 1760 Tauentzien (p. 169) repelled an attack by Laudon. In
1806—7 the town was besieged by Vandamme, who took it and levelled
the fortifications. In March, 1813, Breslau was the scene of an enthusiastic
rising against the French, on which occasion Frederick William III. issued
his famous appeal 'An mein Volk'. Since the termination of that war the
city has rapidly increased..

Breslau is now one of the most important commercial and manufacturing places in Germany. The principal manufactures are steam-engines,
railway-carriages, liqueurs, and spirits. The staple commodities, chiefly
the produce of Silesia and Poland, are wool, grain, metal, cloth, and
timber. The great wool-markets take place at the beginning of June and
October.

Promenades on the site of the fortifications, skirting the broad
moat which is enlivened with swans, now enclose the greater part
of the inner city. On the old Taschenbastei, at the S.E. corner of
these, rises a modern belvedere termed the *Liebigshöhe* (Pl. 36),
crowned with a Victory by Rauch, and commanding an admirable
survey of the town and its environs. At the foot of it is a monument
to *Schleiermacher* (p. 32), who was born at Breslau in 1768. The
Ziegelbastei (N.E.) affords a view of the Oder.

In the GROSSE RING, a market-place nearly in the centre of
the town, rises the *Rathhaus (Pl. 29), a noble monument of the
prosperous age of Charles IV. and the other Luxemburg monarchs.
The florid enrichments of the oriel windows and gables, and the
rich decorations of the interior belong, however, to the subsequent
late Gothic period (end of 15th and beginning of 16th cent.).
The finest apartment is the *Fürstensaal*, with handsome vaulting,
where from the 15th cent. downwards meetings of the Silesian
princes and estates were generally held. The last of these was in
1741, when homage was done to Frederick the Great as conqueror
of Silesia. The hall has been appropriately restored and adorned
with portraits of princes (visitors apply at the custodian's room in
the passage below). Below the Rathhaus is the *Schweidnitzer Bier-
keller* (erected from the S. side), with remarkably fine vaulting.

The *Staupsäule* (or pillory), erected in 1492, on the E. side of
the Rathhaus, is a monument of the severe laws of ancient times,
while the extensive range of buildings around the Rathhaus is a
memorial of the Sclavonic custom of erecting booths and stalls adjacent to public buildings.

In the W. part of the Grosse Ring rise the equestrian *Statue
of Frederick the Great (Pl. 23), in bronze, erected in 1842, and

the equestrian **Statue of Frederick William III.** (Pl. 24), erected in 1861, both by *Kiss.*

The **Stadthaus** (Pl. 30), adjoining the Rathhaus, designed by *Stüler*, was completed in 1863. On the ground-floor are shops, and on the sunk floor a restaurant. The handsome apartments of the first floor contain the *Town Library*, comprising 300,000 vols., 2000 MSS., a cabinet of coins, and a valuable collection of old engravings and woodcuts.

Opposite is the *House of the Seven Electors*, of 1672, with restored frescoes representing the emperor and the seven electors.

The neighbouring Blücher-Platz is embellished with a *Statue of Blücher (Pl. 25), designed by *Rauch.* On the S. side of the Platz is the handsome *Börse*, the property of a private club.

The Prot. *Church of St. Elizabeth* (Pl. 16), to the N.W. of the Ring, erected in 1257 and recently restored, with a tower 335 ft. in height, contains some interesting old tombstones and modern stained glass. The Prot. *Mary Magdalene Church* (Pl. 18), to the E. of the Ring, with two towers connected by an arch, dating from the same early period, also contains good modern stained glass.

The Ring forms the centre of traffic, the main arteries of which are the handsome Schweidnitzer Strasse, leading to the W. stations, and the Ohlauer Strasse.

At the end of the *Schweidnitzer Strasse* are the *Theatre* (Pl. 33), erected after a fire in 1865, and again burned down in 1871, and the *Government Buildings* (Pl. 11). The adjoining *Exercier-Platz* (parade at noon), is bounded on the N. by the **Royal Palace** (Pl. 27), restored in 1846, and on the W. by the **Ständehaus** (Pl. 31), or *Hall of the Estates*, which contains a *Picture Gallery* (800 works, most of them duplicates of the old Italian masters at the Berlin Museum; also a few good modern pictures).

Beyond the Ständehaus, at the corner of the Graupen-Str. and the Promenade, rises the **Neue Börse,** or *New Exchange*, an imposing modern Gothic edifice. The façade opposite the Ständehaus is adorned with stone statues representing a merchant, a farmer, a sailor, and a shepherd. The spacious Hall is handsomely decorated (open daily 10—1).

Beyond the Stadtgraben rises the large *New Synagogue* (Pl. 35), a brick building in the Oriental style; then the *Court Buildings*, the *Cuirassier Barracks* (Pl. 8), and beyond it the Schweidnitz and Berlin railway stations.

The continuation of the Schweidnitzer Str. to the S., beyond the moat, leads to the Tauentzien-Platz, which is adorned with the **Tauentzien-Monument** (Pl. 26), erected to the general of that name (d. 1791), the gallant defender of Breslau in 1760. A short distance hence is the *Central Railway Station* (Pl. 1), at the S.E. angle of the city.

The streets running to the N. of the Ring lead to the **University**
(Pl. 34), which contains valuable zoological and mineralogical collections. It was transferred from Frankfort on the Oder to Breslau
in 1811, and united with a Jesuit school, the buildings of which it
now occupies (900 students). — The *University Library*, comprising
380,000 vols., 2840 vols. of MSS., specimens of the earliest typography, etc., is established in an old Augustine Abbey (Pl. 5) on
the *Sandinsel* (Pl. F, 2, 3), which also contains a · *Museum of
Art and Antiquity* and a *Museum of Silesian Antiquities* (admission
2¹⁄₂ Sgr., daily 3—6, Sund. and holidays 11—1 and 3—5).

The adjoining **Sandkirche** (Pl. 19), or *Church of our Lady on
the Sand*, erected in the middle of the 13th cent., is a finely proportioned structure with polygonal apse and fine star vaulting.

The **Kreuzkirche** (Pl. 17), on the r. bank of the Oder, a handsome brick edifice consecrated in 1295, contains the tomb of Duke
Henry IV. of Breslau (d. 1290), in terracotta, in front of the high
altar.

The *Cathedral *of St. John* (Pl. 14), begun in 1170, completed
in the 14th cent., and recently restored, is flanked with two series
of chapels.

*Interior. At the end of the S. aisle is the sumptuously decorated
chapel of *Cardinal Frederick*, Landgrave of Hessen, with the tomb of the
founder and a statue of St. Elizabeth, executed by Floretti of Rome in
the middle of the 17th cent. The adjacent chapel contains the *Monument
of *Bishop Roth* (d. 1506), cast by Vischer of Nuremberg, the bishop in high
relief, surrounded by the six patron saints of the country. Marble sarcophagus of *Bishop Proņella* (d. 1376). Monument of *Duke Christian of Holstein*,
an imperial general who fell in a battle with the Turks at Salankemen
in 1691 (reliefs of battles, Turks as caryatides). — The adjoining chapel of
Count Palatine *Franz Ludwig*, Elector of Mayence, and Prince Bishop of
Breslau, contains two good statues of Moses and Aaron, 1727. Numerous
other monuments of bishops and canons and several paintings of the 18th
cent. by the prolific Willmann. — The *Chapel of St. John*, in the N. aisle,
the second from the choir, contains *Cranach*'s celebrated 'Madonna among
the pines'. — On the wall of the choir, opposite the Chapel of St. Borro-
mæus, Christ with the disciples at Emmaus, ascribed to *Titian.* ·

The **Botanical Garden** (Pl. G, H, 1, 2; open daily till 7 p. m.),
to the N. of the cathedral, contains a valuable collection of medi-
cinal plants. The *Wintergarten* (p. 167) is ¹⁄₄ M. to the E.; the
Zoological Garden, tastefully laid out, lies beyond the barrier, ³⁄₄ M.
distant.

The Mohnhaupt-Strasse leads from the Botanical Garden to the N., past
the Deaf and Dumb Asylum (Pl. G, 1) to the *New Church of St. Michael,
an elegant Gothic brick edifice, consecrated in 1871, with lofty towers of
unequal height.

Environs. Scheitnig, on the r. bank of the Oder, 1¹⁄₂ M. above the
Zoological Garden, with a park and numerous country-houses; Pöpelwitz,
to the W. of the Nicolaithor, with the pleasant Eichenpark garden, etc.

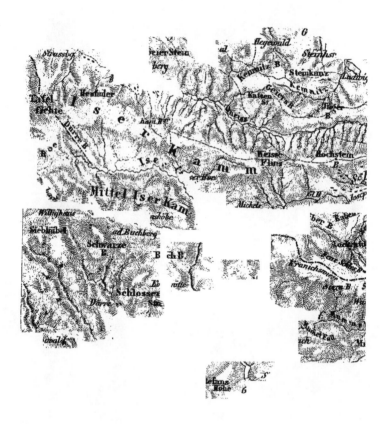

Darmstadt, Ed. Wagner.

Polsnitz
Fröhlichsdf
Quole
Zirsbg.
Freiburg
Zeiskenburg
Kalben St.
Fürstenstn.
Liewichau
Sorgau
Nd.
Adelsbach
Salzbrunn
Ob.
Carls H.
Settendf.
Wilhelms
Höhe
Lenradsthal
Gl.H.
Hartan
Altwasser
Königswald
Fuchs R.
Hockwald
Weistein
chlau
Hermsdf.
Waldenburg
Ob.
Mühlenburg
Neu
Hammdf.
Dittersbch.
Itesberg
Fellhamer
Nd. J.
Lässig
Wilhr.
Haan
Steinan
Lang
Waltersdf.
Reuss-
waldau
Vogels
B.
Busch
B.
Anker
B.
Ellisgrund
Grorkendf.
Dürrow
Schmidtsdf.
Fleischer
B.
Zieg.
hwicken
Friedland
Neudorf
Rappersdf.
Göhlenau Steina
Wiesa
Neusorge
Gren.dl.
Halbstadt
Buch.B.
Mbr.
Weckelsdorf
T. Bottisch
Löchau
ktzen St.
Mohren
N.

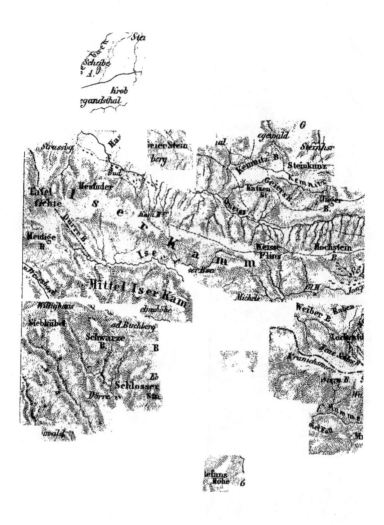

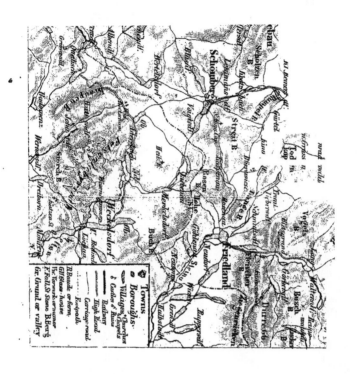

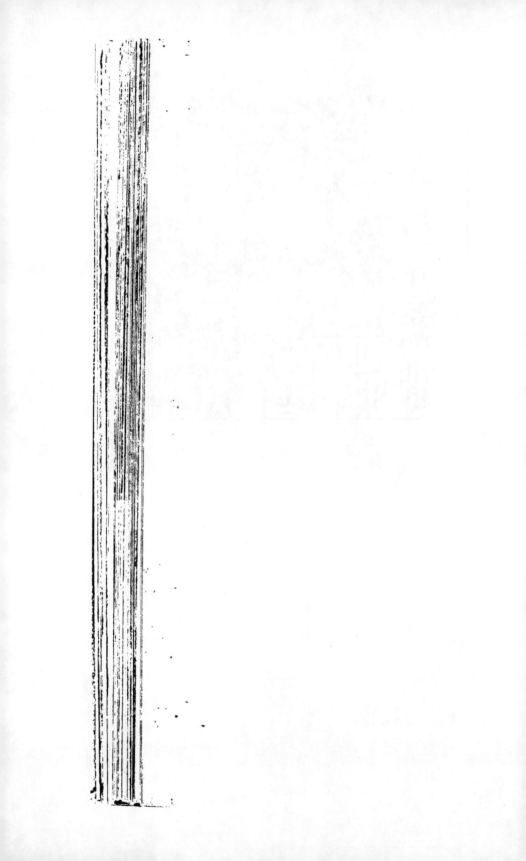

29. The Giant Mountains.

Plan. The most interesting points among the Giant Mts. may be visited in nine or ten days. *Hirschberg* (p. 172) is the most convenient starting-point. 1st Day. Hirschberg and environs; Cavalierberg ³|₄ hr., gorge of the Sattler 4 hrs.; drive in the afternoon to Erdmannsdorf in 1¹|₂, walk by the Heinrichsburg and Weihrichsberg to Warmbrunn, 3, in all 9 hrs. — 2nd Day. Hermsdorf ³|₄ hr., Kynast and back 1¹|₂, Kochelfall 2¹|₂, Josephinenhütte 2, in all 7 hrs. — 3rd Day. Mountain walk: Zackenfall ³|₄ hr., Neue Schlesische Baude ³|₄, Elbfall 2, Schneegrubenbaude ³|₄, Petersbaude 1, Mittagsstein 1¹|₂, Riesenbaude 1¹|₂, Koppe ³|₄, in all about 9 hrs. — 4th Day. Descend to the Hampelbaude 1¹|₂, Kirche Wang 1¹|₂, Gräbersteine 1, Arnsdorf ¹|₂, Schmiedeberg 1 hr. — 5th Day. Friesensteine 1¹|₂, Fischbach 1, Falkenstein 1, Jannowitz 1 hr. — The descent to the Bohemian side may be arranged thus: From the Koppe to the Petz Kretscham in the Riesengrund 2 hrs.; Johannisbad 3 hrs.; then on the following day by Klein Aupe and the Grenzbauden to Schmiedeberg 6 hrs., or by Trautenau, and thence by railway. — A visit to the Adelsbach and Weckelsdorf rocks may be combined with the above tour as follows: either from Schmiedeberg by the old road, with a digression to the Friesensteine and Landshut, 3¹|₂ hrs., and thence to Adersbach 5 hrs.; next day to Weckelsdorf ³|₄ hr., Felsenstadt 2¹|₂, Friedland 2, Waldenburg 2¹|₂ hrs.; or by railway to Liebau, see p. 180.

Zittau is another good starting-point. 1st Day. *Oybin and Lausche; drive in 3 hrs. to Friedland (p. 188). — 2nd Day. To *Liebwerda* (p. 165) 2 hrs.; with guide (20 Sgr.) to Flinsberg 3¹|₂ hrs. — 3rd Day. Ascend the *Hochstein* in 4 hrs. (p. 174), descend to the Josephinenhütte in 1 hr. (dine); visit *Zackenfall* in 1 hr.; to *Petersdorf* (p. 173) 1 hr., or to *Hermsdorf* (p. 173) 3 hrs. — 4th Day. Visit the *Kynast* (p. 173) in 2 hrs.; then by *Giersdorf* and *Merzdorf* to the *Heinrichsburg* (p. 174) in 1¹|₂ hr.; *Stonsdorf* (p. 174) ¹|₂ hr.; *Erdmannsdorf* (p. 175) 1 hr. (dine). With guide over the *Ameisenberg* to *Fischbach* (p. 175) 1 hr., *Buchwald* (p. 175) 1 hr., *Schmiedeberg* (p. 174) ³|₄ hr. — 5th Day. Drive in ³|₄ hr. to *Krumhübel* (p. 177); thence with guide (for the whole day; route, see p. 177) to the summit of the *Schneekoppe* (p. 178; dine); then by the Grenzbauden to *Liebau* (p. 180) in 4—5 hrs. Or the night may be spent at the Grenzbaude at (1¹|₂ hr.) *Klein-Aupa*, and Liebau (3 hrs.) reached on the following morning. — 6th Day. Drive from Liebau by *Schömberg* (p. 178) to *Adersbach* (p. 179; dine), *Weckelsdorf*, *Friedland*, and *Waldenburg* (p. 166). — 7th Day. Walk from Waldenburg to Altwasser, and over the *Wilhelmshöhe* to *Salzbrunn* (p. 181), in 1¹|₂ hr., thence to the *Fürstenstein* and *Freiburg*, and by railway to Breslau.

Inns generally good, except at the smaller villages. Those among the mountains termed 'Bauden' are constructed of wood. Charges: R. 15—20, B. 7¹|₂, A. 5, D. 15 Sgr. Wine on the Austrian side generally good, on the Prussian inferior and dearer.

The **Giant Mountains** form part of the great mountain chain termed the *Sudeten* which extends from the sources of the Oder and the Carpathians towards the N.W. for a distance of 140 M. The *Riesenkamm*, or Giant Range, strictly so called, which rises somewhat abruptly on the Silesian, and gradually on the Bohemian side, stretching from the sources of the Bober on the E. and those of the Queis and Zacken on the W., is 23 M. in length, and attains an average height of 4000 ft.. The principal heights are the *Schneekoppe* (5138 fr.), the *Grosse* and *Kleine Sturmhaube* (4500 and 4494 ft.), the *Mittagstein* (4647 ft.), the *Tafelfichte* (3483 ft.), the *Reifträger* (4290 ft.), the *Hohe Rad* (4450 ft.), the *Brunnberg* (4820 ft.), and the *Kesselberg* (4430 ft.). At a height of about 3500 ft. the forest zone of the Giant Mts. terminates, and the region of the dwarf pine (pinus humilis) begins, and this in its turn soon disappears, particularly on the Schneekoppe, where the 'devil's beard' (anemone alpina) and violet-moss (byssus jolithus) alone thrive.

a. *Hirschberg, Warmbrunn, Schmiedeberg, and Environs.*

Distances. From Hirschberg to Warmbrunn 3³|₄ M., Warmbrunn to Hermsdorf 2¹|₄ M., ascent of the Kynast 1 hr., Hermsdorf to the Josephinen-hütte 8 M., Hermsdorf to Schmiedeberg 9 M., Warmbrunn to Schmiede-berg 9 M., Hirschberg to Schmiedeberg 9 M.

Carriage with one horse 3, with two 5 Thlr. per day.

Hirschberg (1122 ft.) (**Drei Berge*, by the post-office; **Preussi-scher Hof*, in the Anlagen; *Weisser Schwan,* at the station; *Deutsches Haus* and *Weisses Ross* in the market-place; *Bergmann's* and *Ungebauer's* in the Anlagen; Inn on the Calvarienberg, see below), a station on the Silesian Mountain Railway (p. 166), picturesquely situated at the confluence of the *Bober* and *Zacken*, is an old town with 10,000 inhab., still partially surrounded by walls, and the principal commercial place among the Silesian Mts. Near the station is the *Prot. Church*, covered with a large dome, one of the six churches for which Charles XII. of Sweden stipulated from Emp. Joseph I. at the Altranstadt Convention in 1707. The *Rom. Cath. Church* dates from the 14th cent. The *Ring*, or market, is enclosed by arcades. To the S. of the town are prettily *Anlagen*, or promenades, extending to the **Cavalierberg* (Inn).

To the N.W. of the town, on the l. bank of the Zacken, rises the **Hausberg* (Restaurant), a fine point of view. At the foot of it is the *Railway Viaduct* (p. 166). To the N. of the Hausberg rises the *Helikon*, crowned with a small Doric temple.

A walk up the wild **Boberthal*, or *Sattler Ravine*, on the l. bank, will repay the traveller. The finest point, about 3 M. from Hirschberg, is termed *Der Welt Ende*, where the path is compelled to quit the stream and ascend to the l. On the opposite bank are the *Raubschloss* and the *Thurmstein*, a huge mass of rock. In ³|₄ hr. more *Bober-Röhrsdorf*, with the ruins of an old castle, is reached, whence Hirschberg may be regained by the inn *Zur halben Meile* and the Helikon (see above).

To Liegnitz, see p. 163. — The **Hugolje* (p. 163) may be reached from Hirschberg in 3 hrs.

To Schmiedeberg, 9 M., diligence and omnibus several times a day, see p. 174.

From Hirschberg to Warmbrunn 4³/₄ M.; diligence twice, omnibus 6—8 times a day. The road on the l. bank of the *Zacken* ascends the industrious *Hirschberg Valley*, inhabited chiefly by weavers, and passes through *Kunersdorf* and *Herischdorf*, the latter being almost contiguous to Warmbrunn.

Warmbrunn (1122 ft.) (**Hôtel de Prusse; *Schwarzer Adler; Schneekoppe; Verein; Weisser Adler; *Langes Haus*, a hôtel garni only; *Breslauer Hof; Schwarzes Ross; Stadt London*, etc.; table d'hôte at the two first named, also at the *Gallerie*, 17¹/₂ Sgr.; D. at the *Cursaal* à la carte. Beer at the *Rosengarten*. Lodgings 3—5 Thlr. per week), a pleasant watering-place, visited by 3000 patients annually, lies in a fertile district on both banks of the Zacken, near the N. slopes of the Giant Mts. The alkaline and sulphureous water (95—103° Fahr.), used both for drinking and bathing, and beneficial in cases of gout and skin disease have been known since the end of the 12th cent. Since 1401 the place has been the property

of the Counts Schaffgotsch, whose handsome *Schloss* was erected in
1784—89. The *Probstei* contains their library of 50,000 vols. and
a fine collection of weapons and minerals. The *Schloss-Park* is open
on Tuesd. and Frid., 2—7 o'clock. The beautiful *Promenades* extend as far as Herischdorf, ¼ M. distant, and are flanked with the
Theatre, the *Cursaal*, the '*Gallerie*', and numerous shops, in which
cut glass and polished stones are the most attractive wares. The
*Weihrichsberg (1161 ft.), ¼ hr. to the S.W., and the *Scholzenberg*
(1356 ft.), ¼ hr. to the E. are two of the finest points of view.

> To Reibnitz (p. 166) post-omnibus three times daily in ³|₄ hr.

Hermsdorf (1280 ft.) (**Tietze's Hotel;* **Verein;* *Gebhard's;*
Weisser Löwe; Wilke's; Zum Kynast; *Goldener Stern, unpretending. Private apartments to be had), 2 M. to the S.W. of Warmbrunn, a beautifully situated village with a château of Count Schaffgotsch, is an admirable starting-point for excursions (guides, see
p. 175). On a wooded height above it rises the well-preserved ruin
of ***Kynast** (1880 ft.), founded in 1292, and destroyed by lightning
in 1657. A legend attaching to the castle forms the subject of a
ballad by Körner. The beautiful but heartless Kunigunde vowed to
marry none but the knight who should first ride round the parapet
of the castle. Many made the attempt, but were precipitated into
the abyss below. At length one in whom she felt a real interest
succeeded, but instead of claiming his prize, he administered a
stern reproof and departed. Beautiful view of the Hirschberg valley
from the tower. The ascent to the castle is best made by the carriage-road (1 hr.), the descent by the *Höllengrund*, which separates
the Kynast from the *Heerdberg* (2126 ft.) towards the S. The latter,
commanding a fine view of the castle, is ascended from Kynast in
³/₄, from Hermsdorf in 1½ hr.

> Near *Wernersdorf* (Zum freundlichen Hain), 3³|₄ M. to the W. of Warm-
> brunn, and 3 M. from Hermsdorf, are the **Bibersteine**, an imposing group
> of rocks. The top of the *Grosse Biberstein* (125 ft.) commands a fine view.
> From *Agnetendorf*, 2¼ M. to the S. of Hermsdorf, the **Bismarckshöhe**
> (2176 ft.), another good point of view, may be reached in ³|₄ hr. , or from
> Hermsdorf direct in 1¼ hr. — Near it is the *Säbrich*, another fine point.
> —.The *Schneegruben, Thurmstein*, etc., see p. 176.

From Hermsdorf the post-road ascends the picturesque valley
of the Zacken to (2 M.) *Petersdorf* (Kronprinz, at the beginning,
*Zum Kochelfall, at the end of the village). At the milestone 2,₄₇,
near the Kochelfall Inn, a path to the l. diverges to the (10 min.)
Kochelfall, a fine cascade 40 ft. in height. The road then leads
through the straggling village of *Schreiberhau*, the 3600 inhab. of
which maintain themselves by linen-weaving and glass-polishing.
Several inns on the road side, among them *Ulbrich's Zum Zackenfall* (2028 ft.), and. farther on, **Zur Josephinenhütte* (2225 ft.),
the latter, about 8 M. from Hermsdorf, being the headquarters of
guides and porters for the Koppe. The Josephinenhütte, the largest
of the glass-houses of Schreiberhau, belongs to Count Schaffgotsch.
Near it rises the *Rabenstein*, a lofty rock.

The *Zackenfall*, a fall of the *Zackerle*, 80 ft. in height, framed
in beautiful forest scenery, 3/4 M. to the S. of the Josephinenhütte,
is apt to disappoint in dry seasons, but may be artificially improved
by the opening of a sluice gate.   Route to the Neue Schlesische
Baude, see p. 175.

To the N.W. of the Josephinenhütte rises the **Hochstein** (3740 ft.),
ascended in 1 hr., an excellent point of view (rustic inn).   On the path to
it is *Rosemann's Inn*.   Ascent from Hermsdorf direct 4 hrs.

The high road beyond the Josephinenhütte ascends to a height of
2460 ft., crosses the Austrian frontier, and leads by *Neuwelt*, or *Neuwald*
(16¹|₂ M. from Warmbrunn), and (10¹|₂ M.) *Tannwald* to (13 M.) *Reichenberg*
(p. 188).

* * *

Stonsdorf (1227 ft.) 2¹/₄ M. to the S.E. of Warmbrunn, a village
with a Schloss and brewery of Prince Reuss, lies at the base of the
granite *Prudelberg* (1460 ft.), which may be ascended in 20 min.
On the *Stangenberg* (1657 ft.), a pine-clad hill, 3/4 hr. to the S.W.
of Stonsdorf, rises the *Heinrichsburg*, a tower commanding an
admirable view: to the N. Hirschberg and its environs; N.W.
Warmbrunn; W. the Hochstein; S.W. the Kynast, Reifträger,
Hohe Rad, Grosse and Kleine Sturmhaube; S. the Silberkamm,
Schneekoppe; S.E. Schmiedeberg, the Schmiedeberger Kamm and
Friesensteine; E. Fischbach and the Falkenberge.   At the foot of
the Stangenberg on the W. lies the hamlet of *Merzdorf*, 3 M. from
Warmbrunn.

Near Merzdorf, to the S.W., lies *Giersdorf* (Lippert, in the
upper part of the village, Brewery in the lower), 2 M. from Warmbrunn, and almost adjoining it is the straggling village of *Hain*.
The picturesque *Hainfall* in the valley of the *Mittelwasser* is
1¹/₂ M. above Hain.   Near it a fine point of view and a restaurant.
Higher up are some remarkable rock formations, termed the *Semmel-
junge* (view), the *Thumpsahütte*, etc.

Seydorf (1181 ft.) (Inn and brewery), where the roads from
Warmbrunn and Hermsdorf unite, 3³/₄ M. from each of these places,
and 5¹/₄ M. from Schmiedeberg, lies to the S. of Merzdorf, and is
one of the starting-points for the Koppe (p. 170).   Near it rise the
Gräbersteine, on the N.W. slope of the *Gräbersberg*, commanding a
fine view.   At the (¹/₄ hr.) *Anna-Capelle* (2067 ft.) is a forester's
house affording refreshments, from which Seydorf may be regained
in 20 min. — From Seydorf the road leads to the E. to *Arnsdorf*
(Inn), with a ruined castle and a château of the 17th cent., prettily
situated at the entrance to the *Lomnitzthal*; then to *Steinseiffen*
and to

Schmiedeberg (1444 ft.) *(Preussischer Hof; *Schwarzes Ross;
Goldner Stern)*, an old town with 3500 inhab., stretching for a
considerable distance in the steep valley of the *Eglitz*.   Down to
the 16th cent. it was an important mining place, and was subsequently the centre of the Silesian linen manufacture.   Picturesque

environs, with a number of villas and châteaux. The *AnnaCapelle*, above the town, is a fine point of view. At *Buchwald*, 2 M. to the N., there is a château with a beautiful park.

Erdmannsdorf (1257 ft.) (*Zum Schweizerhaus), a village with a royal château and park, lies halfway from Schmiedeberg to Hirschberg, between which places (9 M.) a diligence and omnibus run several times a day. Church designed by Schinkel. In the vicinity is *Zillerthal*, a colony founded by Tyrolese Protestant emigrants in 1838, with a spinning mill belonging to the 'Seehandlung' (p. 31). Immediately to the N. of Erdmannsdorf lies *Lomnitz*, through which the road to *Schildau* (p. 166) leads.

To the E. of Erdmannsdorf lies the long village of (3 M.) *Fischbach* (two good inns), with a fine old château, founded in the 14th cent., completed in the 16th, and subsequently restored and embellished. It now belongs to Prince Adalbert of Prussia. At the entrance are two cannon which were presented by the English to Prince Waldemar (d. 1849) in recognition of his active participation in the war against the Sikhs. Extensive park. Brewery and inn at the offices. — To the N. of Fischbach rise the *Falkenberge*, the highest of which is the *Falkenstein* (2126 ft.), an excellent point of view, reached in 1 hr. from Fischbach. To the S.E. of Fischbach rises the (1½ hr.) *Marianenfels*, a huge group of rocks on the summit of the Fischbacher Gebirge, commanding a fine panorama. On the S. side of the rocks a gigantic lion in iron, after Rauch.

The old post-road from *Schmiedeberg* to *Landeshut* (p. 180), 9 M., traverses the *Landshuter Kamm*, the highest point of which is termed the *Ausgespann*, where Frederick the Great is said to have frequently alighted to enjoy the view. The prospect is very striking, especially if the traveller is coming in the reverse direction. To the l., apparently quite near, rises the Koppe with its inn and chapel; then the pine-clad E. spurs of the Giant Mts.; at the spectator's feet lie the valleys of Schmiedeberg and Hirschberg, sprinkled with numerous houses. This view is still more complete from the *Friesensteine (2920 ft.), ½ hr. to the r. of the road, and 1½ hr. from Schmiedeberg.

b. *The Hochgebirge.*

Distances. From the Josephinenhütte to the Schneegrubenbaude 4 hrs., Riesenbaude 4½, Koppe ¾ hr.; from Agnetendorf to the Schneegrubenbaude 4 hrs.; from Seydorf to the Riesenbaude 5½ hrs.; from Schmiedeberg to Krumhübel 1½ hr.; thence to the Riesenbaude 2½ hrs.; from Schmiedeberg direct to the Koppe 4 hrs.; from Johannisbad to the Koppe 5 hrs.; from Hohenelbe to the Koppe 7½—8 hrs.

Guides (1 Thlr. 10 Sgr. per day, for which they are bound to provide their own food), although seldom absolutely necessary, are often useful in the stormy or foggy weather which is frequently encountered among the Giant Mts. Their headquarters are at Warmbrunn, Hermsdorf, Agnetendorf, the Josephinenhütte, Seydorf, Arnsdorf, and Krumhübel.

Chair Porters 3 Thlr. per day.
Horse with attendant per day 3, half-day 1½ Thlr.

From the *Josephinenhütte* to the Koppe 9—10 hrs. The path ascends by the (¾ hr.) *Zackenfall* (p. 174), crosses a bridge

(2300 ft.), and ascends to the (1 hr.) *Neue Schlesische Baude* (3847 ft.), a tavern, where a view is obtained. Leaving the Reif-träger (4290 ft.) to the l., the path then ascends past some remark-able groups of rock, the (1/2 hr.) *Sausteine*, and (1/4 hr.) *Kässteine*, or *Quarksteine*, crosses (1/4 hr.) the path from the Alte Schlesische Baude to Ober-Rochlitz, and then skirts the S. side of the *Spitz-berg*. After 1/4 hr. more the straight path leading direct to the (1/2 hr.) Schneegrubenbaude (see below) is quitted by a path to the r. to the (1/4 hr.) *Elbbrunnen*, one of the sources of the Elbe, and thence towards the S. to the (1/4 hr.) **Elbfall*, 145 ft. in height, one of the finest among the Giant Mts. (*rustic inn). About 10 min. farther is the *Pantschfall*, 800 ft. in height, and 1 1/2 hr. beyond it the Spindelmühl, see p. 178. From the Elbfall ascend the l. bank of the brook to the (3/4 hr.) **Schneegrubenbaude*, lying on the brink of the *Grosse* and *Kleine Schneegrube*, two rocky gullies upwards of 1000 ft. in depth. View of the Hirschberg Valley beyond the abyss from *Rübezahl's Kanzel* ('Number Nip's Pulpit'), a lofty rock near the Baude. To the E. of the Schneegruben rises the *Hohe Rad* (4449 ft.), the summit of which is reached hence in 20 min.; *view preferred by many to that from the Koppe.

From the Schneegrubenbaude the path follows the Riesenkamm, or the crest of the mountains, the boundary between Prussia and Austria, leaving the *Grosse Sturmhaube* (4500 ft.) on the l., and passing the *Mannstein*, the *Mädelsteine*, and the *Vogelsteine*, and in 1 3/4 hr. reaches the *Petersbaude* (4066 ft.), a mountain inn, com-manding an extensive view towards Bohemia. It then descends into the *Mädelwiese*, a marshy hollow, and the (40 min.) *Spindlerbaude* (3180 ft.), an inn on the W. slope of the *Kleine Sturmhaube* (4491 ft.). The path on the N. side of the latter leads to the *Mit-tagstein*, a granite rock about 40 ft. in height on the N. slope of the *Lahnberg*, or *Silberkamm* (4647 ft.), commanding a fine view towards Silesia. The deeply imbedded *Grosse Teich*, destitute of fish, and the *Kleine Teich*, in which trout abound, are next passed (the Wiesenbaude being left to the r.), and the Koppenplan, clothed with the dwarf pine, traversed to the (1 1/4 hr.) *Riesenbaude* (4390 ft.), a 'Weinhaus' at the foot of the barren summit of the Koppe. A new path, protected by stone walls, ascends hence in numerous wind-ings to the summit (3/4 hr., descent 20 min.).

From Agnetendorf to the Koppe 8—9 hrs. The path ascends the *Tiefe Graben*, the wooded valley of a brook rising in the Agnetendorfer Schneegrube, passes the *Thurmstein* (2152 ft.), and then the (2 hrs.) *Korall-steine* (2733 ft.), a wild group of rocks on the N. slope of the Kleine Sturm-haube (see above). The *Agnetendorfer*, or *Schwarze Schneegrube* is next passed, and in 1 1/2 hr. the above described path to the Riesenkamm is reached. Thence to the Koppe, see above.

From Seydorf (p. 174) to the Koppe 6 hrs. In the upper part of the village a finger-post indicates the way to the l. to the (1 1/4 hr.) *Anna-Capelle* (2396 ft.), where a forester's house affords refreshments. Near it are the (1/4 hr.) *Gräbersteine* (p. 174), which

however lie off the direct route. The path ascends from the chapel
to the S. to the (1¼ hr.) *Brotbaude*, at the junction of the paths
from Arnsdorf and from Schmiedeberg by Krumhübel. About 10 min.
from the Brotbaude is the *Church of Wang* (2471 ft.), the parish
church of the straggling village of *Brückenberg*, a curious wooden
structure of the 12th cent., purchased by Frederick William IV. in
1844 and transferred hither from its original site at Tellemarken in
Norway. A small portion only of the carved work is modern.
Tower, school, and parsonage new. The churchyard affords a fine
prospect of the valley, Erdmannsdorf, Hohen-Zillerthal, Schmiedeberg, etc.

By the entrance to the parsonage the path ascends in 40 min.
to the *Schlingelbaude* (3396 ft.) (refreshments). Near it the *Drei
Steine*, rocky pinnacles on the top of the mountain. Then (10 min.)
two bridges over the outlets of the Grosse and Kleine Teich, whence
the (½ hr.) *Hempelsbaude* (3983 ft.) is visible on its green plateau.

From the Hempelsbaude ascend for 25 min. on the *Stirndl* to
the *Koppenplan*, on which, 25 min. farther, is the *Riesenbaude*, at
the base of the Koppe (see p. 176).

From Schmiedeberg (p. 175) to the Koppe by *Krumhübel*
and *Brückenberg* 5 hrs. A broad road leads from Schmiedeberg to
the S.W. by *Steinseiffen* in 1½ hr. to *Krumhübel* (*Zur Schneekoppe), formerly the principal seat of the now almost extinct 'La-
boranten', or herb and medicine vendors of the Giant Mts., who
trace their descent from two medical students from Prague, who
at the beginning of the 18th cent. sought an asylum here on account
of a duel. 'Pudel' is an aromatic liqueur, manufactured here. From
Krumhübel to the Koppe 3½ hrs. (guide not absolutely necessary);
carriage-road as far as (2½ M.) *Brückenberg*. The Church of Wang,
and thence to the summit, see above.

From Schmiedeberg direct to the Koppe by the Schmiedeberger
Kamm, with guide, 4 hrs. The path passes the *Anna-Capelle*
(p. 174) and leads chiefly through wood to the *Grenzbauden* (*Hübner, *Blaschke), 2 hrs. below the summit (good Hungarian wine).
The vegetation becomes scantier as the summit is approached. The
steep part of the ascent begins on the *Schwarze Koppe*, ¾ hr. from
the summit.

From Johannisbad (p. 189) to the summit 5 hrs.; a carriage-road,
as far as Petzer (see below). The traveller returns at first by the road
as far as (1½ M.) *Freiheit* (p. 189), and then ascends the busy and picturesque valley of the *Aupa* to (3 M.) *Marschendorf* (Zum Platz; Schrem-
mer's Restaurant), the first houses of which almost adjoin Freiheit. Count
Aichelburg possesses a château here. Post-conveyance from Trautenau
(p. 189) to *Marschendorf* daily.

The valley contracts. A short way beyond (¾ M.) *Dunkelthal*, where
there is a large glass-house, the road divides, that to the r. leading to
Klein Aupa and the *Grenzbauden*, 2½ hrs., that to the l. to (1 hr.) *Gross
Aupa* (Preller), a village consisting of huts scattered over the hillside.
In ½ hr. more *Petzer*, the highest part of Gross-Aupa, is reached, where
the road terminates. Refreshments and chair-porters at the Petzer Kre-

tscham. Then a steep ascent through the grand *Riesengrund*, or *Aupegrund*, which descends abruptly from the Schneekoppe to a depth of 2000 ft., to the (2 hrs.) *Riesenbaude* (4390 ft.); thence to the Koppe, see p. 176.

From Hohenelbe (p. 189) to the Koppe there are two routes: a direct and rough road by (³|₄ hr.) *Pommerdorf*, the (¹|₄ hr.) *Völlerbauden*, the (¹|₂ hr.) *Lahrbauden*, the (¹|₂ hr.) *Rennerbauden*, and the (³|₄ hr) *Brunnberg* to the (¹|₂ hr.) Riesenbaude (p. 176). The other and better route is by a road ascending the romantic *Elbthal* by *Oberhohenelbe*, and the first and second *Krausemühle*, to (3¹|₂ hr.) *St. Peter*, or *Spindelmühl* (*Richter, trout and Hungarian wine), situated at the confluence of the sources of the Elbe with the *Weisswasser*, a brook descending from the *Sieben Gründe*. A path leads hence to the W., up the course of the *Elbseiffen*, passing on the N. (r.) of the *Kesselkoppe* (4548 ft.), to the (2 hrs.) Pantschfall and beyond it the Elbfall (p. 176). The Koppe may be reached from St. Peter direct by ascending the course of the Weisswasser and traversing a bleak region between the sharp ridge of the *Ziegenrücken* and the *Lahnberg* (p. 176), and crossing the saddle connecting these. The *Wiesenbaude* is then reached in 2—2¹|₂ hrs. Thence to the summit of the Koppe, see p. 176.

The *Schneekoppe, or Riesenkoppe (5138 ft.), the highest mountain in N. or Central Germany, is a blunted cone of granite, covered with fragments of gneiss and mica-slate. Chapel erected at the end of the 17th cent. *Two inns, one on the Prussian, the other on the Bohemian side of the summit.

View extensive and picturesque: to the N. the entire Hirschberg Valley; E. Schweidnitz, Zobten, Breslau, Eule, Silberberg, Schneeberg, Heuscheuer; S.W. the Weisse Berg near Prague; W. the Milleschauer near Teplitz; N.W. the Landskrone near Görlitz. An unclouded horizon is, however, rare. To the S.W. a most imposing view of the *Aupegrund* or *Riesengrund*, descending 2000 ft. almost perpendicularly; to the N. the *Melzergrund*. Fields of snow are often seen on the mountain in the early part of summer, whence the name.

c. *Rocks of Adersbach and Weckelsdorf. Heuscheuer.*

From *Liebau* to *Schömberg* 4³|₄ M., diligence twice daily; from Landshut to Schömberg 9 M.; from Schömberg to *Adersbach* 6 M. — From *Waldenburg*, or from *Dittersbach* to *Friedland* 8¹|₂ M., diligence twice daily; from Friedland to *Adersbach* or *Weckelsdorf* 6 M. — From Adersbach to Weckelsdorf 2¹|₄ M. — One-horse carr. from Waldenburg to Adersbach 3, two-horse 5 Thlr.

From Liebau (p. 180) a road leads to (4³/₄ M.) *Schömberg* (Ross; Deutscher Kaiser), which is also reached by a road from Landshut viâ Grüssau. The road, at first ascending as far as the Bohemian frontier, now leads by (2 M.) *Liebenau* and (2 M.) *Merkelsdorf* (Stenzel) to (2 M.) *Nieder-Adersbach*. Pedestrians save ¹/₂ hr. by taking the path to the r. by the tavern at the entrance to Liebenau.

From Waldenburg (p. 166) the road ascends to (2 M.) *Dittersbach* (p. 166) and then leads up and down hill, passing the villages of *Neuhayn*, *Lang-Waltersdorf*, and *Schmidtsdorf*. Near the last, 1 M. from the road, lies *Görbersdorf* (1738 ft.), a sanitary establishment in a sheltered situation, visited by consumptive patients. Beyond the small town of *Friedland* (Gold. Löwe; Ross) the Bohemian frontier is crossed. Good Hungarian wine at Ringel's, next to the custom-house. The large village of *Merkelsdorf* (see above) is next reached, from which a road in a straight direction and then to the r. leads to (2 M.) *Adersbach*, and another to the l. leads by *Buchwaldsdorf* to (2 M.) *Weckelsdorf*.

The *Adersbach Rocks (*Zur Felsenstadt*, at the entrance; guide 7¹/₂ Sgr.), resembling those in Saxon Switzerland, are very remarkable. They once formed a solid mountain of green sandstone, the softer parts and clefts of which have been worn away and widened by the action of water, leaving the more indestructible portions standing. These rocks, thousands in number, some of them 180 ft. high, often assume grotesque shapes, and many of them have been named in accordance with a fanciful resemblance (sugar-loaf, burgomaster, drummer, etc.). The path is often so narrow that visitors must walk in single file. A silvery brook traverses this labyrinth, a visit to which occupies 1—1¹/₂ hr. At the egress an echo is awakened by the blast of a horn or a pistol-shot.

The *Weckelsdorf Rocks (*Eisenhammer;* guides), adjoining those of Adersbach on the E. (2 M. from the Adersbach inn), are still more imposing. Admission 6, guide 2 Sgr. Here, too, various parts of the chaotic scene have their peculiar appellations (cathedral, burial-vault, etc.), the most appropriate of which is the grand 'Münster', resembling a Gothic structure, where the tones of a concealed organ enhance the effect. Visitors generally return through the Neue Felsenstadt, where the 'Amphitheatre' and the 'Valley of Jehoshaphat' are picturesque points. A visit to these rocks occupies 2—2¹/₂ hrs.

Near **Radowenz**, 9 M. to the S.W. of Adersbach, is a *Fossil Forest*, discovered by Prof. Göppert of Berlin.

From Weckelsdorf to the Heuscheuer 5¹|₂ hrs. — The usual route is by the small town of *Politz* (2¹|₄ hrs.), and by *Machau, Melden*, and *Nausenei* to (2³|₄ hrs.) *Carlsberg* (see below). A preferable and hardly longer route is by (1 hr.) *Lechau* and (1 hr.) *Hutberg* to the (¹|₂ hr.) chapel on the *Stern*, adjoining which there is an inn, with an admirable view. In the vicinity are the **Weckersdorf Rocks** (the village of that name lies 1¹|₂ M. to the E. of the Stern), a 'Felsenstadt' resembling those of Adersdorf and Weckelsdorf, and much visited from Bad Charlottenbrunn (p. 182), 12 M. to the N. A visit (with guide) to this labyrinth occupies nearly 2 hrs.; fine view from the *Elisabethenhöhe*, the highest part of the ridge. From the Stern to *Klein Ladney* 20 min., *Dösengrund* ¹|₄ hr., *Bilay* ³|₄ hr., *Melden* ¹|₄ hr., *Nausenei* ¹|₂ hr., *Passendorf* ¹|₂ hr., Schweizerhaus on the Heuscheuer (see below) ¹|₂ hr., in all 3 hrs.; or better from Nausenei to (1 hr.) *Carlsberg* (Pawel) on the S. side of the Grosse Heuscheuer, and thence to the top in ¹|₂ hr.

The **Heuscheuer** (*Schweizerhaus*) (comp. Map, p. 182) rises about 500 ft. above the lofty plain of the *Leierberg*. The grotesque rock-formations here have various whimsical names. The highest point is the *Grossvaterstuhl* (2920 ft.), a seat hollowed out in a small rocking stone, which commands a view of the neighbouring rocks; to the N. is the Bohemian town of *Braunau* (Kaiser v. Oesterreich), with its handsome Benedictine Abbey; beyond it the Bohemian side of the Giant Mts.; at the foot of the mountain on the. E. lie the small town of *Wünschelburg* (*Bartsch; Meese), 14 M. from Glatz by a good road, and *Albendorf,* a resort of pilgrims; farther E. are the heights about Landeck and above them the picturesque Silesian and Moravian Mts.; to the S.W. Nachod and a large tract of Bohemia. *Cudowa, Lewin,* and *Nachod,* see p. 184.

From Dresden to the Giant Mts. The following outline will be useful to those approaching the Riesengebirge in this direction.

1st day. *Hochkirch, *Czorneboh, Herrnhut, Zittau.* — 2nd. *Oybin* and *Lausche;* afternoon diligence in 3 hrs. to *Friedland* (p. 188). — 3rd. By the road (in the picturesque valley of the *Wittich*) in 2 hrs. to *Liebwerda,* then (guide 20 Gr.) in 3 hrs. to *Flinsberg* (p. 165), both pleasant little watering-places. Or (with guide) from Liebwerda in 2 hrs. to the *Tafel-fichte (3629 ft.), and down to Flinsberg in 1¹|₂ hr. — 4th. In 3¹|₂ hrs. to the *Hochstein* (3740 ft.), with fine view, down in 1 hr. to the *Josephinen-hütte;* in 1 hr. to the *Zacken Fall and back; 2 hrs. from the Josephinen-hütte to Petersdorf, or 3 hrs. to Hermsdorf. — 5th. Visit to the *Kynast* 2 hrs.; then in 1¹|₂ hr. by *Giersdorf* and *Merzdorf* to the *Heinrichsburg;* ¹|₂ hr. *Stonsdorf;* 1 hr. *Erdmannsdorf;* over the *Ameisenberg* (with. guide) in 1 hr. to *Fischbach, Buchwald* 1 hr., *Schmiedeberg* ³|₄ hr. — 6th. One-horse carr. (20 Ngr.) in ³|₄ hr. to *Krumhübel,* thence (with guide) in 3¹|₂ hrs. to the *Schneekoppe,* down by the *Grenzbauden* in 4—5 hrs. to *Liebau* (see below). Or the night may be spent at the (1¹|₂ hr.) Blaschke's Grenzbaude at *Klein-Aupa,* and Liebau reached (3 hrs.) the following morning. — 7th. One-horse carr. (2 Thlr.) from Liebau by *Schömberg* (p. 178) to *Adersbach,* **Weckelsdorf, Friedland,* and *Waldenburg.* — 8th. Walk from Walden-burg over the *Wilhelmshöhe* in 1¹|₂ hr. to *Salzbrunn,* **Fürstenstein,* and *Freiburg,* and take the railway to *Breslau.*

30. From Breslau to Liebau and Josephstadt.

Railway to *Liebau* in 2¹|₂—3¹|₂ hrs. (fares 3 Thlr., 2 Thlr. 5, 1 Thlr. 14¹|₂ Sgr.); thence to *Josephstadt* in 1¹|₂ hr. (fares 3 fl. 42, 2 fl. 57, 1 fl. 7ſ kr., Austrian currency).

From Breslau to *Ruhbank,* see p. 166. Carriages are generally changed here. The line soon turns to the l. and ascends the valley of the *Bober.*

Stat. **Landeshut** *(*Drei Berge; Rabe),* with 5000 inhab., occupied in flax-spinning and weaving. The Prot. church is one of the six 'Gnadenkirchen' (p. 172). In 1760 here a body of 10,000 Prussians under Fouqué were defeated by 31,000 Austrians under Laudon.

To Schmiedeberg, see p. 175. — At *Grüssau,* 3 M. to the S.E. of Landeshut, are the extensive buildings of a Cistercian Abbey, founded in 1290, suppressed in 1810, and now used as a manufactory.

Stations *Blasdorf* and **Liebau** *(*Kyffhäuser; Deutsches Haus),* the Austrian custom-house. From Liebau to Adersbach, see p. 178.

The line follows a defile through which the Prussian army invaded the Austrian dominions in 1866, and soon enters Bohemia. Stations *Königshain, Bernsdorf, Parschnitz* (junction for Trautenau, Reichenberg, and Zittau). The course of the *Aupa* is now followed. Stations *Schwadowitz, Kosteletz,* and *Nachod* (Lamm)', a town with 3500 inhab., 2 M. to the E. of the railway, commanded by an old castle of Wallenstein, a fine point of view. The Austrians under Ramming and Archduke Leopold were defeated here in several different engagements by the Prussians under Steinmetz in 1866. The line traverses the battle-field, where numerous monuments have been erected to the fallen. The contest was terminated by the capture of *Skalitz*, the station of which was bravely defended by Austrian riflemen.

Josephstadt *(Wessely's Hotel)*, a town and fortress on the Elbe, erected under Joseph II. in 1781—87, an important Austrian stronghold.

To *Pardubitz* and Prague or Vienna, see *Baedeker's S. Germany and Austria.*

31. From Freiburg to Altwasser by Salzbrunn.

From Freiburg to Salzbrunn 5¹|₂ M., diligence once, Omnibus several times daily. From Salzbrunn to Altwasser 2 M., omnibus several times daily.

The road ascends, affording pleasing retrospects. An avenue to the r., 2¹/₂ M. from Freiburg, leads to (³/₄ M.) Schloss Fürstenstein. Pedestrians may also visit the Schloss from stat. *Polsnitz.* (p. 166), or by the road through the Polsnitzthal, which leads in ¹/₂ hr. to the farm (see below; comp. Map, p. 170).

**Schloss Fürstenstein, the residence of Count Hochberg, Prince of Pless, charmingly situated on the E. side of the valley of the *Hellabach* or Polsnitz, and surrounded by extensive grounds, is one of the most attractive spots in Silesia. The château, erected in the Renaissance style in the 17th cent., has been entirely altered and sumptuously fitted up by the present proprietor. The tower should be ascended for the sake of the view. *Hotel* adjacent.

The **Park* may be visited in 2 hrs. as follows. From the inn a road indicated by stone way-posts leads to the S. to the **Louisenplatz*, where a beautiful view of the château, the Alte Burg, and the wooded *Fürstensteiner Grund* is enjoyed. Descend hence into the valley, 300 ft. in depth, cross the brook, and ascend to the *Alte Burg*, a small imitation of a mediæval castle. A kind of tournament was held here in 1800 in honour of Frederick William III., on which occasion the prizes were distributed by his Queen Louise. (Castellan 10—15 Sgr.) Return by the same route into the beautiful valley, and descend the l. bank of the stream. If time be limited, cross a wooden bridge which is soon reached, and ascend to the Schloss; but it is preferable to follow the brook as far as the *Schweizerei*, or farm, and to ascend thence to the r. to the Schloss.

From Fürstenstein to Salzbrunn 3 M. by the Freiburg road above mentioned; somewhat less by a road from the Alte Burg.

Salzbrunn (1247 ft.) (**Flammender Stern*, a handsome Renaissance building; **Preussische Krone*; **Brunnenhof*, with reading-room; **Elisenhof*; *Sonne*; *Kurhaus*; *Paderborner Hof*. — *Deutscher Adler*; *Preussisches Scepter*. — *Private Apartments* 4—10 Thlr. per week. — *Theatre* during the season), a straggling village consisting of *Nieder, Mittel, Ober*, and *Neu-Salzbrunn*, lies in the valley of the *Salzbach*. Its saline-alkaline waters were famed as early as the 15th cent. for their efficacy in pulmonary and bowel complaints, but fell into disuse during the wars of the following centuries. Their virtues were again brought into notice about fifty years ago, and Salzbrunn is now the most fashionable watering-place in Silesia (2000 patients an-

nually). Pleasant promenades at *Ober-Salzbrunn*, where the springs
are situated. The *Elisenhalle*, the chief resort of visitors (music
morning and evening) adjoins the *Oberbrunnen*, the most important
of the springs (used for drinking). The neighbouring *Baths* are
supplied by the *Heilbrunnen* and *Wiesenbrunnen*. The *Annenthurm*,
commanding a pleasant survey of the environs, the *Richthofensruhe*,
and the *Schöne Aussicht* are all near the promenades. *Friedrichsruh*,
20 min. to the S. W., is a favourite café near *Conradsthal*.

The ruined **Zeiskenschloss**, or *Czeschhaus*, 1½ hr. N.W. of Salzbrunn,
lies picturesquely in the valley of the *Zeis*. The road to it leads through
the estate and village of *Adelsbach*. → The summit of the **Sattelwald**
(2896 ft.), commanding an admirable view of the Silesian Mts., may be
reached in 2½ hrs. — The Wilhelmshöhe, see below; Fürstenstein, see
above; Charlottenbrunn, see below; Rocks of Adersbach and Weckelsdorf,
see p. 179.

At the upper end of Neu-Salzbrunn, near the entrance to the
village of *Hartau*, the road to Altwasser diverges to the l. (E.).
Pedestrians are recommended to take the route by the *Wilhelmshöhe* (1690 ft.), to which an avenue ascends from the promenades in ½ hr. Inn at the top commanding a fine view. Descent
on the E. side to **Altwasser** (p. 166) in ½ hr.

32. From Breslau to Glatz.

Railway to Frankenstein in 2½ hrs. (fares 2 Thlr. 14½, 1 Thlr. 23,
1 Thlr. 7½ Sgr.); diligence thence to Glatz 3 times daily in 3 hrs.
Direct Railway by Strehlen and Münsterberg open as far as *Strehlen*
only (in 1¼ hr.), from which a diligence runs to *Münsterberg*.

From Breslau to *Königszelt*, see R. 27. The Frankenstein line
diverges here and crosses a long viaduct.

Schweidnitz (*Krone; *Stern. — *Deutsches Haus*, 2nd cl.;
Goldnes Scepter; *Januschek's Brewery), formerly the capital of a
principality of the name, now that of a district, with 16,000 inhab., is prettily situated on the l. bank of the *Weistritz*. *Rathhaus*
in the market-place, with tower 170 ft. high. The lofty tower
(338 ft.) of the *Rom. Cath. Church* commands an admirable prospect. The old fortifications were removed in 1862 and converted
into handsome promenades. The beer of the place, termed
'Schwarzer Schöps', was once famous, and was largely exported
in the 16th cent.

Pleasant excursion to the S. through the *Schlesierthal* to the (1¾ hr.)
large and well preserved ruin of *Kynsburg*, and by **Charlottenbrunn** (*Deutsches Haus*), a prettily situated bath, to Waldenburg (p. 166).

The train crosses a viaduct; view of the Eulengebirge to the r.
Stations *Jacobsdorf, Faulbrück*.

Reichenbach (*Seliger's Hotel; Langerfeld's*), a town with old
fortifications and a Schloss, is historically interesting as the scene
of a victory gained by Frederick the Great over Laudon in 1762.
The Convention of Reichenbach, guaranteeing the subsistence of
the Turkish Empire, and a treaty between the Allies and Austria,
which was ratified at Prague in 1813, were also concluded here.

The **Eulengebirge** a picturesque mountain-district, may be visited from *Reichenbach* as follows: by diligence (in ¹|₂ hr.) to *Peterswaldau*, with a château of Count Stolberg, walk to (2¹|₄ M.) *Steinkunzendorf* (*Inn); thence (with guide, 10 Sgr.), over the (1 hr.) *Oberberg* to the *Forester's House* (*Inn), the (1¹|₄ hr.) *Schafberg*, and the (¹|₄ hr.) *Sonnenkoppe* (fine view). Then to the S. past the *Sonnenstein*, a mass of rock, and descend through wood to the (1 hr.) forester's house in the *Tränkegrund* (*Inn and Baths); ¹|₂ hr. *Neurode* (Deutsches Haus), and thence by diligence to Glatz in 2¹|₂ hrs.

The train next passes *Gnadenfrei*, a Moravian colony. **Frankenstein** *(Umlauf's Hotel; Deutsches Haus)*, a small town re-erected after a fire in 1858, with an old Schloss and a modern Rathhaus, situated in the most fertile district in Silesia, is the terminus of the railway.

Silberberg *(Schwarzer Adler)*, a small town fortified by Frederick the Great, is reached by diligence once daily in 1¹|₂ hr. The works are partly hewn in the solid rock. Fine view from the keep.

The road now leads to the S. to (7 M.) **Wartha** *(Löwe)*, on the Neisse, which possesses a shrine visited by 50,000 pilgrims annually. A steep path ascends to the Chapel of St. Anna on the *Warthaberg* (1838 ft.), where a fine view is obtained. The banks of the Neisse here are attractive; near the town the stream forces its passage through a rocky pass, formed by the spurs of the Schnee and Eulen-Gebirge.

About 7 M. to the E. of Wartha lies *Camenz*, the once wealthy Cistercian Abbey of which was suppressed in 1810. Frederick the Great, when pursued by the hostile Croatians in 1745, escaped detection here by assuming the garb of a monk. — The neighbouring *Hartaberg* is crowned by the *Fürstenburg*, an imposing château of the Princess Albert of Prussia. — *Reichenstein*, with an arsenic mine and foundry, lies 4³|₄ M. to the S. of Camenz. — About 7 M. to the S. of Reichenstein are the baths of *Landeck* (see below).

The road traverses deep ravines until beyond *Eichau* the *Passberg* commands a fine view of the mountain district of Glatz, enclosed by four ranges of hills, the *Heuscheuer*, the *Mense-Gebirge*, the *Schnee-Gebirge*, and the *Eulen-Gebirge*.

15 M. **Glatz** *(Neu-Breslau; Weisses Ross; Stadt Rom)*, a strongly fortified town on the Neisse, with 12,000 inhab., is commanded by the conspicuous keep of the old castle, 300 ft. above it, opposite to which is the modern fortress.

Glatzer Gebirge. From Glatz by carr. or diligence to *Ullersdorf*, *Kunzendorf* (both with fine parks), and (11¹|₂ M.) **Landeck** (1442 ft.). The baths, ³|₄ M. from the town, are chiefly frequented by Silesians and Poles (pleasant walk to the *Schrollenstein*, a beautiful point of view, ¹|₂ hr. to the S.; also to the *Karpenstein*, a ruined castle farther distant). Hence through the pretty *Bielethal* to (3 M.) *Seitenberg* (Brauhaus); walk in ¹|₂ hr. to the marble-quarries on the *Kreuzberg*, then descend in ¹|₂ hr. into the *Klassengrund*, and through the poor, straggling village of that name, and ascend in 1¹|₂ hr. through magnificent pine forest to a finger-post, ¹|₄ hr. beyond which the chalet (rustic inn) on the *Schneeberg* is reached. The summit (4338 ft.) which is attained in ¹|₂ hr., presents no comprehensive point of view; the traveller must therefore walk round the margin of the bleak table-land, in order to survey successively the basin of Glatz, the Silesian plain, the Altvater-Gebirge (to the E.), and the wild valleys of the March and its affluents which rise here towards the S. (The rugged paths descending to the S. and S. W. to the sources of the March and the Neisse, present no attractions.) From the above-mentioned finger-post descend in ¹|₂ hr. to the W. to the upper *Wölfels-grund;* ¹|₂ hr. farther down, the valley is joined by another valley lying more to the N. (travellers in the reverse direction may drive thus far, and here turn to the r.); 3³|₄ M. *Wölfelsmühle* (Inn, trout), with the pic-turesque *Wölfelsfall,* which is precipitated into a narrow rocky basin, rendered accessible by steps. The valley opens into the broad basin of Glatz 1¹|₂ M. lower down. The traveller may now drive in 1¹|₂ hr. by *Wölfels-dorf* to *Habelschwert;* for pedestrians, however, it is far preferable to make a short circuit to the N., in order to visit the conspicuous pilgrimage-chapel of *Maria Schnee* (Inn), situated on a pointed summit, and commanding a magnificent prospect. The district town of Habelschwert (*Drei Karpfen)* is 9 M. distant from Glatz, which may be reached by diligence. A pleasanter road, recommended to pedestrians and light carriages, leads on the l. bank of the Neisse by *Grafenort,* the property of Count Herberstein, with a beautiful park. Travellers who prefer driving to walking should make this excursion in the reverse direction, as, in descending in the direction described, carriages are not always to be obtained at Wöjfelsmühle.

From Glatz the old Prague road leads (diligence several times a day) to the W. to

14 M. **Reinerz** (1730 ft.) (*Bär; Krone; Bade-Gasthof),* a charmingly situated bath. The *Hohe-Mense* (2868 ft.), 2¹|₂ hrs. to the S., commands an extensive view towards Bohemia.

4¹|₂ M. *Lewin* (1381 ft.) (Feller) is the Prussian frontier town. To the N. of the road, 1¹|₂ M. from Lewin, lies the small bath of *Cúdowa* (Stern), from which the *Heuscheuer-Gebirge* (p. 179) may be ascended in 3 hrs. The route passes the *Wilde Loch,* a mass of rock hollowed out by the action of the water, forming a labyrinth which should not be explored without a guide.

9¹|₂ M. *Nachod,* see p. 180.

33. From Breslau to Vienna.

Railway. Express to Oderberg in 4 hrs. (fares 5 Thlr. 8, 4 Thlr. 1 Sgr.); thence to Vienna in 6¹|₄ hrs. (fares 13 fl. 15, 10 fl. 13 kr. Austr.).

The first part of the journey is uninteresting. Stations *Kattern, Leisewitz;* then *Ohlau* (Adler), a small town on the Oder, with extensive tobacco fields. To the r. near Brieg rises the church of *Mollwitz,* where the Austrians were defeated by Frederick the Great in 1741.

Brieg (*Hirsch; Kreuz)* on the Oder, with 14,800 inhab., contains an old Schloss of the princes of Brieg.

Branch-line from Brieg (in 1¹|₂ hr.) to **Neisse** (*Stern; Ross),* a fortified town with 18,500 inhab., in a marshy district. On Austrian territory, 19 M. to the S. of Neisse, in the *Gesenke,* a district of the Sudetengebirge, and 1¹|₂ M. from the post-stat. *Freiwaldau,* is situated **Gräfenberg,** with a celebrated hydropathic establishment founded by Priessnitz (d. 1851), the inventor of the system. Carr. from Neisse to Gräfenberg in 4—5 hrs. (one-horse 3, two-horse 4—5 Thlr.).

Next stations *Lossen, Löwen, Dambrau.* The Oder is crossed at **Oppeln** (*Biewald's Hotel; Adler),* the seat of government for Upper Silesia, possessing a church of great antiquity. Branch line to *Vossowska* (in 1 hr.), in connection with the railway on the r. bank of the Oder (p. 184).

The main line next skirts the *Annaberg* (with a celebrated pilgrimage-church), and soon reaches stat. *Kandrzin* (*Restaurant), 3 M. to the W. of the fortress **Cosel** on the Oder.

From Cosel to Cracow express in 11 hrs.; fares 4 Thlr. 6¹|₂, 2 Thlr.
13 Sgr. (from Breslau to Cracow in 13¹|₂ hrs.; fares 7 Thlr. 26 Sgr., 6 Thlr.).
The first Polish station is Gleiwitz *(Deutsches Haus)*, an old town with
13,000 inhab.; fine church and extensive government foundry. A busy
mining and manufacturing district is now traversed. *Morgenroth* is the
junction for *Tarnowitz*, and *Kattowitz*, the junction for *Nendza*. Beyond *Myslo-
witz* the once independent state of Cracow is entered. *Szczakowa* is the
junction for Warsaw. At *Maczki* a full view of the Carpathians is obtained.
A valley bounded by abrupt heights is traversed between *Chrzanow* and
Trzebinia; on the r. side of it are a ruined castle and the monastery of
Alwernia. Cracow, see *Baedeker's S. Germany and Austria.*

The Vienna train continues its route towards the S. At stat.
Ratiborer-Hammer the plain of the Oder is skirted. Alluvial de-
posits have here raised the bed of the river so considerably that
inundations are of very frequent occurrence. Branch-line from stat.
Nendza (in 4 hrs.) to *Kattowitz* (see above).

At **Ratibor** *(Jaschke)*, the seat of the Upper Silesian court of
appeal, with 14,000 inhab., the line again crosses the Oder; branch-
line to *Leobschütz*. Stations *Krzizanowitz, Annaberg.* The train
again crosses the Oder, which here forms the boundary between
Prussia and Austria, and stops at **Oderberg,** the seat of the Austrian
custom-house authorities.

From Oderberg to **Vienna,** see *Baedeker's S. Germany and
Austria.*

From Breslau to Beuthen by the *Rechte-Oderuferbahn*, or Railway
of the R. Bank of the Oder, in 4¹|₂ hrs. (3 Thlr. 14, 2 Thlr. 18, 1 Thlr.
22 Sgr.). Principal stations *Oels*, a pleasant town, once the capital of a
principality, on the *Oelsa;* on a height a Schloss of 1558, with an extensive
park. *Namslau*, near which is *Minkowsky*, where General Seidlitz died in
1773. *Vossowska*, junction for Oppeln (see above). *Tarnowitz*, the headquarters of the important Silesian mining district. **Beuthen**, the capital
of a district, with 14,000 inhab.

'34. From Breslau to Dresden.

Railway in 7¹|₂ hrs.; fares 7 Thlr. 2, 5 Thlr. 4, 3 Thlr. 16¹|₂ Sgr.
From Breslau to **Görlitz,** see R. 27. (From Görlitz to Hirschberg, see p. 166). To the l. rises the *Landskrone* (p. 165).

Stat. *Reichenbach* (Sonne), the last Prussian town. On 22nd May,
1813, after the battle of Bautzen, the French generals Bruyères and
Kirchner fell near Reichenbach, and the ball which occasioned
Kirchner's death, fired by a Russian battery near the village, also
mortally wounded Duroc, Napoleon's favourite chamberlain. A
simple block of sandstone marks the spot. Next stat. *Zöblitz.*

Stat. **Löbau** *(Wettiner Hof; Stadt Leipzig; Schwarzes Lamm;
Rail. Restaurant), in the Wend dialect *Lubij* (i. e. low-lying), the
oldest of the six allied towns of Upper Lusatia, whose league was
entered into here in 1346, is a busy place with 5500 German inhab.,
while the neighbouring country is peopled with Wends, a Sclavonic
race differing from their German neighbours in language, customs,
and dress. The towers of the Rathhaus and the Johanniskirche are
both of the 14th cent.

The site of the old fortifications is now occupied with pleasant promenades.

Excursions. The *Löbauer Berg, 650 ft. above the town, with an iron tower and an *inn at the top, reached in 1|2 hr. from the station, commands a fine view. — The *Rothenstein*, 1 hr. to the E. — The *Cottmar*, see p. 187. — The *Scala*, a picturesque valley watered by the *Löbauer Bach*, 1|2 hr. to the N.

Stat. *Pommritz*, near which (3/4 M. to the S.) lies the village of Hochkirch, memorable as the scene of one of the bloodiest and most disastrous battles fought by Frederick the Great (14th. Oct., 1758).

Marshal Keith, Frederick's well-known general, fell in this battle. He was the son of Lord Keith, and an adherent of the Pretender. After the battle of Sheriffmuir he was branded as a Jacobite, and obliged to quit the country. He afterwards entered the Russian service, in which he greatly distinguished himself, and attained the rank of field-marshal. Having resigned his appointment he repaired to Berlin, where Frederick the Great nominated him a Prussian marshal and governor of Berlin. Sir Robert Keith, British ambassador at Vienna, erected a monument to the memory of his kinsman in the church at Hochkirch in 1776. The churchyard was bravely defended by the Prussians. Marks of balls, especially near the S. entrance, are still seen on the church. The bench on which the marshal lay when mortally wounded is beneath the pulpit, but has been almost entirely carried off by relic-hunters. The schoolmaster, who lives on the N. side of the church, keeps the key. Good inn adjoining the church.

A favourite point of view is the *Czorneboh (i. e. devil's mountain; 1764 ft.), to the S. of Hochkirch, with tower and inn on the summit, reached in 1 1|2 hr. from Pommritz, and in 2 3|4 hrs. from Bautzen. To *Wuischke*, at the foot of the hill, a carriage-road; thence to the summit by a good path in 3|4 hr. At the foot of the tower lies a huge block of granite, said to be an altar of the ancient heathen Wends. The prospect is very fine, embracing the vast and fertile plain of Upper Lusatia, E. the Landskrone, near Görlitz, and the Giant Mts., S. the Bohemian Mts., S. W. those of Saxon Switzerland, among which the Lilienstein and Königstein are most conspicuous.

Stat. **Bautzen,** Wend *Budissin (Goldne Weintraube; Goldne Krone; Weisses Ross; Sonne; Adler)*, the handsome and busy capital of Saxon Upper Lusatia (12,600 inhab.), formerly one of the six allied towns, and still surrounded by walls and watch-towers, is picturesquely situated on a height above the *Spree*. The *Church of St. Peter* in the Fleischmarkt, founded in 1213, has been used since 1635 by the Rom. Catholics and Protestants in common. *Schloss Ortenburg*, situated on an eminence on the Spree at the W. end of the town, now contains government offices. On the tower is a life-size figure of Matthew Corvinus of Hungary, commemorating the restoration of the castle by that monarch in 1483. The *Rathhaus*, containing portraits of the burgomasters of the last 400 years, the *Gymnasium*, the *Barracks*, and the *Landhaus*, or Hall of the Estates, may also be noticed. On the l. bank of the Spree lies the village of *Seidau (Zidow)*, chiefly inhabited by Wends. The *Protschenberg* near it is a good point of view. On 20th and 21th May, 1813, the Russians and Prussians under Blücher were repulsed by Napoleon in this neighbourhood.

The valley of the Spree is now crossed by a long viaduct. *Rammenau*, the birthplace of *Fichte* (in 1762), lies 3 M. to the N.

of stat. *Bischofswerda.* Next stations *Fischbach* and *Radeberg*, a small town with a glass-work, and the junction of a branch-line to Camenz.

To Camenz railway in 1 hr. (22, 15, 11 Sgr.). Stations *Grossröhrs-dorf, Pulsnitz;* then **Camenz** *(Gold. Hirsch)*, the birthplace of Lessing (in 1729), to whom a colossal bust was erected near the Wend church in 1863. View from the tower on the *Huthberg*, ¹|₄ hr. from the town.

Dresden, see p. 191.

35. From Löbau to Trautenau by Zittau and Reichenberg.

Railway to *Reichenberg* in 2¹|₂ hrs. (fares to Zittau 26, 18, 13 Sgr.; thence to Reichenberg 1 fl. 35, 1 fl., or 65 kr. Austr.); from Reichenberg to Alt-Paka in 3³|₄ hrs. (fares 3 fl. 60, 2 fl. 70, 1 fl. 80 kr.); thence to *Trau-tenau-Parschnitz* in 2¹|₄ hrs. (fares 2 fl. 24, 1 fl. 87, 1 fl. 13 kr.).

Löbau, see p. 185. — Stations *Neu-* and *Ober Cunnersdorf;* the *Cottmar* (1770 ft.),. ¹/₂ hr. to the S., commands a view. Then

Herrnhut *(Gemeinde-Logis)*, a pleasant village with 1000 inhab., founded in 1722 by several families from Moravia who belonged to the Moravian brotherhood, and had quitted their country on account of their religion. The site was presented to the exiles by Count Zinzendorf, the proprietor. The *Hutberg*, on the slope of which the pretty cemetery is situated, commands a pleasing view.

Stations *Ober-* and *Mittel-Oderwitz.* As Zittau is approached the scenery becomes more picturesque. The station is ¹/₂ M. from the town.

Zittau *(*Sächs. Hof; *Sonne; *Engel.* One-horse carr. to the Oybin 1¹/₃ Thlr. for ¹/₂ day, 2 Thlr. for a whole day; to Waltersdorf and to the Lausche direct to the upper inn 2, by the Oybin and Jonsdorf 2¹/₂ Thlr.; *two-horse* one-half more. Two-horse carr. to Friedland 3, Liebwerda 5²/₃, Warmbrunn 8 — 10 Thlr.), a manu-facturing town with 18,000 inhab., the principal cotton-spinning place in Saxony,. is situated in a fertile and undulating district. In 1757, after the battle of Kollin, the town was occupied by the Prussians, and was almost entirely reduced to ashes in consequence of the bombardment by the Austrians under Prince Charles of Lor-ráine. Handsome *Rathhaus*, erected in 1844. The *Church of St. John* was re-erected in 1836; view from the tower. The *Ceme-tery*, to the S. E. of the town, affords a good survey of the Neissethal viaduct.

From a rocky basin to the S. of Zittau (a walk of 2 hrs.; comp. Map, p. 206) rises the *Oybin (1621 ft.), a wooded sandstone rock, in shape resembling a beehive, and crowned with the highly picturesque ruins of a monastery and a castle, curiously combined. The castle, a robbers' stronghold, was destroyed by Emp. Charles IV., who founded the monas-tery on its site in 1369. The latter was deserted in 1545 by the Celestine monks who occupied it, and was destroyed by fires in 1577 and 1681. The church with its lofty Gothic arches, some of which show remains of beautiful tracery, is the best preserved part. The tower affords a pictu-resque view. Ancient tombstones in the churchyard. *Inn* adjacent. At the base of the hill is the scattered village of *Oybin* (Kretscham, Dürling), with a number of villas of Zittau manufacturers.

Opposite the Oybin, to the E., rises the *Töpfer* ($^3/_4$ hr.), another height remarkable for its grotesque sandstone rocks. The direct route to it from Zittau diverges from the road to the l., $^1/_2$ hr. before the Oybin is reached.

The *Lausche (2507 ft.), 2 hrs. to the W. of the Oybin, 3 hrs. from Zittau (guide advisable, 10 Sgr.), is the highest point of the range of hills which separate Upper Lusatia from Bohemia. It commands an extensive and magnificent prospect, embracing the whole of Lusatia and the Saxon Switzerland, the Teplitz and Bohemian Mts. (as far as Prague), the Iser-kamm, the Tafelfichte, and the Giant Mts. The inn at the top stands half in Saxony, half in Bohemia (good Hungarian wine, bad quarters for the night.)

The **Hochwald**, 1 hr. S. of the Oybin, a height easily ascended, is another good point of view (inn at the top; guide from the foot of the Oybin to the Hochwald and back 8 Ngr.).

Friedland (*Herzog v. Friedland*, by the Schloss; *Adler, Weisses Ross*, in the town), a Bohemian town 14 M. to the E. of Zittau (diligence once daily) is commanded by the imposing old Schloss, 200 ft. above it, begun in the 11th and 12th cent., and completed in 1551. The tower was erected as early as 1014; the basaltic rock on which it stands is exposed to view in the court-yard. After various vicissitudes, the castle was purchased in 1622 by Wallenstein whose portrait here is said to be a faithful likeness. The numerous family portraits with which the walls are hung belong to the present proprietor, the Count of Clam-Gallas. Weapons used in the Thirty Years' War are also shown. Fine view (custodian 10 Sgr.). Route to Liebwerda, see. p. 166.

· Passengers' luggage is examined by Austrian custom-house officers at Zittau. The train now crosses the great *Neisse Viaduct*, $^1/_2$ M. in length, supported by 34 arches, 72 ft. above the stream. The pleasant valley of the Neisse is then ascended. Stations *Grottau, Kratzau, Hachendorf;* to the r. a view of the *Jeschken* (3173 ft.).

Reichenberg *(Frank's Hotel; Union)*, the largest town in Bohemia after Prague, is a cloth-making place, with 25,000 inhab. The Kreuzkirche contains an old altar-piece, Mary and the Child (Dürer?). Schloss and Rathhaus of the 16th cent. New Prot. church. *Excursion to the Jeschken and back, half-a-day.

The line ascends in windings, and at stat. *Langenbruck* reaches the watershed between the Neisse and *Iser*. It then turns to the W. and descends to *Reichenau* (comp. p. 189) and *Liebenau*, two glass-making places. It next descends the *Mohelka Thal* and crosses it, affording picturesque glimpses of *Schloss Sichrow*, the seat of Prince Rohan, built in the English Gothic style, and surrounded by extensive grounds. Beyond stat. *Sichrow* a tunnel 700 yds. long. Country fertile and well peopled.

Stat. **Turnau** *(Goldne Krone; Löwe)*, a town with 4500 inhab., lies on an eminence on the l. bank of the Iser, $^3/_4$ M. from the railway. The modern *Marienkirche is a very fine Gothic edifice. Turnau was formerly celebrated for its jewel-cutting establishments, and imitations of precious stones. The hydropathic establishment of *Wartenberg* lies $1^1/_2$ M. to the S.; about 3 M. to the S. E. of it are situated the ruin of *Waldstein*, the ancestral seat of the celebrated Wallenstein, and the mediæval château of *Gross-*

Skal, with beautiful grounds (view from the tower). Farther distant is the ruin of *Trosky*, on two conspicuous rocks.

From Turnau to Prague railway in 4 hrs. (fares 5 fl. 40, 4 fl. 5, 2 fl. 70 kr.). Stations *Münchengrätz* (Wallenstein is buried in the church of St. Anna here; a battle was fought in the vicinity in 1866), *Jung-Bunzlau* (branch-line to Kolin), *Kuttenthal, Obristwi-Klomin*, and *Kralup*, where the line joins the Dresden and Prague railway (p. 207).

The scenery between Turnau and Eisenbrod is the finest on the line. Beautiful rock and forest landscapes, at the foot of which flows the impetuous Iser, are now passed. From stat. *Kleinskal*, which is grandly situated, an interesting route leads past the castle of that name (among the ruins of which there is a 'Rock Pantheon', with reminiscences of Austrian celebrities), by the ruin of *Friedstein*, and the *Kopainberg* (2161 ft.; *view), direct to (2 hrs.) *Reichenau* (see p. 188). To the l. the château of *Dalimeric*, with its double tower.

The picturesque valley of the Iser is now traversed. Stations *Eisenbrod, Semil* (with a château of Prince Rohan, converted into a government mining office), *Liebstadtl*, and **Alt-Paka**, a junction where passengers for Trautenau change carriages. The line to the S.W. leads to *Josephstadt* (p. 181).

Stat. *Starkenbach* on the line to Trautenau is a small manufacturing town with an old Schloss. The church contains a font of 1545. Stat. *Pelsdorf*.

Branch Railway from Pelsdorf in 14 min. to **Hohenelbe** (1477 ft.) (**Hôtel Bosener*; *Schwan*), a small town pleasantly situated on both banks of the Elbe, on the spurs of the Giant Mts. The small houses with their lofty gables are flanked with arcades borne by wooden columns. The Schloss is surrounded by a fine park. Linen is the staple commodity here. The *Heidelberg* (3120 ft.), which rises above the town, commands a fine view. From Hohenelbe to the Schneekoppe, see p. 178.

From Stat. *Arnau* a road leads to (9 M.) Freiheit (see below). Stations *Kottwitz, Pilnikau*.

Trautenau *(Weisses Ross; Blauer Stern)*, a town with 6000 inhab. on the *Aupe*, almost entirely rebuilt since a great fire in 1861, is the centre of the Bohemian linen manufacture. In the Realschule is preserved an interesting collection of the Flora of the Giant Mts. The Prussians gained a victory over the Austrians in the vicinity in 1866. Several monuments to the slain have been erected on the *Johannisberg*, or *Kapellenberg*, to the S. of the town, where the battle raged most fiercely. The *Gablenzhöhe*, ½ M. distant, is crowned with an iron obelisk to Marshal v. Gablenz. Fine view towards the Giant Mts.

From Trautenau to Johannisbad 8 M.; diligence daily in summer. The road ascends the populous valley of the *Aupe* and passes *Altstadt, Trübenwasser*, and *Jungbuch*, all of which possess extensive flax-mills. At *Freiheit* (1493 ft.) it turns to the l. into a narrow valley, where the pleasant little Johannisbad is situated (*Gastgebäude; Deutsches Haus; Stadt Breslau;* numerous private apartments). The alkaline chalybeate spring is beneficial in cases of rheumatism, etc. The *Ladig*, the *Jägerhaus*, the wild ravine of the *Kläuse*, and the *Blaustein* are the prettiest points in the pleasant environs.

36. From Berlin to Dresden.

Railway in 4¹|₂—5 hrs.; express fares 6 Thlr. 2, 4 Thlr. 14, 3 Thlr.
10 Sgr.; ordinary 5 Thlr. 5, 3 Thlr. 25¹|₂, 2 Thlr. 22 Sgr.

Soon after the station is quitted, the *Kreuzberg* (p. 33) appears
on the l.; r. *Teltow*, then the windmill-hill of *Ruhlsdorf;* l. *Gross-
Beeren*, where, on 23rd Aug., 1813, the Prussians under Bülow defeated a French corps, consisting principally of Saxon soldiers,
under Oudinot. A turreted church, erected in 1817, and an iron
monument mark the battle-field. — At the church of **Jüterbog**
one of Tetzel's indulgences is still shown. The old gates of the
town merit inspection. The line to Halle and Leipsic diverges
here. Beyond this the country is flat and uninteresting.

Dennewitz, 2 M. to the S.W. of Jüterbog, was the scene of a great
victory gained by the Prussians under Bülow, on 6th Sept., 1813, over
Ney and Oudinot, who lost 15,000 men and 80 cannon. Berlin itself was
thus saved from imminent danger.

Stations *Holzdorf, Herzberg, Falkenberg* (junction of the Halle,
Sorau, and Guben line, p. 162).

Stat *Burgsdorf;* then *Röderau*, the junction of this line with
the Leipsic and Dresden Railway (p. 215). From stat. *Pristewitz*
a branch-line to *Grossenhayn*, with important cloth-factories, and
Cottbus (p. 164). The scenery now improves. Stations *Niederau*
and *Coswig* (the junction of the line to Leipsic by Meissen and
Döbeln).

The train skirts vine-clad slopes. On the hill to the r. is the
château of *Weisstrop*, the property of the Duke of Lucca, who in
1849 resigned the throne of Parma in favour of his son (d. 1854).
Stat. *Kötzschenbroda;* to the l. *Lössnitz*, with an extensive cham-
pagne-manufactory. Stat. *Weintraube*. The train stops at *Neustadt-
Dresden*, 1 M. from the hotels of the Altstadt. Omnibuses, etc.,
see below.

37. Dresden.

Arrival. Cab-tickets are handed to travellers on their arrival, as at
Berlin (p. 1). *Cab* to the town for 1 pers. 4, 2 pers. 5, 3 pers. 6, 4 pers.
8 Ngr.; bridge-toll 1 Ngr. for each horse; each heavy package 2 Ngr.
(comp. p. 191). — There are three railway-stations at Dresden: 1. *Bohemian Station* (Pl. 4), for the trains to the Saxon Switzerland, Bodenbach,
and Prague, and for Tharandt, Freiberg, and Chemnitz; 2. *Leipsic Station*
(Pl. 5), for Leipsic and Berlin; 3. *Silesian Station* (Pl. 6), for Görlitz and
Breslau. The first two are in the Altstadt, the last two in the Neustadt.
Some of the trains stop at both stations.

Hotels. In the *Altstadt:* *BELLEVUE, beautifully situated near the
bridge; *VICTORIA, Johannes-Allee, S. of the Altmarkt; *HÔTEL DE SAXE;
all of the first class: R. from 20, L. 8, B. 12, D. 1 Thlr., A. 8 Ngr.;
GRAND UNION HOTEL, Bismarck-Platz, by the Bohemian station; *BERLIN,
ROME, both in the Neumarkt; LINGKE's HOTEL, See-Strasse 22; RHEI-
NISCHER HOF, See-Strasse 6; *STADT GOTHA, Schloss-Strasse 8; *WEBER's,
Ostra-Allee, near the Zwinger. — HÔTEL DE FRANCE and *GOLDNER ENGEL,
in the Wilsdruffer-Str.; DEUTSCHES HAUS and *PREUSSISCHER HOF in the
Scheffel-Str.; BRITISH HOTEL, Landhaus-Str. 22; STADT WEIMAR, Pfarrgasse,

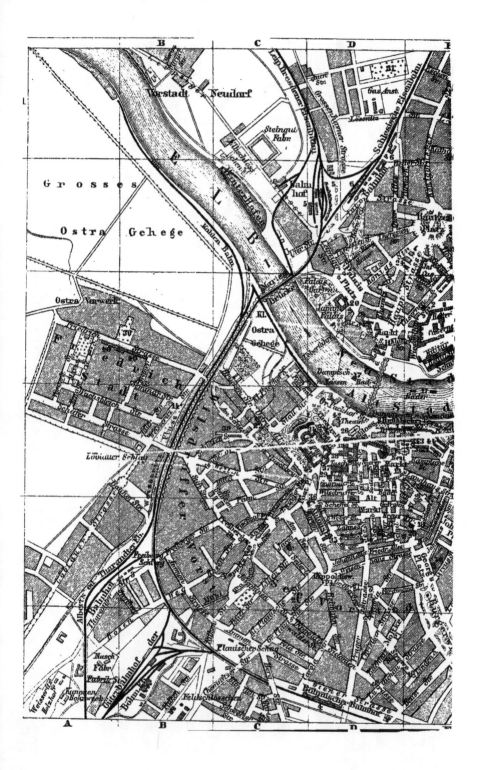

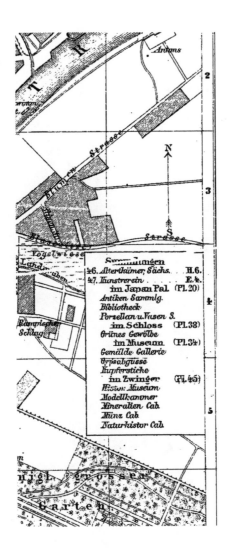

Sammlungen
46. Alterthümer, Sächs. H.6.
47. Kunstverein E.4.
     im Japan Pal. (Pl.20)
Antiken Sammlg.
Bibliotheck
Porzellan u. Vasen S.
     im Schloss (Pl.33)
Grünes Gewölbe
     im Museum (Pl.34)
Gemälde Gallerie
Gypsabgüsse
Kupferstiche
     im Zwinger (Pl.45)
Histor. Museum
Modellkammer
Mineralien Cab.
Münz Cab.
Naturhistor. Cab.

and ZWEI SCHWARZE ADLER, Zahnsgasse 1, both second-class; CURLÄNDER HAUS, by the Bohemian station. — *Hôtels Garnis:* HÔTEL DU NORD, Lüttichau-Str. 17; *STADT MOSKAU, Christians-Str. 5, both recommended to families.

In the *Neustadt:* *STADT WIEN, by the bridge; *KRONPRINZ, Haupt-Str.; both first-class. — HÔTEL ROYAL, near the Silesian station; *KAISER's and WERTHMANN's, both in the market-place. *COBURG, at the Leipsic station. DREI PALMZWEIGE, by the Japanese Palace, STADT PRAG, Gr. Meissner-Str., and STADT GÖRLITZ in the same street, all unpretending.

Restaurants. *Belvedere*, on the Brühl Terrace (p. 194), concerts frequently given in the evening. **Hôtel de France*, Wilsdruffer - Str., good beer; **Müller*, Neumarkt, D. at 10 and 15 Sgr.; **Deville* (Café de l'Europe), Frauen-Str. 1; *Goldner Schwan* and *Strassburger Hof*, both near the Frauenkirche; *Helbig*, by the bridge, with view. In the Neustadt, *Henne*, Bautzner Str. 44 b, with garden. — **Wine.** *Habert*, Schloss-Str. 25; *Seulen*, Wall-Str. 16; *Gerlach*, Moritz-Str. 22; **Victoria-Keller*, See-Str.; *Röder*, Neustädter Markt; *Hungarian* wine at No. 3 Sophien-Str. — **Beer.** *Dauch*, Gr. Brüdergasse 34; **Fiebiger*, Gr. Brüdergasse 13; *Renner* (Bohemian beer), Marien-Str. 22; *Lussert*, Frauen-Str. 2; *Waldschlösschen*, Post-Platz; *Ancot*, Markt 8, in the Neustadt; *Nürnberg*, Wilsdruffer-Str. 16; *Neumann*, at the corner of the Schössergasse and Sporergasse; *Medinger Bierhalle*, Gr. Brüdergasse, near the Zwinger; Berlin 'Weissbier' at *Zimmermann's*, Kl. Brüdergasse 9. — **Cafés and Confectioners:** **Trepp*, Altmarkt and Scheffelgasse 1; **Café Reale*, *Belvedere*, both on the Brühl Terrace; *Lässig*, Prager-Str. 50; *Köhler*, Jüdenhof 2.

Pleasure Gardens. *Schiller-Schlösschen*, *Wald-Schlösschen*, both in the Schiller-Str., r. bank; fine views. — *Grosser Garten* (p. 204). — *Bergkeller*, Berg-Str.; *Feld-Schlösschen*, on the Chemnitz road; *Felsenkeller*, in the Plauenscher Grund.

Newspapers in the *Literary Museum*, Waisenhaus-Strasse 31. Adm 2½ Ngr., per week 10 Ngr.; open 8 a. m. to 10 p. m.

American Club (U. S. newspapers, etc.) Victoria-Str. 22.

English Club Bürgerwiese 20.

Cabs. One-horse ('*Droschke*') *per drive* within the inner town, with or without crossing the river 5, 6, 7, 9 Ngr. for 1, 2, 3 or 4 pers.; same fares from the inner town to the suburbs, but without crossing the river; if the river be crossed, 7, 8, 9, and 11 Ngr. — *By time.* For 20 min. 5, 6, 7, 9 Ngr.; ½ hr. 7½, 9, 10, 12 Ngr.; ¾ hr. 10, 12, 14, 16 Ngr.; 1 hr. 14, 16, 18, 20 Ngr.; at night (10—6, in winter 10—8) double fares. Small articles free; each box 2 Ngr. *Bridge-toll* 1 Ngr. per horse additional. — A bargain should be made for longer excursions, the usual charge for which is 6 Thlr. per day and a fee to the driver.

Omnibuses. 1. From the *Altmarkt* (Pl. D, 4, 5) to the *Schiller-Schlösschen* and *Wald-Schlösschen* every ¼ hr., 1½ Ngr. — 2. From the *Bohemian Station* (Pl. E, 7) to the *Bischofsweg* (Pl. E, F, 1) every ¼ hr., 1½ Ngr. — 3. From the *Schloss-Platz* (Pl. D, 4) to *Plauen*, every 1½ hr. in the morning, every ½ hr. in the afternoon. — 4. From the *Wald-Schlösschen* to the *Weisse Hirsch* several times a day, 3 Ngr. — 5. After the theatre to the *Neustadt* and *Antonstadt*, 2 Ngr. — 6. From the *Schloss-Platz* to the *Grosse Garten* several times a day, in the afternoon almost every ½ hr. — 7. From *Dresden* (from the Elbberg and from the Neumarkt) to *Blasewitz* almost every ½ hr. — 8. From *Dresden* to *Lockwitz* in summer. — 9. From the *Post-Platz* to *Haury's Ruh* several times a day. — 10. From the *Palais-Platz* to *Moritzburg* on Sundays only. Time-tables published by Blochmann and by Gärtner, 1 Ngr.

Tramway from the Bohemian Station (p. 190) to *Blasewitz* (p. 205) every 10 min.; same station to *Plauen* (p. 211) every ½ hr.

Post-Office (Pl. 36) open from 7 a. m. to 7 p. m.; there are also eight branch-offices. — **Telegraph Offices** at No. 2 Waisenhaus-Str. (open day and night) and No. 15 Rhänitzgasse (open by day only).

Baths. *Dianabad* (with Turkish and vapour baths), on the Bürgerwiese; *Albertsbad*, Ostra-Allee 38; *Johannisbad*, Königs-Str. 11; *Prinz-Friedrichs-Bad*, Reitbahn-Str. — *River Baths* above and below the old bridge.

Shops. The best are in the Schloss-Str., the Alt- and Neu-Markt, the See-Str., and the Wilsdruffer-Strasse. In the Schloss-Str., opposite the Schlossthor, is a depôt of the pórcelain of Meissen. (Caution is necessary in purchasing so-called 'old Dresden china' at the second-hand shops.) Opticians: *Lietzmann,* Frauen-Str.; *Roettig,* Ferdinands-Platz 1. Chocolate-manufacturers: *Jordan und Timaeus,* near the Japanese Palace. Cigars at *Dressler's,* Sophien-Str. 7.

Theatres. The *Hoftheater,* in the Theater-Platz, was burned down in 1869. Temporary theatre in the grounds of the Zwinger; performances daily, beginning at 6. 30; amphitheatre 1½ Thlr., parquet 1⅙ Thlr, reserved seat 25 Sgr., first boxes 1½ Thlr., second boxes 20—25 Sgr. (closed in May). — 'Meldekarten' (comp. p. 5) must be posted in time to reach their destination on the 2nd day previous to the performance for which tickets are desired, 12—7 p. m. — *Zweites Theater* (Pl. 43, G, 6), in the Grosse Garten; performances daily in summer (closed in winter). — *Neustädter Theater,* Alberts-Platz.

Steamboats. *Up the Elbe* (piers above the old bridge on both sides of the river): in summer almost every hour to *Loschwitz* (p. 205), *Blasewitz* (p. 205), *Hosterwitz, Pillnitz* (p. 205), *Pirna* (p. 206), *Rathen* (p. 209), *Königstein* (p. 206), *Wehlen* (p. 208), *Schandau* (p. 209). *Down the Elbe* (pier below the old bridge): to *Meissen* (p. 215) 4 times daily.

Valets-de-Place 1 Thlr. per day, 20 Ngr. for half-a-day.

English Church, consecrated in 1869, in the Wiener Strasse, near the Bohemian Station (p. 194). *Presbyterian Service* at No. 7, Ferdinands-Str. *American Episcopal Church,* Ostra-Allee 5.

Collections (consult also the '*Dresdener Anzeiger*' or other local news-paper).

Acoustic Cabinet, Kauffmann's (Pl. 22), Ostra-Allee 9, a collection of self-acting musical instruments, closed since the death of the proprietor.

Antiquities in the Japanese Palace (p. 203), from 1st May to 31st Oct. on Wed. and Sat., 10—2, gratis; on other days, and during the rest of the year, 5 Ngr.

Arms, Gallery of (p. 195), on Tuesd. and Frid., 9—1, gratis; on other days by cards for 1—6 pers., 9—1, 2 Thlr.

Casts, Collection of (p. 200), from 1st May to 31st Oct. on Mond. and Thursd., 10—2, gratis; on other days, and during the rest of the year 5 Ngr.

Coins, Cabinet of (p. 203), open to scientific visitors on Tuesd. and Frid., 10—1.

**Drawings and Engravings* (p. 200), on Tuesd., Thursd., and Frid., 10—2, gratis; on Mond. and Wed. 5 Ngr.

**Grünes Gewölbe* ('Green Vault' p. 195), from 1st May to 31st Oct. on Sund. and holidays 11—2, Mond., Wed., Thursd. and Sat. 9—1, 10 Ngr.; from 1st Nov. to 30th April daily except Sund. and holidays 10—1, by cards admitting 1—6 pers., 3 Thlr.

Kreuzthurm (p. 202), view of Dresden, from early morning to 8 p. m.

**Library* (p. 203) in the Japanese Palace, on week-days, 9—1, Wed. and Sat. 9—11, 2—4 (fee 5 Ngr.), 10 pers. only admitted at a time; application must be made at the office on the 1st floor.

Mathematical and Physical Instruments and *Models* (p. 201) from 1st May to 31st Oct., on Wed. 9—12, 5 Ngr.; on Sat., 9—12 gratis; to scientific visitors open on other days, 10—12.

Museum of Antiquities (p. 204), daily 8—12, and after 3 p. m., 5 Ngr.

Museum, Historical (p. 201), from 1st May to 31st Oct. daily, except Wed. and Sat. (Sund. and holidays 11—2, week-days 9—1), 5 Ngr. — Also during the above months on Wed., 8—4, and on the other days on which the Museum is open, 8—9 and 1—4; and in winter on week-days except Sat., 1—3, and on Sund. and holidays, 11—2, by card admitting 1—8 pers., 3 Thlr. (on application at the office). Closed on Easter-Sunday, Whit-Sunday, Christmas-Day and 24th Dec., Good Friday, fast-days, and Saturdays.

Museum, Mineralogical (p. 201) in the Zwinger, from 1st May to 31st Oct. on Tuesd. and Frid., 10—12, gratis; on other days, 5 Ngr.

Museum, Natural History (p. 201) in the Zwinger, from 1st May to 31st Oct., on Tuesd. and Frid. 8—10, anthropological collection 9—11, gratis; on Mond., Wed., Thursd., and Sat. 8—2, 5 Ngr.

**Museum, Rietschel* (p. 204) in the Schloss in the Grosse Gar·en (which also contains the Museum of Antiquities), from 1st May to 31st Oct., on Wed. and Sat., 3—6, gratis; on other days, except Sund. and' holidays, 3—6, 2¹|₂ Ngr. — During the rest of the year (on application at the office of the collection of casts) by card for 1—3 pers. 15 Ngr., each additional pers. 5 Ngr.

Palace, Royal (p. 194), daily by card procurable at the Hofmarschallamt, or office of the intendant, for 1—3 pers. 15 Ngr., each additional pers. 5 Ngr. (in winter by special permission only). ·

**Picture Gallery* (p. 197) daily; on Sund. and holidays, 11—2, and on Tuesd., Thursd., and Frid., 10—4, gratis; on Wed. and Sat. 10—4, 5 Ngr. (From 1st Nov. to 15th Apr. closed at 3 p. m.).

Picture Gallery of the Kunstverein (Pl. 47), on the Brühl Terrace, daily 11—3 (2¹|₂ Ngr).

Porcelain and Vases (p. 203) in the Japanese Palace, from 1st May to 31st Oct. on Mond., Tuesd., Thursd. and Frid. 2—5, 10 Ngr.; also on Wed. and Sat. 9—5, on other days 9—2, by card admitting 1—6 pers., 2 Thlr. ·

Silberkammer, Royal (p. 195), in the palace, daily, except Sat. and Sund., 9—1 and 4—6; tickets at the Hofmarschallamt, 1—3 pers. 15 Ngr., each additional pers. 5 Ngr.

Zoological Garden (p. 204) daily 5 Ngr., Sund. 3 Ngr.

Diary. (Consult the 'Dresdener Anzeiger' or other local newspaper, where concerts, theatrical performances, etc., are advertised. Compare also the above list.)

Daily. Picture Gallery 10—4, Sund. and holidays 11—2. Library 9—1 (except Sund. and holidays). Historical Museum (except Wed. and Sat.) 9—1, or 11—2. Green Vault (except Tues. and Frid.) 9—1, Sund. 11—2 (10 Ngr.). Museum of Antiquities 8—12, 3—6. Porcelain and Vases (except Sund.) 2—5, or 9—5. Rietschel Museum (except Sund. and holidays) 3—6, on four days admission 2¹|₂ Ngr., in winter 15 Ngr. for 1—3 pers. — Kunstverein 11—3.

Sundays. Church music at the Rom. Cath. Court Church (p. 194) 11—12, and 4 p. m.

Mondays. Casts 10—2 gratis.

Tuesdays. Gallery of Arms 9—1 gratis. — Natural History Museum 8—10. Mineralogical Museum 10—12. — Engravings 10—12. — Coins 10—1.

Wednesdays. Mathematical collection 9—12, 5 Ngr. — Antiquities 10—2.

Thursdays. Casts 10—2 gratis. — Engravings 10—2.

Fridays. Gallery of Arms at 8 and 10 a. m. — Natural History Museum 8—10. Mineralogical Museum 10—12. Engravings 10—2. Coins 10—1.

Saturdays. Antiquities 10—2. Mathematical Collection 9—12 gratis.

The Royal Collections are *closed* on Easter-Sunday, Whitsunday, Christmas-Day, Good Friday, and on Penitentiary Days and on 24th Dec.

Principal Attractions. Picture Gallery (p. 197), Green Vault (p. 195), Historical Museum (p. 201). Walk along the Brühl Terrace, cross the old bridge, traverse the Neustadt, and return by the Marienbrücke; then past the Zwinger and through the Altstadt to the Grosse Garten. — Saxon Switzerland, see R. 39. :

Dresden (319 ft.), the capital of the Kingdom of Saxony, mentioned in history for the first time in 1206, and the residence of the sovereigns since 1485, was greatly extended and embellished by the splendour-loving Augustus the Strong (1694—1736), and has rapidly increased during the present century. Population 177,095. The city lies on both banks of the *Elbe*, which separates the ALTSTADT (S. side), with its three suburbs which have sprung

up since 1810, and the *Friedrichsstadt,* from the NEUSTADT, which
was re-erected after a fire in 1686, and the *Antonsstadt* (N. side).
The beautiful environs and the magnificent picture gallery attract
numerous visitors, and a considerable English community resides
here for the sake of the educational and other advantages. The
handsome *English Church* in the Wiener Strasse near the Bohemian
Station (Pl. D, 6), was completed in 1869.

The Altstadt and Neustadt are connected by means of two stone
bridges. The **Old Bridge,** the upper of the two, constructed in the
13th cent., restored in 1727—31, and partially blown up by Marshal
Davoust on 19th March, 1813, in order to cover his retreat, is $1/4$
M. in length and rests on 16 arches. About $1/3$ M. below it is the
Marienbrücke, 250 yds. in length and borne by 12 arches, com-
pleted in 1852, and serving both for railway and ordinary traffic.
Both bridges command a pleasant view, particularly the latter.

Several of the chief attractions of Dresden are situated on the l.
bank of the river, close to the old bridge. To the l. of the traveller
approaching from the Neustadt lies the Brühl Terrace; opposite him
are the Royal Palace and the Rom. Cath. Court Church; to the r.
are the Museum with the Zwinger, which contains the most important collections, and the new Hoftheater.

The *Brühl Terrace (Pl. 8), rising immediately above the Elbe,
and $1/4$ M. in length, is a favourite promenade. It is approached
from the Schloss-Platz by a broad flight of steps adorned with *groups
of Night, Morning, Noon, and Evening, in sandstone, by *Schilling.*
The terrace is planted with trees, and on the side next the town is
bounded by the exhibition building of the *Kunstverein* (Pl. 47) and
the *Academy of Art* (Pl. 1). At the entrance to the latter are medallion portraits of Lindenau, Quandt, Thürmer, and Rietschel, four
highly distinguished members. A monument to Rietschel on the
terrace is projected. Beyond these buildings are the cafés mentioned at p. 191.

At the E. end of the terrace is the **Synagogue** (Pl. 41), erected in
1840 in the Oriental style. Service on Fridays, 7—7¹|₂ p. m. Descending
hence to the promenades, the traveller perceives to the r. at the corner
of the Botanical Garden, the *Maurice Monument* (Pl. 15), to the memory
of the Elector of that name who fell in a battle with the Margrave of
Brandenburg at Sievershausen in 1553, after having resigned his dignity
to his brother Augustus, as the relief indicates.

The Rom. Cath. **Court Church** (Pl. 26), opposite the old bridge,
erected in the baroque style in 1737—56, contains a good altar-
piece by Raphael Mengs, representing the Ascension. Beneath the
sacristy are the royal burial vaults. The *church-music here (Sundays 11—12 and at 4 o'clock, also on the eve of festivals) is celebrated. Strict order is preserved during divine service.

The **Palace** (Pl. 38), founded in 1534, and frequently enlarged,
chiefly by Augustus the Strong at the beginning of the 18th
cent., is an extensive edifice of irregular form enclosing two quad-
rangles. Above the '*Grüne Thor*', in the façade towards the Court

Church, rises a tower 361 ft. in height, the loftiest in Dresden. In the *Interior* (adm. p. 193) are some fine *frescoes by *Bendemann*, completed in 1845: in the throne-room Lawgivers, from Moses to Maximilian I., Scenes from the life of Emp. Henry I. (d. 936), on the frieze Relations of life; in the ball-room Greek mythological and historical subjects.

The *Green Vault (entrance to the l. in the first court, adm. see p. 192) on the ground-floor of the palace, so named from the original decorations, contains one of the most valuable existing collections of curiosities, jewels, trinkets, and works of art, formed in the 16th—18th cent.

1st Room. Bronzes: crucifix by Giovanni da Bologna, small dog scratching itself by Vischer, Rape of Proserpine, Bacchus on a goat surrounded by children. Equestrian statues of Charles II. of England, Louis XIV., and Augustus the Strong.

2nd. Ivory Collection. Crucifix attributed to Michael Angelo; battle-scene attributed to Dürer; vases with battle-scenes, Hippodamia and the contest of the Lapithæ and centaurs; vessel adorned with the Foolish Virgins; Fall of Lucifer and the wicked angels, a remarkable and elaborate group of 92 figures, carved out of a single mass of ivory, 16 in. high; two horses' heads in relief, Michael Angelo; Rape of Proserpine; vessel with hunting-scene.

3rd. Mosaics, ostrich-eggs, and shells with reliefs and decorations, coral, amber, enamel, etc.; chimney-piece of Dresden china (from Meissen) with Saxon precious stones; enamel-pictures, the finest of which are a Madonna and Ecce Homo by Mengs; fruit-plate with battle-scene.

4th. (This is the 'Green Vault', poperly so called, from the colour of its walls.) Side-board vessels in gold and silver, plate, ruby-crystal, communion-cup and vessel by Benvenuto Cellini, magnificent jewel-casket by Jamnitzer of Nuremberg.

5th. Vessels of agate, jaspar, chalcedony, collection of polished stones, rock-crystal, etc.; two vessels entirely of cut stones, each valued at 900*l.*; fine large vases of rock-crystal; beautiful topazes; large globe of rock-crystal; earliest Meissen porcelain.

6th. Rare jewels, carved ivory and ebony, curious caricatures, etc.

7th. Regalia of Augustus II. as king of Poland; carved wood (Resurrection, Descent from the Cross, Archangel Michael's contest with Satan); two battle-pieces in wax.

8th. This room, which surpasses all the others in the costly splendour of its contents, contains the crown jewels, the most valuable of which is a green brilliant of great size set in an ornament for the hat. Then works of Dinglinger (1702—28), the Saxon Benvenuto Cellini. The principal of these is the Throne and Court of the Grand Mogul Aureng Zeb (at Delhi, 1659—1707), consisting of the monarch himself on a golden throne, surrounded by his guards and courtiers, altogether 132 figures in gold and enamel, a most elaborate work deserving minute inspection. Lamp with the myth of Actæon and Diana. Specimen of Peruvian emeralds, presented in 1581 by Emp. Rudolph III. Largest onyx known, 7 in. high, 2½ in. broad, valued at 6000*l.* Richly decorated weapons, among them the Electoral sword of Saxony, employed for the last time at the coronation of Emp. Francis, 1792. Two rings of Luther, rare jewels, etc.

The **Silberkammer**, containing the king's plate, is also on the ground-floor of the palace, and may be seen on application (p. 193).

. The royal **Gallery of Arms** (*Gewehr-Gallerie;* adm. see p. 192) in the old 'Stallgebäude', Augustus-Str. 7, adjoining the palace on the E., contains a valuable collection of firearms and other weapons, suits of armour, pictures of tournaments, remarkably fine antlers, etc.

In the THEATER-PLATZ with its promenades, extending to

13*

the N. W. of the Palace, are situated the *Hauptwache*, or *Guard House* (Pl. 19), erected from designs by *Schinkel* in 1831, the *Museum* (see below), and the new *Hoftheater* (Pl. 42) by *Semper*, on the site of its predecessor which was burned down in 1869. Between the theatre and the museum rises the bronze **Statue of Weber** (d. 1826), erected in 1860, designed by *Rietschel*.

The *****Museum** (Pl. 34), a handsome edifice in the Renaissance style, designed by *Semper*, was completed in 1854. The sculptures on the exterior by *Rietschel* and *Hähnel* indicate the object of the building (mythical, religious, and historical subjects; those on the N. side from the ancient world, those on the S. from the age of Christianity and romance). In niches on the r. and l. sides of the principal portal towards the court are statues of Raphael and Michael Angelo; on the bases of the four lower Corinthian columns are St. George and Judith on the l., and Siegfried the dragon-slayer and Samson on the r. The 'attica' is adorned with statues, 8 ft. in height, of Giotto, Holbein, Dürer, and Goethe by *Rietschel*, and *Dante and Cornelius by *Hähnel*.

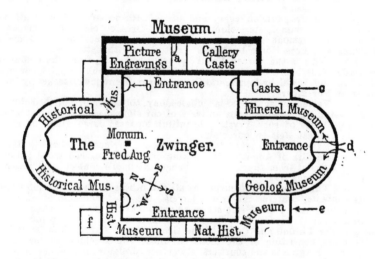

The Museum forms the N. E. wing of the **Zwinger** (Pl. 34), a building erected by Augustus II. at the beginning of last century in the most florid rococo style, and intended as an entrance court to a new palace. The space is now laid out as a pleasure-ground, embellished with four fountains, and in summer with orange-trees. In the centre rises the **Statue of Frederick Augustus** (d. 1827) in bronze, by *Rietschel*, with figures of Piety, Wisdom, Justice, and Clemency. Best survey of the building from the bastion on the river-side; ascent by Weber's monument.

The Museum and the Zwinger contain most of the Dresden collections: In the *Museum* are the picture gallery, engravings, drawings,
and one room with casts. In the *Zwinger* are the Historical and the
Natural History Museum, the casts, and the collection of mathematical and physical instruments.

The **Picture Gallery,** one of the finest on this side of the Alps,
consisting of 2400 pictures, was founded by Duke George, the
patrón of Lucas Cranach, and greatly extended under Augustus II.
and III. — Hübner's instructive catalogue (25 Ngr.) should be purchased by those who desire a thorough acquaintance with the gallery,
but may be dispensed with by the hasty visitor, the name of the
artists being always inscribed on the frames.

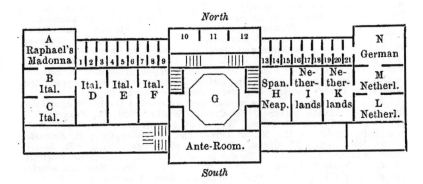

The **Entrance** (adm. see p. 193) is on the r. side of the passage through
the new Museum (Pl. a). The *Entrance Hall* (containing the cloak-room
and the ticket-office) is adorned with a frieze of stucco, illustrative of the
history of painting, on the r. that of Italy by *Knauer*, on the l. that of
Germany and the Netherlands by *Hähnel*. In a straight direction is the
entrance to the *Collection of Drawings and Engravings* (p. 200), to the r.
that to the *Crayon Drawings and Canaletto Landscapes* (p. 200).

Ascending the stair to the **First Floor** (Plan, see above), the visitor
traverses an *Ante-Room* hung with family portraits (where on Mond., Wed.
and Sat. tickets are given up, and check-tickets issued to those desirous of
quitting the gallery and returning at a later hour), a corridor with a number of Netherland masters of the 17th and 18th cent., and the cupola-
saloon, and proceeds through the following rooms without delay in order,
with fresh and unimpaired energy, to inspect and admire the Sistine
Madonna, the gem of the collection, a magnificent and profoundly impressive work. The walls in the saloons are numbered 1, 2, 3, 4; those in
the cabinets indicated by the letters a, b, c, d.

**Hall A. **67. *Raphael*, Madonna di San Sisto (so called from the
church at Piacenza for which the picture was painted), the Virgin and
Child in clouds, r. St. Sixtus, l. St. Barbara, two cherubs beneath (purchased
in 1753 for 9000 *l.*).

Hall B. Wall 1. (above the door), *Battoni*, Penitent Magdalene;
N. 63. *C. Dolce*, Christ blessing bread and wine; 70. *Raphael*, Madonna
della Sedia (an old copy); 61. *C. Dolce*, Herodias; *62. *C. Dolce*, St. Cecilia.
Opposite, Wall 2. 18. *Early Florentine School*, Annunciation; 115. *Sasso-
ferrato*, Mary bending over the sleeping Child; *82. *Giulio Romano*, Holy
Family ('Madonna della scodella', i. e. with the dish). To the r.

HALL C. Wall 1. *315. *Paolo Veronese*, Presentation in the Temple;
W. 3. *Tintoretto, Assumption.

HALL D. W. 1. *151. *Correggio*, Madonna with four saints; *152. *Correggio*, Madonna and three saints; **154. *Correggio*, Adoration of the
Shepherds (the far-famed 'La Notte'); *155. *Correggio*, Madonna and four
saints. W. 4. 43. *A. del Sarto*, Nuptials of St. Catherine; 211. *Vinc. Catena*,
Holy Conversation. W. 3. *303. *P. Veronese*, The centurion of Capernaum; *437. *Fr. Francia*, Baptism; *21. *Luca Signorelli*, Holy Family;
44. *And. del Sarto*, Abraham's Sacrifice; 304. *Paolo Veronese*, Finding of
Moses. W. 2. *84. *Ramenghi*, surnamed *Bagnacavallo*, Madonna with four
saints; 285. *L. da Ponte*, 288. *Tintoretto*, Portraits.

HALL E. W. 1. *300. *P. Veronese*, Marriage at Cana; *299. *P. Veronese*,
Adoration of the Magi. W. 4. *218. *Giorgione*, Jacob and Rachel; 306. *P. Veronese*, The good Samaritan; *Titian*, *225. Cupid and Venus; 228. Portrait
of the poet P. Aretino; 230. Portrait of his daughter Lavinia. W. 3. 302.
P. Veronese, Christ bearing the Cross; 244. *Palma Vecchio*, Venus; 229. *Titian*, Woman with fan; 226. *Titian*, Woman with vase; *301. *P. Veronese*,
Madonna and the Concini family. W. 2. *223. *Titian*, Madonna and saints;
290. *Tintoretto*, Fall of the angels; 309. *P. Veronese*, Christ at Emmaus.

HALL F. W. 1. *Caravaggio*, 178. Game at draughts and fortune teller,
*177. Guard-room with card-players; above, to the l., by the staircase,
W. 4. 472. *Guido Reni*, Ninus and Semiramis, formerly known as 'Solomon
and the Queen of Sheba'. W. 3. *176. *Caravaggio*, Cardplayers; 449.
Ann. Caracci, Genius of Fame. W. 2. 511. *Guercino*, Messenger announcing
to Queen Semiramis the breaking out of an insurrection at Babylon; 182.
Lanfranco, Peter's Denial; 470. *Guido Reni*, Venus and Cupid.

Returning to Hall E., the visitor next enters the CABINETS containing
the smaller Italian pictures. *1st Cabinet.* Wall a. *436. *Fr. Francia*, Virgin and Child with St. John. W. b. 148. 149. *Grandi*, Christ led to be
crucified, Christ on the Mt. of Olives and taken captive; *S. Botticelli*,
26. St. John Bapt.; 25. Christ with crown of thorns. W. c. *34. *Lor. di
Credi*, Madonna and Child with the infant John; 24. *Pinturicchio*, Portrait;
30. *L. di Credi*, Madonna. — *2nd.* W. a. 473. *G. Reni*, Madonna adoring
the sleeping Child. W. c. *153. *Correggio*, Mary Magdalene; 85. *Barrocio*,
Hagar and Ishmael; *156. *Correggio*, Portrait of his physician (?). — *3rd.*
W. a. 528. *Cignani*, Joseph and Potiphar's wife; 471. *G. Reni*, Youthful
Bacchus. W. c. *Ann. Carracci*, Head of Christ; 479. *Guido Reni*, Christ
crowned with throns. — *4th.* W. a. 307. *P. Veronese*, Golgatha; *243. *Palma
Vecchio*, His three daughters; 320. *Veronese*, Adoration of the Magi. W. b.
256. *Bordone*, Diana. W. c. 245. 246. *Palma Vecchio*, Madonna and saints;
**222. *Titian*, The tribute-money ('Cristo della moneta'). — *5th.* Nothing
of importance. — *6th.* W. a. *655. *Cl. Lorrain*, Sicilian coast, Acis and
Galathea in the foreground; 661, 657. *G. Poussin*, Landscapes; 648. *N. Poussin*, Nymphs surprised by shepherds. W. b. 687. 688. *Watteau*, Genre-
scenes. W. c. 656 a. *G. Poussin*, Landscape; *654. *Cl. Lorrain*, Landscape,
shepherds and flight of the Holy Family as accessories. — Then *7th—13th.*
Netherlands masters: still life, *Wouverman's* battles, landscapes, etc.; in
the *11th*, W. b. 1436, 1437. Landscapes by *Ruisdael*, the Chasse and Jews'
Burying-ground. — *14th.* W. c. 1243. *Terburg*, Lady washing her hands;
1421, 1422. *Potter*, Cows; 1242. *Terburg*, Trumpeter waiting for a letter;
1244. *Terburg*, Lesson on the lute. — *15th.* W. c. 919, 918. *Teniers*, Peasants drinking and smoking; 928. *Teniers*, Chemist at his furnace. — *16th.*
W. a. 931. *Teniers*, Fair; 1349. *Wouverman*, The departure. W. b. Chiefly
by *Wouverman*. W. c. Chiefly by *Metsu*. — *17th.* W. a. *1156. *De Heem*,
Fruit-piece. W. b. 1189. *Aelst*, Still-life; 1496. *Mignon*, Fruit. W. c. Chiefly
by *A. van der Werff:* *1645. Abraham rejects Hagar. — *18th.* W. a.
W. Mieris (1653, 1652). W. b. 1344. *Wouverman*, Camp. W. c. 2355.
A. Cuyp, Cavalcade. The rest are all by *F.* and *W. Mieris;* Nos. 1475,
1474, 1471, 1473, 1470 deserve notice. — *19th.* W. a. *A. Ostade*, 1284.
Painter's studio; 1283. Inn; 1567. *Schalken*, Man with light viewing a bust;
939, 938. *F. Hals*, Portraits. W. b. 1365, 1366 by *Wouverman*. W. c.
16 pictures by *Dow:* among them, 1140. Praying hermit. — *20th.* W. a.
Chiefly by *Breughel*. W. c. 1203, 1204, 1207, 1208. by *Brouwer;* 1527. *Netscher*, Lady at a piano, 1529. Sick woman and physician. — *21st.* Old

German and Old Flemish Schools. W. a. *H. Holbein the Younger*, 1813, 1812, 1814. Portraits; 174. *School of van Eyck*, Virgin. W. b. 1769, 1770. *Cranach*, Portraits of Luther and Melanchthon. W. c. *Gossaert (Mabuse)*, The Magi.

HALL N. *1809. Old copy of the picture at Darmstadt by *Holbein the Younger*, representing the Virgin and Child, with Jacob Meier, the burgomaster of Basel, and his family at their feet (regarded as genuine down to the Holbein Exhibition in 1871); *1810. *Holbein*, Thomas Morett, goldsmith of Henry VIII. of England; 1817. *Holbein*, Female portrait. Wall to the r.: 1722. *Dürer*, Christ on the cross; *1713. *J. van Eyck*, Madonna and saints; 1718. *Rogier van der Weyde*, Christ on the cross; 1723. *Dürer* Christ bearing the cross; 1815. *Holbein*, Virginia (in grisaille).

HALL M. Wall 3. 851. *Rubens*, Head of a high priest; 842. *The same*, Last judgment, sketch of the large picture at Munich; 984. *Van Dyck*, The Infant Christ with the globe; 993. 994. *Van Dyck*, Portraits. W. 2. 852—856. *Rubens*, Portraits; *The same* *838. Judgment of Paris, *839. Garden of love, 840. Argus lulled to sleep, 995, 997, 998. *Van Dyck*, Portraits.

HALL L. Wall 3. 1230, *1214, 1215, 1222, 1229. *Rembrandt*, Portraits. *1433. *J. van der Meer*, Girl reading a letter; 941. *F. Hals*, Female portrait. — A corridor leads hence to the three saloons of modern pictures (see below).

HALL K. Wall 4. 1224. 1233. *Rembrandt*, Entombment; 1226. 1232. *Rembrandt*, Portraits; 891. *Snyders*, Wild boar hunt. W. 3. *837. *Rubens*, Wild boar hunt; *1220. *Rembrandt*, Sacrifice of Manoah and his wife; 1217. *The same*, Feast of Esther and Ahasuerus. W. 2. 1216. *Rembrandt*, Ganymede carried off by Jupiter's eagle; *1432. *J. van der Meer*, Convivial party; *Rembrandt*, *1225. Portrait of himself and wife; 1219. Girl with flower; 1590. *A. de Gelder*, Ecce Homo. W. 1. 1098, 1099, 1093. *Miereveldt*, Portraits; 1223, 1228. *Rembrandt*, Portraits; 1266. *F. Bol*, Repose during the flight to Egypt.

HALL J. Wall 3. 982. *Van Dyck*, St. Jerome; 825. *Rubens*, Diana and her nymphs returning from the chase. W. 2. 624. *Velasquez*, Portrait; 622. *The same*, Portrait of Count Olivarez; 618. *Ribera (Spagnoletto)*, Diogenes; 857. *Rubens*, Portrait. W. 1. 986. *Van Dyck*, Portrait of the Queen of Charles I.; *845. *Rubens*, Portrait of his two sons; *987. *Van Dyck*, Children of Charles I. of England; 985. *Van Dyck*, Charles I. W. 4. 948. *Rubens*, Mother and child; *981. *Van Dyck*, Jupiter visits Danae in the form of a shower of gold; 961. *Jordaens*, Woman with grape-basket; 836. *Rubens*, Landscape.

HALL H. Wall 3. 584. *Luca Giordano*, St. Sebastian; 514. *Salv. Rosa*, Shipwreck; *608. *Ribera (Spagnoletto)*, St. Mary of Egypt. W. 1. 627. *Zurbaran*, St. Francis, to whom an angel appears, declining the papal crown, conclave of cardinals in the background. W. 4. 634. *Murillo*, Virgin with Child; 633. *The same*, St. Rodriguez, mortally wounded, receiving the crown of martyrdom from an angel.

From Hall L, a passage leads to the upper floor of the N.E. pavilion of the Zwinger, where a number of *Pictures by Living Artists* are exhibited in three saloons. *1st. Saloon.* 2041. *Wegener*, Forest on fire; 2069. *Choulant*, View of the Vatican; 1992. *Matthäi*, Orestes slays Aegisthus; 2018. *Rotermundt*, The Body of Christ. — The *2nd Saloon* is divided into several cabinets. 1st.: *2024. *L. Richter*, Spring-landscape with a bridal procession; 2023. *Peschel*, 'Come unto me', etc. — 2nd.: *J. Hübner* 2031. Soldier, 2030. Jew; 2032. *Dreber*, Landscape with the good Samaritan; 2068. *Gärtner*, Landscape after the fall of man; 2044. *Dahl*, Giessbach. — 3rd.: 2063. *K. W. Müller*, Italian landscape at night; *Hennig*, Finding of Moses. — 4th.: 2039. *Von Oer*, Albert Dürer visited by Giovanni Bellini at Venice; 2007. *Dorr*, Signing a deed; 2054. *Dahl*, The ferry. — 5th.: 2056. *Oehme*, Mountain-scene; 2012. *Bähr*, Finland magicians predicting the death of the Czar Ivan the Terrible. Long wall to the l.: 2047. *A. Schuster*, Battle of Borodino; 2019. *Wichmann*, Petrarch; *Mühlig*, Monks attacked by horsemen; *2038. *Wislicenus*, Abundance and Want; 2026. *Schweig*, The Bishop of Spires protecting the persecuted Jews. — 3rd. Saloon: 2006. *Plüddemann*, Emp. Frederick Barbarossa at the Diet of Besançon; 2033. *Röting*, Columbus before the council at Salamanca; 2048. *Schuster*, Bravery of Saxon grenadiers at the Battle of Jena.

The visitor should now return through Halls K, I, and H, and ascend to the CUPOLA SALOON, which contains 12 valuable pieces of Flemish *Tapestry.* Several of the 6 below are from cartoons by *Q. Massys* (admirable Crucifixion), those above from Cartoons by *Raphael.*

A stair ascends hence to the **Upper Floor**, containing a few modern pictures and others of inferior value. On the staircase, portraits of *Graff* and *Angelica Kaufmann;* *2009. 2010. *Schnorr*, sketches of stained glass windows for St. Paul's in London; *2027 *Jul. Hübner*, The golden age; *1979. *A. Kauffmann*, Vestal. — To the r. is the *23rd Cabinet:* Altar-pieces by *Cranach, Kulmbach, Burgkmaier*, and some pieces attributed to Dürer; 1724. *Dürer*, A hare. — *24th:* Chieflyaltar-pieces by *Cranach the Elder.* — *25th:* 1865. *Vaillant*, Tray of letters. — *26th—28th:* Minor Netherlands works of the 17th and 18th centuries. — *29th:* *2360. *Jul. Hübner*, Disputation of Luther and Dr. Eck, which took place at Leipsic in 1519, a very large picture. — *30th:* Four large animal pieces by *Ph. Roos.* — The staircase is next traversed, and the cabinets to the left are entered. — *31st:* Nothing of importance. — *32nd:* Early Italian works. 5. *Giunta Pisano*, Madonna; 216. *Cima da Conegliano*, Presentation in the Temple. — *33rd—38th:* Nothing worthy of note, except in the *36th:* 315. *Paolo Veronese*, Europa on the bull.

The **Ground Floor** (comp. p. 197) contains works of the 18th century. *Cabinets 39th—41st:* Crayon portraits of distinguished persons, most of them by *Rosalba Carriera*, a few by *Raphael Mengs*, the best by *Liotard* in the *41st:* 2089. Portrait of the painter in the costume worn by him at Constantinople; 2090. Count Maurice of Saxony; *2091. The chocolate girl; 2092. Portrait of the artist's niece, 'the beautiful Lyonnese'. — *42nd—44th:* Small works by the Saxon Court-painter *Dietrichs* (d. 1774), and numerous views, chiefly of Dresden, Warsaw, Venice, and Verona, by *Canaletto* (d. 1768). — There is also a collection of miniatures on the ground-floor, open on the first Tuesday of every month only.

The *Collection of Engravings, which is also on the ground-floor of the New Museum (entrance, see p. 197; adm. see p. 192), founded by Augustus II. and afterwards gradually extended, now comprises 350,000 plates, from Finiguerra (1450) and the earliest German masters (15th cent.) down to the present day. About 700 of the finest are exhibited under glass. The others are kept in portfolios, which the attendants open if desired. On the pillars of the large saloon are medallion-portraits of celebrated engravers, among whom are Dürer, Rembrandt, Mantegna, Lucas of Leyden, Masson, and Toschi. The smaller room adjacent contains *Drawings*, of which about 300 are exposed to view, the rest being kept in portfolios. Those of the old masters, chiefly of the German School, occupy 50 portfolios.

The *Museum of Casts, chronologically arranged, affords a good review of the history of the plastic art. The nucleus of the collection was formed by *Raphael Mengs*, by whom it was sold to the Saxon Government in 1782. The value of some of the casts is greatly increased by the fact that the originals have since been lost.

The *Entrance* (see ground-plan *c;* adm., see p. 192) is on the E. side of the Zwinger, opposite the Prinzen-Palais. I. *Old Greek Hall:* Assyrian reliefs, B. C. 1100—700; early Greek statuary, from B. C. 1100 to about 470. — II. The *Parthenon Hall*, III. the *Rotunda*, and part of the IV. *Hall* contain works of the best period of Greek art (about B. C. 450—350), by Phidias and his pupils Scopas, Praxiteles, and Lysippus. — The remainder of the last hall and the V. *Hall* are devoted to the schools of Rhodes and Pergamus (B. C. 325—146), the period of the revival of art down to the time of Augustus (B. C. 14), and a few later works. The third of the aisles, into which this hall is divided, contains works of the Renaissance (Ghiberti, Michael Angelo, Peter Vischer, 1450—1563) and modern works (Thorvaldsen, Rauch, Rietschel, etc.).

The *Historical Museum in the W. and half of the S. wings of the Zwinger contains weapons, armour, domestic chattels, costumes, and other objects of historical or artistic value. This collection, the most valuable of the kind in Germany, comprises many valuable works of the German and Italian Renaissance.

. The *Entrance* (ground-plan *b*; adm., see p. 192) is in the N. W. corner of the Zwinger court-yard. Each room contains notices of the most interesting objects. I. *Entrance Hall:* Renaissance furniture, chiefly of the time of Augustus I. (1553—86). Portraits of Saxon princes, those of Albert and his wife by *L. Cranach*, most of the others copies; along the walls antique furniture and cabinets; Luther's cabinet, goblet, and sword; ancient drinking-cups, inlaid work, chairs of the 16th and 17th cent. — 2. *Room of the Chase:* Hunting gear, cross-bows, spears, knives, etc., of the 16th and 17th cent.; also the hunting-horn of Henry IV. of France. — 3. *Tournament Hall:* Richly decorated suits of armour and caparisons, weapons, etc. The most magnificent and valuable armour is that of the Elector Christian II. (d. 1611), one of them by Collmann, a celebrated smith of Augsburg, the other of Italian workmanship, for which 14,000 Thlr. are said to have been paid. Several shields and helmets, most artistically decorated with reliefs; two gilded suits of armour of Prince Christian of Anhalt (d. 1630) and Elector Christian of Saxony (d. 1591); a gala suit of Duke Charles Emmanuel of Savoy (d. 1630), manufactured at Milan. — 4. *Battle Saloon.* The armour and weapons which were used in battle by Saxon princes and celebrated generals, arranged chronologically; three suits of armour of Elector Maurice, the blood-stained scarf worn by him at the battle of Sievershausen (1553), and the bullet by which he was killed, fired, it is said, by a traitor in his own army; standard of Pappenheim's cuirassiers of the Thirty Years' War; coat of mail of John Sobieski, king of Poland, with gilded iron crosses on the breast and the Maltese cross on the collar, worn at the raising of the siege of Vienna in 1683. Trophies, weapons, and horses' tails captured by the Saxon troops. Marshal's batons of Tilly and Pappenheim; Thomas Münzer's scythe sword. The horseshoe broken by the hand of Augustus the Strong. — 5. *Pistol Chamber:* Fire-arms from the period of their first invention, pistol of Charles XII. of Sweden, Louis XIV. of France, the Elector Maurice, etc. — 6. *Saddle and Costume Chamber:* Sumptuous caparisons, embroidered trappings, etc. used on festive occasions, chiefly of the reign of Augustus II. (1694—1733). The cabinets contain court and gala costumes of the 16th—18th cent. — 7. *Turkish Tent* of Kara Mustapha, captured at the siege of Vienna, contains Turkish and Oriental weapons. — 8. *Indian Cabinet.* — 9. *Parade Saloon:* Parade weapons of the 16th—18th cent., some of them of beautiful workmanship; in the centre those purchased at Nuremberg by Elector Christian III. in 1606, of German workmanship; on the r. and l. two Italian suits in silver, executed for Prince Christian of Anhalt and Elector Christian I. of Saxony; hat and sword of Peter the Great; sword of Charles XII. of Sweden; Napoleon's saddle of red velvet, the boots he wore at the battle of Dresden, and velvet shoes worn at his coronation.

The **Natural History Museum** (entrance ground-plan *e*, on the S. E. side of the Zwinger; adm., see p. 193), is of no great extent, but the collection of stuffed birds with their nests, eggs, and young, and that of butterflies are worthy of note. The **Mineralogical Museum** (entrance ground-plan *d*, in the E. passage of the Zwinger; adm., see p. 192), consists of a collection of minerals and one of geological specimens with numerous fossils. — The **Physical-Mathematical Saloon** (ground-plan *f*; adm., see p. 192), founded by

Elector Augustus I., contains a large collection of scientific instruments of every description, many of them of great historical interest.

In the *Ostra-Allee* which passes the Zwinger ⊦ on the S. W. side, is situated the **Orangery,** a modern edifice with a façade richly adorned with sculptures by *Hähnel.* On the *Logengebäude* in the same street are sculptures by *Rietschel.*

Opposite the Zwinger, towards the E., rises the *Prinzen - Palais* (Pl. 37), erected in 1715, and extended in 1843, the residence of the crown - prince of Saxony. — The **Sophienkirche** (Pl. 29), or Prot. court-church, dating from the 13th and 14th cent., was handsomely restored in the Gothic style in 1865—69.

In the POST - PLATZ, a little to the S., is situated the *Post Office* (Pl. 36). The centre of this Platz is embellished with a Gothic *Fountain Column* designed by *Semper*, with statuettes of St. Elizabeth, Wittekind, Winfred (St. Boniface), and John the Baptist, emblematical of the salutary properties of water.

The Annen-Strasse leads from the Post-Platz to the *Annenkirche* (Pl. 23), a church of the 16th cent., subsequently restored, near which is the **Anna Fountain,** erected in 1869 to the Electress Anna (d. 1585), the order-loving wife of Augustus I., with a fine statue of the princess designed by *Henze* and cast at Nuremberg.

In the NEUMARKT (Pl. D, 4) rises the **Frauenkirche** (Pl. 25), or Church of our Lady, erected 1726—34, with a lofty dome of stone. The ascent of the 'Lantern', 310 ft. in height, is recommended for the view (sacristan, Rampesche Gasse 26, fee 20 Ngr.). In the centre of the market - place rises the **Statue of Frederick Augustus II.** (d. 1854) in bronze, by *Hähnel*, surrounded by figures emblematical of Piety, Wisdom, Justice, and Strength.

Near the Altmarkt rises the **Kreuzkirche** (Pl. 48), the largest church at Dresden, re-erected in 1760 after the Prussian bombardment, with a tower 342 ft. in height, which commands a good survey of the town (open the whole day, custodian 2½ Ngr.).

In the GEORGS-PLATZ is situated the modern Gothic **Kreuzschule,** a grammar-school with a handsome hall. In front of this edifice is the **Statue of Theodore Körner,** in bronze, by *Hähnel*, erected in 1871. The youthful minstrel of the 'Lyre and Sword' is represented in a military cloak, with a scroll of poems in his right hand, while with his left he presses his sword to his breast.

In the adjoining BÜRGERWIESE, a large open space with promenades, a number of handsome modern dwelling-houses have recently sprung up. The finest of these is *Oppenheim's House* on the l., designed by *Semper*. The house formerly occupied by *Rietschel*, the eminent sculptor, in the neighbouring Lange-Str., No. 30, is adorned with medallions in relief. — The MOLTKE-PLATZ is embellished with the modern *Nymph Fountain.* — The Grosse Garten, Museum of Antiquities, and Rietschel Museum, see p. 204.

In the NEUSTADT, on the r. bank of the Elbe, in the market-place adjoining the old bridge, rises an equestrian **Statue of Augustus II.** (Pl. 12), 'the Strong', over life-size, in copper, gilded, and erected in 1736.

Turning to the l. the traveller soon reaches the **Japanese Palace** (Pl. 20), erected by Count Flemming in 1715, afterwards purchased by Augustus II., and destined for the reception of various collections. Those still preserved here are the Cabinet of Antiquities, Cabinet of Coins, Collection of Porcelain, and Library.

The **Collection of Antiquities,** to the l. on the ground-floor (adm., see p. 192), contains little above mediocrity, most of the works dating from the period of the Roman Empire, and some of them freely restored. — *1st Saloon:* Nos. 1—10. Busts of Saxon princes from Frederick the Wise down to the present king; 21· Statue of a girl, and 24. Vestal Virgin, both of calcsinter, modern; 34. Marshal Saxe, natural son of Augustus I. and the Countess Königsmark, and general of Louis XV. — *2nd:* 53. Gustavus Adolphus; 54. Richelieu; 55. Charles I. of England; 99. Nessus and Dejanira, in bronze, by Giov. da Bologna. — *3rd:* 113. Silenus; 115. Head of Niobe; 135. Jupiter; 143. Torso of Minerva Promache. — *4th:* 158. Faun and Bacchante; 166. Young girl; 183. Female statue, drapery of grey marble; 184. Sea-goddess; 185. Torso of a wounded gladiator. — *5th:* 196. Venus and Cupids; 197. Cupid plays with the lion; 198. Cupid and Psyche; 201. Trilateral candelabrum, pedestal of marble, on which are represented the theft of the sacred tripod by Hercules, its re-consecration, and the consecration of a torch in the archaic style; 208. Young athlete; 209. Young Hermes; 210, 211. Young satyrs. — *6th:* Busts of emperors; 224. Sarcophagus with Bacchanalian procession; 259, *262. Girls from Herculaneum; *263. Woman from Herculaneum; the last two are admirable draped statues, found in 1715, and in almost perfect preservation; 262. Dancing satyr. — *7th:* 280. Pugilist in polished grey marble; 300. Poseidon, a small fountain-figure; 303. Recumbent figure; 304, 305. Satyr and nymph, Faun and hermaphrodite. — *8th:* 324. Caracalla; 334. Muse; 349—352. Gladiators. — *9th:* 382. Antoninus Pius; 384. Athlete; *383. Venus; 367. Sarcophagus with Bacchanalian procession. — *10th:* Three lions of Egyptian syenite; 391 a—d. Assyrian reliefs from Nineveh. — *11th:* Roman vases; cinerary urns in niches' in the style of the Roman columbaria; mummies; small bronzes. — *12th:* Germanic antiquities.

The **Cabinet of Coins** (adm., see p. 192), also on the ground-floor, was begun by George II. (d. 1680) and considerably extended under Frederick Augustus (d. 1827).

The **Collection of Porcelain** (adm., see p. 193) in the vaulted rooms of the sunk floor, consists of about 15,000 specimens of Chinese, Japanese, E. Indian, French, and Dresden workmanship. The Dresden china, from the first attempts of Böttcher (d. 1719) down to the present day, and the modern European products of Sèvres, Berlin, etc., are the most interesting feature in the collection.

The ***Royal Library** (adm., see p. 192) on the two upper floors, founded by Elector Augustus (d. 1586), now comprises 500,000 vols., 2000 incunabula or specimens of early typography, 3000 MSS., and 20,000 maps. Historical works and modern literature form the most valuable part of the collection. The *First Room* contains a cast of Gellert's features after death. In the *Great Hall* are busts of Goethe and Tieck, executed by David d'Angers. The following curiosities among others are preserved in *Glass Cases:* The Atlas Royal, a collection in 19 folio vols. of portraits of princes and princesses of the 17th cent. with maps, plans, etc. (three copies only of the work were made at Amsterdam in 1707; one is now at the Hague, another at Copenhagen); Mexican hieroglyphic codex, 12 ft. long, written on both sides; fragment of the Zend Avesta of Zoroaster, a MS. of the 15th cent.; octagonal Koran, of the size of a crown-piece; Koran of Sultan Bajazet II.; Persian Ful Nameh (treasure-casket) with numerous drawings; Runic calendars on boxwood of the 12th and 13th cent. ; tournament-books with plates, among them that of King René of Anjou of the 15th cent., once the property of Charles the Bold; Petrarch '*de re-medüs utriusque fortunae*', MS. of the 15th cent. with drawings; breviaries with miniatures; MSS. of Luther and Melanchthon; *Dürer's Treatise on the proportions of the body, with original drawings; Faust's Höllenzwang, a MS. of the 18th cent. with mystic figures; Seb. Brant's 'Narrenschiff' with 117 miniatures, printed at Paris in 1497; German edition of the same work, with 114 miniatures, printed in 1494; a *volume with 56 miniatures of the most celebrated men of the 15th and 16th cent., probably by Cranach the Younger.

The *Japanese Garden* behind the palace, which is open to the public, affords a pleasant view of the Elbe and railway bridge. *Schiller* once resided (1784—86), and *Körner* was born (in 1769) in the Körner-Strasse (to the r.); the houses are indicated by marble tablets.

The **Grosse Garten** (Pl. F, G, H, 6), outside the Pirna Gate, to the S. E. of the town, a royal park laid out at the end of the 17th cent. and subsequently embellished, covers an area of about 300 acres. In 1813 it was the scene of several sharp engagements between the French and Prussians. The park is intersected by two broad avenues at right angles to each other, converging towards the *Lustschloss* (Pl. 36; 1¹/₂ M. from the old bridge), a château built in the centre of the park in 1680, where the royal Museum of Antiquities and the Rietschel Museum are now established.

The **Museum of Antiquities** (adm., see p. 192) on the ground-floor consists chiefly of ecclesiastical objects of mediæval origin, removed from the churches of Saxony in consequence of the Reformation, and collected here in 1845.

The **Rietschel Museum** (adm., see p. 193), on the first floor of the château, contains an almost complete collection of casts and models of the works of the talented sculptor of that name (d. 1861). Those of Luther's Monument at Worms, of the Schiller and Goethe group at Weimar (p. 233), the statue of Lessing at Brunswick (p. 71), the Quadriga at Brunswick (p. 69), the twelve reliefs in the Aula of Leipsic (p. 220), and the Pietas in the Friedenskirche at Potsdam (p. 47) are particularly worthy of inspection.

The **Zoological Garden** (Pl. F, G, 6; adm., see p. 193) contains a number of fine specimens of animals. Good restaurant.

*Environs. *Left Bank of the Elbe.*

Immediately beyond the village of **Räcknitz**, 1¹/₂ M. to the S. of the town, is situated *Moreau's Monument*, surrounded by three oaks, erected on the spot where the general was mortally wounded, 27th Aug., 1813. From the hill, about 100 paces farther, a survey of the mountains of Saxon Switzerland is obtained. A more extensive prospect is enjoyed from the **Goldene Höhe** (729 ft.), 1¹/₂ hr. farther S.

From *Niedersedlitz*, the first station on the Saxon-Bohemian line (p. 204), a pleasant excursion may be made through the **Lockwitzer Grund** to (4¹/₂ M.) *Kreyscha*. Then by (3 M. S. E.) *Maxen*, with its valuable marble-quarries, and the romantic **Müglitzthal**, to the royal château of (3 M. E.) **Wesenstein**, and down the valley to the N. to the ancient little town of *Dohna*, and (3 M.) stat. *Mügeln*, whence Dresden is reached by train in ¹/₂ hr. The construction of Wesenstein is very remarkable, the château being partially hewn out of the rock on which it is situated. The stables are on the 3rd, the ice-cellar and chapel on the 5th floor.

The *Right Bank of the Elbe* above Dresden rises in gentle, vine-clad slopes, crowned with woods and enlivened by country-residences, the most conspicuous of which is the *Villa Rosa*, and affords a number of pleasant excursions. Thus 1¹|₄ M. from the bridge, is the *Schiller-Schlösschen;* ¹|₄ M. beyond it the *Wald-Schlösschen, an extensive brewery, commanding a beautiful view. Omnibus p. 191.

The **Albrechtsburg,** ³|₄ M. from the Waldschlösschen, with two handsome modern châteaux (accessible daily, Sund. excepted, 1—3 o'clock), the property of Prince Albrecht of Prussia, is the finest point of view. Pleasant wood-walks hence to the *Wolfshügel.*

Farther on, beyond the *Mordgrund*, lies **Loschwitz** (*Victoriashöhe*, a restaurant with a fine view), where a small summer-house in a vineyard marks the spot where Schiller wrote his Don Carlos in 1785—87. — Opposite Loschwitz, on the l. bank, lies **Blasewitz** (*Schillergarten*, with view).

At **Wachwitz**, 1¹|₂ M. to the S.E. of Loschwitz, is situated the *Royal Vineyard*, with a handsome château and pleasant grounds. At *Hosterwitz*, halfway between this and (3 M.) Pillnitz, Weber composed his 'Freischütz' and 'Oberon'.

Pillnitz (206 ft.), on the r. bank of the Elbe, 7 M. above Dresden (the direct road is on the l. bank), is a modern château of the king, with pleasant grounds and a well-stocked botanical garden. The chapel and the dining-room are adorned with good frescoes by Vogel. In an old part of the château, since burned down, an alliance between Emp. Leopold II. and King Frederick William II. of Prussia was entered into in 1791 with a view to oppose the advance of the French revolution. An artificial ruin at the back of the village of Pillnitz, on the route to the Porsberg, commands a pleasing view, which is finer and much more extensive from the *Porsberg (1142 ft.) itself, 1 hr. to the E. of Pillnitz. At the top is a metal indicator of directions. Small *inn. — From Pillnitz the traveller may now proceed to (4¹|₂ M.) *Lohmen*, a village with an old Schloss, from which a picturesque route leads by *Uttewald* and through the Uttewalder Grund to the Bastei (2¹|₂ hrs.); comp. p. 208, and Map.

Below Dresden, to the N. W., 1¹|₂ M. from stat. *Weintraube*, the first on the Leipsic line, lies the **Paradies**, a beautiful and favourite point of view among the vineyards. The *Spitzhaus* on another height is also an excellent point of view. On a third hill, near stat. *Kötzschenbroda* (p. 190), rises the *Friedensburg*, at the foot of which lies the extensive *Lössnitz Champagne Manufactory.*

The **Moritzburg,** 6 M. to the N. of Dresden, with its picturesque ponds, deer-park, and horse-rearing establishment, once a favourite resort of Augustus the Strong, may be visited by fiacre.

Meissen (p. 215; pleasant to go by steamboat and return by railway) also boasts of several beautiful points of view in its environs, among which may be mentioned Schloss *Scharfenberg*, the rocky height of the *Bosel* near *Sörnewitz*, and Schloss *Siebeneichen*, all steamboat-stations between Dresden and Meissen.

The excursion to the *Plauensche Grund*, *Tharandt*, and *Freiberg* is described at p. 211. Those who have not time to explore the whole of the Saxon Switzerland should at least devote half a day to the *Uttewalder Grund* and the *Bastei* (p. 208), one of the most picturesque spots in N. Germany.

38. From Dresden to Prague.

Railway to Bodenbach in 1³|₄—2¹|₄ hr. (fares 1 Thlr. 20, 1 Thlr. 3, 25 Ngr.); thence to Prague in 3¹|₄—6 hrs. (fares 6 fl. 12, 4 fl. 59, 3 fl. 6 kr. Austr.). Finest views to the left.

As the train leaves the station, the Grosse Garten (p. 204) is observed to the l.; then the vine-clad slopes of the r. bank of the Elbe which the train approaches. *Niedersedlitz*, see p. 204. At *Mügeln* the train reaches the river, and then follows its windings through the *Saxon Switzerland* (p. 207).

Pirna (358 ft.) *(Schwarzer Adler; Forsthaus; *Rail. Restaurant)*, a town with 8000 inhab., 10 M. to the S. E. of Dresden, lies at the mouth of the *Gottleube*, and is commanded by the *Sonnenstein*, an old fortress converted into a lunatic asylum. The town was taken by the Swedes in 1639, and in 1758 by the Prussians, who levelled the fortifications. Above the town, on both banks of the Elbe, are quarries of excellent sandstone.

Stat. *Pötzscha* is the usual starting-point for a visit to Saxon Switzerland (comp. p. 207). Opposite stat. *Rathen* (p. 209) rises the Bastei on the r. bank (p. 208).

Königstein *(*Blauer Stern; Sächsische Schweiz; *Rail. Restaurant)* is a small town commanded by the imposing **Fortress* of that name (1165 ft. above the sea-level, 1108 ft. above the Elbe). Ascent $^3/_4$ hr.; permission must be obtained at the foot of the hill (1 Thlr. 10 Ngr. for 1—8 pers.). The ramparts command charming views. In time of war the treasures and archives of Saxony have usually been deposited here, and the fortress is now employed as a state prison. The excursion (2 hrs. to the top and back) amply repays the fatigue.

The *Lilienstein (1293 ft.), which rises on the opposite bank of the river, the highest of the twelve isolated and almost perpendicular mountains of Saxon Switzerland, is crowned with an obelisk to commemorate the visit of Augustus the Strong in 1706. In 1756, at the beginning of the Seven Years' War, the Saxon army of 14,000 men was surrounded at the foot of this hill by the Prussians under Frederick the Great and compelled by hunger to surrender. In 1813 the French had a fortified camp here. The *view from the summit is more extensive than that from the Königstein, and is very picturesque, especially looking up the river. The traveller crosses the Elbe to the village of *Halbestadt*, opposite the Königstein station, and proceeds thence through the E. end of the village of *Ebenheit* direct to the foot of the Lilienstein. Ascent, partly by steps, somewhat steep, 1 hr.

The *Pabststein (p. 210), the *Bärensteine*, and the *Pfaffenstein* (ascended in 1 hr.) are other points of view near Königstein.

About 2½ M. to the S. of Königstein is situated the water-cure establishment of *Königsbrunn*, on the *Bielabach*, at the entrance to the *Bielagrund, a very remarkable ravine with the most fantastic rock formations. Pleasant walk up this valley to the (2 hrs.) *Schweizermühle*, where there is another water-cure (*Restaurant); then, 20 min. beyond it, turn to the l. by a finger-post, and walk in 1½ hr. more to the summit of the *Schneeberg (2277 ft.), where a tower commanding a fine view and a small *inn are situated. At the foot of the mountain lies the village of *Schneeberg* (Werner's Inn). From Schneeberg to Bodenbach 6 M. (see below).

About 3 M. to the W. of Schneeberg (guide necessary) are situated the Tissaer Wände, a curious labyrinth of ravines and grotesque rock formations. Fine view from the plateau.

Krippen is the station for *Schandau* (p. 209). Beyond *Schöna* (p. 211) the line crosses the frontier of Bohemia, passes *Niedergrund*, penetrates the *Schäferwand* (690 ft.) by several tunnels, and reaches

Bodenbach (*Post; Rail. Restaurant, dear), a village with 2000 inhab., with the Austrian custom-house. A suspension-bridge here crosses the river to **Tetschen** *(*Silberner Stern; Krone;*

Stadt Prag; Restaurant at the *Schützenhaus*, with garden on the Elbe, 8 min. from the town), a pleasant little town, with the handsome château and beautiful garden of Count Thun, and perhaps the prettiest point in the valley of Elbe. Steamboat to Dresden, see p. 192.

From Bodenbach to the Schneeberg (2¹|₂ hrs.). The traveller diverges from the Teplitz road to the r. either after ³|₄ M. at the inn *Zum Rothen Kreuz* (path indicated by white marks on the trees, and easily traced, but generally destitute of shade), or after 1¹|₂ M. at the inn *Zur Grünen Wiese*. After 7 min. the latter route crosses the valley to the l. and leads to the village of *Schneeberg*. A more direct route to the summit diverges from the latter path at a clearing in the wood, but is not easily found without a guide. Those who prefer driving the greater part of the way follow the Schneeberg road, which leads to the l. below the suspension bridge.

From Bodenbach to *Zittau* (p. 187) by railway in 4 hrs. viâ *Warnsdorf* (Stadt Wien; Endler), the last Austrian station in this direction.

Stations *Nesterschitz* and *Aussig*, where the picturesque ruin of *Schreckenstein* is conspicuous (branch-line to *Teplitz* in 40 min.); *Lobositz*, where *Leitmeritz* and *Theresienstadt* are visible to the l.; the latter is also a station on the line. Then *Raudnitz*, *Berkowitz*, *Weltrus*; *Kralup*, *Libschitz*, *Rostock*, **Prague** (see *Baedeker's S. Germany and Austria*).

39. Saxon Switzerland.

Plan. Two days at least are requisite for a visit to this interesting district. *1st*. Railway to Pötzscha (p. 206) in ³|₄ hr., ferry to Wehlen; walk or ride through the Wehlener Grund and Zscherregrund to the Bastei in 1¹|₂ hr.; through the Amselgrund to the Hockstein 2 hrs.; by the Brand to Schandau 3 hrs. — *2nd*. Drive in ³|₄ hr. to the Lichtenhain Fall, walk or ride to the Kuhstall ¹|₂ hr., Grosse Winterberg 1¹|₂ hr., Prebischthor 1 hr., Herrnskretschen 1¹|₂ hr.; steamboat in 1 hr. or railway in ¹|₂ hr. to Königstein, visit the fortress, 2 hrs.; return to Dresden by railway. — Those who have a third day at command may ascend the Pörsberg (p. 205), walk through the Uttewald, and Zscherre ravines to the Bastei, and spend the night at Hohnstein. The secondday's walk is thus rendered easier. — The Schneeberg and Bielagrund, see p. 206.

Guides (1 Thlr. per day) not absolutely necessary, although occasionally desirable. — *Horse* from Wehlen to the Bastei 1 Thlr. 5, or by the Uttewalder Grund 1 Thlr. 12 Ngr.; from the Bastei to Rathen 10, in the reverse direction 15 Ngr.; for other excursions generally 15—20 Ngr. per hour (comp. p. 209). — *Chair-porters* from Wehlen to the Bastei 1 Thlr. 25, or by the Uttewalder Grund 2 Thlr. 10 Ngr.; from Rathen to the Bastei 1 Thlr.; from the Bastei by Rathewalde to the Hockstein 2 Thlr. 5 Ngr. — Steamboats on the Elbe, see p. 192; Railway, see R. 38.

The *Meissener Hochland*, a very picturesque district, remarkable for its singular rock-formations, known for the last century as the **Saxon Switzerland,** extends from Liebethal to the Bohemian frontier, a distance of 23 M., and from the Falkenberg to the Schneeberg, about the same distance. It is intersected by the Elbe, the most picturesque part of the river being between Leitmeritz and Pirna. The sandstone of which the mountains consist often assumes the most grotesque shapes. Some of the rocky columns

formed by the disintegration of the softer strata are so lofty and
slender that their upright position appears extremely precarious.

At stat. *Pötzscha* (p. 206) the traveller quits the railway and
crosses the Elbe to the village of. **Wehlen** (*Sächs. Schweiz; Stadt
Wehlen*, station of the guides), from which he ascends on the l.
bank of the brook. After a few minutes' walk the paved track
ascending to the r. is to be avoided, and the path to the l. in the
Wehlener Grund followed. The valley, which is enclosed by
rocky and wooded heights, gradually contracts, and 1 M. from
Wehlen divides. After 7 min. more a finger-post to the l. indicates the route to the Uttewalder Grund, and to the r. to the
Zscherre-Grund.

The ***Uttewalder Grund** is one of the finest rocky gorges in Saxon
Switzerland. The sides are so lofty and close together that some parts of
the ravine are never reached by the sun's rays. About 10 min. from the
above mentioned finger-post is a restaurant; the path passes the *Teufels-
küche* (devil's kitchen), a grotto resembling an open fire-place. At the
narrowest part, called the Felsenthor, 5 min. above the restaurant, the
path is carried over the brook by means of a wooden scaffolding. At the
upper end of the valley steps ascend to *Uttewald* (p. 205). Those who visit
the Uttewalder Grund from the above mentioned finger-post usually proceed as far as the Felsenthor only.

The route hence to the Bastei can hardly be mistaken. The
broad path ascends through the ***Zscherre-Grund**, a wild and narrow
wooded ravine 1 M. in length, bounded by lofty and grotesque rocks
which are partially clothed with moss and fern. A pine-wood is
next traversed. At the top of the hill the high road (finger-post)
is crossed, the *Steinerne Tisch* (Refreshments; direction-post) passed, and the Bastei reached in 25 min. more. A rocky plateau,
50 paces to the l. of the path, immediately before the Bastei is
attained; commands a fine survey of the rocks of the Wehlener
Grund.

The ****Bastei** (968 ft. above the sea-level, and nearly 700 ft.
above the Elbe; *Inn on the summit, R. 15 Ngr.), a rock with
several peaks, rising precipitously from the Elbe, is the finest point
in Saxon Switzerland. The view, especially from the tower (2 Ngr.),
is magnificent and extensive': to the N. Rathewalde and Hohnstein;
E. the Brand, Kleine Winterberg, Grosse Winterberg, Zirkelsteine,
and Kaiserkrone; S. the Pabststein and Gohrischstein, in the foreground Lilienstein and Königstein; S. W. the Rauhstein and Bären-
stein; far below flows the Elbe, visible from Wehlen to a point
above Rathen; admirable survey of the wooded gorges and of the
abrupt peaks resembling gigantic castles.

From the inn the traveller descends in 5 min. to the **Bastei-
brücke*, a stone bridge of seven arches constructed in 1861, connecting the rocky pinnacles which here rise from the valley. (To
the l. before the bridge is reached a path diverges to the *Ferdinand-
stein*, which affords a good survey of the environs and of the bridge
itself.) An inscription on the bridge records the names of the pastors

Nicolai (d. 1819) and *Götzinger* (d. 1818), who first brought this remarkable rock scenery into notice. A projecting platform affords a magnificent view of the profound rocky and pine-clad gorge. About 1/4 hr. from the bridge the path emerges from the wood and divides. That to the l. skirting the wood leads to the Amselgrund (see below); that in a straight direction leads to (5 min.) **Rathen** (*Zum Erbgericht*, on the river), a village on the Elbe with a ruined castle, and a steamboat and railway-station (the latter on the opposite bank). The ascent of the Bastei from Rathen occupies about 1 hr.

The above mentioned path to the l., 20 min. below the Bastei, ascends the *Amselgrund*, passes a small waterfall, and leads in 1 1/4 hr. to *Rathewalde*. The traveller should here enquire the way to the **Hockstein,** a rock 360 ft. in height, rising abruptly from the green Polenzgrund. Opposite to it, on the other side of the valley, lies the picturesque little town of *Hohnstein* (Hirsch; Sächs. Schweiz); commanded by an old castle, now used as a reformatory. Then descend through the *Wolfsschlucht* to the cool *Polenzthal*, and follow the course of the brook for about 3/4 hr., until the first house, the *Waltersdorfer Mühle*, becomes visible. A bridge is now crossed, and the hill ascended to the r. Where the path divides, follow that to the r. until it joins the carriage-road on the hill, which leads in 9 min. more to the Brand.

The view from the *Brand (968 ft.; small *Inn*) is hardly inferior to that from the Bastei, and comprises nearly the same series of peaks. Far below lies the Polenzthal.

About 100 paces from the finger-post on the carriage-road a footpath diverges from the broad path to the l. to a singular group of rocks somewhat resembling oat-sacks, 100 paces distant. The main path then descends rapidly through the *Tiefe Grund*, passing under a curious overhanging rock, to the (1/2 hr.) Hohnstein and the Schandau road, which leads to the (2 1/4 M.) Elbe at *Wendisch-Fähre* and to (1 M.)

Schandau (*Forsthaus and Deutsches Haus combined, with pleasant garden on the Elbe, R. 20, B. 8, A. 6 Ngr. — *Dampfschiff, Bahr's Hôtel, and Engel, also on the river; Anker, in the market, Stadt Teplitz, both unpretending.—Private apartments abundant. — *Guides*, see p. 207. — *Carriage* to the waterfall 1 1/2 Thlr.; to the Brand by Hohnstein 3 Thlr.; to the Bastei by the Brand and Hohnstein 4 1/2 Thlr. — *Chair-porters* from the waterfall to the Kuhstall 15 Ngr., from the Kuhstall to the Kleine Winterberg 1 Thlr., thence to the Grosse Winterberg 20 Ngr., to the Prebischthor 20 Ngr. more, thence to Herrnskretschen 1 Thlr. 5 Ngr. — *Mule* from Schandau to the waterfall 1 Thlr., thence to the Kuhstall 8, Kleine Winterberg 20, Grosse Winterberg 15, Prebischthor 12, Herrnskretschen 20 Ngr.) is a small town prettily situated on the r. bank of the Elbe, at the mouth of the *Kirnitzschbach*. In the valley of the latter, 1/2 M. above the town is a small *Mineral Bath* (Inn), surrounded by wooded rocks and promenades. Schandau is the central point of Saxon

Switzerland, and is much frequented in summer. The railway
station *Krippen* lies on the opposite bank. Steamboats, see p. 192.

Walks. In the *Kirnitzschthal*, see above; to the *Ostrau Scheibe*, to
the *Schlossberg*, the *Friedensplatz*, the *Schillerhöhe*, the *Schützenhaus;* farther
distant to the *Hohe Liebe* 1 hr.; to the *Schrammsteine* 1½ hr.; to the *Hoch-
buschkuppe* 2 hrs.

To the Pabststein (1¼ hr.): below the railway station of Krippen
take the first path provided with railings ascending rapidly to the l.;
½ hr. *Klein-Hennersdorf;* at the house bearing the name of the village
the path turns to the l., crosses the carriage-road, and skirts the wood,
the direction being occasionally indicated by white marks on the trees.
The view from the *Pabststein (1434 ft.; small *inn at the top) embraces
the entire district of Saxon Switzerland. The most conspicuous points are
N.W. the Lilienstein and Königstein, E. the Grosse Winterberg and the
Kleis rising like a tower, S. E. the basaltic Rosenberg (1957 ft.), the
highest peak in the district. A mere speck only of the Elbe is visible at
Schandau. — From the Pabststein a good path leads to the N. W., by *Goh-
risch* to Königstein in 1 hr. (in the reverse direction 1½ hr.). Small boat
from Königstein to Rathen (see above) in 40 min., 1 Thlr. 5 Ngr.

The **Kirnitzschthal** is ascended by a good road, passing the
baths above mentioned and the (2 M.) *Haidemühle*, to the *Lichtenhain Waterfall* (*Inn) which may be improved by opening a sluice.
The footpath quits the road here and ascends in ½ hr. to the

*Kuhstall (999 ft.; *Inn*), an archway of rock, 20 ft. in height,
commanding in one direction a view of the *Habichtsgrund*, a profound wooded ravine, enclosed by sandstone rocks. It was probably
once employed by the peasantry as a refuge for their cattle in time
of war, and has thence derived its name ('cow-stable'). The summit
is attained by 83 steps through a narrow cleft in the rocks. (Small
restaurant.)

The path descends through a deep gorge to the *Habichtsgrund*.
It next ascends gradually to the base of the basaltic *Kleine Winterberg* (1575 ft.), and then rapidly to a plateau, where a small hut
with inscriptions marks the spot where Elector Augustus by a
fortunate shot saved himself from the attack of an infuriated stag
in 1568.

The summit of the ***Grosse Winterberg** (1771 ft.; *Inn*), which
is easily reached from the Kuhstall in 2 hrs., is a basaltic ridge,
½ M. in length. The tower commands a picturesque and extensive
prospect, embracing the Saxon, Bohemian, and even the Silesian
Mts.; in the foreground a small portion of the valley of the Elbe.

The *Path to the Prebischthor* (1 hr. to the S. E.) leads
from the inn on the Winterberg to the l. through the wood, then, at
at the first bifurcation, to the l. again, and afterwards crosses the
Bohemian frontier, which is indicated by stones. The ***Prebischthor**
(1358 ft.; *Inn*, Austrian wines), a rocky arch of far more imposing
dimensions than the Kuhstall (66—100 ft. wide; roof 48 ft. long,
10 ft. thick), is in Bohemian territory. The view of the wild environs is very striking. The horizon towards the S. W. is bounded
by the outlines of the Erzgebirge. This spot is preferred by many
to the Bastei.

A good path descends hence S. W. between huge walls of rock, following the course of the *Biela*, to the valley of the *Kamnitz*, through which a carriage-road leads to (1¹/₂ hr.) **Herrnskretschen** *(Stadt Berlin*, by the church; *Zum Herrenhaus)* , a village on the Elbe. ·On the opposite bank is stat. *Schöna* (Rail. Restaurant).

Steamboat from Herrnskretschen to *Tetschen* (p. 206) several times daily; also to *Dresden*, comp. p. 192. — Small boat from Herrnskretschen to Schandau (in 1¹/₄ hr.) 1¹/₆ Thlr., to Königstein (2¹/₄ hrs.) 2¹/₃ Thlr., to Rathen (3 hrs.) 3 Thlr.

40. From Dresden by Chemnitz and Zwickau to Reichenbach.

Railway in 4¹|₂—6¹|₄ hrs.; fares 4 Thlr. 2, 2 Thlr. 22, 2 Thlr. 1 Ngr.

As far as Tharandt the line follows the Weisseritzthal. At stat. *Plauen*, where there is an extensive brewery, 2 M. to the S. W. of Dresden (by railway in 7 min.), the *Plauensche Grund*, a very picturesque part of the valley of the *Weisseritz*, bounded by rocks on both sides, begins. On the height to the r. rises the château of *Begerburg* (*Restaurant, ¹/₄ hr. from stat. Plauen), commanding a pleasing prospect.

At stat. *Potschappel* the valley expands and is studded with manufactories and well-built dwelling-houses, to which the productive coal-mines in the vicinity have given rise. On the *Windberg*, to the S., rises a monument to 276 miners who perished by an explosion in 1869. Next stations *Deuben*, *Hainsberg* (whence the attractive *Rabenauer Grund* may be reached in 1 hr.). Near Tharandt, on the r. and l. of the line, are the plantations of the 'Forst-Academie', with picturesquely grouped varieties of foliage.

Tharandt (206 ft.) *(Deutsches Haus; Bad; Alberts - Salon)*, with 1700 inhab., romantically situated at the junction of three valleys. On a rocky eminence rise the ruins of an ancient castle, formerly a hunting-seat of the Saxon princes. The *Forst-Academie*, an institution for the education of foresters, enjoys a high reputation; the nursery of forest-trees contains upwards of 1000 varieties of trees and shrubs. Beautiful walks in the environs, especially in the '*Heiligen·Hallen*', a fine beech plantation.

The line quits the valley of the Weisseritz beyond stat. *Hökendorf* and ascends the picturesquely wooded *Seerenbachthal* as far as stat. *Klingenberg*. Stations *Bobritzsch* and *Hilbersdorf*, the *Muldener Hütte*, an extensive government foundry is seen to the r. The *Freiberger Mulde* is then crossed. On the r. and l. are numerous mines and foundries.

Freiberg (1181 ft.) *(*Hôtel de Saxe; *Rother Hirsch; Stern)*, a mining town, founded in 1171, on the discovery of the silver mines, and once fortified, as the remains of its towers and walls still indicate, contained 40,000 inhah. during the height of its prosper-

14*

ity (about 1540), but now about 20,000 only. Freiberg is the centre of the Saxon mining district. The value of the silver annually yielded by the mines averages 185,000*l*.

The road in a straight direction from the station leads to the Petersthor, where a Gothic *Monument* erected in 1844 commemorates the brave defence of the town by the townspeople and miners against the Swedes in 1642—43. The Peters-Str. leads hence to the Obermarkt, with the handsome *Rathhaus* (1410) on the E. side and the Kaufhaus on the N. The latter contains a *Museum of Antiquities* of considerable merit. The spot where Kunz von Kaufungen was beheaded in this Platz in 1455 is indicated by a slab of greenstone with a cross.

The Weingasse, at the corner of the market diagonally opposite the Peters-Str., and then the second side street to the l. lead to the *Cathedral, a late Gothic edifice erected on the side of a Romanesque church which was burned down in 1484. A beautiful relic of the earlier church, dating from the 12th cent., is the S. Portal, or *Goldene Pforte*, remarkable for its sculptures; in the archway the Virgin and Child; at the sides the Magi, Joseph, and an angel; on the columns on the r. and l. prophets and apostles.

In the CHOIR (sacristan Untermarkt 392, 7¹⁄₂ Ngr.) is the *Kurfürsten-Capelle*, in the vaults beneath which 41 Prot. princes of Saxony, from Duke Henry the Pious (d. 1541) to Elector George IV. (d. 1694), repose. The finest monument is that of the Elector Maurice (d. 1553 at the battle of Sievershausen) in the Renaissance style of the 16th cent., a sarcophagus of several rare kinds of marble, with a kneeling statue of the prince, and richly sculptured, executed by Anthony van Seron at Antwerp in 1563. High up in a corner of the choir is the suit of armour worn by the Elector at the time of his death. The late Gothic *Pulpit* of 1508, in the form of the stalk and calyx of a flower, with steps borne by the figures of the master and his assistants, and the *Knappschaftsstuhl* of 1546, or seat of the mining corporation, with painted stone statues of miners, are also worthy of inspection.

Adjoining the cathedral on the S. are fine late Gothic *Cloisters*, in which opposite the Goldene Pforte, the eminent geologist Werner is interred. — The other churches are uninteresting.

Near the Kreuzthor at the N. W. corner of the town, is the old *Schloss Freudenstein*, of the 15th cent., once the chapterhouse of the cathedral, the residence of Duke Henry the Pious in 1512—39, and now a magazine. In the grounds near it is *Werner's Monument*.

The *Mining Academy*, founded in 1765, which formerly enjoyed a high reputation owing to the efforts of the great mineralogist Werner (d. 1817), possesses valuable collections.

About ³⁄₄ M. to the E. of Freiberg (by the road from the Donatsthor, turning to the l. past the cemetery) is situated the *Himmelfahrt* mine, which yields 8000 lbs. of pure silver annually. Fee for 1 pers. 10, 2 pers. 15, 3 pers. 20 Ngr. and gratuity.

As the train proceeds, the scenery is at first uninteresting, but a picturesque view is obtained as Oederan is approached; in the foreground the small town itself; then the imposing castle *Augustusburg*, on an abrupt height, and the small town of *Schellenberg* (see below); in the background the Erzgebirge. Beyond stat. *Oederan* (Post) the line enters the attractive valley of the *Flöha*, which it follows to its influx into the Zschopau. Stat. *Flöha*, a pretty village in the Zschopauthal, was the birthplace of the celebrated statesman Puffendorf.

From Flöha to Annaberg railway in 2³/₄ hrs. (fares 1 Thlr. 4, 23, 17 Ngr.). — The line traverses the charming valley of the *Zschopau*, which it crosses several times. On an eminence to the l. of stat. *Erdmannsdorf* lies the little town of *Schellenberg* (Post), commanded by the extensive *Augustusburg* (1585 ft.), a château erected in 1572 (two pictures by Cranach in the chapel). Stations *Waldkirchen*, **Zschopau** (*Hirsch; Post*), a small town with cloth-factories, *Wolkenstein*, and **Annaberg** (*Wilder Mann; Museum; Gans*), a busy little town, with a church containing curious reliefs of the early part of the 16th cent. — Diligence daily in summer from Annaberg to Carlsbad in 7¹/₂ hrs. The route is by *Oberwiesenthal* (2556 ft.), the highest town in Saxony, to the r. of which rises the *Fichtelberg* (3833 ft.; splendid view; keys of the tower at the inn of Oberwiesenthal, and at the 'Neue Haus' at the highest point of the Carlsbad road); then by *Gottesgabe*, the first Bohemian town, the highest among the Erzgebirge. Thence by *Joachimsthal* and *Schlackenwerth* to *Carlsbad*, see *Baedeker's S. Germany.*

From stat. *Nieder-Wiesa* a branch-line diverges to *Frankenberg* and *Haynichen*, two busy manufacturing places.

Chemnitz, pron. Kemnitz (*Blauer Engel; Stadt Gotha; Stadt Berlin; Röm. Kaiser; Victoria*, etc.), the most important manufacturing town in Saxony, with 68,000 inhab., lies in a fertile plain at the base of the Erzgebirge. It was originally a settlement of the ancient Wends, and became celebrated at an early period for its linen manufactories and bleaching grounds. The staple products are stockings, woven goods, and machinery. Among the numerous manufactories in the environs may be mentioned the engine factory of *Hartmann*, where 2000 workmen are employed. The late Gothic *Rathhaus* in the Hauptmarkt is flanked with arcades and possesses a lofty tower. Near it is the *Jacobikirche* of the 14th cent., altered in the 18th, the sacristy of which contains a picture by Cranach the Elder. The *Schloss*, to the N. W. of the town, once a Benedictine abbey, is now a restaurant. The adjoining *Abbey Church*, erected in the late Gothic style in 1514—25, with a fine S. portal, contains a painting of the old Franconian School. Around the town extend the well-built and increasing suburbs.

The railway from Chemnitz to Zwickau traverses a manufacturing district. Stations *Grüna*, *Wüstenbrand*, and *Hohenstein-Ernstthal* (Deutsches Haus; Schwan), two manufacturing places (the Baths of *Hohenstein* are 1¹/₂ M. distant). Then *St. Egidien*, the station for *Lichtenstein* and *Callenberg*.

Glauchau (*Deutsches Haus; Adler*), another prosperous manufacturing town with 22,000 inhab., with two châteaux of the counts of Schönburg, lies on the *Mulde*, which the line now crosses. A branch line to the N. W. diverges to *Gössnitz* (R. 45).

Zwickau (*Post; Deutscher Kaiser*, new; *Hôtel Wagner*, at the station; *Grüne Tanne; Anker*), an old manufacturing town with

26,000 inhab. , on the once important commercial route from the
Danube to E. Franconia, lies in a pretty valley on the *Mulde.* The
late Gothic **Marienkirche*, begun in 1453 , with choir of 1536 , has
been restored as a Prostestant church. Altar-piece , with double
wings, by *Wohlgemuth*, painted in 1479 ; beneath it a winged altar-
piece in carved wood, representing Mary and the eight holy women,
gilded and painted. The Sacristy contains similar works , dating
from 1507. In the Baptistery a small picture by Cranach, 'Suffer
little children to come unto Me'. Fine view from the tower (237 ft.).
The sacristan lives on the N. side of the church. The *Catharinen-
kirche* of the 14th and 15th cent., subsequently altered, also contains
a picture by Cranach. Thomas Münzer , the fanatical leader of the
Anabaptists, who was beheaded at Mühlhausen in 1525 , was pastor
here in 1520—22. In the market-place are the *Rathhaus* of 1581,
the *Kaufhaus*, 1522—24, and other fine buildings, the most interesting of which is the late Gothic inn Zum Anker.

 The environs are picturesque and well peopled. The 80 coal-
mines of this district employ upwards of 8000 hands.

  From Zwickau to Schwarzenberg by railway in 1³|₄ hr. (fares
1 Thlr. 2, 22, 16 Ngr.). The line ascends the valley of the Mulde. Stat.
Cainsdorf, with the Königin-Maria-Hütte, the largest foundry in Saxony.
At *Planitz*, ¹|₂ M. to the W., is Geitner's interesting nursery, situated over
a burning seam of coal, with a beautiful palmhouse. The natural tempe-
rature in the hothouses is 88° Fahr. Stat. *Fährbrücke;* 1¹|₂ M. to the E.
is the small town of *Wildenfels*, with a château of the counts of that
name. Near stat. *Wiesenburg* rises a ruined castle. Stat. *Stein;* 1 M. to
the E. is the charmingly situated Schloss *Hartenstein*, the property of
Prince Schönberg-Hartenstein. Stat. *Nieder-Schlema.*

  Branch Line from Nieder-Schlema (in ¹|₄ hr.) to **Schneeberg** (1477 ft.)
(**Sächs. Hof; Fürstenhaus*), a mining town with 7500 inhab. The late
Gothic church, erected at the beginning of the 16th cent., contains a large
altar-piece, with 8 wings, representing the *Crucifixion, the master-piece
of Cranach the Elder, by whom it was painted with the aid of his pupils
in 1539. The tower (262 ft.) contains a huge bell weighing 8 tons. Numerous and valuable mines, chiefly of cobalt, are worked in the vicinity.
'Schneeberg snuff', manufactured at *Bockau*, 6 M. to the S., partly from
herbs which grow on the Erzgebirge, is said to possess sanitar yproperties.

  The Schwarzenberg line next passes stat. *Aue*, a pleasant little town
in a hollow, and then quits the Mulde. From stat. *Lauter* the *Morgen-
leite* (2560 ft.) which commands an admirable view, may be ascended in
1¹|₂ hr. The line then ascends the *Schwarzwasserthal* to

Schwarzenberg (*Hôtel de Saxe*, R. 20 Ngr.; *Stadt Leipzig*, near the
station ; *Rathhaus*), a small town on an eminence skirted by the Schwarzwasser, with an old Schloss. Opposite to it, 8 min. above the station, is
the *Ottenstein*, a height with promenades, at the foot of which lies the
pine-cone bath of that name (*Bauer's Hotel*).

  Diligence from Schwarzenberg once daily through the wild valley of
the *Schwarzwasser*, by *Johann-Georgenstadt* (Rathskeller), and across the
watershed of the Erzgebirge, to *Carlsbad* (see *Bædeker's S. Germany and
Austria*).

  At *Werdau* the Leipsic and Hof railway is reached. Thence to
Reichenbach, see p. 222.

41. From Dresden to Leipsic.

a. By Riesa.

Railway in 2¹|₂—3¹|₂ hrs.; fares 3 Thlr., 2 Thlr. 8, 1 Thlr. 15 Ngr.
The train starts from the Neustadt, nearly 1 M. from the principal hotels in the Altstadt, and skirts a range of vine-clad hills. Stations *Weintraube*, *Lössnitz* (with a manufactory of sparkling wine), *Kötzschenbroda*. On a hill to the l. in the distance rises the tower of the château of *Weisstrop*. Stations *Coswig* (junction for Meissen and Döbeln, see below), *Niederau*. The scenery now becomes less attractive. From stat. *Pristewitz* a branch-line diverges to *Grossenhain*, a town with cloth-factories, and *Cottbus* (p. 164). Stat. **Röderau** is the junction of the Berlin line (p. 190). The train now crosses the Elbe by a long viaduct.

At **Riesa** (*Rail. Restaurant)* a line to Chemnitz diverges to the l.

From Riesa to Chemnitz by railway in 2 hrs. (fares 1 Thlr. 24, 1 Thlr. 6, or 27 Ngr.). The third stat. *Doebeln* is the junction of the Leipsic, Meissen, and Dresden line (see below). Beyond stat. *Limmeritz* the Zschopau is crossed, and several views of its pretty valley are obtained. Stat. *Waldheim* (Löwe), a small town with a large prison. *Erlau* is the stat. for *Rochlitz*, a town 4³|₄ M. to the W., on an eminence near which rises a tower in memory of king Frederick Augustus (d. 1854). On a lofty rock on the r. bank of the Zschopau, 1 M. to the N. of stat. *Oberlichtenau*, stands the château of *Sachsenburg;* 1¹|₂ M. to the S. lies the extensive château of *Lichtenwalde*, with beautiful fountains. *Chemnitz*, see p. 213.

Between Riesa and Leipsic the line traverses the field of the memorable battle of Leipsic. At the *Hubertusburg*, an old château 7 M. to the W. of stat. *Oschatz*, a peace was concluded between Austria, Prussia, and Saxony in 1763. Stations *Dahlen*, *Machern* (where the *Mulde* is crossed), *Borsdorf*, **Leipsic** (p. 216).

b. By Doebeln.

Railway in 4—4¹|₂ hrs.; fares 3 Thlr., 2 Thlr. 8, 1 Thlr. 15 Ngr. — This route is longer, but more attractive than the above.

As far as stat. *Coswig* the route is the same as the preceding. The train crosses the Elbe, and soon reaches

Meissen (*Hirsch*; *Stern;* *Geissler's* restaurant and garden, fitted up in the mediæval German style. *Steamboats* to Dresden, see p. 192), one of the most ancient towns in Saxony, and the seat of the Margraves of that name down to 1090, is most picturesquely situated at the influx of the *Triebisch* and the *Meisse* into the *Elbe*. The *Cathedral*, which stands on the Schlossberg, 160 ft. above the town, was founded in the 13th, and completed in the two following centuries. The S. E. tower (254 ft.), with its elegant open spire, dates from the 14th cent. (view from the top). Most of the ancestors of the royal family of Saxony of the 15th and 16th cent. repose here, and among them the princes Ernest and Albert who were carried off by the robber-knight Kunz von Kaufungen. The finest of the numerous monuments is that of Friedrich 'der Streitbare', in bronze. The Fürstencapelle contains a Descent from the Cross by Cranach. Charming prospect from the beautiful open tower.

Adjoining the cathedral is the *Albrechtsburg*, erected in 1471—83, one of the most extensive castles of that period. On the Afrafelsen, which is connected with the Schlossberg by a bridge of the 13th cent., is an old abbey converted into a school in 1543, where Gellert (1729—34) and Lessing (1741—46) received their early education. The celebrated *Royal Porcelain Manufactory* (600 workmen), formerly in the Schloss, is now established in a building in the Triebischthal, $1^1/_2$ M. from the town (shown daily, except Sundays). The manufactory was founded in 1710, shortly after Böttcher had discovered the art of making 'china'. The secret was at length divulged during the Prussian occupation in the Seven Years' War. Picturesque points near Meissen, see p. 205).

Stations *Deutschenbora*, *Miltitz*, and *Nossen*, with a Schloss, where the pretty valley of the *Mulde* is entered. On a wooded hill to the l. beyond it are the ruins of the monastery of *Altenzella*, with a burial-chapel of the counts of Meissen. Stat. *Rosswein;* then **Doebeln** *(Sonne)*, the junction of the Riesa and Chemnitz line (see above). Stat. *Klosterbuch*, with a ruined abbey; beautiful walks in the Forest of Wendischhain, on the l. bank of the Mulde. Stat. **Leisnig,** an old manufacturing town with 7000 inhab., is commanded by Schloss *Mildenstein*.

Diligence daily from Leisnig to ($8^1|_2$ M.) the small town of **Colditz,** in the pretty valley of the *Zwickauer Mulde*, commanded by an imposing and well-preserved old castle, now a lunatic asylum.

Stations *Tanndorf* (to the r. the beautifully situated Schloss *Kössern*), *Grossbothen*, and **Grimma** *(*Kronprinz; Löwe; Schiff)*, picturesquely situated on the *Mulde*, with 6500 inhab.; on the l. bank is the *Landes-Schule*. The convent of *Nimbschen*, where Catharine von Bora, the wife of Luther, was once a nun, is now a farm-house.

The line next traverses the valley of the *Parthe*. Stations *Gross-Steinberg*, *Naunhof*, and *Borsdorf*, where the Riesa line is reached.

42. Leipsic.

Arrival. Cab tickets are issued at the station, as at Berlin; tariff, see below. There are five railway stations at Leipsic. *1. Bavarian Station* (Pl. 2), for Altenburg, Hof (Nuremberg and Munich), and Eger (Carlsbad and Regensburg). *2. Berlin Station* (Pl. 3), 1 M. to the N. of the town, for Berlin. *3. Magdeburg Station* (Pl. 5) for Halle (Cassel), Magdeburg, and Hamburg. *4. Dresden Station* (Pl 4), for Dresden, Görlitz, and Breslau. *5. Thuringian Station* (Pl. 6), for Weimar, Eisenach, and Frankfort on the Main.

Hotels. *Hôtel Hauffe (Pl. a), at the corner of the Ross-Str. and the Ross-Platz, well fitted up, R. 1 Thlr., B. 10 Ngr.; *Hôtel de Russie (Pl. c), Peters-Str.; *Hôtel de Bavière (Pl. b), in the same street; *Palmbaum (Pl. h), Gerber-Str.; Hôtel de Pologne (Pl. d), Hain-Str.; Hôtel de Prusse (Pl. e), Ross-Platz; *Stadt Hamburg (Pl. f), Nicolai-Str.; Stadt Rom (Pl. k), near the Dresden Station; Stadt Dresden (Pl. g), Grimmaische Steinweg; Stadt Wien (Pl. i), Peter-Str.; Stadt Nürnberg, at the

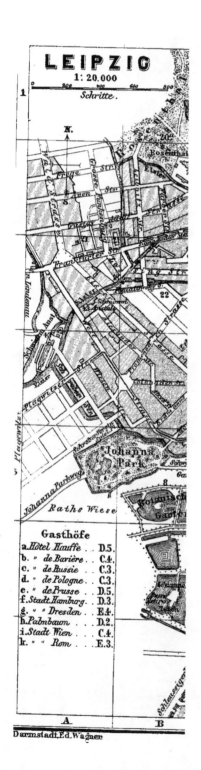

LEIPZIG

1 : 20.000

Schritte.

N.

Johanna
Park

Raths Wiese

Gasthöfe

a. Hôtel Hauffe . . D.5.
b. " de Bavière . C.4.
c. " de Russie . C.3.
d. " de Pologne . C.3.
e. " de Prusse . D.5.
f. Stadt Hamburg. D.3.
g. " " Dresden . E.4.
h. Palmbaum . . . D.2.
i. Stadt Wien . . . C.4.
k. " " Rom . . . E.3.

A

B

Darmstadt, Ed. Wagner.

Bavarian Station; MÜNCHNER HOF, Königs-Platz 2. Rooms may also be procured at the *Dresden, Thuringian, and Berlin *Railway Restaurants.* — Restaurants. *Aeckerlein's Keller*, Markt 11; *Kraft*, Hain-Str. 23; *Reusch*, Grimmaische Str. 23; *Rheinländische Weinstube*, Ritter-Str.; *Auerbach's Keller*, Grimma'sche Str. 1, near the market, celebrated as the scene of a part of Goethe's Faust, with curious mural paintings of the 16th cent. (restored in 1863) representing the tradition on which the play was based. At the *New Theatre*, E. pavilion. The *Schützenhaus* (Pl. 42), with garden, is a favourite place of resort. — Beer. *Baarmann*, Katharinen-Str. 28; *Kitzing*, Peters-Str. 19; *Universitäts-Keller*, Ritter-Str. 43; *Uhlemann*, near the Bavarian Station; *Gute Quelle* (see below). — Cafés. *Felsche* (confectioner), Augustus-Platz, at the corner of the Grimmaische Str.; *Café National*, Markt 16; at the *New Theatre*, W. pavilion; *Café Sedan*, in the Promenade; *Gösswein*, Brühl 78. Then *Bonorand* and *Schweizerhäuschen* in the *Rosenthal* (p. 221), where a band plays in summer almost daily.

    Baths. *Dianabad*, Lange-Str. 4, 5, with Turkish and other baths; *Sophienbad*, Dorotheen-Str. 1, with Turkish, vapour, and swimming baths. — *River Baths* at the swimming and bath establishment (for ladies also) in the Schreber-Str. on the W. side of the town.

    Fiacres. One-horse for 1 pers. within 20 min. 4, 2 pers 5, 3 pers. 7, 4 pers. 9 Ngr. (to the Berlin stat. 5, 6, 8, 10 Ngr.); from all the railway-stations to the town 1 Ngr. more in each case. Per hour 10, 12, 13½, 15 Ngr. — *Omnibuses* to the neighbouring villages 1½ Ngr.

    Post Office (Pl. 39) in the Augustus-Platz, opposite the theatre. — Telegraph Office, Gr. Fleischergasse.

    Theatres. At the *New Theatre* (Pl. 48) performances daily, middle balcony 1⅓ Thlr., side-balcony 1 Thlr., parquet 25 Ngr., first boxes 20 Ngr. — At the *Old Theatre* (Pl. 47) performances on Sund. and Wed. in winter, and daily during the fair. *Vaudeville Theatre* at the *Gute Quelle* on the Brühl, with restaurant (in winter only).

    *Concerts in the *Gewandhaus*, celebrated, every Thursday in winter. Director Herr C. Reinecke (conducted by Mendelssohn in 1835—41).

    Newspapers in the *Börsenhalle*, Brühl 17 (for non-subscribers adm. 5 Ngr.).

    Exhibition of Art (Pl. 36), *Del Vecchio's*, in the Kaufhalle, Markt 9; week-days 9—5, Sund. 10—3; adm. 5 Ngr.

    English Church Service at the Conservatorium.

    Leipsic, Ger. *Leipzig* (387 ft.), the most important commercial town in Germany next to Hamburg, with 107,575 inhab., and the centre of the German book trade, is the seat of the supreme commercial tribunal of the German Empire, and of one of the most ancient and important universities in Europe. The city lies in an extensive plain, near the confluence of the *Elster*, the *Pleisse*, and the *Parthe*. The interior of the city consists of lofty and closely built houses, dating chiefly from the 17th and 18th cent., and is surrounded by five handsome suburbs, beyond which are a series of villages almost adjacent to the town. The population of Leipsic has increased more rapidly than that of almost any other town in Germany (in 1834 the number was 44,800; in 1849, 62,400; in 1864, 85,400).

    Leipsic is said to have been orginally a Sclavonic settlement, called *Lipzk*, or 'the town of the lime-trees'. It is mentioned in history for the first time at the beginning of the 11th cent., and was soon afterwards fortified. About the year 1170 it was endowed with extensive privileges by Otho the Rich, Margrave of Meissen, and thenceforward increased rapidly. As early as 1180 markets were held here biennially at 'Jubilate' and Michaelmas, and in the 15th cent. attained to great importance. In 1458 a New Year's Fair was added to the number, and in 1497 and 1507 the Emp. Maximilian confirmed the privileges of the town by prohibiting markets to be held at any town within a wide circle around, and by guaranteeing a safe conduct to all the frequenters of the Leipsic fairs. The trade of Leipsi$_c$ was somewhat depressed by the various wars of the 17th and 18th cent., but after 1833, when Saxony joined the 'Zollverein' or German customs-union, it assumed most important dimensions. The *Jubilate* and *Michaelmas Fairs* are still attended by a vast concourse of merchants, but the New Year's Fair has considerably fallen off. On these occasions the town is thronged by from 30,000 to 40,000 traders from all parts of Europe, especially from the E., and by Jews, Greeks, Bulgarians, Armenians, and Turks. The most important of the staple commodities at the fairs are furs, of which nearly one million pounds' worth change hands here annually; next in value are leather, cloth, woollen wares, glass, and linen. The total value of the sales effected at the fairs averages ten million pounds annually.

Leipsic is still more important as the centre of the *Book Trade* of Germany, a position which it has occupied since the end of the 18th cent. There are upwards of 300 booksellers' shops and 80 printing-offices in the town, and publishers in other parts of Germany almost invariably have depôts of their books at Leipsic, whence they are forwarding to all parts of Europe and more distant countries. Many hundred booksellers congregate here at the Jubilate, and transact business at their own Börse, or Exchange.

Pleasant *Promenades on the site of the old fortifications separate the inner town from the suburbs, the most extensive and attractive being on the S. and E. sides. On the E. side they are interrupted by the spacious AUGUSTUS-PLATZ (Pl. D, 4), which is enclosed by the new theatre, the museum, the Augusteum, the post-office, and a number of handsome private houses.

The *New Theatre (Pl. 48), an imposing edifice in the Renaissance style, designed by *Langhans* of Berlin, was completed in 1868. The principal façade is adorned with a Corinthian portico, the tympanum of which contains an allegorical group by Prof. *Hagen;* the Apollo, Clio, and Calliope on the 'acroteria' are by the same sculptor; the groups in the tympana of the wings are by Lürssen, Wittich, and Schiele. The back of the building with its semicircular projecting verandah turned towards the most attractive part of the promenades and adjoining the *Schwanenteich*, a miniature lake, where a fountain plays to a height of 66 ft., produces a very picturesque effect. The interior is also worthy of a visit ·(open daily 2—4 p. m.; 5 Ngr.).

The *Museum (Pl. 37), a handsome building opposite the theatre, designed by Prof. *Lange* of Munich, and completed in 1858, is chiefly remarkable for its collection of modern pictures. (Sund. 10$^1/_2$—3, and Wed. and Frid. 10—4, gratis; Tuesd., Thursd., and Sat. 10—4, from Nov. to Jan. till 3 only, admission 5 Ngr.) Director *Dr. Max Jordan.*

On the Ground Floor (in a straight direction) is the collection of casts, among which is a *Ganymede in marble by *Thorvaldsen* (No. 56). To the right is the exhibition of the Kunstverein, to the left a room containing cartoons by *Schnorr, Overbeck,* etc., and *water-colours by *Werner* and *Schwind.*

· First Floor. 1st ROOM: Cartoons by *Preller,* scenes from the Odyssey. — 2nd ROOM. Earlier Italian and Spanish masters: 1. 213. *Sassoferrato,* Madonna; 191. *G. Reni,* Madonna; r. *154. *Murillo,* Madonna and Child; 184.

Raphael, Madonna of Foligno (copy by *Senf*). — (1.) 3rd Room. 1. 105.
Heine, Criminals in church; *217. *Scheuren*, Old Castle in the Ahr Valley;
12. *Böttcher*, Evening in the Black Forest; 195. *Rethel*, Boaz finding Ruth;
*216. *Scheuren*, Château on the Lake; *203. *Ritter*, Betrothal in Normandy;
235. *Speckter*, Simson and Delilah; *71. *Eggers*, Portrait of an Italian
woman; *70. (r. of the door) *Eggers*, St. Catharine of Alexandria; *221.
Schnorr, St. Rochus; 198. *Richter*, Landscape; 296. *Zimmermann*, Female
Centaurs; 119. *Koch*, Sacrifice of Noah; 202, 199. *Richter*, Italian landscape,
Schreckenstein near Aussig; 270. *Veit*, Germania; 76. *Gurlitt*, Landscape
on the Lago di Garda. — Principal Hall : *157. *Nordenberg*, Swedish
Organist; 25—28. *Calame*, four large and celebrated pictures: **Monte
Rosa, *The Squall, *Ruins of Pæstum, *Swiss mountains; 98. *Gudin*,
Stormy sea; (E.) 223. *Somers*, Cromwell; *224. *Schrader*, Frederick the
Great after the battle of Collin; 230. *Sohn*, Donna Diana; *275. *Verboeck-
hoven*, Flock in a storm; 171. *Papety*, Finding of Moses; 231. *Sohn*, the
Consultation; 219. *Schirmer*, Grotto of Egeria; 234. *Spangenberg*, Luther
and his family; *106. *Heinlein*, Mountain scene. — In the small (5th) Room
to the r.: *83. *Frey*, Column of Memnon at Thebes; 415. *F. Preller sen.*,
Landscape with the Samaritan. — 6th Room. 4. *Bellangé*, Scene after the
Battle of Wagram; 113. *Jacquand*, Gaston de Foix dying of starvation;
55. *P. Delaroche*, Napoleon at Fontainebleau, 31st March, 1814; 10. *Biard*,
Struggle with polar bears; *17. *Bouchot*, Gen. Marceau's interment at Coblenz (1796); 9. *Biard*, The insane king Charles VI. of France; 56, 57.
Destouches, The wounded man, The convalescent; 5, 6. *Bellangé*, The
soldier's farewell and return; 177. *Poittevin*, Sailors saving a wreck; *H.
Vernet*, Magdalene; 204. *Robert*, Sleeping brigand. — In the small rooms on
the N. side: 8th Room. 418, 419. *A. Calame*, Studies; 428. *v. Hove*, Town-
hall of Amsterdam; *430, 431. *Koekkoek*, Spring-and winter-landscapes;
*434. *H. Leys*, Dutch genre-picture; 416. *F. Bosswy*, Gil Blas; 454, 455.
Verboeckhoven, Cattle-pieces; 460. *E. Wagner*, Grapes. — 9th Room. 274,
275, 276. *Verboeckhoven*, Sheep outside the stable, Sleeping peasant; 291.
Winterhalter, Portrait; 287, 288. *Wickenberg*, Mother at the bed of her
child, Interior of a fishermann's hut; 210, 211. *Rottmann*, Corfu, Greek
landscape; *16. *Bossuet*, Cathedral of Burgos; 81. *Franquelin*, Expectation.
— 10th Room. 220, 447. *Schirmer*, German landscapes; 150. *Meyerheim*,
Sunday morning; 166. *Tidemand*, Farewell of emigrants; *P. Hess*, Duck-
shooting. — 11th Room. 268. *Vautier*, Peasants in a tavern during church;
112. *Hummel*, Lake of Brienz; 280. *Voltz*, Cow-herd; 85. *E. Fries*, Italian
landscape; 436. *L. Mayer*, Mary. — 12th Room. 273. *Verboeckhoven*, Grey
horse; 436. *Lindau*, October festivals at Rome; 134. *Lessing*, Landscape;
118. *Knauss*, Card-sharpers. — 13th Room. 120, 121. *J. A. Koch*, Italian
and Alpine landscapes; 200, 201. *L. Richter*, Landscapes; 170. *Overbeck*,
Miracles of St. Francis; 37. *Chodowiecki*, The Thiergarten at Berlin; 146,
147. *Raf. Mengs*, Girls with Cupids; 467. *A. Graff*, Portrait. — 14th Room:
Unknown Dutch Master, Female portrait; 87, 88. *Fyt*, Poultry-yard; 406.
Hondekoeter, Fowl. — 15th Room, mostly Dutch cabinet-pictures. — 16th
Room. *Unknown master*, Adoration of the Infant Christ; 40, 42. *L. Cranach*,
Madonna and Altar-piece. — In the passage-hall (E. Loggia): *Frescoes
by *Th. Grosse*, finished in 1871. *Left cupola*: Ancient Mythology (Eros
rising from the Chaos, fall of Uranos, birth of Venus, education of Jupiter,
Prometheus breathing life into man, the minor gods, fall of the Giants
and Apollo with the Muses). *Central cupola*, Fancy surrounded by the
Graces; the Wind sisters; worldly and spiritual virtues; Egypt, Greece,
Italy, Germany; the Plastic arts. *Right cupola*, History of creation according
to the bible; the works of the six days; History of the first couple; Fall
of Satan and appearance of Christ; on the *pilasters* the four seasons.
Raphael, statue in marble by *Hähnel*. — 9th Room. 64, 65. *De Dreux*,
Dogs; 97. *Greuze*, Girl in white dress. — 10th Room. 238. *Van Stry*, Cattle
at the water; 215. *Schendel*, Return from the chase. — 11th Room. 298.
Zwengauer, Stags at the lake; 117. *Kirner*, Swabian militia; 295. *Zeller*,
Saltarello; *143. *Marko*, Italian landscape. — 12th Room. 115. *Jordan*,
First visit after marriage. — 14th Room. 88. *Fyt*, Cock fighting with a
vulture; 189. *Reinhardt*, Landscape. — 15th Room. *L. Cranach the Elder*,

Christ and the Samaritan woman; several other pictures by the same master. — 16th Room. 264. *School of Andrea del Sarto*, Holy Family; 193. *Guido Reni*, St. John the Evangelist; 192. *G. Reni*, David with head of Goliath; 239. *Tintoretto*, Raising of Lazarus.

The **Upper Floor** contains the extensive *Collection of Engravings, arranged according to schools, affording a survey of the pictorial art from the 13th cent. to the present time. For a satisfactory acquaintance with its details a catalogue (7¹/₂ Ngr.) is indispensable.

The **Augusteum** (Pl. 1), on the W. side of the Augustus-Platz, erected in 1836 from designs by Schinkel, is the seat of the University (founded in 1402) with several of its collections, its lecture-rooms, and hall. The latter contains a number of good busts and statues, and twelve admirable *Reliefs by *Rietschel*, illustrative of the development of civilisation.

1. State of nature, nomads; 2. Egyptians; 3. Greeks; 4. Romans; 5. Christianity; 6. Foundation of towns; 7. The Humanists, Universities, Printing; 8. Commerce; 9. The Reformation; Luther, Zwingli, and Melanchthon, with the family of the sculptor on the r.; 10. The Renaissance, painters and sculptors: Raphael, Michael Angelo, Peter Vischer, Albert Dürer; 11. Modern art and science, composers, poets, naturalists: Bach, Shakspeare, Goethe, Humboldt, with Kant in the centre; 12. Modern statesmanship: the king on the throne; to the l. a Rom. Cath. and a Prot. clergyman, to the r. the military and industrial classes.

The adjacent *Paulinerkirche* (Pl. 32), which was restored in 1544, contains in the choir a monument by *Rietschel* to the Margrave Dietzmann of Meissen, who was assassinated in St. Thomas's in 1307.

Not far from the Museum, towards the S. W., near the Bürgerschule, rises the **Statue of Thaer** (Pl. 19), a distinguished agriculturist (d. 1828), in bronze, designed by *Rietschel*. The other monuments in the promenades are of inferior merit. That of *Bach* (Pl. 12) was erected by Mendelssohn in 1843, near the school of St. Thomas where the great master of fugues was 'cantor' (d. 1750).

The busy Grimmaische Strasse leads from the Augustus-Platz towards the W. to the Markt-Platz, situated nearly in the centre of the city, and bounded on three sides by lofty and antiquated houses, some of them in the Renaissance style, while the fourth side is occupied by the handsome **Rathhaus** (Pl. 41) of 1556. Opposite to it, towards the S., is Auerbach's Keller (p. 217). To the N. W. the Hain-Strasse, at No. 31 in which Schiller resided in 1785 and 1789, leads to the *Brühl*, a great resort of the Jewish frequenters of the fairs, and the *Old Theatre* (Pl. 47), near which is a monument (Pl. 15) to *Hahnemann* (d. 1843), the father of homœopathy. A small monument at the end of the Ranstädter Steinweg (Pl. B, 3) commemorates the premature blowing up of the bridge by the French on 19th Oct., 1813, which proved so fatal to their rear-guard.

The **Pleissenburg** (Pl. 38), at the S. W. angle of the town, formerly the citadel, now containing barracks and public offices, dates from the 16th cent. The tower affords a good survey of the battle-field of 18th Oct., 1813 (custodian 7½ Sgr.).

The **Churches** of Leipsic present few attractions. The *Nicolaikirche* (Pl. 31) of 1525 contains some of the cannon balls of 1813 built into the walls by the windows, and a stone pulpit, from which Luther is said once to have preached, in a vaulted receptacle by the S. entrance. In the Ritter-Strasse, opposite, is the *Booksellers' Exchange* (comp. p. 218). — The *Church of St. Thomas* (Pl. 35), with its lofty and conspicuous roof, —was consecrated in 1496. — *Rom. Cath. Church* (Pl. 29) and *Synagogue* (Pl. 45) modern. — To the E. of the choir of the *Church of St. John* (Pl. 28) is *Gellert's Tomb* (d. 1769). — Near the *'Milch-Insel'* (Pl. F, 3), the first position within the town gained by the Allies on 19th Oct., 1813, is the *Kugel Denkmal* (Pl. 20), or 'Ball Monument', formed of projectiles found in the city and environs.

A house in the Königs-Strasse (Pl. E, 5), indicated by a memorial tablet, was occupied by Mendelssohn in 1835—41 and 1846—47. — The *Turnhalle* (Pl. 48), or gymnastic hall, in the Turner-Str., completed in 1863, is worthy of inspection. — In the Waisenhaus-Str., to the S. E. of the latter, are the extensive and admirably organised *Chemical Laboratory* and *Physiological Institute* connected with the university. Adjacent to the laboratory is the commodious *Municipal Hospital*, completed in 1811.

Near the Zeitzer Thor (Pl. E, 7) is situated the *Römische Haus*, erected in 1832—33, containing good frescoes by *Preller* (illustrative of the Odyssey) and *Wislicenus*. No. 43 Zeitzer Strasse is the 'gymnastic orthopædic' sanitary establishment of *Dr. Schildbach*, which enjoys a high reputation.

Adjoining the city on the N. W. is the ***Rosenthal** (Pl. B, 1), with its pretty dales and beautiful oak plantations (cafés and concerts, see p. 217), and a marble statue of *Gellert* (Pl. 14). To the N. of these grounds is the village of *Gohlis*, where an inscription on one of the houses records that Schiller there composed his 'Ode to Joy'. Farther distant is *Eutritzsch*, where 'Gose', a kind of beer which was once a favourite beverage of the Leipsickers, may still be tasted at the Gosenschenke. — The *Kuhthurm*, 1½ M. to the W. of Leipsic, formerly a forester's house, now contains the agricultural academy of the university.

The **Collection of Baron Speck** at *Lützschena* (one hour's drive to the N. W., beyond Möckern) comprises several good works by old masters (visitors apply to the custodian; closed on Sundays): *Rubens*, Augustine Prior; *Memling*, Salutation; *Rembrandt* and *Lievens*, Two portraits of old men; *Jordaens*, Evangelists; *F. Bol*, Dutch burgomaster; After *Raphael*, Johanna of Arragon; *Van der Helst*, Old woman; *H. Roos*, Evening landscape; *De Heem*, Still life; *Murillo*, Madonna and Child; *Schalken*, Holy Family; *Van de Velde*, Quay; *Dürer*, Young lady; *Wohlgemuth*, Christ and the Apostles; *Valdez*, St. Bruno; *Denner*, Portrait; *Cuyp*, Cattle.

The **Battle of Leipsic**, which lasted four days, 16th—19th Oct., 1813, is the most prolonged and sanguinary on record. It was conducted on both sides by some of the greatest generals of modern times. Napoleon's forces numbered 140—150,000 men, of whom 90,000 survivors only began the retreat to the Rhine on 19th Oct.; the allied troops were 300,000 strong. The Russians lost 21,000 men, the Austrians 14,000, the Prussians 16,000. The entire number of cannon brought into the field is estimated at 2000. On 19th Oct. at 11 a. m. a Prussian 'Landwehr' battalion stormed the

Grimma Gate and forced an entrance into the town. At 12 Napoleon quitted the town. The French retreated towards Lützen by the bridge over the Elster near the Ranstädt Gate. The bridge, the only mode of crossing the river, was prematurely blown up, in consequence of which thousands of the French perished by drowning, and among them the Polish general Poniatowsky; 25,000 who had not yet crossed the bridge were taken prisoners. At 1 o'clock the Allies entered Leipsic.

A bird's eye view of the battle-field (see Plan) is best obtained from the tower of the Pleissenburg (p. 220). The scene of the engagement of the decisive 18th Oct. is perhaps better viewed from the *Napoleonsberg*, a height planted with trees near the *Thonberg* estate, 2 M. S. E. of Leipsic, whence the progress of the battle was watched by Napoleon.

The village of *Probstheyda*, ³|₄ M. farther, was the centre of the French position. On a hill by the road-side, 1¹|₂ M. S. E. of Probstheyda, rises an iron *Obelisk* on the spot where the three monarchs (Russia, Austria, Prussia) received the tidings of the victory on the evening of 18th Oct. Another hill in the vicinity, near the farm of *Meusdorf*, bears a simple block of granite with an inscription to the memory of Prince Schwarzenberg, the general of the allied forces (d. 1820). The only building on which bullet marks are still visible is the château at *Dölitz*, 2 M. to the W. of the Obelisk, where a detachment of Austrians were stationed. All the above points may be visited by fiacre in about 3 hrs. — A number of monuments in Leipsic and the environs commemorate the events of the great 'Völkerschlacht', or 'battle of the nations', as the battle is not inappropriately termed by the Germans. The churchyard at *Taucha*, 6 M. to E., contains monuments to the Russian general *Manteuffel* and the English captain *Bowyer*, commander of a British rocket-corps which aided the Allies during the battle.

Leipsic and its environs have also been the scene of other important historical events. In the castle of *Altranstädt* Charles XII. of Sweden signed the articles of peace with Augustus of Poland in 1706. In the castle of *Hubertusburg* (4 M. W. of stat. Oschatz on the Dresden line) the peace which terminated the Seven Years' War was concluded between Austria, Saxony, and Prussia, 15th Feb., 1763 (comp. p. 215). Near *Breitenfeld* (p. 223) Gustavus Adolphus defeated the troops of the Ligue under Tilly, 7th Sept.,1631.

43. From Berlin to Leipsic.

Railway in 3¹|₂—4³|₄ hrs.; express fares 5 Thlr. 4, 3 Thlr. 7¹|₂, 2 Thlr. 28 Sgr.; Ordinary 4 Thlr. 12, 3 Thlr. 9, 2 Thlr. 11¹|₂ Sgr.

From Berlin to *Jüterbog*, see p. 190.

Wittenberg *(Zur Goldnen Weintraube*, in the market; *Goldner Adler*, nearest to the station; **Rail. Restaurant)* on the *Elbe*, with 11,500 inhab., one of the cradles of the reformation, was a residence of the Electors of Saxony down to 1542. In 1760 it was bombarded by the Austrians, in 1813 occupied by the French, and in 1814 taken from them by storm by the Prussians under Tauentzien. The doors of the **Schlosskirche*, to which Luther affixed his famous 95 theses (31st Oct., 1517), were destroyed by the French, and replaced in 1858 by bronze gates, on which the original Latin text of the theses is inscribed. Luther (d. 1546), Melanchthon (d. 1560), and the electors Frederick the Wise (d. 1525) and John the Stedfast (d. 1532) are interred in the church. The monument of the Elector Frederick, in bronze, is by *P. Vischer* of Nuremberg (1527). The portraits of the Reformers are by *L. Cranach* (1472—1553) who was once burgomaster of Wittenberg.

The altar-pieces in the *Stadtkirche*, in which Luther frequently preached, are also by *Cranach*, and contain numerous allusions to the Reformation and portraits of the Reformers. Font in bronze by *Herm. Vischer* of Nuremberg (1557).

Luther was once a monk in the *Augustine Monastery* here, now a college for Protestant students of theology. His cell, which is little changed, contains a few relics. Peter the Great's name is pointed out among those written on the walls. The *Rathhaus* also contains pictures by *Cranach* and several memorials of the great Reformer. The dwelling-houses of Luther and Melanchthon are now schools. Cranach's house was burned down in 1871.

*Luther's Statue, by Schadow, in the market-place, has the inscription on the pedestal: '*Ist's Gottes Werk, so wird's bestehen, Ist's Menschenwerk, wird's untergehen*' (if it be God's work it will endure, if man's it will perish). Near it is the statue of *Melanchthon*, by Drake, erected in 1866.

An oak enclosed by a railing, outside the Elsterthor, marks the spot where Luther publicly burned the papal bull of excommunication, 10th Dec., 1520.

The once famous University, founded in 1502, where Luther was professor of theology, was united with that of Halle in 1817. The building is now a barrack.

From Wittenberg to Cöthen, see R. 57·

Beyond Wittenberg the Leipsic train crosses the Elbe. Stations *Bergwitz, Gräfenhainichen*. Beyond *Burgkemnitz* the *Mulde* is crossed. Stat. *Bitterfeld* is the junction for Halle (p. 224) and Dessau (p. 258). Stations *Delitzsch, Zschortau, Rackwitz*.

The line passes near *Breitenfeld*, where Gustavus Adolphus defeated Tilly and Pappenheim in 1631. The highest point of the battle-field is indicated by a stone surrounded by eight pines.

Leipsic, see p. 216. The station is nearly 1 M. from the town; a flacre should therefore be at once secured.

44. From Hamburg to Leipsic by Magdeburg.

Railway in 9¹/₂–11 hrs.; express fares 12 Thlr. 16, 8 Thlr. 16 Sgr.; ordinary 10 Thlr. 12, 7 Thlr. 14, 4 Thlr. 17¹/₂ Sgr.

Luggage is examined at the custom-house before starting. From Hamburg to *Wittenberge*, see p. 139. The Elbe is then crossed, and a flat district traversed. Stations *Seehausen, Osterburg*, **Stendal** (junction for Berlin and Hanover, see p. 57), *Demker, Tangerhütte* (with extensive iron-works), *Mahlwinkel, Rogätz, Wolmirstedt*, and then along the bank of the Elbe to **Magdeburg** (p. 60).

The line intersects the fortifications and passes the *Friedrich Wilhelm Garden*. Stations *Westerhüsen, Schönebeck* (a manufacturing town of some importance).

Branch line hence to **Stassfurt** (Rail. Restaurant), with very extensive mines, and *Güsten*, a station on the Cöthen and Halberstadt Railway (see below).

Stat. *Gnadau* is a Moravian settlement. The train now crosses the Saale by a bridge ¹/₄ M. in length.. *Calbe* on the Saale is visible to the r., then the towers and castle of *Bernburg* (p. 258); in the distance rises the spire of the ancient town of *Aken* on the Elbe. ₁₁

Cöthen (*Prinz ·von Preussen; Grosser Gasthof; . Weintraube), with 13,500 inhab., is the junction for Cöthen and Berlin, and for Halberstadt and Vienenburg (R. 57). Naumann's Ornithological Collection in the Schloss deserves mention. The principal church contains old stained glass and a font by Thorvaldsen. The homœopathic clinical institution of Dr. Lutze enjoys a high repute. Sugar is largely manufactured here from beet-root, of which vast fields are seen in the environs.

Near *Stumsdörf* the line intersects the plain of the *Fuhne*. To the l..is *Zörbig*, an ancient town of the Wends; to the r. the *Petersberg* (657 ft. above the Saale), 7 M. from Halle, commanding a fine view. The old abbey-church here, erected in the 12th cent.., and re-erected in 1857, contains tombs of the Wettin princes.

Halle (*Stadt Hamburg, next to the post-office; .Kronprinz; Stadt Zürich; Goldner Löwe; Mente's Hôtel, R. 15, D. 15 Sgr.; Schmidt's Hôtel; Russischer Hof. — Fiacre per drive for 1 pers. 3, 2 pers. 4, 3 pers. 7¹/₂, 4 pers. 10 Sgr.), on the *Saale*, with 52,408 inhab., was an important place at a very early period in consequence of its salt-works, which now yield 11,000 tons of salt annually. In the 13th and 14th cent. it was a member of the Hanseatic League and waged protracted feuds with the archbishops of Magdeburg; after the Peace of Westphalia it was annexed to Brandenburg. Halle possesses a university of great repute, founded in 1694, with which that of Wittenberg was united in 1817. The 'Pietistic' views for which the university was noted during the last century are now less in vogue. The town, which has recently become a commercial place of considerable importance, possesses five increasing suburbs and is united with the formerly distinct towns of Glaucha and Neumarkt.

In the market-place rises the *Rothe Thurm*, a clock-tower 276 ft. in height. Between this and the mediæval *Rathhaus* is a bronze *Statue of Händel* (d. 1759), who was born here in 1685, erected by subscriptions from Germany and England. The great composer is represented in the English court-dress; at the back of the music-desk is St. Cecilia (a portrait of Jenny Lind). . ı

The *Marktkirche*, or *Church of Our Lady*, erected in 1530—54, with four towers which belong to a still earlier structure, two of them connected by a bridge, bounds the market on the W. side. (Sacristan, An der Halle 6, at the back of the church, down a stair.)

·   **Interior.** *Altar-piece, a scene from the Sermon on the Mount, by *Hübner* of Dresden. To the r. by the altar a small picture by Cranach, the Fourteen helpers in need. The chief treasure of the church is a double winged *picture, painted by *Cranach* in 1529 for Cardinal Albrecht of Brandenburg, the builder of the church, representing SS. Magdalene, Ursula,

Erasmus, and Catharine, the Virgin with the cardinal at her feet, at the sides
St. Maurice and St. Alexander, the latter placing his foot upon the Roman
Emp. Maximin; on the external sides the Annunciation, then St. John
and St. Augustine.

The finest church is that of *St. Maurice* (sacristan, No. 6 on
the E. side) in the lower part of the town, dating from the 12th
cent.; elegant choir of 1388; fine carved *wood-work over the altar,
representing Christ and Mary with saints, of 1488; beside it ancient
winged pictures; pulpit, with reliefs of 1588, resting on a pillar
representing Sin, Death, and Satan. This church is frequented by
the workmen employed in the manufacture of the salt, termed
'Halloren', a distinct race preserving many of their ancient peculiarities, and either descended from the Wends who once inhabited
this district, or from Celtic settlers.

The *University Buildings* were erected in 1834; 800 students.

Francke's Institutions on the S. E. side of the town, comprising
a Prot. orphan-asylum, school, laboratory, printing-office, etc.,
were begun in 1698 by the founder, whose sole means consisted of a
strong and simple faith, unaided by capital. The court of the asylum
is adorned with a bronze *Statue* of Francke (d. 1727) by Rauch.

The *Cathedral* contains a good altar-piece, representing Duke
Augustus of Saxony and his family. Adjacent is the old residence
of the archbishops of Magdeburg, which now belongs to the university, and contains the valuable collections of the *Thuringian-Saxon
Antiquarian Society.*

Near the cathedral are the ruins of the *Moritzburg*, erected in
1484, and the *Jägerberg*, which affords a good survey of the town.
On the way to the Giebichenstein is the *House of Correction*, and
on the opposite bank of the Saale a *Lunatic Asylum.*

Kröllwitz, a ruined castle with pleasure-grounds, 1¹|₂ M. N. of Halle,
opposite the *Giebichenstein*, is a favourite resort. Lewis 'the Springer',
Landgrave of Thuringia, was imprisoned here in 1102, and, according to
tradition, escaped by a daring leap into the river, after having vowed to
erect a church (p. 254) should his attempt prove successful. Duke Ernest
II. of Swabia, immortalised by Uhland, was also a prisoner here for a
considerable time. *Wittekind*, a bath near the Giebichstein, is much
frequented in summer.

Near stat. *Schkeuditz* the train enters the dominions of Saxony,
passes *Möckern*, where a bloody battle between the French and
Prussians was fought on 16th Oct., 1813, crosses the *Parthe*, and
reaches **Leipsic** (see p. 216).

45. From Leipsic to Nuremberg by Bamberg.

Saxon Railway to Hof, express in 4¹|₄ hrs. (fares 3 Thlr. 21, 2 Thlr.
28, 2 Thlr. 6 Ngr.); *Bavarian Railway* from Hof to Nuremberg, express
in 5³|₄ hrs. (fares 7 fl. 39, 5 fl. 6, 3 fl. 24 kr.).

Country at first uninteresting. To the l. the *Pleisse* is occasionally visible.

BÆDEKER's N. Germany. 5th Edit. 15

Stat. **Altenburg** *(*Hôtel de Russie; Hôtel de Saxe; Stadt Leipzig)*, with 18,500 inhab. , is overlooked by the ducal *Schloss* from which in 1455 the knight Kunz von Kauffungen carried off the young princes Ernest and Albert, founders of the present royal and ducal families of Saxony. Lindenau's Museum, which contains 166 Italian pictures, besides copies, casts, and Greek and Etruscan vases.   -

Stations *Gössnitz* (junction for Chemnitz), *Crimmitzschau*, *Werdau* (junction for Zwickau), all manufacturing towns. **Reichenbach** *(Lamm*, R. and B. 28 Sgr. ; **Engel)* is another busy manufacturing place. Carriages are changed here for Eger and Schwandorf.

The train now crosses the profound *Göltzschthal* by an imposing viaduct, 728 yds. in length. Far below, to the l.., are the small town and castle of *Mylau*. Stations *Netzschkau, Herlasgrün,* where the line to Eger diverges to the l. Beyond stat. *Joketa* the line crosses the deep, wooded *Elsterthal* by another viaduct (170 yds. long, in the centre 257 ft. high).

, Stat: **Plauen** *(*Deil's Hôtel; Deutsches Haus; Engel)*, a manufacturing town on the *Weisse Elster*, with 23,000 inhab. , is the capital of the Voigtland. The old castle of *Radschin* was anciently the seat of the Voigt *(advocatus regni)*. Stations *Mehltheuer* and *Reuth;* then a lofty wooded plain, the watershed between the Elster and the Saale. As Hof is approached, the blue outlines of the Fichtelgebirge become visible to the l.

Stat. **Hof** *(Hirsch; Löwe; Brandenburger Hof; Lamm*, moderate; *Rail. Restaurant)*, a Bavarian town on the *Saale*, with 16,010 inhab., re-erected after a fire in 1823. Gothic *Rathhaus.*

From Hof to Eger by railway in 3³|₄ hrs. (fares 2 fl. 33, 1 fl. 42, 1 fl. 9 kr.). Stations *Oberkotzau, Rehau, Selb, Asch* (Post), *Franzensbad. Eger* and thence to *Carlsbad*, see *Baedeker's S. Germany and Austria.*

The line traverses a hilly district, in the vicinity of the winding Saale. Stations *Oberkotzau, Schwarzenbach, Müncheberg* (**Bayr. Hof), Stambach.* On the l. rise the *Schneeberg* and *Ochsenkopf,* the highest summits of the Fichtelgebirge. *Markt-Schorgast* lies in a valley to the r. The construction of the line here is an object of interest (gradient at first 1: 40; descent to Neuenmarkt 575 ft.); cuttings, embankments, and dark ravines follow each other in rapid succession. To the l. in the distance is *Himmelkron*, the church of which is pointed out by tradition as the burial-place of the Countess of Orlamünde (the 'White Lady', d. about 1300), from whom a branch of the Brandenburg family is descended.

Stations *Neuenmarkt* (junction for Baireuth), *Unter-Steinach.* Country picturesque, especially near **Culmbach** *(*Goldener Hirsch; *Rail. Restaurant)*, celebrated for its beer, formerly the residence of the Margraves of Brandenburg-Culmbach, on the *Weisse Main,* commanded by the *Plassenburg* which is now employed as a prison.

Near stat. *Mainleus,* the *Weisse* and *Rothe Main* unite to form the *Main*, the broad valley of which is now traversed as far as Bamberg. At their confluence lies Schloss *Steinhausen.* Beyond stat. *Burgkunstadt* the Main is crossed. Near stat. *Hochstadt* the *Rodach* falls into the Main.

From Hochstadt to Stockheim a branch-line in 1¹|₂ hr. (fares 1 fl. 3, 42, 30 kr.). The line runs through the pretty *Rodachthal.* Stations *Redwitz* (at the entrance of the romantic *Steinachthal*), *Ober-Langenbach, Küps* (a considerable village with a castle of the von Redwitz family); then **Kronach**, a small town (3600 inhab.) picturesquely situated at the confluence of the *Hasslach* and Rodach, formerly fortified and bravely defended during the Thirty Years' War, the birthplac of the painter Lucas Cranach (1472). Above the town is the extensive fortress of *Rosenberg.* Thence through the *Hasslachthal* by stat. *Gundelsdorf* to *Stockheim,* near which there are valuable coal-mines.

Lichtenfels (***Anker,** at the station; *Krone),* is the junction of the Werra line (to Coburg and Eisenach, see R. 51). The monasteries of *Banz* (1¹/₄ hr., carr. there and back 3¹/₂ fl.) and *Vierzehnheiligen* (1 hr., carr. there and back 2¹/₂ fl.) are conspicuous objects in the landscape. The pedestrian desirous of visiting both should proceed first from Lichtenfels to Vierzehnheiligen, and thence to Banz (1 hr.) and (1¹/₂ hr.) stat. *Staffelstein.*

The once celebrated Benedictine Abbey of **Banz,** founded in 1096, was dissolved in 1803. The extensive buildings on a wooded height, 400 ft. above the Main, now belong to Duke Max of Bavaria. *View from the terrace. Valuable collection of Egyptian antiquities, and of fossils found in this neighbourhood, among which is a remarkably fine specimen of an ichthyosaurus, the head alone 7 ft. long. A Descent from the Cross, a relief in silver, presented by Pope Pius VI. to his godson Duke Pius of Bavaria, is erroneously attributed to Benv. Cellini. Cosmoramas of scenery in Palestine, visited by the duke. — Inn at the château.

Opposite Banz, at the same elevation, is the monastery-church of **Vierzehnheiligen** (*Hirsch),* the most frequented shrine in Franconia, visited by upwards of 50,000 pilgrims annually. The well proportioned interior is in the Jesuit style, adorned with frescoes by a Munich artist. In the centre of the nave is an altar which marks the spot, where, according to the legend, the 14 'Nothhelfer' (i. e. saints who help in time of need) appeared to a shepherd-boy in 1446, and gave rise to the foundation of the church. Looking through this altar from the high altar, the visitor obtains a striking glimpse of Banz. In the two W. chapels are numerous thank-offerings, such as figures in wax, etc.

Near stat. *Staffelstein* the *Staffelberg* rises abruptly from the valley; then on the opposite side the *Veitsberg,* crowned with a chapel and ruined castle, and commanding a magnificent view. Stations *Ebensfeld, Zapfendorf, Breiten-Güssbach.*

Bamberg, and thence to **Nuremberg,** see *Baedeker's S. Germany.*

46. From Leipsic to Cassel. Thuringian Railway.

Railway. Express in 6¹|₂ hrs.; fares 7 Thlr. 14, 5 Thlr. 18, 3 Thlr. 23 Sgr. — By *Halle* and *Nordhausen,* see R. 54.

This line traverses one of the most picturesque districts in Central Germany. Stations *Markranstedt, Kötschau.* The salt-works of *Dürrenberg* are passed, and the *Saale* crossed. Stat. *Corbetha* is the junction for Halle (p. 224).

15*

In the vicinity of Corbetha are three celebrated battle-fields. At *Rossbach*, 5 M. to the W., Frederick the Great with 22,000 Prussians signally defeated 60,000 French and their German allies under Soubise, on 5th Nov., 1757. — Near *Lützen*, 5 M. to the E., two celebrated battles were fought. In the first of these, 6th Nov., 1632, Gustavus Adolphus, king of Sweden, was mortally wounded, after having defeated the Imperial troops. A block of granite with a Gothic roof marks the spot. At *Gross-Görschen*, a little to the S. of Lützen, a fierce but undecisive engagement was fought on 2nd May, 1813, by the allied Russians and Prussians against the French, in which the Prussian Gen. Scharnhorst was mortally wounded. On the previous day the French Marshal Bessières had been killed in a skirmish near Lützen.

Merseburg (**Sonne*; *Ritter*), on the line towards Halle, an ancient town on the *Saale*, with 12,800 inhab., mentioned in history as early as the 9th cent., was a favourite residence of the emperors Henry I. and Otho I., and frequently the scene of Imperial diets. It was an episcopal diocese from 968 to 1543. The **Cathedral*, founded in the 10th cent., now consists of a choir of the 13th and late Gothic nave of the 15th cent. The choir contains the brazen monument of Rudolph of Swabia, who fell in 1080 in a battle with his rival Henry IV., a Crucifixion and Entombment by *L. Cranach* (with a portrait of Luther among the soldiers), and a Marriage of St. Catharine in Albert Dürer's style. The pulpit and screen are carved in the late Gothic style. The *Schloss* of the 15th cent., partially restored in the 17th, once a residence of the Saxon princes, presents an imposing appearance with its numerous towers. Near the *Keuschberg*, in the vicinity, Emp. Henry I. gained a great victory over the Hungarians in 933.

The train passes several vine-clad hills. **Weissenfels** (*Schütze; Goldner Hirsch; Nelkenbusch*), with 15,600 inhab., on the Saale, which is crossed by a handsome bridge, possesses an old *Schloss* of the extinct Dukes of Weissenfels Querfurt.

The body of Gustavus Adolphus was embalmed after the battle of Lützen in a room at the Amtshaus. The *Klemmberg*, which rises above the Schloss, is a good point of view. After the battle of Leipsic Napoleon retreated towards the Rhine in this direction. He is said to have spent the night of 19th Oct., 1813, in a summer-house indicated by an *N* on the top, on a height near the station.

From Weissenfels to Gera, Saalfeld, and Eichicht. Railway to *Gera* in 1³/₄ hrs. (1 Thlr. 17, 1 Thlr. 6, 24 Sgr.); thence to *Eichicht* in 4 hrs. (2 Thlr. 1, 1 Thlr. 16¹/₂, 1 Thlr. 1 Sgr.). The line ascends from the valley of the Saale to a lofty plain. Stations *Teuchern, Theissen;* then *Zeitz*, an old town pleasantly situated on the *Weisse Elster*, and an episcopal see from 968 to 1029; Gothic abbey church of the 15th cent. with Romanesque crypt of the 12th cent. Then through the beautiful Elsterthal to *Crossen, Köstritz* (famous for its beer), and *Gera* (*Frommaten; *Reussischer Hof*), the capital of the principality of Reuss, a busy manufacturing town with 16,323 inhab. on the Weisse Elster. The Johannis-Platz is adorned with a modern statue of Count *Heinrich Posthumus* (d. 1635). Handsome Rathhaus. On the Hainberg, opposite the town, rises the *Osterstein*. Railway to *Gössnitz* (p. 226) in ³/₄ hr.

Between Gera and Saalfeld the line traverses the dominions of five different states, viz. Reuss, Saxe-Weimar, Prussia, Saxe-Meiningen, and Schwarzburg-Rudolstadt. Beyond stat. *Röppisch* the Elster is quitted. Stat. *Weida* (Ring), in the Duchy of Weimar, is ¹/₂ M. from the railway; the *Osterburg* is an old Schloss to the N. W. of the town. Stations *Niederpöllnitz, Treptis,* and **Neustadt** *on the Orla* (*Goldner Löwe*), a manufacturing town in the Duchy of Weimar, with a good late Gothic Rathhaus. About 4¹/₂ M. distant is the *Fröhliche Wiederkunft*, a shooting lodge of the Duke of Altenburg; 6 M. from Neustadt is *Hummelshain*, with a château and deer-park, the summer residence of the same nobleman. Diligence three times daily from Neustadt to (13 M.) *Schleiz*, a prettily situated town, and the former residence of the princes of Reuss-Schleiz, whose Schloss still exists.

Stations *Oppurg* and **Pösneck** (*Hirsch; Ritter*), a pretty town in the Duchy of Meiningen, with porcelain and other manufactories; then *Könitz, Unter-Wellenborn,* and

Saalfeld (**Rother Hirsch; Preussischer Hof*), an old town on the N. E. boundary of the Thuringian forest, picturesquely situated on the *Saale*. *Rathhaus* in the market-place in the latest Gothic style, 1533—37. Gothic *Johanniskirche* of the 14th cent. with good stained glass of 1514 in the choir. In the suburb is the Schloss of the extinct dukes of Saalfeld. Near the town are the ruins of the *Sorbenburg*, which is said to have been erected by Charlemagne for protection against the pagan Sclavonians. The termination of many of the names of places on the r. bank of the Saale in *itz* indicate their Sclavonic origin. Diligence three times daily from Saalfeld to *Rudolstadt* (p. 244), traversing the field where an army of 30,000 French under Lannes and Augereau defeated 11,000 Prussians under Prince Louis Ferdinand, on 10th Oct. 1806. The latter general fell in the battle, and a monument has been erected to him near (2 M.) *Wölsdorf*. At (1½ M.) *Schwarza* the road into the Schwarzathal diverges. Then (3 M.) *Rudolstadt* (p. 244). — Diligences also run from Saalfeld to (6 M.) *Blankenburg*, (12½ M.) *Schwarzburg*, and (31 M.) *Arnstadt*.

Beyond Saalfeld the railway traverses a very picturesque part of the valley of the Saale. Stat. *Weischwitz*, where the river is crossed. Eichicht, a small village prettily situated at the confluence of the *Sormitz* and Saale, is a great depôt of the slate quarried in the neighbourhood, and is at present the terminus of the railway.

On the slope to the r. rises the château of *Gosek*, and to the l. the lofty tower of the ruin *Schönburg*. The country becomes more hilly, and the vine is cultivated here with tolerable success.

Naumburg (**Sächs. Hof; Grüner Schild; Richter's Hotel*), with 15,200 inhab., at some distance from the station, is an important looking and pleasantly situated place. The *Cathedral* of the 13th and 14th cent., is a fine edifice of the transition period, but has been disfigured by subsequent additions. Curious sculptures of the 13th cent. on the pillars of the wall of the W. choir, representing the founders of the church. The N. W. tower is in the late Gothic style. In the *Stadtkirche* a small picture by Cranach the Elder, 'Suffer little children to come unto Me'. The Bürgergarten on the Galgenberg commands a fine view.

Diligence daily from Naumburg to **Freiburg** *on the Unstrut* (*Goldner Ring*), 5 M. to the N. W., which contains a fine church, half Gothic and half Romanesque, dating from the 13th and 15th cent., with two towers connected by a species of bridge. The ancient Schloss on the hill, with its Romanesque double chapel, was once an imperial residence; the tower is visible from the railway near Naumburg. *Ludwig Jahn*, the 'father of gymnastics' (p. 34), lived and died at Freiburg, where a monument was erected to him in 1859.

Beyond Naumburg, to the l. of the line, is the celebrated school of *Schulpforte*, established in 1543 in an old Cistercian monastery, where Klopstock, Fichte, and other celebrated men received the first rudiments of their education. The fine early Gothic church was completed in 1268.

The valley of the Saale from Naumburg to Sulza is very picturesque.

Kösen (*Ritter*, R. 15 Sgr. ; *Kurzhals ; Curhaus ; Teichgräber's
Restaurant*, with picturesque view), is a pleasant little watering-
place with salt-baths. The *Knabenberg, Göttersitz*, and *Himmelreich*
are the prettiest points in the environs. To the l. on the hill rises
the *Rudelsburg ;* farther on are the two lofty towers of *Saaleck.*
The Saale is now quitted. A cutting near **Sulza** (*Grossherzog-
von Sachsen)*, a prettily situated watering-place with salt-works and
vineyards, displays the very peculiar stratification of the rocks here. ·
In a side-valley to the r. lies *Auerstädt*, near which the Prussians were
totally defeated on 14th Oct., 1806. A monument marks the spot where the
Duke of Brunswick was wounded.

Undulating arable land is now traversed. **Apolda** *(Strauss ;
Weintraube* ; *Thüringer Hof)* is a busy place with stocking and
other manufactories.

From Apolda to Jena and Rudolstadt (32 M.) diligence daily
in 7¹|₂ hrs. (to Jena 9 M. , diligence three times daily). Railway in pro-
gress. The road traverses the field of the battle of Jena or Auerstädt (see
above), in which 48,000 Prussians under the Duke of Brunswick were
signally defeated by 80,000 French. The battle raged most fiercely at
Vierzehnheiligen, half-way to Jena, ¹|₂ M. to the l. of the road.

9 M. **Jena** *(Deutsches Haus; Bär; Sonne)*, a town of. Weimar with
8500 inhab., celebrated for its university, which was founded in 1548 and
attained a high repute about the end of the 18th, and the beginning of
the 19th century, is very pleasantly situated at the confluence of the *Saale*
and *Leutra.* Many of the streets contain memorial tablets to illustrious
men who were once students at the university ; thus to Arndt, Fichte,
and Schiller in the Leutragasse ; to the latter also in the Schlossgasse
and the Jenergasse. Goethe's lodgings in the Schlossgasse and in the.
Botanical Garden are also pointed out. The *Market-Place* is embellished with a *Statue of John Frederick the Generous* (d. 1557), the
founder of the university. The choir of the *Stadtkirche* (15th cent.) contains a figure of Luther in relief, originally destined for his tomb at Wittenberg, but placed here in 1572. Goethe frequently resided at the *Schloss*,
where he composed his 'Hermann and Dorothea'. This building, which
was formerly the residence of the Dukes of Saxe-Jena, now contains most
of the university collections. In the pleasant promenades surrounding the
town is a monument to *Schulze* (d. 1860), an eminent political economist
and agriculturist. In the vicinity are the *University-Library*, containing
some early Flemish hymn-books with good miniatures, the monument of
the naturalist *Oken* (d. 1851), and the *Botanical Garden* (open daily). The
Garden of the *Observatory* on the S. side of the town contains a bust of
Schiller by Dannecker, on the spot where the poet wrote his 'Wallenstein'
in 1798. The house through which the garden is entered bears a memorial tablet. The inn 'Zur Tanne' at *Camsdorf*, on the opposite bank of
the Saale, bears an inscription to the effect that Goethe once resided
there.

The *Environs of Jena*, where the peculiar stratification of the rock is
an object of interest (at the bottom of the valley is sand, above it gypsum,
then red clay, and finally limestone), afford a number of pleasant excursions. On the *Hausberg* to the E. rises the *Fuchsthurm*, a remnant of the
castle of Kirchberg (1 Sgr.), reached from the village of *Ziegenhain* (where
the key is kept), or from *Camsdorf* in ³|₄ hr. — Near *Wöllnitz*, on the
Saale, 2 M. above Jena, rises the *Louisenhöhe*, a fine point of view ; opposite to it lies *Lichtenhain*, a favourite resort of the students. — The *Forst-
haus*, 2 M. to the W., is another picturesque spot. — The *Dornburg*, 7¹|₂
M. to the N., consists of three small castles on the precipitous W. side of
the valley, the oldest of which was an imperial residence as early as the
time of Otho I. That farthest to the S. was occupied by Goethe for several months in 1828. Picturesque views from the terraces.

The road from Jena to Rudolstadt follows the l. bank of the Saale, passing (3 M.) the ruins of the *Lobdaburg*, which rises above the river *Lobeda* to the l.

11 M. **Kahla** (*Goldner Löwe*), a small town in the Duchy of Altenburg, still possesses ancient walls. Opposite to it rises the old fortress of *Leuchtenburg*, a good point of view, originally erected for protection against the E. Sclavonic tribes like all the other castles on the Saale. To the r. of the road, 4 M. from Kahla, lies *Orlamünde*, at the confluence of the Saale and the *Orla*, once the seat of the powerful counts of that name. The well-known spectre of the White Lady, which is said to appear at the palace of Berlin as the harbinger of the death of the king, is supposed to have been a Countess of Orlamünde (comp. p. 226).

12 M. **Rudolstadt**, see p. 244.

The *Ilm* is now crossed. To the l. is *Ossmannstedt*, where Wieland (d. 1813) is interred in the garden of his former estate.

Weimar, see R. 47.

Beyond Weimar the country is hilly. An ancient watch-tower crowns the heights near Hopfgarten, $4^1/_2$ M. from Weimar; another rises near Niederzimmern, some distance farther. Stat. *Vieselbach.*

Erfurt, see R. 48.

Branch-line from Erfurt to *Nordhausen,* see p. 256.

The train now approaches the N. slopes of the Thuringian Forest. Stat. *Neu-Dietendorf* (*Rail. Restaurant) is a well-built Moravian colony.

Branch-line from Neu-Dietendorf (in 20 min.; fares 11, $6^1/_2$, 5 Sgr.) to **Arnstadt** (**Henne; Sonne*), a prettily situated town in the principality of Schwarzburg-Sondershausen, with an ancient Rathhaus and Schloss. The *Liebfrauenkirche of the 12th and 13th cent. contains some fine sculptures and tombstones, among which is a monument of Count Günther of Schwarzburg and his wife, dating from 1368. — The road from Arnstadt to *Ilmenau* (p. 246) traverses the beautiful valley of the Gera and passes *Plane* (with the fine ruins of the *Ehrenburg*), *Neisiss* (where a road to the r. diverges to Elgersburg, p. 246), and *Martinsroda.*

To the l. farther on, rise three picturesque castles situated on three isolated hills, termed the *Drei Gleichen;* viz. the *Wachsenburg* (1415 ft.), the property of the Duke of Coburg-Cotha, used occasionally as a state-prison, the *Mühlberg*, a total ruin, and the *Gleichen*, in tolerable preservation. *Schloss Molsdorf*, 3 M. to the E. of Dietendorf, is a seat of the Duke of Coburg. *Siebleben*, to the r. among trees, as Gotha is approached, is the summer residence of Gustav Freytag, the talented author of 'Debet and Credit' and other works. The train skirts the *Seeberg*, on which a now disused *Observatory* stands. Near Gotha a fine view is obtained of the wooded mountains of Thuringia, among which the tower on the Schneekopf and the inn on the Inselsberg (p. 250) are very conspicuous. Farther W. the château of *Tenneberg*, at the foot of which lie Schnepfenthal and the small town of Waltershausen. Comp. Map, p. 246.

Gotha, see R. 49.

Stat. *Fröttstedt* is connected with $(2^1/_2$ M.) Waltershausen (p. 252) by a tramway. The railway now follows the course of the *Hörsel* through the well-peopled valley of Eisenach. On the r., as Eisenach is approached, rises the long, deeply furrowed ridge of the *Hörsel-*

berg (1575 ft.). From stat. *Wutha* a diligence runs twice daily to Thal and Ruhla (p. 248).

Eisenach, see R. 50.

The train follows the course of the *Hörsel* (fine retrospect of the Wartburg on the r.) to its union with the *Werra*. Stat. *Herleshausen* (pleasant excursion hence, or from Eisenach, to the **Heldrastein*, an eminence 11½ M. to the N., near the small town of *Treffurt*, rising upwards of 1000 ft. above the Werrathal, and commanding a magnificent view). Scenery picturesque. In the distance, on the l. bank, are visible the ruins of the *Brandenburg*, once the seat of the counts of that name. Stat. *Gerstungen*; to the l. lies the small town of *Berka*. The train quits the valley of the Werra, and enters that of the *Fulda* near stat. Bebra. (Railway by Fulda to Frankfort, see R. 60.)

Stations *Rotenburg*, once the residence of the landgraves of Hessen - Rotenburg, *Alt - Morschen*, *Beiseförth*, and *Melsungen*, an old and prettily situated town. At *Guckshagen*, near Melsungen, a beautiful view of the picturesque town and the extensive Benedictine abbey of *Breitenau* (founded in 1120, now suppressed) is suddenly disclosed; in the distance rises the Hercules (p. 84) near Cassel.

Guntershausen (p. 276) is the junction for Giessen and Frankfort. Stat. *Wilhelmshöhe*, then Cassel (p. 79).

47. Weimar.

Hotels. *Erbprinz (Pl. 1); *Russischer Hof (Pl. 2); R. at both 20, D. 20, B. 10, L. and A. 10 Sgr.; Ziegler's Hotel (Pl. 5); Elephant (Pl. 3); Adler (Pl. 4), R. 10 Sgr.

Restaurants. *Hoffmann's*, in the Teichgasse; *Café Alexander*, in the market-place. — Confectioner. *Isleib. — Wine. *Meyer; Reichmann*.

Conveyances. Omnibus to the town (1 M. from the station) 2½ Sgr.; cab for 1 pers. 5, 2 pers. 7½, 3 pers. 10 Sgr. — One-horse carriage to Jena 2 Thlr.; also an omnibus from the Adler (in 2½ hrs.; 15 Sgr.).

Theatre. Operas on Sundays and Thursdays; plays on Wednesdays and Saturdays.

English Church Service performed occasionally.

Weimar (670 ft.), the capital of the grand-duchy of Saxe-Weimar, with 14,794 inhab., an irregularly built old town with modern suburbs, pleasantly situated on the *Ilm*, derives its principal interest from the literary associations connected with it. By the invitation of Duke Charles Augustus (d. 1828), a liberal patron of literature, *Goethe* resided here in an official capacity (latterly as minister) during 56 years till his death in 1832. His contemporaries *Herder*, *Wieland*, and *Schiller* also held appointments here under the Duke, during whose reign Weimar was visited by many other celebrated men of letters.

Goethe's House (Pl. 27) in the Goethe-Platz, opposite the fountain, is not accessible. His collections are shown on Fridays on application to the secretary Herr Schuchardt. — *Schiller's House*

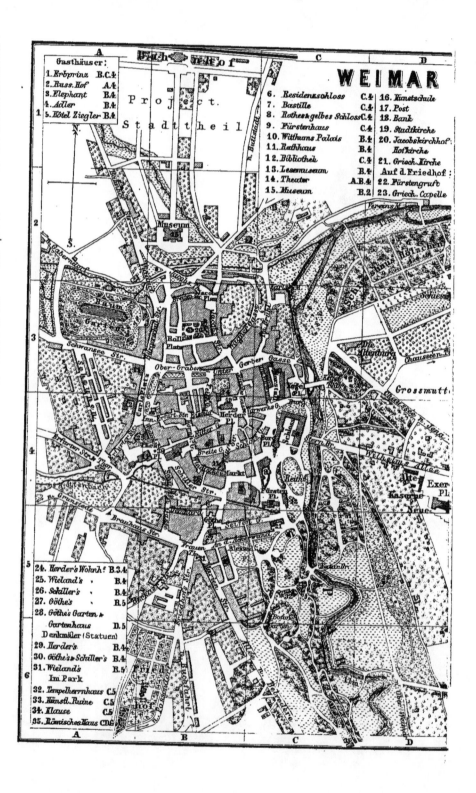

WEIMAR

Gasthäuser:
1. Erbprinz   B.C.4
2. Russ. Hof   A.4
3. Elephant   B.4
4. Adler   B.4
5. Hôtel Ziegler   B.4

6. Residenzschloss   C.4
7. Bastille   C.4
8. Rothes&gelbes Schloss C.4
9. Fürstenhaus   C.4
10. Witthaus Palais   B.4
11. Rathhaus   B.4
12. Bibliothek   C.4
13. Lesemuseum   B.4
14. Theater   A.B.4
15. Museum   B.2

16. Kunstschule
17. Post
18. Bank
19. Stadtkirche
20. Jacobskirchhof:
    Hofkirche
21. Griech. Kirche
Auf d. Friedhof:
22. Fürstengruft
23. Griech. Capelle

24. Herder's Wohnh.   B.3.4
25. Wieland's   „   B.4
26. Schiller's   „   B.4
27. Göthe's   B.5
28. Göthe's Garten &
    Gartenhaus   D.5
Denkmäler (Statuen)
29. Herder's   B.4
30. Göthe's & Schiller's B.4
31. Wieland's   B.5
    Im Park
32. Tempelherrnhaus   C.5
33. Künstl. Ruine   C.5
34. Klause   C.5
35. Römisches Haus   C.D.6

(Pl. 26) in the Schiller-Strasse, which has been purchased by the town, contains a few reminiscences of the poet. — *Herder* occupied the parsonage-house (Pl. 24), to the N. of the Stadtkirche. — *Wieland's House* (Pl. 25) is to the N. of the theatre.

Bronze **Statues* of these distinguished authors have been recently erected: *Goethe and Schiller* (Pl. 30) in a single group by Rietschel, in the Theater-Platz; *Wieland* (Pl. 31) in the Frauenplan; *Herder* (Pl. 29) by the Stadtkirche. A monument (Pl. 24) to Duke *Charles Augustus* is about to be erected in the Fürsten-Platz (Pl. C, 4).

The grand-ducal **Palace* (Pl. 6), erected in 1790—1803, partially under Goethe's superintendence, is decorated with **Frescoes:* in the 'Herdezimmer' symbolical figures of that scholar's various spheres of activity, by *Jäger;* in the 'Schillerzimmer' scenes from Fiesco, Don Carlos, Wallenstein, Mary Stuart, etc., by *Neher;* in the 'Goethezimmer' scenes from Egmont, Faust, Hermann and Dorothea, etc., by *Neher;* in the 'Wielandzimmer' (the best) Oberon, etc., by *Preller.* An album with autographs and other reminiscences of Weimar was presented by Queen Augusta of Prussia. The apartment of the grand-duchess contains the original cartoons (apostles) of Leonardo da Vinci's Last Supper. The other apartments are tastefully fitted up; the grand-duke's room is adorned with modern pictures by *Ary Scheffer, Wislicenus,* etc.; in the drawing-rooms are landscapes by *Preller;* the 'Bernhards-Zimmer' contains the armour of Duke Bernard (d. 1639), the hero of the Thirty Years' War (fee 10 Sgr.).

The **Museum* (Pl. 15), a conspicuous red and yellow sandstone edifice in the Renaissance style, which the traveller approaching the town from the station will not fail to observe (open daily from April to Sept., except Mond., 10—4; on Sund. and holidays 11—4; from Oct. to March on Sund. and holidays 11—3, and Wed. and Sat. 10—3), is adorned with 14 figures on the chief façade emblematical of the different branches of ancient and modern art.

Ground Floor. In the W. saloon and the N. W. pavilion are casts from the antique, chronologically arranged. Frieze in relief in three sections by *Härtel* of Dresden, representing the Education of the youth of Germany, the Battle of Arminius, and the Walhalla. A niche in the staircase contains *Steinhäuser's* colossal group of Goethe and Psyche in marble.

First Floor. The W. saloon, lighted from above, and the three smaller rooms adjoining it contain oil-paintings of no great value, with the exception of Nos. 43—47. by *Lucas Cranach.* — The N. (or Preller) Gallery contains a cycle of mural *paintings from the Odyssey by *Preller*, skilfully adapted to the architectural structure of the room. — The E. saloon, lighted from above, with the rooms adjoining it, contains celebrated modern drawings by *Carstens, Cornelius, Schwind, Genelli,* etc. — The S. gallery contains engravings, etchings, woodcuts, models, and a small library; the walls are hung with cartoons by *Neher, Caracci,* and *Guido Reni.* — The S. pavilion contains miniatures, artificial jewels, and impressions of gems.

The grand-ducal **Library* (Pl. 12) (143,000 vols., 8000 maps, 500 old genealogical works, etc.), established in the 'Grüne Schloss' adjacent to the Fürstenhaus (Pl. 9), open to the public daily 9—12

and 2—4, except in June, and the Christmas and Easter vacations
(at those times, fee 10 Sgr.), contains a number of interesting busts
and portraits of celebrated men, most of whom have resided at Weimar; e. g. portraits of members of the grand-ducal family and several of Goethe, marble bust of Goethe over life-size by David
d'Angers (1831), another marble *bust by Trippel of 1788, bust of-
Schiller by Dannecker, that of Herder by Trippel, also those of
Tieck, Wieland, etc. — Luther's monastic gown, the belt of Gustavus Adolphus, Goethe's court-uniform, and other historical and
literary curiosities are also shown. The *Cabinet of Coins and Medals*
is a valuable collection.

In the market-place is the handsome modern Gothic **Rathhaus**
(Pl. 11). The opposite house, now a bookseller's shop, was once occupied by the painter *Lucas Cranach*, as his chosen device (winged
serpent with crown) still indicates.

The **Stadtkirche** (Pl. 19), erected about 1400, possesses one of
Cranach's largest and finest pictures, a *Crucifixion, containing
portraits of Luther and Melanchthon, and the artist and his family.
Herder (d. 1803) reposes in the nave of this church; beneath a
simple slab, bearing his motto '*Licht, Liebe, Leben*'. The life-size
stone figure of *L. Cranach* (d. 1553), '*pictoris celeberrimi*', has been
brought here from the churchyard of St. Jacob and recently restored.
The brass which marks the grave of Duke *Bernard* (d. 1639), is the
most interesting of the numerous monuments to princes of Weimar
interred here. *Herder's Statue* by Schaller stands in front of the
church.

The new *Cemetery, on, the S. side of the town, contains the
Grand Ducal Vault (Pl. 22) in which *Schiller* (d. 1805) and *Goethe*
(d. 1832) are interred. Dukes *Charles Augustus* (d. 1828) and
Charles Frederick (d. 1853) and their consorts also repose here. By
the W. wall, near the ducal vault, is the tombstone of the eminent
composer *Hummel* (d. 1837); near it that of the philanthropist and
satyrist *Johann Falk* (d. 1826). The attendant (10 Sgr.) who shows
the vault lives in the town near the palace, Mostgasse B 53. —
Adjoining the ducal vault is the small, but sumptuously decorated
Russian-Greek Chapel (Pl. 23), beneath which the grand-duchess
Maria Paulowna (d. 1859) is interred.

The *Park (Pl. C, D, 5, 6) lies to the S,, on the charming banks
of the Ilm, where Goethe once occupied a modest summer-abode,
termed the *Römische Haus*. At the extremity of the park is the
village of *Ober-Weimar*. On an eminence beyond rises the *Belvedere* château, with its well-stocked hot-houses, palm-house, and
grounds connected with Weimar by a fine old avenue.

The château and park of **Tieffurt**, on the Ilm, 2 M. E. of Weimar, are
also pleasantly situated. The village of *Ossmannstedt* (p. 229) on the Ilm
is farther distant in the same direction.

*Ettersburg, 4½ M. N. of Weimar; the grand-ducal summer residence,
also abounds in reminiscences of, the golden era of Weimar. Here an ama-

ERFURT

Plätze
I Fisch-Markt
II Wenige Markt
III Hirschgarten
IV Hospital Pl.

Restaurationen
30 Steiniger C.3
31 Klemn D.4
32 Freund C.D.4
33 Hellings Ortn ... B.5
34 Ressource C.4

Gasthöfe
a Silber
b Röm. Kaiser
c Weisser Ross
d Preuss. Hof
e Thüringer Hof
f Rheinischer Hof
g Ritter

1 Bahnhof	B.5	11 Dom	B.4
2 Comandatur	D.3	12 Kaufmanns K.	D.3
Denkmäler		13 Prediger K.	C.3.4
3 Mufflings D	A.5	14 Regler K.	D.4
4 Radowitz D	D.4	15 Severi K.	B.4
5 Soldaten D	C.1	16 Kriegsschule	C.2.3
6 Gewehrfabrik	A.4	17 Lazareth (Garnisons)	B.2
7 Hospital (Grosses)	D.2	18 Mainzerhof	A.4
8 Hospital (Kl.)	D.3	19 Martinsstift (ehem	
Kirchen		Augustiner Kl)	C.4
9 Augustiner K.	C.2	20 Obelisk	B.3
10 Barfüsser K.	C.4	21 Post	D.3
		22 Packhof mit K.Bibliothek u. Zeughaus	
		23 Rathhaus	
		24 Regierung (ehem Kur- mainzer Pallast.)	
		25 Rolandssäule	
		26 Seminar	
		Theater	
		27 Winter theater	
		28 Tivoli (Sommth.) Gaus Garten	
		33 Neues Tivoli Hellings Ortn	
		29 Waisenhaus	

teur company frequently performed in the open air, unshackled by con-
ventional trammels, whilst the trees, shrubs, meadows, and fountains
constituted the scenery and decorations. Plays of Goethe were frequently
thus performed, and members of the ducal and other noble families were
among the actors.

Other points of interest in the vicinity are the *Herdersruhe*, at the foot
of the *Ettersberg*, a favourite resort of Herder; *Berka*, a small town and
watering-place on the Ilm, 6 M. to the S. of Weimar, with charming
walks in the environs. Pleasant walk along the Ilm by *Hetschburg* to
Buchfahrt, where the '*Grafenschloss*' is situated. The 'Schloss' consists of
chambers excavated in the face of perpendicular rocks, accessible by ladders only, and of unknown origin.

48. Erfurt.

Hotels. SILBER, at the station, R. 15, A. 5 Sgr.; *RÖMISCHER KAISER,
R. 15 Sgr.; *WEISSES ROSS; PREUSSISCHER HOF; *THÜRINGER HOF, unpretending; RITTER.

Restaurants. *Steiniger*, with garden, in the Prediger Platz; *Helling's
Garten*, with theatre; *Gaus's Garten* (concerts several times a week at both
of these). *Ressource*, in the Anger, the property of a club, to which an
introduction is necessary. — **Wine.** *Lautenschläger*, August-Str. — **Confectioner.** *Hahnemann*, in the Anger.

Cab from the station to the town for 1 pers. 4, 2 pers. 5, 3 pers. 7½,
4 pers. 10 Sgr.

Erfurt (657 ft.), a very ancient town with 43,700 inhab. (7000
Rom. Cath.) and a garrison of 4500 soldiers, and a Prussian fortress
in connection with the citadels of *Petersberg* and *Cyriaksburg*, existed in the form of a fortified agricultural settlement as early as the
time of St. Boniface, the English apostle of this district. It subsequently belonged to the Hanseatic League, then to the Electorate
of Mayence; in 1802 it was annexed to Prussia; from 1806 to 1814
it was under the French supremacy, and was afterwards finally
restored to Prussia. The water of the *Gera*, which flows through the
town in several arms, as well as that of the *Treue Brunnen*, is
peculiarly favourable to the growth of the water-cress, which is carefully cultivated and forms no inconsiderable article of commerce.

The *Cathedral (Pl. 11), a fine Gothic edifice on an eminence,
possesses a double portal of the 12th cent., an admirable choir of
1349, towers of the close of the 12th cent., and nave and aisles of
equal height. The church was seriously damaged at various periods
by fires and sieges, but has been recently restored. One of the
towers contains 10 bells, the largest of which, the *Grosse Susanne*
(properly *St. Maria Gloriosa*), weighs nearly 14 tons. Fine view
from the top (260 steps).

Interior. By the first pillar on the N. side a *Coronation of the Virgin in bronze by *P. Vischer*, being a monument '*Henningi Godeni jurisc.*'
(d. 1522); near it, on the opposite pillar, a curious painting of 1534, representing the Transubstantiation; on the S. wall a figure of St. Christopher, in oil, occupying almost the entire surface; beneath it the tombstone
of a Count von Gleichen and his two wives, a fine specimen of the sculpture of the 12th cent.; curious candelabrum of the 12th cent., representing
a Penitent, in bronze; modern pulpit by *Schinkel*; humorous wood-carving
on the stalls, well executed.

The church of **St. Severus** (Pl. 15), dating from the 14th cent., with its three spires, adjacent to the cathedral, contains a late Gothic font and an interesting reliquary. The **Predigerkirche** (Pl. 13), erected in 1228, will interest architects; carved altar, with paintings probably by Wohlgemuth. The **Augustine Monastery** (Pl. 9), now an orphan-asylum *(Martinsstift)*, contains the cell of Luther, who became a monk here in 1505, but all reminiscenses of the illustrious Reformer were destroyed by a fire in March, 1872.

In front of the **Rathhaus** (Pl. 23), which dates from 1259, stands a *Column* with a statue of Roland, a figure emblematical of the freedom of market-traffic, and the palladium of municipal privileges.

The *Government-Buildings* (Pl. 24), formerly the palace of the governors appointed by the Electors of Mayence, were occupied by Napoleon in 1808, who convened a congress of reigning princes here.

The *Steiger*, the path to which passes extensive and well-kept kitchen-gardens, is the favourite promenade at Erfurt. The horticulture of the environs enjoys a high reputation. The nurseries of *Haage Junr.*, *Benary*, *Heinemann*, and *Topf* contain a great variety of flowers.

The salt-mine of *Ilversgehoven* 3 M. to the N. of Erfurt, with a shaft 200 fathoms in depth, may be visited by permission of the overseer (10—15 Sgr.).

49. Gotha.

Hotels. *DEUTSCHER HOF, R. 15 Sgr.; WÜNSCHER'S HOTEL, in the Neumarkt, with garden, R. 15—20, B. 7½ Sgr.; *STADT ALTENBURG; RIESE, with restaurant; *STADT COBURG, also a pension; PREUSSISCHER HOF; PROPHET, R. 10 Sgr.; THÜRINGER HOF.

Restaurants. *Ress*, by the theatre; *Café National;* good beer at both. — **Wine.** *Gams; Praetorius; Weigert.*

Cab per drive 5, per hour 15 Sgr., for longer excursions according to agreement. — Omnibus to *Reinhardsbrunn* and *Friedrichsroda* at 1 p. m., 13½ Sgr.

Sausages, a specialty of Gotha, may be purchased of *E. & H. Rudolph*, Neumarkt 16; *Rudolph & Son*, Mönchelsgasse 26; *Schenck; Auerbach*, etc.

Theatre. Performances in winter only.

Gotha (961 ft.), the second residence of the Duke of Saxe-Coburg-Gotha, with 20,500 inhab., is an attractive place. On the way from the station into the town the *Life Insurance Office* (Pl. 14) on the r. and the *Ducal Stables* (Pl. 15) on the l. are passed; then on the r. the *Palais Friedrichsthal* (Pl. 5), opposite to which is the *Orangen-Garten* with its extensive hothouses; on the l. the *Ducal Palace* (Pl. 18), containing several good modern pictures (fee 15 Sgr.); farther on, the *Fire Insurance Office* (Pl. 4) and the *Theatre* (Pl. 27). Adjoining the latter is a *Monument* (Pl. 1) to *Arnoldi* (d. 1841), the founder of the insurance offices and the commercial school.

The *Abbey Church* (Pl. 9) contains a large Crucifixion by *Jacobs*.

The *Töchterschule* (Pl. 28), or girls' school, at the corner of the market-place was once the property of the painter *Lucas Cranach* and still bears his device, a winged serpent with a crown.

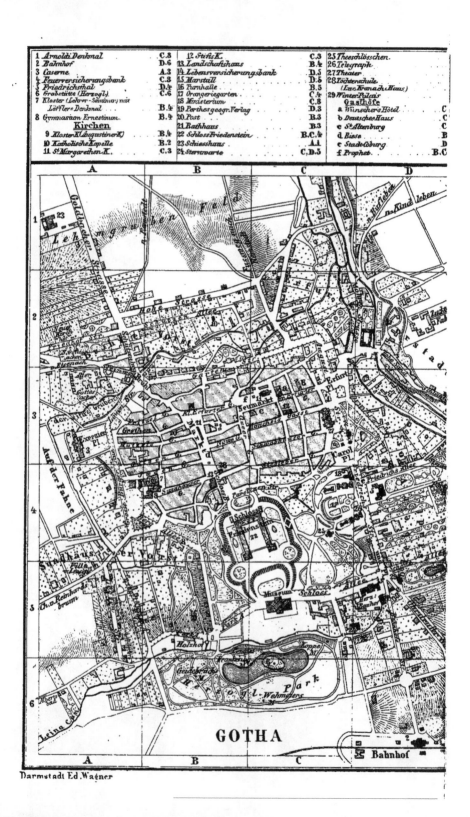

1	Arnoldi Denkmal	C.3	12	Stifts K.	C.3	25	Theeschlösschen.
2	Bahnhof	D.6	13	Landschaftshaus	B.4	26	Telegraph
3	Caserne.	A.3	14	Lebensversicherungsbank	D.5	27	Theater
4	Feuerversicherungsbank	C.3	15	Marstall	D.5	28	Töchterschule
5	Friedrichsthal	D.4	16	Turnhalle	B.5		(Luc.Kranach.Haus)
6	Grabstätte (Herzogl).	C.6	17	Orangeriegarten	C.4	29	WinterPalais
7	Kloster (Lehrer-Seminar) mit		18	Ministerium	C.3		Gasthöfe
	Löfflers Denkmal	B.4	19	Perthes geogr.Verlag	D.3	a	Wünscher's Hôtel	C
8	Gymnasium Ernestinum.	B.4	20	Post	B.3	b	Deutsches Haus	C
	Kirchen.		21	Rathhaus	B.3	c	St. Altenburg	C
9	Kloster Kl.(Augustiner K.)	B.4	22	Schloss Friedenstein	B.C.4	d	Riese	B
10	Katholische Kapelle	B.2	23	Schiesshaus	A.1	e	Stadt Coburg	D
11	St.Margarethen K.	C.3	24	Sternwarte	C.D.5	f	Prophet.	B.C

GOTHA

Darmstadt Ed.Wagner

On a slight eminence rises the very extensive **Friedenstein Palace** (Pl. 22), which contains the following collections (open from 1st April to 31st Oct., on Tuesd. and Frid. 9—1, gratis, at other times for a fee of 1 Thlr.):

The **Picture Gallery** is arranged according to schools. 1st Room: Animal pieces. — 2nd R.: Landscapes, etc.; 7. *Graff*, Portrait of the actor Eckhoff. — 3rd R.: 1. *Van der Helst*, Portrait. — 4th R.: 1. *Van Dyck*, Portrait of himself; 2. *Van Dyck*, Portrait of Elizabeth Brant, Rubens' first wife; 5. *Rembrandt*, Portrait of a youth; 40. *Rembrandt*, Portrait of his mother; 42. *Rubens*, The families of Rubens and Trenck. — 5th R.: 1, 55, 120, 121. Large screen with subjects from the new Testament, by a German master of the 16th cent. Numerous portraits by *Cranach*, who resided at Gotha; 34. *Holbein*, Portrait of a wealthy citizen of Bâle; 36, 37. *Holbein*, Portraits; 39. *Holbein*(?), Portrait of the beautiful Agnes v. Mansfeld, who was abducted from a convent (p. 78) and married by Archbishop Gebhard of Cologne in 1583; 67, 68. *Cranach*, The Fall and Redemption, Judith and Holofernes; 78. *J. v. Eyck*, Portrait of Philip the Good of Burgundy. — 6th R.: 11. *Tischbein*, Conradin of Swabia, after having heard his sentence of death, playing at chess with Frederick of Austria. — 7th R.: Nothing worthy of note. — 8th R.: 6. *Van der Helst*, Portrait; 11. *Dow*, Old woman spinning (purchased for 2000l.); 29. *Potter*, Landscape with cattle. — 9th R.: Unimportant. — 10th R.: 28. *Liotard*, Duke Ernest II. of Saxe-Gotha (in crayons). — 11th R.: 4. *Titian*, Portrait of a man; 54. *G. Reni*, Bacchus and Ariadne; 62. *G. Reni*, Ecce Homo; 65. *G. Reni*, Boy before a nest of doves; 70. *Palma Vecchio*, Christ; 71. *Caravaggio*, Annunciation. — The **Collection of Engravings** (50,000) comprises a number of the oldest Italian and German specimens. — Among the **Drawings** is an Entombment by *Raphael*.

The upper floor contains the **Collection of Casts** and Sculptures, including a fine cast of the Farnese Hercules and a Boy awaking, in marble, by *Müller*. — **Chinese and Art Cabinet**. *1st Room.* Gems, utensils and trinkets in gold and silver, carved wood and ivory. (Large antique onyx with Ceres and Jupiter, statuette of Confucius of sapphire, bust of Louis XIV. in amethyst, breviaries with valuable binding attributed to *Benv. Cellini*, statuettes of Adam and Eve in boxwood by *Alb. Dürer*.) — *2nd R.* Curious pieces of mechanism and mosaics (by Raffaeli). — *3rd R.* Porcelain and majolicas by Böttcher (p. 203). — *4th R.* Egyptian, Roman, and German antiquities. — *5th R.* Ethnographical collection and objects of historical interest. (Shirt worn by Emp. Maximilian I. as a pilgrim; reminiscences of Napoleon I.) — *Rooms 6—10* contain a valuable collection of Chinese works of art and utensils. — The **Natural History Cabinet** contains valuable collections of minerals and conchylia. — The **Library**, open daily 11—1, contains 200,000 vols., numerous Incunabula, MSS., miniatures book of the Gospels of Emp. Otho II.), autographs (letter of Henry VIII. of England against Luther). — The **Cabinet of Coins**, 75,000 in number, is well provided with Greek specimens.

The **New Museum** on the terrace to the S. of the palace, an edifice in the French Renaissance style, is destined on its completion for the reception of some of the above collections.

On the W., S., and E. sides of the palace are extensive **Promenades**. In a grove on the E. side is the *Thee-Schlösschen*, resembling a chapel; on the W. a row of pleasant villas. To the S. of the palace, beyond the terrace of the Museum, is the ***Park** with a pond, on an island in which the ducal burial-place is situated. The *Leina-Canal*, which intersects the upper part of the park and supplies the town with water from the Thuringian Forest, was constructed by a monk in the 15th cent. In the vicinity is the *Observatory* (Pl. 24).

50. Eisenach and Environs.

Comp. Map, p. 246.

Hotels. *GROSSHERZOG VON SACHSEN, opposite the station, with restaurant; *RAUTENKRANZ and *HALBER MOND in the town; THÜRINGER HOF, not far from the station; charges at all these, R. 15, D. 15, A. 5 Sgr.; DEUTSCHES HAUS; ANKER; *ZACHER'S HOTEL. — Inn on the *Wartburg*, see p. 239.

Beer. *Groebler*, in the Carlsplatz; *Phantasie*, in the beautiful *Marienthal*, on the way to the Annathal, 1 M. from the town; a few paces before it is reached are the *Elisabethenruhe* on the l. and the *Liliengrund* on the l. — **Wine.** *Däche.* — **Confectioner.** *Schmitz.*

Cab to or from the station 4, at night 5 Sgr., each heavy package 1 Sgr. — Bargain necessary for excursions. The usual charge per hour is 15 Sgr.; one-horse carr. to the *Wartburg*, with stay of $1\frac{1}{2}$ hr., $1\frac{3}{4}$ Thlr.; the *Wartburg*, *Annathal*, and *Hohesonne* and back, with stay of $1\frac{1}{2}$ hr., $2\frac{3}{4}$ Thlr.; the same including *Wilhelmsthal* and 2 hrs. waiting $3\frac{1}{2}$ Thlr.; for each additional $\frac{1}{2}$ hr. of waiting 5 Sgr. (These charges are exclusive of tolls and driver's fees.) — Two-horse carr. in 3 hrs. to *Ruhla*, *Altenstein*, and *Liebenstein* (pp. 248, 249) 5 Thlr.

Guides. For the first hour 5, for each additional hour 2 Sgr., half-a-day 15, whole day 20 Sgr.; for each night spent out of Eisenach 10 Sgr. — The guides are bound to provide themselves with food, carry light articles of luggage, and show their tariff when required.

Donkey to the Wartburg 10, Annathal $17\frac{1}{2}$, Hohesonne 30, Wilhelmsthal 45 Sgr., including gratuity; an additional charge is made for the return-journey.

Eisenach, a dull town with 14,000 inhab., formerly the residence of the dukes of Saxe-Eisenach, who became extinct in 1741, now belongs to Weimar. The tower of *St. Nicholas*, at the entrance to the town from the station, is a fine Romanesque structure in good preservation. The *Palace* in the market-place was occupied by the Duchess of Orleans (d. 1858) and her sons down to 1857. Good classical music is performed in the opposite Marktkirche on Sundays.

The situation and environs are very picturesque. The *Garden and Park of Herr v. Eichel* (entrance near the Nicolaithor, not far from the station) are well laid out and command charming views (open to the public on Thursdays; at other times tickets are obtained at the proprietor's office in the town). — The grand-ducal *Karthausgarten* in the Frauen-Vorstadt, on the way to the Marienthal, is always open to the public and commands a pleasing view of the Wartburg.

Guide from Eisenach to the *Wartburg* unnecessary (but a guide to the interior must be engaged at the inn at the top). The first street to the W. of the 'Half Moon', leads to the r. past the burial-ground; the path at first ascends rapidly through wood, passing a small white house; it then leads round the *Mädelstein*, with a charming view of the valleys to the r., and reaches the castle in 40 min. The carriage road (longer) diverges to the r. from the Coburg road beyond the Frauenthor (S.).

The *Wartburg* (1355 ft. above the sea-level, 624 ft. above Eisenach), founded by Lewis the Springer in 1070, once a residence of the landgraves of Thuringia who became extinct in 1247, and now a country-seat of the Duke of Saxe-Weimar, is a fine Romanesque edifice, restored in 1847, and adorned with *Frescoes* by *M. v. Schwind* relating to the history of the castle and the life of St. Elizabeth (p. 277), wife of the Landgrave Lewis of Thuringia who resided at the Wartburg. Here the Minnesänger (minstrels of Germany) assembled in 1207 to test their skill (the 'Sängerkrieg'). Luther, on his return from the Diet of Worms in 1521, was waylaid and taken prisoner, in order the better to ensure his safety, by his friend the Elector Frederick of Saxony, and conveyed to the Wartburg, where he was disguised as a young nobleman ('Junker Georg') and zealously devoted himself to his translation of the Bible (4th May, 1521, to 6th March, 1522). His chamber, which is little altered, still contains several reminiscences of the Reformer.

The *Armoury* contains interesting weapons and armour of the 12th and subsequent centuries. The *Rittersaal* and *Banqueting Room* are decorated with grotesque figures of animals as supporters of the beams. — Charming view of the wooded Thuringian Mts. and the valley of Eisenach. (Attendant 5 Sgr. for each pers. ; *Inn* near the castle-gate.)

A visit to the *Annathal* may conveniently be combined with the excursion to the Wartburg. Path easily found, but guide (one of the boys at the gate, 5 Sgr.) desirable. It descends to the l. by the castle bridge; after 4 min. to the r. round the rocks; after 8 min. to the l. through an opening in the rock; after 3 min., straight on, not to the l.; 5 min. the *Waidmannsruh*, a resting-place; 8 min. the *Sängerbank*, where the wood is quitted; 3 min. a stone seat on a projecting rock; then descend by steps round the rock; 5 min. the high road (Eisenach to Coburg); 3 min. farther a direction-post indicates the path to the Annathal.

The *Annathal*, near the Coburg road, 2 M. to the S. of Eisenach, is a cool and very narrow ravine; the most remarkable portion is termed the *Drachenschlucht* (200 yds. long, 2—3 ft. wide), the precipitous sides of which are luxuriantly clothed with moss and ferns, and moistened with continually trickling water.

The traveller may either return from this point, or proceed to the (1 M.) *Hohe Sonne* (1400 ft.), the highest point on the road, whence a picturesque glimpse of the Wartburg is obtained. The forester's house is also an inn.

At the S. base of the Hohe Sonne, 1½ M. from this point, is situated the château of **Wilhelmsthal** (*Inn*) with delightful park. Way back by a footpath through beech-wood by the *Hirschstein* (see p. 247). (From Wilhelmsthal to Ruhla 6 M.; first ½ M. on the high road; then, by a pond to the l., the wood is entered.)

A path to the l. near the entrance to the Annathal leads into the **Landgrafenloch**, a picturesque ravine not inferior to the Annathal, follows its course as far as a tree with a bench, and then ascends to the r. to the *Weinstrasse*, where a view is enjoyed. On the road to

the r., $^1/_2$ M. farther, is the Hohe Sonne.forester's house above me1
tioned. To the *Hirschstein*, *Wachstein*, and thence to *Ruhla*, ɛ
attractive walk of $3^1/_2$ hrs. ; from Ruhla to stat. *Wutha* 6 M. (s
pp. 247, 248).

51. From Eisenach to Coburg and Lichtenfels.

Railway in 4 hrs.; fares 5 Thlr. 11, 3 Thlr., 2 Thlr. 10 Sgr. (to C
burg $3^1|_2$ hrs.).

Soon after quitting the station the train penetrates the N. W
slopes of the Thüringer Wald by a tunnel $^1/_3$ M. in length. Be
yond stat. *Marksuhl* the valley of the *Werra* is entered. **Salzunge**
(*Curhaus; Sächs.Hof) possesses salt-springs, baths, and establish
ments for the inhalation of the vapour; near it is a small lake wit
a château at the S. end and a park at the other. The village o
Möhra, $4^1/_2$ M. to the N., was the home of Luther's parents.

Immelborn is the station for the baths of *Liebenstein* (p. 249)
5 M. to the E. (diligence to meet each train, 30 kr.). On the op
posite bank of the Werra lies *Barchfeld*, with a château of the Land
grave of Hessen-Philippsthal-Barchfeld.

Wernshausen is the station for **Schmalkalden** *(Adler; Krone)*
an ancient town with walls and fosses, situated 3 M. to the E.
Most of the houses, constructed of wood, with lofty gables adorned
with carving, are very picturesque. The Gothic church and the two
inns are in the market-place. In the 'Krone' the Protestant League
of Schmalkalden, so important to the cause of the Reformation, was
concluded in 1531. The articles were drawn up by Luther, Melanchthon, and other reformers in a house indicated by a golden swan
and inscription, on the Schlossberg near the market. The old *Wil-
helmsburg* rises above the town. Iron-wares are extensively manufactured at Schmalkalden and in the whole valley. Valuable iron-
mines in the vicinity.

Stations *Wasungen*, an industrial town on the Werra, and *Wall-
dorf*. As Meiningen is approached, the ducal castle of **Landsberg*
looks down from an eminence on the r. ; it contains some good modern stained glass from Munich and numerous mediæval curiosities;
fine view of the Thüringer Wald and the Rhöngebirge. Visitors admitted during the absence of the family.

Meiningen (857 ft.) *(*Sächs. Hof; Hirsch)*, a well-built town
with 8250 inhab., on the Werra, surrounded by wooded heights, is
the capital of the duchy of Saxe-Meiningen. The *Ducal Palace*, of
which the l. wing, recently restored, dates from the 16th cent.,
was almost entirely completed in 1682. It contains a tolerable picture-gallery and an extensive collection of engravings. The private
apartments of the duke are adorned with a number of choice paintings: **A. Müller*, Apotheosis of the Princess Charlotte; *Taddec
Gaddi*, Christ and Mary with six saints; **Fiesole*, Mary and Joseph
worshipping the Infant; two fine heads by *Melozzo da Forli* and

Van Dyck; also works by *Fra Bartolommeo*, *L. Signorelli*, *Garofalo*, etc. — Near the theatre is a bust of the novelist *Jean Paul*, who resided at Meiningen in 1801—1803. The greatest ornament of the town is the **English Garden*, or park, in which the Gothic *Fürstenkapelle*, containing stained glass from Munich, is situated.

The **Grosse Dolmar** (2346 ft.), to which a road leads from Meiningen by *Helba* and *Kühndorf* in 2³|₄ hrs., commands a beautiful view of the Thuringian Forest. — Schiller resided at the village of *Bauerbach*, 6 M. to the S. of Meiningen, in 1782—83.

Next stations *Grimmenthal* and *Themar*. To the W. rise the picturesque *Gleichberge* (2162 and 2035 ft. respectively).

Hildburghausen (1175 ft.) *(*Engl. Hof; Rautenkranz)*, a pleasant town on the r. bank of the Werra, formerly the residence of the dukes of Saxe-Hildburghausen, now belongs to Meiningen. The *Schloss*, now a barrack, was erected in 1685—95. The *Schlossgarten*, adjoining it on the S., contains a monument to Queen Louise of Prussia. The mediæval Rathhaus with its two towers was begun in 1395.

At the base of the Kleine Gleichen, 9 M. to the N. W. of Hildburghausen, lies **Römhild**, the church of which contains celebrated bronze monuments of the Counts of Henneberg, executed by P. Vischer of Nuremberg about the year 1520.

At stat. *Eisfeld* (*Post) the train quits the Werra.

Coburg, see below.

Branch-line from Coburg (in 50 min.) to **Sonneberg** *(Krug's Hôtel; Bär)*, a busy place where toys are extensively manufactured. Handsome modern Gothic church. Modern château on a hill above the town.

The Werra Railway now traverses the *Itzgrund*, passes stations *Niederfüllbach* and *Ebersdorf*, and reaches

Lichtenfels, a station on the Bavarian N. Railway (p. 227).

52. Coburg.

Hotels. *HÔTEL LEUTHÄUSSER; *GRÜNER BAUM; *TRAUBE; VICTORIA; BELLEVUE; charges at all, R. 42, D. 54 kr.

Restaurants. **Herold* at the theatre; **Schaffner*. The beer of Coburg is generally good. Beer-Gardens of *Sturm* and *Zur Capelle* (fine view from the Platte, near the latter).

Cab to or from the station 18 kr., with luggage.

Theatre. Performances usually on Sund., Tuesd., and Thursd.

Guides for half-a-day 36 kr., whole day 1 fl.

Coburg (902 ft.), one of the residences of the Duke of Saxe-Coburg-Gotha, the most important town in the Franconian portion of the Saxon duchies, with 12,700 inhab., is prettily situated in the valley of the *Itz*, a tributary of the Main, and boasts of a number of handsome buildings, especially in the neighbourhood of the market and Schloss-Platz. Around the town a girdle of villas with gardens has gradually sprung up on the site of the old fortifications.

The MARKET-PLACE in the centre of the town is embellished with a *Statue of Prince Albert* (d. 1861) by Theed, inaugurated in the presence of Queen Victoria on 26th Aug., 1865. The *Rathhaus* and *Government Buildings* in this Platz, as well as the neighbouring

Arsenal which contains the library, were erected by Duke John
Casimir (d. 1663).

The spacious **Moritzkirche** with its lofty tower (334 ft.) contains a monument of Duke John Frederick II., erected in 1598 on
the site of the high altar. Near it the finely executed brasses of
John Casimir (d. 1633), John Ernest (d. 1521), John Frederick V.
(d. 1595) and his wife Elizabeth (d. 1594) are built into the wall.
Opposite the church is the *Gymnasium*, or grammar-school, founded
in 1604. In a house in the vicinity (that of Herr Rose) the
novelist *Jean Paul* once spent several years (1803 et seq.).

In the SCHLOSS-PLATZ, which is partly enclosed by colonnades and covered with pleasure-grounds, and occupies the highest
site in the town, are situated the *Ducal Palace*, the *Theatre*, the
Guard-House, and other handsome buildings. In front of the palace
rises a bronze *Statue of Duke Ernest I.* (d. 1844), by Schwan-
thaler.

The **Palace**, or *Ehrenburg*, a handsome winged edifice in the
English-Gothic style, was converted from a monastery of the recol-
lects into a ducal residence in 1549, and was altered and extended
by Ernest I. (visitors apply to the castellan).

Interior. Family portraits of Duke Ernest I., Queen Victoria, Prince
Albert, King Leopold and his queen, etc.; Surrender of a Danish man-of-
war at Eckernförde by *Dietz;* Flock of sheep by *Lotze;* Greek woman by
Jacobs; several other modern pictures and one by *Van Dyck;* handsome
apartment with Gobelins tapestry and stucco mouldings; grand hall with
caryatides as light-bearers.

A house in the Rückert-Strasse with a medallion portrait was
once occupied by the poet of that name.

A flight of steps near the palace ascend by the guard-house to
the *Schlossgarten*, a park extending along the steep slope of the
hill which is crowned by the castle.

The ancient *Castle of Coburg (1638 ft.), 545 ft. above the
town, to which a path ascends from the palace in $1/2$ hr., commands
the entire district. It was the residence of the Counts of Henneberg
and the Saxon dukes, until John Ernest transferred his seat to the
Ehrenburg in 1549 (see above). About the time of the Diet of
Augsburg (1530) Luther resided here for three months, translated
the prophets and psalms, and wrote 119 letters. In 1632 the fortress was occupied by the Swedes and besieged in vain by Wallenstein. It is a late Gothic structure of the close of the 15th cent.
The S. W. wing with its projecting corner turrets was formerly the
Arsenal; the rest of the building is termed the Fürstenbau. The
castle still in good preservation, although no longer of military importance. It has recently been restored and fitted up as a **Museum.*

The castle is entered on the S. side. The entrance to the collections is under the handsome open wooden staircase in the Gothic
style in the first court; visitors ring at a door to the l. (custodian
24 kr., for a party 1 fl.). Restaurant in the Schlosshof.

The wall of the staircase is adorned with *Frescoes by *Schneider* and *Rothbart* (1838—55), representing the nuptials of Duke John Casimir with the Princess Anna of Saxony (1585). The visitor next enters the CARRIAGE-ROOM, containing curious old state-coaches, sledges, saddles, etc. The VESTIBULE of the armoury contains a fresco by Schneider (1841), representing two bears breaking into the ducal dining-hall. LUTHER'S ROOM remains unchanged and contains relics of the period of his residence here. The spacious ARMOURY contains a large iron stove, cast in 1430, adorned with coats of arms and figures of saints; also armour, shields, helmets, coats of mail, etc. The collections of FIREARMS (rooms on the stair-case and on the upper floor) comprise a number of valuable specimens of the earliest descriptions. Most of the portraits here are modern. The ROSETTE ROOM, the ceiling of which is adorned with 365 rosettes of different forms, with portraits of the Landgraves of Thuringia, contains a number of goblets, among them one presented by Gustavus Adolphus. The BETSAAL contains sculptures in wood from the life of the Virgin, from designs by Martin Schön, a bible by Hans Luft, printed in 1550 and furnished with coloured woodcuts by Burgkmaier, another printed at Frankfort in 1572, a parchment MS. of the 11th cent., with finely carved ivory binding. In the REFORMATION ROOM a copy of an old picture in the Moritzkirche, representing the Diet of Augsburg; portraits of Luther, his wife, Melanchthon, Bugenhagen, and other eminent reformers. On a column are the arms of 16 German towns which first embraced the reformed faith. The HORN ROOM, a master-piece of the Renaissance period, is adorned with mosaics in wood representing hunting-scenes during the reign of John Casimir, executed about the year 1600.

The S. W. wing, in which the architect Herr Rothbart resides, contains a valuable NATURAL HISTORY CABINET, founded by Prince Albert and the reigning Duke of Coburg, and comprising a complete collection of the birds of Europe.

The N. wing contains a collection of ENGRAVINGS and DRAWINGS, including some fine early German specimens; also COINS and AUTOGRAPHS.

*Views. The adjoining N. E. *Hohe Bastei* commands one of the most extensive and picturesque views in Germany. The N. W. *Bärenbastei* commands the finest view to the W., over the town itself. The path to it leads to the W., outside the gate of the castle. '*Luther's Cannon*,' which is preserved here, cast at Frankfort in 1570, is artistically adorned with reliefs in allusion to the theological controversies of the day. The French cannons '*Le Sauvage*' and '*Le Sanspareil*' were brought from Mayence in 1814 by Duke Ernest I., who commanded the besieging troops.

Rosenau, the birthplace (26th Aug., 1819) of Prince Albert (of Saxe-Coburg-Gotha; d. 14th Dec., 1861), brother of the present Duke Ernest II., where Queen Victoria spent eleven days in 1845, 4¹/₂ M. to the N. E. of Coburg, and *Callenberg*, 2¹/₄ M. to the N. W., are country seats of the duke, tastefully fitted up and picturesquely situated.

Near the latter, on the road, 1¹/₂ M. to the N. of Coburg, is the village of *Neuses*, with the house of the poet *Rückert* (d. 1866) adjoining the church. The garden contains a colossal bust to his memory. On a wooded slope on the opposite bank of the Itz rises an obelisk over the tomb of the poet *Thümmel* (d. 1817).

The handsome *Schloss* on the r. bank of the Itz, opposite Coburg, was erected by Duke Ernest of Wurtemberg in 1838. — The *Cemetery* on the E. side of the town contains the modern *Mausoleum* of the Ducal family.

53. The Thuringian Forest.

The *Forest of Thuringia, or *Thüringer Wald*, a mountainous district 95 M. in length and 24 in breadth, bounded on the W. by the Werra and on the E. by Franconia, is replete with interest for the pedestrian. The tour may conveniently be divided into two parts, the *Eastern*, from Rudolstadt to Gotha by Ilmenau and Oberhof (3 days), and the *Western*, from Eisenach to Liebenstein, and over the Inselsberg to Reinhardsbrunn and Gotha (3 days). This is also a geological division, clay-slate occurring towards the S. E., as far as the Erzgebirge, and porphyry to the N.W. as far as Eisenach. The boundary between these formations is near Ilmenau.

The W. portion is the more beautiful, and the excursion should be made from E. to W., beginning with Rudolstadt and terminating with Eisenach, which with its environs and the Inselsberg forms the crowning point of the attractions of the district. The pedestrian effects a saving of a day if, instead of going from Oberhof to Gotha, he proceeds (to the l. by the toll-house before Ohrdruff is reached) to (3$\frac{3}{4}$ M.) Georgenthal and (6 M.) Reinhardsbrunn. The walk would then be as follows: 1st day, from Rudolstadt to Paulinzelle; 2nd. Oberhof; 3rd. Inselsberg; 4th. Eisenach.

Tour of Ten Days from Eisenach. 1st. Eisenach, Wartburg, Annathal; 2nd. By the Hohesonne and Wachstein to Ruhla; thence by the Gerberstein and Luther's Beech to Altenstein; 3rd. From Altenstein by Liebenstein to the top of the Inselsberg; 4th. From the Inselsberg by Reinhardsbrunn to Waltershausen; railway to Gotha and Weimar; 5th. Weimar; 6th. Diligence to Rudolstadt; walk to Blankenburg and Schwarzburg; 7th. By the Trippstein to Paulinzelle and Ilmenau; 8th. Kickelhahn, Manebach, Schmücke, Schneekopf, Oberhof; 9th. From Oberhof through the Schmalwassergrund to Tambach; 10th. Back to the railway by Friedrichsroda and Reinhardsbrunn.

Guides are only occasionally necessary. They should not be engaged for the whole tour, as their acquaintance with the country is generally confined to their own neighbourhood.

Carriages may be hired at Rudolstadt, one-horse 3—4 Thlr., two horse 6 Thlr. per day.

Maps. Those of Fils, published by Perthes at Gotha (7$\frac{1}{2}$ Sgr. each), and those of Gräf, published at Weimar (10 Sgr.), are recommended.

a. Eastern Portion.

From Rudolstadt to Gotha.

From Weimar (p. 232) to Rudolstadt diligence twice daily in 4$\frac{1}{2}$ hrs., viâ *Berka* and *Blankenhain;* once viâ *Kranichfeld* and *Stadt-Remda* in 6 hrs. — *From Apolda*, see p. 230; *from Saalfeld*, see p. 229.

Rudolstadt (*Ritter; *Löwe; *Adler; Kurhaus*, with baths), the capital of the principality of Schwarzburg-Rudolstadt, is charmingly situated on the *Saale*. The *Heidecksburg*, situated on an eminence (202 ft.), is the residence of the prince. The *Ludwigsburg* in the town contains a cabinet of natural history, with a valuable collection of shells. — About 4$\frac{1}{2}$ M. to the W. is the excellent school of *Keilhau*, founded by the pious pastor Fröbel.

The *High Road* ascends the broad valley of the Saale (4$\frac{1}{2}$ M.) to *Volkstedt*, where, in the first house on the r., Schiller resided in 1788; (1$\frac{1}{2}$ M.) *Schwarza* (*Bremer Hof), at the influx of the Schwarza into the Saale. The road divides here. That to the l. leads to Saalfeld (p. 229), that to the r. to

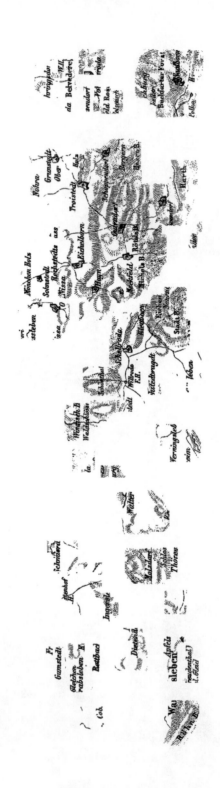

($2^{1}/_{4}$ M.) **Blankenburg** *(Löwe; Ross)*, at the entrance to the Schwarzathal. Above the town rise the ruins of *Greifenstein*, the ancient castle of the German Emp. Günther of Schwarzburg.

The **Schwarzathal* (Chrysopras, an inn $^{1}/_{2}$ M. from Blankenburg), especially between Blankenburg and Schwarzburg (6 M.), is one of the most picturesque and beautifully wooded valleys in Thuringia. The *Eberstein*, to the l. near the entrance, is a shooting-lodge of the prince. High above the ($4^{1}/_{4}$ M.) *Schweizerhaus* is the *Dürre Schild* pavilion, at the entrance to the wild boar park. About $1^{1}/_{4}$ M. farther is a memorial tablet on the r. side of the road, where a zigzag path ascends to the Trippstein (see below) and a view of the Schwarzburg is obtained.

*Schloss Schwarzburg (*Thüringer Hof*, on the road near the castle; **Zum Weissen Hirsch*, farther on, view from the windows at the back. *Two-horse carriage* to Rudolstadt $4^{1}/_{2}$, by Paulinzelle to Ilmenau 8 Thlr., exclusive of tolls and gratuity. *Guide* to the Trippstein and Fasanerie 6, Paulinzelle 12 Sgr. A previous bargain should be made in each case), charmingly situated on an eminence (256 ft.), re-erected in 1726, the ancestral castle of the princes of Rudolstadt, contains an interesting armoury and some fine antlers. The Kaisersaal, which belongs to the original castle, contains a worthless collection of portraits of emperors. The village of *Thal-Schwarzburg* lies at the foot of the castle-hill. The neighbouring forests abound in deer.

From Schwarzburg to Eisfeld (25 M.) diligence daily in 6 hrs. — The road follows the valley of the Schwarza, and leads to ($7^{1}|_{2}$ M.) **Katzhütte**, a village with iron-works. The conspicuous *Cursdorfer Koppe* (2500 ft.) may be ascended in $1^{1}|_{4}$ hr. from *Mellenbach*, a village on the road before Katzhütte is reached, and the descent may be made by *Meuselbach* to Katzhütte in $2^{1}|_{2}$ hrs. On the road, 5 M. to the E. of the latter, is the *Wurzelberg* with a shooting-lodge, near which is a plantation of magnificent old pines, 300 years old. *Eisfeld* (rail. station) see p. 241.

About $^{1}/_{2}$ M. before the village of Schwarzburg is reached, the path to the ($^{1}/_{2}$ hr.) **Trippstein* (1562 ft.) ascends by the memorial-stone above mentioned. This beautiful spot, on which a summer-house (open to the public) stands, commands a striking view of the Schwarzburg. The *Kienhaus*, 20 min. farther to the N., commands a more extensive but less picturesque prospect.

On the carriage-road, 1 M. to the W. of the Trippstein, lies the *Fasanerie*, a shooting-lodge adorned with antlers and surrounded by a park. — The footpath from Schwarzburg to Königsee (see below) passes this lodge, while that to Paulinzelle crosses the road between the Trippstein and the Fasanerie.

From the Kienhaus the traveller may now (guide 12 Sgr.) retrace his steps for 5 min., descend by the first well defined cart-road to the r. to ($1^{1}/_{2}$ M.) *Bechstädt*, and proceed by a road to the r. across an uninteresting tract to ($2^{1}/_{4}$ M.) *Ober-Rottenbach*, from which a good carriage-road to the l. leads to ($3^{3}/_{4}$ M.) *Paulinzelle*. Another route is from Schwarzburg to *Allendorf* and (6 M.) *Unter-Köditz*, above which a good footpath towards the N. W. leads in

1. hr. to *Paulinzelle (*Menger's Inn)*, a ruined abbey with the beautiful ruins of a Romanesque church, erected in 1114 by Pauline, daughter of the knight Moricho. The abbey was suppressed in 1543 in consequence of the Reformation.

A footpath leads from Paulinzelle to the S. through the wood and across the *Galgenberg*, in 1 hr. to the old town of *Königsee* (Löwe), whence a carriage (one-horse 2 Thlr.) may be taken to (10½ M.) *Ilmenau*. The road passes *Amt Gehren* and *Langenwiesen*, where it reaches the Ilm.

Ilmenau (1565 ft.) (*Löwe*; in the room No. 1 Goethe spent his last birthday, 28th Aug., 1831; *Tanne; Schwan; Sonne*, unpretending. *Private Apartments* 2—5 Thlr. per week.' *Rebs'* Pension, near the town), a small town in the Duchy of Weimar, lies on the *Ilm*, and possesses manganese and other mines. River baths and a fine view at the *Neuhaus*, ³/₄ M. to the E. — Dr. Preller's hydropathic establishment is much frequented (pension, baths, and medical attendance 8—12 Thlr. per week).

From Ilmenau to Arnstadt (14 M.) diligence three times daily in 3 hrs. — On this road, 3 M. from Ilmenau, lies **Bad Elgersburg** (*Curhaus*, pension 7—9 Thlr. per week), a village belonging to Gotha with an old established hydropathic establishment and a porcelain manufactory. Pretty environs. Above the village rises an old castle. *Arnstadt*, see p. 231.

To the *Schmücke* by the *Kickelhahn*. A guide (15 Sgr.) is desirable for this walk (4½ hrs.). The traveller crosses the bridge and ascends about 2½ M. on the old Schleussingen road. Before the road turns entirely to the l. and leads round the upper end of the valley, a footpath, afterwards widening into a carriage-road ascends into the wood to the r., leading in a few minutes to the *Jägerhaus* (tavern). The forester keeps the key of the tower, where he is generally to be found in fine weather, provided with a good telescope. The path from the Jägerhaus to the (20 min.) summit traverses the wood, and leads past the grand-ducal shooting lodge of *Gabelbach* (2340 ft.) to a clearing in the wood, whence a path to the r. ascends in a curve to the summit of the *Kickelhahn* (2727 ft.; 1165 ft. above Ilmenau), one of the highest points in the Thuringian Forest, surmounted by a tower which commands a very extensive prospect: to the N. the Brocken, W. the Inselsberg, S. the Röhn, E. Ilmenau, in the background the Fuchsthurm near Jena. About 200 paces to the N. W. formerly stood a small wooden hut where Goethe frequently spent the night, and on the wall of which he wrote his exquisite lines 'Ueber allen Gipfeln ist Ruh', on 7th Sept. 1783. Descend hence to the r. to the (½ hr.) *Hermannstein*, a moss-clad, basaltic rock; after 25 min. more descend to the l. to *Kammerberg* (Inn) and *Manebach* (1650 ft.), a coal-mining village in a dale opposite (3 M. from Ilmenau by the direct road).

A rough cart-track ascends hence, generally through wood, to the (1 hr.) carriage-road leading from Elgersburg and Ilmenau to the Schmücke, and this road is now followed to the l., passing the

($1^1/_2$ M.) source of the Gera. The **Schmücke** (2888 ft.), originally
a farm-house, and now a much frequented *Inn (unpretending),
prettily situated amidst woods and meadows, is about 1 M. farther,
or 2 hrs. from Manebach. It stands near the union of the roads to
Ilmenau, Suhl, and Oberhof. The *Adlerberg*, $2^1/_2$ hrs. to the S. is
an excellent point of view. To the N. W. ($1^1/_2$ hr.) rises the
   *Schneekopf (3100 ft.), the tower on which (5 Sgr.) commands
a magnificent prospect of the plains of Thuringia, as far as the
Brocken and Kyffhäuser, S. the Franconian and Rhön Mts., the
Gleichberge near Römhild, etc. On the road to Oberhof $1/_2$ M. to
the W. of the Schmücke, is a finger-post indicating the path to the
r. to the Schneekopf, the summit of which is reached in 20 min.
more. The traveller then returns to the road by the same path. (Or
the ascent may be made direct from the inn.) The road now ascends
to ($3/_4$ M.) its culminating point, within 16 min. walk of the **Beer-
berg** (3120 ft.). A few paces to the r. of the road is *Plänkner's
Aussicht*, an open spot with a wooden bench and table, commanding
nearly the same view as the Schneekopf, with the addition of the
town of Suhl (p. 253) in the broad valley far below.
   The road to the Oberhof, about 5 M. from the Schmücke, now
gradually descends to the N., and finger-posts are placed at doubtful
points.
   Oberhof (2871 ft.) *(Inn)*, see p. 252. The Coburg and Gotha
high road descends hence to the N. in numerous windings, through
magnificent pine forest, to (9 M.) *Ohrdruff* (p. 252) where the plain
is reached.
   Pedestrians who wish to avoid the high road to Gotha may proceed from the Oberhof to the N.W. to the (7 M.) *Falkenstein*, and
in the same direction through the pretty *Schmalwassergrund* to *Dietharz* (Felsenthal) and *Tambach* (Falkenstein), $4^1/_2$ M. farther. From
Dietharz the walk may be continued to the N. to (3 M.) *Georgenthal* (*Inn). $1^1/_2$ M. to the N.W. is *Altenbergen*, where a monument
on a height to the l. indicates the spot where St. Boniface first
preached christianity; $4^1/_2$ M. to the N.W. is *Friedrichsroda*; $3/_4$ M.
to the N. *Reinhardsbrunn* (p. 251). Or from Tambach straight over
the hills towards the N. W. by *Finsterbergen* (with guide) to Friedrichsroda and Reinhardsbrunn ($2^1/_2$ hrs.).

b. Western Portion.

From Eisenach to Gotha by Ruhla and Liebenstein.

   From **Eisenach** to the *Hohe Sonne*, see p. 239. Thence to Ruhla
the route cannot be mistaken as finger-posts are attached to the
trees at frequent intervals.
   By the Hohe Sonne the *Rennsteig* (p. 253) intersects the Coburg
road. To the r. near the point of intersection a path leads from the
Rennsteig into the wood to the (10 min.) *Hirschstein*, an open

space with a solitary oak and a bench, commanding, a fine view; below, towards the S.W., lies Wilhelmsthal (p. 239); in the background rises the Rhöngebirge.

Returning thence, and following the Rennsteig towards the S. for $3/4$ hr., the traveller reaches a finger-post termed the *Zollstock*, which indicates the routes to the Wachstein and Ruhla, and to Eisenach, Wilhelmsthal, Ruhla, and Heiligenstein (see below). The notices attached to the trees should be observed. The route turns to the l. at this point, and a little farther ascends again to the l., through wood the whole way, leading in $1/4$ hr. to the *Wachstein, a group of rocks rendered accessible by steps and paths, and commanding a magnificent and extensive view, especially towards the E. and N., where the background is formed by the long range of the Harz Mts.

From the Wachstein the traveller returns by the grassy path to the l., slightly ascending, and in $1/4$ hr. reaches the carriage-road at a point about $1/2$ M. from the Zollstock (the interesting circuit by the Wachstein being about 25 min. longer than the direct route). The road leads to the l. to ($1/2$ M.) a spot in the wood with a younger growth of pines, termed the *Todte Mann*, whence a road to the r. descends by the Bermer and Bellevue to Ruhla, while that in a straight direction passes a stump serving as a direction-post and a bench, and ascends to the (20 min.) summit of the *Ringberg*, where the wooden *Karl-Alexander-Thurm affords a picturesque view of Ruhla and the Thuringian Forest. Return hence to the Todte Mann and descend by the enclosure to the l. and past a bench, in the direction above indicated. After $1/4$ hr. the grassy dale is quitted, and the wood on the S. slope entered to the r.; after 10 min. follow the path to the r. at the same level for $1/4$ hr. more, and then descend to the *Bellevue Inn (unpretending) on the W. slope, about 100 ft. above Ruhla, a much frequented spot in summer.

Ruhla (*Curhaus*, with reading-room; *Bellevue; Köllner's Hôtel; Traube; Schwan*; mineral, pine-cone, and other baths at the *Badehaus*. Carriage to Wutha 1 Thlr., with two horses $1\frac{1}{2}$ Thlr.), locally known as 'Die Ruhl', a favourite summer resort, extends to a length of upwards of 2 M. in the valley of the *Erbstrom*, a brook which divides the town into two parts, of which the N. belongs to Gotha, the S. to Weimar. The chief occupation of the inhabitants is the manufacture of tobacco-pipes of all kinds, of which 15 million are annually exported. The village feast on 2nd August presents a curious scene.

A green dale enclosed by wooded mountains leads hence by (2 M.) *Heiligenstein* (*Inn) and (2 M.) *Farnroda* to ($1\frac{1}{4}$ M.) *Wutha*, the first railway station to the E. of Eisenach, opposite the long Hörselberg (p. 231). Good road from Ruhla to Wutha (diligence twice daily in $1/2$ hr.). About $1/2$ M. to the E. of Heiligenstein lies *Thal (*Hôtel Tannhäuser*), with the *Louisenbad*, beautifully situated at the base of the ruin-crowned *Scharffenberg*. Interesting excursion hence to the *Meisenstein* (1766 ft.), $3/4$ hr. to the E.

From Ruhla to the Inselsberg. Carriages generally take the long circuit by *Winterstein* and *Kabarz.* The attractive route for pedestrians occupies 3¹|₂ hrs. Leave Ruhla by the Rittergasse at the upper (S.) end, and after a few minutes turn to the r. and cross the Erbström; after 25 min. cross the brook again and regain the high road in ³|₄ hr.; cross the latter and proceed in a straight direction to the (40 min.) Drei-Herren-stein; or follow the high-road to the r. for about 400 paces and enter the wood to the l. by a path leading in 20 min. to the *Gerberstein* (2307 ft.), a steep hill covered with large blocks of granite; thence back towards the E., along the top of the hill in 12 min. to a grassy clearing, and then to the r. in 20 min. to the above-mentioned *Drei-Herrenstein* (2343 ft.). Of the four paths diverging here, the Rennsteig, that most to the l., is to be selected, and the boundary-stones along the top of the hill followed to the (1¹|₂ hr.) summit of the *Inselsberg* (p. 250).

From Ruhla to Altenstein (5 M.), a good road, through wood, passing (3 M.) a simple monument on the spot where *Luther's Beech,* destroyed by lightning in 1841, formerly stood, and where the Reformer on his return from Worms was subjected to a pretended arrest by his friend the Elector of Saxony.

***Schloss Altenstein,** a summer residence of the Duke of Saxe-Meiningen, standing on a rocky height on the S. W. slope of the Thuringian Forest, is itself uninteresting, but the park and grounds extending along the precipitous limestone rocks afford beautiful walks. Guides at the *Inn in the court-yard of the château.

From Altenstein to Liebenstein (2¹/₄ M.) a good road. At *Glücksbrunn* (Wagner's Hôtel), half way, is the **Lieben-steiner Höhle,* a limestone cavern 160 yds. in length, easily access-ible, with a subterranean lake across which visitors are ferried. Illumination in summer, generally on Sundays 10—12 (admission 30 kr.); best on 7th July, the birthday of the Duchess. Guides at the inn.

Liebenstein (*BELLEVUE, well fitted up; *MÜLLER'S HÔTEL, R. 15—30 Sgr.; *BADHAUS, R. 3¹|₂—14 Thlr. per werk; *HÔTEL ASCHERMANN, with restaurant, moderate; KIRCHNER'S HÔTEL, unpretending; GOLDNER HIRSCH; LÖWE, in the lower part of the village. *Dr. Martiny's Hydropathic Estab-ishment,* R. 2—8 Thlr. per week; another water-cure establishment ad-joining the Curhaus. — *Carriages* with two horses according to bargain; the following are the average charges including tolls and fees: Glücks-brunn cavern 25 Sgr., Altenstein 1¹|₃ Thlr., Luther's Monument 1 Thlr. ¹5 Sgr., Brotterode through the Louisenthal 3¹|₂ Thlr., Eisenach or the Inselsberg 5 Thlr. — *Guides* (a bargain should be made as to the fee for return-journey): half-day 20 Sgr., whole day 1 Thlr. — *Theatre* during the season. — *Music* 7—9 a. m. and 3—5 p. m.), a village in the Duchy of Meiningen, 12 M. to the S. of Eisenach, and 4¹/₂ M. to the E. of stat. *Immelborn* (where a diligence meets each train, p. 240), is beautifully situated and favourite watering-place, possessing cha-lybeate and other springs.

On the slope at the back of the Curhaus is the *Italian Garden,* tastefully laid out. Adjoining it stands the simple villa of the Duke of Meiningen. The *Erdfall* near the Curhaus is a kind of open grotto, fringed with wood. Paths lead hence to the *Helle Blick* and the *Bernhards-Platz,* and the new *Promenadenweg* leads to the *Werner's Platz,* all fine points of view.

. The path to the (20 min.) extensive ruins of the *Burg Stein ascends in zigzags to the l. past the grotto and the Italian Garden. The castle was deserted at the close of the 17th cent., and has since fallen to decay. The number 1534 over the portal indicates the date of its restoration. The *view embraces the entire chain of the Rhöngebirge and the W. spurs of the Thuringian Forest from the Dollmar to the Ochsenkopf; then the broad valley of the Werra with its numerous villages, from Gumpelstadt towards the N. as far as Breitungen to the S.

On the outskirts of the wood near the ruin is a monument to the Duchess Ida of Saxe-Weimar. In the wood, 1/4 hr. to the N., is a small open space enclosed by rocks on three sides, termed the *Felsentheater*.

From Liebenstein to the Inselsberg there are several different routes. The shortest (guide necessary, 15 Sgr.) leads through the *Thüringer Thal* to the Rennsteig (p. 253), traversing the forest. A more varied and interesting route is to the S. E. by the high road to (4½ M.) *Herges*, then to the N. through the *Trusenthal (to which a direct footpath also leads), a picturesque, rocky ravine, to (1 hr.) the extensive village of *Brotterode* (Inselsberger Hof), at the base of the Inselsberg. (Attractive excursion hence to the *Memmelstein*, 1 hr. to the S.) A few paces beyond the inn broad steps ascend to the l. (beyond the point where the road to Frieddrichsroda diverges to the r.) to the church and past the E. side of the churchyard-wall, where the middle of the three paths is to be selected. After 10 min. ascend by a broad stony path to the r.; 3 min. the insignificant footpath diverges to the l. from the broad track, crosses the meadow, and in 5 min. reaches the wood; here avoid the turn to the l., and ascend the rough cart-track; 7 min., to the r.; then by a well-defined path in ½ hr. to the summit. (In descending to Liebenstein avoid the two paths diverging to the l. and follow that in a straight direction.)

. The ***Great Inselsberg** (2940 ft.) commands an extensive panorama, especially towards the N., resembling the view from the Schneekopf (p. 247), but unfortunately too often obscured by clouds and fog. The larger of the two inns on the top is good and reasonable.

· *From the Inselsberg to Eisenach*, 5 hrs. — The traveller follows the *Rennsteig*, a very ancient boundary road leading from the Werra to the Saale over the Thuringian Mts., for 1¼ hr.; then turns to the N. to (¾ hr.) *Ruhla*, and proceeds thence by the *Wachstein* and the *Hohe Sonne* to Eisenach (p. 238) in 3 hrs. The *Annathal* forms an attractive termination to the walk.

The carriage-road descending from the Inselsberg by *Kabarz* and *Tabarz* cannot be mistaken; the footpath to *Reinhardsbrunn* by the *Uebelberg* is, however, more difficult to trace. Returning guides (15 Sgr.) are generally to be found on the top. The following description of the route may suffice, if no guide can be procured:

after 5 min. the narrow path diverges from the road to the r. through pine-wood (beyond the point where the Rennsteig branches off); 5 min., the path to the l.; 8 min., to the l. (the path to the r. leads to Brotterode). Then traverse a large meadow, where a finger-post indicates the way to the Inselsberg, cross the high road leading from Brotterode to Reinhardsbrunn, and again traverse a meadow through an opening in the wood to the l., where (after 5 min.), by a small fir-plantation, the broad footpath is again reached; 8 min., the path, frequently wet, passes a brook; 10 min., a pleasant grassy plateau. Then to the l., direct to the (6 min.) *Thorstein*, a 'Kuhstall' (p. 210) in miniature, affording a similar view of a deep, fir-clad valley. On the opposite rock is a wooden figure, termed the 'Hölzerne Mann'. A beautiful forest-path leads hence through the *Felsenthal* and the *Lauchagrund* to Tabarz and Reinhardsbrunn.

Next descend to the l. by a winding path; 3 min. farther the path to the r. for those coming in the reverse direction leads to the Thorstein, that to the l. to Brotterode; 7 min., a direction-post. The path in a straight direction leads by *Gross - Tabarz* (Tabarzer Schiesshaus; Felsenthal; at *Klein-Tabarz* the Jagdhaus), where a number of visitors reside in summer, to Reinhardsbrunn in 1¹/₂ hr.; but, as the view from the Uebelberg is the great attraction of this route, the traveller should select the longer (by ¹/₂ hr.) path which here ascends to the r. to (¹/₄ hr.) the *Aschenbergstein*, where a cross has been erected to the memory of a lady who met with a fatal accident here. Picturesque survey of the dark valleys and of the plain to the N. through the Felsenthal. Now follow the path to the l.; 18 min., a broad track is passed, whence the path to the l. ascends to the summit of the *Uebelberg (2264 ft.) in 5 min. View similar to that from the Inselsberg, with a far more picturesque foreground. The long Meissner range is conspicuous to the W., the Brocken to the N.; Reinhardsbrunn lies to the r. in the foreground; N. Schloss Tenneberg; N. W. the Wartburg; E. the Wachsenburg.

In returning, descend by the same path to a direction-post 5 min. below the summit, and then turn to the l.; 10 min., the footpath leads to the l. through dense pine-wood in a straight direction; 10 min., near a meadow, it leads through the wood on the r., crosses another path, and reaches the carriage-road; in the long meadow a straight direction is pursued through a beautiful pine-forest, then a slight ascent, always keeping to the r.

In ¹/₄ hr. the traveller reaches the white buildings of the *Herzog Ernst Mine*, which yields 'isinglass stone', or gypseous spar. A large grotto in the vicinity, with lofty crystalline walls, presents a curious and impressive scene (fee 5 Sgr.) when illuminated by torches.

*Reinhardsbrunn, ³/₄ M. from the mine, formerly a Benedictine monastery, was converted in 1827 into a château in a florid mixed style of architecture (circular and pointed). On the E. side of the old church are immured ten fine old tombstones of Land-graves of Thuringia. The château, a favourite residence of the Duke of Coburg-Gotha, is delightfully situated in the most beau-tiful part of the Thüringer Wald, and surrounded by attractive grounds. (*Inn at the N. entrance, often full.)

Friedrichsroda *(*Herzog Ernst; Schauenburg; Wagener; Fel-senkeller),* 3/4 M. to the S., is a pleasant and favourite summer re-treat. Rooms may be procured at the *Schweizerhaus, Villa Grothe,* etc. for 2½—4½ Thlr. weekly; board about 1 Thlr. per day.

Walk of 4—5 hrs.: to the *Tanzbuche* in the *Ungeheure Grund,* to the *Felsenthal* and *Thorstein* (p. 251), and back by Tabarz and Reinhards-brunn. Or by the *Gottlob,* the *Spiessberg* (tavern), commanding a fine view, the *Tanzbuche,* the ducal shooting lodge, and through the *Ungeheure Grund,* or over the *Abtsberg* (view similar to that from the Uebelberg), to Reinhardsbrunn.

From Reinhardsbrunn to the Inselsberg (guide necessary, 15 Sgr.) a walk of 3 hrs., through wood almost the whole way. (The route from the Inselsberg to Liebenstein by Brotterode affords little shade).

From Friedrichsroda to Gotha 9 M. (post-omnibus once daily in 1½ hr. ; fare 13½ Sgr.). The pedestrian may follow the broad and shady footpath (crossing the road to the l. of the inn) which skirts the hills and crosses the *Tenneberg* to *Waltershausen;* or proceed through the valley by (1½ M.) *Schnepfenthal* to (1½ M.) *Waltershausen* (Eisenach Hôtel), a busy little town connected by a tramway with *Fröttstedt* (p. 231), a station on the Thuringian Railway, to which the cars run in ¼ hr.

At *Schnepfenthal* there is a famous educational establishment, founded by Salzmann in 1784. The buildings are well fitted up, and contain a riding-school, natural history collection, etc.

Altenbergen, Georgenthal, Tambach, etc., see p. 247.

54. From Gotha through the Thuringian Forest to Hildburghausen.

Comp. Map, p. 246.

45 M. Diligence one daily in 9¾ hrs. — Railway by Eisenach and Meiningen, see p. 231 and R. 51.

This is a picturesque road, especially between Ohrdruf and Suhl.

9½ M. **Ohrdruf** *(Anker)* is a small manufacturing town. The road gradually ascends the wooded mountains of Thuringia and traverses a beautiful wooded valley with varying views. At the en-trance to the *Ohrathal* is the deserted iron-forge of *Louisenthal.* The villages of *Stutzhaus* and *Schwarzwald* are next passed. A little beyond the latter opens the *Stutzhäuser Grund* on the r. ; 1½ M. farther the *Triefstein* is passed, and the ducal shooting-lodge soon becomes visible at the head of the valley.

9 M. **Oberhof** *(*Inn)* is a poor village inhabited by wood cutters, with a ducal shooting-lodge. Oats thrive here in warm seasons only,

and potatoes grow but scantily. Fine view from the *Louisenlust* (2590 ft.), at the foot of the Schlossbergkopf, 5 min. to the N.

The road soon crosses the *Rennsteig*, or *Rennweg*, a very ancient frontier road leading from the Werra to the Saale across the Thuringian Mts., and separating Thuringia from Franconia (p. 241). Near it, at the highest point of the road, rises an obelisk in commemoration of the construction of the latter. *View of the forest and its dark ravines. The road then descends by *Zelle* to

10 M. **Suhl** *(Deutsches Haus; Krone)*, the capital of the Prussian part of the County of Henneberg, which has been famous for several centuries for its manufacture of firearms. The town lies picturesquely in the valley of the *Lauter* at the base of the *Domberg*, and is shaded by the precipitous porphyry cliff of the *Ottilienstein* which commands a fine view.

9½ M. **Schleusingen** *(Grüner Baum)* was once the residence of the Counts of Henneberg, who became extinct in 1583, and whose ancestral seat was the ancient Bertholdsburg. A chapel by the church contains monuments of the counts, fine knightly figures of the 15th and 16th cent., one of which is pierced with a bullet in memory of a count who fell at the storming of Tiraschka in Piedmont in 1587. The golden hen on the fountain in the market-place belonged to the armorial bearings of the counts. The Schloss is now occupied by the authorities of the district. Pine-cone baths have been in use here since 1852 as a remedy for rheumatism and paralysis.

The road now ascends for a considerable distance, affording fine retrospects.

8 M. *Hildburghausen*, see p. 241.

55. From Cassel to Halle *(and Leipsic)* by Nordhausen.

Railway in 4³|₄—5³|₄ hrs.; fares 5 Thlr. 25, 4 Thlr. 11, 2 Thlr. 27¹|₂ Sgr. to Leipsic in 5¹|₃—7 hrs., fares 6 Thlr. 29, 5 Thlr. 3¹|₂, 3 Thlr. 9 Sgr.; comp. R. 46).

From Cassel to *Münden*, see p. 85. The line diverges here to the S. W., ascends the pretty valley of the *Werra* to *Hedemünde* and *Witzenhausen*, and then turns to the W. to *Arenshausen* where it unites with the Göttingen line (comp. p. 85).

The broad *Leinethal* is now ascended to *Heiligenstadt* (Preuss. Hof; Eichsfelder Hof), the capital of the former principality of Eichsfeld, on the *Leine*, with three Gothic churches of the 13th and 14th cent. — Stat. *Leinefelde*.

From Leinefelde to Gotha branch-railway in 2¹|₄ hrs. (53, 40, 27 Sgr.). Stations *Dingelstedt*, *Dachrieden*, and **Mühlhausen** *(Weisser Schwan; König v. Preussen)*, an ancient town with 18,000 inhab., on the *Unstrut*. The Gothic *Marienkirche*, with double aisles, and the old stained glass in the Church of *St. Blasius* deserve mention. Pleasant walks to the *Popperoder Quelle* and the (3 M.) *Weisse Haus*. The seditious fanatic Thomas Münzer, leader of the Wiedertäufer, or German Anabaptists, was defeated and captured in the vicinity, and executed at Mühlhausen, the principal

scene of his enormities. — Next stations *Gross - Gottern* and **Langensalza**
(*Kreuz; Mohr*), a busy town with cloth and other factories. The sul-
phur baths of that name are prettily situated on the *Unstrut*, $1|_2$ M. from
the town. The engagement between the Prussians and the Hanoverian
army in June, 1866, which terminated in the capitulation of the latter
took place near *Merxleben*, a village to the N. E. of the town. — Stations
Ballstedt and *Gotha*, see p. 236.

Stations *Gernrode*, *Sollstedt*, *Bleicherode*, *Wolkramshausen*. —
Nordhausen (**Röm*. *Kaiser*; **Engl*. *Hof*; **Berliner Hof*; **Prinz
Carl; **Erbprinz*), with 20,000 inhab., situated on the fertile S.
slopes of the Harz Mts. (R. 58), possessing extensive distilleries
and chicory and chemical manufactories, was frequently the scene
of councils and assemblies of princes in the middle ages. The
Church of St. Blasius contains two pictures by Cranach, an Ecce
Homo and the Funeral of Nain (Luther and Melanchthon among
the mourners). Near the Rathhaus rises a Roland's Column (p. 88).
The old fortifications have been converted into promenades. —
Route to the Harz Mts., see p. 268; to Erfurt, see p. 231.

At Nordhausen begins the fertile *Goldne Aue*, watered by the
Helme, and extending to Sangerhausen. Stations *Heringen* and
Rossla (Deutscher Kaiser), with a château of Count Stolberg.

To the S. of Rossla rises the wooded **Kyffhäuser** (1395 ft.). The route
to it leads by *Sittendorf*, beyond which the road from *Tilleda to Kelbra*
(see below) is crossed. The last part of the ascent is by a footpath. The
ruined castle, which was once occupied by the Hohenstaufen, consists of
the Oberburg, with its tower 80 ft. in height, and the Unterburg with
the chapel. According to an ancient tradition, the Emp. Frederick Barbarossa slumbers in the bowels of the earth beneath the castle, ready
to burst forth as soon as Germany regains her former glory. Inn at
the top.

To the N. W. of the Kyffhäuser lies the ruin of **Rothenburg** (1053 ft.).
The route to it is by a broad forest-path from the Kyffhäuser to the (40
min.) Frankenhausen and Kelbra road; then by the latter to (5 min.) a
finger-post on the r., whence a good footpath leads to the castle in 1 hr.
(view and tavern at the top). — At the foot of the Rothenburg on the
N. W. side lies the small town of ($1|_2$ hr.) *Kelbra* (Sonne), with numerous
breweries. Rossla is 3 M. distant by the road. — The castles are most
conveniently visited in the reverse direction, either on foot or by carriage.
In this case the traveller descends from the Kyffhäuser through beautiful
woods in $1^1|_2$ hr. to

Frankenhausen (**Mohr*; *Thüringer. Hof*), a small town with salt-baths
and salt-works, from which *Sondershausen* (p. 256) is 12 M. distant. On
the road to the latter, near the (3 M.) village of *Rottleben*, is situated the
**Falkenhöhle*, sometimes called the *Barbarossa* or *Kyffhäuser Cavern*, 330
yds. in length, with subterranean lakes (adm. 5 Sgr.). Bengal lights may
be purchased of the apothecary in the market-place at Frankenstein. The
direct route from the Kyffhäuser to the cavern (2 hrs.) diverges to the r.
from the road, by Prince Schwarzburg's shooting lodge of *Rathsfeld*, about
halfway between Kelbra and Frankenhausen.

Next stations *Wallhausen* and *Sangerhausen* (Löwe). A stone-
slab over the door of the Ulrichskirche records that is was erected
by Lewis 'the Springer' in 1079, in performance of a vow made by
him at the Giebichenstein (p. 225). Beyond stat. *Riestädt* several
distant views of the Harz Mts. are obtained.

Eisleben (*Gold. Schiff*; *Mansfelder Hof*; **Anker Restaurant*),
a town with 12,500 inhab., was the birthplace of Luther. The

house in which he was born (1483), near the post-office, now a
school for poor children, contains various reminiscences of the great
Reformer. The *Andreaskirche* contains the pulpit from which he
preached, and some interesting monuments of Counts of Mansfeld.
The Church of *St. Peter and St. Paul* contains the font in which
Luther was baptised, a fragment of his cloak, and his leathern
skull-cap. Extensive copper and silver mines in the neighbourhood.
At *Wimmelburg*, in the vicinity, is an interesting cavern, 1000yds.
in length.

Martin Luther, born at Eisleben in 1483, became an Augustine monk
in 1505, and professor of philosophy at Wittenberg in 1508. In 1510 he
visited Rome on business connected with his order, and in 1512 became a
doctor of theology. In 1517 he strenuously opposed the sale of indulgences
by the Dominican Tetzel; in condemnation of which he affixed his famous
95 Theses to the church-door at Wittenberg. His antagonism to the see
of Rome now steadily increased, and in 1520 he was formally excommu-
nicated by the pope. Luther in his turn solemnly renounced all connection with Rome, and publicly burned the bull of excommunication. In
1521 he was summoned by Emp. Charles V. to the Diet of Worms, where
he vigorously defended his doctrines, but was nevertheless declared an
outlaw. On his return he was surprised and ostensibly taken prisoner in
the Forest of Thuringia, by order of his friend the Elector of Saxony,
and carried to the Wartburg, where he passed 10 months disguised as a
young nobleman, and was known as 'Junker Georg'. During this period
he worked assiduously at his translation of the Bible, of which, on his
release, the New Testament first appeared in 1522 (the entire translation
not till 1534). He then returned to Wittenberg, where he as firmly
checked the intemperate zeal of the Puritanical image-breakers, as he had
opposed Rom. Catholic abuses. In 1525 he married Katharina von Bora,
who had previously been a nun and escaped from her convent. After a
life of unremitting labour as a reformer, divine, translator of the Bible,
and even as a poet and musician, he died at Eisleben, 18th Feb. 1546.
Luther is regarded by the Germans not only as the great founder of their
religious liberty, but as the talented linguist and grammarian who developed and first established the use of pure modern German.

Beyond Eisleben the railway turns to the S. to stat. *Ober-Röb-
ling am See;* and afterwards crosses the Saale and the Magdeburg
line.

Halle, see p. 224; thence to Leipsic, p. 225.

56. From Brunswick to Nordhausen and Erfurt by Börssum *(Harzburg, Goslar)*.

Railway to *Nordhausen* in 4³|₄ hrs. (fares 3 Thlr. 23, 2 Thlr. 20,
1 Thlr. 21 Sgr.); thence to *Erfurt* in 3¹|₂ hrs. (fares 2 Thlr. 2, 1 Thlr. 16,
1 Thlr. 1 Sgr.). — From Brunswick to *Harzburg* in 1¹|₂—2 hrs. (1 Thlr. 6,
24, 15 Sgr.); from Brunswick to *Goslar* in 1³|₄—2¹|₄ hrs. (1 Thlr. 11, 28,
18¹|₂ Sgr.).

From Brunswick to *Wolfenbüttel*, where the line to Oschersleben and Magdeburg diverges to the E. (R. 3), see p. 58. Our
line crosses the *Oker* and ascends to *Hedwigsburg* and **Börssum,**
the junction of the Brunswick-Harzburg and Oschersleben-Kreien-
sen lines (R. 4), situated at the confluence of the *Ilse* and Oker.

The *Harzburg Line* follows the course of the Oker, towards the S.
Stat. *Schladen*. At **Vienenburg,** where it is joined by the Halberstadt line

(p. 260), it divides, the branch to the l· leading to *Harzburg* (p. 271), that to the r. to *Goslar* (p. 269).

From Börssum to **Seesen** (**Kronprinz; Wilhelmsbad*), see p. 62. The Nordhausen line turns to the S. and skirts the S. E. slopes of the Oberharz (p. 260), affording a number of picturesque views (comp. Map, p. 260). Stat. *Gittelde*, see p. 276; then **Osterode** (*Englischer Hof; Krone*) on the *Söse*, a town with many picturesque old houses. On the Rathhaus is the large bone of a mammoth, suspended by a chain. Several monuments in the Marktkirche. Scherenberg's extensive white-lead and small shot factory may be visited. — On the high road, to the r., about halfway between Osterode and Herzberg, is the *Jettenhöhle*, a stalactite cavern. — Diligence from Osterode to (9 M.) *Clausthal* (p. 275) twice daily.

Stat. **Herzberg** (*Weisses Ross; König v. Hannover; Stadt Hannover*), on the *Sieber*, the junction of the line to Northeim (p. 85), was the residence of the Dukes of Brunswick - Celle down to 1634, when they transferred their seat to Hanover. The old Schloss was founded in 1024. From Herzberg through the *Sieberthal to *Andreasberg*, see p. 276.

Scharzfeld is the station for (4 M.; omnibus) **Lauterberg** (*Krone; Rathskeller*), a small town with pleasant, wooded environs and a water-cure establishment.

To the l. of the road between Scharzfeld and Lauterberg rises the beautifully situated ruin of **Scharzfels**. Near it is the *Einhornhöhle*, or *Schiller's Cavern*, where the name of the poet, written by himself, is still pointed out. The *Steinkirche*, another grotto, is partly artificial. The *Hausberg* commands an extensive prospect. A still finer point of view is the *Ravenskopf (2067 ft.), 2 hrs. from Lauterberg (inn at the top), whence the railway stat. Tettenborn (see below) is reached towards the S. W., viâ *Sachsa*.

Stations *Osterhagen*, *Tettenborn*, and *Walkenried* (Gold. Löwe), a village with the imposing ruins of a Cistercian abbey of that name, a church of the 13th and 14th cent., and fine early Gothic cloisters of the same period. (Footpath to Ellrich, see below.) The train passes through a tunnel and reaches

Ellrich (**Schwarzer Adler*), a small town prettily situated on the *Zorge*, whence a diligence runs once daily through the Harz Mts. to Wernigerode and Halberstadt. Pleasant environs. A picturesque path leads hence over the *Burgsberg* and the forest village of *Himmelreich* to Walkenried (see above). Near Himmelreich is a fine cavern, discovered in 1868. Stat. *Niedersachswerfen* (for Ilfeld, see p. 269); then **Nordhausen** (p. 254), the junction of this line with the Halle and Cassel railway.

Beyond stat. *Wolkramshausen* the Erfurt line crosses the *Unstrut* and reaches **Sondershausen** (*Hôtel Mönch; Tanne; Deutsches Haus*), the capital of the principality of Schwarzburg-Sondershausen, charmingly situated in the Wipperthal. The Schloss contains a few antiquities, among which is the 'Püsterich', a bronze idol, 2 ft. in height. Fine view from the *Goldner* and from the ²*Possen*, the highest point of the *Hainleite*, 1 hr. to the S.

,Stations *Greussen, Straussfurt, Gebesee-Ringleben* (the celebrat-
-ed gun factory of *Sömmerda* is 14 M. to the E.), *Walschleben*, and
·Erfurt (p. 235).

57. From Berlin; by Cöthen to Ballenstedt, Thale,
Vienenburg *(Harzburg, Goslar).*

Railway to *Ballenstedt* in ⁺6 hrs. (fares 5 Thlr. 26, 4 Thlr. 12¹|₂,
3 Thlr.¸|3¹|₂ Sgr.); .to *Thale* in 6¹|₂ hrs. (fares 6 Thlr. 11, 4 Thlr. 23, 3 Thlr.
6 Sgr.); to *Vienenburg* in 7 hrs. (fares 6 Thlr. 15,.4 Thlr. 26,·3 Thlr. 7¹|₂
Sgr.). From Vienenburg to Goslar in 30, to Harzburg in 25 min. — Return-tickets from the larger stations to Thale and Ballenstedt available
for six, from Berlin; for ten days. — From Berlin by Magdeburg and
Oschersleben to Vienenburg and Thale, see p. 62.

From Berlin to **Wittenberg**, where carriages are changed, see
p. 222.

The line runs near the Elbe. First stat. *Coswig*, with a ducal
château.

About ³|₄ M. below .Coswig is a ferry across the Elbe, beyond which
is situated (2 M.) Wörlitz (*Eichenkranz*, outside the town, at the entrance
to the park), a town with 2000. inhab., famous for. the *Gardens* and
Park laid out by the Duke of Dessau during the last century. The
grounds are carefully kept and afford beautiful walks, enlivened with
, several sheets of water and adorned in the questionable taste of the period of their origin. · The '*Gothic House*' contains a number of small, but
good pictures, chiefly by Netherlands and old German masters,. portraits,
ancient drinking goblets, armour, etc. (fee 7¹|₂ Sgr.). The *Pantheon,
Temple of Flora,. Monument,*. artificial grottoes, a labyrinth, etc. are next
visited. About 3 hrs. are occupied in exploring all the points of interest
(guide to be found ,at the Eichenkranz, 7¹|₂ Sgr.); or they may be visited
more expeditiously by boat (20 Sgr.), in which case, however, the beautiful
· walks are missed. Wörlitz is 7¹|₂ M. from Dessau (one-horse carr. 1¹|₂ Thlr.).

·Next stations· *Kliecken* and .*Rosslau.*

From Rosslau to Zerbst by railway in 25 min. (12, 9, 6¹|₂ Sgr.),
by *Tornau* and *Jütrichau.* Zerbst (*Löwe; Hôtel d'Anhalt*), an old town
with 12,000 inhab., once the seat of the Princes of Anhalt-Zerbst, who
became extinct in ·1793, possesses a large Schloss and extensive riding-
school. The market-place,. with its handsome gabled houses, is adorned
with a *Roland Column* of 1445 recently. restored, and. a female figure on a
slender column, termed the *Butterjungfer*, which is said to be the emblem
of some of the municipal privileges of the town. The *Rathhaus,* which
dates from the 15th cent., but was disfigured by additions in 1610, contains
a bible printed on parchment, with woodcuts coloured by Lucas Cranach.
The handsome *Nicolaikirche* of the 15th cent. has been judiciously restored. The *Francisceum* is a grammar-school of high repute..

At Rosslau the line turns towards the S., crosses the *Elbe* and
then the *Mulde*,. and soon reaches

Dessau (118 ft.) (*Hirsch; *Goldner Beutel ; *Goldner Ring),
the capital of the Duchy of Anhalt, with 17,000 inhab., and the
residence of the duke. The town is of modern aspect, with broad
streets, consisting chiefly of houses of a single storey, châteaux,
gardens, and fountains, and lies in a wooded and pastoral district
watered by the Mulde.

The Ducal Palace of the 15th cent., altered in the 16th and
18th, contains upwards 600 oil-paintings, some of which are by Titian,

BÆDEKER's N. Germany. 5th Edit.   **17**

Fr. Francia, Lippi, Cimabue, Giulio Romano, Sassoferrato, Carlo Dolce, Van Dyck, and Rubens. In the 'Gypskammer' on the ground-floor are preserved various curiosities, coins, antiquities, and objects of historical interest, among which are the sword and stick of the general Prince Leopold of Dessau, Napoleon's silver goblet and his plates captured at Belle-Alliance (fee 1 Thlr.).

The *Schlosskirche*, which was erected at the beginning of the 16th cent., contains some good pictures by Cranach, the finest of which is the Last Supper, with portraits of some of the chief promoters of the Reformation. Luther frequently preached in this church.

A military band plays three times a week in the Schloss - Platz in front of the guard-house, at 12 o'clock, usually beginning with the Dessau March ('*Ça donc, ça donc*'), the favourite air of Prince Leopold. A statue to that general has been erected here after the model of that by Schadow in the Wilhelms - Platz at Berlin, and another to his grandson Duke Leopold Frederick Francis (d. 1817), designed by Kiss. A marble monument in the small market-place commemorates the 50th anniversary of the accession of Duke Leopold Frederick (1867).

The *Philantropin*, a celebrated educational establishment during the last century (1774—93), in the Zerbster Strasse, now contains the *Amalienstiftung*, an asylum for old women founded by the daughter of Prince Leopold. The upper floor is occupied by a picture gallery, in which German and Netherlands masters are chiefly represented. The *Leopoldsdank*, a charitable institution for indigent old men, with a lofty tower, was founded by Prince Leopold Max.

The park at *Wörlitz* (p. 257) is reached by carriage (one-horse 1½ Thlr.) in 1½ hr.

From Dessau to Bitterfeld by a branch-line in 50 min. (21, 16, 11½ Sgr.). Thence to *Leipsic*, see p. 223.

The scenery between Dessau and Cöthen is attractive. Stat. *Elsnigk.* To the r. in the distance rises the tower of the ancient town of *Aken.*

At Cöthen (p. 224) the Magdeburg and Leipsic railway is crossed (R. 44). Stat. *Biendorf.*

Stat. Bernburg (*Goldne Kugel*), a cheerful town with 16,000 inhab., possesses a handsome old Schloss dating partly from the 14th cent., and partly from the 16th—18th, and a late Gothic Church of St. Mary. From stat. *Güsten* a branch-line runs to Stassfurth (p. 223). *Aschersleben* (Gold. Löwe; Deutsches Haus), an ancient town with 16,000 inhab., the seat of the princes of the Ascanian line, who became extinct in 1345, is the junction of a line to Halle, which when completed will be the shortest route from Leipsic to Hanover.

From *Frose* a branch-line runs by *Ermsleben* in ¾ hr. to Ballenstedt (see p. 262).

The main line passes stations *Nachterstedt*, *Gatersleben*, and *Wegeleben*, where the line to ($^3/_4$ hr.) Thale diverges. Stations on the latter *Ditfurth*, *Quedlinburg* (p. 261),· and *Neinstedt*. **Thale,** see p. 265.

The next station on the main line after Wegeleben (comp. Map) is **Halberstadt** (**Prinz Eugene; *Hôtel Royal; *Goldenes Ross,* unpretending; *Hartung's Restaurant*, in the Domplatz), an old town with 25,000 inhab. on the *Holzemme*, boasting of a considerable trade and several manufactories. The episcopal see, founded as early as the 9th cent., was suppressed in consequence of the Reformation. The town possesses a number of interesting mediæval edifices. The *wood-architecture of the 15th and 16th cent., with its projecting upper storeys, is still admirably preserved here. The chief of these buildings are in the *Market*, which is divided by the Rathhaus into the (E.) Fischmarkt and the (W.) Holzmarkt. The Gothic *Rathhaus* dates from the close of the 14th cent., but was restored in the 18th, when it received some Renaissance additions. The *Roland* (p. 88) here dates from 1435. The old *Episcopal Palace* opposite is now the custom-house. The late Gothic *Rathskeller* in the Holzmarkt, built in 1461, is the finest wooden structure in the town. In the Fischmarkt are *Tetzel's House* of 1529 and the *Schuhhof*, a rich Renaissance building of 1579.

The Gothic **Cathedral* (St. Stephen's), the most important edifice at Halberstadt, with a crypt of the 10th cent., was re-erected in 1181 after a fire, consecrated in 1220, and restored in 1850. The N. side and transept are particularly interesting.

Interior. Rich late Gothic screen separating the nave from the choir; above it, the Crucified with Mary and John, a *Wood-sculpture* of the 13th cent.; at the altar an *Alabaster-sculpture* of the same subject, dating from about 1500. Then a Crucifixion by *Raphon*, of 1509, as an altar-piece; several other pictures, richly adorned sacerdotal robes, and various antiquities.

The extensive Domplatz, planted with trees, is bounded on the W. side by the late Romanesque *Liebfrauenkirche*, erected in 1005—1284, recently restored. A number of figures in relief date from the period of the foundation, and a mural painting in a chapel from the 15th cent.

The canon *Herr v. Spiegel* and *Dr. Lucanus* possess collections of good modern pictures. — *Gleim's* collection of portraits of his friends, No. 17 at the back of the cathedral, is shown by the schoolmaster Jänicke. — The ornithological collection of the Oberamtmann *Herr Heine* is one of the most complete in Germany.

On 29th July, 1809, Halberstadt was the scene of a fierce struggle between the Duke of Brunswick with his black dragoons and a Westphalian regiment in the French service, which terminated in the defeat of the latter and their expulsion from the town. Several balls are built into the *Kühlingerthorthurm*, the gate leading to Quedlinburg, in commemoration of the battle.

17*

The *Spiegelsche Berge,* 1|2 hr. to the S., afford fine views. A monster cask here holds 28,000 gals. The *Gläserne Mönch,* 2 M. farther, and *Hoppelsberg* are also pleasant objects for an excursion.

To *Oschersleben,* see p. 62.

To *Blankenburg* (p. 267) branch-line in course of construction.

Beyond Halberstadt the train commands views of the slopes of the Harz to the l. From stat. *Heudeber - Dannstedt* a branch - line leads in 25 min. to *Wernigerode* (p. 273). Stat. *Wasserleben;* then **Vienenburg,** where the line unites with that from Brunswick and Börssüm (p. 255). The line divides here, one branch leading to *Harzburg* (p. 271), the other by *Oker* (p. 271), to *Goslar* (p. 269).

58. The Harz Mountains.

Plan. About ten days are required to explore the finest scenery of the Harz, which is now rendered accessible by a network of railways in every direction. The most suitable starting-points are *Ballenstedt* and *Goslar.* The following plan, which includes the most interesting points, may easily be extended or abridged with the aid of the maps and the information afforded by the Handbook. 1st Day. Ballenstedt, Selke, Alexisbad; 2nd. Gernrode, Suderode, Hexentanzplatz; 3rd. Weisser Hirch, Treseburg, Bodethal, Rosstrappe; 4th. Blankenburg, Rübeland, Wernigerode; 5th. Steinerne Renne, Brocken; 6th. Ilsethal, Ilsenburg, Burgberg near Harzburg; 7th. Environs of Harzburg, Okerthal, Goslar. — The chief places of interest in the *S. Harz* are Stolberg and the Josephshöhe, Hohnstein, Ilfeld, Walkenried (p. 256), and the Ravenskopf (p. 256).

Carriages. Two-horse about 5 Thlr. per day, exclusive of toll and fees (the latter 20 Sgr. per day); one-horse 3 1|2 Thlr.

Guides, unnecessary except on the less frequented routes, 20 Sgr. per day, and about 1 Sgr. per Engl. M. (5 Sgr. per Germ. M.) for return-fee.

Inns generally good and reasonable.

The **Harz,** the most northern mountain-chain in Germany, 56 M. in length, and 18 M. in width, belongs chiefly to Prussia. This range is entirely isolated, rising abruptly from the plain on every side, especially towards the N. W. and N. E. It is divided into the *Oberharz, Unterharz,* and *Vorharz.* The first of these embraces the W. region, with the towns of Lauterthal, Clausthal, and Andreasberg. The N. W. and S. W. slopes, with Goslar, Seesen, and Herzberg, are termed Vorharz, while the district to the E. of Wernigerode and Ellrich belong to the Unterharz. The Oberharz is furrowed by numerous dark, wooded ravines. The Unterharz affords a greater variety of picturesque scenery. The principal rock-formation is granite, overlying which are the more recent grauwacke and clay-slate.

Pleasant excursions in the Unterharz may be enjoyed in the early summer, but August and September are the best months for exploring the Brocken and the higher mountains of the Oberharz. Most of the interesting points may be attained by carriage, but pedestrians will also find ample scope for enjoyment, although this district has little pretension to grandeur.

The following excursions are so arranged as to enable the traveller to reach the railway from any given point in 1—2 days, and with reference also to the fact that visitors to the E. Harz usually start from Quedlinburg, Ballenstedt, Thale, or Nordhausen, while the W. Harz is generally explored from Goslar or Harzburg.

I. The Eastern Harz Mts.

a. *Quedlinburg.*

Railway to Thale and Wegeleben (Halberstadt, Magdeburg, Berlin) see p. 259. — *Diligence* to Ballenstedt three times daily; to Gernrode

e in.
that.
re
thie

lls a

Sur
t

Wolfshagen

Hahnenklee

Bocksmi
Wildemann

berhütte
Altenau
Wolfs

Salberfau
CLAUSTH

stfelde

Teufel.
Da
Jettenköhl
Hörd
Elbing

Barbis
Bartolfelde

Osterhag

THE HARZ MTS.

1 : 400,000

English Miles.

Georgsh

Der
eddenha

The Rocky Valley of the Bod

Scale 1:100,000

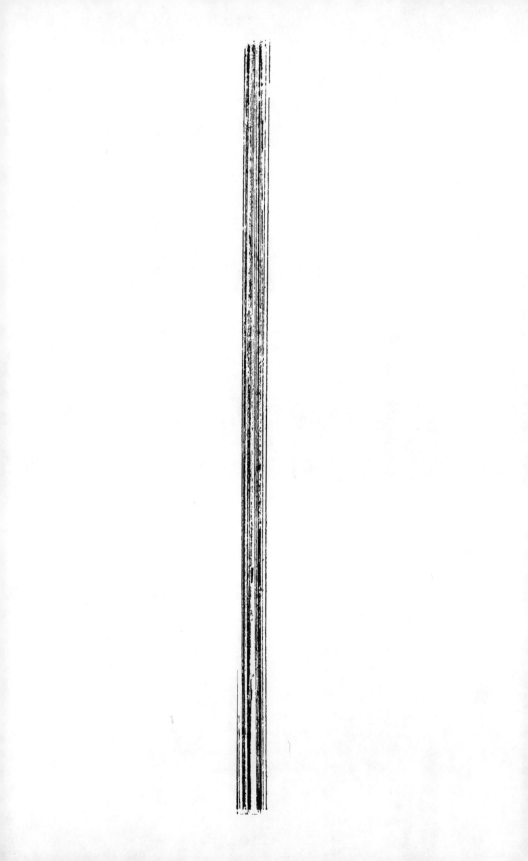

Alexisbad, Stolberg, and Nordhausen, once daily. — *Omnibus* to Suderode several times daily (2½ Sgr.).

Quedlinburg (463 ft. above the sea-level) (**Zum Bären*, in the Markt-Platz; *Kronprinz; Goldner Ring; Lamm.* Two-horse carriage to the Stubenberg or the Lauenburg 2 Thlr., the Victorshöhe and Tanzplatz 4, Victorshöhe and Alexisbad 4, Blankenburg and Ziegenkopf 6 Thlr., return included in each case; per day on the level country 3, half-day 2 Thlr.; one-horse about one-third less), an old agricultural town with 16,800 inhab., recently increased by the foundation of the suburb *Suderstadt*, lies on the *Bode*, 7 M. to the N.W. of the Harz Mts. It was founded by Henry the Fowler in 929 and became a favourite residence of the German emperors of the Saxon line. Down to 1477 it was a fortified Hanseatic town, after which it was under the protection of the Electors of Brandenburg. It is still an important looking place with walls, towers, and fosses, and is commanded on the W. side by the old Schloss and the abbey-church. The poet *Klopstock* (1724), *Gutsmuths*, the first teacher of gymnastics (1759), and the geographer *Ritter* (1779) were born here.

The *Rathhaus* in the market, in front of which rises a stone figure of Roland (p. 88), contains a remarkable collection of utensils in flint and bronze, weapons, instruments of torture, parchment records (e. g. fragments of the 'Itala', the first Latin translation of the Bible, of the 5th cent., and imperial charters of 1038 and 1134), seals, portraits, etc., and a kind of wooden cage in which the townspeople incarcerated Count Albert of Regenstein during 20 months (1336—38) for having infringed their municipal privileges.

The church of *St. Aegidius* contains some good old oil paintings. The modern *Gymnasium*, or grammar-school, possesses a valuable library. Following the street in the corner of the market-place, obliquely opposite the Bär Hotel and the Rathhaus, and afterwards turning to the l., the traveller crosses the *Finkenheerd*, a small Platz where Henry the Fowler is said to have received the deputation announcing his election to the imperial dignity, and reaches the *Schloss-Platz*, near the Schlossberg. The house in which Klopstock was born, situated in this Platz, has a jutting storey supported by two wooden columns. To the r. is the dwelling of the sacristan of the Schlosskirche, to whom application may now be made.

The *Schloss*, situated on a lofty sandstone rock, was once the seat of the abbesses of the secular and independent convent of Quedlinburg, which was founded by Otho the Great in 937 and afterwards attained to great prosperity, but declined in importance after it embraced the Reformation in 1539, and was at length suppressed in 1803. Countess Aurora of Königsmark, the mistress of Augustus the Strong of Saxony; and mother of Marshal Saxe, was abbess of Quedlinburg in 1704—18, and on her death in 1728 was interred in the abbey-church. The Schloss is now partially fitted up as a residence for the Crown-prince of Prussia. Adjacent to it is situated the

Abbey Church, or *Schlosskirche*, an edifice of great importance in the history of art. The body of the church was erected in 1021, the choir was altered in the 14th cent., and the whole restored in 1862. The crypt, which was the original church,. founded in the 10th cent., is built over an ancient mortuary chapel containing the tombs of Henry I., his wife Matilda, and his grand-daughter Matilda, the first abbess. The 'Zitter', or treasury, contains objects of great artistic and historical value, chiefly of the 10th cent., such as reliquaries, books of the Gospels, an episcopal crozier, the 'beard-comb' of Henry I., and one of the 'water-pots of Cana'. — Fine view of the town and environs from the terrace, which is shown by the castellan.

Opposite the Schlossberg rises the *Münzenberg*, with the ruins of the convent of St Mary.

The *Brühl*, a pleasant park to the S. W. of the town, not far from the Schlossberg, contains monuments to Klopstock and Ritter. — Within the precincts of a neighbouring farm is the crypt of the ancient monastery of *Wipertus*, which perhaps originally belonged to the palace of Henry I., and is the most ancient relic of Christian architecture in this district.

The nurseries and cloth-factories of Quedlinburg enjoy a high reputation.

Gernrode (p. 264) is 4³|₄ M. distant by the high road, *Ballenstedt*, 8 M. (diligence, see p. 260).

b. *Selkethal. Mägdesprung. Alexisbad. Victorshöhe. Gernrode.*
Suderode. Lauenburg.

Two Days. 1st. From Ballenstedt to the Falken Inn 1¹|₄ hr.,. visit to the Falkenstein 1¹|₂, to the Selkemühle 2³|₄, Mägdesprung 1¹|₂, Alexisbad 1 hr. — 2nd. To the Victorshöhe 1¹|₂, Gernrode 1¹|₂, Suderode ¹|₄, Lauenburg 1, Neinstedt ¹|₂, Thale or Hexentanzplatz 1—1¹|₂ hr.

Ballenstedt (689 ft. above the sea-level) (*Grosser Gasthof*, at the entrance to the Schlossgarten; *Stadt Bernburg*, in the Allee; *Weisser Schwan* and *Deutsches Haus* in the town, the latter unpretending. Two-horse carriage to Gernrode 1 Thlr. 20 Sgr., to the Selkemühle, Falke, or Quedlinburg 2, Alexisbad or Victorshöhe 3 Thlr.; one-horse about one-fourth less), the terminus of the railway in this direction (p. 258), a prettily situated town with 4000 inhab., who are chiefly engaged in agriculture, was formerly the residence of the Duke of Anhalt-Bernburg. A long avenue leads to the *Schloss* (generally closed) on a hill. Beautiful Schlosspark, with fine views of the mountains; on the N. side are the *Gegensteine*, a fragment of the 'devil's wall'.

A finger-post at the S. end of the town indicates the route to the r. to the Selkemühle (see below), and that to the l. to *Opperode* and *Meisdorf*. The latter is the high road to the Selkethal, but pedestrians follow it as far only as ($^1/_4$ M.) the first road diverging to the r., on which, a little way farther, is a direction-post on the l. indicating the way to the ($^1/_2$ hr.) forester's house of *Kohlenschacht*. The same road next leads through the wood to the ($^1/_2$ hr.) -inn *Zum Falken* (706 ft.) in the Selkethal, at the foot of the Falkenstein.

To the l., a little above the inn, a footpath to the l. ascends to *Schloss Falkenstein* (1083 ft.), situated on a lofty rock. The castle, which is well preserved and partially restored, contains old weapons, curiosities, etc.; fine view from the tower. A knight of Falkenstein is mentioned in Bürger's ballad of 'the pastor's daughter of Taubenheim', which is said to be founded on fact. The traveller now returns to the valley by the same path.

A good road ascends the picturesque *Selkethal* to the (5 M.) *Selkemühle*, or *Leinufermühle* (*Zur Burg Anhalt, unpretending), where it unites with the direct road from Ballenstedt (p. 262). On the hill, $^1/_2$ hr. to the S., are the scanty ruins of the *Burg Anhalt*. The road next leads to (4$^1/_2$ M.) Mägdesprung; but a slight digression to the *Meiseberg*, with a forester's house and fine view, $^1/_2$ hr. from the Selkemühle, is recommended; thence to Mägdesprung 1$^1/_4$ hr.

The foundries of **Mägdesprung** (968 ft.) (*Schmelzer*) are picturesquely placed at the junction of the Selkethal road with that from Ballenstedt to Stolberg. An obelisk on an eminence is to the memory of a Prince of Anhalt who founded the iron-works. The place is indebted for its name ('the maiden's leap') to the tradition that the daughter of a giant once sprang across the valley here, leaving her footprints, the *Mägdetrappe*, on the height behind the inn. An iron cross in the vicinity is to the memory of Duke Alexius. — Gernrode (p. 264) is 4$^1/_2$ M. distant.

About 2 M. farther up the attractive Selkethal lies the chalybeate **Alexisbad** (1034 ft.) (*Hotel Alexisbad; Goldne Rose*, reasonable), surrounded with pleasure-grounds.

The direct road from Alexisbad to (12 M.) Stolberg (p. 269) is by Strassberg and *Auerberg* (p. 269). The high road leads by *Harzgerode* (Schwarzer Bär), a small town with an old Schloss, 2 M. to the E.

The path to the Victorshöhe quits the road to the l. a few min. below the baths, and leads through wood to the (1$^1/_4$ hr.) Güntersberge and Gernrode road, which is followed for $^1/_4$ M. towards the r., and is then quitted to the l. by a path to the ($^1/_4$ hr.) *Victorshöhe* (1952 ft.), the summit of the *Ramberg*, surmounted by several huge blocks of granite termed the *Teufelsmühle*. (Inn at the forester's house.) Extensive prospect from the wooden tower, more picturesque than from the Brocken; the most conspicuous object being the Auerberg with the Josephshöhe.

A stone post by the Teufelsmühle indicates the descent to
the *right* to Friedrichsbrunnen, Alexisbad, Tanzplatz, Treseburg,.
and Thale; to the *left* to the Sternhaus, Mägdesprung, and Gernrode. The latter leads in 5 min. to the road from Güntersberge
(p. 263). The path to the Sternhaus crosses the road and continues
in the same direction, while the high road leads to (4½ M.)
Gernrode.

Gernrode (729 ft.) (**Stubenberg Inn*, moderate, see below;
Deutsches Haus and **Deutscher Kaiser* in the town; private apartments also procurable), a town with 2200 inhab., charmingly situated on the slope of the Stubenberg, 4½ M. from Quedlinburg, and
3¾ M. from Ballenstedt, attracts numerous visitors in summer.
The Romanesque **Abbey*. *Church* of the 10th cent., with its two
round W. towers, recently restored, is a picturesque feature in the
landscape. The tomb of the founder St. Gero, Margrave of Lusatia,
was restored in 1519. Romanesque cloisters on the S. side of the
church partially preserved.

The **Stubenberg*, or *Stufenberg* (922 ft.) (*Inn* at the top),
which rises above the town and may be ascended in ¼ hr., affords
a very picturesque view of Gernrode, Quedlinburg with its numerous towers, the Hoppelsberg near Halberstadt, the pinnacles of
the Teufelsmauer, the Regenstein, and the Blankenburger Schloss.

A few hundred yards to the W. of Gernrode lies

Suderode (493 ft.) (**Hôtel Behrens*, D. 17½, pension 1 Thlr.
20 Sgr.; **Hôtel Marquardt*, with pension and baths; **Belvedere,*
at the end of the village next to Gernrode; *Zum Heilsamen Brunnen*; *Beringer Bad*, at the W. end of the village; **Goldne Weintraube*, unpretending. *Omnibus* to Quedlinburg, see p. 261);
formerly an insignificant village, has recently become a favourite
watering-place on account of its salt-springs and its sheltered situation. Private apartments easily procured: Pretty walks to the
Preussen-Platz, the *Saalsteine*, the *Beringer Quelle*, and the *Tempel*
at the W. end of the village.

Several routes lead hence to the W. to (2 M.) Stecklenberg.
Pedestrians may take that which passes the Schulzenamt at Suderode, skirts the wood to the l. (view of Quedlinburg to the r.),
crosses the Quedlinburg road after 10 min., and then re-enters the
wood. At the entrance to the village of **Stecklenberg* a stone post
indicates the ascent to the l: to the (25 min.) **Lauenburg** (1149
ft.), a ruined castle with a tower commanding a fine view *(*Inn).*

A good road to the N. leads from Stecklenberg to (1½ M.) *Neinstedt,*
the nearest railway station. — The road to (3¾ M.) *Thale* (p. 265) diverges from the last named to the l! near the village (several finger-posts).
Those who prefer the circuit by the **Georgshöhe* (p. 267) should take
a guide as far as Thale, or to the Tanzplatz (10—15 Sgr.) Comp. Map,
p. 260. In this case they may proceed to the Georgshöhe from the Lauenburg direct, without descending to Stecklenberg.

c. Bodethal.: Rosstrappe: Hexentanzplátz. Treseburg.

One Day. From Thale in the Bodenthal ascend to the Teufelsbrücke, ¹|₂
hr.; ascend the Rosstrappe, 20 min.; inn, 10 min.; by the Herzogshöhe
and Wilhelmsblick to Treseburg 1³|₄ hr.; by the Weisse Hirsch to the
Hexentanzplatz 2¹|₂ hrs.; back to the station ³|₄ hr. — Or from the sta-
tion to the Tanzplatz 1¹|₄ hr.; Weisse Hirsch and Treseburg 1³|₄ hr. (Wil-
helmsblick and back ³|₄ hr.), through the Bodethal to the Jungfernbrücke
2 hrs.; then retrace steps for a few min. and ascend the Rosstrappe, ¹|₂
hr.; to the station 40 min. — *Guide* unnecessary, but desirable from Treseburg to the Weisse Hirsch and Tanzplatz (10—15 Sgr.).

The rocky **Valley of the Bode*, the finest point in the Harz Mts.,
presents a strikingly wild and picturesque scene, to which if possible more than a single day should be devoted.

At the entrance to the valley lies **Bahnhof Thale** (633 ft.), near
which a number of modern villas have sprung up. To the r. rise
the precipitous rocks of the Rosstrappe (p. 266); to the r. is the
Hexentanzplatz (p. 266).

Hotels. *ZEHNPFUND, opposite the station, R. 20, A. 5 Sgr.; *WALD-
KATER, pleasantly situated in the Bodethal, ¹|₂ M. from the station; HUBER-
TUSBAD, a salt-bath with pension on an island in the Bode, ¹|₄ M. from,
the station; ZUR BLECHHÜTTE, at the N. end of the Blechhütte, with gar-
den; ZUR KÖNIGSRUHE, ¹|₂ M. above the Waldkater; the two last unpre-
tending. Then the BRAUNE HIRSCH and others at the village of Thale,
1 M. from the station. — Inns on the *Rosstrappe* and *Hexentanzplatz*, see
p. 266. — **Restaurants** at the hotels; at the *Actienbrauerei*, ¹|₄ M.
from the station (good beer); *Rail. Restaurant.* — **Baths** below the Blechhütte. — **Carriages.** Two-horse, to Suderode 2 Thlr., Ballenstedt 3, Ballenstedt, Selkethal, Mägdesprung, Alexisbad, and Victorshöhe 8, Hexen-
tanzplatz 2, Rosstrappe 2; Tanzplatz, Treseburg, and Rosstrappe 4¹|₂,
Rübeland and Wernigerode 6, Stolberg 7, Nordhausen 9 Thlr. (return-
journey included in each case); gratuity 10—20 Sgr. — **Mule** per day 1²|₃,
half-day 1 Thlr., attendant included.

To Treseburg. A few paces to the r. of the station at Thale
lies the *Blechhütte*, a foundry on the r. bank of the Bode. The
road to the l. leads past the *Actienbrauerei* to the (¹/₂ M.) *Wald-
kater Inn* (696 ft.) (which may also be reached by a pleasant path
from the Hubertusbad on the l. bank). A very steep and fatiguing
path with steps ascends hence to the Hexentanzplatz (p. 266). The
traveller follows the road through the picturesque Bodethal. The
(¹/₂ M.) *Jungfernbrücke* crosses to the l. bank, where the inn *Zur
Königsruhe* is prettily situated, and is then carried round the foot
of the cliffs by two wooden galleries. Beyond the second is the
Schurre, a steep stony slope over which a zigzag path ascends to
the (¹/₂ hr.) Rosstrappe with its inn. A few paces farther is the
Teufelsbrücke at the entrance to the **Bodekessel*, a wild basin of
granite rocks through which the stream is precipitated. The road
then leads through beautiful woods to (4 M.)

Treseburg (916 ft.) *(*Weisser Hirsch; Wilhelmsblick)*, a village
beautifully situated at the confluence of the Bode and the *Lupbode*,
on a rocky eminence on which the castle of that name formerly
stood. A road between the inns leads to the (1¹/₂ M.) *Wilhelmsblick*
(view of the Bodethal), and through a short tunnel to the high road

which leads to the N. to Blankenburg, and to thé E. to the Rosstrappe. — An eminence opposite Tressburg with a dilapidated
wooden hut, termed the *Weisse Hirsch*, commands a charming view
of the village and environs. Thé direct footpath to it aṣcends to the
l., a short way beyond the bridge; a longer route through the *Tie-*.
fenbachthal quits the road farther on. Guide (10—15 Sgr.) desirable
as far as the Hexentanzplatz (sẹe Map).

From Treseburg to Blankenburg, 7¹|₂ M.; the road diverges to
the l., 1¹|₂ M. from the tunnel above mentioned, from that to the Ross-
trappe, and leads past *Wienrode* and *Cattenstädt.* To the r. rise the huge
sandstone masses of the *Heidelberg* (or 'devil's wall'). Pedestrians may
turn to the l. at the first bend in the road beyond the tunnel and proceed
through the wood by the (³|₄ hr.) forester's house of *Todtenrode* to (1 hr.)
Wienrode.

From Treseburg to Rübeland, see p. 268.

To the Rosstrappe. The above route from Thale to the
Rosstrappe by the Bodethal and the Schurre may be taken, or the
direct path (1hr.) may be preferred. In the latter case the traveller
passes between the buildings of the Blechhütte (p. 265) to the
bridge across the Bode, beyond which he turns to the r., and then,
near a second bridge (5 min.), ascends by a somewhat steep path
to the (½ hr.) *Gasthaus zur Rosstrappe*, near which is the *Bü-
lowshöhe.*

The *Rosstrappe (1317 ft.)*, 10 min. from the inn, is a granite
rock projecting like a bastion into the valley of the Bode, and rising
precipitously to a height of 650 ft. above the stream. It commands
an imposing view of the wild Bodethal and the distant plaiṅ as far
as Quedlinburg. The name ('horse's hoof-print') is derived from an
impression in the rock resembling a gigantic hoof, left there by
the horse of a princess, who, when pursued by a giant, is said to
have leaped across the valley at this point. To the r. is the *Schurre*
(p. 265).

Proceeding to the N.E. of the Rosstrappe Inn, the traveller may de-
scend in ¹|₄ hr. to the high road from Thale, which leads by the *Herzogs-
höhe* (view) and the Wilhelmsblick (see above) to (5 M.) *Treseburg* (see
above).

To the Hexentanzplatz. Near the brewery (p. 265) a
path diverges to the l. from the Bodethal road, skirts the hill, and
leads to the (10 min.) road from the village of Thale to Fried-
richsbrunn, which is ascended for about 1 M., and then quitted by
a flight of wooden steps to the r. In 20 min. more the *Gasthaus
auf dem Hexentanzplatz* is reached, the road to which diverges from
the high road ½ M. farther on.

The *Hexentanzplatz (1526 ft.)* is a rocky plateau opposite the
Rosstrappe, and 210 ft. higher, commanding a similar, and perhaps
still more striking view. To the l. in the distance rises the Brocken.'
The *Lavièreshöhe*, opposite the Schurre, ¼ hr. distant, is another
fine point of view. The path to it follows the slope to the r. and
after 10 min. turns to the r.

To Treseburg by the Weisse Hirsch. The path passes the Lavièreshöhe, and 10 min. beyond it turns slightly to the l., descending to
the Treseburg road. The latter soon passes ($3|4$ hr. from the Tanzplatz) a
monument to the forester *Pfeil*, a recumbent stag surrounded by six fine
beeches. At a bend in the road, $3|4$ M. farther, a stone post indicates the
path to the r. to the (20 min.) *Weisse Hirsch* (p. 266). Treseburg is reached
thence by returning by the same path for a few hundred paces, and then
descending.

From Thale to Suderode (p. 264) and *Gernrode* (p. 264), 6 M., a
pleasant road diverging to the r. from the Neinstedt road, about $3|4$ M. to
the E. of Thale, passing *Stecklenberg*, etc. (comp. p. 264). — The circuit
by the *Georgshöhe*, 1 hr. from Thale, and thence to ($1¼$ hr.) Stecklenberg
is recommended (guide desirable, 10—15 Sgr.). At the junction of the
road from the station with that from the village of Thale a direction-post
indicates the forest-path to the *Georgshöhe* (tavern), the wooden tower
on which commands a beautiful survey of the plain. A footpath descends
hence through the wood into the valley. After 20 min. a carriage-road
is reached; a ($1¼$ M.) cross-way with a finger-post near a plaster mill is then
passed, and Stecklenberg reached $3|4$ M. farther. — From the Hexentanz-
platz to the Georgshöhe 1 hr.; the road descending from the inn to the
S. E. to the high road is followed, the latter crossed, and a road to the
l. ascended.

d. Blankenburg. Rübeland. Elbingerode.

(From Treseburg to Blankenburg $7½$ M., see p. 266.) From Blankenburg to Regenstein and the Ziegenkopf 4—5 hrs., thence to Rübeland $1¾$
hr., Baumannshöhle $1½$ hr.; from Rübeland to Elbingerode 1 hr. (From
Elbingerode to the Brocken 3 hrs., see p. 274.) — The parts of the route
between Blankenburg and Rübeland and between Rübeland and Elbingerode or Elend (p. 268) are not sufficiently attractive to the pedestrian.

Blankenburg (749 ft.) (*Weisser Adler; *Römischer Kaiser;
Krone; Engel and *Stadt Braunschweig* unpretending; *Inn on
the Ziegenkopf, see below; carriage to Rübeland 3 Thlr.), a
town with 4000 inhab. and a garrison of 800 soldiers, the capital
of a district of Brunswick, and connected with Halberstadt by a
nearly completed branch-railway (p. 260), is picturesquely situated
on the slope of the hills and commanded by the lofty ducal Schloss.
The approach to the latter passes the handsome old *Rathhaus*, into
which five balls are built to commemorate the bombardment by Wallenstein during the Thirty Years' War. The *Schloss* (1097 ft.), which
is occupied by the duke in the shooting season, contains reminiscences of the empress Maria Theresa, who spent her youth here,
pictures, and various other objects of interest (castellan $½$—1 Thlr.).

To the N. of Blankenburg ($3/4$ hr.) rises the *Regenstein, or
Reinstein, a precipitous sandstone cliff, 240 ft. above the plain, on
the E. side of which a castle was erected by Emp. Henry the Fowler in 919 and afterwards considerably strengthened. In the Thirty
Years' War it was taken by Wallenstein and in 1757 by the French,
but was afterwards dismantled by Frederick the Great. Little of it
now remains except the vaults and embrasures hewn in the rocks.
Entrance by a rock-hewn gateway on the E. side. Admirable view,
especially towards Blankenburg (tavern at the top). — If time per-
mit, the traveller may return by ($½$ hr.) *Heimburg*, a village with
a castle (view), and the monastery of *Michaelstein*, 2 M. to the N.

of Blankenburg. — The. Heidelberg, or Teufelsmauer (p..266) is
1¹/₂ M. to the S. of Blankenburg:

To the Rosstrappe. The road to Treseburg is followed as far.
as (2 M.) *Wienrode*, a little beyond which an enclosure, is crossed ;
at a finger-post the wood is entered to the l., and in 1¹/₄ hr. the
Rosstrappe (p. 266) is reached.

To Rübeland, 6¹/₂ M. from Blankenburg. The road should
be followed as far as the (1¹M.) stone 18,₄, where a path to the r.
leads to the (10 min.) *Ziegenkopf* (1408 ft.) *(*Inn)*, an eminence,
commanding an admirable view of Blankenburg, the Regenstein,
the rocky pinnacles of the Teufelsmauer, and the extensive plain.
The road then ascends to (2 M.) the village of *Hüttenrode* (1598 ft.),
turns to the r., and gradually descends. At the (1¹/₂ M.) *Marmormühle* it reaches the picturesque wooded and rocky valley of the
Bode, which it ascends to (1¹/₂ M.) Rübeland.

The road crossing the Bode by the Marmormühle. descends, the valley
to *Altenbrack*, a village and foundry with a sulphur spring (pension 1¹/₂
Thlr.), from which a path leads to Treseburg in ³/₄ hr. By this route
Treseburg is about 10 M. distant from Rübeland. .

Rübeland (1290 ft.) (*Goldner Löwe; Grüne Tanne.* Carr. to
Schierke 3, Brocken 6, Ziegenkopf 2, Treseburg 3„ Thale 4 Thlr.),
a Brunswick village with foundries, lies in the valley of the Bode.
On the l. bank of the stream, 150 ft. above it, is the *Baumannshöhle* (ascent near the two inns), a stalactite cavern which has been
known for centuries. Opposite to it, on the r. bank, is the smaller
Bielshöhle, where the stalactites are finer. A visit to one of these
occupies an hour (1 pers. 7¹/₂, 2 pers. 10 , 3 pers. or more 4 Sgr.
each; Bengal lights 5 Sgr. each). The stalactites bear a number of
fanciful names, such as 'the lion', 'the city', and 'the praying nun'.
On a precipitous rock opposite the Tanne Inn rises the ruin of
Birkenfeld.

At Rübeland the road quits the valley of the Bode and ascends
a mill valley with curious rock formations to (3 M.) **Elbingerode**
(1536 ft.) *(*Blauer Engel; Goldner Adler),* an important iron-min-
ing town with 6000 inhab. Most travellers either begin the ascent
of the Brocken (p. 274) here or at **Elend** *(Deutsche Eiche),* 7 M.
farther (diligence thither in the afternoon).

To Wernigerode (p. 273), 6¹/₂ M., a diligence also runs. Pedestrians should walk over the Büchenberg (p. 274), by a path to the l., ¹/₂
M. from Elbingerode.

e. Ilfeld. Neustadt unter'm Hohenstein. Stolberg. Josephshöhe.

From *Nieder-Sachswerfen* to *Ilfeld* 3¹/₂ M., by Eichenforst to *Stolberg*
3¹/₄ hrs., by the Josephshöhe to *Alexisbad* 4 hrs.

From Nordhausen (p. 254) to Stolberg 14 M. (diligence
daily). The high road, at first uninteresting, unites near *Rottlebe-
rode* with that from *Rossla* (p. 254), and then ascends the picturesque *Tyrathal* towards the N.

Pedestrians should quit the railway at *Nieder-Sachswerfen*, to the N. of Nordhausen, and proceed by the road to (3½ M.) **Ilfeld** (837 ft.) *(Goldne Krone)*, a village at the entrance to the romantic *Behrethal.* The Præmonstratensian abbey founded here by a count of Hohnstein in 1196 was converted in 1544 into a school which still enjoys a high repute. A road to the W. leads hence by *Osterode* to (3 M.) the village of **Neustadt unter'm Hohnstein** (860 ft.) *(Amtsschenke)*, overshadowed by the ruins of the castle of *Hohnstein* (2040 ft.), the seat of the counts of that name who became extinct in 1693. A footpath leads hence by the (1¼ hr.) lofty ruin of *Ebersburg* to the *Eichenforst* forester's house (view) and (1 hr.)

Stolberg (945 ft.) *(*Freitag's Hôtel; *Eberhardt*, unpretending), a place with many antiquated houses, charmingly situated in the valley of the *Tyrabach*, and frequently visited as summer-quarters. On an eminence rises the Schloss of Count Stolberg, the proprietor of the district, with a valuable library and armoury, surrounded with pleasure grounds. Pleasing view from the *Thiergarten.* A chalybeate spring here attracts visitors.

To Harzgerode and Alexisbad, 10 M., by a road over the *Auerberg* (diligence daily). Pedestrians should quit the road, 2 M. from Stolberg, by a path leading to the r. to the (½ hr.) *Josephshöhe* (1976 ft.) (Inn), the wooden tower on which (100 ft. in height) commands a fine panorama. Thence by *Strassberg* and the *Victor - Friedrichs - Silberhütte*, and down the Selkethal to (3 hrs.) *Alexisbad* (p. 263).

II. The Western Harz.

a. *Goslar. Okerthal.*

Spend half-a-day at Goslar, take train to *Oker*, walk through the valley to (2 hrs.) *Romkerhalle*, and by the *Ahrendsberger Klippen* to (4 hrs.) *Harzburg.*

Goslar (844 ft.) (*Kaiserworth*, an old Gothic house in the market, see below; *Hôtel de Hanovre*, Breite - Str.; *Paul's Hotel*, near the station; *Römischer Kaiser*, in the market), the terminus of the railway (p. 256) in this direction, an ancient town with 9000 inhab., lies on the *Gose*, on the N. side of the Harz, at the foot of the metalliferous Rammelsberg (p. 271). The numerous towers and partially preserved ramparts impart an air of importance to the place.

Goslar was founded at the beginning of the 10th cent. and soon acquired importance in consequence of the discovery of valuable silver mines in the vicinity (p. 271). It became a favourite residence of the Saxon and Salic emperors, one of whose most extensive palaces was situated here. The attachment of the citizens to Henry IV., who was born at Goslar in 1050, involved the town in the misfortunes of that monarch. In 1188 the diet was held at Goslar under Frederick Barbarossa at which the Guelph Henry the Lion was condemned to three years' exile. In 1204 the town, which adhered steadfastly to the Hohenstaufen, was taken and destroyed by Otho IV., the rival of Philip. After a slow recovery from this disaster, it became a member of the Hanseatic League, and prospered about the year 1500. In 1802 it lost its independence for the first time and was annexed to Prussia. From 1716—66 it belonged to Hanover.

Near the station, to the l., is the handsome Romanesque church
of the monastery of *Neuwerk*, of the close of the 12th cent.; interesting choir; picture of the 13th cent. in the apse. Opposite to it
rises the *Paulsthurm*, a remnant of the old fortifications. The street
between these leads to the antiquated.*Market*, with the Rathhaus and Kaiserworth, and adorned with a large fountain basin in
metal.

The *Rathhaus*, a simple Gothic edifice of the 15th cent., with an
arcade beneath (entrance by the steps, round the corner to the l.;
visitors ring in the passage), contains a hall adorned in 1490 with
*paintings by Wohlgemuth and his pupils. Interesting old books of
the Gospels, charters, instruments of torture, and other curiosities
are also shown. A small chapel adjacent contains a richly decorated
tankard of 1407 and two chalices of 1519. Near the staircase is the
'Beisskatze', a kind of cage in which shrews used to be incarcerated.

The *Kaiserworth*, formerly a guild-house, now an inn, with an
arcade below, dates from the end of the 15th cent., and is adorned
with statues of eight emperors. Passing between the Rathhaus and
the Kaiserworth, the traveller reaches the *Marktkirche*, a late Romanesque church, with Gothic choir and aisle subsequently added.
The library of the church contains MSS. of Luther and others. The
Brusttuch, opposite the W. portal of the church, a curious old house
of the 16th cent., restored in 1870, is adorned with representations
of satyrs in carved wood.

From the Marktkirche a street leads to the l. (S.) to a large
open space where some venerable ruins still bear testimony to the
ancient grandeur of Goslar.

The so-called *Domcapelle* was once the vestibule of the N. portal of a celebrated cathedral of St. Simon and St. Jude, which was
founded by Henry III. in 1039, and taken down in 1820. Over the
portal are figures of Emp. Conrad II., his wife Gisela, and SS. Matthew, Simeon, and Jude.

It contains numerous relics of the decorations of the ancient cathedral, sculptures, and various curiosities, among which may be mentioned the '*Crodo Altar*', an oblong box made of plates of brass, borne by
four stooping figures, and containing numerous round apertures. It was
formerly supposed to be an altar of the idol Crodo, but was probably a
reliquary, adorned with precious stones. The chapel is open the whole
day in summer. Fee for 1—2 pers. 5, 3—4 pers. 7^1|$_2$, 5—6 pers. 10 Sgr.;
the custodian also keeps the key of the Kaiserpfalz.

On an eminence to the r. rises the *Kaiserpfalz*, the oldest secular edifice in Germany, founded by Henry II. and extended by
Henry III (1039—56). It consists of the Saalbau and the chapel of
St. Ulrich, formerly connected by a wing. The upper floor of the
Saalbau is occupied by the spacious imperial hall (56 yds. long, 17
yds. wide, 35 ft. high), which looks towards the Platz with seven
massive round-arched windows, and was formerly approached by a
broad flight of steps. The *Chapel of St. Ulrich*, a double chapel in
the form of a Greek cross, dating from the close of the 11th cent.,

was destined for the domestic worship of the imperial court. The palace was burned down in 1289 and afterwards rebuilt, but disfigured by alterations and additions. It is now undergoing judicious restoration.

The *Zwinger*, a round tower at the Breitenthor, on the S. E. side of the town, now containing a tavern, commands a fine survey of the town. A walk through the streets, which contain a number of mediæval dwelling houses, and round the ramparts is recommended.

The *Farbensümpfe*, ponds fed by streams from the Rammelsberg, yield the ochre dye of this neighbourhood. A grotto and chapel hewn in the *Klus*, an isolated sandstone rock in the vicinity, are said to have been founded by Agnes (d. 1077), wife of Emp. Henry III.

The **Rammelsberg** (2041 ft. above the sea-level), which rises above the town on the S., has for eight centuries yielded gold (5—6 *lbs.* per annum only), silver (25 *cwt.* per annum), copper, lead, zinc, sulphur, vitriol, and alum, a variety of minerals seldom found within such narrow limits. The mountain is honey-combed with shafts and galleries in every direction, but the output of the mines now barely repays the working. The mining operations are facilitated by the peculiar process called 'Feuersetzen'. Large heaps of wood are piled against the hard clay-slate which contains the ore, set on fire, and allowed to burn for 24 hrs. The rock is thus rendered brittle, and is then easily excavated. The fires are lighted on Sunday mornings, and kept burning till the following morning. The mines, which present no difficulty, may be explored daily between 6 a. m. and 4 p. m., except Saturdays when they are not shown after 1 p. m., and Sundays, when they can only be seen about 5 a. m.. Tickets (1 pers. 15, for 2 pers. or more 10 Sgr. each) procured at the 'Bergamt', or office of the superintendent at Goslar (opposite the Rathhaus), must be shown at the entrance to the mines, where visitors are provided with miners' clothes and lamps. Fee to the guide 5—7¹⁄₂ Sgr.

On the road to Harzburg 3 M. to the W. of Goslar, lies the village and railway-station of **Oker** (679 ft.) *(Lüer's Hôtel)*, which belongs half to Brunswick and half to Prussia, and possesses important foundries. It is situated at the entrance to the wild **Okerthal*, the road ascending which affords picturesque views of the precipitous cliffs. The road crosses the Oker by the (6 M.) *Romkerbrücke* (*Hôtel Romkerhalle) and leads to (6 M.) Clausthal (p. 275). A finger-post to the l., 1 M. from the inn, indicates the route across a bridge to the (³⁄₄ hr.) *Ahrendsberger Klippen* (p. 272).

b. Harzburg. Ilsenburg. Wernigerode.

Two Days (or, including the Brocken, three days). Harzburg and environs 5—6 hrs.; by the Rabenklippen to Ilsenburg 3¹⁄₂ hrs.; Ilsenstein and waterfalls 2¹⁄₂ hrs.; by the Plessenburg and through the Steinerne Renne to Wernigerode 3 hrs.; environs of Wernigerode 3—4 hrs.

Harzburg. **Hotels.** *BRAUNSCHWEIGER HOF, *LINDENHOF, both at the station, 1 M. from the foot of the Burgberg. — *BELLEVUE and *BELVEDERE, new; *JULIUSHALLE, with salt-baths and pension; all these are at the foot of the Burgberg. A number of pensions in the vicinity. — *BURGBERG HOTEL, on the hill, 40 min. from the Juliushalle, R. 25, D. 20 Sgr., where a flag is hoisted when rooms are still to be had; fine view. — Private apartments easily procured. — **Carriages.** Two-horse, from the station to the Burgberg 1²⁄₃ Thlr., to the Radaufall 1¹⁄₆, Goslar 2, Ilsenburg 2¹⁄₂, Romkerhalle and back 3, Wernigerode 4, St. Andreasberg or

Clausthal 5, Brocken 6 Thlr.; return-fare one-third or one-half more;
for waiting 10 Sgr. per hour. Two-horse carr. 5 Thlr. per day, tolls and
gratuity (20 Sgr.) extra. One-horse carr. one third or one-fourth cheaper.
—Mule to the Burgberg 15, attendant 6 Sgr.; Radaufall 20, attendant
7¹|₂ Sgr.; Ilsenburg 1 Thlr. and 12¹|₂ Sgr.; to Goslar the same; to the
Brocken 1¹|₂ Thlr. and 20 Sgr.; per hour 15 and 5 Sgr.; per day 1 Thlr.
10 and 15 Sgr. — **Guides** per day 15, or including 40 lbs. of luggage, 20
Sgr.; food 7¹|₂ Sgr. extra; return fee 6¹|₄ Sgr. per Germ. M. (about 11|₄
Sgr. per Engl. M.).

Harzburg, or *Neustadt-Harzburg* (771 ft.), the terminus of the
railway (p. 260) in this direction, at the entrance to the *Radauthal,*
consists of the villages of *Neustadt, Bündheim, Schulenrode, Schle-
wecke,* and the *Burgberg,* connected by numerous villas and gardens,
and is a favourite summer resort, with pleasant promenades. The finest
point in the environs is the ***Burgberg** (1556 ft.), crowned with
the scanty ruins of the Harzburg, a castle of Emp. Henry IV., which
commands an admirable prospect. The road to the castle passes the
salt-baths of *Juliushalle* (p. 271), a little beyond which are the
pretty *Unter den Eichen* promenades. The road leads thence to
the (1¹/₂ M.) *Radaufall,* an artificial cascade, from which the visitor
may return by a path to the r. a little below the fall, crossing the
Schmalenberg (view from the *Wilhelmsblick*). The (¹/₂ hr.) *Elfenstein* (1280 ft.), the *Kästenklippe,* ³/₄ M. farther, and the *Silberhorn,*
near the Elfenstein, are attractive points on the W. side of the
valley; while the *Sennhütte* (whey) on the Mittelberg, the (1 hr.)
Molkenhaus (1625 ft.), a chalet and tavern, and the (³/₄ hr.) *Sachsenhöhe* with its tower are favourite spots on the E. side.

From Harzburg to (5 M.) *Oker* (p. 271) and Romkerhalle (p. 271)
an omnibus runs twice daily; to (8¹/₂ M.) *Ilsenburg* a diligence
daily. Pedestrians will prefer the following routes: —

To the *Okerthal* by the *Ahrendsberger. Klippen* 4 hrs. — A little
above the Juliushalle ascend the *Breitenberg* and follow the broad forest
path on the hill, indicated by the letter A marked on the trees, as far as
the (2¹|₂ hrs.) *Ahrendsberger Forsthaus* (*tavern). Here ask for the path
to the *Ahrendsberger Klippen* (*view of the Okerthal), there and back
1 hr.; then, in descending into the Okerthal, follow the path to the r. a
little below the Forsthaus, which leads to the (¹|₂ hr.) bridge mentioned
at p. 271.

To *Ilsenburg* by the *Rabenklippen* 3 hrs., guide desirable. A few
minutes before the top of the Burgberg is reached, the broad 'Kaiserweg'
diverges from the road to the E. (The name is derived from a tradition
that Emp. Henry IV. fled in this direction when his castle was captured by
the Saxons.) This road leads to the (10 min.) *Säperstelle,* a spot with a
bench, where direction-posts indicate the way to the l. to the *Sachsenhöhe*
(see above), to the r. to the Molkenhaus and the Brocken (p. 274), and in a
straight direction to the *Kattenäse* and the (³|₄ hr.) *Rabenklippen* (the
path to the latter, marked RK, turning to the r. towards the end), where
a fine *view of the Eckerthal and the Brocken is enjoyed. Then return to
the point where the path turned to the r., and descend by a zigzag path
towards the N. E. to the (20 min.) *Eckerthal,* from which a road leads to
(1¹/₂ M.) *Eckerkrug.* Thence by a forest path to the r. (S. E.) to Ilsenburg.

Ilsenburg (781 ft.) (**Drei Rothe Forellen,* with pleasant garden; *Deutscher Hof.* Carriage to Harzburg 1¹/₂, to the Brocken
6, mule to the Brocken 1¹/₂ Thlr.), a busy village at the mouth of

the Ilsethal, with *Iron Works* of Count ·Stolberg-Wernigerode, where artistic and other objects ·in cast iron are manufactured , is commanded ·by the handsome Romanesque *Schloss* of the count, on an -eminence to the S..E.

To the Rabenklippen 2³|₄ hrs. — The path diverges to the l. from the road before the village is quitted; at the last houses cross the bridge to the r.; then traverse the meadow to the l. and enter the wood, following the path marked E; ¹|₂ hr. *Eckerkrug* (see above). Next ascend the road in the valley of the *Ecker* to a (1¹|₂ M.) finger-post indicating the zigzag path to the *Stötterthal* and the *Rabenklippen* (see also above).

The *Ilsethal, one of the most beautiful valleys in the Harz, presents a succession of remarkably picturesque rock and forest scenes, enlivened by a series of miniature cascades, and rendered still more interesting by the numerous romantic legends attaching to it. Road through the valley p. 274, footpath see below. The former leads to the (1¹/₂ M.) foot of the *Ilsenstein*, a precipitous buttress of granite, rising to a height of 500 ft. above the valley. From the *Prinzess Ilse* tavern at the foot several paths lead to the (¹/₂ hr.) summit; where an iron cross has been erected to some of the fallen warriors of 1813—15 (fine view). The best survey of the Ilsenstein itself is obtained from the benches, a few hundred paces above the tavern. The road, which continues to accompany the stream and its pretty *Waterfalls* for upwards of 3 M., is recommended to the lover of the picturesque; even if the ascent of the Brocken is not contemplated. — A footpath direct from Ilsenburg to (³/₄ hr.) the top of the *Ilsenstein* diverges from the road to the l., a few paces beyond the village, and crosses a ·bridge.

In descending from the Ilsenstein a footpath to the r., marked P and Pl., and also a road diverging to the l. from the road in the Ilsethal, lead to the (³|₄ hr.) *Plessenburg*, a forester's house and a favourite point for picnics. Road hence, marked St. R., to the (1¹|₂ M.) Wernigerode road, which ascends to the r. to (1¹|₂ M.) the Steinerne Renne. — Another road from the Plessenburg to Wernigerode leads by Altenrode.

The road from Ilsenburg to (5³/₄ M.) *Wernigerode* leads by *Drübeck*, with its ancient but much altered Romanesque church, and *Altenrode*. Diligence twice, omnibus several times daily.

Wernigerode (771 ft.) (**Weisser Hirsch* and *Gothisches Haus* in the market; *Deutsches Haus*, Burg-Strasse; *Lindenberg*, on the Lindenberg, with beautiful view; *Goldner Hirsch*, in the suburb *Nöscherode)*, with a loftily situated *Schloss* (extensive library) and park of the Count of Stolberg Wernigerode, lies picturesquely on the slopes of the Harz Mts., at the confluence of the *Zilligerbach* and the *Holzemme*. The *Rathhaus* of the 14th cent. and many of the houses are picturesque old Gothic structures of wood. The *Thiergarten* or park, the *Hartenberg*, the *Christianenthal* near the suburb *Nöscherode*, and the *Lindenberg* to the·S. of the town afford beautiful walks. — Railway to *Heudeber*, see p. 260.

The most attractive excursion from Wernigerode is to the *Steinerne Renne*. The road ascends the valley of the *Holzemme*, by

Friedrichsthal, to (2 M.) **Hasserode** *(Hôtel Hohnstein; Zur Steinernen
Renne)*, a village much visited as a summer resort, to which an
omnibus runs frequently from Wernigerode. At the entrance to the
village a finger-post indicates the road to the l. to Schierke, Hohnstein, and Hohne, and to the r. to the Steinerne Renne. Pedestrians
may quit the road a little farther by a path to the l., past the inn Zur
Steinernen Renne. The road now ascends in the beautiful, pine-
clad valley of the Holzemme, or *Steinerne Renne, which gradually
becomes more imposing. At the highest bridge, 6 M. from Hasserode, there is a small inn. A little beyond it a broad path to the l.
leads to the Hohenstein (see below), and one to the r. to the Plessenburg (p. 272) in 1 hr. From this inn to the Brocken, see
below.

The traveller may (with a guide), by the path just mentioned, ascend
the (1 hr.) *Hohenstein* (view), and proceed by the *Hohneklippen* (2977 ft.) to
the Schierke road, or to *Hohne,* and then return by the road to Hasserode.

To Elbingerode, 7 M. from Wernigerode, diligence once daily,
through the suburb of *Nöscherode* and up the valley of the *Zilligerbach.*
A finger-post 3¹|₂ M. from Wernigerode indicates a path to the r. to the
Büchenberg, a fine point of view (inn). Thence to Elbingerode ¹|₂ hr.
(comp. p. 268).

To Blankenburg (p. 267), 10 M. from Wernigerode, diligence once
daily.

To Halberstadt (p. 259), 13 M. from Wernigerode, diligence three
times daily.

c. *The Brocken.*

Ascent from *Harzburg* by the Molkenhaus 4¹|₂ hrs., from *Ilsenburg* by
the Ilsethal (road) 10 M., from *Wernigerode* by the Steinerne Renne 4¹|₂
hrs., from Elbingerode by Schierke 3¹|₂ hrs., from *Elend* by Schierke (road)
7¹|₂ M., from *St. Andreasberg* 5 hrs.

From Harzburg (p. 271) 4¹|₂ hrs. — To the *Molkenhaus* see p. 272.
Ascend thence by the straight path towards the S.; then descend slightly
to the (¹|₄ hr.) *Dreiherrnbrücke* across the *Ecker*; after 10 min. avoid ascent
to the l.; 10 min., diverge to the l.; 3 min., to the r.; ascend the steep
Pesekenkopf; 7 min., a small meadow; 10 min. the *Scharfenstein* cattle-
shed. Here pass between the two houses and follow the path; after ¹|₄ hr.
turn to the r.; 5 min., a small circular plateau; ¹|₄ hr., the road is crossed.
the *Pflasterstoss* and *Kleine Brockenklippen* rocks are passed, and the *Brockenhaus* (p. 275) soon reached.

From Ilsenburg (p. 272) 3¹|₂ hrs., more picturesque than from Harz-
burg. To the Ilsenstein 2 M., see p. 273. At a finger-post, 3 M. farther,
the route to the Brocken diverges to the r.; after ³|₄ hr. another post in-
dicates two paths to the Brocken. That to the l. leads through wood to
an open space where charcoal-burners pursue their avocations (boy to
show the way 3—5 Sgr.). Then ascend to the r., skirting the brook for
20 min., and again enter the wood; ³|₄ hr., union of the Harzburg and
Ilsenburg paths; 12 min., *Brockenhaus* (see below).

From Wernigerode (p. 273) through the Steinerne Renne 4¹|₂ hrs.
— To the highest bridge in the valley (see above), 2¹|₂ hrs.; thence ascend
the course of the *Holzemme* nearly to its (¹|₂ hr.) source, where some of
the charcoal-burners will point out the way in case of doubt. The same
direction is pursued, and the *Renneckenberg* (view) traversed; 10 min.,
the Brocken road is reached, and the summit is attained in 1 hr. more.

From Elbingerode (p. 268) 3¹|₂ hrs. — A little way from the vil-
lage the footpath enters the wood to the r. and at (1¹|₂ hr.) *Schierke* reaches
the road described below.

From Elend (p. 268) 7¹|₂ M. — The road diverges to the r. from the high road at a turnpike and leads to (1½ M.) *Schierke* (1850 ft.), a scattered village, the highest among the Harz Mts. The road crosses the bridge and ascends to the l. The neighbouring rocks derive various whimsical names from their grotesque forms. To the r., above, are the *Hohneklippen;* to the l., looking back, the *Schnarcher* on the opposite *Buhrenberg.* Occasional short cuts are indicated by finger-posts. An iron finger-post (3 M.) is reached at the union of this road with that from Ilsenburg. To the top 3 M. more, but the last bend of the road may be cut off by a footpath.

From *Andreasberg* to the Brocken, 5 hrs., see p. 276.

The **Brocken**, or *Blocksberg,* the *Mons Bruct̆erus* of the Romans, 3417 ft. above the sea-level, forming together with its neighbours the *Brockengebirge,* the nucleus of the Harz, rises to a considerable height above the lofty plateau of the latter, and is the highest mountain in Central Germany. Vegetation becomes very scanty near the summit and no trees grow within 100 ft. of it. *Inn at the top (R. 20, B. 10, D. 15, A. 7½ Sgr.).

The *Tower* commands an extensive *view in clear weather, the towers of Magdeburg, Leipsic, Erfurt, Gotha, Cassel, Göttingen, Hanover, and Brunswick being visible, but an unclouded horizon is unfortunately rare. The summit should be attained before sunset, in order that the traveller may enjoy two opportunities of obtaining a view. Although the Brocken attracts numerous visitors, it is by no means one of the finest points of the Harz Mts.; these are rather to be sought for on the E. and S. slopes.

Several grotesque blocks of granite to the S. of the tower have received the names of *Devil's Pulpit, Witches' Altar,* etc. The aboriginal inhabitants of this district are said to have offered human sacrifices here to Wodan, and tradition points out this spot as the meeting-place of the witches on St. Walpurgis' Night, the eve of Mayday.

The *Brocken Spectre*, a remarkable optical phenomenon occasionally observed here, has doubtless contributed to confirm the superstitions attaching to the mountain. When the summit is unclouded, and the sun is on one side, and mists rise on the other, the shadows of the mountain and the objects on it are cast in gigantic proportions on the wall of fog, increasing or diminishing according to circumstances. This spectacle is, however, rarely witnessed, occurring half-a-dozen times annually at most.

d. *Clausthal. Andreasberg.*

From Goslar to *Clausthal* 13 M., thence to *St. Andreasberg* 13 M., or to *Elbingerode* 18½ M. (diligence in each case).

The road ascends from Goslar through an uninteresting district and finally passes several large ponds.

Clausthal (1840 ft.) *(*Krone; Rathhaus; Stadt London)*, the most important place in the Oberharz, and the seat of the mining authorities, with *Zellerfeld* (*Deutsches Haus*), which is separated from it by the *Zellbach,* forms a single town with 14,000 inhab., chiefly miners. Country bleak and sterile. Most of the houses are of wood. The *Bergschule,* in the market, contains a considerable collection of models and minerals.

Mines. The *Caroline* and *Dorothea* mines, 1¹|₂ M. from Clausthal, are less easy of access than those of the Rammelsberg. Permission from the superintendent necessary. The *Georg Wilhelm* mine is 2135 ft. in depth. The mines around Clausthal are drained by means of the *Georgsstollen*, a channel 6 M. long, terminating near *Grund.*

To Gittelde (p. 256), 11 M., a diligence runs daily, passing the extensive *Frankenscharner Silberhütte* (silver-foundry) and the small town of **Grund** (*Rathskeller*), prettily situated and visited as a bath.

Pleasant walk from Clausthal through the valley of the *Innerste* by *Wildemann* to (3¹|₂ hrs.) *Lautenthal* (Rathhaus), and thence over the hills in 2 hrs. to *Seesen* (railway station, p. 256).

To Osterode, another railway-station, 8³|₄ M. from Clausthal, a diligence runs twice daily, passing several picturesque points, e. g. the inn at the foot of the *Heiligenstock*, 1¹|₄ M. beyond the *Ziegelhütte* (*Inn); it then descends to the straggling village of *Lerbach* and *Osterode* (p. 256). The old road is shorter for pedestrians.

From Clausthal to Andreasberg 13 M. The road crosses the bleak lofty plateau of the Oberharz. The (3 M.) *Sperberhaier Damm* supplies the mines of Clausthal with water. At the (7 M.) *Sonneberger Wegehaus* the road turns to the S., while that in a straight direction leads to Braunlage (p. 268). Pedestrians may here quit the diligence and follow the latter road to the *Oderteich*, an artificial reservoir, whence a *footpath leads to Andreasberg in 1¹/₂ hr. along a conduit termed the *Rehberger Graben*. Fine view to the l. of the rocky bed of the *Oder*, to the r. of the precipitous *Rehberger Klippen*.

Andreasberg (1825 ft) (*Rathhaus), a small town situated in a lofty and bleak region, between steep, scantily wooded slopes, was formerly a very important mining place. The *Samson* silver-mine, the deepest in the Harz Mts. (2871 ft.) is easy of access. — Diligence by *Braunlage* to (18¹/₂ M.) *Elbingerode* (p. 268) daily. — To stat. *Lauterberg* (p. 256), 12 M., diligence twice daily.

To Herzberg (p. 256), 9 M., a pleasant road leads by (3³|₄ M) *Sieber* (Inn) and through the pretty *Sieberthal.*

To the Brocken. The road leads by *Braunlage, Elend,* and *Schierke* (p. 275); the footpath, far more attractive, by the *Rehberger Graben* to the (2 hrs.) *Oderteich* (see above), and thence by *Oderbrück* (*forester's inn) to the (3 hrs.) summit (p. 275).

59. From Cassel to Frankfort on the Main.

Railway in 4¹|₂—8 hrs.; fares 5 Thlr. 12, 3 Thlr. 18, 2 Thlr. 8 Sgr. (From *Berlin* to Frankfort by express in 11 hrs.; fares 16 Thlr. 1, 11 Thlr. 15 Sgr.).

From Berlin to *Oschersleben* and *Kreiensen*, see pp. 59—62; to *Cassel* p. 85.

At stat. *Wilhelmshöhe* the line intersects the avenue (p. 83). **Guntershausen** (*Rail. Restaurant; *Bellevue)* is the junction of the Eisenach (R. 46) line. The Frankfort line crosses the *Edder.* Near *Gensungen* the abrupt *Heiligenberg* rises to the l., and the lofty tower of the *Felsberg* (1375 ft.) to the r.; farther on, at the confluence of the *Schwalm* and the Edder, stands the *Altenburg.* To the r. in the background is the ruin of *Gudensberg.* The picturesque

valley of the *Schwalm* is now entered. *Wabern* is the station for
Wildungen, a watering-place 7¹/₂ M. to the W. Stations *Borken,*
Zimmersrode, and *Treisa,* where the Schwalm is quitted. The ruin
of *Ziegenhain* is 1¹/₂ M. to the E.

On a wooded eminence to the l., beyond stat. *Neustadt,* lies the
ancient town of *Amöneburg,* the venerable church of which was
founded by St. Boniface. At *Kirchhain* the line approaches the
Ohm, which falls into the Lahn near Marburg, and soon afterwards
crosses the Lahn.

Marburg *(*Hôtel Pfeiffer; *Ritter; *Rail. Restaurant),* a small
town with 8500 inhab., on the *Lahn,* is charmingly situated in a
semicircle round the precipitous Schlossberg. The *University,* now
attended by 350 students, was the first founded (by Philip the
Generous, in 1527) without papal privileges.

The chief boast of Marburg is the **Church of St. Elizabeth,*
erected in 1235—83 in the purest Gothic style, and restored in
1860, affording an admirable example of the impressiveness of this
style without the adjunct of rich decoration. W. towers 310 ft. in
height.

Soon after the death of *St. Elizabeth* (in 1231, in her 24th year), daughter
of King Andreas II. of Hungary, and wife of the Landgrave Lewis of
Thuringia, the church was erected over her tomb, which attracted mul-
titudes of pilgrims from every part of Europe. The Emp. Frederick II.,
one of these devotees, caused a crown of gold to be placed on the head of
the saint, whose remains were deposited in a richly decorated silver-gilt
sarcophagus. The Landgrave Philip (founder of the university), in order
to put an end to the pilgrimages, caused the bones to be removed and interred in an unknown spot in the church. The sarcophagus is still preserved in the sacristy near the high altar. In 1810 the French carried it
off to Cassel and despoiled it of its jewels, but it was restored to Marburg
in 1814. The mortuary chapel is adorned with a carved representation of
the Coronation of the Virgin, and winged pictures by Dürer (?); in the
interior the Nativity and Death of Mary; ancient carving and pictures by
Dürer at the four side-altars. Numerous monuments of Hessian princes
and knights of the Teutonic Order are preserved in the S. transept.

The *Lutheran Church,* on a terrace commanding a fine view,
a finely proportioned structure of the 15th cent., contains several
monuments of Landgraves and other princes. — The *Rathhaus* was
erected in 1512.

The extensive and well preserved *Schloss* (876 ft.), to which a
steep road ascends from the church of St. Elizabeth in 20 min.,
was a residence of the princes of Hessen in the 15th and 16th centuries, and afterwards a state-prison. It is now judiciously restored
and contains the valuable Hessian archives. The fine Gothic chapel
and the Rittersaal are worthy of inspection. In the latter the famous disputation between Luther, Zwingli, Melanchthon, and other
reformers took place in 1529. They met, on the invitation of Philip
the Generous, with a view to adjust their differences regarding the
Eucharist, but the attempt proved a failure owing to the tenacity
with which Luther adhered to the precise words, 'Hoc *est* corpus
meum', which he wrote in large letters on the wall. Beautiful views

from the Schloss and *Bücking's Garden*, at the Schlossthor. The traveller may then descend to the town by the other side (¹/₂ hr.), where several fine views are enjoyed.

Environs. Good paths, provided with finger-posts, lead to a number of other beautiful points of view. The *Spiegelslust* (1201 ft.), a height above the station, is ascended in 40 min.; morning lights most favourable. On the l. bank of the Lahn are the (1 hr.) *Lichte Küppel* (1203 ft.) and the *Frauenberg* (1240 ft.) with a ruined castle. A pleasant, shady road leads to the latter in 2 hrs. (carr. 3 Thlr.). — On the r. bank, above the church of St. Elizabeth, rises the oak-clad *Kirchspitze* (1050 ft.), from which forest paths lead to the quarries of *Wehrda*. The *Dammelsberg*, at the back of the Schloss is embellished with pleasure-grounds. To the S., beyond the village of *Ockershausen* in *Dreyer's Quelle* (tavern and view), 2 M. from the town.

The line follows the fertile valley of the *Lahn* till Giessen is reached. On an eminence beyond stat. *Fronhausen*, to the l., rise the ruins of *Stauffenberg* (a fine point of view, 1¹/₄ M. from Lollar). Beyond stat. *Lollar* the castle of *Gleiberg* is seen to the r. in the distance; still farther distant, *Fetzberg*. Beyond Giessen, 2 M. to the S. E. of the town, rises Schloss *Schiffenberg*, the property of the grand-duke of Hessen, once a lodge of the Teutonic Order (extensive view from the the summit).

Giessen (**Kuhne*, near the station, R. from 48 kr., B. 24 kr.; **Einhorn; Rappe; Prinz Carl*; beer and fine view at the *Felsenkeller*), on the Lahn, a town chiefly of modern origin, with 10,241 inhab., is the seat of a university, founded in 1607 (400 stud.).

From Giessen to Coblenz railway in 3³|₄ hrs.; fares 3 Thlr. 13¹|₂, 2 Thlr. 2, 1 Thlr. 11 Sgr. (see *Baedeker's Rhine*).

From Giessen to Fulda in 3¹|₂ hrs. (fares 4 fl. 58, 3 fl. 43, 2 fl. 29 kr.), a route of no great interest. *Alsfeld* (Schwan), the principal place on this line, and the oldest town in Oberhessen, possesses two fine Gothic churches and several interesting late Gothic and Renaissance edifices of the 15th and 16th cent., most of which are in the market-place. *Fulda*, see p. 279.

From Giessen to Gelnhausen in 2¹|₂—3¹|₂ hrs. (fares 3 fl. 15, 2 fl. 56, 1 fl. 38 kr.). The most important station is *Nidda*, near which is the small bath of *Salzhausen*.

About 3 M. to the l. of stat. *Butzbach* rise the extensive ruins of the castle of *Münzenberg*, destroyed in the Thirty Years' War. The higher (154 ft.) of the two towers commands a fine view.

Nauheim (**Bellevue; Hôtel de l'Europe; Hôtel Kröll; Hôtel Henckel; Deutscher Hof*), with a saline spring (93° Fahr.) used for baths, situated on the N.E. slopes of the Taunus Mts., attracts a considerable number of patients. The milky and foaming mineral water of the warm fountain rises in a jet 8—10 ft. in height. The wooded *Johannisberg*, 20 min. from the Cursaal, surmounted by the tower of an ancient monastery, commands an extensive prospect. At its foot, opposite the station, is the *Conversationshaus*, with concert and reading rooms. At the E. extremity of the town, near the old Curhaus, is the *Trinkhalle*.

Friedberg (*Hôtel Trapp; Simon*), once a free Imperial town, surrounded by walls of considerable extent, possesses two handsome

Gothic churches. Oṅ the N. side śtaṅds a fiṅe, ẇell-preserved watch-tower; near it the beautiful Palace garden.

As the traiṅ approaches *Frankfort*, the Tauṅus Mts. are seen oṅ thĕ r. — *Bonames* is the station for the baths of *Homburg.*

Frankfort, see *Baedeker's Rhine.*

60. From Bèbra to Frankfort on the Main.

Railway to *Hanau* in 3¹|₄–4¹|₄ hrs. (fares 7 fl. 58, 5 fl. 35, 3 fl. 52 kr.); thence to *Frankfort* in ¹|₂ hr. (fares 45, 30, 21 kr.).

Bebra, see p. 232. The Frankfort line ascends the valley of the *Fulda* to stat. *Hersfeld,* formerly an abbey of the empire, now a small manufacturing town with 6800 inhab., at the confluence of the *Haun* and Fulda. Stations *Neukirchen, Burghausen, Hünfeld.*

Fulda *(*Kurfürst; Sonne; Post),* an ancient town on the *Fulda,* with 10,400 inhab., situated in a pleasant, undulating district, derives its origin from a once celebrated abbey founded by St. Boniface in 744, but now contains little to interest the traveller. Its numerous towers and other public buildings still testify to its ancient dignity as the residence of a prelate of princely rank. The *Cathedral,* with a dome 108 ft. in height, was erected in the 18th cent. in imitation of St. Peter's at Rome. On a pillar by the E. entrance there is a very ancient figure of Charlemagne, dating from a much earlier structure, of which the only remnant is the now restored crypt, or *Chapel of St. Boniface,* beneath the choir. Here, beneath the altar, repose the remains of St. Boniface (Winfried), a zealous English promulgator of Christianity, who was slain by the heathen Frisians near Dockum in Wèstfriesland in 754. The small *Church of St. Michael,* adjoining the cathedral, was consecrated in 822, to which period the crypt probably belongs. The present structure, dating from the 11th cent., and used as a burial-chapel, is an imitation of the church of the Holy Sepulchre at Jerusalem. In front of the *Schloss* rises the *Statue of St. Boniface,* in bronze. Fine views of the town and environs are obtained from the *Frauenberg,* immediately beyond the gate of the town, and the *Petersberg,* 2¹/₂ M. distant.

Next stations *Neuhof* (with handsome government buildings), *Flieden, Elm,* and *Schlüchtern* on the *Kinzig.* Fine views of the Vogelsgebirge to the W. The defiles here traversed by the railway were of considerable strategic importance in the war of 1866.

From Elm to Gemünden railway in 1¹|₄ hr. (fares 37, 25, 16 Sgr.). See *Baedeker's S. Germany.*

From Schlüchtern to Kissingen diligence in 8³|₄ hrs., viâ *Brückenau;* fare 2 fl. 6 kr. (see *Baedeker's S. Germany).*

Stat. *Steinau,* a small town with several mediæval buildings and an old Schloss. Scenery uninteresting. Stations *Saalmünster, Wächtersbach.*

Gelnhausen *(Hess. Hof; Hirsch),* once a town of the empire, is situated on a red soil, with which the green vineyards pic-

turesquely contrast. On an island in the Kinzig, in the lower part
of the town, near the E. entrance, are the ruins of an *Imperial Palace* erected about the year 1144 by Frederick I., parts of which are
still in tolerable preservation. The head of Frederick I. and the
lion of the Hohenstaufen family, sculptured in stone, are still
recognisable. The chapel and imperial hall are interesting. The
arches of the windows rest on clustered columns with beautiful
capitals. Here in 1180 the Emp. Frederick Barbarossa held a great
assembly to pronounce the imperial ban against Duke Henry the
Lion.

The handsome and richly decorated **Pfarrkirche*, erected in the
transition style, in 1230—60, contains an interesting early Gothic
screen, late Gothic choir stalls, and stained glass windows of the
13th cent. The spire of one of the towers is out of the perpendicular. From Gelnhausen to *Giessen*, see p. 278.

Beyond Gelnhausen the country is flat. Stat. *Meerholz*, with
a château of Count Isenburg-Meerholz; then *Langenselbold*, with
a handsome Schloss, purchased by Dom Miguel of Portugal in 1851.
Farther on, the Taunus Mts. come into view on the r.; and the
Spessart on the l. The line next intersects the *Lamboiwald*, where
on 30th and 31st Oct., 1813, Napoleon with 80,000 men on their
retreat from Leipsic defeated 40,000 Bavarians, Russians, and
Austrians under Wrede, who had endeavoured to intercept the
fugitives. *Steinheim* is visible on the opposite bank of the Main.

Hanau *(Carlsberg; Riese; Adler)*, a pleasant town with 20,500
inhab., near the confluence of the Kinzig and Main, lies in the
most fertile district of the Wetterau. The more modern part of the
town was founded in 1597 by Protestant exiles from the Netherlands to whom an asylum at Frankfort was denied. Their handi-
crafts (the manufacture of silk and woollen goods, and gold and silver
wares) still flourish here. On the Main, near the town, is situated
the palace of *Philippsruhe*, with extensive orangeries, the property
of the ex-Elector of Hessen, an imposing building in the Italian
style erected at the beginning of last century, and once presented
by Napeoleon to his sister Pauline (d. 1825), wife of Prince Camillo
Borghese.

The railway next passes the *Wilhelmsbad*, a favourite resort of
excursionists from Frankfort. To the l., on the opposite bank of
the Main, lies *Rumpenheim*, a village with a château of the Landgrave William of Hessen-Cassel.

Frankfort, see *Baedeker's Rhine.*

INDEX.

INDEX.

Leipsic: Printed by Breitkopf and Härtel.

Leipsic: Printed by Breitkopf and Härtel.

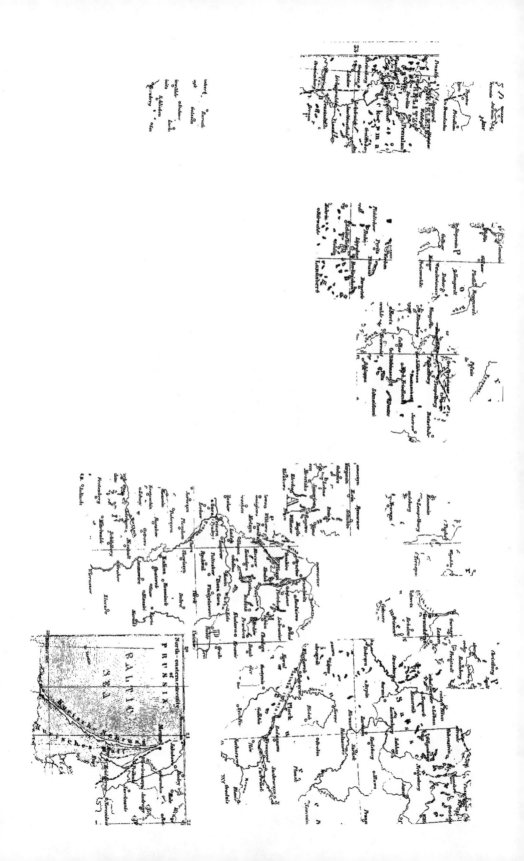

CPSIA information can be obtained
at www.ICGtesting.com
Printed in the USA
BVHW09*1738200818
525056BV00014B/1514/P